Knights of Spain, Warriors of the Sun

Knights

Hernando de Soto

# of Spain,

and the South's

Warriors

Ancient Chiefdoms

of the Sun

CHARLES HUDSON

The University of Georgia Press   Athens and London

Published in 1997 by the University of Georgia Press
Athens, Georgia 30602
© 1997 by Charles Hudson
All rights reserved

Designed by Sandra Strother Hudson
Set in Palatino by G&S Typesetters
Printed and bound by Maple-Vail Book Manufacturing Group
The paper in this book meets the guidelines for permanence
and durability of the Committee on Production Guidelines
for Book Longevity of the Council on Library Resources.

Printed in the United States of America
01 00 99 98 97 C 5 4 3 2 1

Library of Congress Cataloging in Publication Data

Hudson, Charles M.
   Knights of Spain, warriors of the sun : Hernando De Soto
and the South's ancient chiefdoms / Charles Hudson.
       p. cm.
   Includes bibliographical references and index.
   ISBN 0-8203-1888-4 (alk. paper)
       1. Soto, Hernando de, 1500–1542.   2. Southern States—
Discovery and exploration—Spanish.   3. Indians of North America—
Southern States—History—16th century.   I. Title.
E125.S7H85   1997
970.1'6—dc20   96-24255
British Library Cataloging in Publication Data available

This book is for Joyce

Contents

Afterword *441*

Notes *483*

Index *555*

Illustrations

MAPS

Preface

Between 1539 and 1543 Hernando de Soto led a small army on a desperate journey of exploration of almost four thousand miles through the southeastern quadrant of the United States. According to Spanish usage, Hernando de Soto should be referred to as Soto, but to English speakers he is De Soto, and that is what he shall be called here. The name De Soto is perhaps known to people of the older generation because the Chrysler Corporation named a now defunct line of automobiles after him. Most others know him as the Spanish conquistador who discovered the Mississippi River, died there, and was interred in its waters. For the most part, De Soto has been cast as a romantic hero by American artists, as in William H. Powell's depiction of him discovering the Mississippi River in a painting that hangs in the capitol in Washington, D.C.; by novelists, as in Andrew Lytle's *At the Moon's Inn*; and by poets, as in Lily Peter's *Great Riding: The Story of De Soto in America*.[1] Those who read my book will be disabused of any notion of De Soto as a romantic hero. He was a man of the age in which he lived, and a cruel age it was.

The De Soto expedition has evaded historians partly because reconstructing its precise path has been so difficult. The expedition is principally known to us through four chronicles, three firsthand and one secondary. The authors of the firsthand documents are Rodrigo Rangel (De Soto's secretary), Luys

Hernández de Biedma (royal factor for the expedition), and an anonymous Portuguese gentleman of Elvas, who is usually simply referred to as Elvas. The fourth chronicle is a long, romantic secondary document by Garcilaso de la Vega, who was born a mestizo in Peru—styling himself "el Inca"—and who in later life became a literary figure in Spain. Most of what can presently be learned about the De Soto expedition is contained within these four documents. As is discussed in some detail in the afterword to this volume, each of these documents has its uses, and each has its problems of interpretation.

The De Soto expedition begs to be told in the form of a narrative, and in a narrative, swiftness is all. Hence, I relegate most problems of interpretation, meaning, and inconsistencies in the sources to endnotes and to the afterword, the greatest exception being Garcilaso, whom I sometimes cite by name in the text, and almost always with either an explicit or implied caveat. Because this book is a narrative that is set in an exotic place and time, with two sets of exotic actors, I have necessarily had to write it as a "braided narrative."[2] That is, it tells a story, but it is a story into which I have woven pieces of geographical, archaeological, and ethnological explication. I have also attempted to narrate the short-term events that constitute the expedition within the context of longer-term, slower-moving historical phenomena.[3]

All the units of measurement used by sixteenth-century Spaniards were different from the ones used today. An actual year is 365.242199 days long, but the year of the Old Style Julian Calendar used by Spain until 1582 was 365.25 days long—too long by eleven minutes and fourteen seconds. Consequently, as the years passed by, the calendar date fell earlier and earlier than the actual date. Thus, by 1539–43, the dates cited by the De Soto chroniclers run about ten days earlier than actual dates. In this book it has seemed best to retain the Old Style dates cited in the chronicles. Those who wish to convert a particular date to the actual date can do so by adding ten days to the Old Style date in question.

Sixteenth-century Spaniards reckoned distance on land by two different league measurements. The *legua legal* (4.19 kilometers, or 2.59 miles) was ordinarily used in juridical matters, as in measuring large areas of land; the *legua común* (5.572 kilometers, or 3.46 miles) was often used in measuring itinerary distances traveled by land.[4] But sixteenth-century Spaniards in the New World rarely specify which of these two leagues they are using, and one is frequently in doubt about what their measurements mean. Juan Pardo, who retraced part of De Soto's route in 1566–68, appears to have used the legua común. His notary frequently recorded how far they traveled each day, and often it was 5 leagues, or about 17 miles per day. When Pardo's route is laid on a map in day-by-day fashion, this 17 miles per day of travel works quite well.[5]

The problem is that of all the De Soto chroniclers, only Garcilaso and Elvas bother to mention league measures. But the inaccuracy of Garcilaso's quantitative estimates are legendary, and no one has been able to make sense out of Elvas's estimates of distances. Hence, in reconstructing De Soto's route, the length of the league or leagues used by the chroniclers was not particularly germane. When he was on the march, De Soto could have traveled no further in a day than his footmen and his herd of hogs could walk. Because his army was much larger than that of Pardo's, De Soto probably traveled a little more slowly, perhaps fifteen miles on a good day.[6] Certainly any reconstruction of De Soto's route that requires them to have averaged more than fifteen miles per day is to be regarded with suspicion. At the same time, on particular days, under unusual circumstances, they could and did travel more than fifteen miles.

Another measure used by sixteenth-century Spaniards was the *vara*, literally a "staff" or "prod" about .835 meters, or about 32.9 inches. The *braza*, used to measure the depth of water, was two *varas*: 1.68 meters, or 66.1 inches, or 5.5 feet. A *palmo*, rarely used by the chroniclers, was one-fourth of a *vara*, or about 8.2 inches. The *fanega* was a unit of volume of about 1½ bushels, and the *arroba* was a unit of weight of about 25 pounds.

Another difficult measurement problem posed by the chroniclers is that as military men they often estimated short distances in terms of crossbow shots. But the ambiguity that arises is whether they intended to indicate the most extreme distance a crossbow could cast a bolt—about 390 yards—or whether they meant the distance at which a crossbowman could consistently hit a target—a distance of perhaps 65 to 70 yards. Or they may have meant the distance at which they could sometimes hit a man—perhaps 200 yards or so.[7]

The chroniclers rarely agree on the spelling of Indian place-names. I have generally adopted the spellings of Rangel, and after his narrative ceases, I generally use Elvas's spellings. I list the variant spellings in endnotes. For the benefit of English readers, I have substituted z for ç. In two instances, bowing to southern usage, I have anglicized place names, substituting Apalachee for Apalache and Coosa for Coza.

One of the principal claims of this book is that the route of exploration set forth in it is close to the one the expedition actually followed. This does not mean that my colleagues and I claim to have found the ghostly footprints of De Soto and his men across the southern landscape, but that the general line of march indicated here is near the one De Soto and his men followed. In some instances I mention modern highways and railroads that lie on or near their line of march. In describing the location of Indian towns, I frequently do so by referring to modern town locations, always specifying, for example, *present-day* Newport or *present-day* Knoxville, so that no hasty reader should picture an army of Spaniards hoofing it down I-40 from Newport to Knoxville.

A second claim this book makes is that it links this episode in the early history of the Southeast with the late prehistoric era. Hence, often in endnotes, but more frequently in the text than some readers might prefer, I discuss archaeological cultures (occupying regions), archaeological phases (occupying subregions), and finally specific archaeological sites. In endnotes I frequently specify site numbers, that is, combinations of numbers and letters used by archaeologists to unambiguously refer to archaeological sites. While these archaeological particulars may interrupt the narrative for those who have no particular interest in specific localities in the South, there are many who do have such an interest, and it is for them that I have included this information.

Acknowledgments

When I first planned the project on which this book is based, I intended to do the research and writing in no more than four years. But reconstructing the route of the De Soto expedition proved to be far more difficult and ramifying than I imagined it would be. The project has now gone on for more than fifteen years, and even with the completion of this book there continue to be loose ends. The list of people and agencies playing a role in this research is so long that faulty memory and stale notes will surely fail some of them. To these I apologize.

First of all I am grateful to the Center for the History of the American Indian at the Newberry Library for a Senior Fellowship in 1977–78 that gave me a gloriously unencumbered year in which I had time to assess what I understood about the native Southeast and to determine what I needed to do next.

This research would probably not have succeeded had I been deprived of my earliest collaborators—Chester B. DePratter and Marvin T. Smith—who as graduate students were the main players in a seminar on the De Soto expedition that I taught at the University of Georgia in 1980. Our collaboration was very close in working out a method of reconstructing the De Soto route and in working out the first three segments of the expedition. Quite early in the research it became difficult for us to recall who thought what first.

As our reconstruction of De Soto's route proceeded, a number of scholars played crucial roles in reconstructing particular segments of the route. Richard Polhemus's comprehensive knowledge of the late prehistoric Tennessee Valley was indispensable in our work on the first two segments of the route that we tackled—from Apalachee to Chiaha and from Chiaha to Mabila. The route through northern Georgia depends heavily on the archaeological research of David Hally, and his theoretical refinement of the concept of the chiefdom has been important in the entire undertaking. The route through Florida was so intractable we at first laid it aside, and it was only after Jerald Milanich began collaborating, drawing upon the considerable resources of the Florida Museum of Natural History, that a solution became possible. Vernon J. Knight Jr.'s knowledge of Alabama archaeology was crucial in whatever success we have had in reconstructing the route through that state, and he played an important role in shepherding into print modern critical translations of the principal De Soto documents. Our route through the state of Mississippi has benefited from conversations and correspondence with James Atkinson, Richard Marshall, and Rufus Ward, though not all of them agree fully with our interpretation of the evidence.

Dan and Phyllis Morse helped us find our way to the Mississippi River. Previous to the time we began our research, their identification of the town of Casqui as the Parkin archaeological site was nothing short of brilliant. They have been unsparingly generous and supportive of our research.

For help in precisely locating the point where the expedition crossed the Mississippi River, we are indebted to David Dye and Gerald Smith. Hester Davis, Michael Hoffman, and Gloria Young facilitated the research in Arkansas in more ways than one, including organizing two public symposia that provided a forum for public debate. John House was generous with his knowledge of the lower Arkansas River. Ann Early helped make sense of De Soto's travels in the Ouachita Mountains, and she was crucial in locating the province of Tula. Frank Schambach took on the difficult task of working out the final segment of the land route of the expedition, and he was unstinting in sharing his knowledge of the "Trans-Mississippi South." James Corbin helped me understand the importance of the old trail in Texas that became the Camino Real, and Timothy Perttula was invaluable in helping me refine the route in eastern Texas. Finally, Roger Saucier was generous in sharing his knowledge of the habits of the great river that was so important in the last half of the expedition.

The De Soto route reconstructed by my collaborators and me has stimulated spirited and at times heated debate. While responding to this criticism and argumentation has greatly added to the time I have had to spend on this project, insofar as it has sharpened and clarified my scholarship, I am grateful to those who have disagreed with me, the principal ones being Alan Blake, Clifford Boyd, Jeffrey Brain, Caleb Curren, Patricia Galloway, David Henige, Keith Little, and Gerald Schroedl.

The social and natural world explored by De Soto and his men in the sixteenth century differed greatly from the Southeast of subsequent historical eras. Indeed, the social texture of the native Southeast had changed greatly by the eighteenth century, and in most places the natural world of the Southeast had been greatly changed by the late nineteenth century. My desire for this book is that it evoke the sixteenth-century Southeast and make it palpable, not only in words but also in illustrations. Finding photographs of characteristic vegetation types along the route has been particularly difficult, and in many instances I have had to settle for pictures of secondary growth that no more than resemble the original vegetation. And in some instances the photographs that were available to me do not do justice to the magnificent forests that covered the Southeast in the sixteenth century.

Many individuals have helped me in the time-consuming task of assembling illustrations: F. E. Abernethy, Libby Bell, Jefferson Chapman, James C. Cobb, Donald E. Davis, Hester Davis, John D. Davis, Paul Delcourt, Raymond J. De-Mallie, David Dye, Ann M. Early, Ellen Garrison, Thomas J. Green, John Hall, David Hally, Fritz Hamer, Timmy Hill, William R. Iseminger, Douglas Jones, J. Dwight Kirkland, Vernon J. Knight Jr., Kathleen L. Manscill, Lawrence May and the men of Calderon's Company (Dale Beremond, Bill Burger, Timothy Burke, David Elkins, Floyd Johnson, and Ron Prouty), Bonnie McEwan, Bob McNeil, Linda Meyers, Jerald Milanich, James J. Miller, Jeffrey M. Mitchem, Nola Montgomery, David Moore, Dan Morse, Jerry Oldshue, Felicia G. Pickering, Janet Rafferty, David Riskind, Roger Saucier, Frank Schambach, John H. Slate, Marvin T. Smith, Vincas P. Steponaitis, Paul Thompson, Billy Townsend, Stephen Williams, and Concha Worth.

I graciously extended the opportunity to support my research to several granting agencies, but for such a risky, controversial, and evidently unfashionable venture, I had no takers. Thus I have largely paid for it out of pocket. Most of my summers since 1978 I have devoted fully to research on this project, as I have also done with most holidays and weekends. For this I acknowledge the patience and support of my family, whose sacrifice has been considerable. I also absorbed the expenses in 1984 when over a period of six weeks my wife, Joyce, and I drove the De Soto route (as I understood it then), from beginning to end. The journal she kept on this trip is the basis of her book *Looking for De Soto: A Search through the South for the Spaniard's Trail* (University of Georgia Press, 1993). All along the way the two of us depended upon the kindness of archaeologists. It was a tremendously enriching experience, and I thank all of those who extended us their help and hospitality. I am also grateful to the University of Georgia Research Foundation for Senior Faculty Research Grants in 1988 and 1993.

I am not, alas, a technically prepared Hispanic scholar. My knowledge of the Spanish language is limited, and I have therefore frequently had to call upon Hispanic scholars for assistance. In this regard, I owe enduring debts to Paul Hoffman, Carmen Chaves Tesser, and John Worth.

For particular assistance, I am grateful to Scott Akridge for finding a saline where I hoped a saline would be; Gene Black for showing me the Chickasaw-hatchee Swamp in all its beauty; Donald Davis for advice on the dominance of chestnut trees in the old Appalachian forest; Paul Delcourt for his knowledge of the environmental history of the Southeast; Penelope B. Drooker for useful information on *henequén*; Byron J. Freeman and Charlene Keck for fish identifications; Lowell Kirk for advice on the lower Little Tennessee River; Beth Misner for advice on horses and dogs; Julie Smith for drawing the maps; Roger Smith for information on Spanish small craft; Mark Williams for helping to discover a native occupation of the Oconee River basin where I hoped one would be; and John Worth for discovering a similar native occupation on the Flint River.

I gratefully acknowledge the comments of my two anonymous readers at the University of Georgia Press, and I offer sincere thanks to Carmen Chaves Tesser, who generously gave me a critical reading of the entire manuscript, and to Doug Jones and John Worth, who read parts of it. All of my readers should appreciate those who have labored to transmute my manuscript into a book, and most especially Kelly Caudle, Anne Gibbons, Walton Harris, and Sandra Hudson.

Knights of Spain, Warriors of the Sun

1

Separate Worlds

Spain and the American Southeast in the Sixteenth Century

What visitor to the forests of the southeastern United States has not imagined the native people who used to inhabit this landscape? In a southeastern forest in the 1700s one might have seen a mysterious Creek or Cherokee walking silently in the gloom of an old-growth forest, dressed in a breechcloth, buckskin moccasins, a cloth hunting shirt, a brightly colored cloth turban, and armed to the teeth with a steel tomahawk, a razor-sharp scalping knife, and a flintlock rifle.

But a full two centuries earlier than the time when such a Creek or Cherokee might have been seen, there were two sets of even more mysterious people who collided with each other in the vast forests that blanketed the Southeast. In the 1500s Spanish adventurers explored the interior of the Southeast and made first contact with many of the native chiefdoms that dominated the region. These Spaniards were more medieval than modern. They were fighting men who wore body armor and fought with crude matchlock guns, crossbows, lances, and even more with steel swords. Above all they regarded themselves as Christians who were pitted in a great struggle against infidels and devil-worshippers everywhere, both at home and abroad.

The native chiefdoms these Spaniards encountered in the Southeast also fielded fighting men, with a centuries-old military tradition of their own. The chiefdoms to which they belonged were dominated by chiefs who claimed descent from the gods of their universe, and most particularly from the Sun. These chiefs had power over people who made their living by hunting, fishing, and gathering wild food, but what they relied upon even more was farming. When they went to war they preferred to fight almost naked. A Southeastern warrior wore a breechcloth and moccasins of brain-tanned deerskin. He wore leggings when traveling in the woods, and he wrapped a mulberry cloth, deerskin, or fur mantle about his body when the weather was cold. He was adept with the bow and arrow, but his principal martial weapon was the war club, his weapon of choice in hand-to-hand combat.

These chiefdoms were largely self-sufficient, and the people were greatly circumscribed in their knowledge of the larger world. Frequently a chiefdom found itself at war with one or more neighboring chiefdoms, and because of this the members of such a chiefdom could not have traveled widely or inquired into the larger world even if they had wanted to. The chiefdoms of the Southeast were small, intricately structured, self-contained worlds, whose members would have found our imagined eighteenth-century Creek or Cherokee hunter almost as alien as they found the Spaniards who appeared so rudely in their midst in the sixteenth century.

The first sustained encounter between the separate worlds of Europeans and the native people of the southeastern United States occurred in the middle years of the sixteenth century. Between 1539 and 1543 Hernando de Soto led a small army to explore a vast area of the continent. The principal motive that impelled De Soto and his followers was the possibility of discovering a rich, populous society, like that of the Aztecs or Incas. When judged in terms of how well he achieved his objectives, De Soto's expedition was a colossal failure. But along with Francisco Vázquez de Coronado's simultaneous exploration of the southwestern United States, De Soto's exploration of the Southeast was one of the most important historical events in sixteenth-century America. Members of his expedition traveled thousands of miles through about a quarter of the present territory of the United States, a vast portion of the continent, and they visited a large number of native societies, most of whom had had no previous firsthand experience with Europeans.

But for all this, the De Soto expedition has won only a small place in American history. Everyone knows that De Soto discovered the Mississippi River, and that he later died on the banks of that river and was buried in its waters. An automobile was named after him. His name dots the southern landscape, attached to towns, bridges, waterfalls, caverns, pecan houses, and so on. But where did his expedition go? What sort of people did it encounter? And how did it affect these native people?

It is easy to speak of the De Soto expedition as an instance of "first contact" between the Old World and the New. But this is at best a lazy and imprecise characterization. The Indian chiefdoms De Soto encountered did not think of themselves as a collectivity. They were first and foremost Apalachees, or Coosas, or Chicazas. And since they had no knowledge of Europe, Africa, and Asia they surely did not think of themselves as constituting a New World. They were parochial to a degree that few modern people can imagine. Moreover, there is little evidence that De Soto and his men thought of themselves as emissaries from the Old World. They had nothing so grand in mind. They spoke of themselves as Christians, but more fundamentally they were entrepreneurs and adventurers. They were officially charged with evangelizing the Indians, but even more they hoped to acquire wealth, power, and social honor.

"Spaniards"

Referring to De Soto and his men as "Spaniards" is little more than a convenience.[1] In fact, it is historically inaccurate. In 1539–43 the polities to which De Soto and his men owed their allegiance were not modern nation states, and De Soto and his fellows were not modern people. The Iberian peninsula as a geographical entity (map 1) had been referred to as *Hispania* throughout the Middle Ages, and as time went on the people of the Iberian peninsula had a growing sense of being a people as opposed to, say, Frenchmen or Englishmen. Their primary social identification was to their town or region, and they identified only weakly with one of three Christian crowns: Castile, Aragon, or Portugal.

In 1469, with the marriage of Ferdinand of Aragon to Isabela of Castile, two of these crowns were joined together. Their long reign set in motion a remarkable cultural florescence, and for some decades Spain became the greatest power in Europe.[2] During their reign, Spain succeeded in two stupendous achievements that reverberated in world history for centuries. One was that in 1492 Ferdinand and Isabela completed the centuries-long reconquest of their land from the Muslims, who had invaded in 711 and had overrun the Iberian peninsula in a humiliating conquest. The second achievement, in that same miraculous year, was that Ferdinand and Isabela backed Columbus's discovery of the New World and initiated the conquest and settlement of that vast unknown land.

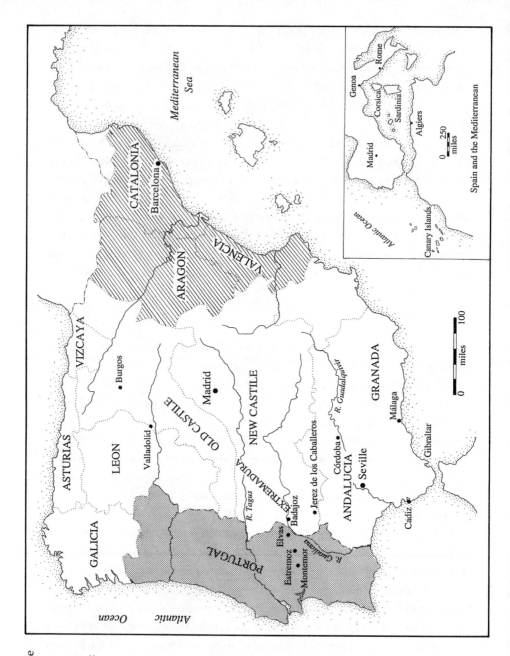

Map 1. Spain in the sixteenth century. The kingdom of Aragon in eastern Spain is hachured; the kingdom of Castile, including Navarre and the Basque Provinces, is left blank.

The royal houses of Castile and Aragon were linked together by marriage, but the two kingdoms were not effectively joined together. They remained politically distinct patrimonies and their economies were not integrated with each other. Their political histories were different and they were unequal. Castile was larger and more populous than Aragon and was therefore dominant. Moreover, their interests were different. Castile looked toward the Atlantic for opportunities, while Aragon looked toward the Mediterranean. With the discovery of the New World, America belonged to Castile, and the inhabitants of the kingdom of Aragon were technically foreigners in this new land. In fact, if Isabela had had her way, only Castilians would have conquered and settled the New World.[3]

The kingdom of Aragon, comprising the states of Catalonia, Aragon, and Valencia, was fundamentally a commercial empire, trading textiles to Africa and Sicily, as well as to other provinces in the Iberian Peninsula. The Aragonese economy was dominated by an emerging bourgeoisie, and their government was a constitutional system with limits on the power of the rulers and with protection against arbitrary power. The Aragonese oath of allegiance to the king was "We who are so good as you swear to you who are no better than we, to accept you as our king and sovereign lord, provided that you observe all of our liberties and laws; but if not, not."[4]

The political and economic character of Castile was quite different. The Castilian economy was heavily pastoral, with wool being the principal export, and in Castile the Reconquest was more protracted and bitter than in Aragon, and it shaped the character of the Castilians to a greater degree than it did the Aragonese. The Reconquest was more than a political action. It was a crusade against infidels. And insofar that plunder could be won, it was an avenue to wealth. Huge grants of land reconquered from the Muslims strengthened the hereditary noble class in Castile. Reconquering land and picking up and moving from one place to another went hand in hand, and migration became familiar to Castilians. Moreover, because Castilians conceived of the Reconquest as a religious crusade, the church in Castile became heavily involved in military affairs, and as a consequence, a series of powerful Christian military orders emerged—Calatrava, Alcántara, and most especially Santiago. The latter was named after St. James (i.e., Santiago), the patron saint of Spain, who was believed to have miraculously appeared after great battles were fought. The church and the military were intimately combined in these orders, or brotherhoods, and in time they came to possess vast estates with many vassals. Being admitted to the Order of Santiago was a very high honor. One had to document a "pure" Christian genealogy for three to four generations, and one had, of course, to possess sufficient wealth.

The ideal Castilian *hidalgo*—"a somebody"—was a man who was never so happy as when he was at war. For such a man, the most esteemed wealth was not to be won by the sweat of his brow, but through booty and land taken in warfare with infidels. Victory was not to be won so much through military technology as through faith, valor, and the exercise of will. The ideal hidalgo was a man who was contemptuous of inherited wealth and a comfortable, settled life. If one had to be tied to property, then let it be sheep, which could be herded from place to place. Moreover, in Castile the bourgeoisie did not grow strong enough to serve as a check against the power of the nobility. Indeed, the power of the Castilian aristocracy made for constant managerial problems for Ferdinand and Isabela.

In the fourteenth and fifteenth centuries Aragon was hit hard by a series of epidemic diseases and went into steep population decline. As Aragon's population fell precipitously, the mercantilist economy shrank. Hence, at the time when Castile found itself master of the Iberian peninsula at the close of the fifteenth century, Aragon found itself unable to provide the skills in banking and overseas trading that Castile needed. Providing these skills fell instead to the Genoese, who quickly became entrepreneurs in Seville, Cadiz, and Córdoba and were important actors in Spain's rise to world power.[5] And so it was that Christopher Columbus, a Genoese, was backed by two Iberian monarchs who, flushed with victory after more than seven centuries of struggle with Muslims, were looking for new infidels to conquer.

The profound political disunity of sixteenth-century Spain was one of the reasons why Christianity was so important. Like nothing else, the idea of the religious crusade mobilized Castilians to risk their lives and to pay taxes. Belief in the Christian mystery was a way of rising above real-world divisions to bind together Castilians, Aragonese, and Catalans. Christianity was so important that Spaniards conceived of Christian ancestry as something one inherited in one's "blood." It was Christian blood that made Spaniards different from others. Thus, their concern with *limpieza de sangre* (purity of blood) was not the racism that came to exist in the nineteenth century, but rather a conception that set Christians apart from people of other religious persuasions, especially Jews. And one purpose of the Spanish Inquisition instituted by Ferdinand and Isabela was to determine whether the *conversos*—Jews who had been coerced into converting to Christianity—had truly become Christians.[6]

Thus it was that De Soto's men thought of themselves collectively not so much as "Spaniards," but as Christians.

The social structure of Castile and Aragon was strongly hierarchical. At the very top were twenty-five Grandes de España, descendants of the oldest families, whom the king addressed as *primo* (cousin). These grandees did not remove their hats in his presence. They all knew each other and acted as a group. There were other titled aristocrats—*títulos*—who possessed somewhat less exalted status.

The next tier in the hierarchy was occupied by the lesser nobility, a class, rather than an organized group. These were caballeros and hidalgos, who might be addressed as *Don,* and who could be rich or poor. Some were descended from nobles, while others were rich merchants or successful military men. They were exempt from paying taxes to the crown, could not be tortured or sentenced to serve as oarsmen in the galleys, and could not be imprisoned for debt. These advantages made *hidalguía* highly coveted, and people went to great lengths to achieve this status. Some even risked falsifying their genealogies.

At the bottom of this Castilian hierarchy were the peasants, who constituted about 80 percent of the population. Some were well off, but most of them were extremely poor. To them fell the task of agriculture, and theirs was a backward agricultural system.[7]

In the sixteenth century the Spanish military was superb. Through experience in the Reconquest, the men of the military were accomplished at laying siege, and they were notable for their ability to endure and overcome the rigors of hunger and hardship. Technically they were not soldiers, because military men were not set apart from civilians in sixteenth-century Spain. Most sixteenth-century Spaniards were skilled at using arms, and even clergy were capable of wielding arms if need be. Those who went to the New World to improve their fortunes were not paid salaries; instead, they expected to be given a share in the conquest. They were *compañeros* (partners, or companions) in the enterprise. Perhaps because the characteristic military engagements throughout the Reconquest were skirmishes and surprise attacks, Spanish footmen were superb, individualistic fighters.[8] And just as the skills of Spanish footmen had been tempered in the crucible of the Reconquest, so had the skills and tactics of Spanish horsemen. The tactical advantage conferred by the horsemen in the conquest of New World peoples can hardly be overstated. When the Inca treasure was divided up among Spanish conquistadores at Cajamarca, horsemen were given twice the share of footmen.[9]

Much of the legal apparatus employed by Spain in the exploration and conquest of the New World was based upon medieval Iberian institutions that had been modified to meet new circumstances. The preponderance of the military actions against the Moors, for example, had been privately financed, but always with authorization by the crown, granted in a document known as a *capitulación,* with specific rights and interests affirmed and reserved by the crown; similar arrangements were made with the conquistadores in the New World. The medieval title of *adelantado,* conferring extraordinary powers to a military leader, was used in the New World.[10] An adelantado might expect to share in wealth procured through conquest and in rights to conquered land, as well as being granted a noble title. Cortés, for example, at the end of his life was made Marqués del Valle de Oaxaca, and Francisco Pizarro was also made a marqués. There was hardly a higher honor to which a Spaniard could aspire.

Castilian men were tough, arrogant, quick to take offense, undaunted by danger and hardship, and extravagant in their actions. They would suffer hunger, hardship, extremes of climate, and still fight savagely against great odds. Compared to their English contemporaries, they were intensely bureaucratic and given to drawing up documents that gave accounts of their actions and detailed their merits with respect to the crown. Their literary tastes tended toward extravagance. Some of them had read—and many more had heard read aloud—romances of chivalry that ran to hundreds of pages. *Amadis of Gaul,* first published in 1508, was the most famous of these romances. Sixteenth-century Spaniards were fascinated with heroic stories, the adventures of perfect knights, ceremonious and courtly behavior, and strange and magical happenings.[11]

But given to religion and extravagant imagination as they were, they came to the New World in search of riches, fame, and power. Many of them were from modest or poor families, and they were willing to risk their lives to become rich.

The Spaniards never doubted their own superiority over the native peoples they encountered in the New World. They saw themselves as a specially favored people who were carrying out a divine mission. But they justified their actions not merely in terms of their belief in their own superiority, but in terms of notions and legal conceptions that emerged from their experience in the Reconquest. In particular, they had evolved a complex code of rules about waging a "just war," which defined the rights of victors over vanquished. A just war, for example, conferred on victors the right to enslave the vanquished. There were, however, problems of interpretation. These just-war principles were unambiguous when applied to the Moors, who knew what the Christian religion was and explicitly rejected it. But what about people such as the Indians, who had never heard of Christianity? Did their being outside Christianity entitle Spaniards to enslave them? Isabela did not think so, and in 1500 she prohibited enslaving Indians, although exceptions were made when Indians attacked Spaniards or when they engaged in abominable acts, such as cannibalism, or prohibited sexual practices, such as sodomy. In practice, few Spaniards in the New World found difficulty in getting around Isabela's prohibition.[12]

Skin color and racial differences were not particularly notable to De Soto and his men. A black skin did not necessarily mean that one was a slave, and a white skin did not necessarily mean that one was free. The notion that the peoples of the world could be graded in an evolutionary scheme of skin color from the highest to the lowest was not elaborated into an ideology until the eighteenth and nineteenth centuries. Rather, if De Soto and his men inquired into the nature of the Indians, they would probably have followed Aristotle in asking whether the Indians in question lived in polities, as social and political beings. If so, they were by definition human beings, though they might be infidels. At the same time, there were people in the New World who seemed not to live in polities. They were people such as the Chichimecas of northern Mexico, tribal people who lay beyond the Aztec periphery, whom the Spaniards could not control by their usual means. In time, in North America "Chichimeca" became synonymous with "savage, barbarous."[13] Later, in the seventeenth century, the Spaniards in Florida would apply this term to some of the troublesome Indians who lay on their northern frontier.

De Soto and his followers were not relativists. It seemed quite reasonable to them to measure people in terms of the degree to which they lived like Spaniards.

The member of a civilized polity, then, as conceived by a sixteenth-century Spaniard, was a town-dweller who was dressed in doublet and hose, and wore his hair short. His house was not overrun with fleas and ticks. He ate his meals at a table and not on the ground. He did not indulge in unnatural vice, and if he committed adultery he was punished for it. His wife—who was his only wife and not one among several—did not carry children on her back like a monkey, and he expected his son and not his nephew to succeed his inheritance. He did not spend his time getting drunk; and he had a proper respect for property—his own and other peoples.[14]

When De Soto and his men judged some of the people they encountered in the Southeast to be more civilized than others, as they sometimes did, they were probably employing criteria like these.

In accounting for customs and actions that seemed truly aberrant or abhorrent, sixteenth-century Spaniards were quick to invoke God's great adversary—Satan. Cannibalism, and even drunkenness, could be seen as the work of Satan. Satan deprived men of reason; hence, they became as children, and they might even become as beasts. The Spaniards had not yet questioned the assumption that European people were the measure of men everywhere, and by so easily explaining cultural differences as having been caused by Satan, they had little reason to inquire into the specific ways in which Indian cultures differed from their own.[15] When French and English Protestants came into contact with North American Indians in the 1580s, their approach to the Indians was notably more objective and descriptive.

A great debate about the rights of the Indians raged in Spain in the first half of the sixteenth century. Bartolomé de las Casas, a conquistador who participated in the conquest of Cuba, developed pangs of conscience and came to champion the Indians, arguing that if the Indians were subjects of the Spanish crown, they should have the same rights as Spaniards and should not be enslaved. The contrary position was championed by Juan Ginés de Supúlveda, who argued in favor of Aristotle's doctrine of natural slavery. The Indians, he argued, were naturally inferior to Spaniards and on this basis alone could be enslaved by them. Eventually, in 1542, slavery of Indians was prohibited by a royal decree that went beyond the earlier injunction of Isabela.[16] But this came too late to soften De Soto's treatment of Indians.

De Soto and his men were more medieval than modern in the way they thought and acted. They came from a society that was basically agricultural and pastoral. Theirs was a world that was slow-moving and seemingly immutable. For them, the calendar was not comprised of a series of equivalent units of measurement; instead, the year played itself out as a kind of circle whose various parts were qualitatively different. It was an ancient circle punctuated by Christian festival days. This is why De Soto and his men frequently named the places they discovered after these days. Hence, they would name Tampa Bay Bahía del Espíritu Santo, and a large lake they came to soon after departing from Tampa Bay they would name the Lake of St. John. They remembered events more in relation to these festival days than by the calendar. Moreover, clocks were still extremely rare, and people had little awareness of hours of the day.[17]

De Soto's men were from a Spain that still retained considerable areas of wilderness. Forests were extensive, and there were few fences so as not to impede the free passage of shepherds and their flocks. It was a land where bears and wolves were still numerous. To travel from Madrid to Barcelona could take fifteen days. And travelers always had to be on the lookout for bandits. People in Spain would often travel in caravans in order to protect themselves against bandits. When bandits were killed, their severed heads would often be impaled on poles alongside the road.[18]

Spaniards dreamed of acquiring wealth, and the quicker it could be obtained and enjoyed the better. They disdained labor. Wealth was not merely to be possessed or carefully invested for profit; it was to be used in display, finery, and diversion, or to buy slaves or pay servants who were themselves items of display. Something of this spirit may be seen today on festive occasions in Valencia, where at great expense the people build *fallas,* large artistic floats made of wood, paper, and wax, and then in a single night they burn them all to cinders to the delight of the crowd. Sponsoring a festival was a way of displaying wealth and prestige. For such people, bourgeois values were contemptible.[19]

De Soto and his men grew up in a small-scale society in which relationships were intensely personal. Honor or reputation, a constant preoccupation, was esteemed above all else, even life itself. Mere life ended with death, but one's reputation (whether honorable or dishonorable) lived on after death. Honor was something that could be sought and increased, and once a man possessed it, he sought to retain it and was worried that he might lose it. Honor was one's public reputation, and it was a vital concern of both men and women of all classes. Honor could be called into question by a public insult, and it could be tarnished by slander. A Spaniard would kill to preserve honor.[20]

"Indians"

Just as "Spaniards" is not an accurate label for De Soto and his army, neither is "Indians" an accurate label for the people De Soto encountered during the course of his expedition in the southeastern United States. Through a well-known geographical misconception, Columbus called the islands he discovered the Indies, and he therefore called the natives of these islands *indios*—"Indians." In time Europeans would realize that "Indians" was not only a misnomer but also a word that glossed over a host of differences. Despite their remarkable genetic homogeneity, the people of the New World differed one from another in their languages, their cultures, and their social institutions.

But the misnomer "Indian" is not corrected by merely substituting "Native American." In terms of their biological ancestry, the people De Soto encountered in the Southeast were the progeny of immigrants: they were descendants of people who had migrated from Siberia to the New World more than twelve thousand years earlier than the second wave of immigrants from Europe and Africa—the one that included De Soto. The term "Native American" is as problematic a cover term as "Indian." "Native American" is as much a conquerors' term for a conquered people as "Indian" is. The problem is that we have no reason to think that any of the native people of North America had a word that referred to the continent on which they all lived. In fact, their knowledge of the wider world was quite limited. Misnomer though it be, the word "Indian" does have the advantage of being long established, and variants of it are used in many of the languages of the world.

But it is important to understand what kinds of cultural and social entities are subsumed under the label "Indian." The fact is that by the time of first European contact in the sixteenth century, these immigrants from Siberia had been in the New World long enough to have developed some considerable differences among their languages and cultures. The Indians of the Southeast alone spoke languages belonging to at least seven different language families—Muskogean, Iroquoian, Catawban, Caddoan, Algonkian, Tunican, and Timucuan—and each of these families comprised several languages. Languages belonging to these several language families were as different from each other as English is from Chinese. Moreover, some of the languages within these language families were mutually unintelligible. For example, Cherokee and Tuscarora belong to the Iroquois language family, but a Cherokee speaker could not understand a Tuscarora speaker. In addition to these major language families, there were an unknown number of language "isolates" in the Southeast that are not definitely related to any known language family. Some areas of the Southeast, such as the southern half of Florida, appear to have been extraordinarily diverse linguistically. Spanish missionaries in this area in the late sixteenth century complained bitterly about their problems in missionizing Indians whose languages were so diverse.

Differences existed among the Indians of the Southeast, but there were also ways in which they were similar. Although it is difficult to document, it appears that all the Southeastern Indians, as well as some Indians outside the Southeast, shared certain basic assumptions and thought patterns. This includes notions about how the cosmos was put together, as well as very general "theories" about why things happen. For example, many Indians in North America believed they lived in a world divided into four cardinal directions (see figs. 31, 55), with each of these directions being associated with distinct symbolic associations, such that the east was associated with life, the west with its opposite, death, and so on. Similarly, North American Indians believed that the cosmos was peopled by a panoply of spiritual beings, and when one's relationships with these spiritual beings were disturbed, then various kinds of misfortunes would occur. Thus, even though the Southeastern Indians differed among themselves in terms of culture and language, they shared some deep assumptions, and they probably grasped the meanings of each others' visual symbols.[21]

A second basis for similarities among the Indians of the Southeast was a fundamental social transformation that began occurring among them at about A.D. 800 to 1000 and by 1539–43 had affected most of the people De Soto and his army encountered. Evidence for this transformation was unearthed by archaeologists, who coined the word "Mississippian" to denote both a distinctive culture and the time period in which it existed, that is, from about A.D. 800 to 1600. This Mississippian transformation appears to have been set in motion by a growing dependency on corn agriculture. But whatever cause was decisive in setting it in motion, the most notable consequence was that it stimulated the development of chiefdoms, a new kind of social order in the Southeast in which social power, probably for the first time, was concentrated in the hands of chiefs who ranked above the people. Hand in hand with this concentration of power, the populations of the chiefdoms began to expand, and the level of military competition increased greatly.

De Soto and his army would meet up with the first of these Mississippian chiefdoms in northern Florida, and from this point on they encountered one chiefdom after another as they traveled through the area that in the nineteenth century would be the cotton-growing states of the Old South. They would probe along the northern and western boundary of the Mississippian area until they came to hunter-gatherers in eastern Texas who lay outside the Mississippian sphere.

These Mississippian chiefdoms were important to the Spaniards. For one thing, they concentrated political power in the hands of the chiefs, which meant that if the Spaniards controlled a chief they could control his people. Another advantage for the Spaniards was that the chiefdoms concentrated wealth in the form of stored food, most particularly corn. De Soto and his army needed these stores of corn. Like other premodern armies, they did not carry their own food with them. Their itinerary, therefore, was determined by the locations of the chiefdoms, for they could only go from storehouse to storehouse if they were to survive.

The Southeastern Indians began supplementing the wild foods they hunted and collected with cultivated foods many centuries before the Mississippian transformation occurred. These older cultigens included squash and sunflower, still cultivated today, but also some native southeastern plants—chenopodium, marsh elder, and smartweed—that the people mostly ceased cultivating after they obtained corn. Corn made its appearance in the Southeast at an early date, but at first it was not cultivated on a large scale. Even in the Mississippian period, the Indians of the Southeast continued to supplement their cultivated foods with wild foods gained through hunting, fishing, and collecting. But in the Mississippian period, dependency on corn increased. This in itself may have shaped many of the cultural changes that came about in the Mississippian transformation. Corn is a plant that produces a great quantity of storable nutritious grain, but it is also a plant that places great demands on farmers. It cannot be cultivated casually, and it quickly takes its toll on the fertility of soils. To cultivate corn successfully, the Indians had to modify their way of living.

But even with this increased dependency, the native farmers of the Southeast did not produce quantities of corn that greatly exceeded what they themselves consumed as food. Each farmer did produce some surplus for his chief, who used this corn to support himself and those close to him and also to "redistribute" it to his people in various ways. The corn taken by the Spaniards, then, was not corn the Indians had to spare.

During the Mississippian period, and probably for all the many millennia of his existence in the New World, the Southeastern Indian's most fundamental allegiance was with his kinsmen. These were the people whom a person counted as "blood relatives," the linkages among whom were based purely on the fact of being descended from particular parents. If the kinship organization of Southeastern Indians in the eighteenth and nineteenth centuries can be taken as a guide to earlier conditions, then most of the Indians whom De Soto encountered in the Southeast traced their descent matrilineally (fig. 1). That is,

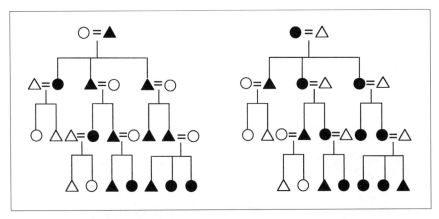

Fig. 1. Patrilineal descent (*left*) and matrilineal descent (*right*). Triangles represent males; circles represent females; equal signs represent marriage; horizontal lines link siblings; and vertical lines link the generations. Shaded triangles and circles represent "blood" relatives.

an individual traced his blood relatives only through his mother and through her female relatives. In a matrilineal kinship system, one's father was not a blood ancestor, and he was not a male authority figure in one's life; that role fell to one's mother's brother. In a matrilineal society the avuncular relationship between nephew and maternal uncle was very important (fig. 2). By the same logic, in a matrilineal society a man's own children were not his blood descendants.

Because De Soto and his men did not make a special effort to inquire into the culture of the Indians, one cannot be certain that matrilineality prevailed everywhere in the Southeast. And in fact, a few of the chiefdoms De Soto encountered—particularly those just west of the Mississippi River, in what is now Arkansas, may have been patrilineal in their kinship reckoning. If so, in these societies descent was traced through males, and the most important male authority relationship was between father and son (fig. 1).

Most of the social needs of the Indians were satisfied through membership in lineages and clans founded on the basis of their kinship organization. Lineages and clans were the context for the production and raising of children; the production of food, housing, and clothing; "legal defense" and support in the event of conflict with others; health care; and many other activities.

The chiefdom introduced a new kind of organization into the Southeast. Societies can be organized solely on the basis of lineages and clans, with each of the constituent groups existing on a par with each other, and the Indians of the

Fig. 2. The matrilineal avuncular relationship. Tomo Chachi Mico, an important Indian in early eighteenth-century Georgia, and his nephew Tooanahowi. Mezzotint by John Faber after a portrait painted by Willem Verelst in 1734, when uncle and nephew visited London and met the king. This is an excellent rendering of South-eastern Indian physiognomies. (National Anthropological Archives, Smithsonian Institution)

pre-Mississippian Southeast appear to have been basically egalitarian. Each member of such societies probably felt himself to be as worthy as any other. But with such egalitarianism, the ability to organize large numbers of people, as in a military organization, was limited, and the ability to make difficult decisions on behalf of the society at large was very limited. Moreover, in egalitarian societies there was no mechanism to even out risks among the people. For example, when a lineage or clan lost its supply of stored food through some calamity, to whom could they turn for assistance? The chiefdom provided a means of dealing with all these problems.

With the advent of chiefdoms, inequality was institutionalized in the Southeast. The chief and his blood kinsmen had the power to demand economic support from the people. They justified their eminence by claiming descent from their deities, and judging from the eighteenth-century Natchez Indians, the chief might claim to be the actual earthly kinsman of the Sun. Hence, the chief's person was sacred, and in rituals he represented the sacred. He was also first in warfare. One of the functions of the chiefdom was to organize people so that warfare could be waged more effectively. Hence, all across the Southeast during the Mississippian period, warfare and the weapons and symbols of warfare were frequently represented in various art forms.

The Mississippian military was made up of part-time specialists: all males were normally hunters and farmers as well as warriors. Many of the skills they employed in warfare they also employed in hunting and in other pursuits. One of their principal military weapons, the bow and arrow (fig. 3), was also their favorite hunting weapon. The bow and arrow may have been adopted in the Southeast somewhat earlier than the Mississippian period, but it was during this period that this weapon became widespread and popular. The characteristic Mississippian projectile point was a small triangular or ovoid (see fig. 61) arrow point.

The males born into Mississippian chiefdoms no doubt began mastering the bow and arrow when they were children. There is ample evidence in the documents of the De Soto expedition that Southeastern Indian archers were large in stature, well built, and in superb physical condition. They could shoot accurately and with great force.

East of the Mississippi River the Indians made self (or simple) bows out of hickory, ash, or black locust. West of the Mississippi River the bows were commonly made of Osage orange, the very best bow wood in North America. Until the nineteenth century, when its range was purposefully and deliberately

Fig. 3. Mississippian archer. Drawing by Charles Hudson III after a design etched onto a shell drinking cup found at the Spiro site in Oklahoma.

extended, the range of Osage orange was restricted to a tiny area in east Texas. On the dry western margin of the Southeast, bows were often backed with sinew, an elastic material taken from animals, which made the bows stronger, increasing their range. The typical Southeastern bow was a moderately long D-bow—with a length of about fifty to sixty inches—and with a pull weight of about fifty pounds. Such bows had a long pull, and they would cast an arrow a long distance. Occasionally bows were made with slightly recurved tips.

Cabeza de Vaca, who experienced Southeastern Indians about ten years earlier than De Soto, came to know them well. He reports that their bows were as thick as one's arm (presumably one's wrist), measuring from eleven to twelve spans long, and the Indians could shoot an arrow that was capable of hitting a target at two hundred paces. Cabeza de Vaca saw one of these arrows penetrate as much as six inches into the base of a poplar tree. The Indians often slept with their bows strung and with some arrows near at hand. When an alarm was given, they could be up and about in an instant. They fought in a crouching position, darting from side to side, dodging missiles fired at them, and they did it so well that the Spaniards had difficulty hitting them with their crossbows and arquebuses.[22]

A weapon even more closely linked with Mississippian warfare was the war club. Unlike the bow and arrow, the war club, so far as anyone knows, was used exclusively in warfare. Most Mississippian clubs were probably made of hickory, though many other woods—such as ash, ironwood, and black locust—were suitable. War clubs were one to three feet long, and they were carved into a variety of shapes. Some had roughly the shape of a cutlass (called *atassa* by later Creek Indians), complete with a V-shape edge, while others had a ball carved on the distal end. Both of these forms enhanced the ability of a war club to impart skull and bone fractures. Other war clubs were mounted with stone celts or else spikes made of sharks' teeth (see fig. 84), animal bone, antler, or flint set into their distal ends. Still others had their distal ends carved into spatulate (see fig. 5) or "mace" (fig. 4; also see fig. 48) shapes. Some of the more elaborate clubs are thought to have been wielded by the warrior elite in Mississippian societies, and some may have been reserved for very high-status individuals among these elites.

The war club was both the principal implement and dominant symbol of Mississippian warfare. The warriors must have undergone long training in the art of hand-to-hand fighting. Some of the moves they learned appear to have been incorporated into ritual dances celebrating warfare. The clubs were often decorated with potent symbols, and the clubs themselves became symbols not only of warfare but also of deities such as Thunder. War clubs themselves were sometimes represented artistically. They were made out of sheet copper (see fig. 48), carved out of stone, or even cut from sheets of mica, and as such they were completely nonfunctional. In some respects, the war club must have been for the Southeastern Indian warrior what the sword was to the knight in Arthurian legend. Indirect evidence of the war club's effectiveness has been found in archaeological contexts. That is, the skeletal remains of males at several Mississippian sites have shown fractured skulls, cracked collar bones, and lower arm breaks, the latter probably sustained in holding up their arms to ward off blows from war clubs.[23]

Southeastern Indian warriors were at their best when they wielded offensive weapons in individualistic, hand-to-hand combat. They expended relatively little energy in defensive military technology, except that under some conditions Mississippian people encircled their towns with defensive log palisades (see figs. 6, 41, 49, 53). At certain times and places, Mississippian warriors may have worn woven cane and wooden slat body armor, though the

Fig. 4. A Mississippian warrior running with a "mace" war club in his left hand and a severed human head in his right hand. The design is incised on a gorget made from a disc cut from a seashell. (National Museum of the American Indian, Smithsonian Institution)

evidence for this is minimal. They possessed shields, but there is little evidence that shields played an important role in combat. Mississippian warriors wore minimal clothing when they fought—sometimes wearing only a breechcloth—and their emphasis was on speed and agility (see fig. 4). In contrast, Spanish foot soldiers wore elaborate defensive body armor, and they had the advantage of matchlock guns, crossbows, and steel weapons (see fig. 10). They were at risk, however, when they got separated from their horsemen and fell under attack by the agile warriors of the Southeast.

In addition to their individualistic fighting, the Southeastern chiefdoms

Fig. 5. The formation of several companies of bow- and club-wielding warriors under the Timucuan chief Outina (1565). Engraving by Theodore de Bry after a watercolor drawing by Jacques Le Moyne de Morgues. Theodore de Bry, *Americae*, part 2, 1591. (National Anthropological Archives, Smithsonian Institution)

were capable of mobilizing large numbers of warriors (fig. 5) and mounting co-ordinated attacks. This included forming men up into companies, each with its own leader, with the chief acting as a kind of commanding officer. When Indians fought Spaniards in such contests, however, they found that their military organization was decidedly inferior to that of the Spaniards.

If De Soto or any of his men inquired deeply into the thought or character of the Indians they encountered, extant documents do not record it. A priest on the expedition, Sebastián Cañete, may have done so, but only a very brief account by him has survived.[24] What can be said about the social institutions and belief systems of the Indians of the sixteenth-century Southeast must be inferred from Spaniards' written accounts of their actions; from what is known about them in later times (assuming that their belief systems were not completely obliterated by the passage of two or three centuries); and, with all due caution, from observations anthropologists have made on people living in chiefdoms in other parts of the world.

Perhaps the most notable influence on the character of the Indians of the

Southeast is that they lived in very small societies. People were born into a village that might contain no more than about three hundred to five hundred people, and they might live out their entire lives in such a village (see fig. 49). Beyond one's village, one's chiefdom might contain no more than about five thousand people, and one could feasibly have some knowledge of a very large percentage of *all* the individuals in the total population of one's chiefdom. In some places in the Southeast, chiefdoms were incorporated into larger paramount chiefdoms. In such instances, one would have some knowledge of individuals in the larger paramount chiefdom, which might contain as many as fifty thousand people. Beyond one's paramount chiefdom, there were societies of people on all sides who were enemies, or potential enemies. Beyond this, one's knowledge of more far-flung people was apt to be strongly colored by notions embedded in one's belief system.

But most of one's effective relationships were with the people living close by, in one's own village. In a social universe of five hundred people, all relationships were many-stranded. People had relationships with other individuals in their village in many social contexts. Because of this, any action by anyone in one's social universe very often had implications for oneself. In such intense social contexts, people came to regard each other's behavior with extreme interest. They inquired closely into the intentions and motives behind acts both public and private. And for the same reason, they tried to conceal their own intentions and motives as much as possible.

There was a social group even smaller than the village—the lineage or clan—to which Southeastern Indians owed their primary allegiance. Lineages and clans were groups of blood relatives who provided a person's primary support. They took care of their own. It is likely that in the sixteenth century, as in the eighteenth century, the members of a clan sought their own "justice." They never forgave the killing of one of their own. If a person in one's clan were killed, one was obliged to kill the killer, or else a member of the killer's clan. A balance had to be exacted to set the matter straight. Vengeance was very much a part of the social world of the Southeastern Indians, and they would go far to exact it.[25]

And just as their social worlds were small, bounded, and composed of intricate, many-stranded relationships, the philosophical knowledge with which the Southeastern Indians interpreted their world was similarly organized. They believed that they existed—literally—in the center of the world. And all around them, in the four cardinal directions as well as above and below, were spiritual beings who were attentive to what went on among the people—the principal people—who lived in the center of the world. One sought to keep these spiritual beings balanced off against each other, so that none got the upper hand.

Just as people inquired into the motives and intentions behind every act in their village, using various techniques of divination the Indians sought to inquire into the motives and actions of spiritual beings. The Indians believed that some individuals possessed the power to divine the intentions of spirits and in so doing were able to explain why mysterious or threatening events occurred. In the eighteenth century it puzzled Europeans when a group of Indian warriors would suddenly decide to cancel a planned attack. But if the omens were bad, warriors would not hesitate to abort a mission and go back home.

Sixteenth-century Spaniards noted that Southeastern Indian societies were structurally similar to their own society in one respect: some Indians possessed more social honor than others. Some appeared to be nobles (see fig. 5), while others were commoners. But in fact the Indians were not organized into social classes, as were the Spaniards. Rather, they were ranked in terms of their closeness of kinship to the chief. Closest of all to the chief were his or her siblings, and the more senior of these siblings ranked higher than did the younger. Moreover, the children of higher-ranked siblings ranked higher than those of lower-ranked siblings, and these principles applied uniformly through the generations. This concern with precise degrees of ranking was probably greatest in the chief's clan, for these individuals were the ones who had most to gain from their rank, but to some degree all members of a chiefdom had some awareness and concern with ranking. In principle, this ranking was conferred upon a person by birth, and it was inalterable.

Most of the important matters in a Southeastern Indian's life were determined by the fact of being born into a particular clan, at some ranked distance from the chief, and from the fact of marrying a person who likewise belonged to a particular clan, different from one's own. Beyond this ascribed social status, obtained simply by being born, one of the principal ways in which a man could improve his social standing was in the arena of warfare. In the sixteenth century, possibly even more than in the eighteenth century, the darling passion of young Southeastern Indian males was to attain skill and achievement in war. By performing meritorious acts against the enemies of his chiefdom, a man could ascend in status. Judging from the high proportion of martial symbols in relation to all other symbols recovered from Mississippian archaeological sites, the young men were heavily propagandized to become warriors.[26]

Even though Mississippian chiefdoms were capable of placing large forces of fighting men on the field of battle, the brash, one-on-one, lightning ambush of an enemy was the most favored kind of combat. The creatures Southeastern Indian men admired were hunters who killed by cleverness or stealth, and most particularly by a swift attack. They admired the spider, the rattlesnake, the cougar, and most especially the peregrine falcon. The peregrine kills other birds on the wing, in a lightning attack, and it will not hesitate to attack a bird twice its size. With its rakish beak, unwavering stare, and V-shape eye marking (see fig. 4), its face is death itself.

Southeastern Indians strongly identified with their chiefdom, and they were protective of their chiefs. When De Soto's men interrogated their prisoners, asking them to which chiefdom they belonged, they sometimes answered indignantly, as if someone had dared to imply that they belonged to any other. And when De Soto would occasionally seize their chiefs and hold them as hostages for the good behavior of their people, the chiefs' subjects would sometimes make a move to rise up and free them. In at least one instance, one of De Soto's prisoners committed suicide rather than betray his chief.

Archaeologists are only just now beginning to grasp the overall shape of the long-term development and short-term dynamics of Mississippian societies. It is now clear enough that the developmental path of any particular Mississippian society was not onward and upward forever. The Mississippian archaeological record is full of beginnings and endings, sites built and abandoned, times of feast and times of famine, and in much of this adversity one suspects that Mississippian peoples' greatest adversaries were themselves. Mississippian societies were neither utopias nor peaceable kingdoms.

Nascent Mississippian chiefdoms began forming at a number of locations across the Southeast between about A.D. 800 and 1100. Most notably, one of these chiefdoms, Cahokia (fig. 6), arose in the fertile American Bottom, east of present-day St. Louis. And at the same time, or shortly afterward, chiefdoms began forming in the central Mississippi Valley and along the Arkansas River. To the south they arose in the Mississippi delta and along the Black Warrior River in Alabama. And southeast from the American Bottom they arose on the Tennessee River in eastern Tennessee, and along the Etowah, Chattahoochee-Apalachicola, Ocmulgee, and Oconee Rivers in Georgia. It is likely that these earliest, or "pristine," chiefdoms arose very gradually and with little evident artistic or ideological elaboration. There is no archaeological evidence of a high level of warfare during this early period.

It was during the Middle Mississippian period, from about A.D. 1100 to 1350, that these pristine chiefdoms developed elaborate art and community

Fig. 6. Artist's reconstruction of the largest Mississippian community, the Cahokia Mounds site, circa A.D. 1150. The Monks Mound is at the upper end of a large plaza, and the complex is surrounded by a bastioned palisade nearly two miles long. The circle of posts to the left is the "woodhenge." Painting by William R. Iseminger. (Cahokia Mounds State Historic Site)

forms and, it is not to be doubted, elaborate ideological justifications for the authority of the chief and his lineage. During the Middle Mississippian period the chiefdoms produced their most elaborate artistic expressions, and warfare became a grim concomitant of Mississippian life.

The population of existing Mississippian chiefdoms expanded during this middle period, and it was at this time that some few of the chiefdoms achieved their most elaborated form. This was the period in which the massive mounds at Cahokia were built, as well as the very large palisaded town; and it was at the end of this period that Cahokia went into steep decline and dissolution. This is the period in which the Spiro mounds were built in eastern Oklahoma, and a spectacular array of artifacts including superbly incised marine shells were interred in them (see fig. 8). This was also the time when numerous mounds were constructed at sites such as Moundville in Alabama (see fig. 53), Etowah in Georgia (see fig. 46), Hiwassee Island in Tennessee, and Lake Jackson in northern Florida.

In all of these large Middle Mississippian chiefdoms there is evidence that notable effort was expended in justifying and sanctifying the legitimacy of the ruling lineage. This was the period during which the largest and most elaborate mounds were built; it was also the period during which the most impressive artistic productions of the Mississippian period were realized (e.g., fig. 7). It would seem that the leadership in Middle Mississippian societies expended great effort in instituting and perpetuating a sacred order. That is, they sought to persuade their people to obey, and to think the sacred order and do the sacred order, not from threat or coercion but because it was the only way to think and act. The Sun was in her heaven, blazing her way daily across the sky, and the chief and his blood kinsmen were the Sun's representatives on earth. Hence, it may be that Mississippian ideology was not based on newly developed knowledge but was an elaboration of some of the Southeastern Indians' oldest, most unquestioned assumptions.

It is in this way that some of the art motifs of the Southeastern Ceremonial Complex might be explained. Many years ago archaeologists realized that all across the Southeast during the Middle Mississippian period the same symbolic motifs were used in the various art forms (fig. 8). These symbols were not carried from one place to another by traveling religious missionaries or by means of a sudden nativistic movement, as was once thought. The similarity exists because all Mississippian societies found themselves faced with devising symbolic responses to similar social and political problems, and they all drew upon the same ideological substratum.

Fig. 7. Sculpted stone statues of a female (*left*) and male (*right*) from the Etowah site at Cartersville, Georgia. The male sits in lotus position while the female has her legs tucked beneath her. (Etowah Indian Mounds State Historic Site, Georgia Department of Natural Resources)

The Mississippian mode of organization spread rapidly, between about A.D. 1100 and 1350, and in marginal areas it continued to spread and become stronger until the time of Spanish exploration. This is thought to have occurred by means of two processes. In some cases, chiefdoms segmented into two parts, and one part moved away to settle an unoccupied area. In other cases, societies outside the Mississippian area adopted Mississippian organizational and cultural trappings, probably as a defensive measure. The chiefdoms that formed in the central Mississippi Valley appear to have been the earliest (map 2). Subsequently, variant Mississippian cultures developed in all directions: to the southwest, the Arkansas Valley culture of Arkansas and the Caddo culture in what is now northwestern Louisiana and east Texas; the Plaquemine culture along the lower Mississippi Valley and in adjacent areas of Louisiana and Mississippi; and the Moundville culture of the Tombigbee and Black Warrior Rivers. Further east the Hiwassee Island culture developed in the Tennessee Valley; the Savannah culture dominated a broad swath of

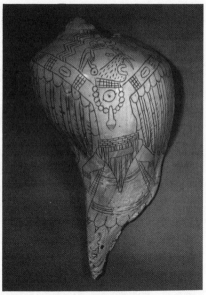

Fig. 8. Incised shell drinking cup from the Spiro site. Southeastern Ceremonial Complex motifs depicted here include the pointed apron or pouch; the barred oval; the shell columella worn dangling on a necklace; the dangling, beaded forelock; and a man in the costume of a bird, probably a raptor. The stepped design above the man's head may represent the several levels of a stepped, bowl-shaped upper world. (National Museum of the American Indian, Smithsonian Institution)

northeastern Alabama and northern and eastern Georgia; the Pisgah culture dominated the Blue Ridge Mountains; and the Peedee culture was in central South Carolina. And from west to east, coastal variants of Mississippian include the Pensacola, Fort Walton, Alachua, Safety Harbor, and St. Johns cultures.[27]

At the same time Mississippian societies were attempting to consolidate and solidify themselves, they were faced by serious challenges. Because chiefs inherited their positions, and because it was a desirable position, it is likely there were rival claimants and that struggle and even insurrection may have occurred. Perhaps the Fort Walton chiefdom on the Apalachicola River split during the Middle Mississippian period because of such a conflict.

Another challenge was that during the Middle Mississippian period, the number of chiefdoms in the Southeast increased. The competition for resources, perhaps most especially for fish and game, contributed to an increased level of warfare among the chiefdoms. Some warfare may have had purely social causes. The most dramatic testimony to this increased warfare is the appearance in the archaeological record of impressive defensive structures—

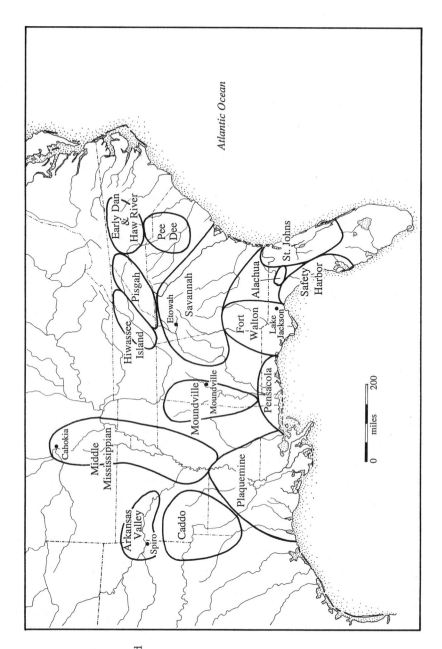

Map 2. Archaeological
cultures of the Middle
Mississippian period.
Bold lines enclose the
areal extent of the more
important Middle
Mississippian cultures.
The locations of selected
archaeological sites are
indicated by dots.

Atlantic Ocean

Early Dan
&
Haw River

Pee
Dee

Pisgah

Savannah

Hiwassee
Island

Etowah

St. Johns

Alachua

Fort
Walton

Lake
Jackson

Safety
Harbor

Moundville

Moundville

Pensacola

Middle
Mississippian

Cahokia

Plaquemine

Arkansas
Valley

Caddo

Spiro

0   200
miles

strong wooden palisades, sometimes with towers, and often surrounded by ditches.

Corn was the principal cultivar of Mississippian farmers, and as a grain grown gigantic, corn depleted nitrogen from the soil. And even though Mississippian farmers had their pick of the richest 1 percent of soils in the Southeast, repeated tilling of land depleted it, and over the long term productivity fell. Such declining fertility may have underlain a long-term secular trend powerful enough to have destabilized the pristine chiefdoms of the Middle Mississippian period.[28]

Finally, the climate worsened worldwide at around 1350 to 1450, becoming colder by several degrees. At the time of the De Soto expedition it was notably colder than it is today. And between 1300 and 1600 there were several decades-long dry periods. Both of these climatic changes must have posed serious challenges for Mississippian farmers and may in turn have exacerbated the level of social conflict.

Perhaps one or more of these challenges proved to be too much for the old pristine Mississippian chiefdoms. Around 1350 the people ceased adding more earth to the largest mounds. Their elite artistic productions became less spectacular, though they continued making pottery that was technically very good and pleasing to the eye. Some pristine chiefdoms evidently stagnated. Both Etowah and Moundville went into decline. Some failed spectacularly. Cahokia went into steep decline, and the vast area it had dominated became a wilderness—the so-called Vacant Quarter—an area that was still uninhabited at the time of the De Soto expedition. In another instance, the chiefdoms along the Savannah River collapsed. In 1540, except for a chiefdom that remained on its headwaters, the Savannah River ran its entire course through unpopulated wilderness.

Archaeologists do not currently have evidence for an absolute decline in population all across the Mississippian region after 1350. De Soto and his men certainly encountered substantial populations of people, and there is evidence that some of the people in this Late Mississippian world were engaged in building societies above the chiefdom level. These were paramount chiefdoms, that is, constellations of chiefdoms under the sway of a particular chiefdom that was dominant or paramount. These paramount chiefdoms could be multicultural and multilingual. Although the great Middle Mississippian societies may have faded, the Indians of the Late Mississippian period were not necessarily in decline when De Soto and his army entered the Southeast. It seems rather that they may have just been embarking on the task of building larger social entities and developing new social and political forms.[29]

Early Spanish Exploration of North America

As the Reconquest of Spain came to a close, its military impetus carried over in two directions—southward and westward. To the south, Spaniards launched a crusade across the strait of Gibraltar into North Africa. The people of North Africa were in political disarray at the close of the fifteenth century, and they were a tempting target for Spaniards flushed with their victory over the Moors. Spain achieved significant victories in North Africa in 1497 and in 1505, but it was only in 1509–10 that a substantial Spanish army was sent across the strait. Africa, however, proved not to be so easy to conquer. Perhaps this was because Ferdinand and Isabela would only commit themselves to achieving a limited occupation along the Mediterranean coast, leaving the interior to the Moors. This left the Spaniards in North Africa vulnerable to persistent depredations by Barbary pirates and periodic attacks by Moors. When Charles V mounted an expedition against Algiers in 1541, it was a disaster for Spain. The nature of the land and people of North Africa were such that a simple continuation of the tactics of the Reconquest would not work. The terrain in North Africa was difficult, and there was little booty to be taken. Spain's crusade southward into Africa foundered.[30]

It was Spain's thrust toward the west, across the Atlantic, that was to be so fateful for the Southeastern chiefdoms, and for the world generally. After Spaniards recaptured Seville from the Moors in the thirteenth century, a community established itself at this city, with merchants and investors looking for commercial opportunities. They first set their sights on the Canary Islands (see map 1), which appear to have been discovered by the Genoese in the fourteenth century. The conquest of the Canaries began in earnest in 1482, and it continued until 1493.

With the conquest of the Canaries, Spaniards began putting together the legal and economic mechanisms they would later use in their conquest of the New World. They thought of their campaign against the non-Christian native people of the Canaries as a holy war against infidels, and the assault was a thoroughgoing blend of private and royal initiatives. Although the ventures were privately financed, they had to be authorized by the crown in a capitulación, in which the leader (and often principal investor) of an expedition was granted the right to certain rewards. He might be appointed adelantado, and he was granted a substantial share in the spoils of the conquest, in land and slaves, as well as other concessions. But the crown reserved for itself rights to any conquered territory, so that, for example, the only way a town in a conquered territory could secure its rights and privileges was through a royal charter. The crown was able to retain impressive control over a world empire that in time became very extensive and far-flung.[31]

Not only were the Canary Islands a place in which the techniques used in the conquest of the New World were pioneered, the islands were to become a vital way station in that conquest. From the very first oceanic voyages, the Canaries were a convenient stopover for ships sailing from Spain to the New World. Columbus, for example, on all his voyages to the New World put in at the Canaries to resupply and make repairs.

After Columbus made his discovery of the New World in 1492, the conquest of Hispaniola, Cuba, and other Caribbean Islands was completed in about another two decades (map 3). In 1519 Panama was conquered, and in that same year Hernán Cortés began his conquest of the Aztec state. More than anything else, the conquest of the Aztecs inspired Spanish adventurers to look for other states to conquer. Cortés proved that there existed in the Indies populous states whose people possessed precious substances that could be seized and taken to Europe as instant wealth.

The Spanish colonists in the Caribbean were slow to realize that an entire continent lay to the north. Although Juan Ponce de León was surely not the first European to sight the coast of eastern Florida, documentary evidence attests to his sighting it in 1513, on Easter (Pascua Florida); hence, he named his discovery La Florida.[32] He sailed southward along the coast, rounding the southern point of the peninsula, and landed briefly on the western coast in the vicinity of Charlotte Harbor. He returned to La Florida in 1521 and attempted to found a colony, probably at Charlotte Harbor, but he was attacked by Indians and his colony failed. He himself was wounded and later died. Ponce de León assumed that the Florida peninsula was simply another island in the Caribbean, an error that was perpetuated on maps for some years.

The principal impetus for the Spaniards' exploration to the north of their Caribbean colonies was their need for slave labor. The native population of the islands on which Spanish colonies were founded was quickly decimated by Old World diseases, forcing the Spaniards to look further afield for Indian slaves to work their mines, sugar plantations, and cattle ranches. They began raiding the Bahamas for slaves. At some time between 1514 and 1515, Captain Pedro de Salazar sailed from Hispaniola to the Bahamas to capture slaves. But venturing further, he landed at a place that lay to the northwest of the Bahamas—on the coast of present-day South Carolina—and there he captured some Indians who were very large in size, much larger than Indians of the Caribbean or of Central America.[33] Again, Salazar assumed that the place where he made his landfall was the coast of a large island.

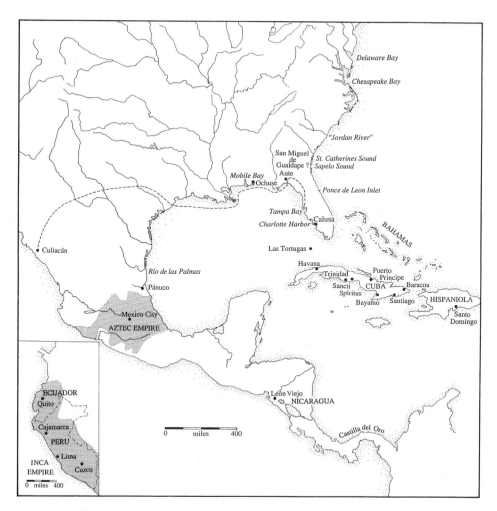

Map 3. The New World in the sixteenth century. Included are important locations of Spanish activity. The dashed line shows the approximate route followed by Panfilo de Narváez and Alvar Núñez Cabeza de Vaca.

Salazar took his cargo of enslaved Indians back to Hispaniola, and in this way the existence of what was at first called the Island of Giants became known to Lucas Vázquez de Ayllón, a judge in the colonial government of Hispaniola. In 1521 a slaving ship commanded by Pedro de Quejo, partly financed by Ayllón, met up with a second such ship commanded by Francisco Gordillo, who was at that time slaving in the Bahamas. When, after much searching in these islands, they were unable to find any Indians to enslave, they sailed northward and then westward, and on June 24 they sighted the coast of the continent that was Salazar's Island of Giants. Their landfall appears to have been the mouth of the Santee River, which they named the River Jordan, but they soon discovered Winyaw Bay to the north, and they sailed there. They gave presents to the Indians—items of clothing, axes, "false pearls," iron tools, and combs. The Indians gave them, perhaps in exchange, a quantity of pearls and some "terrestrial gems."[34] These pearls and gems were to pique the interest of Spaniards and other Europeans in the Southeast for many years to come.

Quejo and Gordillo carried out limited exploration of the coast, learning that the people who lived there were subject to a powerful native ruler known as Datha (also known as Du-a-e or Duhare). The chiefdom ruled by Datha was probably Cofitachequi, a native polity that would figure prominently in the De Soto expedition.

On July 15, just before departing, Quejo and Gordillo enticed about sixty Indians aboard their ships, promising them gifts. But once the Indians were on board, the Spaniards hauled in their anchors and set sail, condemning their guests to slavery. When they reached Santo Domingo with their human cargo, the people gathered to gawk at the tall, brown-skinned slaves who were dressed in animal skins. The enslaved Indians were put to work on plantations. Some of them died from disease, and some escaped into the interior of the island. One who survived became a pearl-diver. But the one who is of most interest was a native of a town or polity named Chicora (probably in present-day South Carolina), whom they named Francisco.[35] Francisco learned Spanish and became a personal servant to Ayllón, who is said to have treated him as if he were his own son.[36] He became Ayllón's principal source of information on the newly discovered land.

Ayllón and several others decided to petition the king for a capitulación to explore and colonize the new land. Accordingly, later in 1521, Ayllón sailed to Spain to deal with some problems of governance in Hispaniola and to pursue his own interests. Ayllón took Francisco with him. While the two of them were in Valladolid, seeking an audience with Charles V, they were for a time guests of the Italian humanist and historian Pietro Martiere d'Anghiera, known to English speakers as Peter Martyr. Martyr interviewed Ayllón and Francisco, inquiring into the nature of the newly discovered land and its peoples, and he took notes that he incorporated into a later edition of his book *De Orbe Novo—The New World*. Using this information from Francisco, Martyr wrote the first ethnographic description of the culture of the native people of North America.

In many respects the account of the people of South Carolina Martyr got from Francisco is consistent with what archaeologists have reconstructed about the Mississippian culture. Francisco told of the existence of Datha, a powerful chief in the interior. Datha and his kinsmen were said to be physically much larger than their subjects. Datha had many tributaries under his power or influence, his domain extending, it was said, for some way up and down the Atlantic coast. Francisco said the people of Duhare were "white," but he may have been alluding to a symbolic attribute of the people of Duhare rather than a literal description of their skin color. That is, in much of the Southeast *white* was symbolic of authority and peace. Datha was carried upon the shoulders of his subjects when he wished to travel from place to place. As sovereign, Datha lived in a special house (though not of stone, as Martyr says), and in his dwelling there were statues (which Francisco called *Inamahari*) of a male and a female, carved at about the size of three-year-old children (see fig. 7). These were periodically exhibited at agricultural rituals. The people built earthen mounds whereon orators stood to deliver speeches and eulogies for the dead.[37] All of these are aspects of Mississippian culture that have been corroborated by archaeological and historical information.

But distortions of various kinds are present in the stories Martyr got from Francisco and Ayllón. Some of these distortions are no doubt due to the fact that Francisco came from a small, preliterate society with a constricted worldview encapsulated within a religious belief system. For example, Francisco told Ayllón a story about the people of Inziganin, who were once visited by people who had tails as thick as a man's arm and a yard long, so that they had to dig holes in the ground in order to sit down. They had scaly skin and fingers that were as wide as they were long, and they only ate raw fish. In relating other matters, Francisco may have exaggerated the advantages of the land to make it more attractive to the Spaniards, so that he might have occasion to return to his homeland. He told, for example, of the province of Xapira, near Datha, where quantities of pearls and gems could be obtained.

Some of the distortions in what was told to Peter Martyr may have been deliberately introduced by Ayllón. For example, Martyr was persuaded that the people of Chicora kept herds of deer and used their milk; that they kept chickens, ducks, and geese; and that they tended orchards of figs, almonds, and spice plants. Even though Quejo had taken a solar latitude reading of 33° 30' north at the place where they anchored, back in Santo Domingo, Ayllón claimed that the new land was located at about 34°, and when he was in Spain, Ayllón stated on various occasions that it lay at 35°, 36°, and 37°, the parallels in which Andalucia lay. Ayllón's motive in shifting this measure of latitude northward may have been to make the new land seem more attractive to people in Spain, because at that time Europeans generally assumed, incorrectly, that places situated at the same latitude anywhere in the world should have similar plants and animals. Ayllón also claimed the Indians were cannibals and sodomites, thereby justifying enslavement.[38] Thus, the new land was depicted as a land of milk and honey, begging for colonization. Ayllón specifically wanted exclusive rights to the pearl fisheries he expected to find at Xapira.[39]

After Ayllón returned to Santo Domingo, he sent Pedro de Quejo back to the land of Chicora to explore the coast. In 1525 Quejo took two caravels and sixty men with orders to explore two hundred leagues of coast (about 240 nautical miles), taking soundings and bearings. He was to take possession of the land and erect stone markers. Quejo did in fact spend about two and a half months exploring the coast from about Fernandina Beach, in Florida, northward to about Delaware Bay.[40]

Based on information collected by Quejo, Ayllón determined that the most favorable place to locate his colony was at the Jordan River, the probable site of the 1521 landfall, and the river that led to Duhare and the gems of Xapira. He assembled about six hundred colonists, recruited from Spain and the Indies, including women, children, and some black slaves. He took along cattle, sheep, pigs, and horses. Father Bartolomé de las Casas and others watched the little fleet of ships depart from Santo Domingo.

On August 9, 1526, the fleet approached the entrance to what they took to be the Jordan River—either the South Santee River or Winyaw Bay. But as they crossed the bar at the entrance, their main ship ran aground and sank, destroying much of their food and supplies. Moreover, they soon found that the place they had chosen for their colony was unsatisfactory. They found no soil suitable for farming, and few Indians lived nearby. To make things worse, a few days after landing, Francisco and their other Indian interpreters fled the colony and were never seen again.[41]

Ayllón sent at least three parties by boat to explore to the south to try to find a better location for a colony. They explored inlets as far south as Ponce de León Inlet, finally settling on Gualdape, a bay with a "very powerful" river, possibly Sapelo Sound. This was the territory of a well-documented early historic Indian population—the Guale—living at Pine Harbor, Saint Catherines Island, and other nearby sites. The Guale were farmers, as well as hunters and fishermen. Ayllón loaded most of his colonists on board ship, while he and the able-bodied men, the horsemen, and possibly the livestock went by land. The two parties rendezvoused at the new location—possibly Harris Neck—

and they built a town: San Miguel de Gualdape.[42] But they soon ran short of food, and many fell ill. Ayllón himself fell ill and died. With Ayllón's death, the colony disintegrated and the survivors sailed back to the Caribbean Islands. Only about 150 of them survived.

Martyr's writings became the basis of an alluring legend about the land of Chicora and the "nation" of Duhare. It was fancied to be rich in pearls and other "terrestrial gems." It was said to be a land like Andalucia—the best of Spain—and it was there for the taking. After Ayllón's experience, however, it should have been clear to Spaniards that Chicora was no Andalucia. No easy wealth could be obtained on the coast, and settlement would be hard. But what about the interior? Ayllón and his men had explored inland from Gualdape, but had they gone far enough to reach Duhare and Xapira? There was no assurance that they had, and this part of the legend continued to excite Spaniards for many years. Later, Frenchmen and Englishmen fell victim to its enticement.[43]

In 1528 a second initiative to found a colony on the southeastern coast was led by Pánfilo de Narváez. In his capitulación Narváez secured the right to colonize from the Soto de la Marina River in northern Mexico around the Gulf coast to the southernmost point of the Florida peninsula. Narváez may have intended to establish his colony in northern Mexico, where he might have been positioned to challenge Hernán Cortés, but a storm that blew up as he was approaching Havana forced him to land on the west coast of Florida (see map 3).[44]

Narváez's fleet sighted land on April 12, 1528. They meant to land at Tampa Bay, but they apparently landed north of the entrance to the bay, possibly near present-day John's Pass. When they began exploring they found that from where they put ashore on the coast, the waters of Tampa Bay were less than a day's march to the east. When they made plans about what to do next, they were confused about where the entrance to Tampa Bay was located. Some of Narváez's seamen erroneously thought the entrance to Tampa Bay lay to the north of where they put ashore. To compound their problems, Narváez then made the error of separating his men from their supplies. He and his soldiers began marching northward, intending to rendezvous with the supply ships at where they thought Tampa Bay lay. Not only was Narváez now separated from his supplies, he did not have the services of a good Indian translator. Hence, he was not able to obtain reliable intelligence about the lay of the land.

Narváez and his army of 40 horsemen and 260 footmen marched northward, paralleling the Gulf coast, through very poor, sparsely populated country. Their food supply dwindled, and they were reduced to eating the inner leaves of palmetto. They crossed the Withlacoochee and Santa Fe Rivers, learned of the existence of the Apalachee Indians, and then they turned westward. They crossed the Suwannee River and came to the Aucilla River, which was the boundary of the territory of the Apalachees. When Narváez seized an Apalachee chief, his subjects became hostile, launching repeated attacks on the Spaniards.

Some scholars are of the opinion that Narváez did not reach the central town of Apalachee, but rather one of the lesser towns, perhaps near the Aucilla River. Narváez and his army remained at this Apalachee town for just over three weeks, sending out several parties in various directions to learn the lay of the land. Nothing is recorded about what lay to the north, but to the west the land did not look promising. Narváez learned that a village—Aute—lay to the south, near the coast, and that supplies of food could be obtained there.

After a journey through difficult terrain, they arrived at the end of July at Aute, finding that the natives had set it on fire. But they did find some supplies of food. After a short time, they traveled about a day's journey from Aute to an inlet on the coast where they began building five crude boats in which they intended to sail to Mexico. Many of the men were ill. They sent periodic raiding parties into Aute to procure food, and every third day they killed a horse and butchered it, giving most of the meat to those who were ill and to those who were building the boats. They called this place—probably the mouth of the St. Marks River—the Bay of the Horses.[45]

Finally, in September 1528 they rowed their clumsy boats out into the Gulf and began sailing along the coast. They soon began starving and suffering from dehydration, and their vessels were not seaworthy. Near Mobile Bay some Indians paddled out in a canoe and met them peaceably. Doroteo Teodoro, a Greek, accompanied by a black man went ashore with the Indians to look for drinking water. But the two did not return, and the others presumed they had been killed by the Indians.[46]

Some of the boats were later lost in a storm. Others were cast up on a barrier island off the Texas coast. Some of those who reached shore were killed by Indians. Some of the starving men cannibalized each other. After years of extreme hardship, only Alvár Núñez Cabeza de Vaca and three others managed to walk westward across Texas to safety in Mexico. They were the sole survivors. It is principally from Cabeza de Vaca's writings that we know of these events.

2
Hernando de Soto
The Man Who Would Be Marqués of La Florida

Hernando de Soto was born in Extremadura of parents who were hidalgos, though of modest means. Two towns—Badajoz and Jerez de los Caballeros (see map 1)—claim to be the site of his birth. All that can be said with certainty is that as a child he spent time in both, and in his 1539 will he specified that his body be interred at Jerez de los Caballeros.[1] There is uncertainty as well about his date of birth, but it appears to have been in the year 1500.[2]

Extremadura, in southwestern Spain, was a region of poverty and hardship, and like many young Extremadurans, De Soto chose to seek his fortune elsewhere.[3] Vasco Núñez de Balboa, the first European to cross the Isthmus of Panama and see the waters of the Pacific Ocean, was born in Badajoz, and perhaps Balboa's fame influenced De Soto's decision to seek his fortune in the New World. It was said of him that he went to the New World possessing nothing but his sword and shield. This was true as well of other Extremadurans—Francisco Pizarro, Hernán Cortés, Pedro de Alvarado, Pedro de Valdiva, and Francisco de Orellana—who went to the New World to gain wealth and fame.[4]

De Soto had his first schooling in the art of conquering Indians in the expedition of Pedro Arias de Avila in Castilla del Oro (see map 3), modern-day

Panama. Pedro Arias de Avila—whose name is usually shortened to Pedrárias—was an aged, cruel veteran of the campaign in North Africa. De Soto sailed from Spain bound for Castilla del Oro on February 25, 1514, and arrived in the New World when he was about fourteen years old. As such, he was an entering freshman in an exceedingly hard school. Hundreds of the early Castilla del Oro colonists died of starvation. Others learned to raid Indians and extort food from them, often with great brutality. At first serving as a page for Pedrárias, within a very few years De Soto began to rise in prominence, and people began calling him "Captain," a term that referred not so much to a military rank as to the ability to command men. While still a very young man—perhaps seventeen or eighteen years old—he formed a *compañia*, or "universal partnership," with two others, Hernán Ponce de León and Francisco Compañón. In this partnership, the three members agreed that they would hold all their property in common, so long as they should live. They became, in effect, brothers, living together, eating at the same table, and defending each other's interests in a context in which one's acquaintances could quickly become one's mortal enemies; hence it was important to have at least a few staunch allies. In particular, the tyrant Pedrárias was notorious for executing his subjects, and he went so far as to execute Balboa, his own son-in-law, whom he accused of treason and conspiracy. De Soto and his two compañeros shared everything equally among themselves—all that they possessed and would possess in the future.[5]

A few years later when Compañón died from an epidemic disease, De Soto and Ponce de León handed over his third of their commonly owned wealth to public officials and to Compañón's heirs. Ponce de León and De Soto remained in the partnership. The two of them amassed a small fortune in the conquest of Panama and more particularly in the conquest of Nicaragua, where Spaniard vied with Spaniard in a bloody scramble for power. De Soto served as *alcalde* of León (now called León Viejo), the most important town in Nicaragua. He built a house fronting the plaza of León Viejo, and he took a mistress, Juana Hernández, a commoner. De Soto took full advantage of his position as alcalde, but holding a municipal office did not satisfy him. He had learned well the art of surviving under the paranoid rule of Pedrárias, but what he longed for was more independence.

Between 1524 and 1528 an opportunity began to materialize when a series of nautical explorations financed by Francisco Pizarro, Diego de Almagro, and Hernando de Luque probed the northwestern Pacific coast of South America. In 1528 they entered the Gulf of Guayaquil and reached the Inca city of Tumbez. They quickly realized they had touched the fringe of an advanced civilization complete with domesticated animals, clothing made of woven fabric, and wealth in precious metals. Francisco Pizarro returned to Spain and procured a capitulación to discover and conquer Peru.

In 1530 Francisco Pizarro sailed from Spain to Central America with a small army of recruits, including his half-brothers Hernando, Juan, and Gonzalo Pizarro. When Pizarro arrived, Diego de Almagro learned to his disgust that he had been slighted in the capitulación, but he was mollified by the promise of a territory of his own further south than that which was to be conquered by Pizarro.[6]

By about 1530 De Soto and Hernán Ponce de León were among the half-dozen richest men in Nicaragua. They amassed their wealth by ferreting out modest amounts of precious metals in Nicaragua, but even more by the brutal enslavement and sale of local natives. They owned a ship, the *San Gerónimo*, which they primarily used to transport slaves, and they planned to build others. Needing ships as well as men, Hernando Pizarro invited De Soto and Ponce de León to assist in the exploration of Peru. They signed on, and in December 1531 De Soto sailed from Nicaragua in two ships with a contingent of about a hundred men and twenty-five horses. De Soto expected to be second in command of the conquest.

It so happened that Pizarro invaded Peru during the midst of a dynastic struggle and civil war among the Incas. Between 1526 and 1527 the Inca Huayna-Capac had extended the Inca empire from southern Chile to southern Columbia. He died from a plague, perhaps smallpox, and he left his empire under the control of two of his sons, Atahualpa and Huascar. Atahualpa was in charge of the imperial army in the north at Quito, and Huascar succeeded his father as ruler in the south at Cuzco, the capital city of the Inca empire. Both had claimed the throne, and a hard-fought civil war had broken out between their supporters. Huascar had sent his militia north to attack Atahualpa, but Atahualpa had repelled them and had sent his own Quitan troops southward to attack Cuzco, and they succeeded in capturing Huascar. One of Atahualpa's generals, Quisquis, set about exterminating all members of Huascar's family. Huascar was captured and taken northward to Atahualpa's court, but he was assassinated en route, almost certainly by Atahualpa's order.

Pizarro took full advantage of this civil war in conquering the vast Inca empire with an army that was very small, but that nonetheless possessed a vast military superiority. The Incas were slow to realize that this army of hundreds intended to best an army of hundreds of thousands and to conquer an empire numbering in the millions. Plague and anarchy were the Spaniards' allies, but it was the mounted lancers who won the day, time after time, routing the Inca armies. And Hernando de Soto, commanding the vanguard of the best horsemen, was often in the very thick of these encounters. It was he who led the small contingent of horsemen who first met Atahualpa near Cajamarca. When the two met, Atahualpa was seated on a low stool, and he kept his eyes averted as De Soto rode up on his horse. In order to intimidate Atahualpa, De Soto rode up so close to him that breath from his horse's nostrils buffeted a fringe, a badge of office, the Inca wore on his forehead. But again the Inca never blinked an eye, and pretended to be unimpressed.

In an outrageously bold maneuver, with 168 Spaniards pitted against thousands of Incas, Pizarro contrived to slaughter Atahualpa's retinue and to capture him, and De Soto played an important role in this capture. Later, desperate to purchase his freedom, Atahualpa commanded his subjects to collect together an entire room full of gold and silver, though Pizarro executed him anyway. When this wealth was divided, De Soto received a portion that was the third largest after Francisco Pizarro and Hernando Pizarro. De Soto later added to this fortune by looting and extorting all the gold and silver he could lay his hands on.

De Soto played a leading role in the march southward from Cajamarca down the Inca road to Cuzco, at times advancing ahead of the others, putting himself and his men in harm's way in doing battle with the valiant Inca general Quisquis. After Cuzco fell, De Soto again led a contingent of horsemen and five thousand Inca warriors in pursuit of General Quisquis. De Soto failed to kill him, but later Quisquis was killed by his own troops who wished to surrender when Quisquis was unwilling to do so.

For a time De Soto served as lieutenant governor of Cuzco. After putting down the disorder among Spaniards after Cuzco fell and the men began looting, he oversaw the creation of a city council, courts, and a police force. Living in a spectacular palace that had been built by the emperor Huayna-Capac, he took as his mistress a beautiful Incan noblewoman, Tocto Chimpu, who was renamed Leonor, after De Soto's mother. They had a daughter, who was also given the name Leonor.

In 1535 the king granted Diego de Almagro rights to a portion of South America that lay to the south of the 270 leagues specified in Pizarro's capitulación. Essentially, Almagro was to have the territory of modern-day Chile. De Soto offered to buy into this expedition as an investor, but Almagro rejected his offer, and De Soto was deeply humiliated.

When De Soto went to Peru with Pizarro, his partner Ponce de León remained behind in Nicaragua for a time to look after their interests there. But when he later joined De Soto in Peru, the two again lived in the same house, and their partnership continued as before. They formally renewed their partnership in Cuzco on June 27, 1535.

Evidently, De Soto's agreement with the Pizarros was ambiguous, because later it became clear that he and the Pizarro brothers had different ideas about what was De Soto's due under the terms of their agreement. The Pizarros claimed that De Soto and Ponce de León only contributed their ships to the enterprise, and for this the two of them were due *encomiendas*, grants of Indian land entrusted to them as colonists. In addition, De Soto was made lieutenant governor of the main city of the land they conquered. But De Soto thought the fact that he supplied crucial men and horses for the conquest entitled him to be second in command of all Peru. Hence, he had been angered when he arrived in Peru and found that Francisco Pizarro's own brother, Hernando, was second in command. De Soto knew his position in the conquest of Peru was on shaky ground, and Almagro's spurning him was the last straw. It was clear to him that if he was to have his own command, he would have to find it elsewhere.[7]

De Soto's greatest ambition was to be marqués of a territory in the New World. He had failed to win a place on Almagro's expedition to Chile. If he remained in Peru, he would forever be a subordinate, and given De Soto's thirst for power, it is doubtful whether Pizarro was altogether comfortable with having him as a subordinate. The overarching strategy of the Pizarros in Peru was to push aside, expel, or if need be, destroy all the men who might challenge them. Hence, after the initial conquest of Peru, many prominent men returned to Spain, including De Soto's men from western Extremadura.[8]

According to a deposition made by Luís de Moscoso in Tenochtitlan in 1547, when things began going badly in Peru, both De Soto and Ponce de León began to talk of returning to Spain. Then De Soto became so annoyed and angered that he decided he would proceed immediately to Spain with Luís de Moscoso, one of his most valued subordinates, leaving Ponce de León behind to attend to their possessions and enterprises. De Soto took with him the gold and silver they had accumulated up to that time in their partnership. They did not divide it between them. Ponce de León authorized De Soto to use it as he saw fit to obtain concessions from Emperor Charles V at the court at Valladolid. In the Peruvian village of Gualuchiri, Luís de Moscoso saw De Soto take possession of this gold and silver, which he estimated to be about a hundred thousand ducats. Whatever De Soto might succeed in gaining through his negotiations at court was to be shared between him and Ponce de León, and De Soto was to return to Peru. All of their real property in Peru and all that was owed to them was to remain in the hands of Ponce de León.[9]

De Soto arrived in Spain in 1536. Though perhaps he and Ponce de León were not yet aware of it, the two had already begun diverging. De Soto wished for new lands to conquer, while Ponce de León wished to return to Spain to enjoy a comfortable life.[10]

In returning to Spain, De Soto claimed to be doing business on behalf of his partnership with Ponce de León.[11] Ponce de León agreed to this action by De Soto, and he authorized him to spend as much as a 110,000 *castellanos* on the initiative.[12] Whatever the precise amount, De Soto arrived in Spain with an immense fortune. In Seville he employed a retinue of servants: a mayordomo, grand master of ceremonies, pages, equerry, a chamberlain, footmen, and other servants.[13] But he found that wealth and the pleasure of displaying wealth did not satisfy him. What he wanted was honor and power. In November 1536 he married Isabel de Bobadilla, daughter of the now-deceased Pedrárias, and he received as dowry the cattle Pedrárias had owned in Panama, along with the slaves who tended them. With this marriage, De Soto gained access to the political influence of the Pedrárias family.[14] He petitioned Emperor Charles V to have his ancestry examined—his proof of the "purity" of his blood—and he was admitted into the elite military Order of Santiago. De Soto wished to be a governor, a marqués, the equal of Cortés and Pizarro.[15] He did not covet any particular part of the Indies. He first asked for the governorship of Quito, from whence he could launch an expedition into the Amazon basin. But this governorship fell under the aegis of the Pizarros, and it was denied him. He next failed to secure the governorship of Guatemala, from whence he could have launched an expedition along the Pacific coast. Perhaps concerned about reprisals by the Pizarros, he asked the court of Charles V to officially confirm his title to the Indians and property he and Ponce de León owned in Peru.[16]

When De Soto first reached Seville, his gold and silver were seized by the Casa de Contratación so that an accounting could be made. When it was returned to him, the crown had held back a reported fifty thousand ducats as a "loan." A year or so later, a portion of this was paid back to De Soto in the form of *juros*, Granada silk annuities.[17] In 1537 Charles V granted him the right to conquer La Florida, and he was appointed adelantado of that venture, as well as governor of Cuba. And to some of the lands he would conquer, he would bear the title marqués.[18]

All previous royal contracts that had granted lands in La Florida were invalid by the time De Soto arrived in Spain because all previous colonization schemes in the Southeast had failed. All three previous contracts were consolidated in De Soto's contract; so he fell heir to Juan Ponce de León's peninsular Florida (the land originally named La Florida), Narváez's Gulf coast, beginning at the Rio de las Palmas, and Ayllón's south Atlantic coast, as well as all the vast territory contained within these areas. The three together were named La Florida by royal decree.

In some of its stipulations, De Soto's capitulación resembled those of Ayllón's and Narváez's. He had four years in which to explore La Florida at his own expense before creating a permanent colony and selecting his own land for settlement, which was to have as a boundary two hundred leagues of the coast (about 640 nautical miles). And within this area, any twelve square leagues could be his personal estate. Unlike Ayllón and Narváez, he was granted authority to confer encomiendas, an enticement that was presumably intended to offset La Florida's reputation as a place that was unhealthy for Spaniards. This authority must have been an extraordinary incentive for investors. He was also granted tax incentives, and after first taking out the crown's customary fifth of any loot or ransom he collected, he could keep for himself one-seventh of what remained, the other six-sevenths going to his men. He was adelantado and governor of Florida for his lifetime. And an important provision in his contract was that he was named governor of Cuba, from whence he could extract the necessary provisions and supplies to get his colony underway, this being a very considerable advantage that Ayllón had lacked.[19]

A few months after De Soto received his capitulación, Cabeza de Vaca returned to Spain, as if back from the dead, with stories and a written account of what he had experienced as a survivor of the Narváez expedition. He and the three others who had gotten out alive had done so by walking westward from the coast of Texas and then southward to Mexico—a remarkable story of human endurance.[20] He described the hardships he and his comrades had suffered, but at the same time he conveyed a strong impression that riches could be obtained in La Florida. In part he encouraged this impression by his refusal to directly answer questions put to him by some of those who were thinking of going with De Soto, who asked him whether there was a rich society in this new land. He would only say that some of the information he possessed was for the king's ears only. Both from what he said and what he refused to say, some drew the conclusion that he himself wished to govern La Florida, and that it was indeed a very rich land.[21]

But De Soto had already been granted the contract to colonize La Florida. He offered Cabeza de Vaca a place in his expedition, but Cabeza de Vaca declined when De Soto would not give him money to purchase a ship. Two of Cabeza de Vaca's relatives—Baltasar de Gallegos and Cristóbal de Espindola—decided to go with De Soto on the basis of what Cabeza de Vaca had told them. When Cabeza de Vaca backed out, Gallegos and Espindola asked him whether they should remain with the expedition. He replied that he had withdrawn because he expected to govern a different territory, and he did not wish to be subservient to another. He advised them to sell their estates and go with De Soto.

Cabeza de Vaca obtained an audience with Emperor Charles V and told him about what he had suffered and seen in the Southeast. The marqués of Astorga gained access to some of the information in the report Cabeza de Vaca gave to the emperor, and on the basis of it he decided to send his brother, Don Antonio Osorio, on the expedition. Two of his kinsmen—Francisco and Garcia Osorio—went along as well. Don Antonio disposed of an income of six hundred thousand reales, which he received from the church, and Francisco Osorio disposed of a village of vassals he owned in the district of Campos.[22]

Cabeza de Vaca seems to have thought one could have a future in La Florida, though precisely what he thought it could have been is unclear. Perhaps it was because in the course of his long walk to Mexico he had encountered people possessing both cotton cloth and turquoise, and had not Cortés first found cotton cloth and turquoise and then gold and silver as he marched toward the Aztecs?[23] Also, in spite of Ayllón's bitter experience with the realities of the Southeast, it is possible that the legend of Chicora and Xapira still lingered in Spain. Whether intentionally or unintentionally, Cabeza de Vaca fostered the mirage of another Peru, another Mexico, in the unexplored land of La Florida. Around De Soto and his associates, hopeful expeditionaries swirled in a kind of frenzy. More wanted to go—some of them wealthy—than could be accommodated.[24]

What was the character of this man who played important roles in the Spanish exploration and conquest of all three major geographical regions in the New World: Central America, South America, and North America? De Soto could sign his name, and he was probably literate, though he did not advance himself through learning, and he shows little of the legalism of some of his contemporaries. He did, however, insist on exact and complete fulfillment of what was stipulated in written documents.[25] At a very young age he became a superb horseman, and he became one of the best lancers in the New World.

From an early age he was fearless and impetuous, and if there was an enemy to be fought, he wanted to be first into the fray. He was a brilliant military leader who won the respect of his men, or at least their obedience. He won high offices in the New World, but he repeatedly abandoned them in favor of further adventures.

His character and personality were shaped by two harsh parents: the Reconquest of Spain and the conquest of Latin America. And he had been schooled by a brutal mentor—Pedrárias. His associates described him as being passionate (*apasionado*), given to snap judgments (*corto de razones*), and as one who did not suffer fools gladly (*mal sufrido*).[26] De Soto may not have been altogether comfortable in society after he returned to Spain. His frontier manners and impetuous personality may have put him at a disadvantage. He had spent his entire adult life in the New World. In Spain, De Soto did not choose to marry a woman from Badajoz, but rather Doña Isabel de Bobadilla, daughter of Pedrárias, a woman of the New World.[27]

De Soto has generally been depicted as a hero in the popular culture of the United States. In his defense it could be said that he shows less savage cunning and vindictiveness than that of the Pizarros. But he was no less ambitious and greedy than they were, and he wished to be their equal. He wished to conquer and govern a portion of the New World comparable to Mexico and Peru. He was like most of his contemporaries in having no compunction about killing anyone whom he defined as an enemy, and when he thought it necessary, he had no apparent qualms about subjecting people to mutilation, torture, and horrible death.

Organization of the Expedition

De Soto selected some of the principal officers for his La Florida expedition before he went to Valladolid for an audience with Charles V. Indeed, several of the most trusted of these officers had served under him in Peru and had come to Spain with him. These included Luís de Moscoso y Alvarado, who was to serve as master of camp and as field marshal. De Soto often put Moscoso in charge of the main army, and he assigned important tasks of leadership to him. De Soto held in high esteem Nuño de Tovar, another veteran of Peru, appointing him captain general. Still another, Juan Rodríguez Lobillo, served as one of the captains of footmen.[28]

Other important officers were recruited in Spain. Juan de Añasco from Seville appears to have been well educated, and he would be both active and effective throughout the expedition. He was appointed *contador*, the royal accountant who was entrusted by the crown with keeping account of any treasure they discovered. He was one of De Soto's favorites, often serving as captain of horsemen, and he understood something of the art of navigation. He alone procured a royal permit to trade with the natives of La Florida.

Baltasar de Gallegos was a kinsman of Cabeza de Vaca. He sold all his property in Spain in order to go on the expedition. De Soto made him chief constable, and he relied on him for important assignments almost as much as he relied on Juan de Añasco.

Others recruited in Spain were to play important military roles. Arias Tinoco and Alonso Romo de Cardeñosa, both relatives of De Soto, and Pedro Calderón of Badajoz were captains of horsemen. Francisco Maldonado was a captain of footmen, and Cristóbal de Espindola, another kinsman of Cabeza de Vaca, was captain of the halberdiers who served as De Soto's guard.

Still others recruited in Spain were to serve as officials. Luís Hernández de Biedma served as the royal factor, and Rodrigo Rangel served as De Soto's private secretary. Both of them wrote accounts of the expedition. Juan Gaytán, veteran of North Africa and a nephew of the cardinal of Cigüenza, served as treasurer. Maestro Francisco, a boatwright from Genoa, was not well liked by the men, but he was to play an important role in the expedition.

Several of the more prominent men had servants. De Soto had a steward, Prado; a chamberlain, Fuentes; and three pages, Pibera, Viota, and Juan López Cacho. Don Carlos Enríquez had a female servant, Ana Méndez. Several black men were included. Some of them were slaves, but others, perhaps former Moorish slaves, were freemen. One of these, Bernaldo Loro, was a servant of Pedro Calderón. Isabel de Bobadilla took with her three white slaves—possibly Moors—who had been Christians since before they were twelve years of age.[29]

To a degree that is surprising to modern people, De Soto's army was held together by powerful bonds of locality and kinship. It was not an army of strangers. De Soto began forming up his army after he returned to Seville from Valladolid. Of 257 known survivors of the expedition, the place of birth of 240 are known. This represents a sample of over a third of the people who went with De Soto to La Florida. A full 41 percent of the survivors were from Extremadura. The next most important province was Andalucia, a poor second with 12 percent, and after that León with 11 percent. Others were from Castilla la Nueva (7 percent), Galicia (3 percent), Viscaya (4 percent), and Portugal (5 percent). There was also one French and one Italian survivor, as well as several who were from unknown foreign countries.[30]

Many members of De Soto's army were connected by kin ties. Moscoso took along two of his brothers, Juan de Alvarado and Cristóbal de Mosquera. Don Carlos Enríquez married De Soto's niece, Isabel de Soto, and he took her to the New World with him. Several of De Soto's relatives went along, including Diego de Soto (his nephew), Arias Tinoco, Alonso Romo, and Diego Tinoco.[31]

A substantial company of Portuguese, some of whom had fought in North Africa, elected to go with De Soto. They may have first learned of the expedition when Moscoso visited Elvas. On that occasion André de Vasconcelos approached Moscoso and asked him to put in a good word for him with De Soto. He sent papers along with Moscoso to De Soto, and on the basis of these papers De Soto invited Vasconcelos to join the expedition, promising him that he would be favored and would have men to command. Others from Elvas joined the expedition: Fernan Pegado, Antonio Martínez Segurado, Mem Royz Pereyra, Joam Cordeiro, Estevan Pegado, Bento Fernández, and Alvaro Fernández.[32]

The Portuguese under the leadership of Vasconcelos departed from Elvas on January 15, 1538, and proceeded to Seville. Upon arrival, they went to the inn where De Soto was staying, entering a patio that was surrounded by balconies. As they mounted the stairs to one of these balconies, De Soto came out to meet them. He ordered that chairs be brought for them, and Vasconcelos introduced himself and his company. De Soto expressed pleasure in their joining the expedition, and he invited them to dine with him. He sent his mayordomo out to arrange for lodgings for them nearby.[33]

After initial arrangements had been made, De Soto proceeded from Seville to San Lúcar, and there he made the final selection of those who were to go with him to La Florida. He ordered a muster of those who wished to go with him. The Portuguese showed up wearing their armor, but the Castilians were dressed in finery. De Soto was displeased, and he ordered that another muster be held the next day, and *all* were to be wearing armor. At the next day's muster De Soto made his selection.[34]

It is impossible to know precisely how many people were included in De Soto's army because the various lists and estimates of the total number do not agree. One list of those who signed on puts the number at 657, but this list does not include De Soto himself, nor his entourage, and perhaps others were not included. Slaves, for example, were often omitted from such counts. In sworn testimony two survivors of the expedition put the number at 700.[35] Hence, it can only be said that the number of people departing with De Soto from San Lúcar was between 650 and 700.

Judging from what is known about the survivors, they were a young army. Two were less than 15 years old, and none was older than De Soto, whose age was about 38. The average age was 24.6 years. Six of the company are known to have been women.[36] Only 5 percent of the survivors could not sign their names, perhaps indicating a very high literacy rate for De Soto's army. A wide range of occupations was included: a farrier, a trumpeter, several tailors, shoemakers, carpenters, ironsmiths, a swordsmith, a caulker, and at least seven religious. Most of De Soto's personnel were commoners; some were hidalgos; and a few were from the lower nobility.[37]

Whether De Soto spent the entire fortune he had accumulated in the New World on his Florida venture is not known, but clearly he invested a significant portion of it. Perhaps more important, he was not the only investor. In a sense, all who went with him except the priests were investors. Those who had been to Peru invested their wealth in the enterprise. Baltasar de Gallegos sold his estate in Spain and purchased arms, horses, and provisions for several servants.[38] None of the principals were salaried; instead they expected to receive one or more shares of any booty that might be gained during the course of the expedition.

Departure from San Lúcar

In April 1538 De Soto delivered the ships he had purchased to the captains whom he had appointed to command them.[39] As admiral of the fleet, De Soto himself commanded the *San Cristóbal,* a new ship that was to serve as the flagship of the fleet.

Along with De Soto's ships the fleet also included twenty large ships bound for Mexico. Until they reached Cuba all ships were under the general command of De Soto. Afterward, the fleet of twenty ships was to proceed to Vera Cruz under the command of Gonzalo de Salazar, one of the conquistadores of Mexico who was returning to serve as factor of the Imperial Resources of the City of Mexico.[40]

The fleet of ships departed the bar of San Lúcar on Sunday, April 7, 1538, the feast day of St. Lazarus.[41] They left with high expectations and celebration, with trumpets sounding and with many salvos of artillery. For four days they sailed with good wind, and then they were becalmed for a week and could make very little headway.[42]

An incident occurred on the first night after they set sail that could have hindered the expedition from the start. De Soto had commanded the sentinels on his ship to keep a particularly close watch, and the chief gunner was to be ready to fire on any enemy that might threaten them. All the ships were to keep in strict formation.[43] De Soto commanded that the penalty for breaking these orders was death.

A little past midnight, the ship that was to be the flagship of the Mexican fleet under the captaincy of Gonzalo de Salazar, edged out in front of De Soto's ship to about the distance of a cannon shot. Whether through negligence or through someone's order, this was a breach of fleet discipline. Gonzalo Silvestre, who was in charge of the sentinels, alerted the gunner and asked him whether the ship out in the lead was one of their own or an enemy. They concluded it must be an enemy ship, because all crews in their fleet knew that to pull out of formation was a capital offense.[44]

They fired a cannon shot at the supposed enemy ship and pierced all its sails from stem to stern. A second shot likewise damaged its sails, and with this the ship lost speed. As they were making ready to fire a third shot, they heard people on the distant ship crying out for them to cease fire. They were friends, not enemies. Everyone in the fleet was awake by this time, and other ships had their guns trained on the errant ship.

The damaged ship slowed further, and because De Soto's *San Cristóbal* was in close pursuit, it fell rapidly to the leeward of the damaged ship, and the crewmen of the two ships realized they were on a collision course. When the two frightened and angry crews realized their predicament, they seized up a great number of pikes and applied them to each other's ships, trying to keep them apart. A great number of pikes were broken, but they prevented a violent collision as the two ships brushed against each other. Now, however, the rigging and sails of the two ships became entangled, and they were in danger of sinking. In the darkness there was great confusion.[45]

Finally the sailors cut the rigging of the two ships and disentangled them, and the *San Cristóbal* pulled away. Now that the catastrophe was averted, De Soto cast about for who was to blame. He concluded that the incident was caused by the disrespect and malicious intent of Salazar, and he considered beheading him. But Salazar pleaded that he was not at fault in what had occurred, and the men in his crew affirmed that what he said was true. Others aboard the *San Cristóbal* counseled De Soto to show restraint. In the end De Soto pardoned Salazar, and all seemed healed between them, though Salazar never forgot De Soto's accusation. Afterward in Mexico, whenever the subject came up, Salazar would say that he would like nothing better than to meet De Soto in combat man to man. He would make him eat the angry words he had heaped upon him that night. With two such strong-willed men, with anger a stranger to neither, a confrontation such as the one that occurred was probably inevitable.[46]

Sailing in the sixteenth century was a dangerous business, and other smaller accidents occurred as the voyage continued. A few days out of port, two sailors got into a fight, and as they wrestled with each other, they fell overboard and drowned. As they approached the Canary Islands, a mishap occurred when Tapia, an hidalgo of Arévalo, lost his very fine greyhound when it fell over-board. Because the wind was so favorable, they could not afford to turn back and retrieve the dog.[47]

On Easter Sunday, April 21, fifteen days after they departed from San Lú-car, they reached the Canary Islands. The governor of the Canaries, the Count of Gomera, was a cousin of Isabel de Bobadilla. He came out to meet them dressed, from cap to shoes, entirely in white. To the Portuguese, he seemed to be as gaudily dressed as a Gypsy count. He received De Soto's army well, and provided lodging for all the men at no expense. De Soto purchased wine, bread, meat, and other provisions for the remainder of the journey.[48]

The Count of Gomera had a seventeen-year-old bastard daughter, Doña Leonor de Bobadilla, who was exceedingly beautiful. De Soto prevailed upon the count to give Doña Leonor to Doña Isabel as a waiting maid, promising that in the course of his conquest of La Florida a favorable marriage for the girl might be arranged. Confident that De Soto should succeed in his venture, the count agreed, and Leonor was given to Isabel's keeping, to care for as if she were her own child.[49]

While they were in the Canaries, Tapia, whose greyhound had been lost overboard, was startled to see his dog in the possession of a citizen of the is-lands. He learned that his dog had swum in the ocean for perhaps five hours before a local boat chanced upon him and had taken him aboard. But as finder of the dog, the new master, arguing that finders are keepers, refused to return him to Tapia.[50]

They departed from the Canaries a week after they had landed, and they sped forward, favored by a good wind. It so happened one day that the un-lucky Tapia walked over and stood at the rail of the ship on which he was sailing. The boom of the ship swung and struck his head. He fell overboard and sank like a stone, never to be seen again.[51]

Cuba

The fleet approached the harbor of Santiago, on the eastern end of the island of Cuba (see map 3), on Whitsuntide, June 7, 1538.[52] As they approached the harbor, they saw a man on horseback rush out from the town and gesture anxiously at them. He shouted in a loud voice: "To port! To port!" They seem not to have had a pilot who was familiar with the port of Santiago, because at this horseman's behest the flagship veered, and some of the others followed. But then the man on land seemed to have second thoughts, and he frantically signaled them to veer in the opposite direction, shouting: "Return, return to the other side before all of you are lost!"

They later learned that Cuba had recently been under attack by French corsairs. The residents assumed that the approaching ships were pirates, and they sent the man out to try to decoy the ships onto some rocks. When the man at last realized they were not corsairs, it was almost too late. The flagship took a sharp turn, but a violent shudder went through the ship. The men rushed to the pumps, seeing what looked like water in the hold. Some on board panicked. They put a small boat into the water, and Doña Isabel, Leonor de Bobadilla, and the wives of Baltasar de Gallegos and Don Carlos Enríquez were put ashore, as were several panicky young men who had rushed to escape the ship. But when the sailors went below to inspect the damage more closely, they found that the ship was intact. The liquid in the hold was a large quantity of wine, vinegar, oil, and honey that had spilled from ceramic jars broken by the lurching of the ship.[53]

A different kind of misfortune now befell Nuño de Tovar. During the voyage from the Canary Islands, he somehow managed in the close quarters of the ship to have an affair with the beautiful Leonor de Bobadilla, and he got her pregnant. De Soto was furious when he learned of it, and he demoted Tovar from the post of captain general. Tovar married Leonor, but doing so did not mitigate his fall from grace. He determined to go on the expedition to La Florida and try to restore himself in De Soto's esteem.[54]

Upon coming ashore, a gentleman of Santiago sent to De Soto a roan horse for his personal use and another steed for Doña Isabel. All of the foot soldiers and cavalry of the town came down to welcome the newcomers. De Soto and some of the men were quartered in the town while others went out into the country, where they were quartered in groups of four and six at no expense to themselves.[55]

Cuba must have seemed exotic to those in De Soto's army who had never been to the New World. There were only six towns of Spaniards on the island of Cuba: Santiago and Havana, each with about seventy or eighty houses, and Baracoa, Bayamo, Puerto Principe, and Sancti Spiritus, with thirty to forty houses each. Most of these houses were built of boards and had thatched roofs. Only the houses of the wealthy were built of stone, with lime mortar, and were roofed with tiles. Santiago, the principal town in Cuba, had a Franciscan monastery and a church with a parish priest and seven secular priests.[56]

Many of the trees and plants growing on the large farms around Santiago were unfamiliar to the Spaniards. These included pineapples, growing on low plants whose leaves they thought resembled aloe, and a tree that produced *anona* fruit, the size and shape of a small pineapple, but with a pulp said to be as tasty as a curd. Other trees produced guava, shaped like a hazelnut, but the size of a fig, and the *mamei* fruit, which grew to the size of a peach and was considered by Spaniards to be the most delicious of the island's fruits.[57] They saw plantains, which grew in bunches of twenty or thirty on a single stalk that bent over as the fruit grew larger. Figs and oranges introduced into Cuba from Spain produced fruit all year long because of the tropical climate. Most of the people, and especially the slaves, subsisted on yams and cassava, the latter a root that was deadly until it was leached of its poisonous acid, as one of De Soto's sailors found to his misfortune, when he foolishly ventured to taste an unprocessed cassava root.[58]

The planters of Cuba produced great numbers of horses, cattle, and pigs. The horses were of good quality, and some individuals in Santiago owned herds of as many as fifty or sixty.[59] Many of the cattle and pigs escaped to the wild, where they had created a maze of trails through the forests. They multiplied greatly in the wild, because on the island of Cuba there were no wolves, bears, or cougars to prey upon them, only feral dogs. It sometimes happened that a Spaniard would get lost and wander around in this maze of animal trails for days or even weeks at a time.[60] The roads between towns had to be kept cleared by men wielding machetes. If they were not cleared regularly, they would quickly grow up in vegetation and be lost to sight.[61] In Cuba it was dangerous to travel unless one had an Indian as a guide.

The Spaniards had mined a considerable quantity of gold in Cuba, but the slaves they used as miners were in short supply. The labor regimen was so severe and the work in the mines so hard and brutal, many of the slaves had hanged themselves rather than keep on. Vasco Porcallo de Figuerora, a wealthy planter who lived near the town of Trinidad, had used slaves to mine gold. On one occasion, it was said, one of his overseers heard that some of the slaves had determined to hang themselves. This overseer went to where the slaves were to do this. He had with him a noose, and he told them that if they hanged themselves, he would do the same, and if they thought they had it hard in this world, they would see what he would do to them in the next world. With this dismal prospect, so the story goes, they decided to forgo meeting a devil they did not know and to stay in this world with the devil they knew.[62] There was a distinct and well-perceived labor shortage on the island of Cuba.

The people of Santiago were twice pleased at the arrival of De Soto's fleet. Not only had it turned out that they were not under renewed attack by French pirates, but the new governor of Cuba had arrived. The celebrations lasted for several days, with dances and masquerades at night, and various games during the day. They played at *juegos de cañas*, a game introduced by the Moors, in which teams of horsemen charged at each other, throwing cane lances, which they deflected with their shields. They sponsored bullfights in which men rode their horses and wielded their lances. Those who excelled at arms, at riding, or at games were given prizes of gold and silver trinkets or silk and brocade. Those who did least well were given booby prizes.[63]

De Soto visited other towns in the vicinity of Santiago, appointing ministers of justice to represent him. And he and his men began purchasing the horses that would be so important in the course of the expedition.[64]

While he was at Santiago, De Soto was visited by Vasco Porcallo de Figuerora, the wealthiest man in Cuba. He was over fifty years old and was somewhat the worse for wear after many military campaigns both in Europe and in the Caribbean. But the new expedition caught his enthusiasm. As later became plain, one of his motives was to capture Indian slaves for his plantations and mines. He reached an agreement with De Soto that he would go with him to La Florida, and De Soto appointed him lieutenant general of the fleet and army.[65]

Vasco Porcallo promised to take a number of servants along on the expedition, as well as stores of food—especially cassava bread—and equipment. He brought along a large number of horses for his own use, and he donated others to be used by De Soto's men. And not least in importance, Vasco Porcallo supplied a herd of pigs to be taken along on the hoof as a mobile larder.[66] That Vasco Porcallo elected to go with De Soto probably inspired a number of other

Cubans to join the expedition. These newcomers compensated for the loss of several individuals who came from Spain with De Soto but who, for various reasons, decided to remain in Cuba.

De Soto ordered Don Carlos Enríquez to go with the ships as they sailed on to Havana, taking Doña Isabel and most of the men. About 150 of the men were ordered to travel overland from Santiago.[67] They bought horses and set out for their first destination, Bayamo, where the inhabitants took the men into their houses in groups of four and six.[68] Their only expense was corn for their horses, since De Soto, as governor of Cuba, was empowered to levy a tax on tribute and services as they traveled along. These uninvited guests must have imposed a considerable burden on the local population.

The Spaniards made particular note of the river that ran past Bayamo, remarking that it was infested with giant lizards—actually alligators—that preyed on people and animals swimming in the water. They also encountered large snakes, as thick as a man's thigh, but that moved sluggishly and were not to be feared.[69]

From Puerto Principe, De Soto went by dugout canoe along the coast to the house of Vasco Porcallo de Figuerora to get some news of the ships that had sailed for Havana. Upon arriving, he learned that a storm had come up while the ships were en route, and they had become separated and blown out to sea. De Soto proceeded immediately to Havana by boat to see what damage had been done. He learned that there was in fact little damage, but the ships had been forty days in reaching Havana, and all on board had suffered from want of food and water. They had been blown very far off course, so much so that two of the ships had in fact sighted the Florida peninsula.[70]

The party of horsemen continued traveling overland. They divided themselves into two companies so as to not overburden the people among whom they traveled. They took along a supply of cassava bread, but because this bread dissolved when it became moist, it did not travel well. Consequently, the men had to rely mainly on wild pork or beef, which was killed by a native hunter who had brought along a pack of dogs. From Puerto Principe they continued on to Sancti Spiritus with its groves of orange and lemon trees. Half the men stopped off here for a rest; the others continued on to the coastal town of Trinidad.

As they traveled along they were plagued by mosquitoes, which were especially bad when they crossed a swamp they called the Marsh of the Watering Trough. It was a half a league wide, and in passing through it, they had to swim the distance of a long crossbow shot. The rest of the distance they had to wade, often in mud up to their knees and in water up to their waists. Embedded in the mud were sharp clam shells that cut through their shoes and into their feet. They towed their clothes and saddles on small makeshift rafts, so that they were almost naked. Slapping at the mosquitoes swarming over them, they became covered with welts, bruises, and blood.[71] From Trinidad they proceeded on to Havana, crossing a long stretch of country in which there were no Spanish towns. They reached Havana at the end of March 1539.

Final Preparations

After De Soto reached Havana by boat, he began making final arrangements for the expedition to La Florida. During the winter, De Soto sent out Juan de Añasco, Francisco Maldonado, Juan López (the chief pilot), and fifty men in a caravel and two *bergantines* to explore the bay where the expedition was to make its landing. They were also to capture Indians to serve as guides and interpreters.

They spent a considerable time sailing up and down the coast, exploring the inlets and searching for a bay where they could land.[72] Añasco and his men experienced considerable hardship on this mission. At times they subsisted on what shellfish they could gather, as well as on birds on the offshore islands, which were so tame they could easily be killed with clubs. After about two months this exploring party returned to Cuba, and upon disembarking, they crawled on their hands and knees to the church at Havana to give thanks for their safe return.[73] Añasco brought back several Indians he had captured on the coast, who were to serve as guides and interpreters. The Spaniards showed these Indians rings and objects of gold and asked them whether this metal could be obtained in Florida. The Indians indicated by signs that much of it could be had there. They also indicated that corn could be obtained there.[74] With this good news, De Soto and his men looked forward to getting under way, for La Florida promised to be a very rich land.

While De Soto was still in Havana, he received the alarming news that Don Antonio de Mendoza, the viceroy of Mexico, was making preparations for a second expedition into North America, one that would depart from Mexico. De Soto and his men were afraid the two expeditions would come into contact with each other and that conflict would break out between them, like the quarrels that had occurred in Nicaragua and Peru. De Soto decided to send word to Mendoza, apprising him of the royal capitulación under which he operated, imploring him to not proceed with a second expedition.[75]

De Soto chose Antonio de San Jorge, a trusted Galician soldier, to be his envoy to Mexico. San Jorge went and delivered his message and in due course returned with a message from Mendoza that La Florida was a vast land, and that Mendoza's own expedition would reach places far from where De Soto planned to go. He assured De Soto that the two expeditions would not meet up with each other and offered assistance for De Soto's expedition. De Soto was satisfied with this.[76]

In fact, Mendoza had been disturbed when he first heard news of De Soto's planned expedition, and he had received an order from the crown that he was not to intrude into the area reserved for De Soto. His anxiety was compounded on September 2, 1539, when Fray Marcos de Niza returned to Mexico City from an expedition to the north claiming that great wealth existed at Cibola, the Zuñi Pueblos. By this time De Soto and his men had already begun their expedition, but Mendoza was afraid that this news from Fray Marcos would reach Havana, and attempting to suppress it, he issued a decree forbidding anyone from departing from Mexico without a license. In spite of Mendoza's decree, the news reached Havana in November.[77] Going forward with his own plans, on February 23, 1540, Mendoza sent Francisco Vázquez de Coronado north from Mexico to search for the gold of Cibola.

De Soto proceeded with final preparations. For two thousand ducats he purchased a cattle ranch complete with slaves and a well-furnished house, which he left in the care of Doña Isabel.[78] He appointed Doña Isabel to serve in his absence as governor of the island of Cuba. The wives of Don Carlos Enríquez, Baltasar de Gallegos, and Nuño de Tovar remained in Havana with her.[79] De Soto appointed Juan de Rojas to serve as her deputy in Havana, and he appointed Francisco de Guzmán to serve as her deputy in Santiago. Both of these men had served in this same capacity before De Soto arrived.[80]

A short time before the fleet was to embark for La Florida, a ship fleeing a storm took refuge in Havana harbor. People in Havana watched this ship approach the entrance to the harbor three times, and each time it fought its way back out to sea, suggesting that it was trying to avoid coming into port. The storm, however, was so great that the ship finally had to enter the harbor to find a safe haven.[81]

On board the ship was Hernán Ponce de León, De Soto's compañero. But this was no joyful reunion. Ponce de León had liquidated some of their holdings in Peru, and he had a considerable fortune on board ship. He knew De Soto was in Havana and was governor of Cuba. He also knew that De Soto, seeking to finance his expedition, would claim his share of this treasure—and perhaps more than his share—and for this reason he attempted to avoid the harbor. Once in port, Ponce de León warned his seamen to conceal the fact that this treasure was aboard ship. If anyone should ask, they were to say that it had been left behind at Nombre de Dios.[82]

When De Soto learned that Ponce de León had landed, he went to greet him. They exchanged pleasantries, but Ponce de León said he was exhausted from the storm and wished to remain aboard ship for one more night. De Soto sensed that something was amiss, and upon taking his leave he commanded that guards patrol the area where the ship was moored that night.

Ponce de León came up with a plan. He would leave the silver he was carrying aboard ship, so that he would have something to show De Soto, but he commanded two black slaves to load two chests of gold and precious jewels onto a small boat and take them to the house of a friend for safe keeping. He would retrieve them before departing for Spain. But as the boat carrying the treasure came ashore during the night, De Soto's sentinels spied it and silently waited. When the men from the boat had carried the two chests for some distance, the sentinels rushed them. Ponce de León's slaves dropped the chests and fled back to their boat. The sentinels seized the treasure and took it to De Soto, who hid the treasure and then waited to see what his partner's next move would be.[83]

The next day, Ponce de León came ashore and went to visit De Soto. As best he could, he tried to conceal his pain over what he had lost. They conversed for a while about various matters, and finally the conversation turned to what had occurred on the previous night. De Soto complained to Ponce de León about his lack of faith and his lack of loyalty. To prove his own good faith, De Soto commanded that Ponce de León's treasure chests be brought to him. De Soto reminded him of their partnership, and he let it be known that he could produce witnesses to all its stipulations. De Soto invited Ponce de León to go along as a participant on the expedition to La Florida. He would share the conquest with him.

De Soto made it plain to Ponce de León that he wanted half the treasure, as was his due. But Ponce de León countered that De Soto had already spent *all* the money he had taken from Peru to Spain, half of which belonged to Ponce de León. Moreover, he said that *all* the treasure seized by De Soto belonged to him alone because it had come out of the sale of his estate and slaves. But De Soto would not relent. If Ponce de León would not cooperate, he would destroy his ship and take him and his retinue to La Florida by force. Alonso de Heredia and others advised Ponce de León to give in to De Soto, seeking

the best terms he could get. He could protest later, when he was in a more secure position.[84]

Ponce de León relented, and he signed a document on May 13, 1539, drawn
up on this occasion by the notary Francisco Cepero. Ponce de León agreed in
writing that De Soto's expenditure in Spain (here set at 130,000 castellanos)
was justified. He agreed to turn over to De Soto 8,000 castellanos of the treasure he had attempted to hide. Moreover, he again reaffirmed the lifetime
partnership that existed between them. Thus, if De Soto realized any gain in
La Florida, Ponce de León would be entitled to half of it. De Soto also got from
Ponce de León—whether by seizure or by gift—a fine Peruvian tent made of
wool and cotton, which he took with him on the expedition.[85]

On May 10, De Soto made out a will. His first concern was that he be buried
and memorialized in such a way as to recognize his attainments and to bring
honor on his kinsmen. He wished for his corpse to be taken back to Spain to
Jerez de los Caballeros, to the church of San Miguel, there to be interred
alongside his mother and father, and if the corpse of either or both of them
were in Badajoz, they should be moved to Jerez de los Caballeros. He set aside
funds to build a chapel and altar at the church of San Miguel, and he provided
funds for its furnishing, as well as a salary for a chaplain, who was to be a
kinsman, if possible. His sepulchre and that of his mother and father were to
be within the chapel, adjoining the altar, and he specified that the altar be covered with a piece of fine black broadcloth bearing the red cross of the order of
the Knights of Santiago. His coats of arms were to be used to adorn the interior of the chapel, and he specified in great detail the many masses that were
to be said in his memory.

He provided in his will for his wife, Isabel, his nephew Pedro de Soto, his
bastard son, Andrés de Soto, his bastard daughter, Doña Maria de Soto in
Nicaragua (whose mother was probably Juana Hernández), his mayordomo,
his carver, and his secretary, Rodrigo Rangel. He provided nothing in his will
for his daughter Leonor, born to Tocto Chimpu in Peru. He specifically stated
that his compañia with Hernán Ponce de León was in effect and had recently
been reaffirmed in Cuba. And finally, as a charity, he stipulated that a portion
of his silk revenues in the city of Granada be spent providing dowry for poor
orphaned girls of his lineage, to the fifth degree, and if there be none, then
poor orphaned noble daughters of the city of Jerez de los Cabelleros. The will
was witnessed by Fray Juan de Gallegos and Fray Francisco de la Rocha.[86]

De Soto gave the order to load up the ships. Those boarding included a few
men from Cuba who had volunteered or had been coerced into going. As gov-

ernor of Cuba and adelantado of La Florida, De Soto had the power to impress people into serving against their will. He forced a certain *bachiller* (an educated man) to join the expedition, as well as a barber, a master shipwright, and several seamen and soldiers. The financing of the expedition must have been a considerable drain on the Cuban economy.

Ponce de León watched De Soto's fleet sail out of the harbor. He remained in Havana under the pretense of waiting for more favorable weather. But eight days after De Soto departed, Ponce de León filed suit with Juan de Rojas, testifying that it was because of his fear of De Soto that he had handed over ten thousand pesos to Doña Isabel. He contended that he did not in fact owe this money to De Soto, and it should be refunded to him. If he received no satisfaction, he would present his suit to His Majesty, the emperor.

Doña Isabel countered that Ponce de León owed much more than ten thousand pesos to De Soto and that he should be put in jail until the records could be examined. But Ponce de León either heard about Doña Isabel's threat or anticipated what it would be. As soon as he could, he boarded ship and set sail for Spain.[87]

3

La Florida

De Soto's fleet departed from Havana Harbor on Sunday, May 18, 1539. It consisted of nine ships: five large ships (*naos*), two caravels, and two bergantines. The naos were stout, beamy vessels with a length-to-beam ratio of about 3 to 1, and they were deep in the hold. Rigged with square mainsails, foresails, and topsails, and with a lateen mizzensail, they were designed to carry men and cargo, but still they were relatively fast. One of the naos was the worm-eaten *Santa Catalina* in which Hernán Ponce de León had sailed into Havana harbor.

The caravel, incorporating both Iberian and Muslim nautical traditions, was crucial in the early exploration of the Atlantic. The caravel was long, with a length-to-beam ratio of 3.3 to 1, or even more. It was fast and maneuverable, and had a shallow draft so that it could venture into unknown shallow waters. It was a medium-size vessel, typically rigged with square mainsails and fore-sails and with a lateen mizzensail. The bergantín was a large open boat that was used as a service vessel. It had one, occasionally two, masts, and it could be propelled by oars as well as by sail. Equipped with seven benches, more or less, and with two rowers to each bench, the bergantín was used for river travel and also to ferry men and freight from ship to shore. On voyages they were ordinarily towed behind caravels and naos. A bergantín could carry thirty to fifty people in addition to its crew.

De Soto's fleet enjoyed good weather and favorable winds, and on Sunday, May 25, the Feast of Espíritu Santo, they sighted a string of low, sandy islands that lay off the coast of La Florida. They anchored their fleet at about one or two leagues from shore in four brazas or less of water (about twenty-two feet).[1] They were afraid to approach any closer for fear of shoals, reckoning that they were at this time due north of the island of Tortuga, which lay at the mouth of the Bahama Channel.[2] Rangel describes their position as being ten leagues west of the Bay of Juan Ponce (Charlotte Harbor).[3] Presumably he meant they were ten leagues west of the longitude of Charlotte Harbor. Since longitude could not be accurately measured in this era, this could have been no more than a guess, but as it turned out, a good guess. At about the same time the ships sighted land, the Indians on shore sighted the ships, and the Spaniards soon saw smoke from many fires rising above the trees, this being one of the ways the Indians signaled alarm.[4]

Evidently, Juan de Añasco did not recognize landmarks on the coast he had reconnoitered the previous winter. They were looking for a harbor that Luís Hernández de Biedma called Bayahonda (i.e., Bahía Honda), the "deep bay."[5] In order to determine better where they were, De Soto, Añasco, and Alonso Martín, the pilot for the fleet, got into a bergantín with several others and sailed toward the shore. When they came in close to the shore, Añasco still did not recognize any landmarks. Because it was getting dark, they turned around and attempted to sail back to the ships, but the wind was against them. They were forced to drop anchor near the shore. When they went ashore, they saw many indications of Indians and then came to a village consisting of one large house—probably a public structure—and several small ones.[6] Evidently the inhabitants had run away.

Those on board the ships were concerned for De Soto's safety. If he came under attack in the dark of night, they would not be able to go to his aid. As always, De Soto was long on courage, short on prudence. He was more than ready to throw himself into the middle of a situation, no matter what the danger, and in so doing perhaps raised himself in the eyes of the men under his command, though in exposing himself to injury or death, he was putting his men at risk.[7]

The next morning, May 26, the men on the ships could see the bergantín again attempting in vain to approach them. Baltasar de Gallegos shouted to

Vasco Porcallo, the lieutenant general, who was aboard the flagship, saying that he should go out and try to learn what De Soto wanted them to do. But if Porcallo heard and answered, Gallegos did not hear him. Gallegos then ordered the caravel he captained to sail out to meet the bergantín. De Soto was heartened that Gallegos had tried to help him, but he was distressed that by doing so he had put his caravel into some hazard in the shallow Gulf waters.[8]

By this time the entrance to the harbor had been located. They were anchored off the coast of Longboat Key, about sixteen miles south of the entrance to Tampa Bay. De Soto ordered that Gallegos's caravel be stationed on one side of the entrance to the channel, and that the second bergantín be stationed on the opposite side of the channel. The bergantín occupied by Añasco and him then acted as a pilot boat, guiding the ships through the channel and into the harbor. It is likely that they used the Southwest Channel, which lay southwest of Egmont Key and had a minimum depth of perhaps 22.5 feet. The ships were anchored at four or five leagues from the entrance. One at a time they began their entry under sail, constantly sounding the depth, because there were many shallow places in the bay. Even though they proceeded with great care, two of the ships scraped bottom, but because it was a silt bottom no damage was done. De Soto had difficulty containing his anger at Añasco, whom he evidently felt had been derelict in locating a deep entrance and passage within the bay.[9]

Perhaps because the information they had on the channel into Tampa Bay was so poor, it took them five days to pilot the ships into the harbor—from Monday, May 26, until Friday, May 30—and even though they constantly sounded the lead, the ships continued to sometimes scrape the soft bottom. It is possible that as they proceeded further into the harbor they used the bergantines, rowed by the men, to tow the ships in, the water being too shallow to proceed safely under sail. While this maneuver was in progress, some of the men went ashore in small boats to procure fresh water and fodder for the horses. They also brought back some wild grapes. These were not ripe enough for the men to eat, but they were nonetheless a good omen, because such grapes were not to be found either in Mexico or Peru.[10] Impeded by the shallow water, they anchored their ships about four leagues from the village where they intended to land.[11] The dominant chief of the region they were in was Ozita, and the village they had picked for their camp was subject to him.[12]

De Soto had chosen to land on what was geologically the youngest part of the North American continent, the shoreline of the Florida peninsula. In 1539 much of the shoreline of Tampa Bay was lined with stands of red mangrove

Fig. 9. Red mangrove forest at Tampa Bay. Photograph by Lawrence May.

(*Rhizophora mangle*), a tree remarkable for its ability to send out a tangle of stilted roots into shallow salt water (fig. 9). When the leaves of these trees fall into the tangle of roots and seawater, they rot to form soil and build land. Red mangrove trees grow as high as seventy feet tall, though today, because sea-front land is so valuable, much of the red mangrove forest in Florida has been cleared.[13]

For De Soto these dense stands of red mangrove trees would have been a formidable barrier to getting his men and horses ashore. The stands of these trees must have been especially dense around the estuary of the Manatee River. Fortunately there was a stretch of mangrove-free sandy beach at present-day Piney Point, and this area was doubly attractive because it lay only about a half mile from the channel they were following as they eased their way into the bay. From the channel the water rapidly becomes shallow as one moves toward the shore.

On May 30 they began winching the horses up out of the holds of the ships and swimming them ashore to the beach. While the unloading of the horses was still underway, Vasco Porcallo de Figuerora, Juan de Añasco, Francisco

Osorio, and five others went ashore and rode from the beach into the woods to see what they could see.[14] Some of the vegetation they encountered was like that on the island of Cuba. Inland from the shoreline, and especially in the salt flats, the trees were black mangrove, and inland from these were white mangrove, as well as buttonwood, poisonwood, and other salt-tolerant plants.

Vasco Porcallo, Añasco, Osorio, and the others reconnoitered the land for about a half a league around the place where they had come ashore.[15] It is probable that Vasco Porcallo was already hunting for slaves. They chanced upon some Indians who were coming to have a look at the strangers on their shore. These Indians put up a resistance, and in the fighting that ensued, two Indians were killed and one horse was killed before the remaining Indians turned and ran.[16] The Spaniards' horses were weak from the voyage, and they became mired in the swamps and floundered in the water and mud. After they returned to camp, Vasco Porcallo's horse fell to the ground and died. It had been struck by an arrow that passed through its cloth, saddletree, and pack saddle and still carried enough force that more than a third of the arrow penetrated into its rib cage.[17]

They evidently continued unloading the horses on May 31. To further lighten their ships, they also put an unknown number of men ashore at Piney Point. Vasco Porcallo and about a hundred men went ahead in the bergantines to scout out the village where they intended to land. Gómez Arias later returned in one of the bergantines, reporting that it was a good country and that the Indians had all fled from their village.[18] Pánfilo de Narváez had been in the vicinity of Tampa Bay in 1528, and the natives thereabouts had good reason to fear and detest the Spaniards.

Base Camp

On June 1 the men who had been put ashore began marching toward the village they had selected for their base camp. Their guides were four of the Indians Juan de Añasco captured when he had reconnoitered the coast the previous winter. The Spaniards soon lost their bearings, although it is not clear whether this was because they could not understand their guides or whether the guides were intentionally trying to mislead them. De Soto and a contingent of horsemen went ahead to scout the way, but they found it difficult going, and their horses became very tired after winding around along deer trails and slogging their way through swamps for what seemed like twelve leagues.[19] But finally they found themselves at an inlet of the harbor, the mouth of the Little Manatee River, which lay between them and the village selected for the landing place, the place where they would establish their base camp. The men reached the inlet at the end of a long day, exhausted, unable to cross over to the base camp without boats. That night they slept scattered about, here and there, in an undisciplined way, and would have been vulnerable had the Indians attacked.[20] The next day they were ferried across the inlet.

After the men and horses had all been put ashore, the seamen began ferrying the cargo ashore in small boats. As the ships grew lighter, they drew less water and could gradually be maneuvered closer to the landing site. The mouth of the Little Manatee River lay at about one and a half miles from the main channel in Tampa Bay, but a lesser channel about eight or nine feet deep connected the main channel to the river's mouth, providing safe navigation for small boats.[21] This unloading continued for several days.

It is not possible to be precise about the number of people and horses De Soto landed in La Florida. But the number of people appears to have been about six hundred, and the 243 horses that were loaded on the ships in Havana harbor had been reduced by the 19 or 20 that died en route.[22] Horses fared badly aboard ship. They were often transported by means of belly bands suspended from the roof of the hold, so their hooves were held several inches from the floor, preventing them from rearing.

To native people who observed the Spaniards unloading their ships and boats, it must have been an amazing spectacle. The Spaniards brought their food and supplies ashore in wooden barrels and casks, and in large and small earthenware containers. Their clothing and other dry goods were packed in baskets and panniers. The Indians had seen the strange clothing and weapons before, when Narváez had come. Sixteenth-century Spaniards did not wear the uniform clothing of modern armies. Rather, their clothing was individualistic and colorful (fig. 10). Their upper garments were doublets of cloth and leather, perhaps with fashionable slashed sleeves and rolls at the shoulders. They wore short breeches, which may have been puffed out with stuffing. On their legs and feet they wore tight-fitting stockings. Some of them wore boots that reached to their thighs, but that were ordinarily worn rolled down to below their knees. They loved color—green, blue, black, and especially red.

The footmen wore steel helmets. One popular type was the morion, a helmet that rose up to a keeled peak, with a short down-turned brim that was likewise peaked in front and in back. The horsemen wore the heaviest armor, though not the full armor of the medieval knight (see fig. 12). Riding *a la jineta*, they wore a helmet, a cuirass to protect their chest, abdomen, and back, and

Fig. 10. Men of Calderon's Company, a living history group at Bradenton, Florida, demonstrating replicas of sixteenth-century arms and armor. *Left to right:* an arquebusier wearing padded (*escaupil*) armor, stockings, and leather shoes; a swordsman, wearing chain mail, leg armor, and boots; a crossbowman, wearing padded armor and sandals; and a halberdier, wearing a morion helmet, gorget, chain mail, gauntlets, leg armor, and boots. Photograph by Lawrence May.

armor to protect the outsides of their arms and thighs. Some wore only shirts of chain mail and gauntlets. A shirt of chain mail could weigh as much as fifteen to thirty pounds, but it was evenly distributed on the body, and on horseback, one could bear it. The horseman was armed with a lance consisting of a steel point mounted on a small-diameter wooden shaft nine to twelve feet long, and he carried a small shield made of metal or wood covered with thick leather.

Footmen wore lighter armor. They wore steel helmets like the horsemen, but they were more likely to protect their bodies with sleeveless linen garments to which small steel plates (*brigandine*) were riveted. Even lighter defensive garments were made of two layers of heavy cotton cloth, stuffed with two or three fingers of cotton fiber and then quilted. Such garments could stop arrows more effectively than chain mail. Padded doublets were worn in sixteenth-century Europe, but this attire may owe something to the Aztecs, who wore larger, looser-fitting padded (*escaupil*) garments as armor.[23] Some of the footmen were armed only with sharp, double-edged swords (see fig. 85g) and small shields. Some also carried crossbows (see fig. 85a), matchlock guns, or halberds. The latter is a polearm consisting of a long wooden handle with a steel head that could be used to impale, hack, or hook one's opponent.

The Spaniards established their camp near the shore of the bay that ran inland to the village of Ozita.[24] This village was a small one with only seven or eight houses, which were built of wood with roofs of thatched palm leaf. The chief's or headman's house stood on a high artificial mound near the beach. On the opposite side of the town was a temple that had on top a wooden bird with gilded eyes. They found nothing of value to them in the houses or in the temple, only some pearls, which the Indians had ruined by exposing them to fire. The Indians valued these fire-marred pearls, wearing them strung about their necks and arms.

The chroniclers' description of the town of Ozita is consistent with what archaeologists have learned about the Safety Harbor culture of the people who lived around Tampa Bay in the late prehistoric period. More than a hundred Safety Harbor sites are known to archaeologists in an area of west Florida stretching from Charlotte Harbor in the south to the Withlacoochee River in the north, but most particularly around Tampa Bay in Manatee, Hillsborough, and Pinellas Counties. The Withlacoochee River appears to have been a particularly important boundary separating Safety Harbor culture from cultures that lay to the north. The Safety Harbor people lived in clusters of small villages that were under the power of chiefs. The larger sites had temple mounds and burial mounds, and many sites had large accumulations of discarded shell, mainly oyster. Much of their food came from the Gulf, and from the estuaries at the mouths of the rivers. Unfortunately, most of these shell heaps have been bulldozed in the twentieth century and the shell used to pave roads, effectively destroying many Safety Harbor archaeological sites. Archaeologists have thus far learned next to nothing about the houses built by the people of the Safety Harbor culture.

Like many people in the late prehistoric Southeast, the Safety Harbor people practiced secondary burial. That is, when someone died, they would remove the flesh from the skeleton, and the skeleton was then bundled up in a fabric wrapping or placed in containers and then stored inside a temple or charnel house. These temples were often built on top of low mounds. Some of these remains were subsequently interred in burial mounds (see fig. 16), perhaps reserved for particular kin groups, located out in the woods, away from the villages. Similar low and generally circular burial mounds were also built in northern Florida and along the coast of Georgia. Periodically the temples were razed and the bundles of bones inside were buried or placed on the surface of the mound. The mound was then covered over with a layer of sand or dirt, and a new temple might then be built on top of the enlarged mound. The event that occasioned the emptying and rebuilding of a temple-ossuary is unknown, though here as elsewhere, one such occasion might have been the death of an important chief.

The town of Ozita, where the Spaniards had established their base camp, may have been the Thomas mound site, on the north side of the mouth of the Little Manatee River. This site had a burial mound measuring six feet high and sixty feet in diameter, and it included an extensive shell midden along the bank of the river. European artifacts have been recovered from this site, but the site has been destroyed, and the evidence to prove conclusively that it was where the base camp was located may no longer exist.

The Safety Harbor people who lived on the eastern side of Tampa Bay had been touched by the Mississippian way of life, but they were not fully Mississippian. The Mississippian way of life was dynamic and transforming, and one of its most potent factors may have been a new, more highly organized kind of warfare. Safety Harbor people did make and use small triangular arrow points similar to those made by Mississippian people elsewhere, but as De Soto and his men marched through northern Florida, the Indians they encountered greatly feared the Apalachees, a Mississippian people in northwestern Florida. It is reasonable to think that if the Apalachees could pose such a military threat to their neighbors, then their neighbors would thereby be encouraged to organize themselves along more Mississippian lines in order to meet this threat. The military might of the Apalachees may have been felt as far south as the Calusa in extreme southern Florida. The societies De Soto encountered between Tampa Bay and the territory of the Apalachees existed in a kind of gradient, with those who were most Mississippianized being nearest the Apalachee.

Thus, the Safety Harbor people possessed some but not all of the trappings of Mississippian societies. They built small platform mounds adjacent to plazas in their main towns. They made great use of cups made of Busycon shells from the Gulf and probably traded them to people in the north. They made sand- and grit-tempered ceramic vessels in the form of open, cazuela, and globular bowls. Their everyday ware was plain, but their fancier ware was incised with rectilinear and curvilinear motifs reminiscent of those used by the Apalachees. Safety Harbor pottery, however, was less well made than Apalachee pottery.

The people of the Safety Harbor culture were more dependent on wild foods than were people north of the Withlacoochee River. Archaeologists have not yet found any substantial evidence of corn agriculture at any Safety Harbor site, although the historical records indicate that some of the people in the interior of the Florida peninsula were farmers.[25]

De Soto never met the chief who held power over Ozita, and because of this it is difficult to delineate his territory. But it probably included the coast of Tampa Bay from the mouth of the Little Manatee River to the entrance to the bay, and it included a hinterland that extended some distance into the interior.

Had the Spaniards but noticed, they could have inferred that the people of Ozita were not agriculturalists because their village was closely surrounded with a dense and lofty forest. De Soto ordered that the trees around the village be cut down and cleared away to about the distance of a crossbow shot so the horses could be used for tactical advantage over any Indians who might attack, particularly if they should attack at night. He posted foot soldiers in pairs as sentinels on four-hour watches along the trails and around the perimeter of the camp. At intervals during the night, mounted soldiers made their rounds, visiting these sentinels to see if everything was all right.

They could have used the trees they cut around the perimeter of the base camp to build a fortification, but unfortunately, the documents are silent about this. A large store of supplies guarded by a small contingent of men would eventually be left here, and so a fortification would have made sense. In this connection, it may be notable that the Thomas mound site is known to have been enclosed by segments of ditches and embankments forming three sides of a rectangle, with two legs of this rectangle measuring about five hundred feet and the third segment shorter than this. The river formed the south side of the rectangle.[26] We do not know whether these ditches and embankments were the work of De Soto's men.

De Soto and the men who had marched from Piney Point evidently spent June 2 being ferried across the mouth of the Little Manatee River to reach the landing site on the opposite side.[27] On June 3 De Soto took formal possession of the country for Emperor Charles V. De Soto renamed the bay they had been calling Bayahonda; the new name was Puerto del Espíritu Santo, in honor of the holy day on which they had made their landfall.[28]

De Soto took up residence in the chief's house, along with Vasco Porcallo and Luís de Moscoso. Baltasar de Gallegos took up residence in a house in the center of the town, and provisions from the ships were stored in other houses. The temple and the remaining houses were torn down, and the materials salvaged from them were used to build small shelters for the rest of the men, who lived together in groups of three and four.[29]

After some time had passed, De Soto sent a letter back to Santiago, Cuba, reporting what had occurred. He reported having heard rumors of pearls and precious metals, but he said he was skeptical of their truth.[30]

Horses, Dogs, Pigs

De Soto's men had as allies a triad of domesticated animals—horses, dogs, and pigs—that served them in peace and in war. These three animals were thoroughly integrated into Spanish life, and particularly so for Extremadurans. Horses conferred a tremendous military advantage on the Spaniards, carrying goods for them and allowing them to travel farther and faster than they could have on foot, and with much less expenditure of energy. The dogs formed social bonds with the Spaniards, perhaps regarding them as dominant members of their own pack; thus they would search out, herd, harass, or attack and kill anything their masters sent them after. The pigs, tended by swineherds and dogs, were a mobile larder for the Spaniards. The herd belonged to De Soto, who butchered them only occasionally, for feasts and at times when his men had no other source of food.

The interlocking roles of these three animals in Spanish culture can be seen most dramatically in the wild boar hunt (fig. 11), a very popular sport among the nobility in sixteenth-century Spain. The favorite time for a hunt was a moonlit night in autumn, when the pigs were feeding on acorns that had fallen to the ground. The hunters would go out on their horses armed with lances. They took along dogs to locate the pigs, drive them to the hunters, and worry the pigs until the hunters could ride them down and lance them. It required considerable equestrian skill, as well as bravery on the part of both rider and horse, to lance wild pigs from horseback.

The horses that De Soto brought with him were probably like the "Barb" of today, so called because they were first bred on the Barbary Coast of North Africa and introduced into Spain by the Muslims. In many ways the Barb resembled modern Arabian horses. They were small horses, with exceptionally

Fig. 11. A wild boar hunt. The lancers are riding in the *a la jineta* style. Photograph of a plate in George Millar's *Orellana Discovers the Amazon*, facing p. 40.

hard bones and strong tendons. They could carry heavy loads for long distances at surprisingly fast speeds. They were able to travel long distances with little sustenance, and they were famous for continuing to perform after being grievously wounded. The Spanish horse had a broad forehead, and a face tapering to a small muzzle with large, flaring nostrils. It had an arched neck with a long mane and a flowing tail set high. The color was variable. De Soto started out riding a dappled gray called Aceytuno, named after Mateo de Aceytuno of Havana, who had given him the horse. Nuño de Tovar also rode a dappled gray. Juan López Cacho rode a toasted bay with a black mane and tail. Gonzalo Silvestre, who bragged shamelessly about the virtues of his horse, rode a chestnut with a stockinged left foot and a white stripe from its forehead to its muzzle. This horse, by scent only, was able to follow a trail through a swamp along which De Soto's army had passed earlier.[31]

De Soto and his men rode their horses in the *a la jineta* style, after the manner of Moors, with their legs slightly flexed, so they could maneuver their horses better and wield their lances more effectively. In this way they could hold the lance level alongside their thigh, parallel to the horse, or they could brace their hand against their chest for a powerful thrust. Also, they could thrust downward with their lance, and they could do likewise with a sword. They used high Moorish saddles and Moorish bits.[32]

Not only could lancers inflict heavy casualties on Indian warriors, they could prevent them from closing in and doing hand-to-hand combat with Spanish footmen. Indians found few places to hide from the horses. If they could make it to a swamp or canebrake they were safe. Lacking these refuges, they could try to seek cover behind a tree, but any attempt to run brought the great danger of exposing their naked backs to the lance.

The Spaniards would sometimes put their men at risk in order to protect their horses. During the course of the expedition, Baltasar de Gallegos once commanded a contingent of men who were detached from the main army and were trying to catch up with them. They were slowed down when three of their horses became ill. The men grumbled, but Gallegos insisted that they continue their slow pace because the horses were the "nerve and sinew" of the army, and the Indians feared them greatly. The chroniclers said the Indians were more intent on killing horses than on killing Spaniards, and when the Indians killed a horse, they were as pleased as if they had killed three or four men.[33]

The Spaniards attached quantities of small copper bells to the trappings of their horses—in the manner of sleigh bells—that jingled when their horses moved. These bells were made out of pieces of sheet copper that were individually formed and then soldered together (see fig. 85c). The bells are spherical, measuring about one and a quarter inches in diameter. An attachment loop of copper was soldered to the top of the bell, and the lower part had a slot cut in it, so sound from a pebble or piece of iron inside would escape freely. The Indians fancied these bells, and archaeologists (who call them Clarksdale bells) have found them in several sites in the neighborhood of the routes traveled by Narváez, De Soto, and Luna.[34] Perhaps the close association of these little bells with fearsome horses was part of their allure for the Indians.

Well before the sixteenth century Europeans had developed several breeds of large dogs (fig. 12) that were used to herd animals, to hunt, and to do battle with and terrorize men (see fig. 20). These were the mastiff (*mastín*), a short-haired, heavily muscled dog that could withstand long marches and hold its own against wolves, and was favored in herding sheep and pigs. The swift, lean, greyhound (*lebrel*) was used to hunt and attack large animals such as deer and wild boars, and it could also be trained as a war dog. A third type of dog,

Fig. 12. A mounted lancer and a dog-handler. Both the dog-handler (*left*) and his two greyhounds wear padded (*escaupil*) armor. The horseman (*right*) wears heavy armor. Note the bells attached to the trappings of his horse. Drawing by Lawrence May.

the *alano*, was a large attack dog, evidently of several breeds, including large mastiffs and Irish wolfhounds.

Such dogs were used against the Moors in the Reconquest, against the Guanches in the conquest of the Canary Islands, and quite naturally they were taken to the New World to be used against the Indians. The most vicious of these war dogs had to be chained and managed by handlers. But these fierce dogs knew the difference between Spaniard and Indian, and some of them could be sent to chase down a particular Indian. Their handlers could send them on the attack by shouting *tómalos!*—"Get them!"—while indicating who was to be the target. To make the dogs even more fearsome, the Spaniards often put spiked leather or wide steel collars around their necks, so the person under attack could not get his hands around the dog's neck to choke it. And when the dogs were exposed to Indian arrows, the Spaniards sometimes protected the dogs' bodies with *escaupiles*, jackets of thick, quilted cotton armor. Typically these war dogs would kill by attacking a man's belly and disemboweling him. Often they would attack a man's genitals.

De Soto no doubt learned to use dogs against Indians while he was in the service of the sadistic Pedrárias. On one occasion in León Viejo, Nicaragua, Pedrárias determined to punish eighteen chiefs who were accused of having killed seven Spanish *encomenderos*. Pedrárias had the captive chiefs brought into the plaza, armed them with short sticks, and set five or six half-grown war dogs against them. The Indians easily beat them off and felt they had withstood their ordeal, but then Pedrárias sent seasoned war dogs against the chiefs. One by one the chiefs were killed and mutilated and their corpses eaten. Citizens of León Viejo watched this affair as sport or spectacle. By the time he died, at age ninety, Pedrárias was called El furor Domini—the Wrath of God—a title he richly deserved.

De Soto was most certainly familiar with another use of dogs in Central America—*montería infernal*—the sport of using dogs to hunt down Indians, including captives who were set free to run into the woods. The dogs chased these Indians down as if they were wild beasts; and when they caught them, they killed and ate them.[35]

Dogs played an important role in the De Soto expedition. Unfortunately, the number and kinds of dogs that De Soto brought with him are not known. All that is known with certainty is that some of them were greyhounds and one was an Irish wolfhound. Dogs were used for the entire duration of the expedition.

The pigs De Soto brought from Cuba may have been descendants of the pigs Queen Isabela enjoined Columbus to take with him on his second voyage. The variety of pig the Spaniards brought with them probably resembled the wild boars (*Sus scrofa*) from which they had been domesticated. They were black or dark gray in color, erect-eared, long-snouted, lean, long-legged, and capable of defending themselves with formidable tusks.

The pig is a primitive ungulate that is remarkably flexible and adaptable in its behavior, and omnivorous in its diet. De Soto did not lack swineherds with so many of his men having come from Extremadura, a province in which swine-herding is historically one of the most important endeavors and that even today is famous for its pork. The pig is a forest animal (fig. 13), and in the sixteenth century *porqueros* normally kept their herds in forests, where they could feed on acorns and chestnuts. Sometimes these herders were called *vareadores*, after the *varas*, wooden flails or sticks, which they used to flail nuts out of trees for the pigs to eat. The value of forests in sixteenth-century Europe were sometimes measured in terms of how many swine they could support.

In general the pigs would fare better on the expedition than the men, horses, and dogs. Pigs can subsist on almost anything they encounter in the forest—

Fig. 13. A fifteenth-century French swineherd, probably in the province of Savoie. It is November and the swineherd is throwing a staff to knock down acorns for the pigs to eat while his dog watches. Detail from the *Tres Riches Heures* of Jean, Duke of Berry.

plants, fruits, seeds, mushrooms, as well as eggs, carrion, lizards, and even poisonous snakes. They have poor eyesight but a keen sense of hearing, and they have an exceedingly keen sense of smell. They eat what is on top of the ground and what is below it. With the cartilaginous discs on their snouts, they can root up the soil to find tubers, worms, and burrowing rodents.

Pigs are the most efficient food producers that can be herded. (Chickens are more efficient than pigs, but no one has ever devised a way to herd chickens.) Pigs can store in their bodies 35 percent of the energy they consume. Sheep and cattle can store only about 11 percent. A pig's carcass yields 65 percent to 80 percent dressed meat, while a cow yields only 50 percent to 60 percent, and a sheep yields a mere 45 percent to 55 percent. A four-ounce serving of pork yields 402 calories, while the same serving of beef yields 369 calories, and lamb yields 367 calories.[36]

Wild boars are not migratory animals, and their domesticated relatives cannot be herded from place to place as easily as cattle or horses. But they are gregarious animals, and they like to stay together. Although they are not easy to drive, they can be led, and they can be conditioned to respond to sound.

They communicate among themselves with a wide range of grunts and squeals, and their hearing is sharp. They normally travel at a trot, but they can hurry along at a fast gallop when need be. They are excellent swimmers and can cross bodies of water a mile or more wide.

Pigs are unusually fecund. A female as young as nine months old may become pregnant, and she can give birth to as many as twelve in a litter. She normally has two litters per year. Thus a herd of pigs can increase prodigiously within a few years. Within a few weeks after birth, young pigs forage with their mothers, but they are mainly dependent on their mother's milk until they are two and a half to three months old. The mothers are unusually alert and protective of their young.

In sixteenth-century Spain shepherds drove herds of pigs along with their much larger herds of sheep. They ate pork not only for sustenance but also to remove any suspicion that they were Jews. These shepherds could drive their herds as much as fifteen to eighteen miles per day over a good road or trail, but if there was no trail, they traveled shorter distances.[37]

The triad of horses, dogs, and pigs conferred an additional advantage on the Spaniards. Each of these animals possesses senses more acute than those of people, and together they added up to a superb early warning capability. This made it very difficult for the Indians to mount effective surprise attacks on De Soto's army.

Juan Ortiz

De Soto and his men found themselves in a country with no adviser or informant who could tell them where anything was located. There were trails, but no one knew which ones to follow. De Soto sent out one of their captive Indian translators to establish contact with the local Indians, but evidently this man did not return. Foolishly, they did not take the precaution of chaining the other three translators, and during the night of June 3, two of them escaped through the carelessness of two soldiers who were supposed to have guarded them.[38]

The Spaniards evidently captured at least one Indian who was subject to Ozita. They interrogated him, presumably using their lone remaining translator. The captive attempted to tell them about a matter that Añasco's captive translators had already told them about in a garbled way. He seemed to say that a Spaniard was living among some Indians near where their camp was. The captive kept uttering the word "Orotiz," which caused the Spaniards much delight, because what he was saying seemed to contain the Spanish word *oro*, "gold," and that is what they all wanted to discover.[39]

De Soto and his men were growing anxious about their lack of intelligence concerning La Florida. The land surrounding their base camp was very swampy and thickly wooded, and they had difficulty getting about. With their one remaining Indian translator and guide unable or unwilling to tell them about the lay of the land, they were helpless to plan what to do next. On June 4 De Soto ordered Baltasar de Gallegos to take forty horsemen, eighty footmen, and their Indian guide and to go find a village, or short of that, to capture some people.

De Soto next ordered captain Juan Rodríguez Lobillo to take fifty footmen and go in a different direction. Lobillo had some arquebusiers and crossbowmen in this company, but most of his men were armed only with swords and shields. After crossing a swampy area impassable to horsemen, they discovered a small village near the river. When the people inside the houses spied them, they ran out and plunged into the river. The Spaniards managed to capture four women. But as they were returning to camp with their captives, they were pursued by twenty warriors who pressed them very hard.

Without horsemen, Lobillo and his men had little if any advantage over the Indians. In this conflict they realized that the Indians of La Florida would be formidable adversaries. They were extraordinarily nimble, and if the Spaniards pressed them, they would flee, but never to more than the distance of an arrow shot. But as soon as the Spaniards turned their backs, the Indians would come after them. They were constantly in motion, running from side to side, so that the arquebusiers and crossbowmen could not get a clear shot. In the time it took a crossbowman to load, aim, and shoot once, an Indian could let fly three or four arrows, and they seldom missed their mark. They managed to wound six of Lobillo's men, and one of them subsequently died.[40]

As for Gallegos and his contingent, they ranged about the countryside for the entire day, often confused because their guide took advantage of their ignorance of the land to lead them in circles. But when Gallegos became certain the guide was deceiving him, he threatened to kill him, and this persuaded the guide to lead them back to a trail.[41] Near sunset they spotted a party of ten to twenty Indians who had painted their bodies with a red pigment they used when they wanted to make a good show. They wore tufts or bunches of feathers (*penachos*) on their heads, and they were armed with bows and arrows. Gallegos and his men charged at this party of Indians and lanced one of them, the others fleeing into a small forest. But one of the Indians separated from the others and brashly approached the Spaniards. As Alvaro Nieto bore down on him with his lance, the warrior adroitly knocked the lance away with his bow and leaped aside. He shouted "Xivilla, Xivilla," which the Spaniards realized was meant to be "Sevilla, Sevilla!"[42] Then to their astonishment the man said: "Sirs, for the love of God and of St. Mary, do not kill me; I am Christian, like you, and I am a native of Seville, and my name is Juan Ortiz."[43] He was the "Orotiz" their captive had told them about. His Spanish was so rusty that Gallegos and his companions could hardly understand him. He begged for the Spaniards to stop attacking his Indian comrades, some of whom had run back to their chief Mocozo with news of the encounter. At Ortiz's prompting, Gallegos sent another Indian messenger to Mocozo, informing him that the attack had been a mistake.[44]

At first appearance, Juan Ortiz was indistinguishable from his Indian comrades. He was deeply tanned by the sun; he was dressed as the Indians were dressed; he carried a bow and arrows; and his arms were tattooed just as theirs were.[45] Because he had not spoken Spanish for the twelve years he had been held captive, he now spoke it haltingly. It was more than four days before he ceased mixing Indian words into his Spanish. Gradually, as he regained fluency in his native language, his story began to unfold.[46]

Not only was Ortiz a native of Seville, he was the son of a noble family. He had first come to La Florida with Narváez but had returned to Havana with the ships after they had unloaded Narváez and his army. In Havana, Narváez's wife eventually ordered Ortiz and twenty or thirty others to sail to La Florida to search for signs of the expedition. They did so, sailing into Tampa Bay to a town of Ozita. On the beach they saw stuck in the sand a stick with its upper end split and with what appeared to be a letter wedged into the cleft.[47]

Ortiz and the others concluded that it had been left by Narváez to inform them of his actions. They asked some Indians who were on the beach to bring it to them, but the Indians, by means of signs, indicated that they should come ashore and get the letter themselves. In a show of friendship, two Indians swam out and climbed aboard the ship. With these two friendly Indians as hostages, Ortiz and another crewman volunteered to go and retrieve the letter, even though the other men counseled them not to do so. As soon as the two Spaniards were on the beach, a great number of Indians rushed out and surrounded them. At the same instant, the two Indian hostages dove overboard and swam underwater for a great distance before surfacing and swimming on to the shore.[48] Ortiz's companion put up a fight and was killed on the spot. The men on the bergantín were so outnumbered they made no attempt to rescue Ortiz. Instead they raised sail and made for the mouth of the harbor.

The Indians led Ortiz to their chief, Ozita. Chief Ozita had good reason to hate Spaniards. A member of the Narváez expedition had thrown the chief's wife to the dogs to be killed and devoured. And they had cut off the tip of the chief's nose (see fig. 20), disfiguring him for life. It was said that every time the chief went to blow his nose, he would remember that Ortiz was his captive. He condemned Ortiz to performing the most menial tasks—carrying water and firewood—which he was required to do unceasingly.[49] When the chief became particularly irritable, he would make Ortiz run back and forth across the plaza of the town for long periods of time. If he tried to stop running, the chief's men would shoot arrows at him. Ortiz's suffering was so great he sometimes envied his companion who had been killed on the beach.

Finally chief Ozita decided to put Ortiz to death by torture. He ordered that a great fire be built in the plaza. When it had burned down to coals, the Indians raked the coals under a grill (see fig. 25), suspended on posts about three feet high. Then they bound Ortiz hand and foot and tied him to the grill. But when Ortiz began shrieking, the wife and daughters of the chief begged that his life be spared. They argued that Ortiz had not been with those who had perpetrated the crimes against Ozita. And how could a single boy be any threat to the people of Ozita? Moreover, alive they had the benefit of his service as a slave. The chief relented.[50]

Ortiz had already been badly burned by the coals. Huge blisters on his body became raw and bloody, and some later became infected with maggots. One entire side of his body became a solid scar.[51] The chief's wife and her daughters nursed him back to health using herbal remedies.[52] When he had recovered his health, he was given the job of guarding the temple at night. Cadavers were stored in this temple, and wolves and other scavengers would sometimes come at night to try to eat the remains.[53] The chief warned Ortiz that if even a part of a body was devoured by an animal, he would roast him for certain. The chief gave Ortiz some javelins to use against scavengers.[54]

One night Ortiz dozed off while on watch. He awoke to the sound of some boards being toppled from a sepulcher, and he thought at that moment that he was as good as dead. A wolf had entered the temple and had dragged out the body of the son of one of the principal men in the town. Ortiz followed a trail for a distance until he heard the sound of an animal gnawing on bones. He threw a javelin into the darkness in the direction of the sound.[55] Though it was too dark to see if he had hit his mark, he was somewhat encouraged because he did not hear the beast flee, and also because his throwing hand was "salty," this being a good sign when one had to make a throw in the dark.[56] He returned to the temple to pray while waiting for the sun to rise. In the first light, he saw that the boy's body was missing, and he became depressed, knowing what the consequences would be. When chief Ozita learned what had happened, he resolved to execute Ortiz. But when Ozita sent a party of men to examine the trail where the wolf had gone, they found the body of the boy, and a little further on they found the wolf dead of a wound from Ortiz's javelin.[57]

This lucky throw of the javelin was impressive to chief Ozita and his people, and because of this their estimation of Ortiz rose. Thereafter they treated him with respect.[58] Ortiz enjoyed this good favor for about three years, until Ozita was attacked by his enemy Mocozo, whose territory was two days distant. As a consequence of those hostilities, Ozita and his people had to flee to a tributary town located on another inlet. For unknown reasons, this attack undercut Ortiz's good standing. He learned from one of the same girls who had saved his life that the chief had decided to sacrifice Ortiz the very next day.[59] She told him he should flee to Mocozo, where he would be safe, because she had heard that Mocozo wished to have Ortiz as a subject.[60]

Ortiz did not know how to find his way to the territory of Mocozo, but the girl offered to help, and that night she led him half a league from the town and put him on the right trail.[61] In order to keep their absence from being discovered, she then returned to the town, presumably after giving Ortiz instructions on how to proceed from there.

Ortiz traveled all night through the darkness, and the next morning he came to the river—the Alafia—that lay on the boundary of Mocozo's territory. Two Indians were fishing in the river. Since they were enemies of Ozita, and since the languages of Ozita and Mocozo were mutually unintelligible, Ortiz was afraid that if they saw him, he would not be able to explain to them who he was and why he had come, and they might kill him before he could make his purpose known. Fortunately, they had not yet seen him, and he crept over to where they had laid their weapons and then let himself be seen. The two Indians responded by bolting and running to their town, even though Ortiz had tried to make them wait and hear him out. But they had no way of understanding him. Shouting loudly, the two Indians raised a great number of warriors to come back with them. As they surrounded Ortiz, intent on killing him, Ortiz cowered behind some trees and shouted to the top of his lungs that he was a Christian who was a prisoner of Ozita. Luckily, one of Mocozo's Indians understood the language of Ozita, and he translated to the others the sense of what Ortiz was trying to say.[62]

They began leading Ortiz to their village, sending three or four ahead to inform chief Mocozo of what was happening. Mocozo came out a quarter of a league from his town to meet them. He was evidently glad to see Ortiz, and he made him swear he would not run away and go to any other chief. For his part, Mocozo promised to treat him with respect, and he said that if any Christians came in their ships, he would release him and let him go to them.[63]

Three years after Ortiz found refuge with Mocozo, some Indians who had been fishing at a distance of two leagues from the village, presumably in Tampa Bay, came to Mocozo and told him they had seen Spanish ships. Mocozo gave Ortiz permission to go to them, and Ortiz said goodbye and went as quickly as he could to where he might see the ships. But when he got there he did not see any ships, and he thought a trick had been played on him. Perhaps Mocozo was testing him.[64]

Ortiz remained with Mocozo for nine years and had given up hope of ever seeing other Spaniards. But as soon as De Soto's fleet approached the coast of La Florida, Mocozo was informed of it. Mocozo told Ortiz that Spaniards were living in Ozita's town. But Ortiz suspected it to be a trick, like the one he thought had been played on him earlier. So he said he no longer thought about Spaniards: his only thought and desire was to serve Mocozo.[65]

Mocozo assured Ortiz that what he told him about Spaniards was true, and that he had permission to go to them. If the Spaniards departed, then he should not blame Mocozo for failing to do what he had promised. Moreover, Mocozo wanted him to put in a good word with the Spaniards for the help and protection he had given to Ortiz.[66] With this, Ortiz believed what Mocozo said, and he could hardly contain his joy. Mocozo asked ten or twelve of his principal men to go with Ortiz, and they were with him when they came upon the scouting party led by Baltasar de Gallegos.[67]

De Soto and his men were delighted with their great good luck in finding Ortiz. Now they had what they so desperately needed, a trustworthy translator and guide. In fact, Ortiz spoke two languages—those of Ozita and Mocozo. Now the expedition could make real progress.[68]

De Soto gave Ortiz a fine suit of black cloth to wear, as well as arms and a beautiful horse. But Ortiz was so unaccustomed to European clothes that for twenty days, while getting used to being dressed, he wore only a shirt, linen pants, a cap, and some shoes.[69] De Soto questioned Ortiz closely about the lay of the land. Was there any gold and silver? Ortiz replied that he knew of none, although he had never traveled more than ten leagues from where he lived. But he said he had heard that thirty leagues away there was the territory of chief Urriparacoxi, to whom Mocozo, Ozita, and the other chiefs of the coast paid tribute.[70] Urriparacoxi's land was reputed to be richer than that near the coast, and his people were said to produce an abundance of corn. Perhaps Urriparacoxi would have information about a place where riches could be found. De Soto put a good light on this news. In such a vast land, there *had* to be a rich society somewhere.[71]

When Chief Mocozo came to the camp to visit with the Spaniards, he told De Soto that he wished to be at peace with him, and that his having given refuge to Ortiz was proof of his good will. De Soto replied that he was grateful to him for what he had done, and he would consider him to be a brother and would protect him. He presented Mocozo with a shirt and other gifts.[72]

Chief Mocozo remained at De Soto's camp for several days. His mother became worried that he was suffering at the hands of the Spaniards, fearing that he might be subjected to the same kind of torture and humiliation Narváez had inflicted on the chief of Ozita. One day she appeared at the camp, obviously terrified, and offered to be tortured in place of her son. She begged De Soto not to do to him what Narváez had done to his victims. Though De Soto reassured her that no harm was to come to her son, she still remained fearful. When she sat down to eat with the Spaniards, she would eat nothing until Ortiz had tasted it first, because she was afraid of being poisoned. When she had been convinced that her son was in no danger and that he was enjoying himself among the Spaniards, she returned home, but not before imploring Ortiz to look out for himself.[73]

On June 7, after Mocozo returned to his village, Juan Ortiz led De Soto and a detachment of men to repay his visit. Mocozo waited for them in his village, with all his relatives and his people present to meet them. Using Ortiz as translator, chief Mocozo complained to De Soto about his political problems. Hirrihigua, Neguarete, Capaloey, and Ozita were neighboring chiefs, and they were all hostile to him because he had protected Ortiz and delivered him to the Spaniards.[74] But De Soto told Mocozo he had nothing to fear from these chiefs. Many more Spaniards would come in the future, and they would be allies of Mocozo against any who should oppose him.[75]

On this same day, back at the camp, Captain Juan Ruiz Lobillo went out on a foray with forty footmen and came upon some settlements.[76] They captured two Indian women. But the kinsmen and neighbors of these women were not willing to give them up. Nine warriors followed Lobillo and his men for three leagues, firing arrows at them. One Spaniard was killed and three or four others were wounded. Even though Lobillo had arquebusiers and men with crossbows, the Spaniards were unable to inflict any casualties on the Indians. Once again the Spaniards learned that on foot the Indians were formidable fighters, fully a match for Spaniards who were also on foot, unsupported by horsemen.[77]

After returning to camp, De Soto ordered General Vasco Porcallo to go to a certain town of Ozita because, through intelligence gained by Ortiz, he had reports that many Indians had come together there. When Vasco Porcallo's contingent arrived, they found the Indians had all fled. Furious, he torched the village, and because the Indian guide they were following had led them badly and had lied to them, they threw him to the dogs.[78] This is the first instance of a practice that seems to have occurred repeatedly on the expedition but that the chroniclers explicitly mention only occasionally. Indeed, dogs are carnivores, and because the Spaniards themselves often went for long periods without having any meat, the dreadful truth must be that there was little else for the dogs to eat but Indians.

While Vasco Porcallo was away on this foray, De Soto sent an Indian messenger on a mission to chief Urriparacoxi.[79] The messenger did not return as ordered, and the Spaniards learned that an Indian woman they held captive had encouraged him not to come back. For this she was thrown to the dogs.[80]

Northward from Tampa Bay

After unloading, the large ships returned to Cuba and the smaller ones remained at Tampa Bay for further service.[81] The leaders of the expedition discussed what to do next. The place where they had landed did not seem to be a good place to found a settlement. The soil was "too barren," and this may mean that from their point of view there were no suitable food-producing native societies to exploit.[82]

The prevailing soils around Tampa Bay, and in much of Florida, are sandy gray-and-black flatwood soils. They are poorly drained, very acidic, and low in native fertility. The water table is typically quite near the surface.

De Soto decided the time had come to look further afield. On June 20 he sent Baltasar de Gallegos with eighty horsemen and one hundred footmen to Urriparacoxi.[83] Their task was to assess the nature of the land and the people, to acquire intelligence about the land that lay beyond, and to report on what they had learned via messengers. De Soto ordered some of the remaining ships to return to Havana with orders to bring back more provisions at a specified time.

Meanwhile, the Indians of Ozita continued harassing and waging war on the Spaniards. In one raid they captured a man named Grajales. But later, in a daring raid on an Ozita sanctuary in a vast canebrake, the Spaniards rescued Grajales. The Indians had already dressed him as one of their own. In contrast to the way in which Ortiz had been treated, Grajales claimed to have been treated well.[84] Perhaps the Indians wanted to gain intelligence from him or to use him as a bargaining chip.

One day De Soto received intelligence that chief Hirrihigua and his warriors were encamped not far from the base camp. He sent Juan de Añasco and some foot soldiers in ship's boats along the shore to locate and disperse them. When Añasco found them on an island, a battle ensued. Añasco used a small piece of artillery (probably a swivel gun) that was on one of the boats to kill and wound ten of these Indians. But the Indians inflicted a similar number of casualties on the Spaniards. Añasco was not able to drive them from the island, so he sent Johan de Vega back to request that a detachment of horsemen be sent to the place where he expected the Indians to flee. Vasco Porcallo came with forty horsemen and some foot soldiers, but by the time he got there the Indians had already escaped.[85]

Vasco Porcallo thought this would be a good opportunity to acquire some slaves, this being one of his principal reasons for coming on the expedition.[86] He recruited some of his horsemen and foot soldiers and they set out. Going along, they came to a particularly bad swamp, and Vasco Porcallo, to set an example for his men, spurred his horse into the swamp. But after taking only a few steps, his horse slipped and fell in the mud and slimy water. Vasco Porcallo was at risk of drowning, but his men were afraid to plunge in after him for fear they themselves would end up in the same predicament. Vasco Porcallo was wearing a full suit of armor, and one of his legs was pinned beneath his horse. With much effort, his men finally extricated him from the mud.[87]

The slave-raiding party only managed to capture a few women before heading back to camp, and Vasco Porcallo was in a dark mood. He realized he had bet a small fortune on a venture that was beginning to seem unsure of success, and even worse, he was beginning to realize he was no longer the man he had once been.

On the way back to camp he muttered to himself, and sometimes he talked aloud. He would repeat the names of the two chiefs Hirrihigua and Urriparacoxi, breaking up the syllables of their names and interspersing Spanish swear words. "Hurri, harri, hurri, higa, burra coja, hurri, harri . . . may the Devil take the land where the first and most continuously spoken names I have heard are so vile and infamous." *Burra coja* refers to a lame she-ass, and *higa* refers to an amulet of a human hand with the thumb held between the fingers, worn to ward off evil. Vasco Porcallo repeated this and other obscenities many times on his way back to camp.[88]

When Vasco Porcallo got back to camp, he and De Soto exchanged angry words. Vasco Porcallo was frustrated at not being able to capture more slaves, and the character of the land did not look promising to him. He decided to return to Cuba and to take with him all the slaves and servants he had brought with him. He left behind the food he had brought, including the herd of hogs. He also gave some promise to give assistance to De Soto in the future if it should become necessary to do so.[89]

Gómez Suárez de Figuerora, the bastard son Vasco Porcallo had sired with an Indian girl, remained with the expedition. Vasco Porcallo supplied him with two horses, arms, and other supplies. Gómez Suárez was a fine soldier, but he was excessively proud. Later, when Indians killed both of his horses, De Soto offered to help him out, but he was too proud to accept help from anyone.[90]

Baltasar de Gallegos and his detachment reached the land of Urriparacoxi in due time. Juan Ortiz went along as translator and guide. They first stopped at Mocozo and asked the chief to go with them to Urriparacoxi, but he declined, saying he did not want to direct strangers to the land of a "brother" and an in-law. He did not want to be on the outs with Urriparacoxi. But after some persuasion, he picked one of his men who had been a friend of Ortiz to serve as an emissary and sent him out in advance of the Spaniards.[91] When they reached Urriparacoxi's land (it is not clear that they ever reached his principal town), the chief and all his people had fled.[92] But the chief sent thirty men to meet with the Spaniards. Gallegos asked that the chief come and speak to him in person. The Indians took this message back to the chief and then returned to say the chief was ill and could not come. They asked Gallegos about his motives. What did he want?

Gallegos asked where he might find a rich land. The Indians told him of a fabulous province, Ocale, which lay to the west of where they were. And they told him many marvelous stories about Ocale. But they were so fantastic that Gallegos suspected them of lying to him as a way of persuading him to leave their land. He was afraid that if he let them go, he would never see them again. So he seized them and put them in chains. Then he sent eight horsemen back to De Soto with letters reporting what he had learned.[93]

4

Apalachee

De Soto used both a stick and a carrot to keep his expedition moving forward and his men performing their duties. The stick was the very considerable power vested in him as adelantado and as governor. The carrot was the prospect of riches and ample food supplies farther on, beyond the next river or mountain range. De Soto had ordered Baltasar de Gallegos to send back encouraging news from Urriparacoxi even if he should be disappointed at what he found. Gallegos obeyed, sending a detachment of eight horsemen back to De Soto carrying two letters, one telling the truth, to be read only by De Soto, and the second, framed in ambiguous but optimistic language, to be read aloud to the men.[1] De Soto explained to his men that the personal letter contained secret information that would be revealed to them in due time, when they would see that what was contained therein was to everyone's advantage.[2] In the letter read aloud to the men, Gallegos promised them nothing specific at Urriparacoxi, but hinted at wonderful things that lay ahead.[3]

In this letter to the men, Gallegos recounted some of the fabulous stories told him by the Indians of Urriparacoxi. They told of the province of Ocale, further on, whose inhabitants kept herds of deer and turkeys in pens and who could shout at birds flying overhead and cause them to drop from the sky.[4]

Ocale was reputed to be a province with traders and with much gold, silver, and pearls.[5] It was a province whose people were at war with a people who lived to the south, where it was summer most of the year. These people to the south were said to possess gold in such abundance they wore hats that seemed to be helmets of gold. If we are to believe that there was any substance to these stories, the people to the south may have been the Calusa, a nonagricultural chiefdom dominating the coastal area from Charlotte Harbor southward (see map 3). They are known to have been at war with people around Tampa Bay and perhaps with people further north, and they recovered gold and silver from Spanish shipwrecks, though their wearing gold hats must be attributed to poor translation, misunderstanding, or falsehood. Gallegos realized these stories were probably false, perhaps a ruse by the people of Urriparacoxi to encourage the Spaniards to move on.[6]

When Gallegos's letter was read to the men at the base camp, they were moved by a great enthusiasm to march immediately into the interior. When De Soto ordered Captain Pedro Calderón and forty horsemen and sixty footmen to remain behind to guard the supplies at the base camp and the ships in the harbor, they were crestfallen over not being permitted to go forward with the others.[7] The stores left behind included enough food to last the men stationed at the base camp for two years.[8] De Soto ordered Calderón and his men to maintain good relations with the Indians even if their patience should be tried.[9]

De Soto and his men did not find at Tampa Bay the supplies of native food needed to sustain them; hence, the promise of more ample supplies of corn to the north was an additional incentive to march into the interior. Juan Ortiz had reported that the quality of land was better in the country of Urriparacoxi and that plenty of corn could be obtained there.[10] As it turned out, the quantities of corn available to De Soto and his men did in fact increase as they traveled northward from Tampa Bay. But it so happened that they were on the move at the very time the green corn was beginning to ripen, so one cannot be sure that all of the increase can be attributed to increased overall corn production and greater dependence on agriculture by the people. Some of the increase may have been due simply to the progressive ripening of the corn.

Departure from Tampa Bay

De Soto announced his decision to move the army forward to Ocale, where he intended to spend the winter.[11] He sent a contingent of horsemen to

Urriparacoxi to inform Gallegos that he should look for the army to arrive in a specified number of days.[12] On July 15 De Soto took his leave from Calderón and the hundred or so men who were to remain behind to guard the base camp. Leading a force of about 320 people, De Soto set out toward the east.[13]

While on the move De Soto normally formed his army up into three units. A vanguard, consisting of horsemen and sometimes a small number of footmen, went in front, clearing the way for the others. De Soto himself usually traveled with the vanguard. Next came the main guard, or battalion, comprising most of the footmen, Indian porters, and servants. A contingent of horsemen traveled with the main guard to protect them. Last came the rear guard of horsemen to protect the rear and on occasion to prevent any stragglers from defecting or escaping from the expedition.

It is likely that the herd of pigs traveled with the main guard, shepherded along by a company of horsemen, according to Garcilaso. Whether De Soto brought along mastiffs to guard the pigs is not known. If not, he might have been able to train one or more of the greyhounds to this task, but doing so would have been hazardous, since greyhounds are chase-and-attack dogs, and the pigs would have been a constant temptation for them.[14]

As they left the base camp, De Soto and his army entered the lower fringe of the vast southeastern pine forest, covering the coastal plain of the eastern Carolinas, southern Georgia, central and southern Alabama, southern Mississippi, and most of Florida; west of the Mississippi it covered central Louisiana and a small portion of eastern Texas (map 4). This southeastern pine forest and all subsequent vegetation zones and landscapes traversed by the De Soto expedition have been profoundly altered during the past 450 years of European occupation, and indeed some changes in the forests had been caused by the Indians. Only fragments of the kinds of forests De Soto and his men explored can be seen today. The landscapes that existed in the sixteenth century must be reconstructed from historical sources and from various kinds of geological information. To imagine the southeastern landscape as it was in the sixteenth century, one must begin by taking away some elements and putting back others.

Some of what one must take away is obvious—the cities, towns, and highways. One must also take away the dams that impound many southeastern streams, creating large lakes in a region where, except for Florida, there were few natural lakes. And one must take away plants introduced into the Southeast from other parts of the world. One must take away bluegrass, plantain, dandelions, honeysuckle, kudzu, and Canadian thistle. One must take away

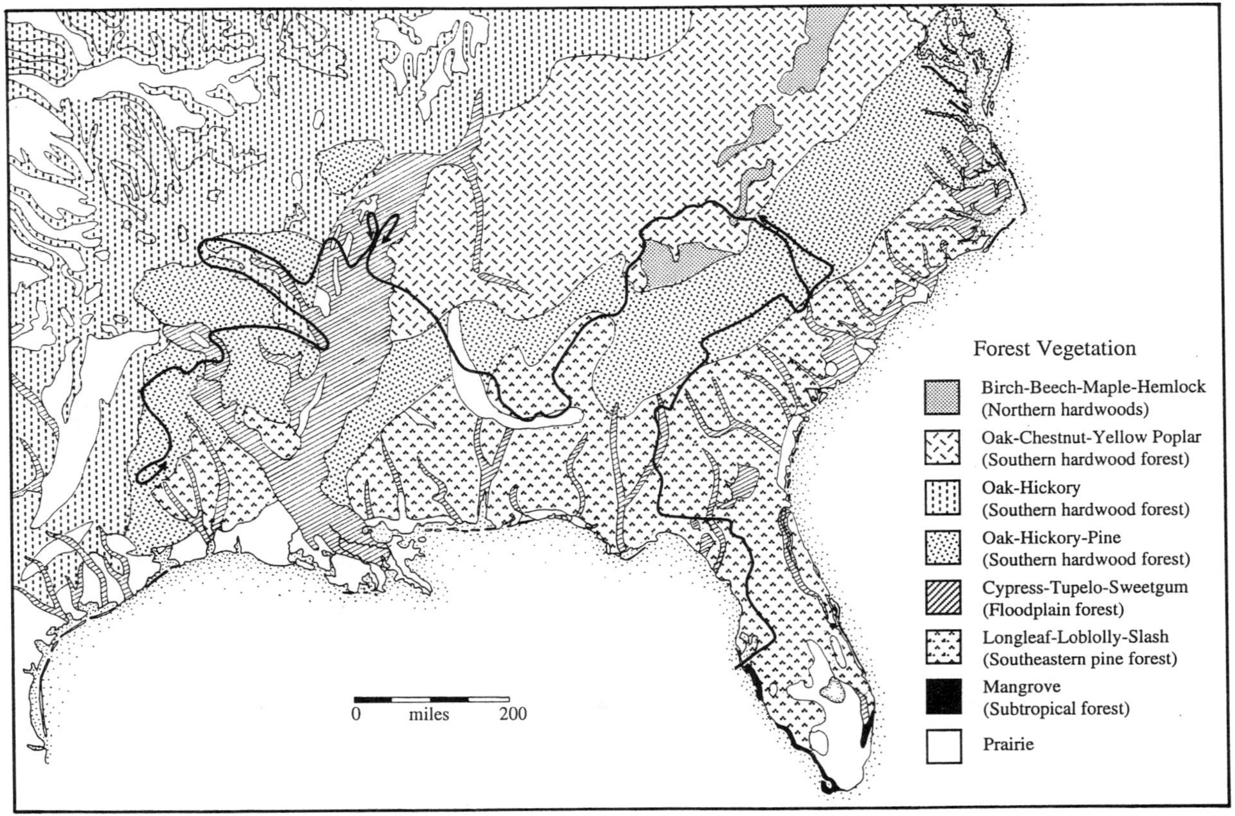

Map 4. Types of forest vegetation in the early southeastern United States. The bold line from Tampa Bay northward indicates the route of the De Soto expedition.

Forest Vegetation

Birch-Beech-Maple-Hemlock
(Northern hardwoods)

Oak-Chestnut-Yellow Poplar
(Southern hardwood forest)

Oak-Hickory
(Southern hardwood forest)

Oak-Hickory-Pine
(Southern hardwood forest)

Cypress-Tupelo-Sweetgum
(Floodplain forest)

Longleaf-Loblolly-Slash
(Southeastern pine forest)

Mangrove
(Subtropical forest)

Prairie

0   200
miles

privet and mimosa. One must take away imported animals such as nutria, starlings, and the Norwegian rat.

One must put back the animals that are now extinct. The passenger pigeon, whose migratory flights once darkened southern skies, the flocks of boisterous green-and-yellow Carolina parakeets, the ivory-billed woodpecker—a giant among woodpeckers—who lived in the depths of forests and hammered large, rotting trees to smithereens. One must also vastly extend the range of the animals that are today almost extinct—the sly and furtive panther, master of the lightning attack, and the gregarious wolves, consummate pack animals and clever strategists. Most of all, one must put back the enormous stands of trees that today can only be seen as remnants of the great old-growth forests that were cut down as American farmers moved west.

The southeastern pine forest was composed of various mixes of several species of pine trees and broadleaf deciduous trees. In some places the pines dominated; in other places the deciduous trees dominated; and in still other places they were intimately mixed together. But as the name implies, vast areas of the southeastern pine forest were covered with longleaf, loblolly, and slash pine trees, a forest of such monotony that eighteenth-century travelers complained of it. The southeastern pine forest became established during the Hypsithermal climatic interval, between about 6000 and 4000 B.C., when prevailing westerly winds made the Southeast much hotter and drier than it is today. The climate was so warm and dry, the treeless prairie vegetation of the West crossed over to the eastern side of the Mississippi River, and the forests in the coastal plain became tinder boxes. For thousands of years they were swept by hot forest fires (mostly started by lightning) that killed off most of the deciduous trees, leaving only pine trees, which withstand fire handily. And these effects were compounded later by an Indian cultural practice. One of the principal ways in which the Indians modified forests was by intentional burning to clear farmland of weeds and brush, to drive game, and perhaps to clear away litter on the forest floor to make way for the tender herbage that would sustain larger numbers of white-tailed deer.

The principal deciduous trees in the southeastern pine forest are the southern magnolia, ancient of trees, with its large leathery leaves and fragrant white flowers; the sweetgum, with its masses of star-shaped leaves and its fragrant storax gum, valued by Europeans as a medicine and perfume; the white oak, a medium-size tree with heavy, hard wood and sweet acorns; and particularly in the northerly part of the forest, the beech, with strong wood and edible nuts.[15] A minor tree, to which the Spaniards probably initially paid no notice, was the yaupon holly from whose parched leaves the Indians of the Southeast brewed a caffeinated beverage. This tea (called "black drink" by eighteenth-century Englishmen) was used by the Indians as a sacramental beverage in many social and ritual contexts. The Spaniards may also have paid no notice to cabbage palmetto, but they would soon come to appreciate some of the uses to which it can be put.

Because Ozita and Mocozo were at war with each other, the territory between their domains—that is, between the Little Manatee and Alafia Rivers—may have been uninhabited. By the end of the first day of travel the vanguard reached the River of Mocozo—the Alafia River—where they bivouacked (map 5). This was probably somewhere between Buckhorn Creek and present-day Bell Shoals Bridge, and perhaps at Bell Shoals itself. They built two footbridges in order to cross the river. These footbridges were probably no more than tall pine trees, stripped of their branches. The Alafia River is about seventy or eighty feet wide at this point. If the crossing was at Bell Shoals, they may have laid one bridge from the near bank to a promontory in the middle of the river and a second one from the far bank to that same promontory. It is also possible they constructed the two small footbridges so the army could cross the river more rapidly.

They entered Mocozo's territory, the area between the Alafia and Hillsborough Rivers, but they did not go out of their way to visit his towns because they were situated too far afield from their line of march.[16] On July 16 they continued on, coming at the end of the day to a place they called the Lake of the Rabbit, probably one of the small lakes near present-day Plant City, Florida. They gave the lake this name because after the horsemen had dismounted near it, leaving their horses untethered, a rabbit suddenly jumped up and frightened all the horses, stampeding them to over a league away. This incident placed the Spaniards in a very dangerous situation because they depended so heavily on their horsemen for military superiority over the Indians. Even if only a few Indians had attacked them at this moment, they could have inflicted much harm. The Spaniards scattered out and retrieved their horses as quickly as they could.[17]

They had come to the western edge of the central lake district that runs north and south in central Florida. It is a sandhill karst terrain, composed of ancient sand dunes supporting a scrub ecosystem with many rare and now-endangered plants and animals (fig. 14). These remnant scrub forests are home to the scrub jay, the Florida sandhill crane, the gopher tortoise, and the Florida panther. It has been called a "concealed desert" because it is covered by

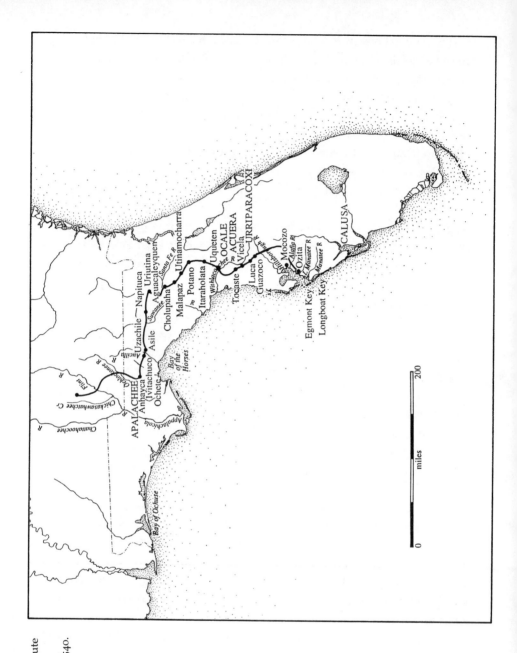

Map 5. De Soto's route
from Ozita to
Apalachee, 1539–1540.

Fig. 14. Scrub forest two miles west of Plant City, Florida. Photograph by Roland Harper, April 22, 1909. (William Stanley Hoole Special Collections Library, University of Alabama)

vegetation and enjoys ample rainfall, but when it rains in this area, the water drains from the surface very rapidly, leaving virtually no standing water except where there are lakes.[18]

On July 17 they continued on to a lake they named St. Johns Lake. This could have been any of the lakes near present-day Lakeland, the largest being Lake Parker and Lake Gibson. As they headed out from St. John's Lake the next morning, De Soto and his men again found themselves in a situation that could have been disastrous. As they set out in a northwesterly direction, the country must have looked innocent enough. But the entire day would be spent traveling through a stretch of sandhills and scrub forest. It was very hot, and they found to their discomfort that there was no drinking water to be had: no springs, no creeks, no standing water.[19] One of De Soto's pages, Prado, died of thirst or sunstroke, and others would have died had they not been riding horses. At the end of the day, they arrived, much fatigued, in the probable vicinity of present-day Lumberton. They bivouacked near the upper Withlacoochee River, where they were probably able to obtain water.

The next day they came to Guazoco, where they found a large open field with green corn growing in it, the first they report seeing.[20] Guazoco, in the vicinity of present-day Dade City, was probably a town subject to the chief of Urriparacoxi. Here they came to the southern edge of the well-drained sandy and loamy soils that lie in Sumter, Marion, and Alachua Counties. These desirable agricultural soils lie on the southeastern edge of the Ocale Uplift District, with its diversified low ridges, plains, and swamps.

The next day, July 20, after traveling only a short distance, they came to Luca, a small village probably in the vicinity of present-day Lacoochee. This was near a place where a large number of trails evidently crossed each other. De Soto and his men bivouacked at Luca, and Gallegos rode in from the main village of Urriparacoxi to meet with him. The main town of Urriparacoxi was probably located somewhere east of the upper Withlacoochee River, perhaps in present-day Sumter County, where there are soils suitable for native agriculture, but it also could possibly have been in Lake or even Orange County. The following day, Gallegos's contingent of men came to Luca and rejoined the army.

De Soto sent a message summoning chief Urriparacoxi, who was still hiding in one of the large swamps that lay near his principal towns. The chief did not reply.

Chief Urriparacoxi is shrouded in mystery. None of the Spaniards ever laid eyes on him, and the precise location of his town is unknown. We cannot even be sure of his name or the name of his chiefdom. *Irri* is Timucuan for "war," and *paracusi* is "chief," so *Urriparacoxi* may simply be a Timucuan title meaning "war chief." It does seem clear enough that Urriparacoxi and his people had access to good agricultural soil, and he clearly dominated the nonagricultural people around Tampa Bay. This is consistent with the hypothesis that practicing agriculture produces enough surplus food to underwrite a military organization that confers an advantage over people who are hunter-gatherers. Hence, the preeminence of Urriparacoxi would seem to give us some insight into why the Mississippian transformation was so dynamic and why it spread so rapidly throughout the Southeast.[21]

On July 23 De Soto and his men resumed their march. They reached the village of Vicela, which must have been a small place, because they continued on beyond it to bivouac, probably in the vicinity of present-day Nobleton or Istachatta.

The next day, July 24, they came to Tocaste, located beside a large lake. They were at this time near present-day Floral City, which lay on the southwestern edge of the cove of the Withlacoochee, a wetland comprising Lake Tsala Apopka and its associated swamps in the sixteenth century. The cove of the Withlacoochee measured about twenty-five miles from north to south, and it was about six miles wide. The depth of the water in this wetland varied from a few inches in parts of the swamps, to several feet in the channel of the Withlacoochee River.

In 1539 the cove of the Withlacoochee was far different from what it is today. At that time over half of all the land in Florida was covered in forested wetland. But draining, clearing, and filling has reduced this area until today only about 10 percent of Florida is in forested wetland.

Remnants of the swamp forest in the cove can be seen today (fig. 15). But in 1539 the stands of cypress were vast, and the trees were very tall. Other trees

Fig. 15. Swamp at Lake Panasofkee. Photograph by Roland Harper, April 23, 1909. (William Stanley Hoole Special Collections Library, University of Alabama)

in the swamps were Atlantic white cedar, cabbage palm, dwarf palmetto, slash pine, black gum, water tupelo, coastal plain willow, and several oaks. On the forest floor there were many shrubs, often with evergreen leaves, such as wax myrtle and yaupon holly. And everywhere there were vines, the most common being thorny bamboo-vine and poison ivy. The swamps were no doubt full of birds—limpkins, white ibis, many kinds of herons, wild turkeys, and now rare wood storks.[22]

The same day they reached Tocaste, where they established camp, De Soto continued on, leading a detachment of eleven or so horsemen, including Rodrigo Rangel. De Soto knew they were not far from Ocale, and he wanted to press on, expecting to find riches there. After he and his men had traveled for some distance, they came to a place where the trail widened appreciably. Thinking this must indicate a populous society ahead, De Soto ordered Rodrigo Rangel to ride back to camp with the order to send reinforcements forward. Rangel saw the danger to himself in this assignment, but he bowed his head and submitted, refusing to stoop to asking for others to go along with him. As he backtracked, he did in fact encounter hostile Indians who were following along after De Soto and his contingent of horsemen. But he managed to reach camp safely, and then he made the return journey with fourteen additional horsemen, which raised De Soto's total contingent to twenty-six.[23] For all of this to have occurred in the course of a single day means De Soto could not have traveled far beyond where the main part of the army had bivouacked.

On July 25 the main part of the army began moving forward to catch up with De Soto, but two horsemen bearing a message intercepted them, telling Luís de Moscoso, the master of camp, to return to the place where they had bivouacked the previous night. The two horsemen said De Soto and his men had had a skirmish with hostile Indians; several Spaniards had been wounded and a horse belonging to Carlos Enríquez had been killed. The news of this skirmish must have been distressing because the Spaniards were beginning to suffer for want of food. They had become so desperate that when they chanced upon any little field of corn, they would pull the immature green ears from the stalks and wolf them down, cobs and all.[24]

The next day, July 26, De Soto found the trail to be wider, and the nature of the terrain improved. This may have been the day when De Soto and his men came to a village whose people had fled. But they spied several of the inhabitants out in dugout canoes in a shallow swamp. Ortiz persuaded one of them to come ashore and serve as a guide.[25]

De Soto sent Gonzalo Silvestre back to the main body of the army with an order for thirty additional horsemen to be sent forward to join him. The remainder of the army was to resume moving forward.[26] De Soto asked that some biscuits and cheese be sent to him with the detachment of horsemen. Silvestre was to accomplish this mission and be back by the following night (i.e., by July 27).[27] De Soto told Silvestre that he could select one other horseman to go with him. Silvestre chose Juan López Cacho, one of De Soto's pages, who was reluctant to go, but who nonetheless mounted his horse and rode away with Silvestre.

Because it was late in the day when they started out, Silvestre and Cacho had to travel much of the way through darkness. They had to retrace precisely the same difficult trail by which they had come, and once daylight had faded, they had to depend upon the ability of their horses to stay on the trail. In sniffing their way the horses gave out such snorts Silvestre and Cacho were afraid the Indians would hear them. Finally, they gave their horses full rein. Silvestre was confident that his own horse, a dark chestnut, was superior to Cacho's toasted bay.

The two young men—both under twenty years old—were famished from having eaten so little food during the past two days, and they were very tired. In several places along the way, they saw Indians dancing by the lights of their fires. But even though the Indians' dogs sensed the Spaniards and began barking, the Indians, perhaps assuming that no Spaniards could be moving about at night, paid them no heed.

Later, Cacho became so exhausted he told Silvestre they had to stop for a while so he could rest; either that, or else Silvestre should lance him to death on the spot. Silvestre insisted they had to press on and cover as much distance as possible. But Cacho could go no further. He fell from his horse onto the ground as if he were dead. Silvestre remained on his own horse, holding Cacho's horse by the bridle. A very hard rain fell during the night, but it did not waken Cacho. Finally, quite suddenly, the rain ceased, the clouds dispersed, and it quickly became light. Day came so abruptly that Silvestre realized he himself must have fallen asleep in the saddle. He called out to Cacho, who failed to stir, and he had to prod him with the butt of his lance to waken him.

Now in the light of day, they again moved forward, riding at half speed. The Indians quickly spotted them and set up a great noise, shouting, beating drums, and trumpeting on conch shells, and whenever other Indians heard this alarm, they too set up a clamor.

The two riders saw so many canoes moving through the reeds, it was as if the leaves that had fallen into the water had been transformed into canoes.

The Indians were not only hostile, they were angry, because the two men had succeeded in traveling so far undetected. The Indians in the canoes were heading toward a deep water crossing where they would attempt to intercept the two horsemen. But the two pressed forward through the danger, and even though a shower of arrows rained down on them, neither was wounded. Now they were nearing the camp, and when the soldiers there heard the Indians shouting, a large party of horsemen led by Nuño de Tovar rushed out to assist Silvestre and Cacho. As the two came onto higher ground, the Indians were in hot pursuit, but when the warriors saw the horsemen, they turned on their heels and fled back to the safety of the swamp.

Following the orders delivered by Silvestre, Luís de Moscoso selected thirty lancers to go forward under the leadership of Nuño de Tovar, along with two mules loaded with a supply of biscuits and cheese. Silvestre had time to eat only a couple of mouthfuls of boiled, half-ripe corn and a small amount of cheese. Less than an hour after he arrived, he set out with the lancers. Cacho, however, remained behind, saying: "The General did not order me either to come here or to return."[28]

This force of horsemen was large enough to intimidate the Indians, and not a hand was raised against them along the way. They did not reach the location from which Silvestre had departed until two hours after nightfall. Upon arriving, they found that De Soto had already moved forward. Not knowing where he had gone, they could travel no farther. Fearing an attack, they organized a watch and spent an anxious night at the abandoned camp.

When daylight came, they were able to see the trail De Soto had taken, and they moved forward to join him. Because in places they had to travel through water up to their chests, they were afraid they would be attacked by Indians in canoes. They were only armed with lances—no crossbows or arquebuses with which to hold the Indians at bay. In swamps, this made them especially vulnerable to arrows. But no attack was made, and they caught up with De Soto without incident.

The Swamp of Ocale

On this same day, July 26, the day of Saint Anne, De Soto and his contingent of horsemen entered the Swamp of Ocale—the cove of the Withlacoochee.[29] The location of the place where they crossed the Withlacoochee River may have been on a trail that lay near present-day Turner Camp Road, which runs from Inverness northeasterly across the cove.[30] Why they chose to take this difficult crossing of the Withlacoochee River is not clear. They could have evaded it by crossing into the territory of Urriparacoxi, southeast of the cove of the Withlacoochee, or they could have continued skirting the western side of the cove to about present-day Dunnellon, where the Withlacoochee River was relatively free of swamp. Perhaps De Soto was impatient to reach Ocale, or perhaps their Indian guide deliberately led them into difficult terrain. In any case, those who made the crossing still remembered it vividly many years later.

As De Soto and his men made their way into the swamp, small parties of Indians would rush out from concealment, fire arrows at the Spaniards, and then melt back into the cover of trees and bushes. The Spaniards did, however, succeed in capturing a few of them, whom they coerced into serving as guides. But whether through necessity or malice, these guides led De Soto and his men into difficult crossings and into ambushes. De Soto suspected malice, and he threw four of them to the dogs. One of the Indian captives, seeing his comrades killed and devoured, and fearing a similar fate, led them to a good clear trail. They followed it to a place where they could wade an expanse of swamp where the water came only to their chests, and this led to a place where the Withlacoochee River could be crossed.[31]

Some were of the opinion that it was the same place where Pánfilo de Narváez and his army crossed the Withlacoochee in 1528, but in fact Narváez's crossing may have been closer to the Gulf coast.[32] In places in this swamp, they would step onto what appeared to be solid land, but it would tremble and shake for a radius of twenty or thirty feet, and sometimes they would plunge through this "land" into the water and mud underneath.[33] What they were walking upon were thick floating masses of peat with plants growing on top.

De Soto and his advance guard constructed a footbridge across the channel of the Withlacoochee River by taking advantage of a fallen tree that already spanned it. They built a footbridge across a portion of the stream that this tree did not span.[34] De Soto ordered Pedro Morón and Diego de Oliva, mestizos from Cuba, to go out with axes and chop away some limbs of the tree to make their passage across it more convenient. But as they were at work, some Indians who had been hiding in reeds near the opposite bank rushed out in a fury and fired arrows at them. Both men dove into the water and swam back, staying underwater as much as possible. They were only slightly wounded because the arrows were slowed by the water. After this minor ambush, the resistance of the people of Ocale faded away.[35]

Upstream from the bridge, they found a place where they could get their horses across.[36] At this spot the Withlacoochee River was broad—more than three crossbow shots (*más de tres tiros de ballesta*) from side to side—and the current was swift, but it was a place where the river could be forded.[37] Some of the men crossed by wading, though in places the water came up to their necks. They held their clothes and saddles on top of their heads, and they used a rope and tackle to help the horses swim the swift current.[38] When Nuño de Tovar arrived with his thirty horsemen on the following day, he first attempted to swim his horses across the river. But the first one he drove in drowned, and after that they resorted to using a rope and tackle to pull the horses across. De Soto again sent two horsemen back to tell Luís de Moscoso and the others to hurry forward because they had a long way to travel, and there was little food to be had along the way.[39]

Commanding a contingent of over fifty horsemen, De Soto set out in search of Ocale.[40] The first village of Ocale they came to, Uqueten, was abandoned by its people, but nearby they captured two Indians who were spying on them.[41] They found some supplies of corn and beans, as well as some "little dogs."[42] Tovar and his men found De Soto encamped among lush cornfields, some stalks bearing three or four ears, which they snatched off and ate green while still on horseback. De Soto explained to those who caught up with him that he had moved forward because his men were starving, and for all he knew, his messengers Silvestre and Cacho had been killed by Indians.[43]

De Soto sent some horsemen back with mules loaded with corn and other provisions to supply Moscoso and the rest of the army.[44] This came as a welcome relief to Moscoso and his comrades, who were making their way through the swamp with hostile Indians hounding them. Some of the Spaniards who chanced to stray away from the main body of the army had been wounded, and a crossbowman named Mendoza had been killed.[45] They were reduced to eating wild greens (*bredos*), which they stewed, and roots, which they roasted and risked eating, although they did not know whether they were poisonous. When they reached the vicinity of the Withlacoochee River, they were able to eat cabbage palmetto, which reminded them of the low palm trees growing in Andalucia.[46] They were much relieved to receive the food sent by De Soto and to learn that ample corn was available in Ocale.

The principal towns of Ocale lay on the eastern side of the Withlacoochee River, clearly occupying land that was good for raising corn. Perhaps their principal towns were located on the small island of fertile soils from about Gum Slough up to Ross Prairie and westward toward Dunnellon. The archaeological culture of Ocale appears to be similar to that of the Safety Harbor culture found in the cove of the Withlacoochee River and around Tampa Bay.[47]

De Soto sent an Indian they had captured to the chief of Ocale to ask him and his people to come out of hiding, threatening reprisals if they did not show themselves.[48] The chief sent back a reply, whose words were no doubt different from these reported by Elvas, though the sense may have been the same:

> I have long since learned who you Castilians are . . . through others of you who came years ago to my land [i.e., Pánfilo de Narváez]; and I already know very well what your customs and behavior are like. To me you are professional vagabonds who wander from place to place, gaining your livelihood by robbing, sacking, and murdering people who have given you no offense. I want no manner of friendship or peace with people such as you, but instead prefer mortal and perpetual enmity. Granted that you are as valiant as you boast of being, I have no fear of you, since neither I nor my vassals consider ourselves inferior to you in valor; and to prove our gallantry, I promise to maintain war upon you so long as you wish to remain in my province, not by fighting in the open, although I could do so, but by ambushing and waylaying you whenever you are off guard. I therefore notify and advise you to protect yourselves and act cautiously with me and my people, for I have commanded my vassals to bring me two Christian heads weekly, this number and no more. I shall be content to behead only two of you each week since I thus can slay all of you within a few years; for even though you may colonize and settle, you cannot perpetuate yourselves because you have not brought women to produce children and pass your generation forward.[49]

De Soto made further attempts to communicate with the chief of Ocale, but to no avail. The Spaniards were afraid to venture as much as a hundred yards from camp for fear of falling into the hands of the Indians. The Indians of Ocale succeeded in killing several Spaniards, decapitating them as promised. When the Spaniards buried the bodies, the Indians would come at night, dig up the corpses, cut them into pieces and hang the body parts in trees for the birds to eat. The Indians moved with such stealth, the Spaniards were able to kill only a few of them.[50]

From Ocale onward the Spaniards met stiffer resistance than they had previously encountered. This began when De Soto sent a contingent of men to Acuera to seize food. Acuera appears to have been located to the east of Ocale, in the vicinity of Lake Weir and Lake Griffin.[51] On two occasions the Indians of Acuera attacked, killing three Spanish soldiers, wounding several others, and killing a horse. The people of Acuera appear to have been the carriers of the St. Johns archaeological culture, and they presumably resembled Timucuan-speaking people living to the northeast along the St. Johns River.[52]

When the Spaniards collected together all the food they had seized at Ocale, it amounted to only enough to last them for about three months.[53] So far, they had not captured many Indians to serve as slaves, so the soldiers had to attend to their own needs. They had to collect their own firewood and pulverize their own corn, using the mortars and pestles they had found in the towns of Ocale.[54] Some of them used their coats of chain mail to sift the coarse meal and then cooked their bread on flat pieces of pottery that were laid on the fire. Others, who were put off by the difficulty of reducing corn to meal in this way, parched the grains and stewed them whole.[55]

De Soto Leads a Contingent Northward

The Indians the Spaniards captured at Ocale told the Spaniards about Apalachee, a very large province abounding in corn, which lay seven days' travel away.[56] All of the Indians they met were in awe of the Apalachees, though their impressions and expectations of such distant places exceeded their direct experience: in fact, none of the men they had captured could serve as guides beyond two leagues from where they had been captured.

On August 11 De Soto set forth from Ocale in search of Apalachee with fifty horsemen and one hundred footmen. He ordered Luís de Moscoso to remain at Ocale with the remainder of the army. Here they could be sure of having at least a meager supply of food. By the end of their first day of travel De Soto and his contingent came to Itarraholata, a small village with a plentiful supply of corn.[57] It was located somewhere west of present-day Ocala, probably along a trail that led north through present-day Cotton Plant to Wetumpka Hammock and Lake Orange.[58] As they traveled northward, beneath a canopied forest of huge hardwoods and pines, the foliage was so clear beneath the vaulted trees, they could safely gallop their horses. They were relieved to have entered country that was less swampy and marshy than that which they had just traversed.[59] The farther from the sea they traveled, it seemed to them, the more fertile and populous was the land.[60]

The next day, August 12, they came to Potano, where they spent the night. This town was possibly located on the western side of Orange Lake. Potano appears to have possessed a considerable power or influence over other populations living in the surrounding region. In the late sixteenth century, Spaniards in Florida used the name Potano to refer to all the Indians living in present-day Alachua County.

Itarraholata, Potano, and other towns up to about the Santa Fe River embodied the Alachua archaeological culture. Alachua sites appear to be concentrated in a narrow band of fertile soils that run from about Lake Weir northward through present-day Ocala, Orange Lake, and Gainesville to the Santa Fe River. People of the Alachua culture almost always built their villages on high ground near lakes or ponds. Their houses were of flexed construction, built of poles inserted into the ground and then bent over to form a dome-shaped roof, and the circular floors averaged 7.6 meters in diameter. A fire pit inside was used for heat, light, and cooking. Sleeping platforms were raised up on posts around the inside walls of the houses. Their pottery was sand-tempered, with the surface of the vessels scratched or impressed with corncobs. In addition to the foods they cultivated, they caught a variety of small fish—catfish, blue gill, bream, and sunfish—probably using nets. They principally hunted deer, but also opossum, rabbit, raccoon, muskrat, squirrel, and bear. They also collected palm berries, acorns, and hickory nuts. They built small burial mounds (fig. 16), interring certain of their dead beneath the mounds and also in the eastern slopes of the mounds, so that with several such burials the mounds gradually became oval in shape.[61]

On August 13 De Soto and his men reached Utinamocharra, a village located

Fig. 16. Burial of a Timucuan chief in a mound, with his shell cup placed on the mound surface. Note the circular, dome-shaped houses, which were intentionally set on fire when a person died. Perhaps because this is a chief, they have also set the town house on fire. Theodore de Bry, *Americae*, part 2, 1591. (National Anthropological Archives, Smithsonian Institution)

in the vicinity of present-day Gainesville, and then they continued on to a town near present-day Alachua, which they named pueblo de la Malapaz—village of Bad Peace—because of an incident that happened there. The incident came after the course of the day's travel, during which Juan de Añasco had captured about thirty Indian men and women.[62] That night an Indian man came to him in peace, saying he was the chief and if his people were released, he would make peace and serve the Spaniards well, providing them with food and guides.[63] De Soto released the slaves and put a close guard over the man who claimed to be chief. On the morning of the next day, August 14, many armed Indian men were seen to come near the town, where they took up positions in the woods. The presumed chief asked to be taken near them, so he could speak to them and assure them that everything was all right. He told the Spaniards that the Indians would do whatever he ordered them to do. But when several Spaniards took the man who pretended to be the chief to his armed comrades, he suddenly attacked his guards and ran away. Other Indians joined him, and they all ran to a densely wooded hill. But De Soto ordered that they loose Bruto, an Irish greyhound (*lebrel de Irlanda*) already accustomed to the Indians' scent. The dog ran past several of the fleeing Indians; he seized the pretended chief by the fleshy part of his arm, throwing him to the ground and holding him until the Spaniards came up and captured him.[64] Bruto was one of the Spaniards' principal war dogs, and the Indians soon came to know and fear him.[65]

The next day, August 15, De Soto and his men arrived at Cholupaha, which had such an abundance of corn they named it Villafarta—City of Plenty. It was also at this place where they acquired a quantity of delicious dried small chestnuts, which grew on low bushes rather than on the large trees with which the Spaniards were familiar. This was the Florida chinkapin (*Castanea alnifolia* Nutt.), a dwarf chestnut that grows in northern Florida. Cholupaha was probably located in present-day northern Alachua County, near the Robinson Sinks area.

Cholupaha lay near the Santa Fe River. This is normally a small river, and except when the water is high, there is a natural bridge in the vicinity of their crossing place. That is, when the water in the river is low it flows underground for a distance before emerging from the ground again. But on August 16, 1540, the waters of the Santa Fe must have been swollen and the bridge under water, because they had to spend the entire day building a bridge to cross it. And they spent all of the next day getting across the river, describing their crossing as being as difficult as their crossing of the Withlacoochee.[66] Some of the men may have begun arguing at this time about whether they should abort the expedition and return to Tampa Bay. In any case, because of an unspecified quarrel among themselves, they named the Santa Fe River the River of Discords.

On April 17 they continued on to Aguacaleyquen, which appears to have been located on the Ichetucknee River.[67] This town was larger than the ones they had just visited, but its inhabitants had fled to the woods.[68] When the horsemen went out to search the surrounding country for the Indians, Rodrigo Rangel and Villalobos captured a man and a woman in a cornfield. The woman showed them where the supply of corn was hidden, and the man took Baltasar de Gallegos to a place where he captured seventeen Indians, including the daughter of the chief.[69]

On August 22 a large number of Indians of Aguacaleyquen appeared, including their chief, who wanted his daughter freed. The chief promised De Soto he would supply him with interpreters and guides, but when the man did not honor his promise, De Soto took him prisoner. As it turned out, he was a personage whose importance extended to other neighboring polities. Here, north of the Santa Fe River and east of the Aucilla, the Spaniards encountered a series of Indian societies that appear to have possessed a more effective political and military organization than did the Indians they had previously encountered, but who still fell short of the Mississippian type of organization they would encounter for the first time in Apalachee. The societies that were party to this alliance appear to have been Aguacaleyquen and several polities soon to be encountered: Uriutina, Napituca, and Uzachile. These societies would defend each other against an outside aggressor (e.g., De Soto), but none of them appears to have been notably paramount over the others, as would be the case later on when the Spaniards encountered societies with more marked Mississippian organization.

The Indians of Apalachee referred to this alliance of polities as "the Yustega," and the Timucuan-speaking Indians of the St. Johns River called them "Houstaqua." Either the alliance was organized in terms of a segmentary lineage system, with all the parties to the alliance being more or less equal to each other, or else one of the chiefs actually was paramount and his being so either eluded the Spaniards or was not mentioned to them.[70] There is abundant evidence that the Yustega were at war with the Apalachees and also with the Indians living along the St. Johns River; they may also have been at war with the people living to the south of the Santa Fe River. Their ceramics are somewhat distinctive—the Suwannee Valley complex—but relatively little is presently known about their culture.[71]

The Spaniards were notably suspicious about the intentions of the Indians around Aguacaleyquen. On one occasion, one of the messengers sent out by De Soto had come back with four young Indian men whose heads were bedecked with feathers and who appeared to be men of some importance. The Spaniards suspected they had come as spies to observe what manner of men the Spaniards were. But De Soto decided to divert them with a friendly reception. He gave them gifts and invited them to dine with him. The four Indians did so, but when the Spaniards ceased to pay close attention to them, they rose up as one and raced away as fast as they could to the safety of the forests. They ran so fast the Spaniards could not catch them on foot, and the horsemen were not prepared for action. However, Bruto was close by, and when he heard a Spaniard shout and saw the Indians running away, he set out in pursuit. According to Garcilaso, whose storytelling pushes the envelope of the credible, Bruto raced past three of the Indians and leapt upon the fourth, knocking him to the ground, holding him until the next man approached. Then, one after the other, he knocked all three of them to the ground, and going back and forth from one to the other, he held them captive until the Spaniards arrived.[72]

Heartened by finding a moderately large population and more ample supplies of corn at Aguacaleyquen than they had found before, De Soto was in favor of pressing on. But an Indian informant they had captured told them some distressing news about Apalachee. This man told them that years earlier Pánfilo de Narváez had gone there, but because he found only a single town, and no road that led beyond Apalachee, and because water lay in every direction, he had built boats and had quit the country. This discouraged some of De Soto's men, who argued that they should abandon their expedition and turn back, lest they come to the same terrible end as Narváez.

But De Soto would not hear of this. He told the men he doubted what the Indian had said; he would not believe it until he saw it with his own eyes. He ordered a party of eight horsemen to ride back to Ocale to summon Luís de Moscoso to immediately move forward with the men under his command. Before leaving Ocale, Moscoso buried there a quantity of horseshoes and iron artifacts he planned to retrieve when they returned to the base camp. Evidently he was of the opinion they would eventually have to retreat from Apalachee and return to Tampa Bay.[73] The journey to Aguacaleyquen was a difficult one for Moscoso and his men, not the least because the villages through which De Soto and his men had passed had been ravaged and stripped of corn.

Moscoso and his contingent rejoined the others at Aguacaleyquen on September 4, much to the relief of De Soto's men, who feared that the Indians would attack and attempt to free the chief of Aguacaleyquen.[74] On September 10 the reunited army set out from Aguacaleyquen, taking along the chief and his daughter as hostages, as well as a guide named Guatutima, who claimed to know a great deal about the territory through which they would have to pass.[75] During the course of this day, they built a bridge of pine trees across the river of Aguacaleyquen—the Ichetucknee—and they reached a small village where they spent the night.[76]

On September 11 they continued on, coming at the end of the day to Uriutina, a pleasantly situated village with an abundant supply of food.[77] Within this village there was an open plaza, a large town house (*bohío*), and a large population.[78] This town was probably in the vicinity of Indian Pond in present-day western Columbia County.[79] After De Soto and his men departed from Uriutina, messengers playing flutes to signal their peaceful intentions began coming from the chief of Uzachile, taking messages back and forth.[80] They told the Spaniards that further on the chief of Uzachile waited for them with gifts. The chief of Uzachile was a relative, they said, of the chief of Aguacaleyquen, whom they were holding captive. The messengers implored the Spaniards to set the man free. But the Spaniards were afraid that if they released this man, the Indians would cease cooperating and would refuse to supply them with the guides on whom they depended. De Soto kept the chief captive, but he soothed the messengers as much as he could while denying their request.[81]

The captive chief sent a message to the chief of Napituca.[82] It was, in effect, as follows: "These Spaniards cannot be defeated in war, for they are very brave, and they are sons of our own gods, the Sun and the Moon. They came from the direction of the rising of the sun, and they came upon animals . . . which are so swift, brave, and strong, one can neither resist them nor escape from them. We beg you to not resist."

To this, the chief of Napituca replied to De Soto's captives, in effect:

Your saying that these Spaniards are valiant sons of the Sun show you to be mere boys. Your giving yourself up to be slaves is making you talk like women, praising people you ought to vituperate. These Spaniards are the same people who committed cruelties against us in the past [i.e., Pánfilo de Narváez's army]. They are demons, not sons of the Sun and Moon, for they go about killing and robbing. They do not bring their own women, but prefer to possess the wives and daughters of others. They are not content to colonize a particular piece of land because they take such pleasure in being vagabonds, living upon the labor of others. They are thieves and murderers. Warn them not to enter my land, for no matter how brave they are, they shall never leave it, for I shall destroy them all. Half of them I will bake, and the other half I shall boil.[83]

Other messengers came, blowing conch shell trumpets as they approached. The warnings became ever more threatening. The chief of Napituca said he would cause the earth to open and swallow up the Spaniards. The hills through which they had to pass would collide together and bury the Spaniards alive. Strong winds would blow the huge trees down on them. A great flock of birds with venom in their beaks would fly overhead and drop the venom down upon them, causing their flesh to rot, with no remedy. The water, the grass, the food would be poisoned, so that all would die. Because the Indians of the Southeast believed their chiefs possessed extraordinary powers over the cosmos, these threats may have been issued in all seriousness. But the Spaniards merely laughed at them. And as they continued to march westward, the messengers from the Indians became more friendly and conciliatory. They apologized for their harsh threats, promising to serve the Spaniards when they arrived.[84]

On September 12 the Spaniards came to a village they named Many Waters (*Muchas Aguas*) because it had rained so much they were unable to travel beyond it. This place was probably in the Peacock-White Lake area, near present-day Wellborne; they arrived there after what may have been a short day of travel, remaining at this place on September 13 and 14.[85] On September 15 they resumed travel, crossing a wide, difficult swamp and arriving at Napituca, a pleasant and well-situated village with a plentiful supply of food.[86] Napituca was probably located in the general vicinity of present-day Live Oak.[87] De Soto and many of his men took up residence in the house of the chief, and the Indians made a great show of friendship.[88]

The Battle at Napituca

At first De Soto may not have realized how important the chief of Aguacaleyquen was. Seven chiefs from the area through which they were traveling came to the outskirts of Napituca and told De Soto they were subjects of the chief of Uzachile.[89] Their chief had ordered them to come to the Spaniards with an offer of friendship. They said they were willing to join forces with the Spaniards in waging war against the Apalachees, who were their enemies. Perhaps in exchange for this promise of alliance, they asked De Soto to free the chief of Aguacaleyquen. De Soto replied that he was not holding the chief as a prisoner; he merely wanted him to accompany his army as far as Uzachile. The Indians indicated that they wished to return at a later time to discuss the matter further. They said they would not wish, however, to come into the Spanish camp for fear they themselves would be taken prisoner.[90] De Soto agreed to meet with them on a small plain nearby and promised to bring along only a small number of soldiers. He also promised to bring the chief of Aguacaleyquen to the meeting.

As the Spaniards would later learn, the chief of Napituca was plotting in all of this a surprise attack. At one point the chief took aside four of the Indian interpreters who were traveling with De Soto and told them of his plan. He said the Spaniards foolishly thought that he, Napituca, and his allies were their friends, and the Spaniards were thereby becoming careless. When De Soto came out on the plain to meet the chiefs, a surprise attack would be launched against him and all the Spaniards. According to the plan, a dozen men were to seize De Soto and carry him bodily into the midst of the warriors, who would kill him. Other warriors would hurl themselves against the Spanish soldiers, who being unprepared, would be easily killed or captured. The chief of Napituca planned to use all the modes of execution the Spaniards had found so amusing. Some Spaniards he would roast; others he would boil. Some he would bury, with just their heads remaining above the ground. Some he would poison, so they could see their flesh decay and decompose. Some he would hang by their feet from trees, where birds would eat them.[91]

He asked the interpreters to tell him what they thought of his plan, and he asked them to guard his secret. Later, if they wished to remain in his land, they would be honored and would be given beautiful wives. But if they wished to return to their own lands, they could do so, and he would provide a guard for them as they made their way home. They had, after all, been brought forcibly away from their homes by the Spaniards, and now, being so far from home, they would be unable to return through the lands of their enemies. Now, he said, was the time to repulse the Spaniards, who if unopposed, would deprive them of their lands and women, would take away their liberties, and impose tribute payments upon them.

The four interpreters assured the chief of Napituca that his plan was a good one. But later, when they had time to reflect on it, they realized it probably would not work. They had never seen the Spaniards so poorly disciplined that they could be taken by surprise. Nor were the Spaniards easy to deceive.

If the interpreters participated in this venture and it failed, they would surely be executed. With these thoughts, they informed Juan Ortiz of the planned attack, and Ortiz immediately went to De Soto with the news.[92]

De Soto informed his captains, telling them they should be vigilant but give the appearance of being careless.[93] On the day on which the meeting was to take place, De Soto ordered his men to make ready for combat, but to do so secretly. His horsemen were mounted and made ready, concealing their horses among the houses in which they were quartered. The attack was to begin when a trumpet was sounded.

On the appointed day, an estimated four hundred Indians armed with bows and arrows were seen to come and take up positions in a woods within sight of the camp. Two Indian men came to the camp and asked De Soto to release the chief of Aguacaleyquen. De Soto, perhaps seeming to comply, took the chief by the hand and walked along with him, talking all the while, to put the Indians at ease. Only six footmen accompanied him.[94]

De Soto took a saddle along with him to serve as a stool, but no sooner did he sit down on it than the Indians poured out of the woods from many directions. Some were magnificently dressed, wearing tall feather headdresses.[95] As it often happened, De Soto had placed himself in grave danger. Even before the note from the trumpet sounded, Luís de Moscoso whipped his horse, shouting the battle cry: "Come on, knights, Santiago, Santiago—at them!" The horsemen raced down to the small plain, lancing Indians as they rode. For a time the Indians fought valiantly, but faced with the dreaded lancers they took to their heels.[96] De Soto mounted his favorite horse, Aceytuno. But the Indians took careful aim, striking Aceytuno with several arrows in the chest, in the knees, and on both sides, and he fell as if he had been hit by a cannonball.[97] The horsemen swept down to where De Soto had fallen, giving him protection. One of De Soto's pages, Viota from Zamora, dismounted and gave De Soto his own horse to ride.[98]

Thirty or forty Indians were lanced during the fighting. Others fled to the safety of a nearby forest.[99] The rest of them fled to two "lakes" that were close by each other. Diving in, they swam out to some distance from the shore, where they stayed out of reach of the Spaniards, treading water. The water in these lakes was more than head-deep at only a short distance from shore, which means they were probably lime sinks, numerous in the karst topography of this part of Florida.[100] One of these sinks was small enough for the Spaniards to surround completely. The other was too large to be surrounded.[101] The arquebusiers and crossbowmen shot at the swimming Indians, but they were at too great a distance from shore to be harmed. While their strength lasted, the Indians managed to shoot back. Three or four Indians would lift an archer up out of the water, who would shoot several arrows at the Spaniards, though to no effect.[102]

As darkness drew near, De Soto ordered his horsemen and footmen to keep guard all the way around the smaller of the two lakes. Some or all of the Indians in the larger lake may have escaped under cover of darkness. The Indians in the smaller lake also tried to escape by putting lily pads on their heads and swimming silently toward shore. But when the Spanish soldiers saw the pads moving, they would dash into the water with their horses, until they were chest deep, driving the Indians back out into the lake.[103]

Juan Ortiz shouted to the swimmers in the lake, telling them that escape was impossible and they should surrender. As the night went on, the swimmers suffered more and more from fatigue and from the cold water. By midnight, they had been in the water for about fourteen hours.[104] One by one they began to surrender, approaching the shore and shouting to Juan Ortiz that they were giving up. By daybreak all had surrendered except twelve of the principal men. De Soto sent the Indians whom they had enslaved at Urriparacoxi—who now went about unchained—to swim out into the lake and bring in the remaining ones. These Indian slaves did as they were ordered, pulling the half-drowned men to shore by their hair.[105]

The last remaining Indian in the lake was the chief of Uriutina, who was finally pulled out by some Indians of Uzachile. When he came ashore, he asked for a messenger to be sent back to his people bearing the following message, interpreted by Juan Ortiz:

> Look you, go to my people and tell them that they take no thought of me; that I have done as a brave man and lord what there was to do, and struggled and fought like a man until I was left alone; and if I took refuge in this [lake], it was not to escape death, or to avoid dying as befits me, but to encourage those that were there and had not surrendered. I did not give myself up until these Indians of Uzachile, which are of our nation, asked me to, saying that it would be best for all. Wherefore, what I enjoin upon them and ask is, that they do not, out of regard for me or for any one else, have anything to do with these Christians who are devils and will prove mightier than they; and that they may be assured that as for me, if I have to die, it will be as a brave man.[106]

All told, the Spaniards took as many as three hundred Indian prisoners from the lake. Among these were five or six chiefs, including the chief of Uriutina.[107]

The Spaniards tied the hands of their prisoners behind their backs and put them into a building in the town of Napituca.[108] The next day the bulk of the prisoners, the ones who were commoners, were divided up among the Spaniards to be their slaves. As for the chiefs, De Soto went among them and talked to them, trying to persuade them to accept his friendship. He ordered that they be released from their bonds and treated with civility.[109]

But the captives were not interested in peace. They had agreed among themselves that should an opportunity present itself, they would rise up in revolt. When De Soto released the chiefs from their chains, one of them, perhaps the architect of the revolt, turned his body from one side to the other, extended his arms with his fists clenched, and then brought his fists back to his shoulders.[110] Then he shook his arms once or twice with enough force to make his joints crack. This was a gesture the Indians of the Southeast commonly performed when they were about to undertake something that required strength.

This man then sprang over to where De Soto was sitting, grabbed him by the collar, and with a loud shout struck him a ferocious blow in the face. De Soto toppled backward, chair and all, and landed on his back, unconscious. The chief then fell upon him, trying to kill him with his bare hands, but De Soto's guards drew their swords and killed him.[111]

The chief's shout had been a signal for all the Indian prisoners to rise up in revolt. They grabbed up whatever was close at hand, whether a sword, a burning firebrand, or a pot of hot food, and tried to kill those Spaniards who stood nearest. One Indian felled his master with a club and then commenced to beat him with his fists until his face was swollen. When the fallen man's comrades came to his aid, the Indian seized a lance that was propped against a wall and climbed up into a corncrib, shouting so loudly it sounded as if ten men were inside. He defended the door of the corncrib in such a way that none could enter. Finally, Diego de Soto, a relative of the governor, came with his crossbow. When the Indian saw him take aim, he threw the lance, which glanced off Diego de Soto's shoulder and knocked him to his knees, though not before he loosed the bolt from his crossbow. The lance penetrated deeply into the earth and stood there, quivering, while the bolt from the crossbow struck the Indian in the chest and killed him.[112]

The Spaniards—especially those who had been injured in the attack—began killing every Indian they could lay their hands on. Others, however, had no stomach for killing Indians who had surrendered or who had been serving as slaves. They took these to the plaza and handed them over to De Soto's guard. The fate of those who had rebelled was not good. Only the very youngest ones were kept as slaves, and these were only given to masters who possessed strong chains. Many of the older ones were slain with halberds and pikes. Some were tied to posts in the plaza and shot with arrows by Indians who had been enslaved during the march north from Tampa Bay. The Spaniards forced the enslaved Indians to do this so they would be ineradicably defined as enemies of the Indians who had rebelled and therefore would not dare try to escape and return to their homes.[113]

Francisco de Saldaña had no appetite for killing the slave who had been assigned to him. He tied a cord around his neck and led him to the plaza. But when this Indian saw what was happening there, he grabbed his master's collar with one hand and the seat of his trousers with the other, and lifting him up in the air, smashed him to the ground head first. As Saldaña lay stunned, the Indian began jumping up and down on him. Other Spaniards rushed to assist, but the Indian seized Saldaña's sword. Swinging it around himself with great force, bellowing like a bull, he held off fifteen or twenty swordsmen, until the halberdiers came and killed him.[114]

Several Spaniards had been killed, and many had been seriously wounded.[115] When De Soto came to, more than half an hour after the chief had toppled him with the blow to his face, he was bleeding at the nose and mouth. His upper and lower lips looked as if he had been hit in the face with a club, and two of his teeth had been knocked out.[116] For many days thereafter he could eat nothing that had to be chewed. This surprise revolt would have been much worse for the Spaniards had not many of the Indians been in chains.

Anhayca, Principal Town of Apalachee

On September 23 De Soto and his army departed from Napituca and traveled to the Suwannee River (fig. 17), probably coming to it in the vicinity of present-day Dowling Park.[117] They called the Suwannee the River of the Deer because messengers from Uzachile met them at this point bearing a gift of deer meat. This was noteworthy, because throughout the entire expedition they seldom ate deer meat. But for some reason, deer abounded in this area.[118]

In spite of this gift, the people of Uzachile were not kindly disposed toward the Spaniards. When De Soto and his men went to look at the river with its steep limestone banks, a great number of warriors appeared on the opposite side of the river, shouting and firing arrows at the Spaniards. They shouted, according to Garcilaso: "So you thieves, vagabonds, and foreign immigrants want a bridge. You will not see it built with our hands."[119] Because of the great width of the river, their arrows did little damage. However, the war dog Bruto

Fig. 17. The Suwannee River. (Florida State Archives)

escaped from one of De Soto's pages who was holding him on a leash. Bruto plunged into the river and began swimming over to attack the Indians on the opposite side. The Spaniards called for him to return, but he would not. The Indians began shooting at him, their arrows striking him in the head and back, delivering mortal wounds. He reached the opposite bank before he died, and the Indians no doubt rejoiced at his death. The Spaniards, on the other hand, were distressed over the loss of a dog who had been so effective against the Indians.[120]

A bridge had to be built to cross the Suwannee. When its framework was ready to be placed in the river, De Soto built several rafts and sent a contingent of arquebusiers, crossbowmen, and horsemen across to secure the other side. The horsemen's mounts were driven into the river and made to swim across.[121] With the opposite side of the bank thus secured, they completed construction of the bridge, which was three tall pine trees long and four wide. The entire army made it across to the other side on September 25. On this same day, traveling through level, clear land, skirting around the northern end of San Pedro Bay, they passed through two small villages and one very large one named Apalu, and came by nightfall to the main town of Uzachile, probably in the general vicinity of Sampala Lake.[122]

The main town of Uzachile had been abandoned by its people, who must have had full knowledge of the occurrences at Napituca. They were hiding out in the surrounding countryside. The Spaniards remained in this place for three days, commandeering an abundance of corn, beans, and pumpkins. The pumpkins were said to be tastier than those that were grown in Spain. Small parties of Uzachile warriors began attacking the Spaniards, guerilla fashion. With this the Spaniards began killing Indians wherever they found them, sparing very few.[123] After a time, De Soto sent out two slaving parties in different directions, who captured about a hundred men and women of Uzachile.[124]

On September 29 they continued traveling, passing through a woods of very tall trees, coming at nightfall to a pine woods, where they bivouacked. Without obtaining De Soto's permission, a boy named Cadena left camp and backtracked to retrieve a sword that had been lost. When he returned, De Soto threatened to hang him for leaving the army without permission. The boy's life was saved only through the good words of some who intervened on his behalf.[125]

On September 30 they came to Asile, the first town subject to Apalachee, and the people there were taken completely by surprise. Their having no forewarning that De Soto was coming was a sure sign they were not in amity with the people of Uzachile. When De Soto and his men approached, the people of Asile fled to the surrounding woods, but the Spaniards succeeded in capturing some women. Asile was probably located on the eastern side of the Aucilla River, in the southwestern corner of Madison County.

Immediately upon entering the territory of the chiefdom of Apalachee, the Spaniards realized they were up against a military force that was more organized than any they had seen up to this point. Indians all along the way had warned the Spaniards about the fierceness of the Apalachees.[126] Even the women were tough. This was brought home to a young soldier named Herrera, who lagged behind his comrades with a woman of Asile.[127] Herrera probably tried to assault the woman sexually.[128] But she grabbed him by his genitals and had him at her mercy and might have done him great damage had he not yelled and been rescued by his comrades.

On October 1 they departed from Asile and soon arrived at the river and swamp of Ivitachuco—the Aucilla River and its adjacent floodplain.[129] The point at which they came to the swamp and river was a few miles southeast of present-day Lamont. The channel of the Aucilla River was not wide, but it was too deep to be forded. On both sides of the river lay broad backswamps with shallow water, and bordering both backswamps was a dense jungle of tall trees, with vines and undergrowth of cane so dense that from a distance it looked like a solid wall.[130] The Indians had cut a footpath, just wide enough for a single person—or at most two abreast—to pass through this morass of foliage, water, and mud.

As the Spaniards made their way through the backswamp on the eastern side, with water coming up to their thighs and waists, the Apalachees contested every inch of their progress. The Spaniards used their hatchets and axes to widen the trail as they passed along it. By the end of the day, on October 1, they had reconnoitered the swamp and were in a position to pass on to the channel of the river. They spent an anxious night because of the threat of the Apalachees.

Two hours before dawn of the next day, De Soto roused his men and moved silently toward the river. The Apalachees had not expected them to be up and about while it was still dark, and they had relaxed their vigilance. When they heard the Spaniards moving about, the Indians rushed toward the place where they intended to cross, shouting in a fury. But the Spaniards were ready and met them blow for blow, shot for shot. The Spaniards built a crude bridge across the river near a tree that lay across the channel. The army began crossing to the other side on October 2. The night of October 2 was spent in the swamp in an area they laboriously cleared. None of the Spaniards slept that night because the Indians whooped and created diversions to upset them. De Soto and his men were aware that this was the same swamp through which Narváez had crossed with such difficulty, years earlier. And perhaps the Apalachees had learned a thing or two about tactics from their encounter with Narváez.

At daybreak the Spaniards continued their crossing of the river and swamp, finding on the western side another backswamp with another very narrow footpath. And still the Apalachees kept up their resistance. With their horsemen useless, the Spanish footmen had to push the Indians back a little at a time. Arrows flew at the Spaniards from both sides. In the time it took a crossbowman or arquebusier to reload his weapon, an Apalachee was able to fire six or seven arrows. An arrow had hardly hit its target before another was nocked in the bowstring.

When the forest finally opened up, the Spaniards found that the Apalachees had built barriers against the horses by tying poles horizontally to the trees. But once the Spaniards got past these barriers, they took the offensive with their horsemen, lancing the Indians without mercy. When they reached the first cornfields of Apalachee, they continued to ride down and lance to death any Apalachee they encountered, particularly those who made any show of resistance.[131] All the army had succeeded in making the crossing by noon, October 3. Their only loss was a horse, which drowned while crossing the river. By nightfall they had reached the town of Ivitachuco, which the Apalachees had set afire.[132] This town was probably located near Lake Iamonia.

Evidently they rested in Ivitachuco on October 4.[133] Throughout the night the Apalachees shouted and fired arrows into the camp.[134] The next day the army traveled in a northwesterly direction. Following a trail that lay near present-day Highway 27 or State Road 36, they passed through fields of corn and vegetables as far as the eye could see, with many houses scattered about. They passed near Lake Catherine and Lake Waukeenah before coming to a small entrenched stream—probably Burnt Mill Creek—where the Apalachees put up a particularly stiff resistance. In the dense floodplain vegetation that grew along this stream, the Indians had constructed fences and barricades against the horses. The Spaniards had to fight their way to the other side on foot until they could cut through the barricades. The Apalachees fought with great desperation. This was their last hope of stopping the Spaniards, and they failed.

By the end of the day on October 5, De Soto and his men reached the village of Calahuchi, possibly on the St. Marks River southeast of present-day Chaires.[135] Here they captured two men and a woman, and they found a large quantity of dried deer meat.[136] On this same day, the guide who had brought them this far escaped and ran away.[137]

The next day, October 6, they got nowhere at first, following a new guide, an old man who led them at random. Then an Indian woman led them to Anhayca, the principal town of the chiefdom of Apalachee.[138] Anhayca was located within the present-day city of Tallahassee. All the people of Apalachee had fled from this and all the other towns, seeking refuge in the swamps.[139]

Luís Hernández de Biedma estimated the distance from the landing point at Tampa Bay to Anhayca to have been 110 leagues.[140] The actual distance is about 320 miles.[141]

5

Winter, 1539–1540

De Soto established his winter camp in Anhayca, the principal town of Apalachee, a site located within the city limits of present-day Tallahassee. Luís de Moscoso, the master of camp, was able to find lodging for the entire army in this town, and De Soto himself took the chief's house to be his own.[1] Later the Spaniards would have to build additional houses when the men who had remained behind at the base camp at Tampa Bay marched northward to join their comrades. They also constructed a fortification of unknown form and dimensions around their camp at Anhayca.[2]

Along with being militarily powerful, the Apalachee chiefdom was richer in stores of food than the societies the Spaniards had previously encountered. In these Apalachee towns they found stored large quantities of corn, pumpkins, beans, and wild foods. Even meat—venison and fish—was more abundant here than in some places they had been. In the surrounding Apalachee towns and homesteads they found enough food to support them through the winter, and they took it back to Anhayca for safekeeping.

At Uzachile, and more particularly at Ivitachuco, they had come to the southern margin of a more elevated part of the coastal plain, the Tifton Upland, with its low, eroded hills. The reddish clay and sandy loam soils of this area are the best agricultural soils in Florida. Another attractive feature of this Tallahassee red hills region is that it contains many lakes, large and small. De Soto's men were impressed with the large quantities of fish the Apalachees took from these waters. All of these lakes are shallow and flat-bottomed, and some of them are connected to rivers by small streams, so that when the water level in the lakes is high, they drain into the rivers through these streams. They also drain into the underlying limestone substratum through sinks, vast drain holes eroded through the limestone, and they feed underground streams, some of which come to the surface in spectacular outflows, such as Wakulla Springs. These sinks sometimes become clogged up, and when they do, water levels in the lake may remain high for a time. But by the same token, new sinks can open up, and a lake can drain in an amazingly short time. The great eighteenth-century naturalist William Bartram observed these sinks and springs and described them in his beautiful prose. This in turn inspired the opening lines of Samuel Taylor Coleridge's "Kubla Khan."[3]

In Xanadu did Kubla Khan
A stately pleasure-dome decree:
Where Alph, the sacred river, ran
Through caverns measureless to man
Down to a sunless sea.

Several kinds of forest covered the Tallahassee hills. Perhaps the most distinctive type was that made up of very large magnolia and beech trees, accompanied by various understory trees. A second type, and the one most favored by the Apalachees, was the pine-oak-hickory forest, with stands of shortleaf pine, post oak, Spanish oak, and mockernut hickory, with a lush understory of grasses, shrubs, saplings, and numerous dogwoods with their spring displays of white flowers. On the margins of these deciduous forests, and perhaps particularly on the margins of Apalachee agricultural fields, were clumps of red mulberry trees; wild plum trees, with their tart, red-skinned, yellow-fleshed fruits; black cherry trees with their small, almost black, slightly bitter fruit; and sassafras trees with their fragrant leaves and roots, which would in time be treasured by the European newcomers. The Apalachees sun-dried the wild plums, and to the Spaniards they seemed tastier than those that grew in Spain.

De Soto's men noted the variety of nuts produced by the trees in Apalachee country. In addition to the chinkapins they had already encountered, there were American beechnuts, the acorns of white oak and live oak, and two varieties of hickory nuts: mockernut and pignut. The hickory nuts, with their oily

Fig. 18. Pine barrens in Franklin County, Florida. Photograph by Roland Harper, June 11, 1909. (William Stanley Hoole Special Collections Library, University of Alabama)

kernels, were admired by the Spaniards, who said they were "all oil." They were valued by Indians throughout the Southeast as one of their most important wild foods.

A fourth type of forest, reaching into Apalachee country from both the north and the south, was the pine barrens (fig. 18), a southern pine forest comprised almost exclusively of very tall, widely spaced longleaf pines with a thick blanket of fibrous wiregrass on the forest floor. The pine barrens were created and sustained by frequent fires, most of which were started by lightning strikes that could leave a fire smoldering for days inside the rotted trunk of a tree before it broke out into a conflagration. Longleaf pine trees, with their thick fire-resistant bark, can withstand hot fires, and even when incinerated as seedlings, they will send up a new shoot the next spring. Deciduous trees, on the other hand, are easily killed by forest fires. Hence, longleaf pines, wiregrass, and fire are the best of friends. There was so little understory in the pine barrens, they seemed almost parklike to Europeans, though it was a depressingly monotonous park.

The forest cover of the Tallahassee hills had probably been altered by Apalachee agricultural practices. That is, before the Mississippian period, the principal forest cover in the Tallahassee hills was pine and wiregrass. The magnolia-beech hammocks were restricted to ravines and the margins of lakes, and the pine-oak-hickory woods ringed these magnolia-beech forests. Because wiregrass was easily removed from loosened soil, and there was no other undergrowth to speak of, southern pine forest land would have been the most desirable land for corn cultivation. But as the fertility of these fields was exhausted and they were left fallow, the pine-oak-hickory forests would gradually creep back in with tall broom sedge as a ground cover.

But the impact of the Apalachees on the forest cover was as nothing compared with the impact of early and middle nineteenth-century American cotton plantations. Erosion and gullying were so great on the cotton plantations in the Tallahassee hills that the land lost as much as three-quarters of its topsoil by 1860. Subsequent sharecropping and timbering into the 1900s has affected almost all the vegetative cover of the Apalachee hills. Today, the magnolia-beech and pine-oak-hickory forests can be seen only in small remnants. And the longleaf pine–wiregrass forests are long gone, although small remnants may still be seen in southern Georgia.[4]

Like Mississippian peoples elsewhere in the Southeast, the Apalachees had a mixed economy, combining agriculture with hunting and gathering. In addition to the wild foods already mentioned, the Apalachees, like other Southern Indians, collected several edible roots: *kunti*, the root of the smilax vine that tore at Spanish clothing and flesh, arrowhead (*Sagittaria*), groundnut (*Apios*), and *ache* (possibly *Peltandra virginica*), a large tuber that grew in swampy areas and that, unless properly processed, could set one's mouth on fire and perhaps even be poisonous. They also collected palm berries, blackberries, and blueberries.

The Apalachees, like other Mississippian peoples, were also fond of edible oils. They rendered vegetable oils from acorns and hickory nuts by mixing the pulverized nutmeats with water, then skimming the oil off the top with a large feather. Their main animal fat was bear oil. During the Spanish Mission period they soon learned to substitute butter and lard for these native oils.

Corn, however, was the staff of life. The Apalachees burned their agricultural fields in January to clear away brush and weeds. This burn was the occasion of a particular kind of hunt, which the Spaniards in the Mission period called *hurimelas*, or *junumelas*. The field to be burned was surrounded by people of all ages and sexes, who killed any animals that came running out of the smoke and fire. Later the men prepared the soil for planting, and the women planted and tended the fields.

Like other Mississippian cultures, the Apalachees made their corn into hominy by treating it with lye made from wood ashes. Then they used large wooden mortars and pestles to pound the hominy into a meal like the grits used in contemporary southern cuisine. (See fig. 91. These mortars and pestles were used by Southeastern Indians until well into the twentieth century.) They cooked this meal into a thin gruel (called *onsla*) or into a thick gruel, and they also made it into a dough for making fried cakes, or fritters. Some of their corn they parched and then pounded into meal. This parched cornmeal, sometimes mixed with dried persimmons, blueberries, and other fruits, was the food they carried with them when they traveled. They would simply add water to it to make a cold gruel that needed no further cooking.[5]

The territory of the Apalachee chiefdom lay between the Aucilla River to the east and the Ochlockonee River to the west and north. The Asile people, just east of the Aucilla River, were under the control of Apalachee, but they appear to have been Timucuan-speaking. The southern boundary of Apalachee territory was the Gulf of Mexico. The Apalachee population was not evenly spread across the land. The Tallahassee hills were divided from the sandy low country by the Cody Scarp, and this low country was very thinly inhabited. It was used mainly for hunting, collecting wild plants, and fishing. The great mounds of discarded shellfish along the coastal strand are testimony to this particular aspect of the Apalachee economy.

Archaeological evidence suggests that the Apalachee chiefdom was pioneered by a people who segmented off from an early Mississippian chiefdom centered in the Apalachicola River valley. Between A.D. 1100 and 1500 the Apalachees developed a complex chiefdom based on cleared-field agriculture. Although typical Mississippian chiefdoms farmed the alluvial soils on the margins of rivers, thus favoring the development of long, narrow territories, this was not the case with Apalachee. The rivers in Apalachee territory are coastal plain rivers that form swamps rather than well-drained levees; therefore they were not centers of population. Rather, the Apalachees farmed the hilltops, and their territory was blocklike, or compact, measuring almost forty miles from east to west, and about the same from north to south. The land between the Ochlockonee and Apalachicola Rivers was uninhabited, indicating that it was a buffer zone. This implies that the Apalachees were as hostile toward the people of the Apalachicola valley as they were toward the Timucuan-speaking Yustega on their eastern boundary. But in spite of the high level of warfare in the Apalachee area during the Mississippian period, external trade did occur. For example, the Apalachees obtained copper from the north, and they traded Gulf shells toward the north.

The Apalachees developed a hierarchical settlement system of principal villages dispersed throughout their territory and surrounded by satellite villages. Hence, their population was spread over the landscape rather than being concentrated in compact towns defended by palisades, as was the case with many Mississippian chiefdoms. The smallest Apalachee social unit was the homestead, consisting of a matrilineal kinship unit with male spouses coming in to live with their wives and the wives' kinsmen. These homesteads were built in clusters, in named communities. Communities that had single platform mounds were minor ceremonial-administrative centers, and the multimound Lake Jackson site was the principal ceremonial-administrative center.

It is thought that the principal Apalachee chief lived at the Lake Jackson site (fig. 19), and subsidiary chiefs lived at single-mound centers and perhaps elsewhere. For much of Apalachee's existence, there may have been two major

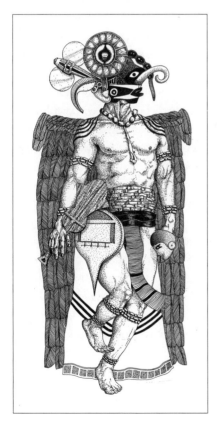

Fig. 19. Apalachee falcon dancer. After a repoussé copper plate found at the Lake Jackson site. Drawing by Theodore Morris.

centers of power—one in the western part of Apalachee's territory, another in the eastern part. Seemingly, just prior to the Narváez and De Soto entradas— in about 1500—a major change occurred within the Apalachee chiefdom. At this time the Lake Jackson site was abandoned and the seat of power of the principal chief moved to Anhayca, the center encountered by De Soto and his men. From the chroniclers' accounts it is clear that Anhayca had a plaza surrounded with houses, like Mississippian towns elsewhere.[6] But it evidently had no mound, a fact revealed to us by archaeology, and that is somewhat perplexing, given the town's importance. We do know, however, that Mississippian mounds were a part of Apalachee culture. They exist at the Lake Jackson site and at other Apalachee sites, and it is in northern Florida where Garcilaso de la Vega first describes the kind of mounds the expedition encountered in their later travels through Mississippian chiefdoms.

According to Garcilaso, the Indians of northern Florida built the houses of their chiefs and lords on platform mounds, which they constructed by carrying in large quantities of earth that they packed down by stamping on it with their feet, forming mounds as much as forty-two feet high. The tops of these mounds were flat, and here they built the dwellings of the chief and his family and retainers. At the foot of the mound they built a plaza, around which the most important people built their houses. Garcilaso noted that people preferred to live close to where the chief lived.

One or more courses of steps were built up the sides of the mounds. These steps were fifteen or twenty feet wide, and they were bordered with walls constructed of thick posts that were set into the earth, according to Garcilaso, to a depth of more than a man's height. Other pieces of wood were laid crosswise between these, forming the steps, and the Spaniards easily rode their horses up and down them. The sides of the mounds were so steep they were difficult or impossible to climb except by the steps, which added to their defensibility.[7]

It is likely that in De Soto's day, as in the seventeenth century, the Apalachee polity comprised two clusters of settlements divided by a sparsely inhabited area that lay along the margins of the St. Marks River. In the seventeenth century the two seats of power, Anhayca and Ivitachuco, were ruled by two brothers, of the dominant lineage, with one of these brothers having a stronger claim to power than the other. It is possible that the Apalachee were organized into moieties. That is, the entire society may have been divided into two like parts, between which a kind of complementary opposition existed, like the opposition between one's two hands.

The principal chief presided over communal religious ceremonies; he was spokesman for his people; and he might be a leader in war. He could mete out punishment to those in the chiefdom who behaved badly. His people greeted him ceremoniously by holding their hands together—as Christians do when they pray—while uttering the vocable *gua*. Fields of corn were set aside and cultivated by the people to support the chief and his family, and also certain others, such as his translator and perhaps his most outstanding warriors.

Because descent was matrilineal, the principal chief could not be succeeded by his son. The office passed to his sister's son. However, the children of chiefs—called *usinulo*—were accorded some social honor, and they performed certain ceremonial tasks.

In addition to being entitled to agricultural products, the chief also expected other kinds of tribute. He was given dressed deerskins, and he was entitled to all the bearskins brought in by hunters. He was also entitled to booty captured in raids against the enemies of Apalachee, which he perhaps later dispensed to his subjects.

None of the De Soto chroniclers learned the names of Apalachee political offices, or if they did they did not think it noteworthy. Nor is much light shed on this by the Spaniards of the Mission period, who too often simply called Apalachee leaders *cacique*, an Arawakan word for "chief" that came into Spanish usage throughout Latin America. Although the missionaries did not record the Apalachee word for "principal chief," the word *nico* (similar to Muskogean *mico* [or *miko*]) appears in Apalachee myths, and it may have signified their highest office. In any case, it is clear that the Sun, their principal deity, was *nico* in the cosmos. We do know from the missionaries that, as among several other Southeastern societies, *holata* was the Apalachee word for a subsidiary chief. Much of the routine administrative duties fell to the chief's second in command, the *inija* (or *heniha*) who, for example, supervised the posting of sentinels and the work in the communal fields. He may also have been responsible for preserving the town's traditions, functioning as a kind of historian. Finally, another Apalachee official was the *atequi*, who served as translator and perhaps performed other functions in which skill in language was prized.

The Spaniards were impressed with the fruitfulness of Apalachee country. They found plenty of corn, beans, and squash, enough to feed the entire army, the servants, and the horses for five months without going a league and a half from Anhayca. The forests were abundant with mulberries, and the oak trees covered the ground with acorns; several kinds of stone fruits abounded; and the fish were excellent.[8]

As soon as they were settled at Anhayca, De Soto sent out three parties of men to explore the country. He sent Captain Arias Tinoco and Captain André de Vasconcelos in two different directions to the north. Both were gone eight or nine days, and they returned to report having seen many villages as well as forested land free of swamps.[9] Tinoco and Vasconcelos may have penetrated as far north as present-day Grady or Thomas Counties in Georgia.[10]

The Bay of the Horses

De Soto commanded Juan de Añasco to lead a third party of horsemen and footmen to find a trail to the coast, which he had heard was ten leagues away.[11] Following a guide whom they captured at Apalachee, they traveled for some distance over terrain that became more difficult the further south they went and came to the town of Ochete, perhaps located on the Wakulla River near its junction with the St. Marks River.[12] The inhabitants had fled, but the town was well stocked with food.[13]

Moving on beyond Ochete, toward the coast, they encountered dense woods, where they sank into mire and were torn by thorns and brambles— probably smilax and blackberries—which spread out over the ground. Eventually the Spaniards realized their guide was intentionally leading them into swamps and coastal marshes.[14] Several times they could hear the surf, but they never saw the water because their guide kept leading them inland.

Eventually they turned around and headed back to Ochete to obtain more food. They did not confront their guide with their suspicions about him because they had no one else to lead them. After replenishing their food supplies at Ochete, they again set out for the coast. They had not gone far when their guide, perhaps realizing he was under suspicion, picked up a burning log from a fire and struck a Spaniard in the face. The others seized the man and were about to kill him when they reconsidered and spared him because he was still their only guide. Later in the same night he attacked another Spaniard, and again they gave the man a beating instead of killing him. Before dawn the guide attacked a third Spaniard. This time they beat him with cudgels, shackled him, and put him under guard.[15] When they resumed their journey the next day, the guide made a desperate attack on the guard who was leading him by a chain. The Spaniards went after him with swords, lances, and a dog. The man put up a terrific fight, including holding off the dog by locking its jaws open with his thumbs. But he was finally killed.[16]

With their guide dead, the Spaniards were at a loss about which way to go.

Fortunately, they had with them an Indian they had captured when they re-turned to Ochete. Because the false guide had threatened him, this captive had pretended to be mute, but when he witnessed the torture and death the Spaniards had inflicted on their false guide, he began to communicate. Using signs and a few words, he indicated that he could lead them to the place where Narváez had built his boats. But first, he indicated they would have to return to Ochete to pick up the correct trail. They were already so close to the Gulf they could hear the surf, but the man was firm in what he said. On their return to Ochete, they seized two more Indians, who confirmed that what their new guide had said was true.

The day after they returned to Ochete for the second time, they set out on a clear trail that led them to the bay where Narváez had built his flatboats. They only had to cross one narrow swamp, where their horses hardly sank above their hooves in the mire. Eventually they came to a broad bay, which they skirted until they came to the place where the boats had been built.[17] This was quite likely at the St. Marks Wildlife Cemetery site on the lower St. Marks River, where a number of early sixteenth-century Spanish artifacts—including sev-eral copper Clarksdale bells (see fig. 85c)—have been found.[18] The Spaniards themselves found a great quantity of charcoal at the remains of the forge where Narváez's men had recycled all their spare iron to make nails for their boats. They searched for letters from Narváez that might have been concealed for Spaniards who would come later, but all they found were some crosses carved into the bark of trees.[19] They found horses' headpieces and a large tree that had been felled and hollowed out to form a trough in which to feed horses. They also found heaps of horse bones, confirming that Narváez's men had eventually butchered their horses and eaten them.[20] They named this place the Bay of the Horses.[21]

They continued on to where they could see the open water of the Gulf. Here they found some old dugout canoes that had been beached. At low tide, ten or twelve swimmers swam out into the bay to test the depth of the water, and they found that it was deep enough to accommodate large vessels. Añasco or-dered the men to place flags up in the tallest trees where they could be seen by mariners who were searching for the entrance to the Bay of the Horses.[22]

Marcos and Perico

Along with sending out small parties of men to explore the country surrounding Anhayca, De Soto also interviewed captured Indians about what they knew of the interior, using Juan Ortiz as translator. He learned from some of the captives that among their number was a boy of sixteen or seventeen who had been associated with some Indian traders who had traveled many leagues into the interior, and that this boy might have the information De Soto was seeking. When De Soto questioned this boy—whom they named Marcos—he told them that what had been said of him was true. He said he would guide De Soto for a twelve to thirteen days' journey into the interior, the limit of where he had knowledge. De Soto ordered that the boy be placed under a special guard, but such precautions were unnecessary because the boy became a willing ally of the Spaniards.[23]

In addition, Juan Gaytán learned that one of his slaves, a young Indian boy who had been captured during the fighting at Napituca, was also a trader. This boy, whom they called Perico (and sometimes Pedro), was about the same age as Marcos. He was from a distant province called Yupaha, whose location was in the direction of the rising sun, "on another ocean"—the Atlantic.[24] Yupaha was ruled by a female chief—whose province, as they were to discover, was Cofitachequi. Perico said the female chief collected tribute from a great many subjects. Some paid her in cloth, but according to Perico others paid her in gold. Perico indicated that he knew what gold was by pointing to the rings and jewelry worn by the Spaniards. When he saw a pearl set in a ring, he said these too could be obtained in great quantities in Cofitachequi.[25] But he said the principal concern of the traders with whom he traveled was a trade in yellow and white metals. The boy seemed to describe how the gold was taken from mines, melted, and refined. He described the process so vividly the Spaniards were persuaded he had seen it done.[26] Perico's powers of persuasion may have been considerable, though any small glimmer of light could be magnified into a beacon by the greed of De Soto and his men.[27]

The Return to Tampa Bay

Perico persuaded De Soto and the other Spaniards that the gold and silver and precious stones they desired could be obtained at Cofitachequi. To some it may have seemed that Perico was describing the fabled province of Xapira reported by Francisco of Chicora and Lucas Vázquez de Ayllón. Now thinking ahead to his entry into the interior, De Soto ordered Juan de Añasco to take a detachment of twenty-nine horsemen and retrace the path the army had followed from Tampa Bay. When he reached the base camp he was to tell Captain Calderón to come north to Apalachee with his detachment of horsemen. Then Añasco was to sail with the boats northward to the Bay of the Horses, bringing the greater part of Calderón's footmen and what supplies he could carry.[28]

This was an assignment that was to be as difficult as it was hazardous. They had to retrace their way along a forested trail with several difficult river and swamp crossings. They had to do it in the early winter season, making the water crossings harsher because of the cold. They had to pass as a small force back through the territory of Indians whom, their first time through, they had brutalized, enslaved, and robbed of their food. This time the Indians would not only be better prepared for them militarily, they would also be seeking revenge.[29] Moreover, they had with them no crossbowmen or arquebusiers who could keep the Indians at bay. Hence, if the horses became mired, the Indians could attack them at close range. Traveling as lightly as possible, they wore helmets and coats of mail over their clothes, and in their saddle bags they carried horseshoes, some nails, and whatever food they could pack.[30]

Añasco and his detachment of horsemen departed from Apalachee well before dawn on November 17.[31] They traveled as rapidly as possible, running their horses whenever it was feasible. They lanced to death two Indians they encountered on the trail to prevent them from warning the people ahead that they were coming. On the first day they crossed the Aucilla River and its floodplain swamp with no opposition from the Indians.[32] When night fell, they paused and rested in an open area some distance beyond the swamp.

The next day, November 18, they were again on the move before dawn, crossing the unpopulated area that lay between the Aucilla River and Uzachile. They traveled slowly, however, because they did not want to pass through Uzachile in the light of day. They stopped short of the town. Then, when night fell, they rushed through the town at half speed and traveled some distance beyond the town before stopping. When they rested, one-third of the force stayed awake in shifts, serving as sentinels, while the other two-thirds slept.[33]

At dawn the next day, November 19, they were again on the move, running at half speed because Indians were out and about, at work in their fields. They came to the Suwannee River, where they had crossed it previously.[34] The river was even harder to cross than before because the water was up and quite turbid. Presumably, the bridge they had previously built had been destroyed, either by Indians or by the river itself. Moreover, they had to contend with hostile Indians on both sides of the river, who called out to each other to kill the Spaniards while they were making their crossing. After much difficulty, they succeeded in dispersing the Indians and crossing the river on rafts.

The general strategy of Añasco and his detachment of horsemen was to travel rapidly and surprise the Indians, to preclude their organizing an effective resistance. Whether knowingly or unknowingly, as they traveled they took advantage of existing hostilities among the Indians to impede the news of their coming. News did not pass easily or quickly across Mississippian buffer zones. Often they would pass through Indian towns and settlements at night, when surprise would be greatest, and they would pause to sleep and rest a little in uninhabited places. In many places—such as when they later came to Uzachile—they found the Indians had relaxed their guard and had become careless. The Spaniards could have captured and enslaved many of them, but they did not do so because the slaves would have slowed down their progress.[35]

Traveling so rapidly, they sometimes surprised small parties of Indians as they went along. On one occasion they chanced upon two Indian men who were out hunting. They lanced one, but the other took cover behind a tree and nocked an arrow in his bow. Añasco told his men to ride on, unwilling to risk casualties for the sake of a single Indian. As they rode by, the Indian aimed his bow at each one, threatening to shoot, and he hurled insults at them. They were thirty in number, and on horseback, and he was a single man. The Spaniards had to grit their teeth, swallow their pride, and ride on.[36]

After their cold, wet crossing of the Suwannee River, they spent the remainder of the day in a town whose people had fled, drying out their saddles and clothing. They stuffed their horses with corn, and the men ate their fill as well. They found a variety of vegetables and dried fruit in this town, but they packed their saddlebags full of corn, because that was what it took to fuel their horses, and they could eat corn also.[37]

When darkness fell, they stationed pairs of sentinels at some distance from the town, to patrol and keep watch for Indians. When two of these sentinels heard the low noise of people approaching in the darkness, one of the pair returned to camp to put the Spaniards on guard. The other moved closer to investigate; in the moonlight he saw a large, dark mass of people muttering low, ferocious sounds. He galloped back to camp with the news that an attack was imminent.

The thirty Spaniards departed from the town before the Indians arrived. By dawn they had traveled many leagues. When they reached Napituca they beheld a chilling spectacle. The Indians had burned and laid waste to the entire town. The houses had been leveled, and the bodies of the Indians who had been killed in the battle and executed afterward lay piled up, unburied. Perhaps because of the horror of the battle and because the enormity of their loss was such a great tragedy, the Indians may have concluded that Napituca was a doomed place. It was uncharacteristic of the Indians to allow their dead to lie unburied, to be eaten by vultures and scavengers. They may have concluded that because so few Spaniards had killed so many Indians, the calamity could not have been simply due to the Spaniards, but to the malevolence of the place itself.[38]

On about their sixth day of travel (November 22), they came to the fringe of the territory of Ocale. On the seventh day, Pedro de Atienza became ill, and when he complained of his illness, the others refused to slow down. He died upon his horse. They paused briefly, cut wood with their axes, and made a sepulchre for him.[39]

At sunset of the seventh day, they came to the swamp of Ocale.[40] That night, as they bivouacked at the edge of the swamp, a very cold north wind blew in. The Spaniards built large fires, even though they realized these fires might attract the Indians. Even as few as twenty Indians in dugout canoes could have blocked the Spaniards' passage, since they had no crossbowmen or arquebusiers and could not use their horses in the swamp.[41]

During the night Juan de Soto died suddenly. Because he was a friend of the man they had just buried, one of the Spaniards became afraid that Atienza and Soto had died of plague. But when this man in his fright made a move to flee the camp, Gómez Arias ridiculed him: "You already carry enough pestilence with you in your flight not to be able to escape it, no matter how much you may try. If you flee from us now, where do you propose to go? You are not on the sandy beaches of Seville, nor are you among its hills."[42] The man returned to camp, but he would not go with the others to bury Juan de Soto's body.

Early the next morning they began crossing the swamp. When they reached the Withlacoochee River, eight of the Spaniards who could swim went out to repair the handrail of the bridge of fallen trees that spanned the deepest part of the water. Then those same eight carried across the saddles and gear of the entire company. This left the other twenty to drive the horses into the water. But because the water was so cold, the horses balked, even though the men beat them mercilessly. Some would start to swim, but because of the coldness of the water, they would turn back, dragging the men with them. The Spaniards struggled with their horses for hours. It was three in the afternoon before all had made it to the other side. The men were so fatigued from their labors and from exposure to cold, they could hardly stand. But they counted themselves fortunate that the Indians had not come to contest their crossing. The reason was that the place where they crossed was far from any Indian settlement, and being in the cold season, the Indians were in the habit of remaining near their houses. Añasco and his men traveled to just beyond the swamp and bivouacked in an open area. They took comfort in the knowledge that from this place to their destination they would encounter no more such difficult river crossings.[43]

Before dawn the next day (their ninth day on the trail), they were up and on the move. They encountered a party of five Indians and killed them all to keep them from carrying forward the news of their approach. The horses of Pedro de Atienza and Juan de Soto were stripped of their saddles and bridles and allowed to run free.[44]

The next day they started forward at dawn, and very early in the morning they went past the vicinity of the town of Urriparacoxi.[45] By nightfall of this tenth day of their journey, they bivouacked just three leagues from the town of Mocozo.[46]

A little past midnight they began traveling again. After they had gone about a league, Pedro Morón, who possessed a great sense of smell, said: "Be on the alert. I smell a fire not far from where we are heading."[47] They traveled for another league and Morón told them they were very near the fire. A short distance further they came to a place where there were many Indians of Mocozo cooking some skates they had caught.

The Spaniards rode into their midst, capturing eighteen or twenty women and children. Terrified by the horses, the men ran to safety in the woods. Those who were captured wept and shouted the name of Ortiz, reminding the Spaniards of the way they had taken care of him and had saved his life. But their cries had no effect on the Spaniards.[48] The Spaniards then dismounted and ate the skates, without even dusting off the sand that had been kicked up on the food during the melee. They were so hungry, they said the grains of sand tasted as sweet as sugar and cinnamon.[49]

They continued on toward Ozita. After they had traveled about five leagues, the horse of Juan López Cacho became exhausted and would go no further. Nothing they could do would make Cacho's horse continue. They removed the saddle and bridle, placing them up in a tree, and they left the horse to forage for itself in a meadow. They were sure that when Indians came upon this horse, they would kill it.

Another five leagues and they came to within a league of Ozita. They examined the ground, but they found no horse tracks, and they became worried that Calderón and all his men had been killed by the Indians or else had sailed away in the boats. This was a depressing thought, because with the Indians now on the alert, their return to Apalachee by way of the trail they had just followed would be extremely difficult without Calderón's horsemen to re-inforce them. And without boats, they would simply be marooned. They re-solved that if Calderón and his men were not there, they would rest up for a few days, kill one of the horses and dry the meat for food, then set out for Apalachee.

With this resolve they continued on toward Ozita.[50] Still they saw no horse tracks. But when they came to a small lagoon that was less than half a league from Ozita, they saw horse tracks and also evidence that water had been boiled with ashes where the men had washed their clothes. When their horses scented other horses, it gave them new life, and they galloped forward at a good pace.

On November 27, the eleventh day after they departed from Apalachee, they caught sight of the village of Ozita.[51] As they approached the town, a pa-trol of several horsemen with bucklers and lances came out of the camp two by two. Seeing this, Añasco formed up his own men in pairs, as if they were entering the start of a game of jousting. With great shouts they galloped to-ward Ozita, arriving grandly and in regular formation. Their shouts brought out Pedro Calderón and his soldiers, who were very glad to see their com-rades. But the first thing they asked about was not the health of De Soto nor of any of their friends at Apalachee. The question was, "Is there much gold in the land?"[52]

Several days after Añasco arrived at Tampa Bay, chief Mocozo came and brought with him Cacho's horse. Mocozo remained at peace with the Span-iards in spite of the fact that they apparently did not release the women they had captured.[53]

Between the time De Soto and his army had taken their leave from Tampa Bay and the time when Añasco and his men returned, one man under Captain Calderón's command had been killed by Indians, a second had been wounded, and two had been captured.

The Spaniards now prepared to abandon the base camp. The supplies that could not be carried away by the men or placed on board the brigantines were burned, though some may have been given to chief Mocozo and his people.[54]

At some time earlier, Gómez Arias had been ordered by De Soto to sail to Havana in the caravel. He was to convey to Doña Isabel news of what had oc-curred thus far on the expedition. Perhaps as evidence of the riches to be had in La Florida, he took with him some of the Indian slaves they had captured.[55]

The two bergantines still remained, and Juan de Añasco ordered that they be repaired to make them seaworthy. Then he loaded these and a small boat with men and supplies and set sail for the Bay of the Horses.

Between them, Añasco and Arias took with them thirty men on the bergantines. This left Calderón with forty additional horsemen and twenty-five or so footmen.[56] As Calderón and his men made their way to Apalachee, the Indians put up hardly any resistance until they approached the river and swamp of Ivitachuco—the Aucilla River. On the day they reached this place, they bivouacked in an open area near the swamp. The next day they moved through the narrow path that led through the swamp. The foot soldiers repaired the bridge while the horsemen swam their horses across the deepest part of the channel. After they had crossed, Calderón ordered ten horsemen to carry five crossbowmen and five shield bearers on the backs of their horses and to move rapidly through the narrow path on the other side. But when they began this maneuver, a large number of Apalachee warriors jumped up from where they had been concealed and began shooting arrows. They killed the horse of Alvaro Fernández and wounded five other horses. The attack was so sudden the horses bolted, turned around, and headed back for the channel of the river, without their riders being able to control them. All of the ten footmen were spilled from the horses and almost all fell into the water. Most of them were wounded. With this, the Indians closed in for the kill, shouting for others to join them.

The suddenness of the attack panicked the Spaniards, who were in a situation in which their horses were of limited usefulness. But then they recovered and rushed forward to try to protect the footmen who were being pressed very hard by the Indians. On their left flank a large group of Indians advanced, led by a bold man wearing a large feather headdress, evidently a war captain. Both Gonzalo Silvestre and Antón Galván were among the footmen who had been caught in the attack and had been spilled into the water. Seeing the war captain, they went after him. Galván put a bolt into his crossbow and walked along behind Silvestre, who protected the two of them with a half-shield. The war captain loosed three arrows at them in quick succession, but Silvestre deflected them with his shield. Galván waited until they were quite close, took careful aim, and shot a bolt striking the war captain in the center of his chest. The bolt passed completely through his body. He did not fall at once, but turned and cried words interpreted by the Spaniards as, "These . . . wretches have slain me!" When he fell, his comrades picked up his body and carried it away.[57]

Another group of Apalachees attacked on the right flank, closing in with great ferocity, shooting at the parts of the Spaniards' bodies where they were vulnerable. Andrés de Meneses was felled with four arrows to his thighs and genitals. Five others were seriously wounded. The Spaniards fought desperately, and gradually the Indians began to fall back. In part the Apalachees may have been demoralized at the news that their war captain had been killed.

The Spaniards were able to regroup, and they pressed forward, driving the Indians before them. Eventually they reached the path through the woods on the western bank and moved through it to the place they had cleared for a camp their first time through. They found that the Indians had fortified this place for their own uses. Here the Spaniards remained for the night, treating their wounded. The Indians shouted at them all night long, allowing them no rest.

The next morning, the Spaniards moved on, driving the Indians ahead of them. They reached the more open woods beyond the swamp, where the Indians had built barricades to defend against the horses and to offer themselves some protection. As the Spaniards moved through this area, the Indians alternated shooting arrows from the left and right sides of the trail to keep from injuring each other. The Indians wounded many of the Spaniards, while losing few or none of their own. But once the Spaniards reached the place where the woods opened up, the Indians fled, because they could not stand against the horsemen.

After traveling through open woods for some distance, the Spaniards bivouacked and attended to their wounded. When darkness fell, the Indians came closer and harassed them, shouting insults and provocations. According to Garcilaso, they said: "Whither are you wretches going now that your Captain [De Soto] and all of his soldiers are dead? We have quartered them and put them up on the trees, and we will do the same with you before you arrive there. What do you wish? Why do you come to this land? Do you think that we who inhabit it are so vile as to abandon it and become your . . . slaves? Let it be understood that we are men who will kill all of you as well as those of your people who remain in Castile."[58] The Indians kept shouting and threatening them all through the night.

The next day the Spaniards arrived at the ravine of Burnt Mill Creek, where the Apalachees had put up such a determined resistance when De Soto had first passed through. They had constructed wooden barriers at different intervals. The horsemen, who wore the best armor, dismounted and advanced as a vanguard against the barriers with shields, swords, and axes. Some of them also formed a rearguard in case the Apalachees attacked from the rear. The footmen, with their lighter body armor, mounted the horses and occupied the center of the formation along with the servants.

The Apalachees periodically attacked, but the Spaniards advanced along the narrow path through the ravine. They chopped their way through the barriers built of poles and withes (*bejucos*). Several of them sustained wounds, and Alvaro Fernández of Elvas had a second horse shot out from under him. As soon as they got through the dense undergrowth, the Indians melted away for fear of the horses. But whenever there was forest cover, the Apalachees would attack from ambush. And they continued to torment the Spaniards with their taunts that De Soto and all his men were dead. Some of Añasco's men began to fear that this was true, and particularly as they approached Anhayca, where their shouts at first brought no response. But then De Soto's soldiers replied, and they greeted Calderón and his men with gladness, though they were saddened at the losses Calderón had endured: two killed, including Andrés de Meneses, many wounded, and seven horses lost.[59]

Añasco had not arrived at the Bay of the Horses in the bergantines by the time Calderón arrived in Apalachee, and this worried De Soto.[60] He ordered men to proceed to the Bay of the Horses to saw planks and build a piragua large enough to hold thirty well-armed men. They were to row out into the Gulf each day where they could be lookouts for the bergantines. On several occasions when they went out in the piragua they were attacked by Indians in canoes. Añasco, for his part, was not able to spot the flags he had left up on the trees at the entrance to the inlet.[61] Finally, on Sunday, December 28, he arrived in the bergantines with his men, who were much fatigued.[62]

Apalachee Resistance

The Apalachees kept up a constant military pressure for the entire time the Spaniards were in their homeland. The Spaniards learned to respect the boldness and courage of the Apalachees. Repeatedly they ambushed the Spaniards, killing several of them. Twice they set fire to Anhayca. Especially damaging was the fire on Saturday, November 29, when an Apalachee slipped by the sentinels and ignited some of the houses. Fanned by the strong wind that was blowing, two-thirds of the camp was destroyed.

No torture the Spaniards imposed upon Apalachee warriors would dissuade them from their loyalty to Apalachee nor deter them from their hostilities. The Spaniards burned several of them to death. They would cut off hands or noses (fig. 20), and the maimed warriors would act as if nothing had

Fig. 20. A compendium of sixteenth-century Spanish cruelties. *Foreground:* cutting off hands; *upper right:* cutting off noses; *upper left:* dogs attacking an Indian. Theodore de Bry illustration for a German edition of Bartolomé de las Casas's *Brevísima Relación de la destruyción de las Indias,* 1552. (Lessing J. Rosenwald Collection, Rare Book and Special Collections Division, Library of Congress)

happened.[63] None would conceal his identity. "From whence am I? I am [a man] of Apalachee." And they were insulted if anyone thought they were not Apalachee.

Apalachee warriors smeared red ocher on their bodies and wore multi-colored feathers on their heads, and they were avid in taking the scalps of their victims (fig 21; also see fig. 55). A scalp was proof that one had killed an enemy, and they advanced themselves through their warrior organization by taking scalps. A warrior who had killed an enemy was a *tascaia*. One who had taken three scalps was a *noroco*. The highest title a warrior could attain was *nicoguadca*. Attaining this fabled title required one to have killed ten enemies, and three of these had to be warriors who were themselves more than *tascaias*.[64]

The Apalachees became so bold they would come to within two crossbow shots of the camp to kill Spaniards. On a day in late December, De Soto sent eight horsemen out to punish and intimidate the Apalachees for a distance of two leagues around Anhayca. The horse patrol came upon two Indian men and a woman gathering beans in a field.[65] Although the two men could have escaped, they would have had to abandon the woman, who was the wife of one of them.

The Spaniards succeeded in killing both the men, but one of them, perhaps the husband of the woman, fought with singular ferocity. Wanting to take him alive, the Spaniards closed upon him rapidly and trampled him with their horses. Just as he was about to get to his feet, another trampled him. But the more they assaulted him, the more ferocious he became. He managed to fire arrows into three of the horses, one of which died several days later.[66] Finally he took his bow in his hands and swung it like a staff, striking Estevan Pegado of Elvas a blow on the head, which caused blood to run down his face and nearly knocked him out. When he regained his senses, Pegado took his lance and ran the man through, killing him. They returned to camp astounded at this Apalachee man who had the audacity and strength to stand up against eight horsemen.[67]

On another occasion, a detachment of horsemen and footmen went from Anhayca to a neighboring town to seize some corn. The Apalachees had fled the village before the Spaniards arrived. After they had taken the food they wanted, Diego de Soto, a nephew of the adelantado, concealed himself in a temple and waited to see whether he could capture an Apalachee. Eventually a man appeared in the main plaza, and Diego de Soto galloped out. At first the man attempted to outrun Soto's horse, but although he was very fast, the

Fig. 21. A compendium of Southeastern Indian cruelties. *Right:* smoke-drying a scalp; *left:* scalping, dismembering, and desecrating the body of a dead enemy; *above:* returning home with war trophies. Theodore de Bry, *Americae,* part 2, 1591. (National Anthropological Archives, Smithsonian Institution)

horse gained on him. The man ducked behind a tree and nocked an arrow into his bow. Soto rode close past the tree and attempted to thrust a lance into the man. But the man dodged the thrust, stepped out, and fired an arrow that struck Soto's horse between the cinch and the knee so hard the horse stumbled for fifteen or twenty feet before falling down, then expired without moving a foot.[68] Diego Velásquez, a skilled horseman, approached at half-speed and attempted the same maneuver. The Indian stepped from behind the tree and loosed an arrow at him that struck his horse in the knee; this horse also fell down, further injured himself, and died. The two Spaniards made a move to attack the Indian with their lances on foot, but the man sped off into the woods, jeering at the Spaniards. To add insult to injury, he ran not at full speed, but only just fast enough to keep ahead of the Spaniards.[69]

Because of their ferocity, the Apalachees effectively confined the Spaniards to their camp for the entire winter.[70] If Apalachees heard the sound of firewood being cut with axes, they would come running, intent on killing and scalping. If they chanced upon the Spaniards' slaves, they would remove their chains and release them. Spanish reinforcements, answering cries of alarm, could seldom arrive before the damage had been done.[71] The Apalachees attacked in frequent small ambushes from concealment, rather than in frontal assaults. And they constantly set up alarms at night, to keep the Spaniards on edge.[72]

The Chief of Apalachee

The chief of Apalachee was a man named Capafi. It was De Soto's practice to capture the chiefs of the provinces he traveled through and hold them hostage to insure the good behavior of their subjects. This would be the way he would try to subdue the Apalachees. But try as he might, he could not lay hands on Capafi, who had taken refuge with some of his subjects in a dense swamp several leagues from Anhayca, probably in the Ochlockonee Valley.[73] De Soto sent go-betweens with gifts and kind words to Capafi, but Capafi would not come to see him.

De Soto began to make a determined effort to learn where Capafi was hiding, and in time he did find out. To reach the hiding place one had to pass along a very narrow path through dense woods. At intervals along the path the Apalachees had, as before, built barricades of thick poles of wood, bound together with willow withes. These barricades were defended by very determined warriors, and Capafi was surrounded by others who would die before they would see him captured or harmed.

De Soto went out with some of his men to try to force their way to the chief. As they began traveling along the path, there was only room for two soldiers to go abreast. A rain of arrows flew at them. Nonetheless, they made headway, cutting through barricade after barricade. The Apalachee warriors fought valiantly, but because they wore no body armor, the Spaniards killed many of them.

When De Soto and his men approached the refuge, and when it became clear they would succeed in killing or capturing Capafi, the chief commanded his men to cease fighting. The Apalachees knelt before De Soto begging him to kill them and spare their chief. But De Soto had come for Capafi, and he took him prisoner.[74]

In many Mississippian chiefdoms the chief was so sacred there were occasions in which he was not to walk on the earth with common people. Rather, his subjects transported him on a litter, which they carried on their shoulders. Consistent with this, Capafi's subjects carried him on a litter back to Anhayca.[75] But his capture did not cause the Apalachees to cease their hostilities; they continued their alarms and ambushes. Spaniards who strayed only a short distance from Anhayca were attacked.

De Soto spoke to Capafi, telling him that if the hostilities did not cease, he would lay waste to the country; he might even execute him. De Soto made it clear to Capafi that he should command his subjects to cease their hostilities. Capafi replied that he could only do so if he could go in person to his people to speak to them directly. They would not believe any words brought to them by go-betweens.

Capafi persuaded De Soto to send a detachment with him to the south, where some of his people were hiding. De Soto complied, and a detachment of horsemen and footmen went with Capafi to the place he designated.[76] When they reached this place, ten or twelve Indians appeared whom Capafi instructed to go and command his principal men to appear before him the next day. He wished to give them an important message.

The Spaniards posted a special guard. But during the course of the night, Capafi escaped, and he was picked up and carried away by his people. When dawn came, the Spaniards were astonished that he was able to escape in spite of their best efforts at security. The fact is, the guards were tired, and they had fallen asleep and become careless. Also, they had been lulled by Capafi's words of friendship and assurance. His people carried him to an even more secure place, and the Spaniards never saw him again.[77] As the contingent of Spaniards responsible for Capafi returned to Anhayca empty-handed, the Apalachees jeered and ridiculed them. The men who had lost Capafi told De Soto he must have been carried away by devils. De Soto, seeing that nothing could be gained by berating his men, pretended to believe them, avowing that the Indians were in fact great sorcerers and that they could have got back their chief by this means.[78]

Maldonado Reconnoiters the Gulf Coast

Shortly after Añasco arrived at the Bay of the Horses in the bergantines, De Soto ordered Francisco Maldonado, captain of the foot soldiers, to take fifty men in the two boats and to coast along the shore and explore all the coves, inlets, creeks, and rivers until he arrived at a river with a good entrance and harbor and that had an Indian town on its shore.[79] Presumably De Soto was thinking ahead to the water transport needed to supply colonies that would be established in the interior. Maldonado was to return within two months with an account of all that he had discovered.

Maldonado presumably departed in late December and explored the coast to the west of Apalachee Bay. About sixty leagues west of the Bay of the Horses he succeeded in discovering an excellent harbor—Pensacola Bay—which he sounded and explored.[80] It was safe from all winds, and it was large enough to accommodate a fleet. It had good depth very near shore, so that ships could come in close to land to disembark.[81] And there was an Indian town there named Ochuse, from which he seized by trickery a man from a group of several who had come out to trade with the Spaniards.[82] The captive from Ochuse was taken back to Apalachee to serve as an informant and perhaps as a guide, should the occasion arise. Maldonado also brought back a blanket of "sable" fur that was of better quality than the others they had seen in Apalachee.[83] What this "sable" was is not known, but they would repeatedly encounter it on their travels. Perhaps it was muskrat, or even otter or beaver.

Maldonado returned four days past the two months allotted to him by De Soto, which to men anxious to move on in search of promised riches seemed like a thousand years.[84] De Soto had determined that he would have waited only three more days before quitting Apalachee to march into the interior.[85]

While in Apalachee, De Soto was still planning to found a colony in the southeastern United States. He intended to explore this territory by heading northward and then looping around to the west and then south to the port of Ochuse.[86] Here he would rendezvous with Maldonado, who would arrive from Cuba with fresh supplies in two bergantines, the caravel in which Gómez Arias had sailed to Cuba, and in other ships if they could be procured.

De Soto ordered Maldonado to sail to Cuba from the Bay of the Horses, taking news to Doña Isabel of all that had happened so far on the expedition. De Soto gave him written instructions of what he was to do. He was, for example, to collect together crossbows, arquebuses, lead, powder, footwear, and other supplies for an army.[87] He was to order Gómez Arias to accompany him. He was to rendezvous with De Soto at Pensacola Bay late in the summer or in the fall.[88] If necessary, he was to sail along the Gulf coast all the way to the Río del Espíritu Santo searching for De Soto and his army.[89] On February 26, 1540, Maldonado sailed away in the bergantines under these orders, and Juan de Guzmán replaced him as captain of the footmen.[90]

6

Cofitachequi

In early spring 1540, De Soto began making plans for his march into the interior of the Southeast to discover the riches of Cofitachequi and other provinces. Presumably because of what the Indians told him about the land ahead, he carried enough corn to feed the army while they marched through an extensive uninhabited area. They loaded this corn onto the backs of the horses and also the footmen, who had to perform this labor because so many of their poor Indian slaves, who were naked and in chains, had died during the winter.[1] In addition to suffering from exposure, the slaves probably were not given adequate food during the winter, and some may have succumbed to disease.

What lay before De Soto and his army was a considerable expanse of pine barrens and sandy soils, the same longleaf pine-wiregrass vegetation they had already seen in north Florida (see map 4). All of the eighteenth-century and early nineteenth-century travelers who described the pine barrens spoke of the depressingly monotonous stands of widely spaced, immense pine trees, with very little foliage except wiregrass growing underneath. Deer, turkey, and bear shunned the pine barrens, and even smaller animals—cottontails, squirrels, opossum, and raccoons—were scarce. The pine barrens were home to animals with unusual adaptations, such as the gopher tortoise and the red-cockaded woodpecker. The gopher tortoise digs burrows as much as fifteen feet deep, a defense against predators and forest fires. The red-cockaded woodpecker builds its home by pecking a hole into a large pine tree that has a rotten core but is still capable of drenching the entrance to the hole with sticky sap, a defense against tree-climbing snakes. Both of these species are now threatened.

The pine barrens were also shunned by the native people. No large Mississippian sites occur in areas once dominated by pine barrens. The monotony of the pine barrens was only relieved by the floodplain forests, which grew adjacent to the rivers cutting through the coastal plain, particularly the larger rivers whose headwaters lay in the higher, geologically older interior. In these moist floodplains the partnership between fire, longleaf pines, and wiregrass was broken. In contrast to the open forest of the pine barrens, the floodplain forests were ribbons of dense forest consisting of bald cypress, tupelo gum, sweetgum, willow oak, and water hickory, as well as luxuriant shrubs. These were overgrown by peppervine, rattan vine, cowitch vine, and smilax vine, growing so thick in places they choked out small trees. Likewise, large stands of cane grew in floodplain forests so densely they excluded all competition from other plants.[2]

On March 3 the army departed from Anhayca and began marching northward (map 6).[3] De Soto, along with Rodrigo Rangel and others, traveled out in front with the horse vanguard, and they reached the River of Bacuqua, the Ochlockonee, by nightfall.[4] Then, a day and a half later, on March 5, passing near present-day Cairo and Camilla, Georgia, the vanguard arrived at a large river in the vicinity of present-day Newton.[5] The remainder of the army caught up with the vanguard on March 6 or 7, after a march of four or five days.[6]

The Spaniards found themselves standing on the bank of the Flint River, deep and swift, and so wide—about 250 feet—that Cristóbal Mosquera, the best stone-thrower among them, could not throw a stone to the opposite bank. They cut down some trees, sawed them into planks, and built a piragua, which was a simple, flat-bottomed boat, usually long and narrow in shape, used to transport people and goods, mainly on rivers and lakes. They at first attempted to pull the boat back and forth across the river using their slave chains, the segments of which they connected together with iron S-hooks. But the current of the river was so strong that twice it broke the chain. Finally, they twisted several ropes together, forming them into two hawsers. They fastened one hawser to the bow and the other to the stern of the boat, and in this way they pulled the boat back and forth across the river, ferrying the men and

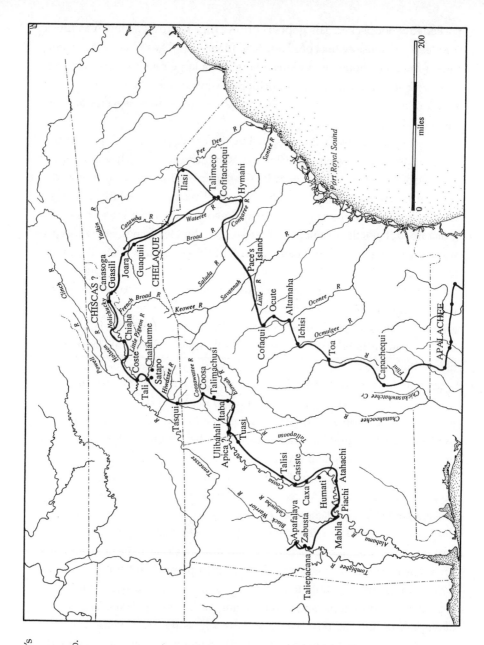

Map 6. De Soto's route from Apalachee to Apafalaya, 1540.

supplies across. They got the horses across by tying ropes around their necks and pulling to assist them while they swam.[7] Had they not been anxious about obtaining food, De Soto and his men could have traveled due north up the eastern side of the Flint River, thereby avoiding this river crossing.

Capachequi

By March 10 the entire army had been ferried to the western side of the river, and on this day they traveled for some distance before bivouacking in a pine woods. The next day, March 11, they came to the first village of the chiefdom of Capachequi, where they found good stores of food, though the people had all run into nearby swamps to hide. This village was among some densely wooded hills (*arboledas*), probably the line of hills, rising as much as seventy feet, that lie along the southern edge of the Chickasawhatchee Swamp. These hills are densely wooded with cherry laurel as well as deciduous trees, which contrast sharply with the pine uplands surrounding the swamp.[8] As they traveled, they saw native towns they could not reach because they could not cross the wide expanses of swamp with their stands of bald cypress, tupelo, willow oak, and other wet-adapted trees.[9] By the end of the day they approached a second town of Capachequi. But to get to it they had to cross a difficult swamp with a strong current running through it, probably Kiokee Creek. They had to ford a wide expanse of water, with the water coming up to the cinches and saddle pads of their horses. Darkness fell before all the men were able to make this crossing.[10]

They had come to the central town of the chiefdom of Capachequi, probably the Magnolia Plantation mound site. At places around the town the natives had built small wooden footbridges across some of the wet areas.[11] Capachequi was a small chiefdom occupying the territory in and around the Chickasawhatchee Swamp—the largest and most well-developed expanse of floodplain bottomland in the entire Flint River drainage. This swamp is a vast wetland, with many flood channels. In addition to the Magnolia Plantation mound site, there is a second multimound site in the swamp, as well as several nonmound sites. To date, very little archaeological research has been done in the Chickasawhatchee Swamp. But existing evidence testifies that this area was occupied in the first half of the sixteenth century, and the ceramic culture of the people of Capachequi resembles that of the people of Apalachee. This need not mean, however, that Capachequi was politically affiliated with Apalachee.[12] The relationships between Capachequi and its nearest neighbors to the south, west, and north are unknown. The fact that Marcos, the Spaniards' guide, led them to Capachequi may indicate that this place lay on the trail between the Apalachees and the people to the north with whom they traded.

On March 12 five of the Spanish soldiers went on foot to look for some of the wooden mortars (see fig. 91) the Indians used to pulverize corn and hominy into meal. Not far from the main camp, they came to several houses surrounded by woods.[13] Exploring the environs, they happened upon several Indians who were hiding in the woods to spy on the Spaniards. Five of these Indians came out to do battle with the like number of Spaniards, deliberately making the contest equal, as if to measure their own military prowess against that of the invaders. Being lightly clothed and agile, they jumped about in front of the Spaniards, taunting and deriding them.[14] They attacked one Spaniard with their bows, swinging them as clubs, breaking one man's shield into pieces and striking him across the forehead, laying it open to the eyebrows.[15] One of the five Spaniards broke away and ran back to the camp, sounding the alarm. When several horsemen arrived at the scene, they found one Spaniard dead and the other three badly wounded. The Indian attackers, seemingly unharmed, fled into the densely wooded swamp, where the horses could not enter.[16]

Toa

Having rested for six days, on March 17 the Spaniards departed from Capachequi and marched toward the northeast. They probably followed a trail that paralleled the western side of Kiokee Creek, coming at the end of the day to White Spring, a beautiful spring (*fuente*) with a voluminous flow of water, teeming with fish. This was possibly James Pond, a large, isolated lime sink in southern Lee County. This pond measures about twenty-five hundred feet across, and it has streams flowing into and out of it.[17]

By nightfall of the following day, they came to the River of Toa—again the Flint River. They spent the next three days traveling along a trail paralleling the western bank of this river. The trail probably skirted the edge of the floodplain forest that lay along the course of the river. Hence, as they traveled along, they would have had open longleaf pine-wiregrass forest on their left side, and dense floodplain forest on their right (see map 4). There would have been few animals to be seen on their left, except perhaps occasional flocks of turkeys. Being a large and noisy army, they probably saw few to their right, either, but from this direction they were surely seen by floodplain forest fauna: deer, bear, panthers, cottontails, raccoons, squirrels, and by many kinds of birds.

On March 21 they arrived at a place where they could cross to the eastern side of the Flint River. The most likely location is at an old fording place approximately five miles south of where Georgia State Road 127 crosses the river. This lay at the southern end of the fall line meander zone of the Flint River. The fall line is an imaginary line across the southeastern landscape that divides the geologically older hilly piedmont from the geologically younger flat coastal plain. As the piedmont rivers spill into the coastal plain at the fall line—often through rapids and shoals—they embark on a sinuous path through a meander zone flanked by rich levees and backswamps. In the eyes of the Mississippian Indians, these meander zones were very good places to hunt, fish, and farm.

De Soto and his men came to the Flint River at a point where this meander zone pinches in and where the channel of the river is particularly narrow. It is where the first good fording place occurs south of the Flint's fall line meander zone.[18] It is unclear what time of day they arrived there, but it may have been early enough for them to begin constructing a bridge. Somewhere in their travels on this day, the horse belonging to Lorenzo Suárez, son of Vasco Porcallo, drowned.[19] The entire distance from Capachequi to where they crossed the river was through an uninhabited land, presumably a buffer zone between competing polities.[20]

Had they taken a left turn and marched westward at this point, they would have come to a Mississippian chiefdom that occupied the fall line meander zone of the Chattahoochee River. But their destination was Cofitachequi, and so they took a right turn instead. Unfortunately, none of the expeditions that followed De Soto in the later sixteenth century visited the Chattahoochee River. Hence, although archaeologists have learned quite a bit about the chiefdom that occupied the middle Chattahoochee River in the sixteenth century, we cannot be sure about what name these people called themselves, nor can we be sure about what name any other people might have used to refer to them. But perhaps they were called Apalachicola, the name used by seventeenth-century Spaniards to refer to people on the Chattahoochee River.[21]

To span the Flint River, the Spaniards built a footbridge of pine poles lashed together.[22] But the current in the river proved to be very strong, and two of their attempts at building a bridge were washed away. Finally, at the suggestion of Nuño de Tovar, they used crisscrossed timbers, and with this third attempt, the bridge held. By nightfall on March 22, they all got across to the eastern side of the river, and they camped in a pine woods.[23] The men got separated from each other in the course of this crossing and were too disorganized to bivouac in good order. Had they been attacked, they would have been vulnerable.

The next morning, March 23, they arrived at a town of the chiefdom of Toa. It was a large town; in fact, it seemed to them to be larger than any they had seen up to this point.[24] After having traveled through the small villages of peninsular Florida and the dispersed settlement pattern of Apalachee and Capachequi, they were beginning to encounter the compact, often walled towns that occurred in many parts of the Mississippian interior of the South-east. Toa was a small chiefdom whose towns lay adjacent to the floodplain of the Flint River, from just below the fall line to about fifteen miles downstream. Two mound centers—Hartley-Posey and Neisler—lay in the northern part of this area. Most of the larger sites lay on the western side of the river.[25]

At Toa they had come to the fringe of the Lamar (or South Appalachian) area, a distinctive subarea of Late Mississippian culture. It developed out of an earlier Middle Mississippian culture called Savannah that occupied approximately the same wide geographical range (see map 2). It included chiefdoms on the Coosa, Coosawattee, Etowah, and Tallapoosa Rivers in Alabama and Georgia; on the Hiwassee River in southeastern Tennessee; on the small rivers in the mountains of eastern Tennessee and western North Carolina; on the upper courses of the Chattahoochee, Flint, Ocmulgee, Oconee, and Savannah Rivers of Georgia; on the Broad, Catawba-Wateree, and Peedee Rivers of South Carolina; and in delimited areas along the sounds and estuaries of the Georgia and South Carolina coast.

The Lamar culture was first identified by archaeologists on the basis of its distinctive pottery. This was first produced at about A.D. 1350, at a time when notable changes were occurring in many Mississippian cultures. Lamar pottery was made by forming coiled clay vessels, the soft exteriors of which were often decorated by being paddled with wooden paddles with specific design motifs carved on them (fig. 22). These design motifs were paddled into the clay rather randomly, and then the potters often smoothed them over a bit. Archaeologists call this complicated stamped pottery. The potters thickened the rims of their vessels by folding them outward or by adding on a thin strip of clay. They then typically decorated these rims by incising small notches, or by pinching up small ridges with their thumb and index finger, or by punching in shallow holes, often with the end of a small piece of cane. Later on—at about A.D. 1450—Lamar potters began incising designs on the upper portions of their vessels (see fig. 22). Like the stamped motifs, these incised motifs vary from region to region within the Lamar area, and they changed through time. It is notable, even striking, that throughout the four-century life span of the Lamar period, stylistic changes in making pottery tended to diffuse rapidly

Fig. 22. A Lamar complicated stamped jar (*right*) and a Lamar bold incised bowl (*left*), both from the Irene site at Savannah, Georgia. Photograph by S. Dwight Kirkland. (University of Georgia, Laboratory of Archaeology)

throughout the Lamar area. In addition to these decorated wares, plain-surfaced vessels were used throughout the Lamar period.

Archaeologists are generally of the opinion that the advent of the Lamar pottery style was a reflex of deeper economic or ecological dynamics. What these dynamics could have been has been difficult to discern, and the problems of evidence are such that all proposed solutions are likely to be contestable. But several things are becoming clearer. For one thing, Lamar agriculturalists had a knack for finding and exploiting the soils that were richest and easiest to till, namely, the soils that lie along the Coosawattee and Etowah Rivers where they emerge through the Great Smoky Fault; along the Chattahoochee, Flint, Ocmulgee, Oconee, and Wateree just below the fall line; and along the small levee ridges that lie along the rivers that course through the Piedmont. But like Apalachee farmers, Lamar farmers were also capable of farming up-land soils when need be, and some even farmed the soils near the tidal marshes and on the barrier islands of coastal Georgia and South Carolina. No matter how rich the soil, however, the Indians did not add fertilizer, and their intensive farming would, over the course of time, deplete the fertility of their farmlands. Their heavy use of wood would also have depleted local forest resources, making the territories occupied by the old pristine chiefdoms more and more undesirable. Such long-term trends could have produced the fundamental changes evident in Mississippian culture a century or two before De Soto arrived.[26]

It is probable that like eighteenth-century American frontiersmen, the Indians judged the suitability of soils for corn cultivation in terms of stands of river cane (*Arundinaria gigantea*) (fig. 23). Like corn, river cane is a grass, and the richer the soil the taller it grows. The rule of thumb for the eighteenth-century frontiersman was that if the cane grew five to ten feet, the soil was ordinary; if it grew twenty to thirty feet, the soil was excellent. In addition, river cane probably served the material needs of the Southeastern Indians in more ways than any other resource in their environment. Cane is a hard, flexible, water-resistant material that they used to manufacture a host of artifacts, including baskets, woven mats, knives, arrows, fish spears, blowguns, houses, and so on. Its leaves stay green the year around, and it therefore attracted herbivorous animals in winter, where they could be hunted. Likewise, bears often took

Fig. 23. Interior of a dense canebrake in Tuscaloosa County, Alabama. Photograph by Roland Harper, March 4, 1913. (William Stanley Hoole Special Collections Library, University of Alabama)

up residence in canebrakes, as did carnivores such as red wolves and cougars. Canebrakes were superb places of refuge. They were very dense, and the dry leaves and stalks betrayed any intruding movement. When pursued, the Indians would head for the nearest canebrake. Some canebrakes were vast, covering thousands of acres. But over the centuries American farmers have eliminated them, and today few large stands of river cane survive.

In addition to farming, the Lamar people depended upon hunting for a substantial portion of their diet, most particularly white-tailed deer, which they mainly hunted in late fall and winter. Turkey and bear were next in importance, and they killed and ate the smaller animals as well. The abundance of game was quite as important to Lamar people as the success of their agriculture. They may have intentionally set fire to the woods at optimal times in the fall and winter to increase the growth of browse, thus providing more food for deer and artificially increasing their numbers. The extensive wildernesses that lay between Lamar societies, while having primarily a defensive purpose, had the perhaps unintended benefit of providing refuges where deer and other game animals could keep their numbers up. Lamar people also drew upon the wild aquatic resources to be found in the lakes, oxbows, rivers, and estuaries. And when they could not find abundant sources of fish, turtles, and shellfish close to their agricultural fields, they would travel considerable distances to good fishing spots, where they lived temporarily in lightly built shelters. Fishing was especially good along the shoals of the rivers. Protein from aquatic sources was probably most important to the Lamar people during the summer months.[27]

Lamar archaeological sequences appear to be oldest and most continuous in the interior river valleys, and they are youngest and least continuous on the southern and eastern margins of the Lamar area. This implies that for whatever reason and by whatever means, Lamar culture expanded from the interior to the east and south. Warfare among Lamar chiefdoms was a fact of life at the time of the De Soto expedition, and there is reason to think that it had been so for some time. But in addition to fighting each other, Lamar chiefdoms also conducted among themselves at least a low level trade in exotic substances—copper (see fig. 48), Atlantic and Gulf coast shell (see fig. 8), greenstone, mica (see fig. 31), and so on. This, after all, was the enterprise that had caused Perico and Marcos to be in northern Florida when De Soto and his men arrived.

And as De Soto would soon discover, Lamar chiefdoms were attempting to build larger polities, organizing wider spans of people who were at peace with each other, but who might be at war with other societies. These were the paramount chiefdoms De Soto would visit in coming months. Because the

Spaniards' dealings with Toa were so brief and uneventful, nothing is known about Toa's wider political relationships. Toa may have been an independent chiefdom, subject to no other, or it may have been affiliated with paramount chiefs to the west or east.

De Soto's men noticed that the houses and way of life of the people of Toa were different from what they had seen at Apalachee and Capachequi. The houses they had seen thus far had thatched roofs, whereas the houses of Toa had roofs covered with canes (perhaps cane mats) laid overlapping, as tiles are laid. Most, perhaps all, the houses they had seen up to this point were of flexed construction, constructed of slender flexible poles set individually in the ground and then bent over to form a dome- or conoidal-shaped structure. But from Toa onward the houses were of rigid construction, with distinct walls and interior posts supporting a separate roof structure (see figs. 35, 42). The houses of Toa probably had walls made of wattle-and-daub construction, consisting of a basketlike framework of vertical wooden posts interwoven with horizontal cane or wood withes, neatly plastered with clay and straw to keep out the cold. In the Lamar area as elsewhere in the interior of the Southeast, the Indians built houses for cold weather with small doors, which they shut tightly at night, so that with a small fire it heated up like an oven inside and remained so all night. They were warm enough that one had no need to wear clothing while inside. In addition they built lighter structures—porticos or arbors—often little more than posts with sunshade roofs for use during the day and when the weather was fair. The fires where they did much of their cooking were in or near these porticos and arbors. In addition, they kept their grain and other stores in barbacoas, storehouses raised up on four posts, timbered like a loft and with a floor of cane (see fig. 49). *Barbacoa* is an Arawak word that the Spaniards applied to any weight-bearing framework raised up on posts, whether a grill for roasting meat or the floor of a structure. The areas beneath these storehouses were also shady places where people socialized during the day, when the weather was fair.

The chiefs, their relatives, and the more important people of the community lived in buildings that were larger than those of the common people. Moreover, they sometimes had large porticos built in front of their houses with benches made of cane where people sat. Nearby were large barbacoas in which they gathered the tribute paid them by their subjects. This tribute consisted of corn, dressed deerskins, and shawls woven out of the inner fiber of mulberry trees, as well as other fibers. The mulberry fiber shawls had the appearance of white linen, and the fabric was sometimes very thin. They also made cloth from the fiber of woods nettle and from a plant whose leaves

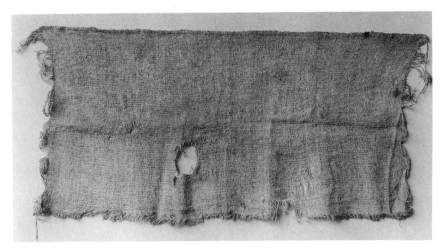

Fig. 24. A twined shawl from Clifty Creek rock shelter, Morgan County, Tennessee. It is woven from woods nettle, *Laportea canadensis*. (Smithsonian Institution)

had a growing habit the Spaniards could only compare to daffodils (*abroteas*) (fig. 24). When the leaves of these latter plants were pounded, they produced a fiber like flax. This plant was probably button snake-root (*Eryngium yuccifolium* or *E. aquaticum*).

The Indian women clothed themselves in these white mulberry fiber shawls, wrapping one around their waist, forming a short skirt, and wearing a second draped over their shoulder, with the right arm uncovered, so that they reminded the Spaniards of Bohemians or Gypsies in Spain.

In places the Indian men wore a mulberry fiber shawl over their shoulders in something of the same manner. And they wore a breechcloth made of dressed deerskin in the same way that breechcloths were formerly worn in Spain. Their moccasins were also made of dressed deerskin. They dyed these deerskins various colors. Those that were dyed vermillion had the appearance of a closely woven cloth, and those they dyed black were likewise attractive. Some of their mulberry fiber shawls were also dyed red and black.[28]

Ichisi

De Soto wanted to push on to the next chiefdom without pausing at Toa. But there was some dissension in the ranks. Perhaps the land they were exploring did not look promising to the men. They had had a brush with starvation in the swamp of Ocale, and perhaps they were afraid something similar or worse might lie ahead. Whatever the reason, some members of the army were balking. But De Soto knew how to inflame their avarice. At midnight of the same day they arrived at Toa (March 23), De Soto abruptly departed with forty horsemen including Rodrigo Rangel, heading eastward.[29] With Perico serving as guide, they followed a trail that lay on or near present-day Georgia State Road 127.[30] Beyond present-day Perry, Georgia, they probably followed a trail that led to the Ocmulgee River in the general vicinity of the present-day town of Westlake.[31]

This was one of the most extraordinary maneuvers of the entire expedition. On March 24 De Soto and his detachment of horsemen traveled from midnight to dawn, and they continued for that entire day and night, arriving on the morning of Holy Thursday, March 25, at the Ocmulgee River.[32] They had traveled continuously for about thirty-five hours, covering approximately thirty-four miles.[33] Ordinarily they only traveled about fifteen miles per day.

They crossed a broad arm of the Ocmulgee, wading and swimming, and arrived at a village on an island in the river. This was the first town they came to that was subject to the chiefdom of Ichisi. De Soto and his men surprised the people of this town and captured several of them, who seemingly had no knowledge that these Spaniards were present in the land.[34] The Spaniards found some turkeys and pieces of venison roasting on a barbacoa with the coals of a fire beneath it (fig. 25). Hungry after their long journey, they ate this meat for breakfast, in spite of it being Holy Thursday. For southerners, it is a matter of some interest that it is from this use of the word *barbacoa* that barbecue takes its name and that this was the first barbecue in Georgia to be recorded in the annals of history.[35]

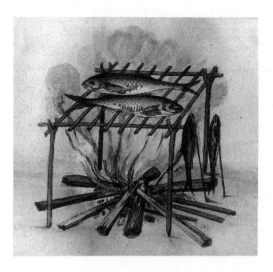

Fig. 25. Broiling fish on a *barbacoa,* coastal North Carolina. Barbecue takes its name from this Spanish word, and most Southerners will recognize the technique. (Watercolor by John White, British Museum)

Among the Indians they captured, there was one who understood Perico's language. This was a relief to De Soto, because they had passed through the territories of some Indians—presumably Capachequi and Toa—whose languages Perico did not understand. Because Perico could converse with this person, De Soto and the others were more willing to give credence to what the boy said.[36] The Indians they captured were cooperative, informing them that this was the chiefdom of Ichisi, and so De Soto released most of them, keeping only a few to serve as guides and interpreters.[37] Because the island was isolated and vulnerable to attack by Indians who might come in dugout canoes, the Spaniards returned across the arm of the river to the bank. Then De Soto sent one of the Indians he had captured to go upstream to notify the chief of Ichisi that the Spaniards were on their way.[38]

They traveled along a trail to the north, paralleling the western bank of the Ocmulgee River. It seems that this trail must have lain close to the river. They passed through several villages. In one place, where they had to travel through a swamp, several horses forced to swim with their saddles on almost drowned. The Spaniards made the crossing by walking across a tree trunk that lay across the channel, but Benito Fernández fell off the log and, weighted down by his armor, was drowned.[39] In La Florida, death could come, most innocently, at any time. This incident may have occurred on the lower course of Thompson Mill Creek or Sandy Run Creek.[40]

Later on March 25, which was Maundy Thursday and the Day of the Incarnation, they came to a village in the vicinity of present-day Warner Robins, where they waited for the rest of the army to catch up. While they were there, the chief of Ichisi sent a delegation of principal men bearing gifts of deerskins and woven shawls. This was the first instance in which De Soto and his men were met with gifts of peace. The messenger asked four measured questions of the Spaniards: "Who are you; where did you come from; what do you want; where are you going?"[41]

De Soto replied that he was a captain of the great king of Spain and that he had come to bring the holy faith of Christ to the Indians. They should acknowledge Christ and be saved. They should obey the Apostolic Church of Rome and the supreme pontiff and viceroy of God. And in their worldly affairs they should acknowledge themselves as being vassals of the emperor, king of Castile, and if they did so, they could expect peace and justice.[42] This language may have been that of the *Requerimiento*, a legal formula that Spaniards were supposed to utter to the people they encountered. It is to be doubted that the Indians of Ichisi were able to understand much if anything of the dreadful import of De Soto's answer.[43]

De Soto and his men were not merely met in peace by this delegation of the chief of Ichisi, they were met in accordance with a ritualized protocol. Up to this point, they had seen little of such formalities in their travels. But now they had entered an area where the Indians were familiar with visits by powerful people—their own paramount chiefs. Paramount chiefs probably periodically visited the people whom they claimed as tributaries or allies. The paramount chief probably traveled about with a retinue. The tributaries and allies came out to meet the visiting paramount, offering to carry the chief to their town on a litter. Formal speeches were made by both parties. The tributaries offered food to the visiting paramount and his retinue, and gave them gifts and tributes of dressed animal skins, woven shawls, and stores of food. The tributaries made available a place for their visitors to sleep. And when the visitors departed, the tributaries offered them porters. There are hints that they may also have made a practice of offering them women.[44]

In a short time, no doubt fueled by their curiosity about the secrecy surrounding De Soto's foray to the east, wondering what he had found there, the rest of the army followed and joined the vanguard on the west bank of the Ocmulgee River. On Monday, March 29, the entire army began marching northward, paralleling the west bank of the Ocmulgee. They marched in very hard rain through a floodplain forest much as they had seen before, and while they were fording a small stream—probably lower Echeconnee Creek—the water rose very fast, and had not the army crossed it quickly they would have been in danger of drowning.

As they neared Ichisi, men and women came out to meet them in peace. The women of Ichisi, clad in their white mantles, made a fine appearance. They gave the Spaniards corn cakes and bunches of young wild onions as big as the end of one's thumb, similar to those in Castile. The Spaniards relished these corn cakes, and they ate the onions raw, roasted, and boiled.[45] They came to a small village of Ichisi where they found abundant food.[46] Here they spent the night and also rested the following day.[47]

On Wednesday, March 30, they resumed their march. They came to the bank of the Ocmulgee River, and here they were met by the subjects of the chief of Ichisi, who ferried them to the other side in a large fleet of dugout canoes (fig. 26). They were met on the other side by the chief of Ichisi, a man who had only one good eye. His principal town was at the Lamar mound site, about a mile south of the fall line, in the swampy floodplain of the Ocmulgee River. The site has the channel of the river on its western side, and it has an old channel of the river—Black Lake—on its eastern side. In 1540 the site may

Fig. 26. A small dugout canoe, coastal North Carolina. The Indians often paddled standing up in these tippy craft. Several fishing techniques are illustrated. (Watercolor by John White, British Museum)

have been encircled by water, or nearly so. Now as then, the Lamar site is surrounded by lush floodplain vegetation. Measuring about twelve hundred feet
from east to west and about one thousand feet from north to south, the Lamar
site has two moderately large mounds. One is rectangular and roughly ori-
ented to the four points of the compass. The second, on the opposite side of
where the plaza lay, is a truncated cone, with a spiral ramp circling it four
times in a counterclockwise direction. At one time in its existence the site was
surrounded by a defensive palisade and ditch, though none of the chroniclers
mentions a palisade at the time of their visit. The culture of the people of Ichisi
was similar to that of other Lamar people. They built square houses, some
with drainage ditches dug around them. Clearly, the people of the chiefdom
of Ichisi had adapted to life in a swamp.[48]

The chief of Ichisi gave the Spaniards a large quantity of food and fifteen
Indians to serve as porters. Because the people of Ichisi had been peaceable,
De Soto did not want to make burdensome demands on them. The Spaniards
remained in Ichisi the next day, April 1, when they set up a cross made of wood
atop a mound in the village.[49] The Spanish priests tried to explain something of
the significance of the cross to the people of Ichisi, who gave the appearance of
understanding what was being said and who appeared to worship the cross.[50]
But in fact, they could have understood very little of what was told them.

Ocute

It was De Soto's practice always to ask the Indians about the nature of
the country that lay ahead. He would ask where he could find the greatest
lord and the richest province. When asked these questions, the chief of Ichisi
said that a great lord—in fact a paramount chief—lived nearby, and his
province was called Ocute. He provided De Soto with a guide and an interpreter (implying that the languages of Ichisi and Ocute were different), and
because the chief of Ichisi had been so cooperative, De Soto set free the Indians he had captured at the island village of Ichisi.[51]

On April 2 De Soto and his army set out traveling toward the northeast,
probably following a trail that in the eighteenth century was known as the
Lower Creek Trading Path. They may have followed Old Hawkins Road, which
ran through southern Jones County and Baldwin County, where it intersected
the Oconee River.[52] They bivouacked in open country at the end of their first
day of travel. On April 3 they came to the bank of a large river, the Oconee,
where they found some deserted cabins (*bohíos*), possibly a fishcamp.[53] All of
their travel since departing from Ichisi was through unpopulated country.[54]

The Spaniards were under the impression that the Oconee River was the first stream they had encountered that ran not southward but eastward into the Atlantic and that its mouth was at a place that had been visited by Lucas Vázquez de Ayllón.[55] On at least one point they were wrong—the Ocmulgee River, not the Oconee, was the first river they came to that ran into the Atlantic. Since this confusion could not have been based on firsthand experience, it had to have been information they got from Indians, who may have regarded the Ocmulgee as a tributary of the Oconee.[56] While it is possible that Ayllón explored the mouth of the Altamaha River, it is unlikely that his town, San Miguel de Gualdape, whose site has so far eluded archaeological discovery, was located there.[57] But because of these rumors of Ayllón, they gave even more credence to what Perico told them.[58]

Some Indians from Altamaha came and met them at the river. They took De Soto and his army to a village where they found plenty of food and where they spent the night.[59] The next day a messenger from Altamaha came bearing a present for De Soto and also many dugout canoes in which to ferry the Spaniards to the eastern side of the river.[60] The principal town of Altamaha is thought to have been at the Shinholser mound site (fig. 27), though it is not certain that De Soto visited this place.

De Soto sent word for the chief of Altamaha, a man named Zamuno, to come and meet with him.[61] The messenger warned De Soto that Zamuno went about armed both night and day because his territory bordered that of Cofitachequi, his enemy. Zamuno would not come unarmed. De Soto said he could come

Fig. 27. The Medlin repoussé copper plate discovered at the Shinholser site (Altamaha). This plate was worn as part of a headdress. From Mark Williams, *Archaeological Excavations at Shinholser (9BL1), 1985 and 1987* (Watkinsville, Ga.: LAMAR Institute, 1990), 232–33.

armed if he wanted to. When Zamuno came, De Soto gave him a large feather that was adorned with silver. Zamuno, who was greatly pleased by this gift, said: "You are from Heaven, and this plume of yours which you have given me, I can eat with it; I shall go to war with it; I shall sleep with my wife with it." De Soto replied dryly that, yes, Zamuno could do all these things.[62]

De Soto questioned the people of Altamaha about Cofitachequi, the fabled chiefdom they were seeking. They told De Soto it would not be possible for his army to go there because there was no clear trail and no food, and they would starve to death if they tried.[63] Could this be believed? De Soto would make further inquiries.

The place to which they had come impressed the Spaniards as being thickly populated, and its inhabitants were cooperative.[64] Zamuno and other chiefs were subject to the great chief (*un gran cacique*) whose name was Ocute. Zamuno asked De Soto whether in the future he should pay tribute to De Soto, or should he continue to pay tribute to Ocute? De Soto, suspecting that Zamuno was trying to take advantage of the situation to get out of his tributary relationship to Ocute, replied that he considered Ocute to be as a brother, and Zamuno should continue to pay him tribute until he was told otherwise.[65]

Somewhere in the territory of the paramount chiefdom of Ocute, De Soto decided that a small cannon (probably only a swivel gun) that had been carried strapped to a mule would not be necessary in the lands they were exploring. Before leaving it in the care of some Indians, De Soto gave them a demonstration of its power. The Spaniards set up the cannon near a chief's house, loaded it, and took aim at an oak tree. The Indians were very surprised when the tree was splintered after being hit with two shots.[66]

De Soto sent messengers to tell the paramount chief of Ocute to come and see him. When the chief made his appearance, De Soto presented him with a shirt and a cap of yellow satin with a feather stuck in it. De Soto set up a wooden cross at Altamaha, presumably in much the way he had in Ichisi, and the Spaniards prepared to take their leave.

Taking the paramount chief of Ocute with him, on April 8 De Soto departed from Altamaha after having spent three days there, and by the end of that day reached a place where they spent the night in some Indian houses.[67] The next day they came to a town of Ocute, at the Shoulderbone archaeological site. For reasons not stated, De Soto became angry at the chief of Ocute, let his feelings be known, and the chief trembled in fear.[68] Perhaps he had been slow to offer De Soto supplies and porters. In any case, as many as two thousand Indians soon showed up, offering to serve as porters. They brought supplies in abundance, including cornbread, many rabbits, partridges, two turkeys, and many dogs.[69]

De Soto remained in the main town of Ocute for two days. Once again he set up a wooden cross, and the Indians fell on their knees before it as they observed the Spaniards to do.

What was the widest extent of the power and influence of the chief of Ocute? It is difficult to say because De Soto passed through his realm so quickly. Altamaha was clearly a tributary of Ocute, and the town of Cofaqui, where they would visit next, probably was also. Ocute seems to have been in amity with Ichisi, on the Ocmulgee River, but they need not have been in a tributary relationship. Was Ocute in amity with the people who lived on the headwaters of the Savannah River? And what about the Guale on the Atlantic coast? They may all have been allies against Cofitachequi. But the documents are silent on these questions, and we may never know for sure.[70]

On April 12 the Spaniards departed from Ocute with four hundred porters in their service. When they reached Cofaqui, probably the Dyar site, west of present-day Greensboro, Georgia, they were met by several principal men who came out with gifts and food. The chief of Cofaqui was an old man who wore a full beard.[71] His nephew, Patofa, governed for him.[72] If Patofa was the son of Cofaqui's sister, his succeeding to the chieftainship was in accordance with the matrilineal kinship that prevailed in much of the Southeast. It is clear enough that Cofaqui and Patofa were at peace with the paramount chief of Ocute and were probably his tributaries. Patofa came to visit De Soto, and he brought along food and porters.[73] He made a speech to De Soto, offering him friendship and support, in effect putting himself into a tributary relationship.[74]

The Wilderness of Ocute

The Indian boy Marcos had guided the Spaniards northward from Apalachee to central Georgia, but here his knowledge gave out.[75] It now fell to Perico to serve as their only guide.

While they were at Cofaqui's town, Perico told the Spaniards that a march of four days toward the east would bring them to Cofitachequi. But just as had the people of Altamaha, the people of Cofaqui informed them that they did not know of any people living in that location. They knew about Cofitachequi, but it lay further away. To the northwest, they said, lay the province of Coosa, a rich land of large villages.[76] But if in spite of their warning, the Spaniards were determined to go on to Cofitachequi, they should know that they would not be able to travel along a clear trail, and they would not be able to find any people who would provide them with food along the way. The people of Cofaqui said that when they went to wage war on the people of Cofitachequi, they traveled through remote parts of the country where they could expect to evade detection by their enemies. On these raids they ate nothing but parched corn and plant food—perhaps collected along the way—and they expected the round-trip to take from twenty to twenty-two days.[77]

The contradiction was all too evident between what Perico said they could expect to find after four days' travel to the east and what the people of Cofaqui said they could expect to find. Perico had been with the Spaniards long enough to know what kind of man De Soto was, and he must have known what De Soto might do if he suspected that he had been misled. Perico had seen Indians beaten, thrown to the dogs, and burned at the stake. Whether real or feigned, one night Perico had what the Spaniards took to be a kind of seizure, falling to the ground and foaming at the mouth.[78] He yelled so loudly the entire army fell to arms, thinking the town they were in was under attack.[79] They found Perico trembling with fear, and he said that a frightful demon and many imps had come to him and forbade him to guide the Spaniards to Cofitachequi. Seemingly, he had been beaten and tussled about.[80] One wonders whether some people of Cofaqui, angry at the prospect of having to accompany De Soto all the way to Cofitachequi, might have come under cover of darkness to give Perico a beating to try to change his mind about serving as a guide. Whatever the real cause of Perico's distress, Fray Juan el Evangelico was persuaded the boy had been possessed by the devil. He prayed over Perico, who then came to his senses.[81]

The people of Cofaqui said that if the Spaniards insisted on going to attack the Lady of Cofitachequi, they would lend their support. Patofa supplied De Soto with guides and some seven hundred porters, as well as enough corn, nuts, and dried fruit to last for four days.[82] A principal man was selected to lead the Indians. He wore a mantle of panther skins, and as a sign of his rank he carried a war club made of hardwood in the form of a broadsword. He performed a kind of dance, leaping from side to side, wielding his war club with grace and dexterity, like a dancing master.[83] This performance greatly astonished the Spaniards.[84] He promised his chief he would wreak revenge on the people of Cofitachequi for the injuries they had perpetrated on Ocute.[85]

They departed from Cofaqui on April 13, traveling first across the watershed of Little River, on whose bank they bivouacked on the night of April 16.[86] The Spaniards and the Indians, not trusting each other, bivouacked separately,

Fig. 28. Oak-hickory-pine forest in Cades Cove. It is secondary growth. Photograph by Jack Boucher, June 7, 1959. (Great Smoky Mountains National Park)

and each posted sentinels.[87] The country for all this distance was devoid of human habitation, contrary to what Perico had promised. Since departing from Ichisi, they had been traveling through the oak-hickory-pine forest through which they would travel for the next several weeks (see map 4). Surely it was a relief for them to emerge from predominantly pine forests into medium to tall stands of several species of hickory, shortleaf pine, loblolly pine, white oak, and post oak, as well as dogwood, sweet gum, tulip poplar, and sourwood (fig. 28).

De Soto ordered the men to eat as little as possible.[88] The next day, April 17, they came to the Savannah River where two very large islands—Winns Island and Paces Island—divided the river into two branches, each wider than a long arquebus shot.[89] In the nineteenth century a ferry—Pace's Ferry—crossed the river between these two islands. All of this area is now beneath the water of Clark Hill Reservoir.

Fording the Savannah River was difficult. The bottom of the stream was covered with flat stones and the current was very swift. The water came up to their stirrups, and in a few places up to their saddle pads. So treacherous was the current, no horseman was willing to carry a foot soldier on the rump of his horse. The foot soldiers crossed by tying thirty or forty men together with a rope, so they could support each other in the current while crossing. The horsemen crossing upstream from the foot soldiers would occasionally help them by allowing them to hold onto the tail of their horse or onto the butt end of a lance.[90] By the end of the day they had all got across to the eastern side of the river, and they bivouacked in a woods. They swam their herd of pigs across the river, but the swift current carried many of them downstream, and they were lost.[91]

They continued on their way, moving as rapidly as they could, on a trail growing ever narrower and more indistinct.[92] On April 18 they bivouacked in a woods, in the vicinity of the present-day town of Saluda, and the next day came to another large river, the Saluda, which they waded across with difficulty.[93] They probably made their crossing near the mouth of the Little Saluda River. Pressing on, they bivouacked on the night of April 20 beside a small stream, and on April 21 they reached a third large river that was very hard to cross and was divided into two branches. They had come to the Broad River where a large island lay in the channel. Possibly it was Boatwright's Island, where a nineteenth-century ford was located.[94] The crossing of this river was especially difficult because the current was very powerful, and in one place the water was so deep the horses had to swim for about the length of a lance.[95] On the eastern side they found a few crude shelters that were used by fishermen or hunters.[96]

They had been on the trail for nine days, and still there were no signs of people or food. They began to fear starvation.[97] De Soto was furious at Perico for having misled them. He made as if to throw him to the dogs, and he would have done so had Perico not been the only Indian who could translate from a Muskogean language into the Timucuan language spoken by Juan Ortiz.[98] This is the only reason De Soto spared his life.[99]

The guides from Ocute who had been leading them had also lost their bearings.[100] De Soto interrogated the Ocute principal man, saying he did not understand how none of the hundreds of Indians who were in the party knew anything about either the public or secret trails between Ocute and Cofitachequi. The principal man replied that neither he nor any of his men had ever been to Cofitachequi. The battles they fought were small ones that occurred when men from the two societies ran into each other when hunting or fishing in the wilderness. Moreover, because the people of Cofitachequi had been militarily superior to those of Ocute, the latter had become intimidated, and they dared not enter the territory of Cofitachequi. That is why they did not know how to get there.[101]

De Soto and his men knew they had been traveling through a vast wilderness—a place where no humans lived—but none of them understood why the wilderness existed (see map 6). It was land and forest as fit for human habitation as any they had traveled through, or would travel through. They had no way of knowing that if they had carried out their explorations a century and a half earlier, they would have found a thriving chiefdom in the Savannah River valley. The area they were traveling through had been abandoned rather abruptly around A.D. 1450.

Mississippian people abandoned town sites for various reasons. One was that their societies ran on wood, as it were, and they depended upon accessible wood for building defensive walls around their towns, for building the houses in which they lived, and for fueling the fires that gave them light, cooked their food, and kept them warm. As time went on, people in a particular town had to walk longer and longer distances to find the wood they needed, which was both tiresome and dangerous, because it exposed them to attack by marauding enemies. At some point the distance would become too great and the town would be abandoned. Sometimes they returned to abandoned town sites after a suitable interval of years, when the forest had grown back. In fact, secondary growth forests may have suited them better than primary growth forests, because of the smaller trees.

But the Savannah River valley was abandoned for a reason other than forest exhaustion. Chiefdoms in general are fragile forms of social organization that are beset with persistent problems. Internally, they are troubled by disputes over succession and by factionalism and rebellion. Externally, chiefdoms were often in military conflict with each other, and the level of violence could become very high. Just prior to the time the Savannah River Valley was abandoned, the people began building especially strong fortifications, suggesting that warfare between chiefdoms was a serious problem.

Finally, analysis of growth rings in bald cypress trees in the Southeast indicates a decline in rainfall between 1400 and 1500. This may have had an effect on corn production, which might have helped destabilize the chiefdoms. It is likely that one or several of these factors caused the collapse of societies in the Savannah River valley, as well as the Saluda and Broad River valleys, and created the wilderness of Ocute.[102]

None of De Soto's men had the slightest idea of which direction to take once the trail had disappeared. De Soto set up camp in a pine woods, and he and his men debated what to do next. Some said they should continue on, but in a different direction. Others said they should turn around and go back to Ocute, but one thing they did know was that the land through which they had come was very desolate.[103] De Soto, aggressive as always, said it was better to go forward, even though they did not know where they were going.

On April 22 De Soto sent out four scouts, each accompanied by eight horsemen, but all failed to find native towns and returned that night, leading and driving their exhausted horses. On April 23 De Soto sent out two scouts, each with contingents of ten horsemen carrying rations to last for ten days. Baltasar de Gallegos went up the Broad River toward the northwest, and Juan de Añasco went along the river to the southeast. Later De Soto sent out Juan Ruiz Lobillo with four horsemen to the north with ten days' rations; he also sent out Alonso Romo, presumably toward the northeast.[104]

The army's situation grew more desperate by the day, both for the men and the horses. The supply of food they had brought from Ocute was exhausted. They were tired, hungry, and drenched from continual rain. It had rained so much the rivers were rising out of their banks. So far as they knew, the land they had come to was devoid of people. As a last resort, De Soto ordered that some of the full-grown pigs be killed and butchered. He issued each man about a pound of pork, which they ate cooked with wild greens and roots that the Indians showed them how to collect.[105] Since he could not provide them with food, De Soto sent the Indians of Cofaqui back home, giving them gifts of cloth, knives, scissors, mirrors, and other articles.[106]

The Spaniards, in spite of their hunger, were still able to joke about their plight. According to a story told by Garcilaso, when their corn supply had diminished until it was hardly more than a fistful, they cooked their last bit, and divided it equally among the men—eighteen grains each. Gonzalo Silvestre wrapped his in a handkerchief and put them inside his shirt. He later ran into Francisco de Troche, who asked whether he had anything to eat. Silvestre said jokingly that he had some very good marzipan recently made and brought from Seville. As Troche laughed, Pedro de Torres came up and asked the same question. To him Silvestre replied that he had a very soft and delicious Utrera bun, fresh from the oven. All laughed, and Silvestre said: "In order to prove that I have not lied, I will offer you something which will taste to one man like [marzipan] if he has a desire for such, and to another like an Utrera bun if that is what he longs for." Then Silvestre fished out his handkerchief, and he distributed the grains of corn among them, so that each had six grains. All of them ate their corn quickly lest others come and ask for a share. Then they went to a stream and drank their fill of water.[107]

On April 25 Juan de Añasco came riding into camp with news that he had found a town of Indians and food to the southeast.[108] He brought with him an Indian woman and a boy he had captured to serve as interpreters and guides. Perico spoke the language of these people, and again the Spaniards were persuaded that what he had told them about Cofitachequi was true.[109] De Soto immediately issued an order that no more pigs be butchered; the men would have to subsist as best they could in order to save the meat for the future. The town Añasco had discovered was called Hymahi or Aymay.[110] De Soto gave the order to prepare to move forward. For the men who were out scouting, De Soto left a letter with instructions buried at the foot of a pine tree. On the bark of the tree he had Juan de Añasco carve the words: "Dig at the foot of this pine tree and you will find a letter." Añasco had marked the trail to Hymahi by cutting blazes on trees along the way.

On April 26 De Soto set out for Hymahi with a contingent of men mounted on the very best horses. De Soto and his comrades reached the town at the end of a long day of travel. They were so hungry they rode forward with their reins loose, and whoever could outdistance the others did so.[111] The remainder of the army straggled behind, bivouacking short of Hymahi, at distances of two to four leagues.[112] To their relief, they found a barbacoa in the town full of corn, and they found more than 25 fanegas (about 37.5 bushels) of parched corn meal, which was rationed among the men.[113] They found many mulberry trees loaded with fruit, as well as other fruit trees, and some very fragrant wild strawberries that tasted as good as those that grow in Galicia.[114] Along the trails were an abundance of fragrant wild roses similar to those in Spain. Because of all this food and beauty, the Spaniards named it Hymahi Soccoro— "succor."

On April 27 Captain Alonso Romo, who had apparently been reconnoitering to the northeast of where they had crossed the river, arrived in Hymahi with four or five captives. De Soto interrogated them, but not one of them would reveal the location of the town of their chief. De Soto burned one of them to death in front of the others, but still they would not talk.[115] De Soto had all of them burned to death.[116]

On April 28 Baltasar de Gallegos, who had gone northwest up the Broad River, arrived in Hymahi with a captive Indian woman and with news of a populated area.[117] On April 29 Johan Ruiz Lobillo, who had been sent north from the camp, came back with no captives, but with news of some trails he had discovered.[118] Lobillo had left two of his men straggling in the rear because their horses had tired.[119] This breach of discipline made De Soto furious. He ordered Lobillo to go back and find the men, and if he failed to do so, De Soto said that he would have him executed. It was not long before Lobillo returned with the two men.[120]

Cofitachequi

The Spaniards learned from three Indians they had captured that the people of Cofitachequi had known for some time that strangers were on their way, and they were awaiting the Spaniards' arrival. On April 30 De Soto set out for their villages, again riding in a vanguard with the best horses. The woman whom Gallegos had captured served as a guide. At the end of the first day they bivouacked near a large, deep river—the Wateree.[121] He sent Juan de Añasco ahead with a few horsemen to seize some interpreters and some canoes for crossing the river.[122] As Añasco and his men traveled northward, it grew dark. They traveled along the trail silently. In the darkness they gradually became aware of a low murmur, and a little further on they emerged from the forest through which they had been traveling. They saw the lights of fires and heard the crying of children, the talk of men and women, and the barking of dogs. Añasco and his men crept forward, hoping to capture some Indians, but then they realized that the town was on the opposite side of the river. They remained for some time at a beach—a canoe landing—before going back to inform De Soto of what they had learned.[123]

The next day De Soto and his vanguard came to the river at the canoe landing, across from one of the major towns of Cofitachequi. This town was at the Mulberry site, a large mound site at the junction of Pine Tree Creek and the Wateree River (fig. 29). It originally had three mounds—two large and one small. The small mound no longer exists, and one of the large mounds, built around 1300 to 1350, has for some time been eroding into the river. At present, the archaeology of the site is poorly understood. It is known, however, that this site was inhabited at the time of the De Soto expedition.[124]

On the eastern side of the river they could see several men.[125] De Soto had Perico shout to the men on the other side of the river that the lord of the province should come across and hear a message. Perico was proving to be quite useful at Cofitachequi. De Soto spoke Spanish to Juan Ortiz, who spoke the language of Moscoso to Perico, who spoke a dialect of Muskogean that

Fig. 29. Diorama of the Mulberry site (Cofitachequi). (South Carolina State Museum)

was intelligible to the people of Cofitachequi. The Spaniards were, at this point, approaching the easternmost extent of the geographical distribution of the Muskogean language family. Muskogean, the most widespread language family in the Southeast, included the language spoken in Apalachee, probably those spoken in Capachequi and Toa, and definitely those spoken in Ichisi and Ocute, as well as in Guale and Orista on the Atlantic coast. As the Spaniards had already discovered, not all of these Muskogean languages were mutually intelligible, since Perico could not understand some of them. The principal language of Cofitachequi was Muskogean, as were the languages north of Cofitachequi to about present-day Charlotte, North Carolina.[126]

The men to whom Perico shouted climbed into four dugout canoes and paddled across the river to where the Spaniards were. De Soto waited for them, seated on a "rest seat" that was carried for his use.[127] The principal men among those in the canoes approached De Soto with grave demeanor. They first made ritual gestures to the four cardinal directions, and then they asked De Soto whether he came seeking peace or war.[128] De Soto replied that he wished for peace, and that he only wanted to be provided with supplies until he could proceed on his travels. A young woman of the ruling lineage came in company with the principal men. She welcomed the Spaniards, saying that her people were assembling canoes in which to ferry them across. She then returned to the other side with the principal men.

The De Soto chroniclers were not interested in the particulars of Indian languages or cultures, and they did not record the names of the positions occupied by these principal men. But when the Juan Pardo expedition visited this same location twenty-six years later, Juan de la Bandera, the notary, recorded the names and titles of the Indians whom they met. There were three levels of political power at Cofitachequi, and the names of these political positions were quite similar to those at Apalachee. In Cofitachequi and vicinity, the *orata* was a "lesser noble," seemingly in charge of a village, or a few villages. The *mico* was a "great noble" who occupied one of the administrative centers of the chiefdom, presumably complete with a mound. Pardo dealt with about eighty *oratas* on his travels, but with only three *micos*. Above both of these was the *gran cacique*, the "grand chief" or paramount chief. Bandera did not record a native term for this position, and there may have been none. Lesser officials were *ynihas*, or *ynanaes*, who were chiefs' assistants, perhaps comparable to magistrates. The *yatikas* were interpreters and spokesmen.[129]

It is clear enough that the chieftainess of Cofitachequi was a paramount chief. And the principal men who greeted De Soto must have occupied various positions in the chiefdom, including some of those mentioned above.

Shortly afterward, a woman the chroniclers call the Lady of Cofitachequi (La Señora de Cofitachequi) was carried from the town to the river's edge on a litter that was covered with a delicate white cloth. One of the Spaniards described this young woman as being "brown but well proportioned." Perico told them later that she was not the ruler, but rather the niece of the ruler.[130] Nonetheless, Rangel and others considered this young woman, the Lady of Cofitachequi, to be the chieftainess. This woman may not have lived at the town opposite them, since Perico said she had come to that place to chastise some of the principal men of the chieftainess who were refusing to pay tribute.[131]

The lady entered a dugout canoe that had an awning over its stern. Beneath the awning a mat was placed on the floor of the canoe, and two cushions were placed on that. She seated herself on the cushions and several of her principal men climbed aboard.[132] Others climbed into several other canoes and they paddled over to the bank where De Soto stood. The lady got out of the canoe and seated herself on a seat that her subjects had brought for her.[133] She, too, welcomed De Soto to Cofitachequi. While she was speaking, none of her subjects uttered a word.[134] De Soto questioned her about the chiefdom, and she answered satisfactorily.[135] She presented him with gifts of dressed animal skins and pieces of cloth. At the end of their conversation, the lady removed several strands of large freshwater pearls from her neck.[136] She held them out to Juan Ortiz, who was serving as interpreter, telling him to present them to De Soto. But Ortiz indicated that she should do it herself, and she arose and placed the strings of pearls about his neck.[137]

She ordered her men in the canoes to ferry the Spaniards to the other side of the river. The lady assigned half the town to be reserved for use by the Spaniards, and she had supplies of food brought to them. This included dry bread fritters, many turkeys, strips of venison, and a large supply of very good salt.[138] The town was pleasantly situated among rich agricultural fields along the margins of the river. The forest, which was cleared from around the town, had growing in it many nut trees and some very large mulberry trees loaded with large berries.[139] The Spaniards were impressed with the people of Cofitachequi. They wore leggings of well-dressed skins and shawls of native fiber and "sable" fur, as well as cougar skins that gave off a strong smell. The people were polite and pleasing in appearance.[140] And they showed subservience in a way that made it seem that they had lived among Spaniards all their lives.[141]

The rest of the army did not arrive at Cofitachequi until May 3, and all of them did not get ferried across the river until the day after that. The Wateree River had perhaps been swollen from rain.[142] Through some of the men's carelessness in not locating a suitable crossing, seven of the horses drowned while swimming across the river.[143] The highest casualties were among the fattest and strongest of the horses, who struggled in the current. The leaner horses, on the other hand, had drifted downstream as they swam across.[144]

The first order of business in Cofitachequi was to ask about the gold, silver, and pearls that Perico had told them were to be found there. He said the traders with whom he had traveled acquired their metals at Cofitachequi.[145] The lady commanded the people to fetch what the Spaniards desired.[146] Sure enough, they came carrying freshwater pearls (fig. 30), but to the Spaniards' great disappointment the gold and silver turned out to be pieces of copper and mica (fig. 31).[147] Apparently the Indians did not distinguish between copper and gold, and the mica must have seemed silvery in color to Perico. The lady said there were no gems to be found.[148] Some of the Spaniards claimed that in some of the celt blades they saw, gold seemed to be mixed in with the copper, but they lacked the means of testing to prove that gold was present.[149] They asked where the copper came from, and the Indians said it came from the land of the Chiscas. But they said that to go there one had to travel through a thinly populated land, including mountains that horses could not

Fig. 30. Freshwater pearls. (Frank H. McClung Museum, University of Tennessee, Knoxville)

Fig. 31. Cross-in-a-circle mica discs from the Mulberry site. Photograph by Tom Charles. (South Carolina Institute of Archaeology and Anthropology)

cross. De Soto decided that when he reached a better-populated land, where travel was easier, he would find out whether what they said was true.

De Soto and the others clamored to find out where the precious things were kept. The Indians took them to a temple where the principal people had been buried and where there was a barbacoa upon which had been placed wooden boxes containing bodies. It was a mortuary house, not a place where the Indians went to pray or to offer up sacrifice. Apparently the Indians did not abhor the smell of death.[150] The bodies inside the boxes had many strands of pearls about their necks, arms, and legs.

As they were removing the pearls, Rodrigo Rangel saw something green, which appeared to be an emerald. De Soto was encouraged by this, and he ordered Rangel to go and fetch Juan de Añasco, who was the contador, and who represented the king's interests. Rangel said, "My lord, let us not call anyone—it may be a precious jewel." But De Soto answered angrily: "Even if it were, do we have to steal it?"[151] When Añasco came to inspect the contents of the mosque, they found that the emerald was, in fact, a green glass bead. Then they found several rosaries, and some *margaritas,* a type of glass bead (still not definitely identified by archaeologists) taken to the Indies to trade with the natives (see figs. 85e, 85f).[152] And they found two iron kindling axes made in Castile. They realized that these artifacts had come from the colony of Lucas Vázquez de Ayllón, and they reasoned incorrectly that the river that ran through Cofitachequi must be the River of Santa Elena.[153] Moreover, they saw other evidences in the behavior of the people of Cofitachequi that they had been in contact with Spaniards. For example, they made and wore leggings (see fig. 87) and moccasins of black leather, but they used ties or laces of white leather and fringes and edging of colored leather, as was the custom in Spain.[154] In general, they seemed to be more "civilized" than any Indians they had met on their travels.[155] From the Indians the Spaniards learned that the coast Ayllón had visited was thirty leagues distant.[156]

The Spaniards looted some two hundred pounds of pearls from the temple, even though most of these had been discolored by lying in the earth and against decaying flesh, as well as having been damaged by heat.[157] When the Lady of Cofitachequi saw what they were doing, she said, "Do you value that? Then go to Talimeco, my town, and you will find so many [pearls] that your horses cannot carry them."[158] De Soto replied, "Let them stay there; to whom God gives a gift, may St. Peter bless it." And for the time being the matter of Talimeco was dropped. The men took this to mean that De Soto planned to claim Cofitachequi for himself, because it was the best place the Spaniards had seen so far. The chiefdom was very good, although there were not many people nor very much corn.[159] The land was excellent, with a pretty river—the Wateree—bounded by excellent fields with groves of hickory, oak, pine, sweet gum, and cedar trees. A rumor spread among the army that Alaminos, a native of Cuba, had found a trace of gold in the river.[160] This heightened their expectations that they would find gold in the country ahead.

Eventually they did go to Talimeco, probably located at the Adamson mound site, about four miles upstream from the Mulberry site, where they found a temple or oratory situated on a high mound that was much revered by the people.[161] The town was devoid of people, perhaps because it was not so much a population center as a mortuary temple where the remains of members of the ruling lineage were kept.[162] Talimeco was a ritual center, and the *caney,* or home, of the chieftainess was very large and was built atop the highest mound.[163] It was decorated above and below with finely woven split-cane mats, which were fitted together so cleverly as to appear seamless. All the other houses of Talimeco were similarly covered with such mats.

The temple was situated in front of the dwelling place of the chieftainess, in the center of the town. It was a large structure, with a high-pitched, vaulted roof constructed of cane and covered with split-cane mats stacked on top of one another.[164]

Upon opening the doors to the temple, one encountered two rows of large wooden statues of ferocious men wielding various kinds of weapons, all held at the ready, as if they were about to assault an intruder. The statues were paired, with the tallest pair at the entrance and descending down to the last and smallest pair. They bore war clubs of various kinds, bows and arrows, and pikes with blades of copper.[165] The statues were all quite lifelike. From the top of the walls upward, the ceiling was adorned with marine shells, strands of pearls, and feather headdresses.[166] Some were suspended on strings, so they seemed to float in the air. Along the two end walls of the temple were two rows of large wooden statues, one above the other, representing men and women. The men held weapons that were decorated with strands of pearls and colored strings, while the women's hands were empty. Everything in the temple was clean, perfectly arranged, and neatly kept. Along the other walls were more wooden benches on which there were chests filled with the remains of dead ancestors. And above each of these chests stood a carved wooden statue representing the man or woman whose remains were in the chest. Again, the Spaniards found a large quantity of pearls and shell gorgets in these chests.[167] In the spaces along the wall between these statues hung excellent shields made of tightly woven cane. They were round and oblong, large and small in size, and they were so strongly made they could stop a crossbow bolt. The Spaniards also found breastplates (*pectos*) resembling corselets and helmets (*capacetes*) made of rawhide with the hair stripped off.[168] All of the various kinds of weapons held by the statues were also found stored in the temple.[169]

At the temple they also found stores of cloth shawls and feather mantles decorated with mosaics of multicolored feathers. And there were many dressed deerskins, both plain white and with designs painted on them (see fig. 87), deerskin leggings and moccasins, as well as panther and "marten" furs.[170]

It did not take the Spaniards long to discover why there were fewer people and less corn in Cofitachequi than they expected to find. Within a league to a league and a half around Talimeco were large uninhabited towns grown up in vegetation. These towns looked as if they had been abandoned for a long time. The people of Cofitachequi said they had been struck by a pestilence two years earlier, and this was what some of the Spaniards took to be the reason why the towns were abandoned and the reason why they were short on stored corn.[171]

Can these statements about pestilence by the people of Cofitachequi be taken at face value? If so, there are some puzzles to be worked out. For example, if the pestilence was a disease that originated in the Old World (and no epidemic diseases are definitely known to have been endemic in the pre-Columbian New World), then the members of the Ayllón expedition would have been the logical carriers of the germs or viruses in question. But the Ayllón expedition took place in 1526—twelve years before the disease struck Cofitachequi. What disease could have taken twelve years to spread from the coast to the fall line? And could Cofitachequi have been so isolated that the disease had not spread from there to other parts of the Southeast, where the De Soto chroniclers report no evidence of the presence of such epidemic diseases?

Some scholars have argued that it was not a pestilence at all but a severe drought that caused a shortfall of food, and this in turn made the people of Cofitachequi less resistant to disease of any sort, including diseases that were already present among them. Others have also argued that no disease had struck, suggesting that the Spaniards had mistaken towns abandoned by Cofitachequi decades earlier, as a consequence of whatever it was that caused the collapse along the Savannah River. The houses they reported being piled high with corpses were no more than the mortuary temples that are well attested in other parts of the Southeast. Cofitachequi was short on stored corn because it was early May, the previous year's corn was giving out, and the new corn was not yet ripe.[172]

And yet Cofitachequi was the only place on all their travels where the De Soto chroniclers mention seeing evidence of an epidemic disease among the Indians. It is amply demonstrated that Old World diseases swept away entire populations in later, better documented, times. De Soto and his men had found plenty of food at Ichisi and Ocute, where the new corn was not as far along as that at Cofitachequi. Hence, in spite of the interpretive problems, it seems imprudent to brush away this reported pestilence as little more than erroneous perception or bad translation.

Cofitachequi may also have suffered from political instability. Some of the principal men were apparently not paying tribute to the chieftainess.[173] But whether this political instability was the cause or the consequence of the pestilence is not known.

The Spaniards consumed the stores of corn at Cofitachequi very rapidly. To help feed his men, De Soto, on May 7, ordered Baltasar de Gallegos and Arias

Tinoco to take a large contingent of the soldiers and go to Ilasi, near present-day Cheraw, South Carolina.[174] Here there were seven barbacoas of stored corn that belonged to the Lady of Cofitachequi.[175]

The chieftainess evidently did not like what she had seen of the Spaniards.[176] After they had been there three or four days, she ran off and hid.[177] De Soto commanded Juan de Añasco to go find her and bring her back. Añasco took a contingent of soldiers with a principal man as a guide who had been supplied them by the lady. He was said to be a blood relative of the chieftainess. She had held him in her arms when he was a baby, and she loved him as if he were her own. He was about twenty years old, a handsome warrior in all respects. He wore a feather headdress and a deerskin mantle. He carried a beautiful bow, which had been so finely polished it shone, and on his back he wore a quiver of arrows.

After they had traveled for about three leagues, they stopped and prepared to eat and rest in the shade of some large trees. The guide had been light-hearted up to this point. But now he became contemplative, sighing deeply. Then he removed his quiver and began examining his arrows, one by one, showing them to the Spaniards. They had various kinds of points, and all were excellently made. The Indians took pride and pleasure in the beauty and polish of their weapons. He handed his arrows to the Spaniards to see. Each was feathered with three feathers in a triangular pattern, so the arrow would leave the bow smoothly. The last one he removed had a sharp flint point. But instead of handing it to a Spaniard, he suddenly thrust the arrow into his own body and died instantly.

It happened so suddenly, the Spaniards were shocked. They questioned other Indians who were with them about the man's motive. These Indians said the man realized that his serving as a guide for the Spaniards was contrary to the wishes of the chieftainess, and the Spaniards might bring her back against her will. On the other hand, if the guide had refused the command of the lady, he would have fallen into disfavor with her. To have offended either the chieftainess or the lady would have been worse than death. Thus, the man saw no alternative but to commit suicide.

Añasco continued on the trail for some distance. But none of the other Indians knew where the chieftainess was hiding. They decided to return without her.[178] Later an Indian offered to lead the Spaniards down the river to where the chieftainess was hiding. Añasco took twenty Spaniards in two canoes. They came to a tree that had fallen across the river in which several of the drowned horses had lodged, but they never succeeded on this occasion in finding the chieftainess. They heard that she had gone further away to hide, and for the time being they gave up their attempt to find her.[179]

Perico told the Spaniards they were beginning to enter the land he had told them about, and since he did in fact speak the language of Cofitachequi they gave him more credence than they had before. They concluded that what he had told them about Cofitachequi he had acquired through hearsay and had enlarged upon it.[180] Perico requested that he be baptized, for he wished to become a Christian. They baptized him and removed the chains they had used to restrain him.

De Soto asked the people of Cofitachequi if there was a great lord further on. They answered that twelve days away was the province of Chiaha, which was subject to the lord of Coosa, whose name the Spaniards had first heard when they were in Ocute.[181]

Many of De Soto's men were of the opinion that they should remain in Cofitachequi and colonize it. If Cofitachequi were settled, ships from New Spain, Peru, Santa Marta, and Tierra Firme could put in at a port of Cofitachequi on their way to Spain. Much profit could be made here. But De Soto wanted another treasure like the one he had won in Peru. Good land and freshwater pearls were not enough to satisfy him. Moreover, De Soto pointed out that there was not enough food in Cofitachequi to last his army for a month. He wanted to continue on according to plan and to rendezvous with Maldonado at Ochuse. If they did not encounter a richer land on their travels, they could always return to Cofitachequi, and in the meantime, the Indians could plant their crops so the Spaniards would be better provisioned.[182] Though De Soto listened to what everyone said, he was a man who was "hard and dry of word." He followed his own desire, and after he made his decision known, he would not be contradicted. He said they would go on to Chiaha, and after he had spoken, no one would say more.[183]

The culture of the people of Cofitachequi was a variety of Lamar culture that was broadly comparable to that of the people of Ocute. Clearly, possessing similar cultures in the sixteenth-century Southeast did not mean that people were in amity with each other. In 1540 there was a high level of expressed enmity between the peoples of Ocute and Cofitachequi. How long they had been at war is not known. But the fact that the Savannah River valley except for its headwaters was abandoned in about 1450 and the Saluda and Broad Rivers were abandoned at about the same time suggests that the two paramount chiefdoms had engaged in a long-lasting, bitter war. It seems likely that this war, rather than some environmental cause, was the principal reason why the Savannah, Saluda, and Broad Rivers had been abandoned, creating the wilderness of Ocute.

What was the maximal territorial extent of the paramount chiefdom of Cofitachequi? It is difficult to say. Arguing on the analogy of other chiefdoms in the Southeast that are known on the basis of better archaeological and historical evidence, the Cofitachequi chiefdom proper lay in the fall line meander zone of the Wateree River, stretching a few miles upstream from the Mulberry site and downstream at least to the junction with the Congaree River. It is the extent of the larger paramount chiefdom that is in dispute. The chroniclers convey a distinct impression that in 1540 Cofitachequi was not what it had been previously. It is, however, impossible to know whether this impression comes from exaggerated ideas about Cofitachequi held by their adversaries, the people of Ocute, or whether the avarice of the Spaniards, stirred by what Perico had told them, led them to expect from Cofitachequi much more than they found when they got there.

Of this much we can be sure: the chieftainess had several barbacoas of corn stored at Ilasi, near present-day Cheraw, and this indicated that in 1540 she still had real power over the people who lived along the middle segment of the Peedee River. Also, as De Soto made his way northward, the Indians they encountered gave the lady at least ritual deference all the way through the piedmont to the mountains. This need not necessarily mean that these people would do her bidding, either in 1540 or earlier, when the power of Cofitachequi may have been greater. The show of deference, however, is attested by Elvas, one of the more reliable of the De Soto chroniclers, and there is little basis for second-guessing him and brushing him aside.[184]

The farthest reach of the paramount chieftainess to the south is problematic. So far as is known, none of De Soto's men went further south than Hymahi, at the junction of the Congaree and Wateree Rivers. The chieftainess definitely had precious objects in her temple that came to her from the Atlantic coast, namely the tools and rosaries that had come from the Ayllón expedition. These artifacts were valuable enough to the people of Cofitachequi to be stored in their most sacred space, which may mean they were extracted as tribute from people on the coast. That this was a tributary relationship may have been substantiated by the testimony of Francisco of Chicora, the Indian whom agents of Ayllón captured in 1521. Francisco described a chiefdom, Duhare (or Duahe), that was ruled by Datha, a powerful chief. According to Francisco, most of the "provinces" known to him, predominantly situated between the junction of the Congaree and Wateree Rivers and the Atlantic coast, paid tribute to Datha. If Duhare was in fact Cofitachequi—and there is archaeological evidence of no other major chiefdom in interior South Carolina—then one may reasonably conclude that Cofitachequi once exercised power over people living on the coast adjacent to the mouth of the Santee River.[185] It does not seem too much to say that in its heyday, some decades before De Soto arrived, the maximal extent of the paramount chiefdom of Cofitachequi reached from the mountains of the present-day Carolinas to the Atlantic coast.

7

Coosa

The corn supply in Cofitachequi was low, and the Spaniards and their horses consumed it very rapidly, so that very little was left for the Indians.[1] Baltasar de Gallegos and the contingent of men he led to Ilasi probably made comparable demands on the food supply there. Now, as before, the Spaniards wished to find gold, but they *had* to find food.

Because the Spaniards had mistreated them, the people of Cofitachequi threatened to rise up in rebellion. The Lady of Cofitachequi did not want to supply De Soto with guides and porters, and she was of a mind to run away. But De Soto learned of her intentions, and he placed a guard over her and treated her harshly.[2]

Joara

On Wednesday, May 12, De Soto and his contingent of men departed from Cofitachequi, heading north up the Wateree-Catawba valley (see map 6) in search of Chiaha, where they hoped to find a plentiful supply of food.[3] To insure the good behavior of her subjects, De Soto forced the Lady of Co-fitachequi to go along with them as a hostage, making her travel on foot.[4] As a paramount chief on tour, she took several of her slave women with her so she

185

would be surrounded by a retinue who would help her command respect. As they traveled from town to town, she commanded some of the people in the towns to serve as porters, and they dutifully obeyed her.[5]

Two days after departing from Cofitachequi (presumably on May 14) they entered the territory (*población*) of Chalaque.[6] This area must have been somewhere southwest of present-day Charlotte, North Carolina, on the edge of the territory occupied by Catawban-speakers. *Chalaque* is no doubt a Hispanicized version of the Muskogean word *chilokkita*, "people of a different language." In later times, an anglicized version of the word—Cherokee—came to refer specifically to Cherokee-speaking peoples.[7] Chalaque impressed De Soto's men as one of the poorest places they had seen in their travels. There was very little corn, and it seemed to them that the people of Chalaque subsisted mainly by hunting and collecting wild vegetables. It should be remembered that the Spaniards were there in the month of May, and very little of the previous year's corn production remained, but there is little question that the people of Chalaque produced less corn than the more "Mississippianized" people to the north and south of them. The Indians thereabouts also seemed to the Spaniards to be less warlike than other Indians they had encountered, and they saw little evidence of political power among them. As the Spaniards approached, many of the Indians fled their villages, leaving only old men and women behind, and many of these were blind.[8] A Chalaque man brought them a present of two deer skins, as if this were a great gift. Another managed to provide them with a large number of turkeys.[9]

On May 15 they evidently traveled to a place where they encamped in a pine woods.[10] This may have placed them to the west of present-day Charlotte, near the town of Otari, which Juan Pardo would visit in 1566–68. It is probable De Soto was traveling with the horse vanguard out in front of the main body of the army.[11] They remained at this place on May 16, Whitsunday (Pascua del Espíritu Santo), when many Indian men and women came with presents and gifts for the Spaniards. On this day De Soto wrote a letter to Baltasar de Gallegos and sent it to him at Ilasi by way of Indian runners. He told Gallegos that he should immediately proceed forward and rejoin the army.[12] De Soto had previously ordered Gallegos to rendezvous with him on the way northward and to bring along as much corn as his men could carry.[13]

The archaeological picture of the Catawban-speaking peoples of present-day Gaston County and Lincoln County, North Carolina, is still not as full as one would wish. And De Soto traveled swiftly through this area, neglecting to record the names of the towns he visited. But as recorded by members of the

Juan Pardo expeditions of 1566–68, these were such towns as Otari, Yssa, Cataba, Uchiri, Dudca, Subsaquibi, and Quinahaqui. The culture of these people was a variant of the Uwharrie culture, which prevailed to the east, in the Carolina piedmont. At the time of the Pardo expeditions, these Catawban-speaking people of the Carolina piedmont were dominated by Guatari Mico, a female chief whose principal town was on the Yadkin River, in the vicinity of present-day Salisbury, North Carolina.[14] They built flexed houses with circular floor plans; platform mounds are absent, or only weakly present; and in general they appear to have been marginal to the Mississippian way of life.

On May 17 the Spaniards continued northward, spending the night bivouacked in a woods. The next day they came to Guaquili, which was probably located on the upper reaches of the South Fork of the Catawba River, in the general vicinity of present-day Hickory, North Carolina.[15] Here the Indians gave them a little corn, many turkeys, which they had roasted on a barbacoa, and several little "dogs" that were good to eat. These "dogs" were small, and they did not bark, and the Spaniards were under the impression the Indians raised them in their homes for food.[16]

They did not stay long at Guaquili. The next day, May 19, they traveled on, paralleling the upper Catawba River, aided by porters from Guaquili, and they bivouacked in a canebrake. The next day they bivouacked in a small savannah, where one of their horses died. Because there was so little corn, the men and the horses suffered greatly from hunger. On this same day, some of Gallegos's foot soldiers caught up with them and told them that Gallegos and his contingent from Ilasi would rendezvous soon. The next day, May 21, they arrived at Xuala—or more properly Joara—a village situated at the foot of the mountains in a plain among several streams.[17]

The chiefdom of Joara was located on the upper Catawba River and its tributaries, and its principal town was probably at the Berry site, north of present-day Morganton.[18] When Juan Pardo visited this area in 1566–68, Joara was the seat of power of an important chief, Joara Mico. The chiefdom of Joara was the northernmost ally or tributary of the chieftainess of Cofitachequi. The principal territory of Joara lay on the upper Catawba River, and its political reach extended for an unknown distance into the near fringe of the mountains. Guaquili, for example, was clearly a subsidiary town of the chiefdom of Joara.

Joara lay on an important crossroads in the native trail system. It lay on a major south-north trail that ran northward through the mountains to the upper Nolichucky River in the Tennessee Valley. And it lay on a second trail that ran east-west—eastward to piedmont North Carolina and Virginia, and westward to the headwaters of the French Broad River. Partly as a function of this strategic location, Joara was actively engaged in trading salt, copper, and perhaps other substances.

Joara was a chiefdom that lay on several borders. Geographically it lay on the border between the upper piedmont and the Blue Ridge mountains. Linguistically it lay on the border between Catawban-speaking peoples to the south and east and Iroquoian-speaking peoples to the north and west, most particularly several dialects of Cherokee. At the time of the Juan Pardo expedition, both Catawban-speaking and Cherokee-speaking chiefs came to Joara to meet with Pardo, as well as people who may have spoken languages whose affiliations are unknown, perhaps including Yuchi.

Joara also lay on a cultural boundary between the Pisgah-Qualla culture of the Cherokee-speaking peoples and the culture that is associated with Catawban-speaking peoples. Joara may have been the namesake of the eighteenth-century Cherokee town Jore. And less obviously it may be the namesake of Swannanoa, the name of the river that ran by the trail that led from the upper Catawba River through Swannanoa Gap to the upper French Broad River. The name Swannanoa is probably derived from the Cherokee word *suwalinunahi*, meaning "the Suwali (i.e., Joara) trail."

Did the people of Joara speak a Cherokee language? Unfortunately, this cannot be determined with certainty. On phonological grounds, "Joara" *could* be a Cherokee word, but it could just as well be Yuchi, or some unknown language.[19]

One should not fall into the trap of thinking that "Cherokee" or "Catawban" refer to the same kinds of social entities in the sixteenth century that they referred to in the eighteenth century and later. For one thing, it is quite clear that Mississippian paramount chiefdoms subsumed peoples who were diverse both culturally and linguistically. Moreover, the Cherokees and Catawbas of the eighteenth century also comprised culturally and linguistically diverse peoples, and the political and economic dynamics that shaped sixteenth-century native polities in the Southeast were quite different from the forces that shaped native polities in the eighteenth century and later. Hence, there is no simple, linear relationship connecting sixteenth-century Cherokee with eighteenth-century Cherokee.

The rendezvous of the Ilasi contingent, under Baltasar de Gallegos, with the main force of the army did not go smoothly. De Soto had given Gallegos orders to depart from Ilasi on a particular date and to rendezvous with De Soto's half of the army while they were both traveling northward.[20] When Gallegos failed to rendezvous at Chalaque, De Soto presumably sent a letter by runners to prod Gallegos along. These runners may have met up with him on the trail a day or two away from Chalaque, or else they missed him entirely. In any case, after departing from Ilasi and spending five days traveling, Gallegos and his men came upon the trail De Soto was following, and they could see from the tracks they found that De Soto had already been there, and not all that recently.[21]

Seeing this, and seeing how little corn there was in the province of Chalaque, Gallegos's men very nearly mutinied. They were afraid they were walking into another area like the wilderness of Ocute.[22] They did not know whether they would rendezvous with De Soto in one day, or ten, or twenty.[23] They began marching very rapidly, and not in good order. But Gallegos did keep his men from panicking, and they arrived at Joara on May 22, the day after De Soto arrived.[24] Many of Gallegos's men were sick and lame, and some of their horses were ill and not able to travel rapidly.[25]

They found more food supplies in Joara than they had found in the country they had just traversed. Hence, the chiefdom of Joara seemed prosperous, and the chief supplied the Spaniards with corn, little "dogs" to eat, porters, and *petacas,* an Aztec word the Spaniards used to refer to cane baskets with lids, in which they could carry their food and possessions (fig. 32).[26] Presumably from the copper they had seen at Joara, they felt they had seen more indications of gold in this area than anywhere else they had yet visited.[27]

Fig. 32. Choctaw split-cane basket with a lid, early twentieth century. (National Anthropological Archives, Smithsonian Institution)

The Cherokee-Speaking Peoples

Even though the men were tired, and some of them were ill, and even though they could see what a high mountain range they were going to have to cross (fig. 33), De Soto rested in Joara for only two days after Gallegos arrived. On May 25 they departed from Joara and climbed a very high mountain, arriving at the end of the day in a woods in the vicinity of Jonas Ridge, where they bivouacked. The next day they continued on to bivouac in a savannah, where they suffered from extreme cold even though it was already the twenty-sixth of May. This is the first indication that at the time of the expedition the climate in the Southeast was significantly colder than it is today. Here they walked in the water of a river, only shin-deep, which at some later point they believed emptied into the Río del Espíritu Santo—the Mississippi River.[28] They were wading in the headwaters of the North Toe River, in the general vicinity of present-day Spruce Pine, North Carolina.[29]

As they traveled northward from Cofitachequi, and more particularly when they entered the mountains, De Soto and his men entered the Appalachian oak-chestnut-yellow poplar forest (see map 4). This was a canopied broadleaf deciduous forest composed of very large white oaks, northern red oaks, and most particularly chestnuts. The chestnut was the tree that dominated the

Fig. 33. The Appalachian Mountains. LeConte Mountain from Greenbrier Pinnacle, ca. 1935. (Great Smoky Mountains National Park)

Fig. 34. Old-growth American chestnut forest, ca. 1910–20. For scale, note the man standing at the base of the tree. (Great Smoky Mountains National Park)

canopy of the Appalachian forests. Mature chestnuts averaged as much as 6 feet in diameter, some reaching 10 to 12 feet, and their branches spanned as much as 120 feet (fig. 34). Properly spaced out, three of these giant chestnut trees could have shaded a football field. They produced a prodigious quantity of delicious nuts, which supported large populations of turkey, deer, and bear. The American chestnut is now sadly insignificant in the Southeast because early in our century the chestnut forest succumbed to the chestnut blight, a deadly fungal bark disease imported from the Old World. For this reason there is no place today where one can see a remnant of this magnificent forest as it was in 1540. No matter how large the oak trees, without the chestnut trees, it is not the same forest.

It was after the army had entered the mountains that the Lady of Cofitachequi excused herself from the others, saying that she needed to go to the woods to relieve herself. She took one of her female slaves with her, and once out of sight, the two women fled from the expedition. The slave woman was carrying a *petaca* full of unbored pearls, which some of the Spaniards claimed were very valuable. De Soto had allowed the lady to keep these pearls for the time being, so as not to take everything from her, though he had intended tc take them from her later. She fled to Joara, joining up with several slaves who had defected from the army between the province of Chalaque and the mountains. These included Rodriguez, a native of Peñafiel, an Indian slave from Cuba who belonged to Villegas, a Barbary slave belonging to Don Carlos Enríquez, and Gómez, a black slave who belonged to Vasco Gonzalez.[30] All of these slaves spoke Spanish. Rodriguez was the first to desert, and the others deserted later.[31] De Soto did not at first succeed in recapturing them.[32]

The Spaniards also thought that Mendoza de Montanjes and Alaminos of Cuba had deserted on May 26. Since Alonso Romo was in command of the rear guard on that day and was therefore responsible for the missing men, De Soto halted the army for a time (May 27), sending Romo back to fetch them.[33] Romo succeeded in finding Montanjes and Alaminos, the latter of whom claimed he had been ill and his horse had strayed from the trail. De Soto was furious, and he threatened the two of them with hanging.[34] Evidently, Alaminos then doubled back and tried to talk the slaves who had escaped into returning to the army, and while the army was at Chiaha, he returned with one or two others.[35]

From those who lagged behind the expedition and then rejoined it, De Soto learned that in Joara the Lady of Cofitachequi had attached herself to a black slave owned by André de Vasconcelos (presumably one of those already named) with whom she was cohabiting, and the two of them planned to return to Cofitachequi.[36] It is not known what the plans were of the other slaves who escaped, though some on the expedition said those who had deserted were infatuated with native women.[37]

While they were traveling along this leg of their journey, it happened that during the hottest part of a day, a foot soldier, Juan Terrón, approached a friend who was riding a horse. Terrón was tired and wanted to lighten his load, even though, according to Garcilaso, he was a big, strong man. Terrón took a linen bag out of his knapsack containing more than six pounds of unbored pearls. Where he obtained them, he never told. He said: "I do not want these pearls; take them and carry them away." But the friend refused to accept them, saying that Terrón should keep them and buy himself some horses when they returned to Havana. But Terrón took offense at this, saying: "Well, since you do not want the pearls, I swear to God that I will not take them either, so they will have to remain here." And with this, he opened the bag, and swinging it like a man sowing seed, he scattered the pearls in the weeds and grass, and he returned the empty bag to his knapsack.

The pearls, according to the story, were as large as hazelnuts or fat chickpeas. His comrades were amazed at what Terrón had done, and several of them scrambled to find as many of the pearls as they could. When they saw how fine they were, they began taunting Terrón with a jingle: "Pearls are not for Juan Terrón."[38] They continued needling him in the following days until finally Terrón said, "For the love of God, do not mention this matter to me again; I assure you that each time you remind me of my stupidity, I feel a desire to hang myself from a tree."[39]

On May 28 the army bivouacked in an oak grove, and on May 29 they continued on down the Toe River, crossing and recrossing it many times because of the narrow passage through which its channel passes. The Toe River flows swiftly, over a series of cascades as it cuts its narrow path down to the Tennessee Valley. They halted near the confluence of the Toe and Cane Rivers and the head of the Nolichucky River.[40] On May 30 peaceful emissaries from Guasili met them on the trail, and later in the day they arrived at Guasili, probably the Plum Grove site near present-day Embreeville, Tennessee.[41] After having traveled through so much deserted country, they felt themselves fortunate to have come to this place, beautifully situated among small streams in the mountains.[42] The Indians gave them a small quantity of corn, many little dogs to eat, and many porters.[43] It was such a fine place that afterward, when they were playing dice, when they made a good throw they would sometimes call out, "The house of Guasili."[44]

"Guasili" is very likely a Cherokee place-name. Juan Pardo traversed the headwaters of the French Broad River in 1567–68, meeting along the way with many chiefs, almost all of whom were Cherokee-speaking. Pardo found the town of Tocae in the vicinity of present-day Asheville. While Pardo was at Tocae, he was met by several chiefs from towns whose names resemble Cherokee place-names, particularly "Senneca" and "Taucoe." In the eighteenth century these towns were located on the headwaters of the Savannah River, though their being located there in the sixteenth century is by no means certain. It is possible that in the sixteenth century they were located closer to Tocae, on the headwaters of the French Broad and Saluda Rivers.

A large number of Cherokee-speaking chiefs met with Pardo in the mountains. And a number of these same Cherokee-speaking chiefs met with Pardo at Joara, but not a single Cherokee-speaking chief met with him at any town on the northern side of the mountains, in the Tennessee Valley. Thus, it would seem that in the sixteenth century, Cherokee-speaking Indians were more specifically located in the mountains and high foothills than they were in later times. Also, it appears that their wider political and perhaps cultural alliances were with the paramount chiefdom of Cofitachequi. Their lack of intercourse with the people in the Tennessee Valley implies enmity.

The social and cultural history of the Cherokee-speaking peoples strongly bears the geographical imprint of the Blue Ridge Mountains. They had been shaped by the Mississippian transformation just as had the people of the Ridge and Valley and the southern Piedmont provinces. But mountains offer impediments to easy travel, and mountain people everywhere tend to be conservative. Thus, the Mississippian transformation first began to occur at about A.D. 800 in the Ridge and Valley province, and at about A.D. 900 in the southern Piedmont, but the earliest occurrence in the Appalachian highlands is not until about A.D. 1100. Hence, it would seem that the Cherokee-speaking peoples began organizing themselves into Mississippian chiefdoms two or three centuries after their northern and southern neighbors did.

The agricultural season is significantly shorter in the mountains than it is in the Ridge and Valley and the Piedmont provinces. Late spring freezes and early fall freezes in the mountains made farming more uncertain. Also, deposits of rich and easily tilled alluvial soils in the mountains are small in area and widely scattered. Perhaps for this reason, the chiefdoms with mound centers that developed in the mountains were much smaller, more recent, and less elaborate by every measure than were those in the Ridge and Valley and the southern Piedmont. And the elaborate paraphernalia and symbolism of the Southeastern Ceremonial Complex is virtually absent from the mountains.

In addition to having a rugged topography that frustrates rapid and easy travel, the mountains possess an unusually varied and rich diversity of plants. At higher elevations in the Appalachian mountains, the plants change significantly from those in the southern Piedmont. Although Cherokee-speaking people in the mountains were farmers, they supplemented this cultivated food with wild foods more so than did the people in the Ridge and Valley and the southern Piedmont. And because the human population in the mountains was low, game was correspondingly plentiful.

Finally, these mountain Mississippians do not seem to have suffered as much from the social and political instabilities that are evident in the archaeological record of the Ridge and Valley and the southern Piedmont. Perhaps because of their mountain isolation, their less specialized (and therefore less vulnerable) food production, and their more egalitarian social structure, they may have been spared some of the internal and external conflicts that plagued Mississippian societies that lay north and south of them.

The Mississippian mountaineers—the Pisgah culture—in many ways resembled their Lamar Mississippian contemporaries elsewhere. Their small villages appear always to have been situated in stream valleys, usually up on the first or second alluvial terrace, to give them security from high water. Their villages were typically surrounded by palisades with overlapping entryways, though these palisades were not as strongly built as those around towns in the Ridge and Valley province (fig. 35). Their houses were square or slightly rectangular, with rounded corners, measuring about twenty feet to the side. The walls were probably covered with sheets of bark or perhaps woven cane mats, and the floors of the houses were dug down to slightly below ground level. In the center of the house floor, centered between four stout roof-support posts, was a clay platform hearth where a fire was kept burning. A roofed entryway, a kind of vestibule, stood in the center of a wall or else at one corner of the house. Roofs were possibly made of thatch or else of sheets of bark, laid down like large shingles.

The larger Pisgah towns had structures for ceremonial purposes that were twenty-four to twenty-eight feet square—somewhat larger than their houses.

Fig. 35. Artist's reconstruction of a Pisgah village. Roy S. Dickens Jr., *Cherokee Prehistory* (Knoxville: University of Tennessee Press, 1976), fig. 15.

These also had sunken floors, and they evidently had roofs that peaked at the center, on which a thin layer of earth was spread. Hence, they are sometimes called earth lodges. The Cherokees continued building these structures into the early historic period, when European observers described them as small, artificial mountains. After a period of time, perhaps after the timbers of an earth lodge became weak, they collapsed the structure and covered it over with a scattering of medium-size river boulders, and then laid a mantle of earth over this, forming a mound. Then they built a new earth lodge on top of the mound, which might in time be again collapsed and covered over, raising up the mound to a new height.

The Pisgah peoples of the Blue Ridge Mountains may have been culturally different in many respects from those in the Ridge and Valley and the southern Piedmont provinces, but all that archaeologists have to work with are those aspects of material culture that can be recovered from the earth. And of what archaeologists have recovered, it must be said that Pisgah material culture is much like that of other Lamar Mississippian peoples. Thus, their arrow points, stone celts, pipes, burial practices, bone tools, and jewelry were not particularly distinctive. What is distinctive about the Pisgah culture is certain elements in pottery decoration. Pisgah pottery was characteristically made of sand-tempered paste decorated by paddling the soft clay walls of the vessels with wooden paddles carved with preponderantly rectilinear designs (fig 36). These were ladderlike designs made of parallel grooves that ran either horizontally or slanted at an angle. The vessels frequently have rims that are formed into collars, which are decorated with incised lines, often at an oblique angle, or else with patterned gash punctations. Some rims are everted and thickened. This way of decorating the rims of pots resembles techniques used by the Iroquois of the northeast and, in an earlier prehistoric era, by people in southern Illinois.

Archaeological evidence shows that the densest concentrations of Pisgah pottery are in the Blue Ridge Mountains on the upper French Broad, upper Pigeon, and upper Nolichucky Rivers. This pottery also occurs in significant quantities on the southern side of the mountains on the upper Keowee, Saluda, and Catawba Rivers, on the northern side of the mountains on the lower Pigeon and French Broad Rivers, and in restricted locations on the upper Holston, Clinch, and Powell Rivers. Further afield, Pisgah pottery occurs as a minority ware on the Tuckaseegee River, upper Little Tennessee River, and upper Hiwassee River, as well as on the Chatooga River and upper Chattahoochee River in Georgia.

Fig. 36. Pisgah jar. Valentine collection from Hayward County, North Carolina.
(Research Laboratories of Anthropology, University of North Carolina at Chapel Hill)

Archaeological evidence argues strongly that Pisgah pottery is ancestral to pottery that has been recovered from early historic Cherokee sites. Hence, *some* of the people who made Pisgah pottery almost certainly spoke Cherokee languages. It is possible that *most* of the people who made Pisgah pottery spoke Cherokee languages. But since there is no necessary connection between the language one speaks and the pottery one fashions, the distribution of Pisgah pottery may not be an infallible guide to the prehistoric distribution of Cherokee-speaking peoples. Nonetheless, the known distribution of Pisgah pottery is not inconsistent with where Cherokee-speaking people may have been living at the time of the De Soto expedition.

Consistent with other parts of their culture, the Pisgah people possessed a simple iconography. In one high-status burial, archaeologists found several circular discs cut out of mica. Some of these had portions excised to form equal-arm crosses. Similar mica discs have been found at the Town Creek site in North Carolina and at the Mulberry and McCollum mound sites in South

Fig. 37. Lick Creek gorget. (Frank H. McClung Museum, University of Tennessee, Knoxville)

Carolina (see fig. 31). The most interesting example of Pisgah iconography is the Lick Creek gorgets (fig. 37), small discs of shell cut out of the walls of large marine shells, with a coiled serpentlike creature cut out and incised in their centers. Some of these creatures have rattles on their tails, and some bear a forked-eye motif that is frequently seen on birds and is specifically thought to be derived from the eye markings of the peregrine falcon. Thus, the Lick Creek serpent depicts not simply a rattlesnake, but one of the anomalous serpentine monsters that haunted the belief systems of Southeastern Indians in later times. It is no doubt significant that the Lick Creek gorget is considered to be a highly simplified version of the much more elaborate and technically better-made Citico gorget (see fig. 44) that was current among the sixteenth-century people of the Tennessee Valley.

At about A.D. 1500 new design elements began appearing in Pisgah pottery. These are stamped designs with bolder and more varied rectilinear stamps, more stamps with curvilinear designs, larger vessel forms, bowls with cazuela rims and with small lugs replacing loop handles. All these elements were derived from the Lamar pottery style of the southern Piedmont. This new style of pottery is termed Qualla, and it is the style of pottery found most plentifully in historic Middle Cherokee towns in the mountains, but also in the Lower Cherokee towns that were on the headwaters of the Savannah River. The appearance of Qualla pottery occurs at about the time De Soto and other early Spanish explorers first penetrated the southeastern United States. The question is, did this change proceed from precontact social and economic dynamics, or did it proceed from the unprecedented instabilities the Spaniards left in their wake?[45]

Chiaha

On May 31 De Soto and his army departed from Guasili, sending a messenger ahead to Chiaha to tell the chief there to send some corn to them. They continued on, paralleling the Nolichucky River, and at the end of the day they bivouacked in the open. The next day they passed near the town of Canasoga.[46] Twenty Indians came out from this town bearing baskets filled with mulberries, which was perhaps the only food they had in abundance in this spring season.[47] They continued on past Canasoga and again bivouacked in open country.

They continued traveling on June 2, sleeping at the end of the day near a swamp or bog (*cienega*), probably in the vicinity of present-day Warrensburg, Tennessee. The next day they followed along Lick Creek to its confluence with the Nolichucky River, which had by now grown very large.[48]

On June 4 they bivouacked in a pine wood, where they were met by Indians of Chiaha, who came with the corn De Soto had requested.[49] These Indians told De Soto that the chief of Chiaha awaited them with twenty barbacoas of corn.[50] This news must have been a relief to the Spaniards, for from Conasoga to this point they had traveled through an uninhabited wilderness.[51] In fact they had not been able to procure a sufficiency of corn since they had departed from Cofitachequi.[52] Moreover, they had endured hunger before they reached Cofitachequi, while crossing the wilderness of Ocute.[53]

The next day they arrived at Chiaha, a fortified town on the upstream end of Zimmerman's Island in the French Broad River (fig. 38), near present-day Dandridge, Tennessee.[54] This was the first place in their travels where they report seeing a fortified town.[55] (Who were the people of Chiaha defending themselves against? Perhaps their enemies included the Cherokee-speaking peoples in the mountains.) The town of Chiaha was about two crossbow shots from the end of the island, the width of which varied from one to two crossbow shots. The river itself was very wide, but fordable, and the fields along the river were excellent in quality, and many of them were planted in corn.[56]

The people of Cofitachequi had told the Spaniards that the chiefdom of Chiaha was subject to the chief of Coosa. When Juan Pardo visited Chiaha in

Fig. 38. Zimmerman's Island. The small rectangular dark spot at the upper end of the island is a mound with a known sixteenth-century occupation. This island is now beneath the water of Douglas Lake. Hardly any archaeological excavation was carried out at the site. (Tennessee Valley Authority)

1567, he noted that the principal town had two names: Chiaha and Olamico, the latter being a Koasati word meaning "chief town," or "head town." It is likely that the towns that constituted the chiefdom of Chiaha were those situated on the islands and margins of the French Broad River for some few miles upstream and downstream from Zimmerman's Island.

The culture of the chiefdom of Chiaha is termed Dallas by archaeologists. Developing out of the Hiwassee Island culture of the Middle Mississippian era, the geographical range of Dallas culture extends south along the French Broad, Little Tennessee, and Tennessee Rivers down to about present-day Chattanooga. In many respects the Dallas culture was broadly similar to the Lamar culture. Both, for example, built square houses with four interior support posts and trenched entryways. Dallas differs from Lamar mainly in its shell-tempered, cord-marked plain, and black burnished pottery (fig. 39), with appliqué strap handles and bifurcated lug handles. Most, if not all, of the

Fig. 39. A negative painted Dallas bottle. It is decorated with representations of living heads alternating with skulls. (Frank H. McClung Museum, University of Tennessee, Knoxville)

languages spoken in this Dallas area appear to have been Koasati, or dialects of Koasati—all members of the Muskogean language family.[57]

The chief of Chiaha met the Spaniards in peace, and he moved out of his own house for the benefit of De Soto and his retinue. The rest of the army camped out in the open. Finding the weather fair and the people peaceable, they slept beneath trees, widely scattered from one another. Had conditions been more difficult, it would have been a great trial to the men, who were extraordinarily hungry and tired from their travels. Their horses had become so thin they could not bear the weight of riders, and so for some distance the horsemen had to walk along leading them by their reins.[58]

De Soto and his men rested and recuperated in Chiaha. They obtained plenty of food from the native people. In addition to the twenty barbacoas of corn at their disposal, they were given an abundance of bear's fat stored in gourds. They described the fat as having the consistency of butter and, when melted, tasting as sweet as olive oil. They also obtained quantities of hickory oil, which was very delicious, though some claimed that it caused flatulence.[59] They were given a pot of honey, a food they had not seen up to this point in their travels and of which they saw precious little afterward. Most likely this honey was from bumblebee nests, where it is produced in small quantities. They were also given generous portions of *sofkee*, a gruel rather like hominy grits.[60]

For a time the Spaniards and the Indians of Chiaha got on well together, even playing games. They swam together in the clear water of the French Broad River.[61] The Spaniards grew fat, and so did their horses, which they put out to pasture a quarter of a league from where the men camped.[62]

The Spaniards also fished in the French Broad River. From Garcilaso we learn the tragic story of Juan Mateos, who one day was fishing in the river with a cane pole. It so happened that up above the bluff of the river, Luís Bravo de Xerez was walking along, lance in hand. Xerez saw a dog, and he threw his lance at the animal, hoping to kill it for food. He missed. When he went down the bluff to retrieve his lance, he found that it had struck Mateos in the temple, killing him instantly. The men were distressed at the death of Mateos, whom they all addressed as "father" because of his age and gray hair. And it must have been driven home to them once again that on this expedition death could come at any time, even in the most innocent circumstances.[63]

The Spaniards took mussels from the river as well as fish. Garcilaso tells us that when the soldier Pedro López bit into one of these mussels, he discovered a round pearl the size of a large hazelnut and with good color. Some of the Spaniards thought it might be worth as much as four hundred ducats.[64]

The peace between the Spaniards and the people of Chiaha lasted for about two weeks, but then De Soto demanded that the chief of Chiaha provide the Spaniards with women.[65] The chief said he would consult with his principal men. Then, on June 19, many of the Indians took their wives and children and ran away to hide from the Spaniards. The next day De Soto made ready to go out and take Indians by force, but a chief came to him and said the people had fled without his permission. He complained to De Soto that he did not have full authority over them. They were under the power of his uncle, who was the legitimate chief until he himself came of age.[66] This implies that De Soto had not met the uncle, the real chief, or if he had, he did not know it. Again, this succession of office from uncle to nephew is consistent with a matrilineal kinship system.

The young chief offered to lead De Soto to where the people were hiding. With the young chief as a guide, De Soto went out with thirty horsemen and thirty footmen. In passing through the villages of some of the principal men, De Soto ordered his men to cut down and destroy their large cornfields. Finally they came to a place on the river where the people had taken refuge on a small island. The water was so deep the cavalry could not make the crossing, so De Soto sent an Indian across with the message that the people should return to their towns. They need not be afraid. De Soto said he would demand no women—because they were so reluctant to give them up—but he wanted to be supplied with porters, in the way that other Indians had supplied him along the way. The Indians of Chiaha talked this over among themselves, and they agreed to return to their towns, making excuses to De Soto for their behavior. They provided De Soto with five hundred porters, and he agreed to leave off the iron collars and chains.[67]

A short time before De Soto was to depart from Chiaha, a chief of Coste, whose town was downriver, came to meet and talk with him. De Soto asked him his customary question about the whereabouts of a rich land. The chief responded that to the north was a province called Chisca, where copper was mined, as well as another metal of that color, except that it was finer and of a more perfect color.[68] The province of Chisca is thought to have been located in the upper Tennessee Valley and adjacent areas. He said his people did not make much use of this metal because it was too soft. Because this seemed to confirm what the Indians of Cofitachequi had told him, De Soto sent two of his men, Juan de Villalobos and Francisco de Silvera, to investigate; they were guided by Indians who spoke the language of the Chiscas.[69] Even though Villalobos and Silvera owned horses, they departed on foot, thinking they could make better time. Later they would come down the river in dugout canoes and rendezvous with the rest of the army at Coste, where they were to report on what they had discovered.[70]

It was in Chiaha that the Spaniards saw how the Indians collected pearls. The chief of Chiaha demonstrated this for De Soto. The Indians went out and gathered up some mussels from the river, and while they were doing this, others piled up a great amount of firewood and burned it down to coals near the river. When the mussels were brought in, they were tossed onto the coals, and the shells immediately opened. From the first ones that opened, the Indians took out several large pearls, which they took to De Soto, though they had already been damaged by the heat.[71]

Coosa

Chiaha was the northernmost chiefdom that was subject to or allied with the paramount chief of Coosa. All of Coosa's subjects and allies lay in the southern part of the Tennessee Valley, the Ridge and Valley physiographic province (see map 6). The Ridge and Valley province, as its name implies, consists of a series of low to moderately high parallel ridges that lie on the western side of the Appalachian Mountains. This band of ridges is narrow where it begins in New York state, widens as it runs southward, and plays out in northern Alabama. From above, these heavily eroded folds of sedimentary rock look like a long strip of coarse corduroy.

From the point of view of Mississippian Indians, the southern end of the Ridge and Valley province was a very good place to live. It had magnificent stands of chestnut and other nut-bearing trees. It had numerous clear, swift rivers running down from the mountains with abundant fish and shellfish. In places, the alluvial soils deposited by these rivers were exceedingly rich and easy to till. This was true of some of the large islands in the French Broad and Tennessee Rivers, as well as the margins of these streams. The margins of the smaller rivers—the Little Tennessee, Hiwassee, and Coosawattee Rivers—at the points where they emerged from the mountains, were likewise bordered by exceedingly fertile soils. Rainfall is abundant in the Ridge and Valley province, and the growing season is significantly longer than that in the mountains, and a bit longer than that in the Piedmont.

In addition to being a rich environment for both domesticated and wild foods, the Ridge and Valley province was a source of several minerals and metals that were important to the Indians. Western Virginia had some quite productive salines, and lesser ones existed at other places. In the areas bordering the upper Nolichucky River there were deposits of mica, and further north there were small quantities of metallic copper. In several places there were deposits of flint and chert that could be used to make flaked stone tools. And there was plenty of stone suitable for grinding into celts and axes, as well as soapstone that could be carved into pipes and ornaments.

The Indians of Coosa were not the only ones who saw the Ridge and Valley province as a desirable place to live. The members of the Juan Pardo expedition, impressed by its beautiful rivers, rich land, wild grapevines, and fruit trees, called it a *tierra de ángeles*—a land of angels. It must have reminded them of their Iberian homeland.

The Spaniards spent twenty-four days resting in Chiaha.[72] De Soto gave the chief of Chiaha some pieces of cloth as a parting gift, and on June 28 the army set out once again.[73] Several men who were ill remained behind at Chiaha; they would wait for Villalobos and Silvera and catch up with De Soto later. Upon departing, De Soto and his men evidently forded a branch of the French Broad River that ran by the island. Their initial course was generally along the south bank of the river, perhaps so they could keep an eye out for the men left behind who would come downriver in canoes. During the course of the day, they passed through five or six villages before again coming to a river— the Little Pigeon—which was wide, swift, and hard to cross. They made the crossing by lining up their horses, head to tail, in the channel of the river, breaking the force of the current, so the men could cross below them, holding onto the tails, stirrups, manes, and breastplates as they waded across.[74] They succeeded in making the crossing, and that night they bivouacked in a pine grove near a village.[75]

Their course took them southward along the southern bank of the French Broad River. They passed through a village, where they obtained some corn, and then bivouacked at the end of the day, June 29, in open country in the vicinity of present-day Shooks. The next day, they forded the French Broad River, went through a village, and then forded the Holston River. They traveled down the northern side of the Tennessee River, bivouacking in open country in what is now southwestern Knoxville. On July 1 they continued down the western bank of the Tennessee, passing by several islands that were part of the chiefdom of Coste. The chief of Coste came out to meet them on the trail, and he took them to one of his villages where they spent the night.[76] Without first obtaining the consent of the chief, some of De Soto's soldiers appropriated stores of corn from several barbacoas in the village. The chief took offense at this, and the next day, July 2, as the army was proceeding to the main town, the chief slipped away and went forward, telling his people to arm themselves.[77]

Later that day the Spaniards arrived at the main town of Coste, which was on Bussell Island, in the mouth of the Little Tennessee River (fig. 40). At this point the Tennessee River is large, swift, and hard to cross, but Lenoir's Shoal stretched all the way across the river to Bussell Island.[78] They made the crossing, but they did so rather carelessly, because they were not sufficiently armed and on guard. Evidently, the settlement pattern of the chiefdom of Coste was similar to that of the chiefdom of Chiaha. That is, its principal town was on an island, and its territory extended for some few miles up and, presumably, down the river.

De Soto picked out a spot where they could bivouac at a distance of about two crossbow shots from the town, and he went with eight of his guard to the town to meet with the chief of Coste. At first, relations were friendly enough, but then some of the Spaniards went from the camp to the town to look for corn. After taking some corn, they began rummaging through the houses to see what else they could find. This angered the Indians, who armed themselves with war clubs and bows and arrows. They were ready for a fight, shaking their arms and brandishing their fists. Some of those who were armed with war clubs attacked five or six Spaniards.[79] De Soto, seeing the hazard in which

Fig. 40. Bussell Island in the mouth of the Little Tennessee River, the smaller of the two rivers. (Tennessee Valley Authority)

his men had placed themselves, picked up an Indian war club and went over to berate his own men, delivering a few blows on them himself, as if he were taking the side of the Indians. But at the same time he secretly sent a message to his camp, ordering the men to come to the town, but to come gradually, so as not to further inflame the Indians.

Thus De Soto defused the situation, cooling down both the Indians and his own men. He began talking to the chief, with Juan Ortiz no doubt translating. Taking the chief by the hand, De Soto walked along conversing with him and ten or twelve of his principal men. Still talking, they left the town and walked along a trail toward the camp. Then De Soto's armed soldiers began to come up, one by one, seemingly innocently. In this way De Soto led the chief and his principal men into the Spanish camp. As they neared his tent, he ordered his men to seize the chief and his principal men and to put them in collars and chains. Then he raged at them, threatening to burn them at the stake for daring to lay hands on his men. He told them he would keep them prisoners until the rest of his men, left behind in Chiaha, came down the river in canoes.

And moreover, before he would release them he would require them to give him a guide and some porters for his departure.[80]

De Soto was afraid the Indians of Chiaha had killed the men he had left behind. But three days later they arrived by canoe. The two who had gone to reconnoiter the Chiscas said that in getting there they had traveled through very rough country that possessed little corn, a mountainous area so rugged it would be impossible for the army to march through it. They came to a small, poor village where they found copper like they had seen before, but they saw nothing else that was interesting, except for a skin as soft as that of a kid, with wool whose softness was between that of a common sheep and a merino. Perhaps it was the skin of an immature buffalo.[81] Since buffalo bones are notably absent from archaeological sites in the Ridge and Valley province in the Mississippian period, this skin had perhaps been obtained in trade from elsewhere. Because they had seen little or no indications of gold, and the trail was getting rough, and time was getting short, they decided to rejoin the army.[82]

The two Spaniards reported that the Chiscas had offered them two young women to sleep with them, but they felt so vulnerable, they dared not touch the women. They were afraid, or so they claimed, that the Chiscas might use this as a pretext for killing them.[83] In fact, the offer may have simply been an act of hospitality.

The remainder of the time the army spent in Coste was seemingly uneventful. De Soto may have sent out cavalry to reconnoiter the countryside, probably including the towns that lay further up the Little Tennessee River, but no specific mention is made of such forays. While they were there, they found a tree with honey in it as good or better than that in Spain.

Counting the day they arrived, they spent eight days in Coste, departing on July 9. Crossing over the eastern channel of the Little Tennessee River, which ran alongside Bussell Island, they proceeded along the eastern bank of the Little Tennessee to the town of Tali, probably the Toqua site (fig. 41), which lay on the opposite side of the river. Here the river was so deep they were not able to ford it. But the Indians of Tali, fearing that the Spaniards were about to cross the river, loaded their women and children and clothing in dugout canoes and began to flee down the river. De Soto, however, forced them to turn back, presumably deploying his arquebusiers and crossbowmen. With this threat, the chief of Tali came and met with De Soto. Submitting to the Spaniards, he provided canoes to ferry them across the river.

De Soto and his men had reached one of the most densely occupied areas in the Ridge and Valley province—the valley of the Little Tennessee River. The

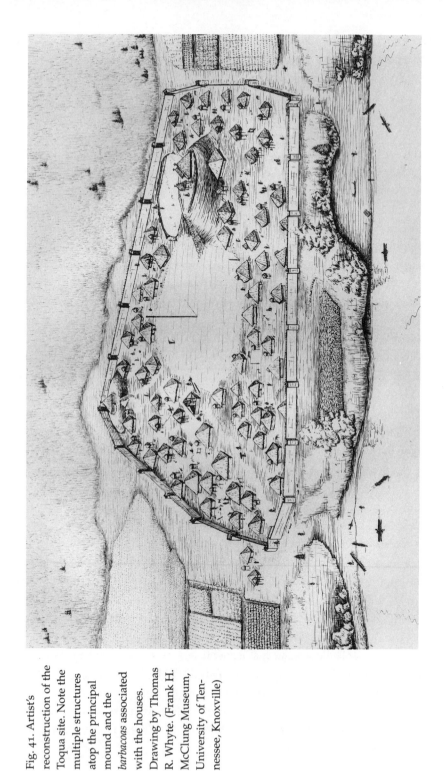

Fig. 41. Artist's reconstruction of the Toqua site. Note the multiple structures atop the principal mound and the *barbacoas* associated with the houses. Drawing by Thomas R. Whyte. (Frank H. McClung Museum, University of Tennessee, Knoxville)

transition to a Mississippian mode of production occurred at an early date in this valley, and the people gradually evolved the Dallas culture that was present there in 1540. Dallas towns were characteristically compact and fortified, and they remained so for a very long period of time, implying that they occupied a land in which warfare with an enemy or enemies was longstanding. The Cherokee-speaking people in the mountains were probably among the enemies of the Dallas people. Characteristically, Dallas towns were occupied for long periods of time, and consequently the people drew heavily on the soils and forests in their immediate environment.

The geological analysis of pollen in cores taken from ponds in the Little Tennessee Valley testifies to modifications of the environment by Mississippian people. Corn pollen first shows up around fifteen hundred years ago. Present also is pollen from the older indigenous eastern cultigens, goosefoot and marsh elder. But what is most notable is that between 30 and 55 percent of all the pollen in these cores was ragweed, a weed that constitutes 5 percent or less of the pollen in areas where the forest has not been disturbed. The implication of this is that as the people cleared fields for agriculture and took wood from the forests, the amount of ragweed expanded. The cores also reveal a sharp increase in particles of charcoal, evidence of the Indian practice of burning off their agricultural fields as well as undergrowth in the woods.[84]

The clearing of forest for farming by the Dallas people and their use of wood for fuel and building materials left extensive areas in the Little Tennessee Valley almost bare of trees. The valley seen by Moravian missionaries in the late eighteenth century may not have been very different from the valley De Soto and his men saw in the sixteenth century. The missionaries describe extensive plains covered with tall grass on the southern bank of the river. Mixed in with the grass were wild strawberry plants so thick that when they were ripe it looked as if the earth was covered with red cloth. The trees that grew in and around these plains were the ones the Indians spared for the fruit they bore—a profusion of plum, mulberry, walnut, honey-locust, persimmon, and red sumac trees. At some distance from the towns and farms the Spaniards no doubt saw stands of pine, hickory, chestnuts, post oaks, and a few black oaks and Spanish oaks, with very little underbrush, but with high grass and a profusion of wild grapes growing below the forest canopy.[85]

The Toqua site, the probable location of Tali, was a large late Dallas site located on the south bank of the Little Tennessee River just upstream from the mouth of the Tellico River. The people of the Toqua site exploited a rich bottomland at least two thousand feet long and as much as six hundred feet wide. Toqua was a compact town with two mounds and a plaza surrounded by closely spaced houses, all of which was encircled by a strong wooden palisade with regularly spaced defensive towers.

At about A.D. 1300 the Dallas phase people began constructing their buildings in a new way. Previously they had employed a flexed mode of construction, in which they had set four long, small-diameter poles in the ground (either in individual holes or in trenches), bent them over the center of the space that was to be enclosed, and then tied the tops of these poles together. Additional poles were closely spaced between these four main poles and similarly tied together at the top. Small split saplings and lengths of river cane were then woven horizontally around this structure, forming, in effect, an inverted basket with no internal support posts. Thus, the walls and roofs of these houses were of the same fabric. On the margins of the Southeast, Indians continued building these flexed houses into the sixteenth century. The Spaniards saw them on their way from Tampa Bay to Apalachee; they probably saw them in the Catawban-speaking area of Cofitachequi; and they would see them again west of the Mississippi River, particularly in eastern Texas.

But like many people in the interior of the Mississippian Southeast, at about A.D. 1300 Dallas people began building *rigid* structures—like those De Soto and his men first saw at Toa—with walls built of posts set in individual holes, with four heavy interior support posts (large buildings had more), and with a separate peaked roof structure resting atop these walls and interior support posts. The typical Dallas house had a sunken floor space measuring about five hundred square feet, dug a foot or more down into the earth. The large interior posts, which were pine, were set at the corners of a square space in the center of the house floor. Weight-bearing timbers, also in the form of a square, connected the tops of these posts. The walls of Dallas houses were low, made of vertical posts with horizontal timbers again set along the tops of the posts. The horizontal beams on the walls and interior posts supported roof poles of pine, hickory, or white oak, the small ends of which joined at the smokehole at the peak of the house. Dallas people used twisted cordage to tie lengths of river cane and split saplings horizontally to these vertical wall and slanted roof members, and both the roof and the walls were thatched with grass. The dirt that had been excavated for the sunken floor was banked up to a height of about one meter around the outside of the walls, diverting rainwater and providing added insulation. A wall-trench entryway kept mud from running into the sunken floor in rainy weather.

The "private" space inside a Dallas house lay between the walls and the public floor area bounded by the interior support posts. Within this private space, couches, supported by posts, were built along the walls. The frames of these couches were made of river cane, and they were covered with split-cane mats. For a modicum of privacy, wooden partitions about four and a half to five feet high were built at the ends of the couches and were plastered with clay mixed with grass and leaves (see fig. 42). The clay surfaces of the partitions were sometimes decorated by punctating, incising, or painting. The inside of the roof above the public space was heavily daubed with clay, no doubt to give the roof some protection from sparks carried up by smoke from the fire. The area beneath the couches could be used for storage, but in the course of time debris from everyday life collected there, out of sight and probably out of mind.[86]

Near the center of the house's square public space, a circular raised hearth was built up out of clay, formed in the shape of a wide, shallow basin. Fires kept in them provided heat and light, and to some extent they were used for cooking, though much of the cooking was done on fires outside the house. In time, these clay hearths became quite hard. The public space in a house was kept clear of debris. Pottery vessels were sometimes left sitting here, but they were never casually left sitting in the hearth itself. The corners of the houses were used for storage. Many tools and raw materials were stored in the northwestern corner of the house, and food was generally stored in the southeastern corner, perhaps implying a symbolic opposition between a male northwest and a female southeast.

The use of space within these houses accorded well with one of the dominant Mississippian symbolic motifs—the equal-armed cross (see figs. 5, 55). That is, everyday life was lived out in the four cardinal directions around a "sacred" central fire. This equal-armed cross motif is so frequent in native Southeastern art, dance, and ritual, it deserves to be called archetypal. It is likely that the couches in the several directions had particular social values assigned to them. Males, for example, appear to have been particularly associated with the western couch; females, with the northern and southern couches.

Like Lamar households, the typical Dallas household also included a second, smaller portico or open structure with a rectangular floor surface of about thirty-five square feet. In some cases these structures were barbacoas, storehouses built up on posts with their floors perhaps six feet from the ground, so that people could sit or stand in the cool shade beneath them. In other cases, the posts of these structures may have simply supported roofs to give shade. The floors of these open structures generally contained baked areas from sustained, hot fires. Food was probably cooked on fires beneath these structures when the weather permitted. And beneath barbacoas, the low cooking fires would have helped preserve food and perishable goods by keeping moisture out of the storehouse, and the smoke no doubt discouraged insects.

The basic architectural features of these two typical domestic structures were also incorporated into the structures built on top of Dallas mounds. A walled, four-sided town house was the principal public structure. It had in the center of its floor a relatively large four-sided public space, surrounded by eight heavy posts rather than four. It had a central raised hearth, and couches were built against the walls. The floor measured about a thousand square feet. The couches along the walls were sometimes partitioned into several distinct sections. Both the walls and floors of these town houses were sometimes covered by split-cane mats. The posts forming the outside wall were often made of rot-resistant cedar and black locust. This town house is the structure in which the elite of the chiefdom—mostly males, in all probability—met to conduct the most important social and religious affairs.

A second walled structure (fig. 42), seemingly little different from domestic walled structures in the town, was built quite near the town house, and the two were connected by means of a roofed and walled passageway. This is thought to have been the residence of the reigning chief and his family. Addi-

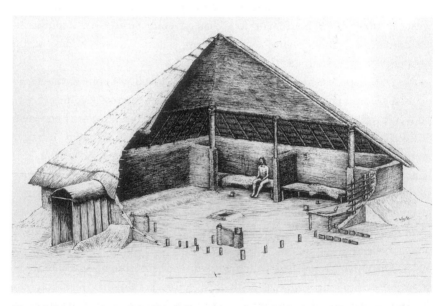

Fig. 42. Cutaway view of the chief's house atop the principal mound at the Toqua site. Drawing by Thomas R. Whyte. (Frank H. McClung Museum, University of Tennessee, Knoxville)

tionally, built quite near the eastern sides of these paired structures was a rectangular open-sided structure that had a floor area of 780 to 1400 square feet. This structure differed from domestic porticos in having internal support posts, like those inside the walled structures. The eastern side of this portico, facing the rising sun, was conspicuously open. The northern, southern, and western sides were sometimes walled, or partially so. And this portico was connected to the town house by means of a trenched entryway.[87]

The De Soto chroniclers barely mention Tali, and they have very little to say about the material culture of any of the chiefdoms comprising the paramount chiefdom of Coosa. Virtually all that we know about the material culture of these people has been patiently accumulated through decades of archaeological research.

Two other large sixteenth-century Dallas towns lay further up the Little Tennessee River from Toqua. A few miles upstream lay the Citico site, and about five miles beyond that, the Chilhowee site. In 1567 Juan Pardo and his small army visited both of these towns. After departing from Chiaha and skirting the eastern side of Chilhowee Mountain, Pardo came to Chalahume (the Chilhowee site), and from there he went to Satapo (the Citico site). It was at Satapo that some Indians told Pardo that other Spaniards—De Soto and his army— had been at Satapo before, both on foot and on horseback. In testimony in 1600, Juan de Ribas, who had been with Pardo, said he had seen paintings of mounted Spanish lancers on the walls of the houses at Satapo. Pardo did not continue on to Tali because it was in Satapo that an Indian informer apprised Pardo of a plot by the people of Satapo, Coste, Chiaha, Coosa, and others. Their plan was to launch an attack as Pardo traveled south to Coosa. With this threat Pardo decided to abort his mission, and he abruptly returned to Chiaha, and then to Santa Elena, on Parris Island, South Carolina.[88]

De Soto and his men remained in Tali on July 10, and some of his horsemen may very well have ridden to Satapo and perhaps Chalahume as well. The next day the Spaniards departed from Tali and continued on, probably taking a trail that paralleled the Tellico River. (The resemblance of "Tali" to "Tellico" is probably not coincidental.) The chief of Tali gave the Spaniards four women and two porters.[89] At the end of the day they bivouacked in the general vicinity of present-day Belltown. On July 12 they crossed a stream—possibly the upper Tellico River—and bivouacked, possibly in the vicinity of present-day Prospect. On July 13 they crossed another stream—possibly Conasauga Creek—and again they bivouacked. On July 14 they crossed a large stream, the Hiwassee River, and they slept in the town of Tasqui, located in the general vicinity of present-day Old Fort or Ocoee. During all these days, the chief of Tali had his subjects bring out to the Spaniards daily rations of *mazamorras* (i.e., hominy grits; called *sofkee* by the Creeks), cooked beans, and other foods.[90] As they traveled, they had Harlan Mountain, Tellico Mountain, and Starr Mountain on their left side, and the Notchy Creek Knobs and other high hills and ridges on their right side. They continued their march on July 15, passing through several small villages.[91] As they approached the principal town of Coosa, in the intermontane valley of the Coosawattee River, just east of present-day Carters, Georgia, messengers began coming to meet them.[92]

On July 16, as they approached to within two crossbow shots of the capital town of Coosa, they saw the chief of Coosa coming out to meet them. He was seated on a cushion on a litter carried upon the shoulders of his subjects. Like the litter on which the Lady of Cofitachequi was conveyed, the litter on which the chief of Coosa sat was covered with the white shawls common in the late prehistoric Southeast. Sixty or seventy of his principal men carried the litter in relays, singing and playing on flutes as they walked along. The chief wore a mantle of "marten" skins the size and shape of a woman's shawl, and he wore a crown of feathers on his head.[93]

The chief of Coosa was twenty-six or twenty-seven years of age. He was intelligent, and he spoke with deliberation. It seemed to some of the Spaniards that it was almost as if he had been brought up at a court in an atmosphere of learning and culture.[94] The chief of Coosa was a paramount chief, and with such diverse peoples within his domain, this could not have been the first difficult diplomatic situation he had faced, only the most serious. Unlike, say, the chief of Apalachee, who seemed only to know to wage war on the Spaniards, the chief of Coosa may have been pursuing a more long-range strategy. Since the Spaniards had departed from Capachequi, they had not met any armed resistance to speak of. They walked through Ichisi, Ocute, and Cofitachequi unopposed, setting up tall crosses made of poles in the plazas. But restraint on the part of the Indians was especially notable in the paramount chiefdom of Coosa. The people of Chiaha had become restive under the demands of the Spaniards, but they attempted to flee rather than fight; the people of Coste put up a small protest when the Spaniards ransacked their houses and barbacoas; and the people of Tali had attempted to spirit their women and children away. But they did not use their superior numbers to wage war on the Spaniards.

The chiefdom of Coosa seemed to the Spaniards to be a very rich province, and they liked the lay of the land. Coosa was populous, with many large towns, and along the banks of streams there were large fields of corn and beans stretching from one town to another.[95] The barbacoas in the towns were full of corn and beans, and the fruits of the country were excellent. The Spaniards especially relished the local plums, which were like the early plums of Seville. Grapes of good quality grew on vines in the trees along the streams, and there were some large sweet grapes with large seeds, perhaps scuppernongs, growing on low stocks away from the streams.[96] There was also a fruit they described as being like small sour apples, like the *canavales* of Extremadura. In many ways, Coosa reminded them of Spain.

The chiefdom of Coosa lay along a stretch of the Coosawattee River. It began in the Coosawattee Valley, where the river and its tributary, Talking Rock Creek, emerge from the Blue Ridge Mountains and where these streams have deposited a wonderfully rich layer of alluvial soil, enriched with the minerals of freshly weathered igneous and metamorphic rock in the hills and mountains. The principal town of Coosa was located in this valley, and as many as eight subsidiary towns, some with mounds, lay along the banks of the Coosawattee River for about ten miles downstream.

The principal town of Coosa was at the Little Egypt site, where mound construction began at about A.D. 1350–1400. Little Egypt had two mounds, each more than two and a half meters high, and it had a third mound that farmers, pothunters, and erosion destroyed before archaeologists could excavate it. The town was about twelve and a half acres in size. It had a plaza, but it does not appear to have had a palisade.

At some time after A.D. 1475, the political star of the Little Egypt site and the Coosa chiefdom began to ascend. The principal mound at the Little Egypt site was enlarged four times, and each of these enlargements perhaps represents a transfer of power from one chief to his successor. In most respects the culture of the people was similar to that of the Dallas culture at Tali and the upper Tennessee Valley. The pottery at the Little Egypt site was distinctive in that it combined features of both the Dallas and Lamar cultures (fig. 43). The population of the chiefdom of Coosa can only be calculated using the crudest of estimates, but it was somewhere between 2,500 and 4,650 people.[97]

The way in which the chiefdom of Coosa was able to ascend to the leadership of the paramount chiefdom is unknown. Archaeologists are not even sure about the nature of the paramount chief's power or influence over the chiefdoms comprised within the paramount chiefdom. It is clear enough that the paramount chief was entitled to receive tribute from some, if not all, of

Fig. 43. Burnished Lamar bowl with conch shell rim elements from the Little Egypt site. Photograph by S. Dwight Kirkland. (University of Georgia, Laboratory of Archaeology)

these chiefdoms. But was this tribute of economic importance, or was it merely given to fulfill a ritual obligation?

The archaeological characteristics of the paramount chiefdom of Coosa are fairly well known. The paramount chiefdom consisted of at least seven and possibly nine or ten clusters of sites that constitute chiefdoms, stretching from Chiaha, in present-day Tennessee, in the northeast, down to Talisi, in present-day Alabama, in the southwest. These chiefdoms were invariably located along the margins of rivers and large creeks, and each cluster included up to eight towns. The radius of these chiefdoms was a maximum of about 12.5 miles. The chiefdoms were separated from each other by considerable distances, with wildernesses in between averaging about 20 miles wide.

It is likely that the truly enduring social units in greater Coosa were the simple chiefdoms themselves. These social units were compact enough so that a chief could walk round-trip from his principal town to any other town in his chiefdom in the course of a day, and he could therefore exercise direct control over all towns. It is this factor that determined the 12.5-mile maximum radius of a chiefdom. The control of the paramount chief over other chief-doms, on the other hand, must have been considerably thinner, more problem-

Fig. 44. Citico gorget. William H. Holmes, *Art in Shell of the Ancient Americas,* Second Annual Report of the Bureau of American Ethnology (Washington, D.C.: GPO, 1883), plate lxii.

atic, and possibly short-lived. As in the paramount chiefdom of Cofitachequi, the paramount chiefdom of Coosa encompassed notable cultural diversity. It also encompassed some linguistic diversity, with eastern Muskogean, western Muskogean, and Koasati languages being represented.

Perhaps the most notable item of material culture that is found throughout the paramount chiefdom of Coosa is the Citico style gorget (fig. 44), an oval or circular disc cut out of a conch shell on which was incised a highly stylized serpentine monster. The monster has a huge circular eye, the teeth of a carnivore or herbivore, eye-markings perhaps of a peregrine falcon, and the body of a rattlesnake. These gorgets have been found exclusively in the burials of adult females and subadults, and many or all of the latter were probably also female. One possibility is that Citico gorgets are somehow associated with the matrilineage of the chief of Coosa. In contrast, shell gorgets in the form of "masks" (fig. 45) tend always to be found with males.[98]

The chief of Coosa ordered his people to move out of their houses to make

Fig. 45. Mask gorget. (Frank H. McClung Museum, University of Tennessee)

way for the Spaniards. De Soto himself occupied one of the three buildings that were on the tops of mounds in the town. Despite the cooperation of the chief of Coosa, De Soto took him and some of his principal people hostage and kept them in collars of iron and chains.[99] Whether it was because of the imprisonment of their chief and principal men or Spanish demands for women and porters, the people of Coosa revolted and fled to the woods. This included the people in the principal town and in the subsidiary towns. De Soto sent out four captains with detachments of men in four directions. They captured many men and women and put them in collars and chains.

Seeing the damage the Spaniards were able to inflict upon them, the people returned to their towns, saying they would do what was commanded of them. Most of those who were captured remained in chains. Upon the pleading of the chief, De Soto released some of the principal men. Some of the slaves were later able to file off their chains at night and escape, and some ran off in their chains when their guards were inattentive.[100]

Modern times have not been kind to sites of the towns of the paramount chiefdom of Coosa. The towns of Chiaha are now submerged under the waters of Douglas Lake, a lake that was constructed before the passage of federal legislation requiring archaeological research on sites that were to be destroyed. The towns of Tali, and most of the main town of Coste, now lie beneath Tellico Lake. Fortunately, many of the archaeological sites on the Little Tennessee River were excavated before the lake basin was flooded. The principal town of Coosa was excavated and now lies beneath Carter's Lake. Other sites have been destroyed by urban sprawl and by the depredations of pothunters.

8

Tascaluza

Since departing from Joara, De Soto had traveled toward the northwest and then the southwest, circling around toward Ochuse at Pensacola Bay, where he intended to rendezvous with Maldonado and be resupplied before winter.[1] When De Soto departed from Coosa, he had to leave behind Robles, a black slave who was too ill to walk. And perhaps because Robles was left behind, a Christian named Feryada, a Levantine, deserted from the expedition to live among the people of Coosa.[2]

South from Coosa

On August 20 De Soto and his army left Coosa and headed south (see map 6). Along the way, De Soto learned that Feryada had deserted and that he was back in Coosa saying that he preferred to remain among the Indians rather than to continue to submit to the insults and abuse of De Soto. De Soto tried to persuade the Indians who were with him to go back and fetch Feryada to him, but they would not.[3] In addition to the slaves and porters acquired at Coosa, De Soto forced the chief of Coosa, his sister, and some of his principal men to go along as hostages to insure the good behavior of the tributaries and allies included within the paramount chiefdom of Coosa. At the end of the first day of travel they passed through a large town, Talimachusi, which had been abandoned by its people. This was somewhere in the vicinity of present-day Pine Log. They bivouacked near a stream, at some distance beyond the town.[4]

Coosa lay just at the southern edge of the oak and chestnut forest (see map 4) that dominated the Blue Ridge Mountains and the southern reaches of the Ridge and Valley province. As the Spaniards traveled southward, they passed out of this forest of chestnuts, white oaks, and northern red oaks and reentered the oak-hickory-pine forest they had traveled through in middle Georgia and South Carolina. As they proceeded on their way, more and more pines grew among the deciduous trees, and in some places the pines predominated.

On August 21 they continued all day with the Blue Ridge Mountains on their left and the hills and ridges of the Ridge and Valley province on their right. They slogged through heavy rain as they traveled to Itaba, located at the Etowah archaeological site, on the outskirts of present-day Cartersville, Georgia.[5] Here they came to the Etowah River, which was running so high from all the rain they could not ford it. They had no choice but to remain in Itaba and wait for the water to subside.

In terms of the size of its mounds and the technical and artistic achievement of its artisans, the Etowah site (fig. 46) ranks among Mississippian archaeological sites below only the Cahokia site in Illinois and the Moundville site in Alabama. Etowah was in its heyday between about A.D. 1200 and 1350, when it was a town over fifty acres in size. At that time it was surrounded by a strong palisade with evenly spaced towers, and this palisade was surrounded by a

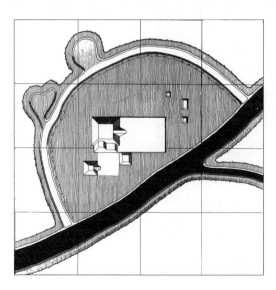

Fig. 46. Schematic map of the Etowah site. From William N. Morgan, *Prehistoric Architecture in the Eastern United States*, 116. (William N. Morgan, architect)

ditch that was in places as much as thirty feet wide and ten feet deep. The site is dominated by three large mounds built on the edge of a plaza. The largest of these mounds is about sixty feet high, with at least two subsidiary terraces off one side and a broad stairway leading up the front. Getting to the top of this mound is a test of the cardiovascular system of anyone who climbs it, particularly in the middle of a Georgia summer. Three smaller mounds in the domiciliary area of the site have fallen victim to the plow and are mostly obliterated. Today the State of Georgia maintains the Etowah site as a park with a visitors center.

From the objects that archaeologists have recovered from burials in and near the Etowah mounds, it is clear the site was a major center of culture and power in the Mississippian Southeast. The artisans at Etowah imparted their symbols and images to stone, copper, shell, and wood. Some of the most important and arresting images and objects of the Southeastern Ceremonial Complex have been excavated at the Etowah site. These include circular shell gorgets with sprightly figures of men with the beaks and wing feathers of raptorial birds, with antlers sprouting from their heads, with clawed hands, and with what seem to be reptilian elements here and there (fig. 47). It is not known whether these gorgets depict mythological creatures in archetypal form or living men dressed up in costume, playing the part of mythological beings. In either case, this is clearly a manifestation of the Southeastern fascination

Fig. 47. Shell gorget of antlered, winged, and bird-footed beings, wielding bi-pointed knives. (Frank H. McClung Museum, University of Tennessee)

Fig. 48. Repoussé copper plate representing a falcon warrior from the Etowah site. He wields a "mace" war club in his right hand, and he holds a severed human head in his left hand. (Smithsonian Institution)

with anomalous beings. On thin sheets of beaten native copper the artisans of Etowah fashioned repoussé depictions of men combined with falcon elements (fig. 48): the open beak, the half-folded wings, the rayed tail. These figures wield stylized war clubs and the severed heads of enemies. With these falcon warriors one can be more sure that they are depictions of men who are dressed in ritual garb, acting out the rapacious killing skills of the peregrine falcon. Warfare is also celebrated at Etowah in the form of very large bi-pointed knives chipped out of flint, war clubs hafted with copper celts, and war clubs with both the celt and handle sculpted out of stone. These are not weapons; rather, they are artistic celebrations of weapons.

The crowning artistic achievement of the people of the Etowah site is the statues of a male and a female carved out of Georgia marble (see fig. 7). The male sits with his feet in lotus position, wearing only a breechcloth, his body decorated with red and black pigment. The woman sits with her feet tucked modestly beneath her. She wears only a short skirt, and on her back she bears what appears to be either a highly stylized infant on a cradleboard or else a pack basket. Both of these sculptured personages stare imperiously at those who view them. These two statues are regarded by some as the finest artistic achievement of any native people north of Mexico.

The reigning chief at the Etowah site must surely have dominated the series of towns occupying known archaeological sites along about a ten-mile stretch of the Etowah River. And it is plausible to think that the influence, if not the actual power, of the chief must have once extended northward up the Ridge and Valley province, and eastward into the Piedmont. If paramount chiefdoms existed in the Middle Mississippian period, then Etowah was surely the seat of a paramount chief.

Etowah rose, and then Etowah fell. The reason for its fall is not known. The two statues, which must have occupied honored places in the town house on the mound, were at some point taken out and buried in the earth. The Etowah site may actually have been abandoned for much of the time between about A.D. 1350 and 1500. At this time the center of regional power in the Ridge and Valley province shifted northward to Coosa.

When De Soto and his army visited the Etowah site in 1540, a village of unknown size existed there, but if the army had not been impeded by high water, it is doubtful that Itaba would even have been mentioned. None of the chroniclers mentions the mounds, which, particularly if they were overgrown with trees and bushes, were not intrinsically interesting to the Spaniards. The chroniclers only mention, in the briefest way, that Itaba was subject to Coosa and that while here the Spaniards bought some women—possibly enslaved enemies—in exchange for some knives and mirrors.[6]

By August 30, nine days after they arrived, the Etowah River could be forded, and the Spaniards moved on. At the end of this day they came to an oak woods, where they bivouacked. The next day they continued on and met up with ten or twelve principal men of Ulibahali, armed with bows and arrows and resplendent in their feathers. They brought greetings from the chief of Ulibahali.[7]

The towns of Ulibahali lay along the Coosa River, from its head (where the Oostanaula River joins the Etowah River at Rome) downstream some fifteen miles to Foster's Bend. De Soto established camp a crossbow flight from one of the upper towns of Ulibahali, perhaps the one that lay at a site that is now beneath the tennis courts and parking lot of the Coosa Country Club. Then he rode into the town with twelve horsemen and a few footmen from his guard. De Soto found that all of the Indians in the town were armed, and from the way they behaved, he expected trouble. The town was palisaded like other towns they had seen earlier and would see later. The walls were made of thick logs the height of a lance, set close together vertically into the ground. Then many long poles were tied crosswise against these vertical posts, and the whole structure was plastered with clay both inside and out. At intervals there were archers' loopholes through the wall.[8]

De Soto ordered all of his men to arms, and taking the chief of Coosa with them, they entered the town cautiously. They found that the people of Ulibahali were ready to rise up and free their paramount chief if he should so order it. But consistent with the restraint shown in the northern and central towns of the paramount chiefdom, the chief of Coosa did not order them to fight, and in fact he told them to put down their arms.

They learned that the chief of Ulibahali was not to be found in the town they entered; he was at a town on the opposite side of the river, perhaps at a now-destroyed mound site that lay at the confluence of the Etowah and Oostanaula Rivers. De Soto sent word to him to come over and show himself, and he did so immediately. The two men exchanged pleasantries, and De Soto persuaded the chief of Ulibahali to supply porters and twenty women to be slaves.[9]

While they were in Ulibahali they realized that Manzano, a gentleman from Salamanca, was missing. Some said he was depressed. He had been lagging behind, and he had asked the others to leave him to be alone with himself. The Spaniards did not know whether he had absented himself from the expedition on purpose, or whether he had gotten lost.[10]

The Spaniards remained in Ulibahali on September 1. They had found some good grapes in Coosa, but it seemed to them that the ones around Ulibahali were even better. The principal wild grapes in this area are fox grape, frost grape, possum grape, summer grape, pigeon grape, and riverside grape.[11]

On September 2 they departed from Ulibahali, reaching a small village near the river, and the next day they traveled to a second village on the river, which was subject to the chief of Ulibahali. This was perhaps the village of Apica, visited twenty years later by members of the Tristán de Luna expedition. Along the way, Captain Juan Ruiz Lobillo learned that his negro slave, Joan Viscaíno, had deserted, and without asking De Soto's permission, Lobillo went back to look for him. De Soto remained in this second village on September 4, waiting for Lobillo to return, and when he did De Soto severely reprimanded him.[12]

This second village was in the general vicinity of the King site (fig. 49), a medium-size Mississippian town situated at Foster's Bend in the Coosa River. The culture of the people of the King site was the same variety of Lamar culture as that of the people of Ulibahali and Coosa. The King site was only occupied for about fifty years until it was destroyed, and as a consequence its structures

Fig. 49. Artist's reconstruction of life at the King site (Apica, "Piachi"?). Note the *barbacoas* positioned among the houses and the tall ceremonial pole in the center of the site. (Painting by Lloyd Kenneth Townsend, National Park Service)

had undergone little rebuilding. The King site, therefore, presents an exceptionally clear archaeological picture, with very little rebuilding of structures. Because the site has been extensively excavated, it provides us with an unusually complete picture of a De Soto-era village in the paramount chiefdom of Coosa.

The King site lay hard against the Coosa River and was surrounded on the land side by a palisade and a ditch. It had a central plaza, with a very large diameter post in its exact center. This post, which was presumably very tall, served as a symbolic center around which dances and rituals took place and where certain games were played. Inside the northeastern edge of the plaza were two large structures, which were the town house and the residence of the chief. There was no mound at the King site, but had the site been occupied by subsequent generations, it is quite likely that a mound would have been built on the site of the chief's house and town house, as old structures were razed and covered over, with new structures built on top of where the old ones stood.

The area between the plaza and the palisade was filled with domestic structures. These were square or rectangular wattle-and-daub houses with circular raised clay hearths in the center of the floor like those at Toqua. In among these were open-air barbacoa–summer house structures. The oldest and largest houses were built next to the plaza, and the smaller and more recent ones were built closer to the palisade. This progression of older, larger houses to newer, smaller ones may represent extended families that were expanding as the daughters married and their husbands moved from their natal houses to the houses of their wives. These clusters of houses often enclose small courtyards that may have been the microcosmic symbolic equivalents of village plazas. The archaeological evidence at the King site suggests that the people had definite plans in mind when they laid out their houses and towns, and in fact, both the houses and the towns were manifestations of the same symbolic scheme.[13]

On September 5 De Soto and his men headed southward, bivouacking at the end of the day in open country. The next day they came to Tuasi, possibly located at the junction of Terrapin Creek and Nance's Creek, in northern Alabama. They remained at this place for six days, during which time they were given porters and thirty-two Indian women.[14]

On September 13 they departed, continuing their march to the south, bivouacking near present-day Jacksonville, Alabama. The next day they again marched through open country and camped without shelter. On September 15 they came to an old village that had double palisades and good towers. The palisades were made like the one at Ulibahali, but built into them were towers and turrets spaced out at strategic distances, making a very strong defense.[15] This old village was in the vicinity of present-day Talladega.

On September 16 they arrived at a new village situated near a stream, probably upper Tallasseehatchee Creek. They rested at this place on September 17. The next day they arrived at the main town of Talisi, in the vicinity of present-day Childersburg, and they found that the chief and his people had fled the town. Talisi was a large town, located near a large stream, and elsewhere on the stream were other towns and many fields of corn. The supplies of corn were very abundant at Talisi.[16]

De Soto sent a message to the chief of Talisi ordering him to make an appearance. The chief came to see De Soto on September 25, and he cooperated in supplying the Spaniards with all they requested: deerskins, supplies, porters, and twenty-six or so women.[17] Once the chief of Talisi showed his obedience, De Soto released the chief of Coosa, but he refused to release the chief's sister. The chief went away in tears, angry because he had been taken so far from his homeland, and angry because De Soto would not release his sister.[18] It is doubtful that De Soto understood matrilineal descent (see fig. 1) and that this woman was quite likely the mother-to-be of the male next in line to be chief. Even if De Soto had understood this, he probably would not have cared. In any case, it is likely that the chief of Coosa would sooner have parted with his wife than with his sister.

De Soto had taken the chief of Coosa hostage to insure the good behavior of his subjects while the Spaniards traveled through their lands. The fact that he released the chief of Coosa at Talisi implies that De Soto perceived Talisi to be the southernmost chiefdom that was subject to or under the influence of Coosa. But just how closely Talisi was allied with Coosa is unclear. Talisi lay quite close to another native lord, Tascaluza, a man whose name the Spaniards would come to know very well. Talisi may have had dual alliances, playing a delicate balancing act between the two native lords, Coosa and Tascaluza.

While the Spaniards were at Talisi, Chief Tascaluza sent a party of emissaries to meet with De Soto. As these emissaries approached the town, De Soto ordered a contingent of horsemen to charge about and blow on trumpets to suitably impress them.[19] Among the emissaries was Chief Tascaluza's son, a boy of eighteen, who seemed a giant to the Spaniards. He was taller than any Spaniard in the entire army. The emissaries told De Soto that Tascaluza was ready to receive him and his army, and he wanted to know where they were going. They told De Soto that from Talisi there were two trails by which the army could reach Tascaluza. They suggested that he send out two Spaniards to go there by one trail and return by the other, so they could pick the trail that was most suitable. Chief Tascaluza would provide guides for them. De Soto agreed to this. One of the two Spaniards who undertook this mission was Juan de Villalobos, who was always the first to volunteer for any exploration.[20] De Soto gave the two instructions to spy on the Indians and bring back as much intelligence as possible.[21] What De Soto may not have known was that Tascaluza had sent his son as a spy, to learn what he could of the curious intruders.[22] As a peaceful gesture, De Soto gave the Indians some glass beads, which they appeared not to value highly, and he gave them some pieces of cloth to take to Chief Tascaluza.[23]

Atahachi

After resting in the central town of Talisi for eighteen days, the Spaniards departed on October 5 and proceeded south in the direction of the Gulf coast, presumably continuing their march toward Ochuse.[24] They came to Casiste, a pretty village alongside a stream, possibly in the vicinity of Sylacauga, and they spent the night there.[25] On October 6 they came to Caxa, a wretched village on a stream bank, perhaps Hatchet Creek, on the boundary between the territory of Talisi and the territory of Tascaluza.[26] On October 7 they bivouacked by the Coosa River (fig. 50), and on the far side of the stream there was a village named Humati, possibly near the mouth of Shoal Creek. On October 8 they arrived at a newly built village, Uxapita, in the vicinity of present-day Wetumpka. On October 9 they crossed the Tallapoosa River.[27] At the end of the day they bivouacked in open country, a league short of Atahachi, the town where Tascaluza lived, a recently built village in the vicinity of present-day Montgomery.[28] De Soto sent a messenger to Tascaluza informing him that he and his army had arrived, and in reply he got a message from Tascaluza saying he could come to hold court with him anytime he wished.[29]

The next day De Soto sent Luís de Moscoso to Atahachi to inform Tascaluza that the Spaniards were coming. Somewhat later, when the entire army reached the town, De Soto found Tascaluza waiting under the portico in front of his dwelling on top of a mound, at one side of the plaza.[30] A mat had been spread for him in front of his house, and Tascaluza went and seated himself on two cushions, one above the other, which had been placed there for him. He wore a beautifully made feather cloak that draped down to his feet, and on

Fig. 50. The Coosa River near lock number 12. Photograph by Roland Harper, February 1, 1913. (William Stanley Hoole Special Collections Library, University of Alabama)

his head he wore a cloth wrapped like the *almaizar* worn by Moors. He was a giant of a man, strong and very powerfully built, a half a yard taller than the Spaniards, who said he was as tall as Antonico, a gigantic guard of Charles V. Tascaluza was as tall as his son, but more strongly built.[31] To Juan Coles he seemed to have as much bone between his foot and his knee as an ordinary man had between his foot and his waist, and his eyes seemed as large as those of an ox.[32]

After Tascaluza seated himself, his retainers took their places about him, forming a kind of courtyard around where he sat. Men of highest social standing stood nearest him. One of these men, always beside him, held a circular sunshade on a long, slender pole. The shade was made of finely dressed deerskin, the size of a shield, and it had neatly painted on it a white cross on a black field. The Indian who held it did so with a ceremonious demeanor, and it was said to be carried as a kind of banner when Tascaluza went to war. This was probably a Mississippian equal-arm cross, perhaps in a circle (see figs. 31, 55). It reminded the Spaniards of the emblematic Maltese cross, also an equal-arm cross, which was prominently displayed by the militaristic Knights of Rhodes and Knights of Malta.[33]

Tascaluza was a powerful paramount chief who had many tributaries, and he was feared by his own subjects and by the people of chiefdoms on his borders.[34] Reserved and dignified in his demeanor, Tascaluza appears to have been ascending in power. He was making overtures to the people of Talisi, who were wavering in their allegiance to Coosa. Tascaluza was evidently not at war with Coosa, but he was expanding his power, and he had caused the people of Talisi to become discontent.[35]

There is no question that Tascaluza was a paramount chief, but the farthest extent of his power or influence is not known. Likewise, the cultural composition of his paramount chiefdom is not altogether clear. His name is almost certainly a Choctaw or western Muskogean word (i.e., *taska* plus *losa*) meaning "black warrior." But the *-hachi* "river, creek" ending of Atahachi would seem to be Creek, or some other eastern Muskogean language. Hence, Tascaluza's paramount chiefdom may have been multilingual, as were Coosa and Cofitachequi.

A dense cluster of protohistoric sites lay between about present-day Montgomery and the falls of the Tallapoosa River, and these must have constituted one of the major chiefdoms subject to Tascaluza. Perhaps it was the chiefdom over which he had his primary power. Events would soon prove that his power extended westward for some distance down the Alabama River. Eastward from Atahachi a dense cluster of protohistoric towns lay along the Chattahoochee River, but there is no way to know whether these towns constituted one or more independent polities or whether they might have been subject to or affiliated with Tascaluza.[36]

After Moscoso talked with Tascaluza, he mounted his horse and commanded his horsemen to gallop about in the plaza. They played at *juegos de cañas*, with teams of horsemen running at each other, jousting with cane lances, charging their horses from side to side, and sometimes feinting toward Tascaluza.[37] De Soto had used this same ploy in 1532, when he tried to intimidate the Inca Atahualpa at Cajamarca. And like Atahualpa, Tascaluza sat seemingly unconcerned, lifting his eyes occasionally to watch the spectacle of the horses, with an expression of contempt. When De Soto approached Tascaluza, the chief remained seated, with the composure of a king, still disdaining the Spaniards and hardly looking at De Soto as he approached. But De Soto took him by the hand and the two of them went and sat together in the shade of the portico.[38] Here they talked for a time, and then Tascaluza said the Spaniards should come and eat food that had been prepared for them. De Soto went with him, and Tascaluza's subjects came to dance in the plaza. These dances were a pleasing spectacle to the Spaniards, reminding them of the dances of rural people in Spain.[39]

Trouble began when De Soto demanded that Tascaluza provide him with porters and women. Tascaluza replied haughtily that he was not accustomed to serving anyone, but rather it was his expectation that all should serve him. With this, De Soto ordered that Tascaluza be taken hostage. Henceforth he would sleep in the house where De Soto slept, and he was not free to come and go as he pleased. Tascaluza expressed his displeasure and surprise at being treated in this manner, but seemingly acceding to it, he dismissed his principal men and remained in De Soto's company, in one of the elite houses inside the town.[40] Some of De Soto's men were quartered inside the town, and others were outside.[41]

The Spaniards began making preparations to move on from Atahachi. De Soto demanded that he be given porters and a hundred women. Tascaluza gave him four hundred porters, and he said he would give him the women when they reached the town of Mabila, where one of his principal vassals lived.[42] To reward Tascaluza for being cooperative, De Soto gave him a pair of boots and a long scarlet cloak, and he provided him with a horse to ride.[43] Even though the Indians were frightened of horses, Chief Tascaluza consented to ride one.[44] They had trouble finding a horse strong enough to carry Tascaluza. Finally they put him on one of De Soto's packhorses, but even on a packhorse his feet hung down to within a few inches of the ground.[45]

Mabila

They departed from Atahachi on October 12, with many principal men accompanying Tascaluza. As always, he was attended by the man who walked or stood behind him, holding his standard as a sunshade, and also by the man who carried his cushions.[46] They traveled along a trail paralleling the southern side of the Alabama River, and at the end of the day they bivouacked in the vicinity of present-day St. Clair.

Earlier, when they crossed the Tallapoosa River just before approaching Atahachi, they had taken their leave of the Piedmont hills. Now as they traveled toward Mabila along a trail paralleling the south side of the Alabama River, to their right they had lush southern floodplain vegetation of tupelo, oak, and bald cypress (see map 4). They had seen small forests like this previously, when they had crossed rivers in Georgia and South Carolina. To their left they began skirting (perhaps without knowing it) an unusual geological and soil zone that was to become famous during the heyday of the cotton plantation economy of the Old South—the Black Belt.

The geological formation that lies beneath the Black Belt is a crescent-shaped deposit of calcareous sediments as much as forty miles wide that begins in northern Mississippi and curves for two hundred miles southward and eastward, encircling the southern edge of the Ridge and Valley and Piedmont hills. This sediment, composed of tiny discs of calcium carbonate, as well as shellfish, was deposited in the bottom of a shallow, warm sea, over 100 million years ago. In places these deposits have compacted to form Selma chalk, a "rotten limestone" that weathers and erodes rapidly. In places the soil above this Selma chalk is formed from grassland humus, and thus has a very dark color. This soil contains a considerable amount of clay that bakes hard when it is dry but soaks up water when it is wet. After a rain this soil is very slippery, and it clings remarkably to anything that touches it. Walking through a stretch of rain-soaked Black Belt soil is an experience one does not soon forget.

The topography of the Black Belt is level to gently rolling. Black Belt soils on higher elevations are acidic, and they were originally covered with stands of oak, hickory, sweetgum, and a few pines, comparable to the forest cover of the Piedmont. But one of the things that made the Black Belt distinctive is that the soil at the lower elevations is alkaline and was covered by open tall-grass prairies. This prairie was mainly composed of grasses, as well as a host of colorful summer and fall wildflowers. Glades of fragrant, rot-resistant cedar grew on the edges of these prairies, and vast canebrakes grew along the rivers and creeks. Some of these prairies were quite large in size and very distinctive, and many Europeans took note of them in the eighteenth and early nineteenth centuries.

The original soils of the Black Belt were very rich, and they were ideal for growing cotton. Particularly after 1830, when the cotton planters devised ways of farming the clays, the Black Belt became the center of cotton growing in Alabama. Cultivation was intense, and because of unenlightened management practices, erosion was particularly severe in this region. In some places today all of the Black Belt topsoil is gone, leaving only the sterile white Selma chalk (fig. 51). Virtually nothing of the original vegetation of the Black Belt prairies remains. Here and there the grasses and wildflowers can be seen on the edges of fields and highway margins, but in recent decades the systematic spraying of herbicides has reduced even this. Virtually all of the original stands of timber have been cut down, and because of the erosion and exposure of chalk, pines and particularly cedars now dominate areas where they did not originally grow.[47]

On October 13 the army came to Piachi, a village situated high above the

Fig. 51. Black Belt topography. The white areas in the prairies are outcroppings of calcareous sediments. This location is about one mile north of Emelle, Alabama. Photograph by Roland Harper, February 27, 1913. (William Stanley Hoole Special Collections Library, University of Alabama)

gorge of a very large, cliff-lined river—the Alabama—in the general vicinity of Durant Bend or Selma.[48] The Alabama River has cut through the soft Selma chalk, and in some places the banks of the river are sheer faces of chalk as much as a hundred feet high (fig. 52). The Spaniards incorrectly deduced that this river flowed into Pensacola Bay (i.e., Ochuse). At Piachi they were shown a dagger that had belonged to Don Teodoro, a member of the Pánfilo de Narváez expedition, who had gone ashore with a black man in search of drinking water as they were attempting to sail to Mexico in their crude boats.[49] De Soto learned that Don Teodoro and the black man had been killed.[50]

The Spaniards began seeing signs of resistance on the part of the Indians of Piachi. When De Soto demanded that he be provided with canoes in which to cross the river, the chief of Piachi told him he had no canoes—obviously a ploy to slow them down. The Spaniards would have to build rafts. They spent October 14 and 15 making rafts out of dry wood and cane, and because there was little current in the river, they were all able to get across without incident.[51]

After they had crossed the river, a Spaniard left the encampment to look for an Indian woman who had run away.[52] And Juan de Villalobos, who liked to go out and explore the country, was also found to be missing.[53] Both of these

Fig. 52. Sheer chalk cliffs lining the Alabama River near Selma. Photograph by Roland Harper. (William Stanley Hoole Special Collections Library, University of Alabama)

men may have been killed by the Indians. De Soto demanded that Tascaluza order that these two men be returned to the army, or else he would burn him at the stake.[54] Several of the principal men traveling with Tascaluza left the expedition at this point.[55] Tascaluza promised De Soto that the missing men would be returned to him when they reached Mabila.[56] Other Indians who were asked about the missing men were more defiant. They asked sarcastically whether they were supposed to be the Spaniards' keepers.[57]

Soon after crossing the river, perhaps on October 14 or 15, Tascaluza sent a messenger to Mabila, ostensibly to let the people know the Spaniards were coming and to prepare to receive and feed them and to provide them with porters and women. De Soto sent Gonzalo Quadrado Xaramillo and Diego Vázquez to Mabila to scout out the situation there.[58]

On October 16 De Soto and his men departed from the river and marched into a woods, where they bivouacked at the end of the day. They were in the vicinity of present-day Selma, Alabama. Sometime during the course of this day, Diego Vázquez returned from Mabila with the news that many armed Indians had gathered there. On October 17 they came to a palisaded town, not far from Mabila, and there they spent the night. It is possible that De Soto expected there would be trouble ahead, and he wished to rest his men and horses so they would be fresh the next day. Many Indian messengers came from Mabila to the palisaded village to see Tascaluza, and they brought him an abundance of cornbread flavored with the chestnuts that abounded in Tascaluza's territory.[59]

De Soto and his men must have arisen early on Monday, October 18. De Soto led the way to Mabila with a vanguard of forty horsemen.[60] He also had with him his guard of crossbowmen and halberdiers, several footmen, as well as a friar, a secular priest, a cook, and several slaves and porters.[61] As they marched along on this day they passed by several small villages and habitations. Mabila was a fertile land, with several large palisaded towns.[62] The houses were scattered about over the land at one or two crossbow flights from each other.[63] It was a settlement pattern that was reminiscent of the pattern they had seen at Apalachee. As they marched along, many of the soldiers lagged behind to forage for food and whatever else they could find. Captain André de Vasconcelos and the rear guard lagged far behind.[64] Even though they had been warned that the Indians might be preparing for a battle, few of them appear to have taken the warning seriously. After all, no Indians had waged war upon them since they had left Apalachee.[65]

De Soto and his advance guard arrived at the outskirts of Mabila at about nine o'clock in the morning.[66] Mabila was a small, strongly stockaded village situated in a cleared field.[67] The palisade around Mabila was built out of thick posts set side by side in the ground. Both inside and outside this row of posts, smaller and more flexible poles were bound crosswise with strips of split cane and fiber cordage. The whole of it was plastered over with a mixture of mud and straw, filling up all the cracks. This coating was quite hard. Spaced at intervals of about fifty feet, the palisade had bastions that were each capable of holding seven or eight fighting men. The wall itself had embrasures at a man's height, through which archers could shoot their arrows. Two gates led into the town, one to the east and one to the west.[68] A plaza was located in the center of the town, with the houses of the most important people encircling it. One of these houses had been reserved for De Soto and a second one for his servants and equipage.[69]

De Soto paused for a short time while outside the town. Gonzalo Quadrado Xaramillo, whom De Soto had previously sent to reconnoiter the town, came out and told him it seemed to him the Indians were preparing for battle.[70] He had seen many Indians gather in the town, and many weapons had been brought in. Also the Indians had worked rapidly at strengthening the palisade, and of the Indians who were to be seen at Mabila, none of them were old, and none were servants—all were young warriors and men of status. Several women were inside, but all were young, and no children were to be seen. To say the least, these demographics suggested to Xaramillo that it was not a normal population. For the distance of a crossbow shot around the town, the Indians had cleared away all growth, even pulling weeds out of the ground.[71] They had also torn down several houses that lay within this area.[72] Finally, on several mornings the Indians had been seen to go out into the field to drill with a leader who harangued them before they engaged in military exercises and skirmishes.[73]

A number of principal men came out and asked De Soto whether he and his men would like to remain outside in the open field, in crude shelters they had built, or whether they would like to enter the town. They said that in the evening the Spaniards would be given the porters they had requested.[74] Luís de Moscoso counseled De Soto to bivouac outside the town, but De Soto said he was tired of sleeping out in the open and he would sleep inside.[75] The primary reason De Soto went inside the town was to show that he was not intimidated.[76]

As De Soto approached the town, the chief of Mabila came out to meet him, accompanied by many Indians singing and playing on flutes. De Soto and his men halted at one of the gates in the palisade. The horsemen tethered their horses there, and the footmen and Indian slaves placed their knapsacks and bundles near the palisade. The chief presented De Soto with three mantles made of "marten skins."[77] Then De Soto went inside with three or four of his horsemen who had dismounted, seven or eight of his guard, and a few others.[78] All were on foot.

Inside they found a plaza surrounded by large houses with thatched roofs. De Soto seated himself under a portico.[79] There were about three or four hundred people in view, and the Indians, seemingly rejoicing, immediately began dancing and singing for the Spaniards.[80] The Spaniards walked about, talking with the people. Afterward they were entertained by fifteen or twenty unusually beautiful young women who danced and distracted the Spaniards.[81]

While this spectacle was unfolding, Tascaluza told De Soto he was tired of marching with the Spaniards, and he wished to remain in Mabila while De Soto continued on. But De Soto let him know he did not intend to leave him behind. Then Tascaluza asked to be permitted to speak to some chiefs, and he got up from where he was sitting with De Soto and went with them into one of the large houses on the edge of the plaza.[82]

When Tascaluza did not come back out of the house, De Soto sent Juan Ortiz to call him out. The Indians denied him entrance to the house, but Ortiz sent the message in by an Indian.[83] Tascaluza replied that he would not come out and that De Soto should leave Mabila in peace. If he did not, Tascaluza and his allies would force him to leave.[84] De Soto tried to talk to Tascaluza, but he remained inside the house and was silent.[85]

Attack

De Soto sent Baltasar de Gallegos into the house to force Tascaluza to come outside. When Gallegos stepped just inside the door, he saw that the house was full to the loft with armed men, ready for battle.[86] Gallegos shouted alarm. De Soto put on his helmet and ordered his horsemen to get to their horses and warn the soldiers outside.

De Soto called out to a principal Indian, clad in a "marten skin" robe, who was entering the door of the house where Tascaluza was. He asked him to tell Tascaluza he could remain behind if he would supply the Spaniards with a guide and porters. The man haughtily replied he would not do it.[87] Gallegos grabbed this man by the arm, but the man pushed him away. Gallegos then seized his robe, but the man let it slip over his head, freeing himself. Gallegos slashed out with his sword and cut off one of the man's arms.[88]

With this, all the Indians rose up with a roar and began to fight. There were perhaps five thousand warriors hidden inside the town.[89] Those who were in the house attacked Gallegos, who stood just inside. Luís de Moscoso was at the door of the house to give Gallegos support. As Moscoso fought the Indians at the door, he shouted for Gallegos to come out, else he would have to leave him alone.[90] The Indians poured out from the other houses, firing arrows, while those inside the houses shot through loopholes they had made in the walls.[91] The Indians quickly blocked the gates of the palisade. Trapped inside were De Soto, Moscoso, Gallegos, Espindola, and seven or eight others.[92]

A young Indian of about eighteen came out of the house where Tascaluza was and fixed his eyes on Gallegos. He quickly fired six or seven arrows at Gallegos, but when he saw that the arrows did not penetrate his armor, he rushed over swinging his bow and struck several blows on his helmet so hard that blood ran down his forehead. Gallegos stabbed the boy twice in the chest with his sword, killing him. De Soto's men surmised that this young man must have been the son of the man who smart-talked De Soto and whom Gallegos had killed.[93]

Taken by surprise, De Soto and his men began retreating from the town, fighting as they ran. They had to abandon their Indian porters and the baggage they had been carrying.[94] De Soto could see that if he ordered his horsemen to come inside the town, the Indians would be able to kill the horses from their positions inside the houses.[95] The Indians quickly killed five of the Spaniards who were inside the palisade. All the others who were in the town, including De Soto, were wounded. De Soto fell to the ground two or three times while running for the gate, but those who were near him helped him to his feet. Along with two of his men, De Soto reached the gate.[96] All of them had been wounded, some of them severely. A great number of Indians were pursuing and striking at them with war clubs. De Soto shouted to all his men outside the town to fall back from the palisade.[97]

Not all the horsemen had time to mount their horses. Some did, but others only had time to cut their horses loose so they could get away. A few of the horses were still tethered when the Indians spilled out of the gate.[98]

Several horsemen rode up to the gate as De Soto and two of his guard came out. The first of these horsemen were Solis and Rodrigo Rangel. Solis was killed immediately. But Rangel was able to hold back some seventy Indians at the gate of the town while De Soto ran to his horse, which was brought to him by a black man.[99]

De Soto ordered Rangel to ride over and give aid to the other two—the captain of his guard and a soldier of the guard—who were wounded and were being pressed very hard by the Indians. Rangel rode over, created a diversion, and the two men were able to escape. Then De Soto ordered Rangel to prevent the Indians from dragging Solis's body inside the gate.[100] Afterward, De Soto pulled out more than twenty arrows that had lodged in Rangel's quilted cotton armor. Luís de Moscoso, Baltasar de Gallegos, and several footmen escaped through the other gate of the town.[101]

Once outside the gate the Indians immediately killed the horses that were still tethered there.[102] Others led the chained Indian porters inside the palisade, removed their chains, and thrust bows and arrows into their hands.[103] Some of these porters took weapons from the packs De Soto's advance guard had been carrying, and others took up the swords and halberds of fallen Spaniards.[104] They also seized the Spaniards' baggage and supplies, which had been placed against the outside of the palisade and in the field next to the palisade.[105] They carried all this gear inside and secured the entrances. They emptied out the bundles, and standing on top of the palisade, held their contents aloft, as if to say, "What was yours is now ours." They raised flags and began beating on drums and shouting.[106]

Not only had the Indians of Mabila dealt De Soto's guard a serious military blow, they had captured many of the Spaniards' possessions—clothing, ornaments, food, and all that was necessary for Christian communion: three bushels of wheat, chalices, and wafer molds. They also captured De Soto's precious pearls.[107] The only articles the Spaniards possessed that were not taken by the Indians were carried by the contingent of horsemen and footmen under the command of Captain André de Vasconcelos, who lagged behind on the trail to Mabila.[108]

Not all of De Soto's people were able to escape from Mabila. When the hostilities broke out several were trapped inside a house: a friar, a priest, a cook, some pages, some Christian women who were slaves belonging to De Soto, and perhaps some footmen.[109] Fighting to save themselves, they barred the entrance to the house with a lattice door, and when the Indians tried to break in, they brandished what weapons they had. The only sword they had among them was owned by one of De Soto's servants. He stood on one side of the door, and the priest and the friar, armed with clubs, stood on the other side.[110] When the Indians saw that they could not come through the door without being injured, they began to tear open a portion of the roof, but they soon aborted their attack, perhaps assuming they could return later, at their leisure, and capture or kill those who were inside.[111]

The Spaniards could only estimate how many Indians were inside the palisade. Biedma, who is probably to be trusted, said there were fully five thousand—a large but not unreasonable number.[112] Garcilaso, who almost always overestimates, sets the figure at six or seven thousand.[113]

De Soto got all his surviving horsemen together in the open field that lay before the main gate of the town.[114] They rode toward the Indians who had positioned themselves in front of the gate, and then, pretending to be frightened of them, galloped away. The Indians, believing their flight to be genuine, ran after them, shooting arrows. But then the horsemen wheeled about and charged the Indians, lancing many of them as they chased them back into the town. As the horsemen approached the palisade, they met a great barrage of arrows and stones.[115] Don Carlos Enríquez charged almost to the gate itself, where his horse was hit in the chest by an arrow, making it impossible for the animal to make a turn.[116] Don Carlos shifted his lance from his right hand to his left, leaned down beside his horse's neck, and tried to pull the arrow out. But in so doing, he exposed his neck, and an arrow struck him there, just above his shoulder, and he fell from his horse. He was pulled from the fray by his companions, but died the next day.[117] The death of Don Carlos saddened the others because they had held him in such high regard, and the more so because of his role among them as a peacemaker and a mediator.[118]

After the horsemen had taken their first toll on the Indians, only the most courageous warriors dared to come out of the palisade. They would run out the distance of a stone's throw but quickly ran back when the horsemen approached.[119] They fought this way for a long time.[120]

While this skirmishing was going on, the Dominican friar, Juan de Gallegos, rode up, trying to give his horse to his brother, Baltasar de Gallegos, who was fighting on foot. But Baltasar was in the thick of the fight, so that even though Juan rode back and forth several times, he could not reach the place where his brother was. Finally an Indian singled him out, took aim, and shot an arrow at him. The arrow struck him in the back, but because it had to penetrate two cowls he was wearing, as well as a felt hat he wore slung over his back, it only wounded him slightly.[121] After this the good friar thought it prudent to put more distance between himself and the Indians.

At the end of this round of fighting, the Indians realized they could not win against the Spanish horsemen, and from this time on none of them sallied out to fight. The Indians inside the palisade, seeing the seriousness of their situation, urged Tascaluza to flee. At first he refused, but they pressed him to do so. Then, with fifteen or twenty of his men, he attempted an escape.[122] Whether he was successful is not known, but it is doubtful.[123] Meanwhile, the Indians closed off the entrances and took up positions around the palisade.[124]

Counterattack

As the battle raged, the main body of De Soto's army and some of his rear guard reached the town. De Soto divided up his men into four squadrons. Included among these were sixty of his horsemen, who wore the best armor; De Soto ordered them to dismount and fight with the footmen in storming the palisade.[125] He then put less well-armored footmen on the horses and ordered them to surround the town and to lance any Indian who tried to escape.[126]

De Soto sent these squadrons against the four sides of the town. In each squadron he had a soldier with a firebrand to set fire to the houses.[127] At the sound of an arquebus shot, the squadrons simultaneously attacked the gates and the palisade, cutting through the clay and straw mortar with axes to expose the wood. Once the horizontal beams were exposed, the Spaniards could help each other climb up and over the palisade, enter the town, and set fire to the houses, which had highly flammable thatched roofs. Realizing that their fortification had been penetrated, the Indians fought furiously, some battling in the streets and others from the roofs of the houses, and several times they drove the Spaniards out of the town. But each time the Spaniards fought their way back.

When Captain Diego de Soto, nephew of Hernando, learned that his brother-in-law, Don Carlos Enríquez, had been mortally wounded by the Indians, he jumped down from his horse and, armed with a round shield and a sword, entered the town seeking revenge. Rashly entering the thick of the battle, he was immediately struck in the eye with an arrow, which penetrated through the back of his skull. As Soto lay dying, Alonso de Carmona placed his knee on his head and tried with all his might to pull the arrow out, but he could not.[128] Hernando de Soto was greatly distressed by his nephew's death.[129]

Many of the Spaniards, weary and thirsty from the fighting, went to a "pond," located near the palisade, where they drank. As they did so, the water in this pond became tinged red with the blood of the dead and wounded.[130]

When the Spaniards began their assault on the palisade, some of the Indians renewed their attack on the Spaniards who were trapped there inside one of the houses. They tore three or four holes in the roof, but the people inside kept them at bay until some of De Soto's soldiers fought their way to the house and got them out, though two footmen were lost in the effort.[131]

After the houses of Mabila had been set on fire, De Soto and Nuño de Tovar quit the fighting, ran out and got on their horses, and then rode recklessly back into the town shouting the names of Our Lady and the Apostle Santiago. Calling out to the soldiers to make way for them, they rode from one side of the town to another, and then rode back through again, lancing many Indians. At one point, when De Soto raised up in his stirrups to make a thrust with his lance, an arrow found its mark in the narrow space between his cuirass and saddle, penetrating deeply into his left buttock. De Soto had to fight the remainder of the battle standing up in his stirrups.[132] In this same action, an Indian's arrow completely pierced the ash lance held by Nuño de Tovar, as if it had been drilled by an auger, so that the arrow shaft formed a cross with the shaft of the lance.[133]

As the house fires grew larger and became hotter, they began taking a toll. The flames and smoke blew this way and that, sometimes to the detriment of the Spaniards and sometimes to the detriment of the Indians. Some of the Indians attempted to escape from the town, but the Spaniards outside were quick to drive them back inside.[134] The Indians fighting from the rooftops sometimes fell into the burning buildings, or else they were forced to jump down into the streets. Some of the Indians, desperate to escape the swords and halberds in the streets, ran into the burning buildings to their deaths. In the flames of the houses, bodies were heaped upon one another. Many women died in the fires.[135] Some of the Indians again attempted to flee from the town, and an unknown number of them succeeded.

By about four o'clock in the afternoon, after the battle had been raging for some seven hours, few of the Indian men were in any condition to fight. Some of the surviving women picked up weapons and began fighting alongside the men. Some used swords, halberds, and lances that had fallen from the hands of the Spanish soldiers. It seemed that some of the women were fighting in order to be killed, this being preferable to enslavement. The women fought fiercely, and even four-year-old boys tried to join the fight. Some of the Indians hung themselves on their bowstrings to prevent being captured.[136]

Some of the rear guard did not reach Mabila until late afternoon. Seeing the smoke rising from the town, they guessed what was happening and hastened to join the last of the battle.[137] Toward sunset the fighting was still going on. Ten or twelve horsemen entered the town to sweep up the remaining resistance. One group of men and women still fought with utmost desperation. All of them were killed, because none of them would surrender.[138]

Finally, only three Indian men were left alive. They joined up with some survivors of the twenty young women who had danced to entertain the Spaniards. Standing in front of the three men, the women crossed their hands, a gesture indicating they were surrendering and the Spaniards should come and get them. But as the Spaniards approached, the young women moved aside and the three men began firing arrows. The Spaniards quickly killed two of them. The third climbed up the palisade, where he could see the Spaniards surrounding the town—escape was impossible. Climbing into a tree that had been left growing in the palisade, he removed the cord from his bow, tied one end about his neck, and hung himself from a limb.[139]

After the Battle

According to Garcilaso, the battle lasted for nine hours, ending as night began to fall.[140] Everything inside the town had burned to the ground.[141] All the Spanish baggage and equipment the Indians had carried inside the town burned also. This included much of the Spaniards' clothing, the nine *arrobas* (about 225 pounds) of pearls from Cofitachequi, the sacramental chalices, wafer molds, and wine for saying the mass.[142]

The most accurate account of the casualties in the battle is probably that of Rangel. After the battle, De Soto must have assessed the damage that had been done to his army, and Rangel was his secretary. According to Rangel, 22 Spaniards had been killed, and 148 were wounded. Altogether they sustained a total of 688 wounds, with many of them wounded more than once. In addition, 7 horses had been killed and 29 were wounded.[143] Among the dead were Don Carlos Enríquez, Captain Diego de Soto, Juan de Gamez de Jaen, Mem Rodríguez (a Portuguese who had served in Africa), Velez, Espinosa, and Juan Vázquez de Barcarrota.[144] All the other casualties were footmen.

Many of the slain Spaniards had been shot in the face, one of the few exposed parts of their bodies. Others had been wounded in the elbow, knee, or ankle. Still others had wounds to the thighs, buttocks, or the fleshy parts of their legs or arms.[145]

The Indians at Mabila suffered a terrible loss of life. Rangel says the Spaniards killed three thousand Indians in Mabila, not counting those who were wounded and later died. After the battle, when the Spaniards began sending forays out into the countryside, they found many Indians dead on the roads and in the houses in the surrounding vicinity.[146] Elvas puts the number of Indian dead at about twenty-five hundred.[147] The son of Tascaluza was found lanced to death. Some said Chief Tascaluza escaped, while others said he died in the fire.[148]

The Indians at Mabila had made two serious miscalculations. They had failed to comprehend the terrible advantage that defensive armor and the horse conferred on the Spaniards. The only defense against the horse in that era was the pike, which the Indians possessed, but they did not possess the knowledge or discipline to stand fast until the horses came within range.[149] They would fight from a distance with bow and arrow, but when a mounted soldier charged at them, they would turn and run, and the mounted soldiers could easily lance them.[150]

The second serious error they made was in thinking that the palisade at Mabila was invulnerable. When they realized they could not prevail against horsemen, they had to depend upon the strength of their palisade. But when the Spaniards succeeded in breaching the palisade, the warriors found themselves too crowded together to fight effectively, costing them their tactical advantage—speed and maneuverability.[151] This was why many of them tried to fight the Spaniards from the rooftops.

The women who survived the battle were divided up among the Spaniards as slaves. From these women, the Spaniards obtained information on some of the events that preceded the battle. Some of the slaves said Tascaluza had planned to destroy De Soto's army when he had first learned of its existence.[152] He had planned the surprise attack at Mabila for a long time.[153] He had sent his son and others to Talisi under the pretext of assisting De Soto, but in reality they were sent as spies to try to detect the Spaniards' vulnerabilities.[154]

Moreover, the Spaniards learned that the people of Talisi had complained to Tascaluza that the chief of Talisi had handed over some of his people to the Spaniards as slaves. One wonders on what basis the chief of Talisi (and other chiefs before and after him) selected men and women to be given over to De Soto. Tascaluza promised the people of Talisi he would not only rescue their people from their Spanish captors but also give them captured Spaniards to serve as slaves.[155]

The women said they had come to Mabila at the prompting of their husbands and brothers. Some were promised Spanish cloth. Others were promised Spaniards as slaves. Some were told they would be given horses, and they would be able to ride these horses in front of the Spaniards, humiliating them. Some were urged to come and see how valiant their husbands and lovers would be in battle, and still others were told that after the Spaniards had been defeated, there would be a great festival as an offering to their god, the Sun.[156]

Finally, the women said that most of them were not natives of Mabila, nor of Tascaluza's chiefdom, but were members of neighboring chiefdoms.[157] Did the Indians from further down the Alabama River take part? Even though the precise location of Mabila has not been established, there is no disagreement that it lay on the north side of the Alabama River, somewhere downstream from Durant's Bend. Archaeologists have established that an extensive series of protohistoric sites lay between Durant's Bend and Mobile Bay. If the same organizational constraints that prevailed elsewhere in the Southeast also prevailed along the Alabama River, there was room for more than one chiefdom in this area. It is reasonable to think that some of the towns and mound centers on the river from Wilcox County northward were members of the same chiefdom as Mabila. In 1559–60 Tristán de Luna traveled to the town of Nanipacana located on the Alabama River in Wilcox or southwestern Dallas County. It was obvious to people who were with Luna that Nanipacana was less than it had been formerly—some houses were "destroyed"—and the people explained that their decline had been caused by Spaniards who had come there earlier (i.e., De Soto). It is reasonable to think that men from these towns participated in the battle at Mabila.[158]

A contingent of Luna's soldiers traveled from Nanipacana to Atahachi (they called it Atache), to Talisi, to Ulibahali, and to Coosa. The fact that Luna's men have so very little to say about Atahachi and other towns along the lower Tallapoosa River implies that these towns had been impacted by the battle. More interestingly, Luna's men had very little to say about Talisi, perhaps implying that the people of Talisi were some of the outsiders who fought at Mabila. And what of the people of the middle and upper towns of the paramount chiefdom of Coosa? Certainly they had grievances with the Spaniards over the way they had been bullied by them from Chiaha southward. Some indications that warriors from the northern towns participated in the battle come to us from the Pardo expeditions. In 1567, when Pardo reached the Little Tennessee River (upstream from Tali), he was told that Spaniards had been there previously (i.e., De Soto), and that the chief of Satapo and his subjects had killed some of them. Additional confirmation comes from Juan de Ribas, who went with Pardo, and who testified in 1600 that he had seen Spanish arms, mail, and clothing at Satapo. Since none of these items were likely to have been given or traded to the Indians, the scavenging of a battlefield is a possible source.

Ribas also claimed he had learned from Almeydo, a Portuguese who had gone with Pardo, that De Soto had taken away the daughter of a chief on a horse, and she had been beaten with a stick, and the chief who was her father had attacked and "killed" De Soto. This is secondhand testimony and dates to twenty years after the event. We can only wonder whether it was a somewhat garbled memory of De Soto taking away the sister of the chief of Coosa.[159]

The day after the battle, October 19, the Spaniards buried their dead and attended the wounded as best they could. They had lost all their medical supplies, such as unguents and bandages. De Soto had only one doctor, and he was not especially skillful, so most of the men had to treat themselves and each other. The wounded were placed in the huts that the Indians, in the show of hospitality that preceded the battle, had built outside the town for the Spaniards to use. The Spaniards now tore some of these down and used the materials to make lean-tos against sections of the palisade that were still standing.[160] For unguents to treat their wounds, they cut fat from the bodies of dead Indians. For bandages, they tore up the shirts of dead Spaniards. They divided up the captured women to serve those who were most grievously wounded. They butchered the dead horses for food.[161]

While their wounds were healing, those who were able foraged in the many towns in the vicinity of Mabila, where they were able to find sufficient food. Some of these towns were palisaded, while in others the houses were scattered out at a distance of a crossbow shot or two from each other.[162] According to Garcilaso, they foraged within a radius of four leagues.[163] This is about the distance to which cavalry could comfortably travel and return in a single day. They could have foraged to the north as far as Selma. Up the Cahaba River they could have gone to about the mouth of Oakmulgee Creek; and to the south, down the Alabama River to about the mouth of Bear Creek.

Within this four-league area, they found many wounded people inside their houses, but seemingly there was no one around to attend to them. The Spaniards concluded that the Indians were hiding in the woods, and they only came into the houses and villages at night to take care of the wounded. They attempted to capture some Indians from whom to obtain information, but for all their efforts, they only succeeded in rounding up fifteen or twenty. They asked them if there were Indians in the area who were planning another attack on the Spaniards. Their prisoners said no—all of the most valiant warriors were dead. And in fact, while the Spaniards remained at Mabila, they were never attacked again.[164] Nonetheless, the Spaniards burned much of the country.[165]

Before the battle occurred, De Soto had received word that ships, presumably captained by Diego Maldonado and Gómez Arias, were waiting for him at Ochuse.[166] This information was confirmed by some of the Indians they captured after the battle. They learned from the Indians that the port of Ochuse was about 40 leagues distant.[167] The actual distance was about 136 miles, or 39.4 leagues.

Before the battle, De Soto appears to have favored a plan of colonization that would have established a colony at the port of Ochuse, thus providing safe haven to Spanish ships. He may also have planned to found another town at some distance inland, where the Indians could be missionized.[168] Certainly this was a part of Tristán de Luna's plan of colonization twenty years later.[169] The battle at Mabila caused De Soto to jettison this plan, although the failure thus far to find silver or gold might also have figured into his decision.[170]

De Soto told Juan Ortiz to keep secret from the men the news of the ships at Ochuse, because he knew they would want to go to Ochuse and end the expedition. Also, he did not want Maldonado to know his whereabouts. He had wanted to send the pearls back to Cuba as evidence that the land contained riches, but when the pearls were destroyed in the fire, he could show no evidence of wealth, and this would deter other Spaniards from wanting to settle in De Soto's country.[171]

But De Soto could not keep the news of the ships from the men. They learned of it and wanted very much to go to Ochuse.[172] The fierceness with which the Indians of Mabila had fought had led some of the Spaniards to think it would be impossible to subjugate such free and bellicose people. They would die before they would be enslaved.[173] The Spaniards had suffered a total of 102 deaths up to this point—1 in 6 of their number.[174] Some of the men talked of going back to Peru or Mexico or even back to Spain, where they would not have to struggle so hard.

Rumors of this talk reached De Soto. He investigated and found the sentiment widespread. Even his treasurer, Juan Gaytán, was talking this way. De Soto realized that if his men learned how to get to Ochuse, his army might disintegrate. If that happened, he would never lead another. He would be ruined and so would the men who had invested everything to come with him to seek their fortunes.[175]

It was at this point that De Soto released the Indian whom Maldonado had captured months earlier at Ochuse.[176] This man had gone with De Soto and his army all the way from Apalachee to Mabila. Presumably, he now returned to his home.

This near mutiny marked a turning point for De Soto. His plan to found a colony was falling apart. He was angry at his men and fearful of failure, but he concealed these feelings as he began to lay plans to continue the expedition. From this time forward, he was a changed man. He ceased asking the counsel and advice of others. He was embittered. He may have seen death as the only acceptable outcome left for him, and he may have been willing to take everyone else down with him. He began to waste the lives of both the Indians and his own men.[177] How De Soto rallied his army and got them on the move again is not known. It was cold at that time of year, and perhaps he told them that to the south, toward Ochuse, food was scarce because, as they had learned on their march northward from Apalachee, the coastal plain was thinly populated. Perhaps he convinced them that their only chance of surviving the winter was to go toward the north.[178]

One of the most crucial problems in establishing the archaeological picture of the route of De Soto's expedition is the location of the site of Mabila. One would assume that a human tragedy of the proportions of the battle at Mabila would leave an easily discovered stain on the face of the land. But such is not the case. The general location for Mabila that fits most of the evidence now available is the vicinity of the lower Cahaba River. Mabila may, in fact, have been located at Old Cahawba, the site of the first capital of Alabama. The capital was located at the mouth of the Cahaba River, but because of its vulnerability to flooding, the site was soon abandoned in favor of Montgomery. Later on this same site the Confederates built a prison for holding Union prisoners. Historical records indicate that a prehistoric mound once stood on the site, and archaeologists have determined that the mound was surrounded by a palisade and ditch and that the site was occupied in the sixteenth century. But only limited excavations inside the palisade at Old Cahawba have been carried out so far.[179]

9

Chicaza

On November 14 De Soto and his army departed from Mabila, heading toward the north (map 7).[1] The men suffered greatly as they marched through a wilderness with a cold rain falling. They only carried a two-day supply of corn with them, so they were hungry as well.[2] They probably followed a trail paralleling present-day Highway 14, skirting the edge of the Piedmont hills. On November 17 they came to a handsome river—the Black Warrior—just south of present-day Eutaw, Alabama. The Spaniards, and presumably the Indians, called it the River of Apafalaya.[3]

They were approaching the southern end of the Moundville archaeological complex, one of the most spectacular Mississippian developments in the entire Southeast. The Moundville chiefdom developed along a thirty-mile stretch of the Black Warrior River, from just downriver from present-day Tuscaloosa, at the fall line, to just northeast of present-day Eutaw. The people who lived in this area had access to an unusually varied environment. What was of greatest importance to the Moundville people was the lush floodplain, varying from about three to five miles wide, that lay along the Black Warrior. This floodplain was covered in bald cypress, sweetgum, holly, black gum, and other hardwoods; it was abundant in edible seeds, fruits, and tubers. Its shallow

Map 7. De Soto's route from Apafalaya to Guachoya, 1540–1542.

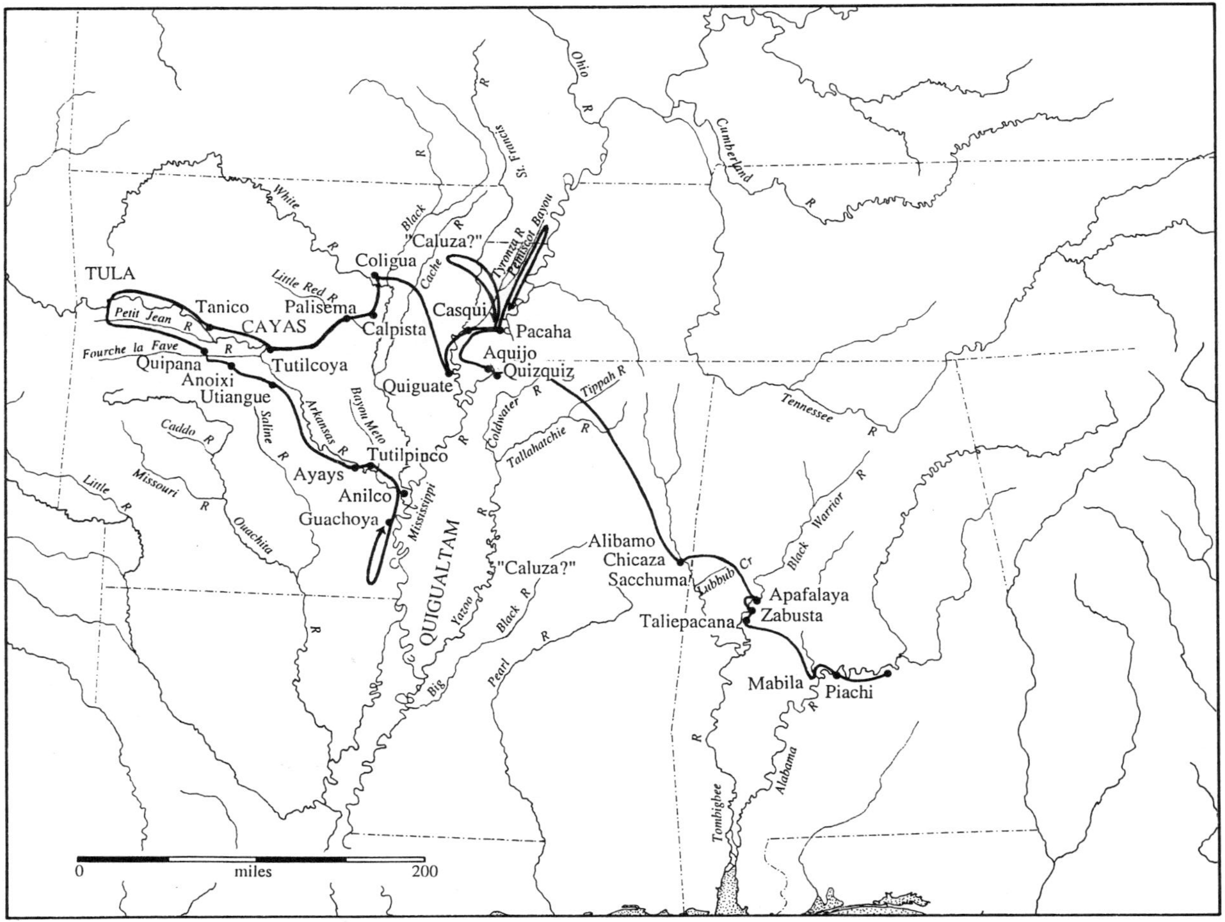

backswamps and curved oxbow lakes were sources of fish, turtle, and water-fowl. The deep sandy loam of the levees was periodically replenished by flooding, and it was ideal soil for growing corn. The water table was high enough that even in droughts it was a virtually fail-safe area for the cultivation of corn. Up beyond the margins of the floodplain lay the fall line hills, covered with hickory and several species of oaks. Further afield, to the north, above the fall line, lay the Cumberland Plateau and Ridge and Valley geological provinces, while to the south lay the Black Belt, curving up toward the Tombigbee River (see map 4).[4]

The precursors of the Moundville chiefdom occupied the Black Warrior River area between A.D. 900 and 1050, building quite small nucleated villages inhabited by perhaps fifty to one hundred people each. They lived in small circular houses, and there is no evidence of political differentiation among their villages. No mounds have been discovered dating to this time period, and no elite burials have been discovered. The archaeological evidence suggests that this was an egalitarian society, composed of more or less autonomous villages. Fancy goods were limited to shell beads, which were manufactured everywhere, even in the smallest villages. The people's subsistence was based on collecting, hunting, fishing, and casual gardening of small quantities of corn, and probably the old southeastern cultigens maygrass, chenopodium, and knotweed. The fact that they lived in nucleated villages may imply that the level of warfare or raiding was high or unpredictable.

It was during the Moundville I period, from A.D. 1050 to 1250, that the fundamental Mississippian transformation occurred in this area. People in the Moundville area began cultivating corn intensively, and they cleared more and more land for field agriculture. The transformation proceeded rapidly, and its consequences were profound. Small pyramidal mounds with structures on top were built at four of the villages along the Black Warrior. As time went on, these mounds were enlarged as additional stages were laid down on top of the old. Late in the Moundville I phase, the Moundville site was laid out and construction began. The principal mound was raised up to a height of ten feet, a defensive palisade was built around the site, and Moundville became a major civic and ceremonial center.

The people of the Moundville site laid out a large plaza and began building at least five and perhaps as many as ten additional mounds around the periphery of the plaza (fig. 53). The two largest mounds are positioned in the northern portion of the plaza, along a north-south centerline. The mounds around

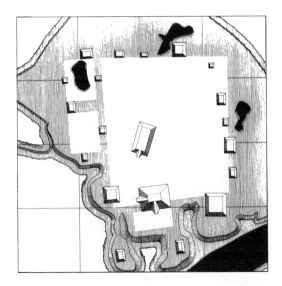

Fig. 53. Schematic map of the Moundville site. From William N. Morgan, *Prehistoric Architecture in the Eastern United States*, 115. (William Morgan, architect)

the plaza are paired residential and burial mounds, with the burial mounds of the pairs generally being smaller in size. During the Moundville II phase (A.D. 1250–1400), most of the resident population moved out, and the site became a vacant ceremonial center and necropolis. During the Moundville II period, all of the truly elite burials of the chiefdom were at Moundville.

The 5 percent or so of the population who were Moundville's elite were buried in or near mounds, and they were interred with lavish grave goods (fig. 54). The shell beads that were previously so important declined, and increasingly elite goods were made out of materials from far-flung places, such as copper, greenstone, and mica. These objects were apparently manufactured in the central town, not in the villages, and the achievements of Moundville artisans and artists are truly impressive. The elite enjoyed better health than the rest of the population, and in particular they suffered from a lower incidence of iron deficiency anemia. They also suffered from a smaller incidence of skeletal trauma—broken and pierced bones—suggesting that they were more protected from physical assault than were common people.

The Moundville elite were apparently supported by the tribute paid them by their subjects in the chiefdom at large. The question is, what did the people get in return? One quite likely benefit was a more secure existence. That is, the ruling chief and his retainers were able to resolve conflicts and maintain a peace among the polities within the chiefdom, so the fear of attack from close at hand was lessened. This is consistent with the fact that in the Moundville I

Fig. 54. Moundville sandstone disc, with two horned serpents encircling a hand-eye design. (University of Alabama Museums)

period, the people of Moundville ceased living in nucleated villages and began living in hamlets and farmsteads that were dispersed in neighborhoods around the mound center. One index of this more secure existence is that the incidence of skeletal trauma during the Moundville I period declined from that of the previous era.

This does not, however, mean that warfare ceased after A.D. 1050. Quite the contrary. The far-flung enemies of Moundville remained. As elsewhere in the Mississippian Southeast, the most prestigious Moundville works of art reflect a strong concern with warfare and the taking of human life (fig. 55). At one point in its history, the Moundville site was surrounded by a defensive palisade, a structure that must have taxed not only the people of Moundville, but also the forest from which the trees were cut to supply the wood. Still, having the people whom one feared living at a distance, rather than in the next village, was a considerable social gain.

Fig. 55. Moundville copper gorget in the form of a scalplock. Note the circle-and-cross motif. (University of Alabama Museums)

Where did these distant enemies live? It is impossible to be certain, but surely it is notable that pieces of pottery manufactured in societies that lay to the south, west, and north of Moundville have been discovered at Moundville sites, while virtually none have been found that were manufactured by societies to the east, northeast, or southeast. Hence, the people of the Black Warrior River valley may have been longstanding enemies of those who lived on the Coosa River (and perhaps further east). This in no way rules out the possibility that the Moundville people had enemies to their west and south.

The Moundville III period (A.D. 1400–1550) appears to have been a time of social change, and perhaps of upheaval. The changes were so dramatic, one infers that whatever it was that the people of the Black Warrior River did successfully before 1400, they did it less well after that time. The causes are obscure. There is no evidence for an environmental catastrophe or for a sharp decline in population, but fewer and fewer people were buried at the Moundville site during the fifteenth and early sixteenth centuries. Other mound centers on the Black Warrior had been kept up during the Moundville II period, but during the Moundville III period two of these centers (one to the north, Apafalaya, and one to the south, Taliepacana) were enlarged, and cemeteries were established near them. Moreover, late in the Moundville III period people began living in nucleated villages, perhaps because it became dangerous to live in a dispersed settlement pattern.[5] During the Mound-ville III phase, only three of the mounds at the Moundville site show any evidence of occupation. The old center had been all but abandoned.

It may be no accident that at about this same time, people who had been living along the Tennessee River to the north of Moundville, and who may have had some relationship with them, moved away, abandoning their former territory. Moreover, this happened at roughly the same time the paramount chief of Coosa was ascending in power, and population was rapidly increasing along the middle and lower Alabama River, an area that was probably under the power or influence of the ancestors of chief Tascaluza. Hence, it is possible the decline of Moundville and the rise of mound centers to the northeast and south were related to larger geopolitical changes in the southeastern region.[6]

After reaching the Black Warrior River, De Soto and his army continued on, probably following a course that lay near the present-day Southern Railroad, and on November 18 they had to traverse some difficult stream crossings and swamps—the flood plains of Big Brush Creek and Fivemile Creek. They came to Taliepacana, the first town in the Moundville chiefdom, where they were no doubt relieved to find ample food.[7] Taliepacana was probably located at the White mound and village site, the southernmost minor ceremonial center of the Moundville archaeological complex. It consisted of a single mound with no more than twenty households clustered around it.[8] Presumably, all the people had fled from this town.

They remained in Taliepacana for several days, sending out small parties of horsemen to explore the country. They came to where they could see a village on the opposite side of the river, which from their vantage point appeared to be beautifully situated.[9] On November 21, half a league from this spot, Vasco Gonzalez found a second village, Mozulixa.[10] Mozulixa was probably at an archaeological site located about nine miles north of the White mound and village site on a high bluff overlooking the Black Warrior River.[11] The people of Mozulixa had taken all the corn from their town and transported it in dugout canoes across the river, where they had piled it up and covered it over with mats. As the Spaniards stood upon the bluff looking across the river, the Indians on the other side shouted loudly at them, threatening that if they dared to cross the river they would kill them.[12]

The Spaniards moved from Taliepacana to Mozulixa.[13] De Soto ordered his men to build a piragua in secret. The Black Warrior was too deep to ford, and De Soto needed a means of getting some of his soldiers across the river quickly. Their location up on a bluff made it difficult for the Indians to spy on them.

And it was an easy camp to defend. They only had to guard the perimeter of the area they occupied, and the steep bank made it difficult for the Indians to infiltrate. The Indians did come at night in small numbers, crossing the river in dugout canoes to attack and harass the Spaniards. But the Spaniards dug foxholes at places near the landing where the Indians could beach their canoes, and when they tried to creep ashore, the Spaniards came out of their foxholes to attack them with swords and arquebuses, inflicting heavy casualties on them. After two or three such attacks, the Indians did not try this again.[14]

The Spaniards sawed lumber and constructed the piragua, completing it in four days.[15] Then they built a large sled on which the boat could be transported to the river. Both the boat and the sled were completed by November 29.

On the night of November 29 the Spaniards used their horses and mules to drag the piragua to the river about half a league upstream from where they built it. In some places the men themselves had to push and pull the sled to move it along.[16] Early on the morning of November 30, they launched the boat into the river. Thirty heavily armed Spaniards boarded it, including a few horsemen, and they made for the opposite bank.[17] The Indians spied them and set up a clamor, filling the air with arrows. But only three or four Spaniards were wounded, and as the boat approached shore, the Indians ran from their positions and hid in a canebrake, where the Spaniards could not pursue them.[18]

The first Spaniard to get his horse ashore and into action was Diego Garcia, son of the governor of Villanueva de Barcarrota. He was so valiant, his comrades named him after one of their heroes, Diego García de Paredes—the Samson of Extremadura—so much did he seem to resemble him in strength, valor, and spirit. The second horseman to go against the Indians was Gonzalo Silvestre.[19] By repeatedly charging and retreating, these two were able to drive the Indian defenders back from the river. As more and more Spaniards were ferried across, the Indians ceased to resist.

It is striking that the warriors of Apafalaya put up such a listless defense against the Spanish invaders. We can never know why they did not resist more effectively, but a host of possibilities come to mind. Perhaps the chiefdom was so weakened by prolonged decline that they lacked the numbers or the esprit de corps to resist. Or perhaps some of their young men had been combatants in the battle at Mabila, and therefore had no illusions about their military capabilities vis-à-vis the Spaniards. Or perhaps they had not fought at Mabila but had heard of the carnage there and did not wish to sustain such losses themselves.[20]

The next day, December 1, De Soto moved the army to Zabusta, at the

Moundville site (see fig. 53), where it was more convenient for the army to cross over to the other side of the river.[21] At its apogee, Zabusta was a great town that included twenty mounds, but in 1540 it was in decline and may have been partially abandoned and overgrown.[22] Here the rest of the army crossed over the river using the boat and also some dugout canoes they had found at the town.[23] Those who had secured the beachhead on the other side of the river had already ridden their horses upstream to the bank opposite to where the crossing was made.[24]

The Moundville site is second only to Cahokia in its overall size and the richness of its artifacts. But for all this, it was based upon a simple economy in which all the local communities of the chiefdom were basically self-sufficient. They all had access to the rich levee soils of the Black Warrior River, as well as the flora and fauna of the oxbow lakes, swamps, and woods. The white-tailed deer was the principal prey animal here as it was elsewhere, with beaver, raccoon, and turkey as lesser prey animals. Throughout the chiefdom, more than 80 percent of the meat consumed was venison. The greater incidence of upper deer leg bones recovered from the mound sites suggests that these choicer parts were supplied, perhaps as tribute, to people who lived in the centers.[25]

There is some evidence of craft specialization in the mound centers and most particularly at the Moundville site itself. This is especially the case with the production of fine ceramic vessels. Everyday vessels were made by simple coiling, but some of the finer bottles (and perhaps some bowls) were made by forming the vessels in molds. These dark gray to black vessels were used for serving and storing food. Close analysis suggests that many of the finer Moundville pottery vessels were made by a small number of individual potters. Moreover, while most stone tools were made out of locally produced stone, the tools that were made of imported stone, particularly greenstone, were crafted at the Moundville site when it was in its heyday. Hence, most of the fancy goods of the chiefdom of Moundville were manufactured at the Moundville site.[26]

After crossing to the other side of the Black Warrior River, De Soto and his army spent the night at a village, where they found a plentiful supply of corn.[27] The next day they continued on to a town commanded by a chief named Apafalaya, which was located at the Snow's Bend site, one of the largest mounds in the Black Warrior Valley outside of Moundville itself. From all appearances, Chief Apafalaya was the dominant political authority in this chiefdom. His town presumably ascended to a position of preeminence after the central town of Moundville declined. The mound at Snow's Bend measures

138.6 by 138.6 feet at the base and is 11.6 feet high. As was his practice, De Soto took Chief Apafalaya captive to serve as guide, interpreter, and as always, hostage. The Spaniards (and presumably the natives) referred to the entire chiefdom as Apafalaya. From the ease with which the Spaniards obtained supplies, it would seem that Apafalaya was an economic center as well.[28]

De Soto and his men rested in this town for a week. Then on December 9 they set out from Apafalaya and headed in a westerly direction, taking Chief Apafalaya with them.[29] On their sixth day of travel, December 14, they came to the River of Chicaza, the Tombigbee.[30] Again, progress had been difficult, because they were traveling in early winter and also because they were crossing many swamps and rivers.[31] Their most likely course was north of Luxapallila Creek, requiring them to cross the Sipsey River (probably near present-day Moores Bridge), Luxapallila Creek (near present-day Millport), Mud Creek, Yellow Creek, and Cooper Creek. This entire distance was through uninhabited wilderness.

The men were suffering greatly from the cold weather and from being repeatedly soaked in cold water. Many of them, both rich and poor, had lost their clothing in the conflagration at Mabila. Don Antonio Osorio, who was brother of the Marqués of Astorga, was reduced to wearing a cloth mantle he had obtained from an Indian. The mantle was too short to begin with, and it was torn on the sides, so his body was exposed to the cold. He was bareheaded and barefoot. He carried a shield on his back and possessed a sword, but he had no scabbard. And if he wanted anything to eat, he had to dig for it with his fingernails. Even though he had two thousand ducats of income through the church in Spain, it was of no use to him whatever in Apafalaya or Chicaza.[32]

It is probable that the trail their guide from Apafalaya was following led them to the Tombigbee River (fig. 56) at present-day Columbus, Mississippi.[33] At this point, high bluffs lie for several miles on both sides of the river, so the channel is narrow even when the water in the Tombigbee is high, and it so happened the water was high when the Spaniards arrived there.[34] With the rainy weather, it is reasonable to suppose that Chief Apafalaya would have known to take them to a place where the river was constricted into a narrow channel.

On the opposite side of the river they could see a large number of warriors, who threatened them.[35] De Soto sent one of the Indians in his company— perhaps the chief of Apafalaya—as an ambassador to the other side of the river to tell the chief there that De Soto wished to have peace. But the Indians on the other side seized this ambassador and killed him in full view of the

Fig. 56. The Tombigbee River near Aliceville, Alabama. Photo by Roland Harper, February 25, 1913. (William Stanley Hoole Special Collections Library, University of Alabama)

Spaniards.[36] De Soto ordered his men to construct a piragua. He also ordered Baltasar de Gallegos to take thirty horsemen who were good swimmers to go upstream, find a place where they could cross the river, and then ride downstream on the opposite side and secure a landing place. Gallegos may have made his crossing a mile or two upstream from where De Soto was building his piragua. Or he may have crossed at the Barton Ferry Crossing, just below the mouth of the Buttahatchee River, about fourteen miles upstream, where the channel of the river would have been narrow.

The Indians on the opposite bank of the river learned of Gallegos's mission perhaps even before he reached the other side, and they abandoned their position. The piragua was ready in two days, and De Soto and his army were able to finish crossing the river in their boat on December 16.[37] Once on the other side, De Soto set out with a company of horsemen in search of the main town of Chicaza, which turned out to be a small town of only twenty houses.[38] The site of the main town of Chicaza has not yet been located by archaeologists, but if the expedition did indeed cross the Tombigbee at present-day Columbus, the town should be somewhere within about an eighteen-mile radius of that point. Hence, it could be in Black Belt terrain in present-day southwestern Monroe County, central or eastern Clay County, eastern Oktibbeha County or Lowndes County, or even northern Noxubee County.[39]

The Spaniards arrived at the main town of Chicaza late at night and found that the place had been abandoned by the chief and his people. The next day Gallegos and his detachment of thirty cavalry rejoined the others.[40] It is likely that Gallegos was delayed because of the floodwater. Crossing the Tombigbee at the Barton Ferry Crossing would have placed them north of Tibbee Creek, which lay between them and the rest of the army, and backwater would have made Tibbee Creek quite wide. Even if Gallegos crossed only a mile or two upstream from where the piragua was built, his men would have been exhausted after swimming the very cold waters of the river. De Soto was wise in stipulating that all the men in this detachment be good swimmers.

10

Winter, 1540–1541

De Soto and his army spent a hard winter in Chicaza. Even though the site of the main town of Chicaza has not yet been located by archaeologists, the territory of the chiefdom is thought to have been west of the Tombigbee River near present-day Columbus, Mississippi, a territory encompassing the watersheds of Magowah Creek and Catalpa Creek.[1] At Christmas a snow fell. The Spaniards said it was as deep as that which might have fallen in Burgos, in northern Spain, and it was as cold as winter in Burgos, or even colder. This was hard on the men, particularly at first, because the main town of Chicaza had such a small number of houses that only some of the men could be quartered inside. For a time, many had to sleep out in the snow.[2]

Fortunately, plentiful food and resources were to be found within the chiefdom of Chicaza. The Chicazas lived in habitations scattered about over the land like the people at Mabila, and much of their corn was still curing in the fields.[3] From the outlying farmsteads, the Spaniards commandeered enough food to see them through the winter. They also tore down houses in the farmsteads and used the materials to build additional houses at the main town.

It is notable that the chroniclers observed that the people of Chicaza and of Mabila lived in settlement patterns with small mound-and-village centers and dispersed farmsteads with quite a lot of land under cultivation. Archaeologi-

262

cal research indicates that this settlement pattern prevailed along the Tombigbee River from the Tibbee Creek area southward to about the mouth of the Black Warrior River.[4] The chroniclers do not say that the Apafalayas of the Black Warrior lived in this manner, and this could be taken to imply that they lived otherwise. Certainly it is consistent with archaeological evidence that in the late Moundville III period the people along the Black Warrior were living in fortified nucleated settlements. And we may speculate that the enmity of the Chicazas and the people of Mabila could have been partly responsible for the defensive posture of the people of Apafalaya, and indeed they may have been at least partly responsible for their long decline in the Moundville III period.

The Chicazas stayed away from the Spaniards at first. Then they came in small numbers to attack at night, and even more frequently to disturb their rest, keeping the Spaniards off balance. Their persistence in this over the course of the winter eventually caused the Spaniards to relax their vigilance.[5] They could not call everyone to arms every time the Chicazas raised a ruckus. Eventually the Spaniards succeeded in capturing a couple of Chicazas, including one who was much valued by the chief. De Soto sent one of these captives to the chief, and using the other captive as a bargaining chip, he persuaded the chief to come and deal with him.[6] After several days messengers from the chief arrived saying the chief of Chicaza would come and see De Soto. On January 3 the chief did come, borne upon the shoulders of his subjects (as was done for the Lady of Cofitachequi and the paramount chief of Coosa), and he was accompanied by two of his tributary chiefs, Alibamo and Miculasa.[7] As gifts they brought as many as 150 rabbits, some shawls, deerskins, and "little dogs."[8] Subsequently they supplied the Spaniards with additional rabbits to eat.

The location of Miculasa is unknown, but later the Spaniards would learn that the territory of Alibamo lay to the northwest of Chicaza, most likely on Line Creek and the western tributaries of Chuquatonchee Creek. Alibamo also included the lower course of Houlka Creek, where there is a concentration of late prehistoric sites.

The overall trajectory of the late prehistoric social development along the Tombigbee River resembles that of the Black Warrior River. At about A.D. 1000 the Tombigbee River area witnessed the same rise in warfare as occurred along the Black Warrior. Here as elsewhere in the Southeast, many burials have arrow points embedded in various bones and parry fractures of lower arm bones. In the Mississippian era the native people constructed a number of mound centers along the central Tombigbee River and its tributaries. Only two of these have been excavated to date, the Lyon's Bluff site on Line Creek near Starkville, Mississippi, and the Lubbub Creek site near Aliceville, Alabama. To date, only the Lubbub Creek site has been adequately reported. Many questions remain to be answered about the chiefdoms of the Tombigbee, but the larger distribution of sites on the landscape resembles that of Coosa, with a number of rather small, simple chiefdoms separated by wilderness buffer zones. But whereas towns in Coosa were typically nucleated and palisaded, the Tombigbee chiefdoms consisted of mound-and-village centers, which were sometimes palisaded, but with their populations dispersed in small farmsteads. The Lubbub Creek site was situated in a meander bend of the Tombigbee River. The neck of this bend had a palisade built across it, and within the area set off by this palisade there was a second palisade with bastions encircling the village itself.

The cultural affiliations of the Tombigbee chiefdoms, particularly as indicated in the ceramics, seem to have been especially strong with Moundville. Greenstone celts and fragments of circular sandstone discs like those at Moundville have been found in sites along the Tombigbee River. Small quantities of copper have been found, including several copper ornaments shaped like arrow points and a copper gorget with a falcon embossed on it that resembles one found at the Shinholser site in Georgia (Altamaha). What is notable, but not yet explained, is that with such similar resources, why did no center comparable to Moundville arise on the Tombigbee River?

As a center, the Lubbub Creek site does not appear to have ever been densely settled. At any particular time, only a small number of houses were built on the site. There were not enough people living there to have constructed and maintained its fortifications, implying that this labor was drawn from the outlying population, who came to the center for social, ritual, and defensive purposes. One of the most important rituals was surely the burial of their dead. Some males had infants buried with them who are thought to have been sacrificed, a form of retainer burial that continued into early historic times among the Natchez Indians. Interestingly, the mound at Lubbub Creek included the bones of several birds that are not likely to have been eaten, and several of these had specific symbolic values for Indians in the early historic Southeast. They are the Carolina parakeet, cardinal, blue jay, crow, mockingbird (or brown thrasher), and merlin. The skins of these birds may have been displayed in the temple or used as parts of costumes.

One advantage of the local center-farmstead arrangement used by people along the Tombigbee may be that it maximized an economy in which small-plot agriculture could be practiced alongside hunting and gathering, while still providing for military defense. There is some evidence that in late fall and winter, the people abandoned their farmsteads, presumably to go where the deer hunting was better, probably for a communal hunt. Since this would have left vulnerable any agricultural produce stored at the farmsteads, much of this food may have been stored in the safety of the mound center. Some of the population—the very old and very young—may also have moved to the mound center while the hunt was conducted. At the Lubbub Creek site, fancy and exotic goods are not concentrated in an elite precinct, as at Moundville; rather, they are spread out among the farmsteads.[9] In all, from what is known of the archaeology of this area, one gets the impression these chiefdoms of the Tombigbee were weakly centralized, and rather independent and self-sufficient. The experience of De Soto and his men is consistent with this interpretation.

The chief of Chicaza frequently came to visit De Soto, and sometimes De Soto would summon him by sending him a horse on which to ride.[10] The people of Chicaza frequently came to De Soto's camp bringing gifts of rabbits and other food.[11] On one occasion the chief of Chicaza gave De Soto guides and interpreters to accompany a detachment of Spaniards to Caluza, a province said to comprise ninety villages, subject only to themselves. It was a rich province whose warriors were bellicose and much feared by other people.[12] The location of Caluza is not specified. We can narrow its possible location, however, by a process of elimination. It could not have been to the north, since archaeological evidence indicates that a vast wilderness lay to the north of Chicaza; the east can be eliminated because the army had already passed through that wilderness area. A considerable population lived to the south, in the Mobile delta, but De Soto had no wish to go toward the Gulf coast because of his fear that his men would mutiny and defect. Hence, the most likely direction for Caluza was to the west. A late prehistoric population occupied the Pocahontas region of the Big Black River, but from all appearances it was a smaller chiefdom than the ninety towns of Caluza.[13] This leaves the Yazoo basin as the most likely location for the people the Chicaza called "Caluzas." The Lake George mound site in the Yazoo Basin is one of the largest mound centers in the lower Mississippi Valley. Whether De Soto actually sent a detachment of his men to reconnoiter the Caluzas is not reported in the documents. Later in the expedition, De Soto and his men became acquainted with the people who lived in the Yazoo Basin, although they came to know them by a different name.

One day the chief of Chicaza came to De Soto complaining that one of his chiefs, Sacchuma, had rebelled and was refusing to pay tribute. He asked that De Soto and his men go with him and offer him protection while he went to Sacchuma to punish the rebels. De Soto suspected this was a ploy. He felt that once his troops were divided, the Indians would launch an attack on one or both sections of his army. But never one to be intimidated, he agreed to go along.

On the appointed day, Chief Chicaza came with two hundred warriors, armed with bows and arrows, and De Soto took thirty horsemen and eighty footmen. When they arrived at Sacchuma, they found a palisaded town that had been abandoned by its inhabitants. The location of Sacchuma is not indicated, but it is thought to have been in an area between the Noxubee and Tombigbee Rivers, including the Lubbub Creek locality.[14] The warriors who were with Chicaza set fire to the houses of Sacchuma, but De Soto thought this was part of their ruse. The Spaniards were so vigilant, however, Chicaza's men had no opportunity to launch an attack, either on De Soto's contingent or on the main army back at Chicaza, where vigilance had also been tightened. Later Chief Miculasa, presumably a Sacchuma, came and pleaded for peace, and messengers from Talapatica came also.[15] Neither the dates nor the number of days consumed by this action are known.

Tensions between the Chicazas and the Spaniards increased through the course of the winter. De Soto invited the chief and some of his principal men to dine on pork; and the meat was so much to their liking, Chicazas began creeping in at night to the pigsty the Spaniards had set up in some houses a crossbow shot from their encampment. They would kill and carry off as many of the hogs as they could. Eventually the Spaniards caught three Indians in the act of stealing hogs. De Soto ordered that two of them be executed by being shot with arrows. The third one had his hands cut off and was sent back to his chief as a warning.

The Spaniards contributed their own share to the worsening relations with the Chicazas. One such incident was set in motion by four Spanish horsemen: Francisco Osorio; Reynoso, a servant of the Marquis of Astorga; Ribera, one of De Soto's pages; and Fuentes, De Soto's chamberlain. The four men rode half a league from the main town of Chicaza to Chicazilla, where the chief was staying. They forcibly took some skins and shawls from the people of Chicazilla, who were so disturbed by this act that they fled, abandoning their houses. When De Soto heard of this, he was furious and ordered that the four men be seized. He sentenced all four of them to the loss of their possessions, and he sentenced Francisco Osorio and Fuentes to be executed, because they were the ringleaders in the affair.

The friars and the secular priests pleaded with De Soto to reduce these sentences, but he would not. As De Soto was giving the order for the two men to be taken to the place of execution, to be beheaded, some Indians from the chief of Chicaza happened to arrive to lodge their complaints against the men. Here the comrades of the condemned men saw an opportunity. Baltasar de Gallegos took Juan Ortiz aside and told him to translate the conversations between De Soto and the Indian emissaries to the advantage of the condemned men. Placing himself at considerable risk, Ortiz complied. The Indian emissaries spoke, and as Ortiz translated, he made it seem that they came to say their chief wanted it known that he did not think the condemned men were guilty as charged and would consider it a favor if they were released. Then, when Ortiz translated for De Soto to the Indians, he told them De Soto had ordered that the men be punished for their crimes as an example to the other Spaniards. The outcome was that the two condemned men were released. It would seem that De Soto's men had resorted to deceiving him because of his excesses and harsh treatment following the battle at Mabila.[16]

At the beginning of March, De Soto began making plans to continue the expedition. When he demanded two hundred porters from the chief of Chicaza, it caused a notable disturbance among the Indians. But the chief promised he would deliver the porters at dawn on March 4, 1541, when the Spaniards planned to take their leave.[17] Later they captured some Indians who came one night feigning peace but who were obviously on a mission to spy on them and see how they slept and kept up their guard.[18] De Soto rode around on the night of March 3 and saw signs that the Indians were planning something. He rode back to camp and announced to all: "Tonight is an Indian night." He let it be known he intended to sleep with his weapons at hand, and he would leave his horse saddled and ready. He ordered Luís de Moscoso, the master of camp, to take extra precautions that night with the sentinels, particularly because this was to be their last night in Chicaza.

But none heeded what De Soto said, another indication of their growing disaffection. The soldiers lay down to sleep without having their weapons at hand. In the opinion of some, Moscoso assigned to the morning watch three of the most worthless horsemen (one of whom was De Soto's nephew), on three of the most worthless horses.[19] None of the other horses had been saddled, including De Soto's.

The Chicazas had collected good intelligence on the Spaniards and their encampment, and they knew where the sentinels were posted. They arrived at some time before dawn, as they had promised, but they came with their own agenda. They approached in four companies, one from each direction of the compass. Creeping up in ones, twos, and threes, they infiltrated the camp undetected, carrying fire concealed in little jars.[20] With this they lit rings woven out of a certain grass, which they twisted around their arrows. These grass rings held fire like an arquebus fuse. Lighting them from their firepots, they shot the flaming arrows into the roofs of the houses.[21] By the time the sentinels became aware of what was going on, half the houses were already on fire.[22] Once they were discovered, the Indians began shouting at the top of their lungs and beating on drums as if, said the Spaniards, they had been Italian infantry.[23]

When this clamor arose, the sentinels did not rush in to defend the camp, but fled to save their own skins. The Indians, perhaps three hundred strong, positioned themselves throughout the town, some of them concealed at the entrances of the houses, and as the Spaniards began tumbling half-clothed from their burning houses, blinded by the smoke and flames, they encountered these warriors at their doors.[24] A cold north wind was blowing, and it spread the fire quickly.[25] In the confusion, the Spaniards were unable to lay hold of their weapons or to saddle their horses. Each tried to find safety without resisting his attackers. Those horses that were able to break their reins fled into the darkness, but many of them could not and burned to death in their stables. Nuño de Tovar, wearing his armor unbuckled, ran out with his sword, shouting for the fleeing men to return. He asked them whether they were running to Córdoba or to Seville. Their security lay not in flight, but in their courage and the strength of their arms.[26]

Everything was on fire, even the pigsty. Hernando Bautista and his wife, Francisca de Hinestrosa, who was pregnant, ran out of their burning house. But Francisca went back inside, reportedly to fetch some pearls she had forgotten. When she attempted to come back out, fire had reached the door of the house, and she was trapped inside and burned to death.[27]

Fortunately the Indians were not immune to the smoke and confusion. Only De Soto and Tapia de Valladolid were able to mount their horses. De Soto donned his armor but did not have time to buckle it on, and his page did not securely fasten the girth of his saddle, so that the first time De Soto lanced an Indian, the force of his thrust toppled him from his horse along with his saddle. But the Indians heard the riderless horses that escaped from their burning stalls and were galloping about, and they thought they were about to be attacked by a large force of horsemen. Fearful, they ran from the camp to the safety of the surrounding woods.[28]

The Chicazas had struck De Soto a severe blow. Twelve Spaniards died of wounds or were burned to death.[29] Two others had been so badly burned that for several days afterward they had to be carried on litters by Indian slaves.[30] Fifty-seven horses had been killed.[31] As many as four hundred pigs had burned to death in their sty, and only about a hundred piglets squeezed through the cracks and escaped.[32] The pigs had grown fat, and the story was told that as they burned up in the fire a stream of lard ran for some distance from the sty.[33]

Many of those who still possessed some clothing after the conflagration at Mabila lost it in the fire at Chicaza. Few of the Spaniards had time to grab up their jerkins when they ran from their burning houses.

The Spaniards had only succeeded in killing a single Indian, the one De Soto lanced. According to Garcilaso, they were furious when they learned that each of their Indian attackers had worn three cords wrapped around his body: one for a horse, one for a pig, and one for a Spaniard.[34]

After the Indians had retreated from the burning town, the half-naked Spaniards who had hidden out in the darkness returned. They stood around the fires in the freezing cold, warming first one side and then the other. In the days after the fire, one of their number, Juan Vego, contrived to weave thick mats out of dry grass, making bedding for himself by placing one mat below and one above, which gave him some warmth. Later he wove many of these for his comrades.[35]

The Spaniards were now thoroughly demoralized. Most of their weapons, saddles, and shields had been burned up in the fire. Somehow they learned that the Chicazas planned to return the next night to attack again. Fortunately, a rain fell that night, wetting the Indians' bowstrings, and because of this, they did not attack.[36] If they had, they might have routed the Spaniards.[37]

The Spaniards buried their dead and treated their wounded as best they could. They butchered the dead horses for meat, and in doing so they found, according to Garcilaso, that almost all the horses had been killed by arrows that had struck their hearts, or very near their hearts. Eleven or twelve horses had arrows directly through their hearts. One was killed by two arrows to the heart, each from opposite sides. The horse of Juan Díaz had been killed most remarkably by an arrow that entered through the thickest part of one shoulder and had penetrated the entire body, protruding on the opposite side the length of four fingers.[38] In stories like this, the Spaniards expressed their admiration of Chicaza archers.

A few days after the attack, the Spaniards moved to Chicazilla, the village about a league distant in an open field—probably Black Belt prairie—on a sloping hillside, where the chief had been staying.[39] De Soto transferred command from Moscoso to Gallegos, having concluded that Moscoso had been negligent on the night of the attack.[40] To cover their nakedness the Spaniards began to improvise clothing out of dressed deerskins. And they built a forge, making a bellows from two bearskins, and used it to reforge those weapons that had lost their temper in the fire.[41] Using local materials they made new shields, new frames for their saddles, and they fashioned lances out of some ash trees found growing nearby.[42]

The Chicazas continued to come at night in small numbers to harass the Spaniards. They inflicted little damage, but they kept the Spaniards on edge with their shouts. De Soto now had his camp well guarded, and the Spaniards inflicted some casualties on the Chicazas. During the day, De Soto took to sending out small groups of cavalry to maraud through the country for four leagues around Chicazilla. They spared no one, and afterward they claimed there were no Indians left alive within a radius of four leagues.[43]

But the Chicazas had not in fact been routed. On March 15 they returned once again on the morning watch to attack the Spaniards and finish them off.[44] They came in three companies, vigorously attacking at three different points.[45] But this time the Spaniards were vigilant, and because Chicazilla was located on an open plain, the horses could be used effectively. Day was already beginning to break when De Soto led three companies against the attackers. The Spaniards killed several of them and would have killed more had not a friar in the camp panicked and called out, "To the camp! To the camp!" De Soto and all his men turned back, allowing the Chicazas to escape. After this, they attacked no more.[46]

11

Quizquiz, Casqui, Pacaha

On April 26, 1541, after they had recovered from the wounds they had sustained in the attack by the Chicazas and had repaired their saddles, shields, and weapons, the Spaniards took their leave from Chicazilla.[1] They continued traveling toward the northwest (see map 7), and at the end of their first day of travel they came to a small village, Alibamo.[2] It was possibly at the Lyon's Bluff site or some other site on Tibbee or Line Creek. They needed a large supply of corn to sustain them until they reached the other side of the wilderness that they expected to spend twelve days crossing.[3] They had little left of the corn they had taken from the Chicazas, and they discovered that the people of Alibamo had hidden theirs.[4]

On April 27 De Soto sent out three captains, each with horsemen and footmen, to search for provisions.[5] Juan de Añasco with fifteen horsemen and forty footmen explored further along the trail De Soto was following. They discovered a very strongly built palisade defended by about three hundred Alibamos.[6] The site of this fortification has not yet been discovered by archaeologists, but it was probably on Line Creek or one of its tributaries. The fortification was built in the form of a square.[7] The palisade wall facing the Spaniards had three doors, one in the center and one near each corner, and all of them were so low a horse could not enter. Subsequently they found that inside there were two additional walls that stretched from side to side, again with small doors. The exterior wall opposite the entrances lay flush against a deeply entrenched stream with nearly vertical banks on either side. Steep banks are characteristic of creeks in the Black Belt, where they erode stream-beds in the soft limestone; hence, many creek and river locations possess the steep banks described here (see fig. 52).

As they approached the fortification, Añasco and his men could see many armed warriors looking over the top of the palisade. Their bodies were painted with red ocher, and their arms and legs were painted with black, yellow, and white stripes, so that it seemed that they were wearing breeches and doublets. Some of them wore elegant feathers on their heads to make themselves appear taller and more formidable.[8] Others wore headdresses with horns and had their faces painted black and their eyes ringed with red pigment, so they appeared to be very ferocious.[9] As soon as they spied the Spaniards they sent up a great shout and began beating on drums. Some of them came out of the palisade in a fury to meet the Spaniards.

It seemed best to Añasco not to attack these Indians, but to pull back and proceed cautiously. He withdrew to about the distance of the flight of a crossbow bolt and sent three horsemen to De Soto with news of his discovery. The crossbowmen and others carrying shields placed themselves between the Indians and the horsemen in order to protect the horses from the arrows the Indians were shooting at them. The Indians began coming out short distances in sevens and eights, to fire their arrows and then return inside the palisade. They built a fire the Spaniards could see, and then they pretended to hit one of their own on the head with war clubs, and seizing him by the feet and by the head, they pretended they would throw him into the fire. The Spaniards had no difficulty understanding what these acts were meant to communicate.[10]

De Soto came forward immediately to join Añasco, and on April 28 all the army was assembled on the open field that lay near the palisade.[11] Though they could have easily bypassed this threat, De Soto, as he was wont to do, decided to take it on, lest the Indians think the Spaniards timid and be emboldened to undertake further hostilities in the future. And of course the Spaniards could make good use of any food and supplies they might find inside the palisade. De Soto ordered his horsemen, who wore the heaviest armor, to dismount.[12] He formed them into three companies, and at the sound of a trumpet they began to advance against the palisade and to chop their way through, the same tactic he had used in the battle at Mabila.[13]

The Spaniards began taking casualties immediately. Both of the men who stood on either side of Gonzalo Silvestre were hit by arrows. Diego de Castro of Badajoz was hit in his right thigh, just above the knee, by an arrow tipped with a flint point. Pedro de Torres of Burgos was hit by an arrow that passed between the two bones of his forearm. In the squadron commanded by Juan de Guzmán, Luís Bravo de Xerez took an arrow in the thigh. In a third squadron, commanded by Captain Alonso de Cardeñosa, Francisco de Figuerora of Zafra also took an arrow in the thigh. The Indians were aiming for the thighs and elbows because these were parts of the Spaniards' bodies on which they wore no armor. The arrows with flint points were fearsome. If they did not penetrate, but only grazed one's body, they would still inflict a wound with their sharp edges. Reportedly, all three of the men with thigh wounds died after the battle.[14] De Soto himself was struck on the helmet by an arrow that Garcilaso said bounced fifteen feet into the air, and with such force it caused De Soto to see stars.[15]

The Indians inside fought ferociously until they could see that the Spaniards were going to succeed in gaining entry. When one wall was breached, the Indians fell back behind another.[16] When the Spaniards began to breach the innermost palisades, the Indians fled from the fortification across narrow footbridges they had laid from bank to bank on either side of the creek.[17] The bridges were high above the water, and some Indians lost their footing and fell while crossing.[18] When the horsemen attempted to attack the Indians on the opposite side, they found that the steep-sided creek was utterly impossible for the horses to cross.[19] The Alibamos had cleverly nullified the advantage the horsemen gave the Spaniards.[20]

The story was told in connection with this battle that one of the Alibamo archers on the other side of the creek began shouting at the Spaniards until they understood that he wished to square off against a crossbowman for a contest of one-on-one. The Spaniards had taken refuge behind some trees to protect themselves from the arrows that had been flying. Juan de Salinas stepped from behind a tree and approached the creek, positioning himself opposite the Indian, standing sideways to present less of a target. Salinas had waved off a shield-bearer who wanted to go and offer him some protection. Alibamo and Spaniard took aim and released their missiles at the same time. The Indian was hit by a bolt in the chest, but before he fell to the ground, his comrades came and picked him up and carried him away. The Indian's arrow struck Salinas beside his ear and penetrated clear through the nape of his neck. Thus wounded, Salinas could have been shot by the other Indians, but they did not attack, because it was a contest of one-on-one. Salinas survived, but his Alibamo opponent almost certainly died.[21]

The Alibamos had not only bettered the Spaniards, they had outsmarted them. More than thirty of De Soto's men had been wounded in storming the fort, and as many as fifteen of them died a few days later along the trail.[22] The Indians only lost three men. And had the Indians not taken flight, many more Spaniards would surely have been killed.[23] When the Spaniards got inside the fort they found it to be empty. There were no houses inside and no stores of food. The Indians had seemingly built it as part of a military ploy. It was a fortification in which the Indians could attack the Spaniards from a protected vantage, and from which they could then flee to a position where the Spanish horsemen could not pursue them. It seemed to betray a strategic ability on the part of the Indians that the Spaniards did not suspect they possessed.[24] But to De Soto's men, Alibamo cleverness did not excuse their losses; they felt this was clearly an instance in which De Soto showed poor military judgment, heedlessly wasting the lives of those under his command.[25]

The Spaniards spent April 29 scouring the countryside of Alibamo, searching for food. They found many small towns of fifteen to twenty houses each.[26] They succeeded in finding a small quantity of food, but it was at great hazard to themselves, and it was not nearly what they needed for their journey across the wilderness that lay before them.[27]

Quizquiz

On April 30 they departed from the fort of Alibamo and began traveling toward the northwest, carrying their wounded with them.[28] They were too short on food to wait for the wounded men to recover, and no doubt because of this, several of them died along the way.

Their path took them from the Black Belt into the red hills of northern Mississippi. At first the tree cover was much as they had seen before, namely southeastern pine forest, but gradually the pines decreased in number and they entered a southern spur of the oak-chestnut-yellow poplar forest that covered parts of Tennessee and Kentucky (see map 4). Their journey from Alibamo was difficult because they had to cross the numerous headwaters of several small westward flowing streams—the Little Tallahatchie, Tippah, and Coldwater Rivers. They marched the entire distance through very rough, wooded country that was laced with wet places, and they often found themselves wading in water. All of these creeks and swamps were fordable except a few swamps they had to cross by swimming.

On the ninth day of being constantly on the march, they came to a trail that paralleled Johnson Creek in present-day western De Soto County, Mississippi, and as they traversed this last stretch of wilderness, they entered one of the most distinctive and richest regions in the Southeast—the Mississippi Valley. They had seen small expanses of southern floodplain forest as they crossed rivers in Georgia and South Carolina, and at Mabila, and yet again at Apafalaya. But in the central Mississippi Valley the floodplain forest was vast, stretching all the way from about present-day Cape Girardeau, Missouri, down to New Orleans (see map 4). In places this forest was as much as a hundred miles wide. The dominant trees were bald cypress, tupelo, and several species of oak, as well as several subdominant species that are tolerant of water. Pine trees were notably absent from this forest. Today virtually all of this vast old-growth forest has been cut down for timber or simply cleared and burned for farming; hence, most of the forest that can be seen in the Mississippi Valley today is secondary growth.

The Mississippi Valley has been powerfully shaped by the magnificent river that runs through it. The Mississippi River, together with its tributaries—the Missouri, Ohio, Arkansas, and Red—drains a vast area of the North American continent. It is one of the largest rivers in the world, and when it floods, particularly in spring and early summer, it can wreak havoc with the land in one place (fig. 57), eroding it away—virtually dissolving it—only to bless other areas as its muddy waters release their particles of soil. The Mississippi

Fig. 57. An eroding outside bend of the Mississippi River in Washington County, Mississippi. Photograph by Roland Harper, June 10, 1911. (William Stanley Hoole Special Collections Library, University of Alabama)

River acquired its meandering habits by about 4000 B.C., and it has frequently changed its course, sinuously, like a giant serpent, within a wide swath of the valley. It has left traces of itself everywhere in its meander zone.

The Mississippi River has meandered over a deep fan of alluvial soil that has been deposited in the valley over the course of many thousands of years. The Mississippi, like other meandering rivers in the Southeast, had characteristic ways of behaving that made certain parts of the Mississippi Valley ideally suited to the Mississippian way of life. Above all, the Mississippi Valley has been shaped by the fact that the river follows a characteristically S-shaped course across a deep bed of deposits of soft soil (fig. 58). Thus, in the outside of a bend in the river the water runs fast and continually erodes the bank on that side, which constantly recedes outward. This is the part of the river that has the deepest water. In contrast, on the inside of the bend the water runs slowest (in fact, on the inside of a bend eddies sometimes flow gently up-river)—and here the water is the shallowest. Water-tolerant willow trees normally grow on the inside of a bend. As time goes on and as erosion proceeds, the loop of the bend becomes longer and longer, and in time it comes to have a very narrow neck. Then, particularly when it floods, the force of the river may cut a new channel through this narrow neck, creating for a time a C-shaped side channel surrounding an island.

The Mississippi, often called the Muddy Mississippi, carries a great load of soil and sediment. When it floods and its waters leave their banks, the heaviest depositions of the coarsest particles precipitate out along the edges of the river, forming natural levees—gently sloping ridges about fifteen to twenty-five feet high and as much as a mile wide that run parallel to the course of the

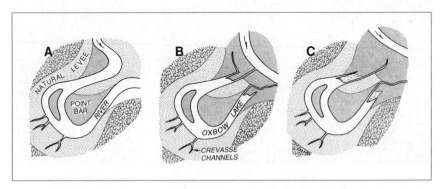

Fig. 58. The formation of an oxbow lake. (Mississippi River Commission)

river. This same process of heavy deposition occurs at the open ends of the cutoff C-shaped bends of the river, so that in a short time they silt up and become C-shaped, oxbow lakes. These oxbow lakes are scattered throughout the meander zone of the Mississippi River, and they were extraordinarily attractive to Mississippian people. The soil of the levee ridges was remarkably rich—superb for growing corn—and because it was sandy, it was easy to till with simple tools. An added feature was that the aquatic resources of the oxbow lakes provided a bountiful supply of frogs, turtles, fish, and seasonal waterfowl. And in an area so subject to flooding, an elevation of any sort was an attractive place to build a house or a town.

A further consequence of the constant aggradation of the Mississippi River—perhaps abetted by occasional earthquakes—is that some areas of the delta became "sunklands," vast swamps. Some of these sunklands are quite large and are normally covered year-round by shallow expanses of standing water.

Two subregions within the Mississippi Valley—the central Mississippi Valley and the Yazoo Basin—supported exceptionally large Mississippian chiefdoms. Both of these subregions within the Mississippi Valley were heavily occupied in the Middle Mississippian era. The Central Valley is principally located on the western side of the Mississippi, stretching for five hundred miles from the mouth of the Ohio River to the mouth of the Arkansas River. It is divided into eastern and western parts by Crowley's Ridge, a long and narrow erosional remnant that runs from north to south, an elevated area supporting a strip of mixed hardwood forest in an ocean of southern floodplain forest (see map 4). On the eastern side of Crowley's Ridge, the St. Francis River runs southward, emptying into the Mississippi River near present-day Helena, Arkansas (see map 7). The western margin of the Central Valley lies against the Ozark Mountains on the west and is drained by the White River, which empties into the Arkansas River near its junction with the Mississippi. The eastern part of the central Mississippi Valley lies in the geologically younger meander zone of the Mississippi River, and it was especially favored by native people.

The Yazoo Basin lies on the eastern side of the Mississippi River, running from an area just south of present-day Memphis down to Vicksburg. It comprises the area between the Mississippi River and the bluff hills of the state of Mississippi. As the name implies, the Yazoo Basin is drained by the Yazoo River and its tributaries.[29]

The first chiefdom De Soto and his army encountered in the Mississippi

Valley was named Quizquiz, and the resemblance of this name to the name of the Inca general who gave De Soto so much trouble probably did not escape him.

The Spaniards arrived at the first village of Quizquiz about midday on May 8, their ninth day of marching from the Alibamo fort.[30] They had crossed a wilderness that was second in extent only to the wilderness of Ocute, and they must have been exhausted and anxious. They took the people of this town of Quizquiz quite by surprise. It was undefended because the men of Quizquiz were away working in the cornfields, perhaps preparing the land for planting. The existence of the uninhabited buffer zone suggests enmity between Quizquiz and the people of Chicaza, and it is therefore unlikely that Quizquiz had received any news of the approach of the Spaniards. De Soto's men found a quantity of shawls and skins that they could use to make clothing, and they captured more than three hundred women, including the chief's mother.[31]

The chiefdom of Quizquiz comprised several towns that lay on the eastern margin of the Mississippi River at and below present-day Memphis. The central Mississippi Valley was the locus of a series of late prehistoric societies, scattered from the southeastern margin of Missouri down to the Arkansas River, as well as along short stretches of the White and Little Red Rivers. All the people in this extraordinarily rich region shared many cultural and social similarities.

They were the inheritors of a long and probably painful experience with the Mississippian transformation. The earliest part of this transformation occurred between A.D. 700 and 1000 in the northern part of the Central Valley, along the upper reaches of the St. Francis and Tyronza Rivers and in the Cairo Lowlands of southeastern Missouri (so-named because they lie south of Cairo, Illinois). This development occurred simultaneously with similar developments at Cahokia to the north and with the Coles Creek culture in the lower Mississippi Valley to the south.

Here, in this extraordinarily rich and diverse region, the native people of the northern Central Valley made the transition to more intensive corn cultivation. In addition to their Mississippi meander zone soils, they had easy access to prairie, hill country, and not so far away, even mountains. For protein they had abundant white-tailed deer, raccoons, rabbits, and turkeys, as well as fish and migratory waterfowl—mallards, Canada geese, teal, pintails, mergansers, shovelers, and cormorants. And wood ducks were present in all seasons. During the early period, the people lived in dispersed, small villages, and at this time there is little archaeological evidence of warfare.

Some of the economic patterns, artifacts, and symbols that were later to occur widely in the Southeast appear for the first time among the early Mississippian cultures of the Mississippi Valley. Because so much of their food was
grain and vegetables, the people of the Mississippian cultures had to trade for
salt from wherever it could be procured. (Hunters, in contrast, gain salt from
the blood of their prey.) Hence, at an early time period archaeologists find at
certain places in this region evidence of ceramic salt pans and ceramic funnels
for extracting grit from brine in the making of salt. Chert and flint were necessary for making cutting tools, and because these substances do not naturally
occur in the Mississippi meander zone, they too were imported from elsewhere, most notably from the Ozarks and from an area south of present-
day St. Louis, where Mill Creek chert (fig. 59) was obtained and traded widely
through the Southeast. This high-quality chert was made into hoes, projectile
points, knives, and purely ceremonial artifacts. Along with these necessities,
the people traded for shells from the Gulf coast, for small amounts of copper
(free copper, not smelted copper), for mica, and for hematite (a red pigment),
and galena (a white pigment). They began making pottery that was notably
superior to any that had been made previously in the Southeast. The best was
made from clay tempered by the addition of mussel shells that had been
burned and then crushed into a powder. This tempering greatly increased the
lightness and strength of vessel walls, allowing the people to make larger
bowls and jars, as well as vessels modeled into a variety of artful shapes, particularly bottles of various kinds. Much of the early pottery in the central
Mississippi Valley has a red film on the interior surfaces.

Arrow points show up for the first time in the Early Mississippian period,
indicating that the people had begun using a weapon that had great potential
for both good and harm. The bow and arrow must have greatly increased

Fig. 59. Mill Creek chert hoe.
(Arkansas Archaeological
Survey)

Fig. 60. A chunkey player incised on a Mississippian shell gorget. (Smithsonian Institution)

their ability to procure meat, increasing the ease with which a wide variety of game could be taken, from rabbit, to fish, to duck, to deer. But it also greatly increased their ability to wage war against each other. Early arrow points in the Central Valley are mostly triangular in shape (Madison points) or else stemmed with serrated edges (Sequoyah points).

The first stone discoidals show up in the central Mississippi Valley in the early Mississippian period. These stone discoidals, about three to six inches in diameter, were used in the game of chunkey (fig. 60), which was still being played in early historic times. In this game two players competed against each other, rolling the discoidal along the ground and then running after it for a distance before each of them hurled a pole that slid along the ground in the direction of the rolling discoidal. The winner was the one whose pole stopped sliding closest to where the discoidal stopped rolling and fell over. This game had great significance in the lives of Mississippian people.

One of the great advantages of the Mississippian way of life over earlier ways of life was that corn produced a grain that could be stored and eaten in the future. In the early Mississippian period of the Central Valley, shelled corn was stored in circular or square pits dug into the ground, each holding an average of about fifty bushels.

The Middle Mississippian period—from about A.D. 1000 to 1350—was the time in which the Mississippian way of life was consolidated and elaborated in the Central Valley. At this time the Cairo Lowland remained the area in which the largest and most elaborate sites were located. Many artifacts belonging to the "Southeastern archaeological complex" have been found by archaeologists in the Central Valley dating to this period. This includes bi-pointed swords (see fig. 47), pear-shaped death mask gorgets (see fig. 45), representations of chunkey players with beaded forelocks, pointed pouches, bi-lobed arrows, and falcons rendered on repoussé copper (see fig. 48). This complex of motifs is found widely across the Southeast in sites that date to the Mississippian era.

But what is most notable about this Middle Mississippian period is that it was a time when the larger towns were fortified with wooden palisades encircled by ditches. Inside these towns the houses were laid out in rows. The polities became hierarchically stratified, with large civic-ceremonial centers, secondary palisaded villages, and small dispersed farmsteads. As time went on, food storage pits declined in number, presumably replaced by more efficient aboveground barbacoas like those already described.

In the Middle Mississippian period there was a pronounced tendency toward consolidating population, which suggests an increase in conflict between polities. Large areas were abandoned, and other areas grew in population. In some cases, entire villages burned down, and there is a strong implication that they were intentionally burned. After about 1350 the entire Cairo Lowland area, the old center of highest development, was abandoned and became a wilderness. It may be no accident that at this time the Nodena arrow point, which was from .5 to 2 inches long and resembled a willow leaf in form, became popular. Central Mississippi Valley people also made arrow points out of the tips of deer antlers (fig. 61).

The chiefdom of Quizquiz was one product of this Middle Mississippian nucleation of populations. The towns of Quizquiz lay like beads on a string on the rich levee ridges along two oxbow lakes—the Norfolk Meander and the Walls Meander. To the south of the levee ridges of these meanders lay an extensive backswamp—the Coldwater Lowland. The first town of Quizquiz was probably the Irby site, which lay near where Johnson Creek empties into the Walls Meander.

Another site that may have been included in the Quizquiz chiefdom was located in present-day Memphis, near the site of the old bridges that crossed the Mississippi River. Only a small area of this site is preserved today as De Soto Park. A few miles to the southwest, however, one can visit the Chucalissa site, which is maintained by the State of Tennessee as a museum and park. In all important respects, Chucalissa resembles the towns of Quizquiz visited by De Soto.

Chucalissa has a large platform mound facing southward across a plaza. A

Fig. 61. A Nodena point (*right*) and a deer antler point (*left*). Both are from the Parkin site (Casqui). (Arkansas Archaeological Survey)

pair of structures once stood on top of this mound, the largest of which was about fifty feet square and had a floor sunk into the earth about nine inches. The roof was held up by cypress posts a foot to a foot and a half in diameter, set in a rectangular pattern in the center of the floor. Several large storage pits (probably lined with cypress bark), about three feet wide and as much as six feet deep, were dug into the floor.

Each time the mound was enlarged, about a foot and a half of earth was spread over it. The buildings on top were torn down or burned and then rebuilt an average of three times before the mound was enlarged again. Several low mounds measuring 1.5 to 2.5 feet high and 30 to 40 feet square were spaced around the plaza, and the houses of elite people were built on top of them. Like the temples on the mounds, when these elite houses burned down or were torn down, the sites on which they stood were sometimes covered over with a layer of dirt before rebuilding took place. In Mississippian towns it was generally the case that the elite people built their houses in close proximity to the house of the chief. The elite houses were 18 to 22 feet square, while the houses of common folk (or perhaps extended kin), situated between the elite houses and the palisade, were somewhat smaller, 15 to 20 feet square.[32]

De Soto's men charged aggressively into the first town of Quizquiz, as if it were a town of Chicaza or Alibamo, whose people had recently inflicted so much damage on them. As the Spaniards came storming in, some of the

Indians fled into a forest that lay outside the town. Others fled to a mound that stood on one side of the plaza. As the people milled around the mound, a very old and ill chief heard the noise made by the people and came out of a house on top of the mound. Seeing what was happening, he seized a war club and with great anger began descending the steps, threatening to kill anyone who dared come into his land without permission. He did not have strength enough to kill a cat, but he acted as if he could kill a lion. His wives and servants held onto him, pleading with him not to go down where the Spaniards were, reminding him of his poor health. These intruders were people the likes of whom they had never seen before, and they had brought with them large and very powerful animals. They told the old chief to feign friendship and bide his time, else he would bring great injury to himself and to all the others. They did stop him from putting up a defense, but they could not make him feign friendship. Instead, he made it clear he wished to annihilate the Spaniards.[33]

De Soto sent one of the Indians they had captured to the chief of Quizquiz, who was still absent, with the news of the Spaniards' arrival. The Indian was to tell the chief that if he would come in peace, De Soto would release his mother and the other captives. The chief, however, sent back a reply that if his people were first released and the seized goods returned, he would come in peace and cooperate. De Soto, because his men and horses were so hungry and exhausted, with many of them ill, thought it best to comply, to see if he would have peace. He ordered the chief's mother and all the others released and the seized goods returned, and he sent them to the chief with kind words.[34]

But the next day the chief came with a large force of armed warriors who seemed to have every intention of attacking the Spaniards. De Soto immediately ordered his horsemen to be ready for action. When the approaching Indians saw that the Spaniards were prepared to fight, they stopped at about the distance of the flight of a crossbow bolt from where De Soto and his men were standing. They stood beside a stream, probably the Walls Meander.[35]

The Indians milled around for about half an hour, and then they sent six of their principal men to meet with De Soto. These emissaries said they had been told a legend by their ancestors that a white race of people would come and subdue them, and they wished to find out what kind of men these were. They gave De Soto six or seven skins and blankets as a gift, and they left, saying they would tell their chief to come and meet with De Soto. De Soto sent word to this chief to supply him with canoes in order to cross the great river that lay ahead of them.[36] But in fact the chief did not come, and he never sent another messenger, and he did not supply the canoes. The Indians who had assembled to do battle departed.[37]

The Mississippi River

The Spaniards found little corn at the first town of Quizquiz. They moved to a second village, probably at the Lake Cormorant site, a league away, where they found an abundance of corn. They also found for the first time small "walnuts" they had not seen before, probably pecans, which they judged to be superior to nuts in Spain.[38] A little later they moved to a third village—probably the Woodlyn site—about a league away, and they also found an ample supply of corn there. They may never have visited the main town of Quizquiz, which is thought to have been the Walls site, located in the narrow neck of the Walls Meander.[39]

At about half a league from the third village of Quizquiz, at some time between May 9 and May 21, they first saw the Río de Espíritu Santo—the Mississippi River.[40] Some of the Indians called this river *Chucagua*.[41] To some of the Spaniards, the river seemed wider than the Danube.

On May 21 De Soto moved his men to a small open field a crossbow bolt flight from the river, where there was an abundance of wood and a good place to establish a camp. This was possibly an old agricultural field that had become overgrown with weeds and grass.[42] It gave them easy access to the water.[43] Here they built temporary houses for themselves and began sawing and squaring planks for the large piraguas in which they would cross the river. To insure their supply of food, they went back and raided the granaries of the towns of Quizquiz they had just visited.[44]

Very soon after the Spaniards began work on their boats, some Indians in dugout canoes appeared and pulled up to the landing. Four principal men got out and approached De Soto. In unison, they all faced the east and bowed deeply toward the sun. Then they turned toward the west and made a lesser bow to the moon. Then they turned toward De Soto and bowed still less.[45] They informed De Soto they were vassals of a great chief, Aquijo, who was dominant over many towns on the opposite side of the river. They said Chief Aquijo would come the next day to talk with De Soto. The next day the chief arrived with a fleet of two hundred very large dugout canoes, full of Indians armed with bows and arrows. The Spaniards counted as many as seven thousand Indians, painted with red ocher and wearing feathers of many colors.[46] Some of them held shields of cane so tightly and strongly woven that a crossbow bolt could hardly penetrate them. Down the center of each canoe, from stem to stern, stood a line of archers, with bows and arrows at the ready.[47]

The chief was in a large canoe, seated beneath a canopy fixed over the stern. It was in such a canopied canoe—though surely a much smaller one—that they had first encountered the Lady of Cofitachequi. This chief gave orders that all the others in the fleet obeyed. Other canoes contained other notable men, who were likewise seated beneath canopies. These canoes were an impressive sight. They were very large, and with the shields and banners and the large crews manning them, they resembled a fleet of miniature galleys.[48]

The fleet massed together and came to within a stone's throw of the bluff where De Soto was walking with several companions. The chief said to De Soto that he had come to serve him because he had heard he was the greatest lord on earth. He asked De Soto what he wished of him. De Soto thanked him and asked him to land his canoe and come ashore so they might converse more readily. Chief Aquijo did not answer, but instead sent three canoes ashore bearing a quantity of fish and brick-shaped loaves made out of the pulp of what the Spaniards took to be plums, though it was probably persimmons. De Soto accepted these gifts and again asked the chief to come ashore. The chief's intent was to see whether he could inflict some damage on the Spaniards, but because the Spaniards were clearly on their guard, the fleet began to withdraw to a safer distance from the shore.

When De Soto's crossbowmen saw this, they shouted and began shooting at the canoes. Their bolts struck five or six of the Indians, but even with these casualties the canoes withdrew in good order, with their crews maintaining perfect discipline. When a paddler fell dead or wounded, the men next to him calmly continued paddling. Then, at a safe distance, the Indians in the fleet taunted the Spaniards with insults and threats and returned to the other side of the river.[49]

The Spaniards continued building four large piraguas, each of which would hold five to six horses or sixty to seventy footmen. While this work was going on, the fleet of two hundred to three hundred canoes would come every day at about three in the afternoon. Protecting themselves with their shields, the Indians would come in close enough to shout threats and loose a hail of arrows toward the Spaniards.[50] The Spaniards dug foxholes along the margin of the river's bank, and from their concealment they would shoot at the canoes when they approached.[51]

The construction of the piraguas was finished in twenty-seven days.[52] When the Indians saw that the boats were almost complete, they informed De Soto that Chief Pacaha, who was their lord, had ordered them to stop resisting and to leave the passage free.[53]

Even without the threat of resistance, the Spaniards were facing a formidable crossing. The river seemed to them to be nearly half a league wide.[54] And in places it was nineteen to twenty brazas deep (about 104 to 110 feet).[55] It was so wide that a person on the opposite bank, unless he were moving, could not be differentiated from a mere object. The current of the river was very strong, and trees and large pieces of wood were constantly being borne down its muddy waters.[56] The banks were steep in places, so that crossings could only be made where there was a suitable landing.[57]

Three hours before dawn on June 18, at approximately 1:50 A.M., under a waning crescent moon, De Soto ordered his men to cross the river.[58] Into three of the piraguas he loaded four horses each, plus a few crossbowmen and rowers. In the fourth piragua he put Juan de Guzmán—now occupying the command previously held by Maldonado—and a number of footmen. Because the current was so strong, they rowed the piraguas for a quarter of a league upstream along the bank of the river. Then they launched themselves into the current and made for the opposite shore. Although the current carried them downstream as they crossed, they reached the other bank more or less opposite their camp. At a distance of about two stones' throw from the shore, the horsemen jumped their horses out of the piraguas and made for land, finding themselves on hard sand that was free of vegetation. They had landed on a sand bar, which could only have occurred in the shallow water in the inside of a bend in the river. There were no Indians there to resist, and the piraguas landed and unloaded the footmen without incident.[59]

Having secured their beachhead on the western side of the Mississippi, the oarsmen in the piraguas returned to the other side and began ferrying the remainder of the army across. Within two hours after sunrise, the operation was complete. The Spaniards had entered the territory of the chiefdom of Aquijo (fig. 62). On June 19 De Soto marched his men upriver about a league and a half to a town of Aquijo, whose people had abandoned it.[60] Soon afterward, they saw about thirty Indians approaching stealthily across an open field, obviously sent to spy on the invaders. But as soon as the Indians became aware that the Spaniards had caught sight of them, they turned on their heels and ran. The horsemen pursued them, lancing ten of them and capturing fifteen others.[61]

A string of archaeological sites are situated on the levee ridge of Horseshoe Lake—the Patoka Meander—which in 1541 may still have been connected to

Fig. 62. A head effigy vessel from the Belle Meade site (Aquijo). Head effigy vessels almost always portray deceased individuals, but archaeologists disagree about whether these are the heads of revered ancestors or vanquished enemies. Photograph by David Dye. (Private collection)

the river, providing access by canoe. Because the town De Soto reached was near the river, he sent a small party of men back to the piraguas with orders to row them upstream. As they made their way upstream, the current was so swift the piraguas could not make any headway if they steered a course very far away from shore. The Indians were now showing more resistance. A company of Spaniards went out to try to drive the Indians away from the river, but because bodies of water frequently prevented them from getting close to the riverbank, they were not able to drive all of them away. Thus it frequently happened that these Indians were able to stand atop the steep bank and shoot arrows down at the men in the piraguas, making their progress upstream difficult and dangerous.[62] But as soon as he could, De Soto sent a contingent of crossbowmen to protect the piraguas, and they were able to do so effectively. When the piraguas reached the town, the Spaniards tore them apart, removing the precious spikes to save them for future use (see fig. 85b).[63]

Casqui

This first town of Aquijo may have been at the Pouncey site, with two large pyramidal mounds and several smaller house mounds arranged around a plaza.[64] The material culture of the people of Aquijo was very similar to that of Quizquiz on the eastern side of the river and, as we shall see, also to Pacaha upriver.[65] On June 21 the Spaniards departed from this village, probably continuing along the levee ridge, and they marched past a second abandoned town, which they said was very beautifully situated.[66] They learned from the Indians they had captured that Pacaha had an enemy, Casqui, whose towns lay at a distance of three days' march from where they were.

De Soto, a devotee of the principle of divide-and-conquer, decided they would visit Casqui before going to Pacaha. On June 22 they came to a small stream, probably Fifteenmile Bayou, and crossed a footbridge the Indians had built. Then they began crossing what they judged to be the worst stretch of swamp they had yet encountered in La Florida. This was the large sunkland swamp at West Memphis, situated between the Mississippi River and the St. Francis meander belts. This vast swamp served as an aquatic buffer zone separating Aquijo, Casqui, and Pacaha.[67] They walked almost the entire day through standing water that was often knee-deep, and their course was generally to the west and to the northwest. At sunset they managed to reach the high ground of some levees, and they were very pleased, having feared they would have to spend the night mired in the waters of the swamp.[68]

At noon on June 23 they entered the first town of Casqui.[69] At this time they were near the St. Francis River, perhaps within sight of Crowley's Ridge. The people they encountered were not on their guard and had not had any warning of the Spaniards' approach. De Soto's soldiers captured many men and women and a quantity of woven shawls and skins, which they needed for clothing. From the vantage of this first town, they could see a second town half a league away, across an open field. The horsemen galloped over to it and seized more captives and goods.[70] The land on which these towns were situated was higher and drier than the terrain they had just crossed.[71] It was the levee ridge that lay along the eastern side of the St. Francis River.

The land near Casqui—and indeed the land of all the chiefdoms in this region—seemed very rich, abounding in food, with very large fields along the margins of the rivers and streams.[72] Many pecan trees grew scattered about in the open fields, and the Indians had large stores of pecans in their houses.[73] They noted that the foliage of these trees resembled that of walnut trees in Spain and elsewhere, except they had smaller leaves. Many mulberry trees grew among the fields, as well as persimmon trees of two varieties. One of the persimmons had fruit that was red, resembling plums in Spain, and the other had dun-colored (*pardas*) fruit that was much better in quality.[74] All the trees were healthy, and scattered about as if tended in orchards or gardens.[75] In clearing trees from land for farming, the Indians evidently spared nut and fruit trees.

On June 23 they continued on, passing through agricultural fields and large villages of fifteen to forty houses. The land was continuously occupied, so that from some villages two or three others could be seen in the distance.[76] A messenger from the chief of Casqui came to De Soto saying he would meet him in peace. After this, in every town they came to, they were given gifts of fish, skins, and shawls. On this same day, as they approached the principal town of Casqui, the chief and his retinue marched out for a certain distance to meet De Soto on the trail, much as the paramount chief of Coosa had done.

The principal town of Casqui was at the Parkin site (fig. 63), on the St. Francis River, a stream the Spaniards said was larger than the Guadalquivir River at Córdoba.[77] The chief of Casqui was a man about fifty years old.[78] He greeted De Soto, and they exchanged friendly words. The chief said he had heard about the Spaniards for a long time, and he knew they were men from heaven, whom his arrows would not harm, and therefore he decided to meet them in peace.[79] He offered the use of his town to De Soto, but De Soto thought that occupying the town might lead to conflict, so he excused himself, saying that because of the excessive heat he preferred to bivouac a quarter of a league from town in the shade of some trees.[80] After their meeting was over, the chief returned to his town.

Casqui—the Parkin site—is situated on the eastern bank of the St. Francis River, just below the mouth of the Tyronza River. Both the St. Francis and the Tyronza flow through old channels of the Mississippi River. The Parkin site is

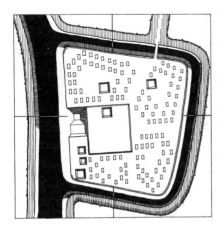

Fig. 63. Schematic map of the Parkin site. From William N. Morgan, *Prehistoric Architecture of the Eastern United States*, 67. (William N. Morgan, architect)

seventeen acres in extent and is laid out roughly in the form of a rectangle. The town was protected on three sides by a palisade and a deep ditch (from which fill was taken to build the mound), and on the fourth side it lay fast against the St. Francis River. It was a site where many people had lived for a long time, so much so that the town came to be elevated on a kind of "tell," built up out of everyday refuse and of fill carried to the site. Eventually it came to stand about ten feet above the surrounding floodplain. The western side of the town was dominated by a temple mound twenty-one feet high, facing a plaza in the center of the town. This plaza, whose surface was somewhat lower than the terrain on all sides of it, was surrounded by a ring of houses with square floor plans.

By great good fortune, the Parkin site has been spared some of the ravages that have destroyed so many of the sites De Soto visited. With great foresight, the Arkansas Department of Parks and Tourism has acquired the site, and it now has a visitors center where people can see a small museum as well as archaeological excavations that will continue under the auspices of the Arkansas Archaeological Survey for many years.

The houses at the Parkin site were furnished with Mississippi Plain, Barton Incised, Burton, Kent, and Old Town Red pottery, and with lesser amounts of other wares (fig. 64). Relatively few of the elaborate ritual vessels (e.g., animal effigies, human effigies, human-head bottles) found at the sites of nearby polities have been found at Parkin phase sites.

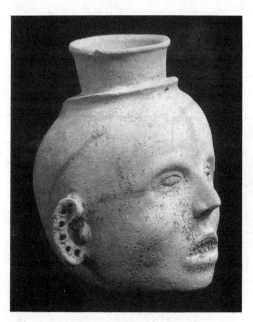

Fig. 64. A head effigy vessel from the Parkin site. Photograph by David Dye.

Other Casqui town sites lay south of Parkin and more lay to the north, up the St. Francis and Tyronza Rivers. Four of these northern sites are medium-size towns (6.5 to 9.25 acres). Three of these four sites are each at a distance of about five miles from Parkin, and the fourth is about twelve and a half miles from Parkin. These medium-size villages and also a much larger number of smaller villages are all thought to have been fortified. No scattered, unprotected farmsteads have been found in the Parkin area. Clearly, this was no peaceable kingdom.

Consistent with its dominant position in the Casqui chiefdom, the Parkin site was situated near the confluence of the St. Francis and Tyronza Rivers, within easy reach of dugout canoes from all parts of the chiefdom. The larger Parkin phase villages were located near the largest expanses of good agricultural soil. Only the Parkin site itself was situated near mediocre agricultural soils, no doubt a sacrifice to its strategic location. The implication of this is that some of the corn consumed by the people of the Parkin site was brought in from other villages as tribute.[81]

At some time after De Soto arrived, the chief of Casqui again came to pay his respects, accompanied by a chorus of singing retainers. All of his people bowed themselves to the ground. The chief brought along two blind men; he said that because De Soto was from heaven, a son of the Sun, and a great lord, he should please restore the health of the two blind men. The blind men rose up and begged De Soto to restore their sight. De Soto replied that he could not, but his Master in heaven had the power to give them health and anything else they might ask of him. De Soto told them that God had created the heavens and the earth and had created man in his own likeness. Christ, his son, had suffered on the cross, and in that he was mortal he died, but in that he is immortal he arose on the third day and ascended into Heaven, where he will welcome all those who convert to him.[82] The chief of Casqui pressed De Soto to give him some kind of sign or symbol to which he could turn for help in warfare and to which he could pray for rain. And indeed, his fields were dry because of a drought, and the children were dying from hunger.[83] De Soto assured him he would come the next day and give him the symbol he desired.

The next day, June 23, the chief returned, complaining about the delay in giving him the symbol he had asked for. He began weeping, asking why it had not been given, and the Spaniards were touched by the man's earnestness. Droughts were one of the greatest hazards Mississippian agriculturalists faced. Some parts of the Southeast went through a particularly dry period from 1565 to 1575; some dry spells occurred in the decades before this period, and 1541 was evidently a drought year.[84]

De Soto ordered Maestro Francisco, their Genoese carpenter and ship-wright, to construct a cross from a large tree. They felled this tree, peeled the bark from it, and cut out two sections of the trunk. The cross was built in the proportion of five and three, and it was placed on the summit of the mound. It was magnificent, standing high above the river.[85] This mound, being the highest point in the area, also served as a lookout from which the people of Casqui could observe activities on the St. Francis River.[86]

The Spaniards and the Indians formed a procession. The chief of Casqui walked along beside De Soto, and his people were scattered out among the Spaniards. Marching in front were the priests and friars who sang litanies, which were answered by responses from the soldiers. The entire procession may have included more than a thousand people. Entering the town they saw that the houses were very well constructed. The largest houses, including the chief's, stood on top of the mound. Above its door it had several stuffed buffalo heads, seemingly displayed as trophies, much as noblemen in Spain mounted the heads of wild boars and bears they had killed.[87] There were several other structures near the mound housing the chief's wives and servants.[88]

When the procession reached the cross, the Spaniards all fell to their knees, and the priests said prayers. Then the priests approached the cross, and fell to their knees, kissing the foot of the cross. Next came De Soto and the chief of Casqui, who kissed the cross. Then came the Spanish soldiers, and finally the Indians of Casqui, who imitated what they had seen the Spaniards do.[89] On the opposite side of the river stood many hundreds of Indians, with their arms stretched out toward the heavens. From time to time they would gesture to the heavens with their hands and faces. Then they uttered the dull, muted cry of people beginning to weep, and their children joined in. Thus the Indians on both sides of the river of Casqui were weeping, seemingly in adoration of the cross. The Spaniards were much moved by this spectacle. When the ceremony ended, the Spaniards returned to their camp in procession, with the priests chanting the "Te Deum Laudamus."[90]

It so happened that later on this day, at midnight, a rain began to fall, and it rained very hard, drenching the parched fields. This pleased the Indians greatly, and they came to De Soto, assuring him that they were indeed his vassals.[91] De Soto told them that from now on they should worship the Lord in Heaven and ask of Him what they needed.[92] The Indians then went immediately and collected a great quantity of river cane, which they used to build a fence around the cross. Such lightly constructed palisades—perhaps to deter children and dogs—have been noted at several Mississippian sites elsewhere in the Southeast.[93]

De Soto soon confirmed that Casqui and Pacaha were indeed mortal enemies and had been so for a very long time. Pacaha appeared to be the more powerful of the two, and from what De Soto could learn it seemed that Pacaha was pushing the chief of Casqui into a corner, so that he did little more than guard his boundaries, neither going beyond them, nor allowing Pacaha to invade. But now the chief of Casqui saw the opportunity that De Soto offered him. He would go together with De Soto and exact vengeance on Pacaha.[94]

Pacaha

De Soto asked the chief of Casqui how far it was to Pacaha, and the man told him that when his people went there it took one day. He said that between his land and that of Pacaha there was a swamp formed by a kind of estuary of the Mississippi River. It was in fact an old channel—a bayou—of the St. Francis River. He said he would send his men in advance of De Soto to build a footbridge on which they could cross to the other side.[95]

On June 26 De Soto and his men departed from the main town of Casqui, passing through several villages and spending the night in one of them.[96] Undoubtedly these were the towns that lay strung along the eastern side of Tyronza River. That night, Casqui and his warriors camped some distance away.[97] On June 27 they passed by several other towns and came to the swamp they had been told about—probably Gibson Bayou—which they found to be half-a-crossbow-flight wide, very deep, and with a current. The Indians of Casqui had just completed building the footbridge, which was cleverly constructed by tying poles from tree to tree—no doubt cypress trees—and with a line of smaller poles at a height convenient for a handrail to support those who crossed. The Spaniards swam their horses across.[98]

The chief of Casqui and some of his warriors accompanied De Soto as he proceeded on to the main town of Pacaha, the Bradley site, a large site with four mounds.[99] The town was on land somewhat higher than its surroundings, namely on Bradley Ridge, a notable levee that lay alongside Wapanocca Bayou.[100] De Soto found the town to be strongly stockaded, with defensive towers, and a ditch had been dug around three sides of the town, connecting with Wapanocca Bayou, which in turn emptied into the Mississippi River.[101] The ditch around the town was wide enough that two large canoes could paddle side by side.[102] Thus the chief of Pacaha had a thoroughfare by which he could send canoes from the outskirts of his principal town to the Mississippi River. A palisade was built to protect the part of the town that was not protected by the ditch.[103]

Evidently the Indians of Casqui were following at some distance behind De Soto, because when the Spaniards came into sight of the town, they saw a large group of Indians approaching. At first the Spaniards thought they were reinforcements for Pacaha, but in fact they were warriors of Casqui.[104] De Soto sent an Indian messenger to Pacaha telling him that he was coming with the chief of Casqui, but that even though Pacaha and Casqui were enemies, no harm would be done to Pacaha and his people if they waited peacefully. De Soto and Casqui would treat him as if he were a brother. But as the Spaniards walked around the outside of the fortification, they could see that the chief of Pacaha and his people were fleeing in dugout canoes from the other side of their town.

De Soto immediately led a contingent of horsemen into the town, hurrying to the place where the people were casting off. By the time they got there, however, almost all the people had fled. There were several large fortified towns at distances of half a league to a league from the main town.[105] Some of the other horsemen rode to a second town a quarter of a league away, where they were able to capture many people. They delivered these people over to the warriors of Casqui, who were overjoyed at having so many of their enemies as prisoners. They led them all back to the main town, but they were disappointed when De Soto refused to allow them to execute them.[106]

Still thirsting for revenge, the Casquis took great pleasure in sacking the house of the chief of Pacaha.[107] Even more, they made a point of entering the temple, where the remains of the Pacaha elite were kept and held sacred. This was the place most venerated by the people of Pacaha. Here the Casquis committed every act of desecration they could devise. They stripped the temple of all its riches. They emptied the wooden chests containing the remains of Pacaha ancestors, strewing the bones and bodies on the ground and stamping on them, smashing them to pieces. When the Casquis found the heads and skulls of their own people impaled on lances by the door of the temple, they removed them and substituted the heads of Pacahas they had just killed. The Casqui warriors wanted to burn the temple, the chief's house, and the entire village, but De Soto would not allow it.[108]

As they marauded through the fields and towns of Pacaha, the warriors of Casqui were also angered when they came across many of their friends and relatives who had been enslaved by the Pacahas. As was the practice elsewhere in the Southeast, these slaves had a hamstring on one foot cut, so they could walk but not run. These slaves were held more as evidence of military superiority than for any economic advantage they might confer.[109] The injured feelings of the Casquis were somewhat assuaged when De Soto let them take home plunder from the towns of Pacaha, including corn, beads made of seashells, and animal skins.[110]

The towns of Aquijo, Casqui, and Pacaha were said to be the best the Spaniards had seen since landing at Tampa Bay. They were large in size, particularly the principal towns, and very strongly fortified with palisades with towers and many archers' loop holes, and they all had subsidiary fortified towns scattered about them.[111] The people of this area impressed the Spaniards as being of "finer quality" than most of the Indians they had encountered on their travels; they considered them to be second only to the people of Cofitachequi.[112] Pacaha was clearly the dominant power in this part of the central Mississippi Valley.

The dominant town of Pacaha was one of a cluster of sites on Wapanocca Lake and Wapanocca Bayou. A similar cluster of towns lay in and around the present-day towns of Joiner and Wilson, Arkansas, and yet another cluster lay along Little River–Pemiscot Bayou in northern Arkansas and southern Missouri. The nature of the relationships between the Wapanocca Lake and Bayou cluster of sites and the clusters at Joiner-Wilson and Little River–Pemiscot Bayou is unknown. There is no evidence they were at war with each other, but neither is there sufficient evidence to say that the people of any of these site clusters were tributary or subservient to the towns on Wapanocca Lake and Bayou.

This area of Pacaha has been so heavily impacted by modern intensive farming and even more by intensive pothunting that little is known about the social geography of Pacaha or its culture. It is clear that Pacaha people lived in compact, fortified towns, similar to those of Casqui. Like other Mississippian polities, the larger towns had multiple pyramidal mounds. At least some of the people used aboveground granaries, and they cultivated a variety of corn that bore unusually large ears. The people were somewhat unusual in burying their dead in cemeteries, possibly clustered in kin groups. Corpses were normally extended full length on a roughly north-south axis. A bowl and a bottle were generally placed near the head as an offering.

The larger sites in this region, such as the Upper Nodena site, occupied as much as 15.5 acres, with an estimated average population of one thousand to fifteen hundred people. Based on the aggregate size of total sites, the population of the Pacaha region seems to have been three to three and a half times that of Casqui. We cannot be sure that all of these people were under the aegis of the chief of Pacaha, but when we consider that Pacaha clearly had command

Fig. 65. Human effigy vessel, possibly from the Bradley site. It represents a male seated with his feet in lotus position. Photograph by David Dye. (Memphis Pink Palace Museum)

over Quizquiz and Aquijo, it is certain that Pacaha had Casqui outnumbered by a large factor.

Like all people of the central Mississippi Valley, the Pacahas were excellent potters (fig. 65). Their domestic and kitchen ware, as at Casqui, was Mississippi Plain—a buff-colored ware with coarse shell tempering and a rather rough surface. But it is the fancy ware, most often found with burials, that most clearly shows the artistry of the potters. This ware includes handsome bottles, some with stirrup spouts, some modeled in various natural forms such as owls, squashes, and human heads (fig. 66). It also includes bowls with rims decorated with small effigies of people, ducks, turkey buzzards, dogs, rabbits, owls, bats, and passenger pigeons. Sometimes the entire bowl was made into an effigy of a fish, opossum, frog, or other creature. A few vessels were decorated with red (hematite) and white (galena or kaolin) slips, and on rare occasion with black (graphite). The favorite painted motifs were broad alternating red and white stripes or a red swastika whorl on a white background. Some jars and bottles were decorated with incising or modeling.[113]

It is difficult to say very much about what languages were spoken in the central Mississippi Valley. The De Soto chroniclers recorded little more than place-names, and these are often linguistically distorted. But there is some evidence the people of Pacaha may have spoken a Tunican language. The languages spoken by Quizquiz, Aquijo, and Casqui are unknown.[114]

Fig. 66. Head effigy vessel from the Shawnee Village site. Note the facial tattooing of an inverted raptorial bird. (Hampson Museum State Park, Wilson, Arkansas)

The people of the central Mississippi River Valley were well off in material things. In their flight from De Soto and his men, the people of Pacaha left behind most of their possessions. The Spaniards found many woven shawls, as well as the dressed skins of deer, bear, and panther. The Spaniards were still poorly clothed, and during their time at Pacaha they used these materials to make new garments. From the shawls they made loose coats, cassocks, and gowns, lining some of them with panther skins. They used the deerskins to make jerkins, shirts, leggings, and shoes, and the bearskins to make cloaks, which they said were very good because they were waterproof. They made armor for their horses from native shields made of raw buffalo skins.[115] While they were at Pacaha, the chief of Casqui frequently sent them gifts of shawls, skins, and a great quantity of fish.[116]

They found an ample supply of the previous season's corn stored in the main town of Pacaha, as well as new corn growing in the fields. Fish could be caught in abundance in the ditch around the main town, especially when using nets the Indians had made. And no matter how many fish were caught, there were always more. There were also plenty of fish in the nearby swamps, but it seemed to the Spaniards that the flesh of the fish they caught in the ditch and in the river of Pacaha (Wapanocca Bayou) was firmer and better than that of those caught in the swamps.[117]

These fish were for the most part different from the freshwater fish of Spain. The fish the Portuguese called *bagre,* a New World Spanish word meaning "catfish," is described by the Gentleman of Elvas as having a head that made up a third of its body, with long sharp spines like a shoemaker's awl on either side of its throat and along its sides. Those in the ditch were as large as a *picão* (a Portuguese fish with a pointed snout), while there were some in the river that weighed up to 150 pounds. Elvas is possibly describing the flathead catfish (*Pylodictis olivaris*). Many of these catfish were taken using hooks.[118] Another fish resembled the Portuguese *barbo*, possibly the shovelnose sturgeon. Another was like the *choupa*, a common Portuguese fish, but with a head like that of the *besugo*, a Portuguese bream. It was colored russet and brown, and this was the fish the Spaniards relished most. Elvas is probably referring to buffalo fishes (see fig. 72): smallmouth buffalo (*Ictiobus bubalus*) and largemouth buffalo (*I. cyprinellos*). Buffalo fish are the most important commercial fishes in Arkansas to this day.

The Portuguese called the spoonbill, or paddlefish, *pexe palla*, literally "spade-fish." It was scaleless and had a snout a cubit long, the upper part of the snout being shaped like a shovel. They called the alligator gar (*Atractosteus spatula*) *pexe pereo*, literally "dog fish." To them it seemed very large, sometimes the weight of a hog, and it had rows of teeth both above and below.[119] The alligator gar can be as much as ten feet long and can weigh as much as three hundred pounds. Good arrow points could be fashioned from its bony scales. Yet another fish resembled the shad.

The chief of Casqui promised De Soto he could deliver the chief of Pacaha into his hands. He returned to his town and ordered that many of his canoes be brought up the river. This was accomplished by paddling from the Parkin site up the Tyronza River to Big Creek, which ran into Wapanocca Lake and Bayou.[120] The chief also brought many of his warriors overland to Pacaha. Once Casqui and his warriors had arrived, De Soto took forty horsemen and sixty footmen and went with them along the bayou.

Reconnoitering in their canoes, the warriors of Casqui found that the chief of Pacaha had sought refuge two leagues away from Pacaha on a small island in the Mississippi River.[121] De Soto and his men made their way to the riverbank opposite the island, and Don Antonio Osorio and four other Spaniards went with some Casquis in a canoe to scout the island. They found there were as many as five or six thousand people there with their chief. But as soon as the people on the island spotted the approaching canoe with Spaniards aboard, the chief and some others fled in three canoes to refuge on the opposite side of the river. Many of those left behind were so terrified of the approaching Spaniards they ran into the water and began swimming, and a number of them drowned, especially the women and children.

From where De Soto stood on the bank of the river, he could not see what was happening to Don Antonio and the others who went to the island. He ordered Spaniards and Indians to follow them in the rest of the canoes brought by the chief of Casqui. The story was later told that as they made the crossing to the island, Francisco Sebastián, a jovial gentleman from Villanueva de Barcarrota, entertained the crew of one of the canoes with witticisms and banter, which, according to Garcilaso, went something like this:

> Evil fortune brought me to these hopeless regions, for God had placed me in Italy, a good land where, according to the usage of the language, I was addressed as your lordship, just as if I had been a lord of vassals. But you people here do not appreciate me sufficiently to address me as "thou." Furthermore the generous and charitable inhabitants of that place regaled and succored me in my needs as if I were their own son. And in both peace and war I fared as follows: if I chanced to kill some Turk, Moor, or Frenchman, I never failed to despoil him of arms, clothing, or horses, which were always worth something to me. But here I have to fight with some naked individual who runs along ten or twelve steps in front of me, jumping and shooting arrows at me as if I were a wild beast, and I am unable to catch up with him. And if my good luck favors me and I do overtake and kill him, I find nothing to take off him except a bow and a feather headdress—as if these articles were of any value to me. And the thing that pains me most is that a famous astrological prophet called "the Morning Star of Italy" has told me to avoid traveling on water since I am to die by drowning, and it appears that misfortune has brought me to a land where we never leave the water.[122]

As the canoe in which Sebastián was riding approached the shore of the island, he stuck the butt of his weapon into the water near the shore to steady the canoe. But when the canoe suddenly pulled back, he fell into the water, which even near the shore of the island was very deep. Because he wore a coat of chain mail, he was not able to surface. His drowning caused great sadness among his comrades.

Once ashore on the island, the Spaniards found stores of clothing, and they captured many Indians of both sexes. The Indians of Pacaha had a quantity of clothing and goods piled on wooden rafts that they intended to take to the opposite side of the river. One of the rafts was set loose and began floating down the river. The Indians of Casqui went after it in some of their canoes, and they retrieved this cargo from the raft. Then fearing that the Spaniards would take it from them, they continued on downstream.[123] This made De Soto furious.

Some Spaniards worried that the Casquis would take all the canoes and leave the Spaniards stranded on the island.[124] But this did not happen. De Soto and his men returned safely to the main town of Pacaha.

De Soto, however, was still furious. He immediately dispatched a party of horsemen on a retaliatory raid against Casqui. They entered Casqui territory and captured twenty or thirty people. But because the horses were tired and it was getting late, they decided to return to Pacaha and to conduct another attack in three or four days.[125] Risking his men in battle and breaking his alliance with the Casquis over a mere pile of clothing was yet another instance of the kind of heedlessness De Soto exhibited following the battle at Mabila.

With this rupture between himself and the Casquis, De Soto, following the divide-and-rule strategy the Spaniards used in the conquest of the New World, set about trying to make peace with the chief of Pacaha. He had captured one of Pacaha's brothers when he had first stormed into the town.[126] De Soto sent a messenger to the chief of Pacaha to tell him he wished to have peace with him so they might conduct war upon Casqui. Chief Pacaha immediately sent a large force of his men to De Soto, accompanied by a man who pretended to be chief Pacaha. However, this ruse was soon exposed to De Soto by the brother of chief Pacaha. De Soto then sent word to chief Pacaha that he was aware of his deception and that he should come make an appearance in person. De Soto gave him to understand he had the ability to anticipate any deception he might attempt.[127]

The next day the chief of Pacaha, who was twenty-six or twenty-seven years of age, came to meet with De Soto. He was accompanied by a large contingent of principal men wearing beautiful feather headdresses, woven shawls, and animal skins.[128] He brought gifts of fish, shawls, and skins, and he was conciliatory, saying that De Soto had done damage to him and his people, but that he had deserved it, and he would henceforth be obedient to De Soto. With this, De Soto released the brother of the chief of Pacaha and some others he had captured.

Pacaha went inside his temple to survey the damage done by the Casquis. He lifted from the floor the bones and bodies of his ancestors and replaced them in the wooden boxes that were their sepulchers. And he straightened up the clutter in the temple as best he could. This desecration was the greatest affront to the Pacahas that the Casquis could have perpetrated.[129] When De Soto proposed that they join forces in attacking the Casquis, Chief Pacaha was more than willing to do so.[130]

The chief of Casqui may have somehow learned about this military pact between De Soto and Pacaha.[131] That same day, before De Soto and Pacaha had time to initiate a joint attack on Casqui, a messenger arrived saying the chief of Casqui would come the next day and beg De Soto's pardon for having absconded with the goods the Casquis had got from the raft. De Soto sent word to the chief of Casqui that he should by all means come in person, and if he did not, the Spaniards would go to his land and give him the punishment he deserved.[132]

The very next day Casqui came with forty of his warriors in full regalia.[133] He brought a gift of many fish, shawls, and skins. Remarkably, he sent ahead of him a clown, who seemingly performed the same function as clowns in medieval European courts. His antics caused everyone to laugh a good deal, undoubtedly in an attempt to defuse a potentially explosive situation.[134] But if De Soto was amused, he nonetheless gave the appearance of being irritated, and he said Casqui should not come into Pacaha's town. Casqui, however, would not be deterred. He said he would come in even if they cut off his head.[135] Pacaha also did not want Casqui to come into his town. He asked De Soto if it would be all right for him to give Casqui a slash on the face with the knife the Spaniards had given him.[136] But De Soto said he should not, and he would be angry if Pacaha did Casqui any harm. He wanted to see what this clever and courageous chief had to say for himself.[137]

Casqui wished to return to De Soto's good graces at all costs. He brought with him one of his daughters, whom he presented to De Soto, begging him to marry her. He wished to form a marriage alliance, joining his blood with that of the general.[138] De Soto told Casqui he had done well to come and place himself back under his protection. If he had not, the Spaniards would have invaded the land of Casqui to burn their towns and kill their people.[139] Then Casqui gave a brilliant speech in which he begged De Soto's pardon, while at the same time both praising and shaming De Soto. Through Juan Ortiz and the other Indian interpreters, Casqui begged De Soto's pardon for having fled from the island with Pacaha booty. He had done so, he said, because he was ashamed at what his people had done without having asked his consent. But Casqui wanted to know how De Soto, after having presented him with the high wooden cross to defend him against his enemies, could have thought of destroying him. And not only that, noting that the warriors of Pacaha were wearing small crosses prominently in their headdresses, how was it that the cross was to be used against him? How could De Soto do this after all the men, women, and children of Casqui had knelt down before a cross, and the rain had subsequently come in great quantities to save his corn from burning up in the drought?[140]

Casqui groveled before De Soto while verbally needling him. Why, after the men, women, and children of Casqui had devoted themselves to the cross and the Christian God, did De Soto intend to treat them so cruelly? Why did the Spaniards wish to do such grievous harm to people who were such good friends of the Spaniards and were friends of the cross?[141]

Some of the Spaniards who had listened attentively to this speech and its translation were moved to tears by Casqui's seeming simplicity and faith. Even De Soto may have had a tear in his eye. Both the Indians and the Spaniards were amazed at the force of Casqui's words.[142]

But if De Soto was at a loss for words, it was not for long. According to Rangel, he replied to Casqui, in effect, as follows:

> Look, Casqui: we do not come to destroy you, but rather to make you know and understand the cross and our God, as you say; and these favors that He has done you are a small thing in respect to many other great ones that He will do for you, if you love Him and believe in Him; and thus hold it for certain, and you will find it and see better each day. And since you went away without my permission, I thought that you held little regard for the doctrine that we had given you; and for the contempt that you had for it, I wished to destroy you, believing that you went away in pride, because this is the thing our God most abhors and for which He punishes us most. Now that you have come humbly, you may be certain that I wish you more good than what you think; and if you have need of something from me, tell me and you will see it, because we do what our God commands us, which is not to lie; and thus believe that I tell you the truth, because a lie is a very great sin among us. And do not be grateful to me or my men for this good will, because if you believe what you say, God Our Lord commands that we love you like a brother, and that we do things for you, because you and your people are our brothers, and thus our God tells us.[143]

Following this, the chief of Casqui and the chief of Pacaha feigned as much friendship as they could muster. They asked De Soto about Spain and also about the other native societies he had encountered during his travels.[144]

As it came time for a meal, De Soto sat down and asked the two chiefs to sit with him. But Pacaha and Casqui began to contend with each other over who should sit at De Soto's right hand.[145] Presumably in this culture of Casqui and

Pacaha, as in that of the Spaniards, the seat to the right was the seat of honor. Pacaha claimed the seat as his own because his lands were vaster than those of Casqui; he was the more powerful chief; and his genealogy was more illustrious than that of Casqui.[146] Casqui granted Pacaha these claims. But he insisted he was older than Pacaha, and age took precedence over youth. Moreover, he was militarily more potent than Pacaha. Casqui said he could contain the people of Pacaha within their walls any time he chose to do so. In fact, the people of Pacaha had never even penetrated inside his own territory. Pacaha objected that if Casqui were dining in his house, he would give him the seat of honor on account of his age, but they were dining with a third party, and the preeminence of his ancestors should be given preference. He insisted that he would have to sit on the right hand if he were to dine.[147] Finally, De Soto interceded and set Pacaha on his right side on the grounds that he was the greater chief, and his genealogy was the more illustrious, and in addition his manners were more like those of a courtier than were those of Casqui, whose manners were coarse.[148] The Spaniards, who doted on fine distinctions of honor and etiquette, were amazed that these two chiefs should have such concerns.[149] And it would seem that this is a measure, however indirect, of the political complexity of the central Mississippi Valley chiefdoms.

Trying to outdo each other, both chiefs supplied De Soto generously with fish, skins, and shawls. Nor did the rivalry between the two chiefs end with this. Casqui had given a daughter to De Soto, but Pacaha would not be outdone. He gave him one of his own wives as well as a sister and another high-ranking woman. One of these, Macanoche, was said to be well disposed, tall, plump, and had the bearing of a lady. A second was named Mochila. She was similarly well disposed, tall, and plump, but she was robust in her behavior. The name of the third was not given.[150]

In all these events at Pacaha it can be seen that these chiefdoms along the Mississippi River were the most complex societies De Soto and his men had encountered in all their travels, Cofitachequi not excepted.

North from Pacaha

While De Soto was at Pacaha, he sent out several expeditions to gain intelligence about the surrounding land.[151] From the Indians he captured at Aquijo, De Soto evidently got the impression that Pacaha lay near Chisca, where there was supposed to be gold.[152] Was this a new rumor, or was it an elaboration of the rumor of gold De Soto first got from the people of the upper

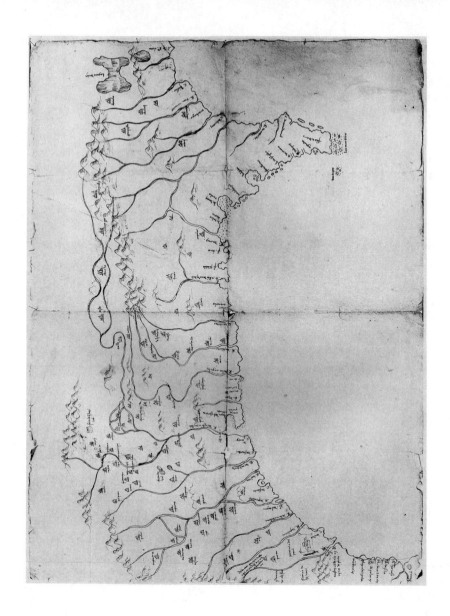

Fig. 67. The "De Soto map." Quizquiz, Casqui, and Pacaha are shown separated by interconnected streams of water at upper left of center. The Mississippi River is represented as running eastward to Tali, Coste, Chiaha, Canasoga, and Guaquili [*sic*].

Tennessee Valley, where he had first heard of the Chiscas and their supposed mines and foundries? The so-called De Soto map (fig. 67), postdating the expedition and evidently based upon it, indicates that De Soto's men thought of the Tennessee and French Broad Rivers as being the upper part of the Río del Espíritu Santo—the Mississippi River.[153] De Soto and his men may have thought that one of their options at Pacaha was to go back eastward toward the Chiscas, the only place where they had heard a strong rumor of gold. Another purpose for the small expeditions was that the Spaniards wanted to determine whether by going north they could discover a passage to the South Sea—the Pacific Ocean.[154]

In the course of several local forays carried out by the Spaniards soon after arriving at Pacaha, they captured an Indian who told them that toward the northwest there were large settlements of people. At some time in the first two weeks of July, De Soto sent a detachment of thirty horsemen and fifty footmen in that direction. They traveled through a wilderness for eight days, through pondy swamps, and eventually they came to some wide expanses where not even trees grew, only a grass—possibly a bluestem or tall-grass prairie.[155] This grassland was reportedly covered with foliage so rank and so tall that even men on horseback had difficulty in traveling through it.[156] Finally they came to the province of Caluza, a small settlement of six or seven huts made out of rushes sewn together and stretched over a framework of poles.[157] When a Caluza man wished to move, he simply rolled up his mats; his wife took down the framework of poles; and together they carried the mats and poles to another location and put themselves up a new house. Because they carried their house on their backs, so to speak, they could move as frequently as they wished.

They learned from these Indians that in this region there were other little settlements similar to theirs. The inhabitants traveled from place to place to fish and hunt for deer. To the Spaniards it seemed that these people planted very little food, preferring to hunt and to fish.[158]

Evidently, this exploring party had entered the lowland area of northern Arkansas that lay over ancient braided streambeds of the Mississippi River, an area that Mississippian people had once occupied but had abandoned by about A.D. 1400. It was at this time that Mississippian people in northern Arkansas began living in medium to large nucleated and fortified villages, and their soil preference was for the sandy loams in the meander belt of the Mississippi, St. Francis, and White Rivers. The soil in the lowland area, therefore, no longer met their needs. So far as archaeologists can determine, this wilderness area was not subsequently occupied by hunter-gatherers coming in from the west. But at several sites in this region, small numbers of Nodena arrow points and end scrapers have been found, artifacts that date to after A.D. 1400. The implication of this assemblage of artifacts is that the farmers of the Mississippi, St. Francis, and White River meander zones periodically went to this lowland area to hunt deer—both for meat and skins—and it is possible that the Caluzas encountered by this Spanish exploring party were such a group of Mississippian people on a communal summer hunt.[159]

The Indians of Caluza said that further north the land was sparsely inhabited because it was very cold, and because the buffalo there were so numerous, agricultural fields could not be protected from them. The Indians who lived there subsisted by hunting buffalo. When the Spaniards returned to Pacaha, they were famished, because on their exploration they had had to subsist on green persimmons and ears of immature corn.[160] Anyone who has ever experienced the mouth-puckering astringency of an unripe persimmon will understand how hungry they must have been.

De Soto sent a second expedition to the north from Pacaha. This was prompted by information gained from eight Indians whom the Spaniards had captured when they stormed the main town of Pacaha. These men were not natives of Pacaha but were traders who traveled about trading salt and other materials. They told De Soto that "forty leagues" away there was a "mountain range" where one could procure a quantity of very good salt. They also said one could obtain there much of the yellow metal in which the Spaniards were so interested. These were probably the Ste. Francois Mountains, where deposits of salt, copper, and other minerals could be procured.[161]

Two Spaniards, Hernando de Silvera and Pedro Moreno, volunteered to go with these Indians to verify what they had said. As articles to be traded to the Indians they would visit, they carried pearls, deerskins, and beans they got from Pacaha, and probably some European trade items as well. Two of the Indian traders went along with them as guides. Eleven days later, after probably having gone as far north as the southeastern corner of Missouri, they returned with a quantity of crystalline rock salt, which had been mined rather than extracted from saltwater. They also brought back a quantity of very good copper. Like the other expedition, they reported that the land they had come to was sterile and thinly populated.[162]

It is reasonable to think that Silvera and Moreno reached the towns of the northernmost inhabitants of the central Mississippi Valley. We know this group by the archaeological sites that have been found on the Little River in northeastern Arkansas and Pemiscot Bayou in southeastern Missouri. Like the lowland Arkansas area, the southeastern Missouri lowlands had mostly been abandoned by about A.D. 1400–50. A cluster of five sites lay on the levee ridges of Pemiscot Bayou. Four of these contained at least one flat-topped mound. Unfortunately, most of these sites were destroyed by farmers and looters before they could be professionally excavated. From one of these sites—the Campbell (or Cooter) site—a substantial number of early European artifacts have been recovered by collectors. Included in these are a Clarksdale bell and at least twenty-four glass chevron beads (see fig. 85). This is the furthest north that such artifacts of sixteenth-century Spanish manufacture have been discovered.[163]

The exploration parties De Soto had sent out returned with very bad news. Although the Spaniards were pleased to have the salt they desperately needed, they were disappointed in not finding what they sought most—the Chiscas and their supposed gold foundries. They were also disappointed to hear that further to the north the land was said to be sparsely inhabited and so poor in corn production the Spaniards could not have traveled in that direction even if necessity had forced them to do so. Hence, even if a northern route to the South Sea existed, travel to it would be virtually impossible.[164]

Hernando de Silvera and Pedro Moreno had no way of knowing they had reached a part of the country that lay on the southern fringe of one of the earliest and certainly the most spectacular Mississippian chiefdoms—Cahokia (see fig. 6). Cahokia was located in the American Bottom, a rich expanse of alluvial soil that lay east of the Mississippi River, just below where the Missouri and Illinois Rivers empty into the Mississippi. The site lies east of present-day St. Louis, Missouri. This marvelously fertile land stretched for about seventy miles from north to south, and it was up to twelve miles wide. The soil of the American Bottom was superb for cultivating corn, and its network of swamps and waterways provided for water transport and access to aquatic resources.

Corn, squash, gourds, and sunflowers were cultivated in the American Bottom between A.D. 600 and 800, and perhaps even earlier. But between A.D. 800 and 1000, the transformation to a dependency on corn occurred, and the first components of the Mississippian way of life began to emerge. The climate during this time was much as it is today. The population increased rapidly at Cahokia, and the first mounds were built there. Between A.D. 1000 and 1200 the climate was warmer and wetter than it is today, and as such it was extremely favorable to corn agriculture. It was during this time that Cahokia grew into something resembling a city.

At the center of the Cahokia chiefdom lay a massive earthen structure—Monks Mound—a mound whose base covered more than fourteen acres and that stood over 100 feet high. It is the largest prehistoric earthen structure in the Western Hemisphere. It had a temple-palace on top that measured 48 feet by 104 feet and was as much as 50 feet high. The mound contains an estimated 22 million cubic feet of dirt that was dug by crude tools and carried there a basketload at a time on people's backs.

Encompassing Monks Mound, the Cahokia site occupied a roughly diamond-shaped area measuring 2.25 miles from north to south and 3 miles from east to west. This area contained over 120 mounds, most of which were flat-topped, but also a small number of conical and ridge-topped mounds. The central part of this area was fortified by a very strongly built palisade with defensive towers, with a total circumference of 2 miles. At its height, the population of Cahokia was perhaps 20,000 individuals. The furthest reach of the power and influence of the chief of Cahokia is unknown, but it must have been considerable.

In most respects Cahokia resembled the Mississippian towns De Soto and his men saw all along their march, only more so. For example, like the people of Tali in the Tennessee Valley, the people of Cahokia were interested in following the passage of the year as calculated by the changing position of the sun at sunrise. But seemingly to more closely follow the changing position of the sun, or perhaps to ritualize its changing position throughout the year, they constructed a "woodhenge"—a large circle of standing cedar posts—such that from the center of the circle, particular posts are aligned with the sun at summer solstice, winter solstice, and the two equinoxes. Near this circle of posts archaeologists unearthed a piece of pottery with an incised circle-and-cross, which may be interpreted as symbolizing the sun and the four cardinal directions.

Like other Mississippian chiefdoms—not to speak of the Natchez Indians of the early eighteenth-century Mississippi Valley—the people of Cahokia thought it right and good to execute and bury a number of retainers when an important man died. Beneath one of the ridge-top mounds at Cahokia, a retainer burial was found that contained a high-status male laid out on a blanket decorated with 20,000 shell beads, piles of mica and sheet copper, more than 800 exquisitely made flint arrow points, and 15 chunkey stones. Along with this individual were the remains of about 300 people, many of whom had evidently been put to death on a single occasion. With justification, some archaeologists have spoken of Cahokia as a small kingdom or nascent state.[165]

If Cahokia had existed in 1541, it is virtually certain De Soto would have gone there. But Cahokia did not exist then. It began to decline in about 1250, with the onset of the climatic decline popularly known as the Little Ice Age. Whether this drop in annual temperature and rainfall was itself sufficient to cause the decline is debated by archaeologists. Clearly, the people of Cahokia had other problems. The fortification they maintained for two hundred years testified to a high level of warfare from without or insurrection from within. And their tremendous demand for wood must have seriously depleted local forests. But whatever the cause or causes, the Cahokia area was essentially abandoned by about 1400.

And the abandonment of territory did not stop there. Archaeologists are mostly agreed now that the Indians who told Silvera and Moreno of a wilderness to the north told the truth. In the century preceding De Soto, a vast Vacant Quarter developed along the Mississippi River from the place Silvera and Moreno had reached up to the old Cahokia area, up the Ohio River to about present-day Evansville, Indiana, and up the Cumberland River to the Nashville Basin. Again, archaeologists debate about whether the Vacant Quarter was caused by climatic, bacteriological, economic, or social causes. One theorist, with tongue in cheek, has even gone so far as to suggest that it might have been caused by a population explosion among passenger pigeons, who pillaged the cornfields and caused the people to starve.[166]

De Soto had no choice but to turn away from the northerly direction he had been following since the battle at Mabila. He decided to lead his expedition westward to see what, if anything, lay in that direction.[167]

12

Utiangüe

Although De Soto learned from his exploration parties that nothing of promise lay to the north, he was told by Indian informants that to the south of Casqui lay Quiguate, a province that was populous and rich in corn.[1] With this prospect, De Soto and his army departed from Pacaha, on July 29, 1541, taking a southwesterly direction that first took them back to Casqui (see map 7).[2]

While they had been in Pacaha, the bridge they had used earlier in coming from the territory of Casqui had fallen into disrepair. It is possible the people of Casqui had destroyed it to discourage Spaniards and Pacahas from suddenly appearing in their midst. But now the chief of Casqui ordered that the bridge be repaired.[3] De Soto and his men made their way unimpeded, and by the end of this first day of travel, they came to a town of Casqui, where they bivouacked.[4] The next day they arrived at the main town of Casqui, and the chief came out to meet them, providing them with a quantity of fish. He brought with him two Indian women, presumably slaves, whom he traded to the Spaniards for two shirts.[5]

The chief of Casqui supplied De Soto with a guide and porters, and on July 31 they continued traveling toward the south, reaching a village of Casqui by nightfall. The next day, August 1, they reached a second village of Casqui,

310

possibly the Rose site, situated on the River of Casqui—the St. Francis—which was an arm of the River of Pacaha, the Mississippi.[6] In size, the St. Francis River reminded the Spaniards of the Guadalquivir River in Spain.[7] The following day, the chief of Casqui sent a fleet of canoes downriver, presumably for a prearranged rendezvous, and they ferried De Soto and his army across to the other side.[8] Afterward the fleet of canoes returned upstream.[9]

Quiguate

On August 3 they continued on their way, coming to a burned town. This was possibly the Big Eddy site, though whether it was a town of Casqui or of Quiguate is not known.[10] On August 4 they came to another village, situated near the River of Casqui, where they found many pumpkins and a good supply of corn and beans.[11]

As they traveled along, the chief of Quiguate sent De Soto gifts of skins and shawls, but the people of Quiguate ran away from their towns before De Soto arrived at them.[12] On August 5 the Spaniards arrived at the main town of Quiguate, probably the Grant site. This town was also located on the River of Casqui.[13] It appeared to them to be the largest town they had seen in all their travels in La Florida.[14] What this perception can mean is unclear, since on archaeological grounds the main town of Pacaha would appear to have been a larger site. Perhaps two or more Quiguate towns were closely contiguous to each other, thus seeming to be a single large town. De Soto and his army occupied half of this town. A few days later, when they spotted some Indians who seemed to be up to no good, De Soto ordered his men to burn down the other half of the town (further suggesting that it was two contiguous towns), so it would offer the Indians no protection in case they came to attack at night and would not provide any obstacle to the free movement of De Soto's footmen and horsemen.[15] De Soto took up residence in the chief's house, on top of a mound.[16]

Quiguate comprised a series of sites on one or both sides of the lower St. Francis River. However, differences in the ceramics from one part of the lower St. Francis River to another suggest that more than one polity may have existed in this area. In addition, archaeologists have discerned both nucleated and dispersed settlement patterns in this area.[17]

A day or so later an Indian came to them in the company of many others, and he said that he was the chief. De Soto placed the man under the care of his guard, ordering them to hold him hostage. Many Indians then came to the

Spaniards bringing gifts of skins and shawls. If he did not suspect it at the out-set, De Soto soon discovered that this chief was in fact a pretender when he sud-denly bolted and ran as the two of them were in company together, emerging from a house. The man ran toward a river or bayou a crossbow shot distant from the town and plunged in, crossing to the other side, where many Indians were walking about. When they caught sight of their comrade, they began to shout loudly, and they shot a hail of arrows at the Spaniards. De Soto went in quick pursuit, leading a party of horsemen and footmen, but the Indians on the other side fled before the Spaniards arrived. As the Spaniards pursued these men, they came to a town whose people had fled. It lay next to a swamp that the horses could not cross. On the other side they could see many women. Some of the foot soldiers managed to cross to the other side of the swamp and captured several of the women and a quantity of clothing. Having accom-plished this, De Soto and his men returned to the main town of Quiguate.[18]

That night, those who were on watch captured an Indian who had come to spy on them. When De Soto interrogated this man, it turned out he knew where the real chief of Quiguate was hiding. At first opportunity, with the captured Indian serving as a guide, De Soto went with twenty horsemen and fifty foot-men to find the chief.

After marching for a day and a half, they came to a dense woods. One of De Soto's soldiers happened upon the chief, and not knowing who he was, he gave him a blow on the head with his cutlass (*cutillada*). The man cried out, saying he was the chief, and begged that he not be killed. De Soto took him prisoner along with 140 of his people, and they returned to the main town of Quiguate. De Soto now tried to force the chief to order his people to come in and serve the Spaniards, but the people would not come. So De Soto sent up both sides of the river (or bayou) a contingent of horsemen and footmen, who rounded up a great number of men and women by force, doing them consid-erable harm in the process. On seeing the brutal treatment they would receive if they continued to refuse to cooperate with the Spaniards, the people of Quiguate began to come in voluntarily and ask De Soto what he wanted of them. After this, they came frequently with gifts of food and clothing.[19]

In the house he was occupying, De Soto allowed the chief and two of his wives to go about unshackled, but only under the guard of his halberdiers. In-quiring of them in what direction he could find a densely populated society, De Soto learned that further down the St. Francis River were large towns with chiefs who held sway over large territories and large populations.[20] Also, to the northwest, near some mountains, was a province named Coligua. The Indians of Quiguate also told him that to the west—though they did not indicate how far—there was a province where the people subsisted on buffalo, and that here the Spaniards could find interpreters who could take them all the way to the other sea, that is, presumably, the Pacific Ocean.[21] This was an attractive possibility. But to De Soto and some of the others it seemed best to go first to Coligua, since its mountainous location might yield silver and gold.[22]

While they were in Quiguate an incident occurred that brought to light the full extent of the rancor De Soto had been harboring since the debacle at Mabila. One night a soldier came to him and reported that Juan Gaytán was supposed to serve the second watch on horseback but had refused to do so on the grounds that he was His Majesty's treasurer. De Soto became furious. In his mind, Gaytán was one of those at Mabila who had spoken against continuing the expedition, although in fact Gaytán had merely spoken in favor of going to Ochuse to rendezvous with the ships. According to Garcilaso, De Soto rose from his bed in a fury and, stepping outside the chief's house onto the mound overlooking the town, he shouted into the darkness in a voice loud enough to be heard by all.

Soldiers and captains! What is this? Do those conspiracies still prevail in which you discussed in [Mabila] the subject of returning to Spain or proceeding to Mexico, so that now on pretext of being officers of the royal exchequer, you refuse to take the watch which has fallen to your lot? Why do you want to return to Spain? Did you leave family estates there to enjoy? Why do you want to go to Mexico? To disclose the baseness and littleness of your souls? Possessed now of the power to become lords of such a great kingdom as this where you have discovered and trodden upon so many and such beautiful provinces, have you deemed it better (abandoning them through your pusillanimity and cowardice) to go and lodge in a strange house and eat at the table of another when you can have your own house and table with which to entertain many? What honor do you think they will pay you when they have learned as much? Be ashamed of yourselves and bear in mind that officials of the royal exchequer or no, we all must serve His Majesty, and none shall presume to absent himself because of any pre-eminences he may possess, for should he do so, I will strike off his head, be he who he may. And be undeceived, for as long as I live, no one is to leave this land before we have conquered and settled it or all died in the attempt.

Therefore, do your duty, and leave off your vain presumptions, for now is not the time for them.[23]

If any of his men had doubts about De Soto's resolve before this night, they had none now. Not only were they under the heel of this man, but they had allowed him to put both distance and a huge river between themselves and the ships that were to meet them at Ochuse.

Coligua

After having spent three weeks at Quiguate, they departed on August 26, heading northwest.[24] They knew they would have to cross an uninhabited wilderness, but they could not have known in advance just how difficult the terrain would be. Leaving the chief of Quiguate to remain in his town, the Spaniards were led by an Indian guide who took them for five days through a pathless lowland that was subject to being flooded by the Mississippi River. Even though it seemed to the Spaniards to be an area that might never before have been seen by humans, their guide led them as confidently as if he were following a royal road, a feat that amazed the Spaniards.[25] They had to cross four large swamps as well as many shallow marshes and small streams of water.[26] The larger swamps lay along the L'Anguille River, Bayou de View, the Cache River, and Village Creek. The shallow expanses of water were full of large fish. The Indians who were in chains stirred things up as their chains dragged through the water, and the fish would rise to the surface. In such shallow water, the Spaniards and the Indians killed these fish by simply clubbing them to death, and they took as many as they wished in this way.[27]

On August 30 they came to the River of Coligua—the White River—and for two days they followed a trail that paralleled this river. On the morning of September 1 they came upon Coligua, a pretty village—probably at the Magness site—situated in the gorge of the White River between two mountain ridges.[28] The Spaniards said the river was about half the size of the Caya River in Extremadura.[29]

After having crossed a vast wilderness of tupelo, oak, and bald cypress in a lowland that had been uninhabited since perhaps A.D. 1350 or 1400, they had reached the edge of the Ozark Plateau. Ever since early May, when they happened upon the people of Quizquiz, they had been in the Mississippi Valley meander zone. At Coligua, both the terrain and the vegetation changed. The hills and low mountains of the Ozark Plateau and Boston Mountains may have reminded them of the hills and mountains they had seen as they traversed the Appalachian Mountains and Cumberland Plateau. The vegetation was oak-hickory-pine forest like they had first seen as they traveled through the piedmont of Georgia and South Carolina (see map 4).

The people of Coligua had not previously heard of the Spaniards and were quite unprepared when they suddenly appeared in their midst. The terrified people ran up along the White River, which flowed through their town, some of them plunging into the water as horsemen charged along both sides of the river, capturing many of them, both men and women, and their chief. At the captive chief's command, his people came three days later with gifts of shawls, deerskins, and buffalo skins.[30] Coligua was a fertile land where the Spaniards found plenty of corn—so much corn, it seemed to the Spaniards, that the Indians had to throw away the corn of the past year to make way for the new. This getting rid of the old corn to make way for the new was in fact a practice widely observed in the eighteenth-century Southeast in connection with the annual Green Corn Ceremony, which celebrated the new year's corn crop. The Spaniards also found in Coligua an abundance of beans and pumpkins, both of which were larger and of better quality than those cultivated in Spain. When these pumpkins were roasted, it seemed to some that they tasted as good as roasted chestnuts.[31] Along with this abundant supply of food, they found here a good supply of salt.

Coligua comprised several sites along the White River near present-day Batesville, Arkansas, some of which were as much as five acres in size. The types of ceramics here resemble Late Mississippian ceramics elsewhere in the Central Valley. The predominant arrow point type along the White River at this time was the Nodena point. Several vessels in the form of effigies of human heads have been recovered in this area. One remarkable vessel appears to have a pair of glasses resting on the forehead. It may seem far-fetched, but Europeans were beginning to wear glasses by the time of the De Soto expedition.[32]

As was his custom, De Soto interrogated the people of Coligua about the land and the people around them. The Indians said that to the north were many buffalo.[33] Some of the Spaniards went out immediately to hunt them, but there is no evidence they ever saw any.[34] The Indians also said the land to the north was cold, and because of this it was sparsely inhabited.[35] The Spaniards questioned them about what lay to the northwest, but the Indians could not tell them of any significant population in that direction.[36] The people of

Coligua told them that if they wished to find suitably large populations of people, they would have to travel to the west-southwest.[37] The best land they knew of was Cayas, and it lay in that direction.[38]

Cayas

The Spaniards now wended their way toward Cayas. Departing from Coligua on September 6, they crossed the White River, apparently bivouacking at the end of the day. On September 7 they marched past some mountains, the Ozarks, which they could see in the distance toward the west. At the end of the day they came to Calpista, where there was a salt spring from which very good salt could be extracted through evaporation. This salt spring was located near present-day Bald Knob, where a Confederate salt works operated in the nineteenth century.[39]

On September 8 they continued on to Palisema, probably on the Little Red River in present-day White County.[40] The house of the chief of Palisema was covered with deerskins decorated with painted designs, and the floor of the house was covered with similar deerskins, as if they were carpets. But the chief and all his people fled before De Soto arrived. De Soto sent out a contingent of horsemen and footmen to hunt them down. The soldiers caught sight of many people, but the country was so rough, they only succeeded in capturing a few women and some children. The towns of Palisema were small and scattered, and there was little corn to be found. For this reason, De Soto remained at this place for only a short time before continuing on.[41]

On September 10 they bivouacked by a body of water (*un agua*), perhaps Cypress Bayou, and the next day they came to Quixila, in the general vicinity of present-day Vilonia or Hamlet, where they remained and rested on September 12. The next day they came to Tutilcoya, near present-day Conway, whose chief served as a guide while they continued on in search of the province of Cayas. On September 14 they came to a village, situated on the River of Cayas—the Arkansas River (fig. 68)—which they later learned emptied into the Mississippi River.[42] The next day they bivouacked near a swamp, perhaps Kuhn Bayou, and on September 16 they came to the town of Tanico, probably in the Galla Rock Bottom or Carden Bottom. This was the first town of the chiefdom of Cayas.[43]

After what they had been told in Coligua, they expected to find a large and wealthy society in the province of Cayas. But instead of the compact palisaded towns to which they had become accustomed at Quizquiz, Casqui, and

Fig. 68. The Arkansas River in Pulaski County, Arkansas, about a mile above Little River. Photograph by Roland Harper, April 26, 1923. (William Stanley Hoole Special Collections Library, University of Alabama)

Pacaha, they found at Tanico a dispersed population. De Soto at first thought the chief of Tutilcoya had misled him and had not guided him to Cayas. De Soto threatened to injure or kill him, but the Indians whom De Soto had captured nearby said this was indeed Cayas, and it was the best society in that part of the country. Although the houses of Cayas were scattered about because of the rough and hilly country, the total amount of land under cultivation was very extensive, and the people grew a lot of corn.[44]

The Spaniards established their permanent camp at Tanico, which lay near the river, and they occupied the larger part of the town. The same day they arrived there, De Soto took some horsemen and continued on for a league further. All the Indians had fled, but along the road they left gifts of many dressed skins as a sign of peace.[45]

The Indians of Cayas were salt-makers and salt traders. This was the first place where the Spaniards found a truly plentiful supply of salt, which was much to their relief, for they had suffered from a lack of it.[46] The people procured this salt from the sand along a stream that emptied into the River of Cayas. This was probably the West Fork of Point Remove Creek, where there is a saline. The people of Cayas would gather up the sand and place it in specially woven baskets that were wide at the top and narrowed at the bottom. They would fill these baskets with the salt-encrusted sand, and then pour water through it, letting the brine collect in basins below. They strained the brine again to remove the remaining sand, and then they poured it into a salt pan and applied heat to evaporate the water. Then they scraped the residue of salt off the salt pan. The Spaniards judged it to be an excellent white salt of good flavor.[47] The people of Cayas carried their salt to other societies, where they traded it for skins and shawls.[48]

The Cayas polity comprised a cluster of sites that lay along the central portion of the Arkansas River from just above present-day Little Rock to a point some miles up the Arkansas River. Our archaeological knowledge of this area suffers from its having been extensively looted by commercial pothunters beginning in the 1920s. What we do know is primarily based on early excavations and on pothunter collections (fig. 69). From this information it appears that late prehistoric occupation was substantial between the lower Petit Jean River and the Arkansas River and that the settlement pattern was quite dispersed. Only one large mound site is known for this area, the Point Remove site on the Arkansas River, near the mouth of Point Remove Creek.

Making sense of the archaeology of the Arkansas River Valley has been difficult. But in coming upon Cayas, De Soto and his men were approaching

Fig. 69. Ceramic bottle from Carden Bottom, Yell County, Arkansas. (National Museum of the American Indian, Smithsonian Institution)

the eastern edge of a distinctive archaeological area—the Arkansas Valley tradition—an area that differed from the Mississippian culture that lay to the east, down the Arkansas River and along the Mississippi Valley, as well as the Caddoan cultures of the Ouachita mountains and the Red River and its tributaries. The territory of the Arkansas Valley tradition extended from the vicinity of present-day Little Rock up the Arkansas River Valley into eastern Oklahoma to the area at the junction of the Arkansas and Grand Rivers.

The Arkansas Valley tradition was based upon cultivating both corn and the plants of the old Woodland period starchy seed complex. They processed these seeds and grains using stone food-grinders, in contrast to the wooden mortars and pestles used elsewhere in the Southeast (see fig. 91). One consequence of this was that their teeth were heavily worn down. Another difference was that by no later than A.D. 1100 bison hunting and the use of bison bone tools were important in the culture. They built flat-topped mounds, but they did not use them as the foundations of temples or other special-purpose structures. They built square to rectangular wattle-and-daub houses with distinctive center posts (two or four in number), a house type that may have had its origin in the Southwest. Unlike people in the Southeast, they made and used coiled basketry. And unlike the people of the Mississippian and the Caddoan cultures, they made plain pottery consisting mostly of simple jars and bowls. Notably, these vessels had flat bottoms as opposed to the rounded bottoms of the central Mississippi Valley. Remarkably, shell-tempered pottery appears to be very old in this area, dating to about A.D. 600.

In many respects, the Arkansas Valley people were marginal to the cultures of the greater Southeast. The Arkansas Valley people were few in number, ate very little corn, and built only small mound centers. But they were positioned geographically to take advantage of an important west-east water route. Downstream from the west came bison skins and perhaps dried meat and tallow, which were attractive to Mississippi Valley peoples who were short on protein and, after about A.D. 1450, were suffering from the cold winters of the Little Ice Age. And upstream from the east came salt, large seashells and shell beads from the Gulf of Mexico, copper finery, and fancy pottery from the cultures of the Mississippi Valley.

Ironically, from a single Arkansas Valley tradition site on the Arkansas River in eastern Oklahoma—the Spiro mound site—archaeologists have recovered as much as 70 percent of the prestige goods of the Southeastern Ceremonial Complex. Though a freak of preservation, the artifacts were recovered from a single mound. These include as many as four thousand shell cups, many of which are carved with intricate etched designs (see fig. 8), carved wooden artifacts, repoussé copper, and even preserved fragments of cloth and feather-work. Hardly any of these artifacts, however, were made by the people of the Arkansas Valley tradition. They were accouterments of the east-west trade conducted by these people.[49]

De Soto and his men remained at Cayas for a little less than three weeks. During this time the horses grew wonderfully fat because of the abundance of corn, and they particularly fed on the leaves of the corn stalks. The Spaniards mention a warm brackish marsh from which the horses drank, swelling their bellies, though it did not seem to hurt them.[50]

The cornfields of Cayas lined both banks of the Arkansas River. The Spaniards were on one side of the river, and the Indians stayed on the other side, not daring to cross. Finally De Soto's men enticed some of them to come over. De Soto asked to see their chief, but they said he was afraid to appear. De Soto told them that if the chief did not come to him and bring a guide and inter-preter to see them to the next province, he would use force to apprehend him, and he would harm his people. De Soto waited for three days, and when the chief did not make an appearance, he went after him. He captured the chief and 150 of his people.[51]

De Soto did not want to spend the winter at Cayas. When he asked where he could find a great chief and the most populous land, the chief of Cayas said he should go to Tula, a fertile province a day and half's travel upriver.[52] He said he could provide De Soto with a guide, but he could not provide an in-terpreter because he was at war with Tula and had been for a very long time, and the people of Cayas and Tula did not communicate with each other.[53]

Tula

On or about September 30 De Soto set out with thirteen horsemen and fifty footmen to reconnoiter Tula.[54] They probably followed a trail that lay near the Arkansas River, with the Boston Mountains to their right and the Ouachita Mountains in the distance to their left. A narrow tongue of southern floodplain forest stretches up the Arkansas River for some distance (see map 4), and therefore the vegetation was more of what they had already seen. But they may have observed, as does anyone who drives westward through the Arkansas Valley today, that the further west one goes the more noticeably one approaches a radically different climatic zone. The average annual rainfall drops rapidly in this westward direction. The trees become notably smaller, and as the moist Southeast begins to give way to the dry West, the vegetation seems to assume a defensive posture.

The Spaniards traveled over some rugged hills (*sierras ásperas*) before arriving at Tula, in the general vicinity of present-day Fort Smith, where they took the Tulas by surprise.[55] As soon as the alarm was raised, however, fifteen or twenty Tula warriors gathered together and came out to attack De Soto's men. They got the worst of the fighting and turned and fled. When the horsemen overtook them, the warriors scrambled up on the tops of their houses, where they tried to defend themselves with bow and arrow. When the Spaniards drove them from one housetop, they would run and climb up on another. While the Spaniards would chase one group of Tula warriors, another group would attack from a different direction.

The Spaniards were surprised at the bravery and skill of the Tula warriors. In Garcilaso the story is told that near the end of the engagement, Juan Páez, captain of the crossbowmen, was fighting from horseback and not as skillfully as he might. He pursued a Tula warrior who was retreating and cast his lance at him. But while running, the fleeing Indian turned around and, using a six-foot staff he carried as a weapon, deflected the lance. Then he took the staff he was carrying in both hands and struck Juan Páez a blow in the mouth, knocking out most of his teeth and stunning him. Then the Indian fled to safety.[56]

The women of Tula fought as bravely as the men, and even more desperately. In another story recounted by Garcilaso, Francisco de Reynoso Cabeza de Vaca entered a Tula house, and climbing into the upper room of the house where food was stored, he discovered four Indian women hiding there. But rather than cower before him, the women suddenly rose as one and came at him in a rush, like mastiffs attacking a bull. Overwhelming him, they seized him by the arms and legs, and one of them grabbed his genitals. Reynoso flailed about, trying to get free of them, but in so doing one of his feet plunged through the cane framework on which he was standing, and his leg went through up to his thigh. Seeing they now had him, the women redoubled their attack, biting and beating him, intending to kill him.[57]

Another Spaniard happened to enter the house at this moment. Hearing the commotion, he looked up and saw the leg sticking through the ceiling. Since the leg was bare, he thought it was an Indian's leg and considered slashing it with his sword. But first he determined to learn about the commotion. He and two companions climbed up into the upper room, where they saw Reynoso's predicament. Even when faced with superior force, the women would not cease their attack, and in the end the Spaniards killed all of them.[58]

To the Spaniards it seemed that the Tulas attacked in packs, like wolves, with alarming ferocity.[59] This fighting continued for such a long time, the horses became tired and could no longer run. The Tulas took heavy losses, but they succeeded in wounding seven or eight Spaniards, and they killed one horse and wounded nine or ten others.[60]

The Spaniards tried to kill every Tula who fired an arrow at them. When the fighting ended, fifteen Tulas were dead, and forty women and young people had been taken captive.[61] De Soto thought it prudent to make his way back to Cayas before the Tulas had time to regroup. They departed, marching into early darkness in order to put distance between themselves and these fierce opponents. Along the way they had to go through a bad pass through a ridge, where they were vulnerable to attack by the Indians.[62] This was probably in the vicinity of present-day Ozark, where hills and high ground come quite close to the channel of the river, making for a narrow passage.[63] They bivouacked for the night in a valley on a terrace of the river. The next day they arrived at the main camp at Cayas. And just as the chief of Cayas had assured them, they could find none of the Indians—neither among the ones traveling with them nor among the Cayas—who could speak the language of the Tula captives they brought back.[64]

In going to Tula, De Soto and his men approached a cultural boundary that was seemingly as distinct as the climatic and physiographic boundary. The Tulas differed in important respects from the Mississippian peoples through whose territory the Spaniards had been traveling for several months, and that included the people of Cayas. The Tulas were culturally affiliated with people to the west. They lived in dispersed agricultural villages, but hunted bison as well as deer. Presumably because they killed bison with lances, the Tulas were not afraid of the Spaniards' horses, and they used their lances against horses and riders in the same way they used them to kill buffalo (fig. 70).[65]

De Soto and his men departed from Tanico on October 5, and on October 7 they returned to the town of Tula they had encountered earlier.[66] The inhabitants had fled from the town, but the Spaniards found plenty of provisions. On October 8, just before dawn, the Tulas came silently to attack, armed with bows and arrows and long poles, like pikes or lances, with sharp points that had been hardened by fire.[67] The Tulas formed themselves in two or three squadrons or bands, each coming from a different direction.[68]

As soon as the Spaniards spotted the Tulas, who by stealth had managed to come in very close, footmen and horsemen ran out to engage them in battle. Again the Tulas fought with desperate courage. They were far and away the

Fig. 70. Plains Indians attacking a buffalo with lance and bow and arrow. Detail from a painting by George Catlin, 1832–33. (National Museum of American Art, Smithsonian Institution, Gift of Mrs. Joseph Harrison Jr.)

most formidable individual fighting men De Soto's men had yet encountered. With the initial advantage of a surprise attack, the Tulas were especially emboldened. Because they were fighting in darkness and in danger of being killed accidentally by their own comrades, the Spaniards made a point of frequently shouting the name of Our Lady and the Apostle Santiago. The Indians, in turn, shouted the name of their province—Tula! Soon, dead and wounded men were everywhere.

According to Garcilaso, the warrior who had struck and wounded Juan Páez with the staff in the first engagement had apparently told his comrades of his exploit. Many of them seemed to have inferred that it was the staff and not the skill of the warrior that had bested Páez, and they had armed themselves with staffs about six feet long, which they were using effectively. Juan de Baeza, a halberdier of De Soto's guard, was fighting with a sword and shield when two Tulas got on either side of him. One of them struck his shield a hard blow and broke it into pieces, and the second struck him across the shoulders so hard it knocked him to the ground. They began to beat him, and had not others rushed to Baeza's defense, they would certainly have killed him.[69]

Once the horsemen began attacking in earnest, especially as it began to grow light, they began breaking up the Tula squadrons and quickly routed them. But even so, the Tulas continued fighting as the horsemen ran back and forth among them, lancing them. After a time the surviving Tulas fled into the trees and brush of a ravine that lay near the town. The Spaniards were much relieved that the Tulas had retreated, and they returned to the town to treat their wounded comrades.[70]

As was their custom after a battle, the Spaniards went out in pairs to examine the dead and wounded of their adversaries. They were particularly interested in the nature of the wounds they had inflicted upon them. A grim story told by Garcilaso in connection with this occasion illustrates the extraordinary valor of the Tula warriors and the respect the Spaniards had for them. As the story goes, one of the Spaniards engaged in this examination of the Tula casualties was Gaspar Caro, who had been knocked off his horse during the battle. His horse had run away. He now borrowed another man's horse and went out to retrieve his own. After a time, he returned driving his horse in front of him. Another of those who were examining the dead and wounded, Francisco de Salazar, mounted Caro's horse to show the others what a fine horseman he was. At this point, yet another of the soldiers, Juan de Carranza, spied an Indian who raised up from behind some bushes. Thinking the Tulas were renewing their attack, he shouted "Indians! Indians!" Immediately the two who were mounted rode in opposite directions to fend off any Indians who might appear. Carranza and one of his companions rushed over to the Indian he had seen, and when this man saw that he could not flee because of the horsemen, he ran out to engage them. He picked up a battle ax that belonged to Juan Páez. This ax was very sharp, and it was mounted on a well-polished handle that was more than three feet long.

Holding the ax in both hands, the Tula warrior swung a savage blow at Carranza, splitting his shield and severely wounding his arm. Carranza was so badly hurt he could offer no more resistance. The Indian then attacked Carranza's companion, Diego de Godoy, with the same effect, splitting his shield, wounding him on the arm, and leaving him incapacitated. Francisco de Salazar then rode over to render assistance to the two wounded Spaniards. He attacked the ax-wielding Indian, but the man ran beneath an oak tree. Salazar could not ride his horse beneath this tree, so he rode around it, making some ineffectual thrusts with his lance. Then the Indian ran out and positioned himself to the left of Salazar, and as he rode by, he took the ax in both hands and struck Salazar's horse across the shoulder, laying him open from his withers to his knee, disabling him.

Gonzalo Silvestre happened upon this fight, but he approached the warrior with more caution than had the other three. The man rushed at Silvestre with the ax, but when he swung, Silvestre positioned his shield so that it took a glancing blow, and the ax continued its swing and stuck into the ground. Then Silvestre struck the Indian with a downstroke of his sword, slashing him from his forehead, down his face, to his chest, striking his left arm and severing his hand at the wrist. Undeterred, the Indian clasped the ax in his right hand, resting it on the stump of his severed left arm, and tried to strike Silvestre in the face. Silvestre, however, now easily deflected the ax with his shield, and wielding his sword from below, gave the Indian a backward slash across his waist. Because the Indian wore so little clothing, the sword cut deeply, but even after this he remained standing momentarily, and then he fell to the ground dead, his body cut almost in two.[71]

At this moment, Gaspar Caro rode up and saw how grievously his horse had been wounded. He was furious, but without uttering a word, he led his horse away. He took it to De Soto and showed it to him, complaining bitterly about the incompetents he had in his service. How, with only three blows of an ax, could one Tula warrior incapacitate two Spanish foot soldiers and a third on horseback! Caro wanted De Soto to brand the three as cowards. De Soto told Caro to swallow his anger and to think of the three Spaniards as victims of bad luck. For Caro's part, De Soto said, he should attend to his horse, which would survive if treated. Then De Soto went to see with his own eyes the corpse of this Tula warrior and the havoc he had wrought.[72]

The Tulas were feared by many of the Indians whose lands bordered theirs. The Spaniards claimed that the Tulas deformed their heads and tattooed their faces hideously to make their visages reflect their fierceness. Even the name of the Tulas was frightening to their neighbors, who would sometimes use it to frighten their children into behaving themselves.

Garcilaso told several stories of the fierceness of the Tula people as exemplified by some of the Tulas the Spaniards enslaved. Cristóbal Mosquera, for example, took a Tula boy away as a slave. In towns where the Spaniards subsequently traveled, where young Indian boys played the game of war, the games were so keenly played that the players often got their heads bloodied. In one of these contests, the Spaniards sent the Tula boy in to join one of the sides. These neighbors of the Tulas knew their reputation and immediately elected him captain, and when he attacked the other side shouting "Tula!" his side began winning. The Spaniards then told him to join the other side, and when he did, his new allies began winning.[73]

According to another story, only one Spaniard, Juan Serrano, took a Tula woman slave. But she was unmanageable, and to the Spaniards she seemed malevolent in the extreme. She would slap them in the face or throw coals at them if they attempted to force her to do what she did not want to do. Eventually she escaped, and Serrano considered himself to be fortunate to be rid of such a slave.[74]

The Spaniards had captured several Tula warriors in the battle. De Soto selected six of them and ordered his men to cut off their right hands and their noses. He then sent these mutilated men back to their chief to tell him that if he did not come and submit to Spanish rule, De Soto would send out his soldiers to similarly mutilate every Tula man they could find. He gave the chief three days in which to come and do his bidding. All of this had to be communicated to the six men through signs, because they had no interpreter.[75]

Three days later the chief of Tula sent an Indian to De Soto with a gift of many dressed buffalo skins. At Tula the Spaniards saw more evidence of buffalo than they had seen in all their travels. They were informed that many of these animals lived toward the north. But, again, the Spaniards did not see any buffalo on the hoof, nor did they venture into their habitat, since the land to the north was poorly settled and there was little corn.[76] The Spaniards had great appreciation for the buffalo skins because they were soft and warm like sheepskins, and they could use them as blankets to protect against the cold.[77] Since cold weather was already upon them, these skins were welcome acquisitions.[78] The Tulas also used buffalo skins as blankets. They also found quantities of buffalo meat at Tula.[79]

The Tulas were not only unusual in having access to buffalo and in their effectiveness as warriors, including their use of spears. Their custom of cranial deformation and facial tattooing of both sexes seemed extreme to the Spaniards, who must have seen both of these customs previously in their travels in the Southeast. The Tulas' heads, sloping upward from their brows to the backs of their heads, seemed incredibly long (fig. 71). They bore tattoos on their faces, including even the exterior and interior of their lips, which made them look abominable to the Spaniards.[80] The Tulas were, in all, an especially memorable experience for the Spaniards.

The cultural and linguistic picture of the Arkansas Valley in 1541 is far from clear. The place-name Tanico may indicate that the people of Cayas spoke a Tunican language. But the people of Tula clearly spoke a language different from that of Cayas. In their practice of ceremonially weeping on certain occasions, the Tulas resembled the Caddoan-speaking people whom the expedi-

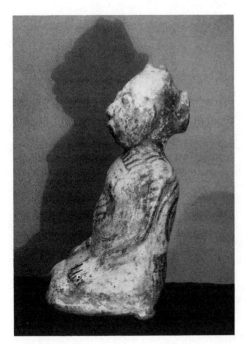

Fig. 71. Mississippian bottle depicting frontal cranial deformation. (Tennessee State Museum, Gates P. Thruston Collection, Vanderbilt University)

tion would later encounter. But since the Caddoan languages lack the consonant *l*, *Tula* cannot be a Caddoan word. It is possible, however, that *Tula* could be a Tunican word that referred to a Caddoan-speaking people.

The cultural affiliation of the Tulas is also surrounded with uncertainty. It is possible that perhaps because of the climatic effects of the Little Ice Age after about A.D. 1450 (or from some other cause), the people of the Arkansas Valley tradition found it expedient to abandon their villages and move eastward, downstream, and the area they vacated was subsequently occupied by enemies of Cayas, perhaps Caddoan-speaking people from the Ouachita Mountains, or else by people who were ancestral to the Wichitas.[81] The only way some of these questions may be resolved is if the actual site of Tula were to be discovered by archaeologists.

The man sent by the chief of Tula with the gift of buffalo skins wept copiously as he came up to De Soto, and he threw himself at his feet. De Soto persuaded the man to stand up, and the man then made a speech, but no one was able to understand what he said. Again using signs, De Soto tried to tell the man he should go back to the chief of Tula and tell him to send an interpreter whom the people of Cayas could understand. The next day three Tulas came from the chief bearing more gifts of dressed buffalo skins. Then, three days after that, twenty Tulas came, and among these was one who could under-stand the language of Cayas. This man gave a long speech in which he made excuses for the behavior of the Indians of Tula, and he praised De Soto and his Spaniards, saying that the chief of Tula would do what was asked of him.[82]

The Spaniards were very happy at having this interpreter, since they could not proceed forward without benefit of intelligence gained along the way. De Soto ordered that the interpreter be placed under guard and that the Indi-ans who had come with him should go back to the chief to thank him for the gifts he had sent and to tell him that he was pardoned. In particular, they should tell the chief he should come to see De Soto the next day.[83]

Three days later the chief of Tula came in the company of eighty Indians. They again brought a quantity of dressed buffalo skins as gifts. Both the chief and his men wept as they came into the presence of the Spaniards. The Span-iards interpreted this behavior as a sign of their obedience and of repentance for their mistakes.[84]

The chief made an eloquent speech in which he excused the behavior of his people, placing his land and his people in service to the Spaniards.[85] Because winter was approaching, and because they could not travel after the rain and snow began to fall, De Soto was especially interested in where he could find a well-populated land in which to spend the winter. He did not think the re-sources in Tula were sufficient to provide food for the winter.[86] He inquired about what lay in all directions from Tula and was told that in the direction in which the Spaniards were traveling—toward the southwest—there was no great society.[87] If they went toward the west, there was a scattering of popula-tion, and toward the northwest there were possibly large towns.[88] But to the southeast there was a province, Utiangüe, where the land abounded in corn.[89] From what the Tulas said, the Spaniards expected they could reach Utiangüe after ten days of travel, and because the Indians said this province was located upon a large body of water, they interpreted this to mean that Utiangüe was situated on an arm of the Gulf of Mexico.[90]

This was an added inducement for De Soto to go to Utiangüe, because he now wished to get word out to his countrymen about his whereabouts and his intentions. No word about De Soto had reached his wife, Doña Isabel, or any-one else, for about two years.[91] The last news of the expedition had been taken to Cuba by Francisco Maldonado, who sailed from Apalachee in the bergan-tines in late February 1540. Since then about 250 men had died and about 150 horses had been lost.[92] None of this was known to the outside world. De Soto determined, therefore, to go to Utiangüe, and the following spring to march to the sea and build two bergantines. One of these would sail to Cuba, and the other would sail to Mexico, in the hope that at least one of them would succeed in taking news of the expedition to other Spaniards. And then De Soto hoped he would have sufficient resources in Cuba to refit the expedition and to explore and conquer further west, where Cabeza de Vaca had gone.[93]

Utiangüe

De Soto released the chiefs of Cayas and Tula, and on October 19 he departed from Tula, heading southeast (see map 7).[94] The path the expedition now followed took them past Pisgah Mountain to the valley of the Petit Jean River. At the end of the first day of travel they bivouacked near two native houses, evidently a very small farmstead. The next day they bivouacked near a single native house, and the next day they did the same. It was at this place that Hernandarias de Saavedra, grandson of the marshal of Seville, who had been wounded in the battle at Tula, died of convulsions.[95] On October 22 they arrived at Quipana, a town situated near the river and among very steep mountains.[96] Quipana was in the vicinity of present-day Nimrod Lake, Arkansas. For this entire leg of their journey they traveled through very rough ridges.[97]

All the inhabitants of Quipana had fled, and the surrounding country was so rough they were at first unable to take any captives. But that night De Soto set an ambush, and when some Indians approached, his soldiers captured two of them. When interrogated, they said that Utiangüe was six days' journey away. They also said that a week's journey to the south was another province, Guahate—later called Chaguate—which was well peopled and had plenty of corn.[98]

The Spaniards evidently spent four or five days resting in the province of Quipana.[99] Then from the main town of Quipana, they proceeded eastward, down the valley of the Fourche La Fave River, coming to the village of Anoixi, which possibly was located in present-day northern Saline County or northern Garland County, Arkansas, near where they would pass through the Ouachita Mountains.[100] From here De Soto sent forward a contingent of thirty horsemen and fifty footmen to surprise the Indians ahead, and they succeeded in capturing many. On October 30 the rest of the army crossed through the mountains to the plains beyond, bivouacking perhaps in western Saline County. On October 31 the entire army reached the town of Quitamaya, in the vicinity of present-day Benton, and they bivouacked in an open field near the town.[101]

Two Indians from Quitamaya showed up with a false message from the chief, their purpose being to discover what the Spaniards intended to do. De Soto instructed them to tell their chief to come and talk with him. The two went away, but they did not return, and De Soto received no further messages from the chief. The next day they entered the town and found it abandoned. They took what food they needed and continued on, passing through a small village and bivouacking in the woods for the night.[102] The next day, November 2, they reached Utiangüe, which they found to be not on an arm of the Gulf of Mexico, but on the River of Cayas, the Arkansas. Utiangüe appears to have been located a few miles downstream from present-day Little Rock.[103]

13

Winter, 1541–1542

In searching out a place where they could expect to find adequate food for the winter, De Soto and his men left behind the Caddoan cultures of the Ouachita Mountains and sought out Utiangüe, on the alluvial plain of the Arkansas River. In so doing they again entered southern floodplain forest and the realm of central Mississippi Valley cultures. The people of Utiangüe offered some resistance as the Spaniards approached their town. A number of them gathered together and fired arrows at the Spaniards from a distance, but they ran when the horsemen sallied out and lanced some of them. Others camouflaged themselves with grass and then jumped up to attack, but some of these were lanced also.[1]

Utiangüe was densely populated, its settlement extending both upriver and downriver. It was one of the several culturally similar Mississippian polities that stretched along the Arkansas River from about present-day Little Rock down to the mouth of the river, and continuing along the western side of the Mississippi—downriver a short distance and upriver to about present-day Helena. Over a dozen major sites have been documented in this area, some with platform mounds, burial mounds, and plazas, and there are many smaller sites as well. The archaeology of this area is still not fully reconstructed, but the culture of the people generally resembled that of Quiguate, Casqui, and Pacaha.[2]

Initially archaeologists designated the culture of this area and time as the Quapaw phase. The name derives from the fact that the Quapaw Indians were discovered living at the mouth of the Arkansas River by Marquette and Joliet in 1673, and they continued to live near the Arkansas River throughout the eighteenth century. But it is now clear there is no archaeological evidence proving a connection between the late seventeenth-century Quapaw and the Quapaw phase people who lived along the Arkansas River in the sixteenth century. It is possible, in fact, that the language of the historic Quapaw, which was a Dhegiha Siouan language, was completely different from the language—possibly Tunican—spoken by the Quapaw phase people. Archaeologists have recently advocated that the term "Menard phase" be used instead to designate the culture of the late prehistoric people of the lower Arkansas River.

Before the Spaniards arrived, the men of Utiangüe had taken their women and children to safety. But the Spaniards were able to capture some of the men who remained behind retrieving clothing. The Spaniards found large quantities of corn and beans in the town, as well as nuts and dried persimmons.

De Soto and his men picked the best part of the town for their camp, which they immediately began to fortify with a palisade, taking care to build it a sufficient distance from their houses so the Indians could not easily attack and set them on fire.[3] De Soto paced off the dimensions of the palisade, and using this measurement he assigned to each of his men a section of it to build in proportion to the number of slaves each man owned. The palisade was built by placing very high poles set close together in the ground and by attaching many additional timbers crosswise. The entire structure was finished in three days.[4]

At first relations between the Spaniards and the people of Utiangüe were peaceful. Indian envoys came from the chief of Utiangüe with gifts of shawls and skins. It became clear, however, that some of these envoys from the chief of Utiangüe were spies. They would, for example, show up at night and ask to speak with De Soto. When the Spaniards showed them in, the Indians could see what kind of guard the Spaniards kept, how they slept, how prepared they were for an attack, whether they had horses ready for battle, and so on.[5]

Nearby was the town of Tietiquaquo, which was subject to Utiangüe. The chief of Tietiquaquo was lame and had to be carried from place to place, and he often came to visit De Soto, bringing gifts. In the beginning the chief of Utiangüe had sent word to De Soto asking how long he intended to stay. But after De Soto had been there three days, the chief of Utiangüe sent no further messages. Instead, De Soto learned from his own spies that the chief of Utiangüe was conspiring with Tietiquaquo to revolt.[6]

De Soto began sending out horsemen into the countryside, and they captured many men and women, as well as the chief of Tietiquaquo. Since the chief of Tietiquaquo had seemingly served him well, bringing him many gifts, De Soto merely scolded him and warned him about what would happen to him if he again plotted rebellion. Then De Soto let him go, giving him two Indians to carry him away on their shoulders.[7]

But the chief of Utiangüe still wanted to drive De Soto from his land, and he continued to send spies. De Soto ordered his men to put the knife to any other Indian envoys who came at night. One night the guard Bartolomé de Argote spotted an Indian stealthily approaching the gate of the stockade. Argote hid behind the gate, and as the Indian entered he rushed out and gave him a thrust with his weapon, knocking him down. The Spaniards took the wounded man to De Soto, who interrogated him about why he had come. But the Indian died before he answered any questions.[8] After this, no further envoys from Utiangüe came to De Soto's camp.[9]

During the winter, the chief of Chaguate, which lay to the west, came to pay his respects to De Soto. He brought along gifts of skins, shawls, and salt.[10] The expedition would later travel to Chaguate, which had in its territory one of the most productive salines in Arkansas. This visit would seem to indicate that Chaguate and Utiangüe were allies, or that they at least had a trading relationship.

As the winter passed, De Soto became fearful that discipline among his men had become lax. One night he instructed one of the guards to sound the alarm that Indians had been seen. In this way De Soto could determine how quickly his men could be at the ready in case of an attack and could see which ones were not up to par. He repeated this false alarm whenever he thought the men were growing lazy or careless. Any who were slow to take their positions could expect a tongue-lashing, which was unpleasant enough that each tried to be the first to take up his position whenever the call to arms was sounded.

The winter of 1541–42 was as cold or colder than the previous one. It was so cold the Spaniards began to fear they would freeze to death.[11] For one entire month the snow was so heavy they could hardly venture out of the palisade. When they had to replenish their supply of firewood, De Soto and the horsemen would go out and beat a trail through the snow to the woods, which were at a distance of two crossbow shots from the town. Then, the footmen and slaves went out single file and carried the wood back through the snow.[12]

Through the winter they had plenty of corn, beans, nuts, raisins (*pasas*), and dried prunes (*ciruelas pasadas*) for food, but as usual, they were hungry for meat. This was alleviated somewhat by rabbits supplied by their Indian slaves, who at this point had been taken so far from their homes they could be allowed to go about unshackled.[13] The rabbits seemed more abundant here than in places the Spaniards had visited previously.[14] The Indians hunted them with bow and arrow and also trapped them with snares. They taught the Spaniards to set their own snares, which consisted of bending over a sapling and attaching a cord noose with a short section of cane threaded on the cord near the noose. When a rabbit stuck his head in the trap, it triggered a release, the rabbit found himself dangling in a noose, and the piece of cane prevented him from chewing through the cord. To the Spaniards the rabbits seemed to be of two varieties. One appeared to be like those in Spain. The other was of the same color, but larger in size, and with longer rear legs. The Indians and the Spaniards snared many of these rabbits in the surrounding cornfields, particularly when it froze or snowed.[15]

The Indians of Utiangüe did not mount a concerted attack against the Spaniards during the winter. As soon as the snows had melted, the Spaniards began to take their horses out to patrol the countryside around the town. At this time, they needed additional Indian slaves, perhaps because some had died during the winter. De Soto sent out a captain with some men to hunt for slaves, but eight days later he returned with only a few prisoners. A second captain made a similar foray, and he too returned with only a few captives. Then De Soto himself went out to a neighboring province, perhaps upstream from Utiangüe.[16] Here the chief of Utiangüe had taken up residence in one of his subject towns. De Soto launched a surprise attack early one morning and captured many men and women of all ages. When he returned to Utiangüe after having been gone for fourteen days, the men who had remained behind were greatly relieved, having feared he had been killed.[17]

The greatest misfortune that befell the Spaniards during this winter was the death of their translator Juan Ortiz.[18] This distressed De Soto greatly, because without good translation the Spaniards would not be able to obtain good intelligence, and without good intelligence they were in danger of getting lost and starving.[19]

14

Guachoya

After the coldest weather of the winter seemed over, De Soto and his men departed from Utiangüe on Monday, March 6, 1542. Their destination was Anilco, which they had learned from Indian informants lay near the Mississippi River.[1] The expedition needed to be resupplied. They were down to fewer than four hundred men, and they only had about forty horses, some of which were lame.[2] The horses had gone unshod for the past year because the Spaniards had run out of iron for horseshoes. Fortunately, the terrain they were in now was flat and alluvial, so horseshoes were not particularly necessary.

Having lost the translating services of Juan Ortiz, De Soto was now finding it difficult to plan their itinerary. For an interpreter they relied upon a young Indian they had seized in Cofitachequi, who had by this time attained some command of Spanish.[3] But what Ortiz could sum up in four words, it took the Indian boy a very long time to say as he stumbled about looking for the right words. Moreover, he was often misunderstood, and because of these misunderstandings, De Soto was often in doubt about where to go next.[4]

Anilco

Departing from Utiangüe, they traveled down the Arkansas River for ten days (see map 7).[5] They appear to have been traveling slowly—perhaps because of the difficulty of getting accurate information—and they may have been stopping briefly at towns along the way. On or about March 15, they arrived at Ayays, probably in present-day southeastern Jefferson or northeastern Lincoln County. Here De Soto ordered the men to build a piragua, which they used to ferry everyone to the eastern side of the Arkansas River.

After they crossed the river, the weather turned very cold. It snowed so hard they could not move from where they were for four days (about March 17–20). After it stopped snowing, they marched for three days (about March 21–23) through a wilderness that was low, swampy, and very hard to cross.[6] For one entire day they marched across a cold expanse of water that in places reached up to their knees, and in others up to the stirrups of the horses, and in some few places they had to swim.[7]

At the end of these three days—on or about March 23—they came to the village of Tutelpinco. It is not clear whether this village had been long abandoned or the people had recently fled to escape the Spaniards. But they found no corn in Tutelpinco. Near the village was a "lake"—probably Bayou Meto—which ran with a strong current and emptied into the Arkansas River. When De Soto sent five men in a dugout canoe to cross to the other side, the canoe capsized. Some of the men saved themselves by catching hold of the overturned vessel, and others climbed up in trees—no doubt cypress trees—that were

Fig. 72. A Menard fish effigy bottle (height 9½″) from the Massey site. It represents a buffalo fish, sucker, or redhorse. Arkansas Archaeological Survey photograph. (Private collection)

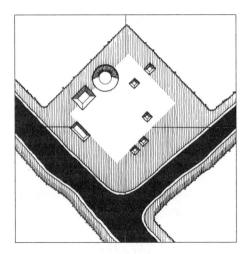

Fig. 73. Schematic map of the Menard site. From William N. Morgan, *Prehistoric Architecture of the Eastern United States*, 76. (William N. Morgan, architect)

growing in the bayou, but Francisco Bastian, a native of Villanueva de Baca-rrota, drowned.[8]

De Soto himself spent a day scouting along Bayou Meto, looking for a cross-ing place, but he did not find one, nor did he find a road leading to the bayou from any other direction. But when he returned to Tutelpinco that night, he came upon two peaceful Indians who took him to the crossing and the trail he should follow. The Spaniards tore pieces of wood from the houses in Tutel-pinco, and putting them together with lengths of cane, they made rafts on which to cross to the other side.

After crossing Bayou Meto (on about March 24) they marched for three days before coming to the town of Tianto, which was subject to Anilco (fig. 72), on or about March 28. In Tianto the Spaniards captured thirty Indians, including two principal men of that town. From Tianto, De Soto quickly sent out a captain with horsemen and footmen to the main town of Anilco to prevent the people from fleeing with their food. This captain and his men marched through three or four large towns before reaching the chief's town, probably at the Menard site (fig. 73) in Arkansas County.[9] As they approached the town, they saw many Indians armed with bows and arrows. When these Indians spotted the Spaniards, they immediately set fire to the chief's house and escaped across a swamp, which lay near the town, so that the Spaniards could not pursue them on their horses.[10] Setting fire to the house of a chief—no doubt situated high atop a mound—may have been a stock Mississippian response to prevent desecration by an invading army.

The next day, March 29, De Soto arrived at the main town of Anilco with all his men. Anilco appeared to be a very fine chiefdom. Elvas thought it was the most populous region they had seen in La Florida.[11] They found more corn here than in any place they had visited with the exception of Coosa and Apalachee. It was very thickly settled, so that the entire area within a quarter of a league around the chief's town was populated, and within the area of a league and a half from the chief's town were other very large towns. They found a great quantity of corn, beans, nuts, and dried persimmons.[12]

After a short time, the chief of Anilco came in the company of several others to deal with De Soto. He gave De Soto the gift of a "marten skin" shawl and a string of pearls. In return, De Soto gave the chief of Anilco a string of *margaridetas*, a type of glass bead that was greatly valued by the native people of Peru, and he gave him some other small gifts. The chief departed, seemingly pleased, and promised to return in two days.[13]

But the people of Anilco came quietly at night in their dugout canoes. They carried away all the corn they could, taking it to the other side of a stream, and stored it in a dense forest. When the chief of Anilco did not return at the designated time, De Soto ordered that an ambush be set up at some of the barbacoas near the swamp from which the Indians had been coming to take the corn. They captured two Indians and took them to De Soto. When these men were interrogated, it turned out that the chief who had been visiting De Soto was not a chief at all, but one who pretended to be chief in order to spy on the Spaniards. They wanted to know whether the Spaniards kept up their guard and whether they intended to settle at Anilco or to further continue their travels.[14] Seeking swift retaliation, De Soto sent a contingent of horsemen and footmen across the stream, but the Indians saw them coming and fled, so they were only able to capture ten or twelve men and women.[15] De Soto sent messengers to the chief of Anilco, trying to persuade him to come and meet with him, but the chief would not speak with the Spaniards, and he was seen to make a gesture with his hands that they should leave.[16]

De Soto learned that Anilco had an enemy, Guachoya, a people who lived not far away and quite near the Mississippi River.[17] The warriors of Guachoya waged war on Anilco by traveling in canoes up the Mississippi River and then up the Arkansas River. The chief of Guachoya sent an emissary to meet with De Soto, saying that he, the chief of Guachoya, was De Soto's servant, and that he would come in two days to formally acknowledge his subservience. The chief showed up as he had promised, accompanied by some of his principal men. With all due courtesy, he presented many woven shawls and deerskins to De Soto, who in return gave the chief some small gifts and treated him well.[18]

De Soto questioned the chief of Guachoya about societies that lay down the Mississippi River from where they were. The chief replied that on his side of the river—the western side—he knew of none except his own. In saying this, the chief surely understood that De Soto was interested in large, corn-producing societies. There may, therefore, have been small societies downstream that he neglected to mention. He said that on the eastern side of the river there was a powerful chief named Quigualtam. After they had finished talking, the chief of Guachoya returned to his town.[19]

Guachoya

A few days later, and about two and a half weeks after having first arrived, De Soto decided to depart from Anilco and go to Guachoya, where he would determine whether the sea were near and whether the resources of Guachoya were sufficient to support them. If the sea were near, he would build bergantines in which he could send some men to sail to Spanish settlements in Cuba and Mexico.[20]

It so happened that just as De Soto was ferrying his army across the Arkansas River, some people in canoes from Guachoya approached, and when they saw that the Spaniards were on the move, they feared that the Spaniards were coming to attack them. They turned their canoes around and carried the alarm to the chief of Guachoya. The people of Guachoya fled from their town, taking away all they could carry. They crossed over to the eastern side of the Mississippi River, which may have put them in enemy territory, but if so, at least it was an enemy they knew.[21] De Soto and most of his men marched overland to Guachoya, while sending fifty men in six canoes down the river.[22] They reached Guachoya on Sunday, April 17, apparently after a single day of travel. De Soto and all his men took up residence in the chief's town, which was defended by a strong palisade and was located a crossbow flight from the river.[23] Guachoya was in the vicinity of present-day McArthur, Arkansas, perhaps near a no-longer-extant channel connecting the Mississippi River and Bayou Macon. The people of Guachoya called the Mississippi River *Tamaliseu*, while those at Anilco called it *Tapatu*, perhaps indicating that they spoke different languages.[24]

The towns of Guachoya lay mostly along Bayou Macon. The ceramics of this area resemble those of both the Menard complex and the Yazoo Basin. Some have argued that the language spoken by the Guachoyas was Tunica, but the actual linguistic evidence is very weak.[25]

After reaching Guachoya, De Soto immediately sent Juan de Añasco with as many men as could be loaded into canoes to go across the river to where the people of Guachoya were. As this party made their way down the river, they saw the huts on the opposite side, which the people of Guachoya had just built. They met no people but raided the huts and returned to Guachoya with their canoes filled with corn, beans, dried plums, and many loaves of dried persimmon pulp.[26]

On that same day—presumably on April 17—an emissary came to De Soto from Guachoya, saying the chief would come the next day.[27] And on the next day the Spaniards observed a fleet of canoes coming up the Mississippi River, bringing the chief as promised. The fleet pulled in at a point on the opposite side of the river and remained there for about an hour, with those on board seemingly debating whether to cross the river and meet with De Soto. Finally, they decided to do it, and the fleet crossed the river, landed their canoes, and the people went to where De Soto was living. Dressed in finery, they brought a large quantity of fish, dogs, skins, and woven shawls, which they presented to De Soto as gifts.

The chief spoke to De Soto through the usual chain of interpreters, begging his pardon for having fled his town, and he asked De Soto what he wished to command of him.[28] De Soto again interrogated the chief about what lay downriver. The chief replied that two leagues from where they were, there was a town that was subject to him, but he reiterated that beyond that subject town there were no settlements on the western side of the river. And he reiterated that on the eastern side of the river there was a chief, Quigualtam, who was the greatest chief in that region. The implication may have been that Quigualtam was also greater than himself.[29] In addition, he said the chief of Quigualtam was located at a distance of three days' travel. Presumably, this was travel by land from a point on the river opposite from Guachoya.[30]

During the course of this interrogation, according to Garcilaso, the chief of Guachoya let out a great sneeze. When he did, his men who were standing around and leaning against the walls, lowered their heads in unison, and making signs of veneration with their arms, saluted the chief with different stock sayings. The murmuring of their voices continued for some time. De Soto remarked that this was exactly what Spaniards do when someone sneezes and was an indication that all people everywhere are similar.[31]

It seemed to De Soto that the chief of Guachoya was lying about who lived where in order to deflect the Spaniards from visiting any more of his towns. So he ordered Juan de Añasco to ride downstream with eight horsemen to see how much population was there, and if he found any people, to ask if they had any knowledge of the sea. Añasco was gone for about a week—from about April 19 through April 25—and when he returned he reported that during this entire time he never found a trail, and he had not been able to penetrate more than fourteen or fifteen leagues because of the great bogs of water extending from the Mississippi River into the countryside, a countryside that was thickly covered with canebrakes and woods. In a word, he found that the chief of Guachoya had told the truth—there were no great towns to the south.[32] This was the Felsenthal region of southeastern Arkansas and northern Louisiana, where the Indians practiced little or no agriculture.[33]

De Soto was deeply grieved by this news. Reaching the Gulf of Mexico by traveling overland seemed hopeless. His men and horses were so run down and exhausted they could not continue the expedition without being resupplied. And he must have realized at this point that the chance of finding a great Aztec-like or Inca-like society in La Florida was very remote. He had searched in every direction and had found nothing. His hopes were at an end.

Quigualtam

This realization must have been almost a physical blow to De Soto. He became ill and took to his bed, no doubt depressed.[34] But before he was felled by illness, he sent a messenger to the chief of Quigualtam. Perhaps because he felt so vulnerable, De Soto was more disposed than he had been to try to bamboozle the Indians.[35] The Indian messenger was to tell the chief of Quigualtam that De Soto was the son of the Sun, and that wherever he traveled people obeyed and served him. He asked the chief of Quigualtam to come to Guachoya and prove his obedience and subservience by bringing a gift of that which was most highly valued in his land. Perhaps De Soto was hoping the chief of Quigualtam would bring a gift of precious metals or gems.

But chief Quigualtam sent De Soto's messenger back to him with the reply that if De Soto was the son of the Sun, as he claimed, then he should dry up the Mississippi River, and then Quigualtam would believe that it was true. Moreover, he, the chief of Quigualtam, was not accustomed to go and visit anyone. Quite the contrary, all the people of whom he had knowledge came to visit him, to serve him, and to pay him tribute. And if they did not do so by their own volition, he forced them to do so. Thus, if De Soto wished to meet chief Quigualtam, then De Soto should come to him. If De Soto would come in peace, he would be welcomed. But if he came under arms, then chief Quigualtam would wait for him in his town and he would not budge an inch. This news was brought to De Soto, who was on his sickbed. He flew into a rage at the most blatant arrogance he had encountered in all of La Florida. He would gladly cross the river and search out Quigualtam and let him know who was most powerful. But in fact he was not able to stir from his bed.[36]

The domain of Quigualtam was one of the most enigmatic native polities encountered by the De Soto expedition. Located on the eastern side of the Mississippi River in the lower Yazoo River basin, it was heir to yet another regional Mississippian development—the Coles Creek culture. The Coles Creek culture emerged at about A.D. 700, and its people eventually dominated the lower Yazoo River basin and the Natchez Bluffs down to the mouth of the Homochitto River, as well as the lower Tensas River basin on the western side of the Mississippi River.

Early Coles Creek sites resemble emergent Mississippian sites elsewhere. The people built small substructure mounds (averaging fifteen to twenty feet in height) and lived in small dispersed communities. The early mound centers were not, however, population centers. They appear to have been the settings for periodic social or ritual occasions. What is also different about early Coles Creek is that there is not only no evidence that these people cultivated corn, there is no substantial evidence that they cultivated any of the old cultigens of the eastern United States, such as sunflower, sumpweed, and chenopodium. For their subsistence they appear to have relied on intensive fishing—particularly for catfish—and on collecting wild foods such as acorns, pecans, and other nuts, perhaps even managing these trees by selective cutting. They also collected persimmons, plums, and probably wild roots, and seeds.

Coles Creek pottery was quite different from the pottery of the central Mississippi Valley. Coles Creek pottery was predominantly brown or gray-brown, tempered with grit and clay particles, and even with tiny bits of organic matter, such as twigs, leaves, or bone. The predominant vessels are simple bowls in a variety of forms and globular jars with constricted mouths. Designs are incised, punctuated, or brushed, and they are predominantly rectilinear and confined to the upper surfaces of the vessels.

As time went on, Coles Creek villages became larger, and evident signs of social rank began to appear, but corn did not appear until around A.D. 1100 to 1200, and even then the quantities were small. The Coles Creek culture spread northward to a point on the Mississippi River opposite to where Guachoya was located. In fact, one of the largest Coles Creek sites—Winterville—was located on a channel connecting Deer Creek with the Mississippi River. (This channel no longer connects the two streams.) By means of this channel, it would have been possible for people to travel by dugout canoe from the lower Yazoo River up Big Sunflower River, and thence via Rolling Fork Creek to Deer Creek and the Mississippi River near present-day Greenville, Mississippi. Seemingly, the location of Winterville mirrored that of Guachoya, which appears to have been located near a similar channel connecting the Mississippi River to Bayou Macon.

The Winterville site was on the northern frontier of the Coles Creek culture. In time the site grew to occupy an area of over fifty acres, and had twenty-three flat-topped mounds measuring from one to fifty-five feet in height. But even though Winterville is a very large site, relatively little cultural debris has been found in the plaza and the areas surrounding the mounds. One interpretation of this absence of debris is that even Winterville was not a population center, but rather a place where people went for ritual or social functions.

The Winterville site was first occupied by Coles Creek people at about A.D. 1000, and for the next two hundred years more and more cultural traits show up at Winterville whose origins lay to the north, in the central Mississippi Valley. This included shell-tempered pottery, made in the forms of a variety of typical Mississippian bowls, jars, and bottles and decorated with a variety of new rectilinear and curvilinear motifs. Between 1200 and about 1350, the culture of the Yazoo basin became a kind of hybrid of Coles Creek and Central Valley Mississippian cultures, and this hybrid is called Plaquemine. The cultivation of corn became well established during this time. At around 1400 many of the structures on the mound summits at Winterville burned down—whether on purpose, by accident, or through warfare is not known. After 1400 mound construction ceased at Winterville, and the site evidently went into decline.

The dominant site in the Yazoo River valley from about 1400 to the sixteenth century was the Lake George site (fig. 74). Including as many as thirty large

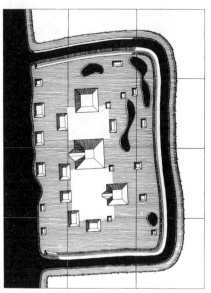

Fig. 74. Schematic map of the Lake George site. From William N. Morgan, *Prehistoric Architecture of the Eastern United States*, 84. (William N. Morgan, architect)

and small mounds, the Lake George site was laid out in a fifty-five-acre rectangular plan that was surrounded by a defensive ditch enclosing a dirt wall surmounted by a log palisade. The site was situated hard against Lake George, an old cut-off channel of the Yazoo River, and the ditch that surrounded it was filled with water from Lake George. The time when Lake George was cut off from the Yazoo River is uncertain, although a remnant channel connecting the southern end of Lake George with the Yazoo River was open as late as 1877–78. Hence, in several respects the setting of this site resembles that of the main town of Pacaha. The Lake George site was built and occupied in a relatively short period of time, perhaps in as few as fifty to one hundred years. The site had a commanding location with respect to the waterways of the lower Yazoo basin. In addition to its advantageous position on Lake George, it lay near Big Sunflower River, Silver Creek, Deer Creek, and the Little Sunflower River, and it was not so very far from the Mississippi River. Many of these streams were connected to each other on their upper courses by small channels that were navigable by shallow-draft dugout canoes; hence, they constituted a veritable maze of waterways (fig. 75).

This maze of waterways was the world of Quigualtam. Sites are scattered throughout this region, but because De Soto's chroniclers left no descriptions

Fig. 75. Bayou in Leflore County, Mississippi, four miles south of Itta Bena. Photograph by Roland Harper, June 8, 1911. (William Stanley Hoole Special Collections Library, University of Alabama)

of this area, we do not know what its internal structure was. From the events that are documented, it is reasonable to infer, however, that the Yazoo Basin was dominated by a complex chiefdom under the sway of a single chief— Quigualtam.

The Lake George site may have been in decline as early as 1500, though some people may have continued to live there as late as the time of the De Soto expedition. The experience of De Soto and his men suggests that Quigualtam was a populous society in 1542–43, and the archaeology confirms that sites dating to that time are scattered throughout the lower Yazoo Basin. The Winterville site may have been completely abandoned by 1542, but the channel that connected Deer Creek with the Mississippi River may have still been open. As members of the expedition would later discover, Chief Quigualtam still maintained a keen interest in activities on the Mississippi as far north as about Winterville.

Where was Quigualtam's seat of power? If we take seriously the Guachoyas' claim that Quigualtam's main town was at a distance of three days' travel— allowing about twenty miles per day—then the location would have been in the general vicinity of the Lake George site. If Lake George had already been abandoned by 1542–43, then Chief Quigualtam's town was somewhere in the neighborhood of the old center.[37]

From his sickbed, De Soto continued waging a war of nerves on the Indians. The people of Guachoya came every day bringing great quantities of fish—so that the town became filled with fish—and in this way they gave the appearance of being compliant. De Soto's men heard that Chief Quigualtam had sworn to the Sun and Moon that he would kill the Spaniards and hang their bodies up in trees for the birds to eat.[38] And the chief of Guachoya told De Soto he had heard that the chief of Quigualtam was going to come across the river on a certain night to attack the Spaniards. But this only made De Soto even more distrustful of the chief of Guachoya, whom he suspected of being party to a plot to drive the Spaniards out. De Soto ordered that the chief of Guachoya be seized and put under close arrest. On the night on which the warriors of Quigualtam were to come, De Soto instituted a very strict watch, a watch that was kept up thereafter.

When Chief Quigualtam did not come with his men on the designated night, De Soto interrogated the chief of Guachoya. Why had chief Quigualtam not come? He had not come, said the chief of Guachoya, because he saw that De Soto was on watch, and he did not dare attack. But Guachoya begged De Soto to order his own captains to attack Quigualtam, and he would send many of his own warriors from Guachoya to join with them. De Soto replied that as soon as he recovered from his illness, he would go after chief Quigualtam.[39]

But De Soto may have been as fearful of an attack from Guachoya as from Quigualtam. He became concerned about the dense population of the land where they were. With so many Indians coming and going from Guachoya every day, what was to keep them from gaining intelligence and conspiring against him?

The openings in the palisade around Guachoya did not have gates that could be closed, sealing off entry. But De Soto decided against making repairs or modifications to make the palisade more secure, because to do so might give the Indians the idea the Spaniards were afraid of them. Instead, he stationed cavalry at each of the openings to stand guard all night. In addition, all of the Spaniards' horses were left bridled all night in case of an attack. He also stationed footmen to guard the trails coming into the town, as well as crossbowmen to guard the dugout canoes where they were pulled up on the river bank. Finally, from each of the companies of horsemen, pairs of mounted men made the rounds all night visiting these sentinels.[40]

The Massacre at Anilco

One wonders how accurately De Soto, lying on his sickbed, grasped his situation. How responsible were his decisions? Was his judgment clouded by sickness and fear because he knew how vulnerable the Spaniards were with so few horses and with such robust native societies on both sides of the river? But whether his judgment was clear or clouded, his willingness to take action, terrible action, was not diminished. In an attempt to put the Indians on both sides of the river in awe of the Spaniards, he decided to launch a terroristic strike against Anilco. Perhaps the people of Anilco had irritated him when they ran from their town carrying away food and supplies. They would be an object lesson in just how terrible he could be. He ordered Nuño de Tovar to take fifteen horsemen by land and Juan de Guzmán to take a contingent of footmen upstream in canoes.[41] In addition, the chief of Guachoya sent many of his own warriors along in canoes.

Tovar and his horsemen stopped two leagues short of Anilco and waited for Guzmán to arrive. That night they crossed the river silently, and they attacked at dawn the next day. It was the horsemen who did the actual fighting, with the others providing backup outside the town. When they came in sight of the town they were spotted by a person of Anilco who ran away yelling loudly to alert the people in the town. But Tovar and his companions gave their horses the spur, and they reached the town before the inhabitants could flee to safety. The houses of as many as five or six thousand people were scattered about in open land a quarter of a league around the town. The frightened people ran out of their houses, or rather they fled from one house to another while attempting to evade the lancers, each of whom found himself in the midst of many Indians.

De Soto had ordered his men to spare the life of none of the males. And the people of Anilco were so taken by surprise and so confused that they offered very little effective resistance.[42] The cries of the women and children were so loud they were painful to the ears of the Spaniards. They killed a hundred or so of the people, and wounded many others with their lances. They intentionally let the wounded live in order that their wounds would strike terror and awe in their fellows. The Spaniards were most cruel, killing without mercy old men and very young boys who offered little or no resistance.[43]

The horsemen used their horses to injure and intimidate the people of Anilco. They would charge into groups of Indians, knocking them down with the breasts and stirrups of their horses, wounding many, and letting them go away wounded. They captured women and children and took them to the footmen for safekeeping. In all they seized around eighty women and children. They also took a quantity of clothing. To many of the soldiers involved in this incident, it seemed that some of the horsemen were so cowardly and cruel as to be inhuman.[44]

The Indians of Guachoya waited outside the town observing the horsemen while they committed these acts. When the people of Anilco were routed, and the lancers were charging about attacking those who were fleeing, the Guachoya warriors went inside the town and looted the houses. They loaded their plunder in their canoes and arrived back at Guachoya before the Spaniards did. Visibly shaken at what had transpired, they reported to their chief all that they had seen.[45]

Even though the warriors of Guachoya may have been astonished and frightened by the ability of the Spaniards to inflict such terrible casualties on their enemies in battle, it is to be doubted they had any sympathy for the people of Anilco. Guachoya and Anilco were at war with each other, and probably had been for a long time.[46] There was only enmity between them.[47]

Did the Guachoyas, as some Spaniards claimed, commit atrocities that rivaled or exceeded those of De Soto's men? If Garcilaso and his sources can be trusted, the people of Guachoya saw this as an opportunity to avenge themselves on Anilco. He says they entered the Anilco temple, took from it the most prized possessions, their battle trophies, including weapons and trophies they had seized from Guachoya, and the heads of their enemies, including some from Guachoya, which had been placed on lance points beside the door of the temple. Just as the Casquis had done at Pacaha, the people of Guachoya removed these heads of their own people and replaced them with the heads of Anilco dead. They took the remains of the Anilco honored dead from chests in the temple and threw them on the ground, trampling and heaping scorn upon them.[48]

According to Garcilaso, the Guachoyas killed people of Anilco indiscriminately and cruelly. They killed both sexes and all ages. They killed old women, and they aimed their arrows particularly at their genitals. They took infants by the leg and threw them up into the air, shooting arrows into them as they fell.[49] In Garcilaso's account, the people of Guachoya tried to conceal these acts from the Spaniards but were found out.[50] He says the Spaniards tried to stop the Guachoyas from burning the town of Anilco, but they had already set some of the houses on fire, though the entire town did not burn to the ground.

According to an account reportedly written by Alonso de Carmona, De Soto tried to make a similar attack on Quigualtam. From his sickbed he ordered a contingent of horsemen to cross the river and strike some terror into the heart of this arrogant chief. Accordingly, his men took some of the larger dugout canoes and joined them together in pairs. They loaded some horses in them, positioning their front legs in one canoe and their hind legs in the other, and in this way reached the opposite bank of the river. Here they succeeded in finding some large towns, but the inhabitants had fled, frustrating De Soto's plan. Later, he received a message, presumably from Chief Quigualtam, that he should not try such a thing again. If he did, none of his men would come back alive. If they should come again, the people of Quigualtam had sworn to their gods they would kill them all or die trying.

According to Garcilaso, De Soto planned, upon his recovery, to cross the river and set up camp in chief Quigualtam's principal town, where he would build two boats to sail to Mexico and Cuba. Then he would decide what to do next.[51]

Survivors of the expedition had the impression that Quigualtam was the richest and most important province they encountered in La Florida. Alvaro de San Jorge said the chief of Quigualtam was reputed to have seventeen chiefs under his command. He thought that if the expedition had reached the province, they would have established a colony there.[52]

The Death of De Soto

De Soto's illness worsened, and his prospects of recovery faded. When he realized that his death was near, he summoned the royal officials and his principal men to his bedside. He told them he was soon to appear before God, where he would have to give an account of his life.[53] He expressed his gratitude to all present, and he thanked them for having been loyal to him, as proven by the hardships they had endured. He had hoped to have occasion later in life to repay them. He asked them to pray to God to pardon him for his sins and to consign his soul to heaven. He asked them to release him from the obligations he owed to them and to pardon any offense he had given them.[54]

De Soto made out a new will, almost in shorthand because of the lack of paper. The will is not known to have survived.[55] In order to forestall dissension that might occur after he died, De Soto asked them to elect one of their own to act as governor, one to whom they would give their oath of obedience. Their doing so would make him feel better about leaving them in a land in which they were lost. Baltasar de Gallegos tried to console him by saying that life is brief and full of suffering, and that those who leave this world earliest are the recipients of God's mercy. Gallegos said De Soto himself should appoint the person who was to succeed him, and they would obey whoever this person might be. With this, De Soto appointed Luís de Moscoso as captain general. Moscoso was immediately elected governor and sworn in.[56] De Soto's captains and principal men swore they would obey Moscoso.

The next day, May 21, 1542, De Soto died. He died a Catholic, asking the mercy of the Holy Trinity, invoking the protection of the blood of Christ and the intercession of the Virgin.[57] It is a measure of his dictatorial command that his soldiers obeyed him until he was dead. But after his death some of them had hard things to say about him. Many did not come to where his body lay to pay their respects.[58] Some of them openly rejoiced at his death, because they knew that Moscoso was fond of living the good life in a Christian land, and he would not want to continue the hardships of the war of conquest in La Florida, which most of them had realized long ago would profit them little.[59]

Moscoso decided they should try to conceal from the Indians the fact of De Soto's death. One reason was that, perhaps more than usual, De Soto had tried to persuade the people of Guachoya and Quigualtam that he was super-natural, possessed of extraordinary powers. The Spaniards thought the In-dians were gullible enough to believe everything that was told to them.[60] De Soto had contrived to make the Indians think that matters they thought they had discussed or done in secret—which he learned about through in-formers—were known to him through his special powers. How did he know these things? In their presence, he would hold up a mirror to himself, which the Indians had never seen before. He would tell them that the face in the mir-ror was his spiritual double, who told him about all that they were thinking and planning. In this way he hoped to dissuade them from attempting any covert action against him. But now that he had set himself up as such an ex-traordinary being, his death might make the people of Guachoya think the Spaniards vulnerable, tempting them to attack.

Moscoso ordered that De Soto's body be hidden in one of the houses for three days. Then, under cover of darkness, he had the men bury it just inside the gate of the town.[61] Another reason for burying De Soto secretly might have been the fear that after the Spaniards departed from Guachoya, the Indians would search out De Soto's grave, dig up his corpse, and desecrate it. They knew full well that in other places the Indians had cut up Spanish bodies into pieces and hung them up in the trees for the birds to eat.[62]

But the Indians knew De Soto had been ill, and when they saw that he was not present any more, they suspected what had happened. Some of them no-ticed the place inside the gate where the earth had been disturbed, and they began talking among themselves. They would point with their chins and wink with their eye in the direction of the grave.[63] When Moscoso learned of this, he ordered the men to dig up the body, again under cover of darkness. They took it from its grave and placed a considerable quantity of sand in the shawls in which it was wrapped. Then they took the body in a dugout canoe to the middle of the Mississippi River and cast it overboard.[64]

The chief of Guachoya asked Moscoso what had happened to his brother and lord, De Soto. Moscoso told him De Soto had gone to the sky, as he often did, and since he was to remain there for several days, he had appointed Moscoso to serve in his place. But in spite of this, the chief believed De Soto was dead, and he ordered two young Indians to be taken to the Spanish camp. It was the custom of retainer sacrifice in his land, he said, that some be killed to accom-pany the dead chief and serve him in the other world. The chief of Guachoya told Moscoso to have the two young men beheaded so they could serve De Soto in death. But Moscoso insisted that De Soto was not dead, he had only gone to the sky, and he had taken some of his own men with him. Moscoso ordered the chief of Guachoya to free the two young men and to cease practicing so evil a custom.[65]

The chief of Guachoya freed the two young men to return to their homes. One of them, however, refused to go. He said he did not wish to remain under the power of one who had sentenced him to a death he did not deserve, and he wished to serve out the rest of his life under the one who had saved him.[66]

Moscoso ordered that the estate of De Soto be sold at auction. His goods consisted of 2 male slaves, 2 female slaves, 3 horses, and 700 hogs. Each horse and slave was priced at 2,000 to 3,000 cruzados, and the hogs were priced at 200 cruzados each, payable to De Soto's estate at the first discovery of any gold or silver or from any other wealth obtained on the expedition. Those who purchased these horses and slaves promised that even if they discovered nothing in the land they were exploring, they would make payment within a year, and those who had no property in Spain gave bond, promising to pay. In general, those who did own property in Spain bought less than those who did not own property there.[67]

After this auction, the Spaniards owned the hogs they had tended for so long, and they began to butcher and eat them as they pleased. This enabled them to resume the then customary Catholic convention of abstention from meat on Fridays and Saturdays and the vespers of holidays. They had left off such observances because they would go for two or three months at a time without tasting meat, and when they did get some they would eat it no matter what day it was.[68]

The most important matter to be settled was what to do next. Moscoso ordered the officers and officials to assemble and discuss what they should do. They had visited most of the population centers in the Southeast, missing very few.[69] There was agreement that they should now return to civilization, but the question was how to proceed—by boat down the river to the Gulf of Mexico, or overland to the west to Mexico. At Guachoya they had made careful inquiry into the populations in all directions. To the south, Quigualtam was powerful but clearly hostile, and he would not be easy to subdue. Moreover, downriver from Quigualtam the country was said to be uninhabited and there was little food available. Toward the west, however, the country was said to be well populated.

Moscoso asked all of those present to express their opinions in writing and to sign it, so that he might be able to decide whether to go south down the river or overland to the west. To some it seemed that going downriver would be the most dangerous course. They might not be able to build ships that would weather a storm; they had no pilot to steer the way in the Gulf of Mexico, nor even a compass or a sailing chart; they did not know how far it was to the Gulf of Mexico; and for all they knew, the river might pass a very great distance through the land and even contain shoals or waterfalls.

Some of them had seen a sailing chart of the Gulf, and they resolved that from where they would exit the Mississippi River it would be about five hundred leagues to Mexico. Hence, travel by water would probably be the shortest way, but the drawback was they would first have to take time out to build boats. They would have to travel a longer distance by land, but they would be able to set out immediately, and unless they came to an uninhabited area that was impossible to cross, they would surely be able to find a place where they could get food enough to survive the winter, and they would reach Mexico the following summer. Moreover, if they went by land they might still discover a rich society where they could yet realize a profit. They resolved to go overland, toward the west.[70]

15

The River of Daycao

On June 5 Moscoso and the army departed from Guachoya, taking a northwesterly direction (map 8) that led them to Catalte, a small polity that lay along Bayou Bartholomew.[1] At first, as they traveled a course that lay between Bayou Bartholomew and the Arkansas River, they traveled through southern floodplain forest. Then in the vicinity of present-day Pine Bluff, they took a westward turn and traveled for six days through an oak-hickory-pine forest wilderness in the upper coastal plain. What they could not have understood, but experience would soon teach them, was that they had begun their departure from the ample rainfall of the Southeast and were approaching the dry West. Moreover, they were entering an area where a culture existed that had been powerfully shaped by this decline in rainfall—the Caddoan area. It was an area they had already briefly encountered when they had proceeded from Tanico up the Arkansas River to Tula and from there had looped southward through Quipana in the Ouachita Mountains.

Chaguate

On June 20 they came to the first town of Chaguate, whose chief had come the previous winter to Utiangüe to pay his respects to De Soto.[2]

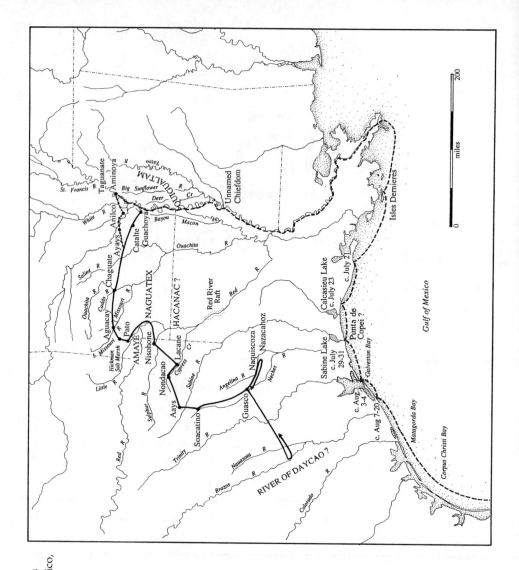

Map 8. Moscoso's route from Guachoya to the Gulf of Mexico, 1542–1543.

Chaguate was one of the cluster of Caddoan sites that lay along the Ouachita River between present-day Malvern and Arkadelphia. The Caddoan area comprised a number of late prehistoric societies in southwestern Arkansas, northwestern Louisiana, eastern Oklahoma, and northeastern Texas. They occupied portions of the area that is sometimes called the Trans-Mississippian South, comprising several forest types of the Southeast that extend west of the Mississippi River, where they are increasingly interspersed with prairies as one moves from east to west (see map 4).

It can be argued that the native societies of the Caddoan area were regional variants of the Mississippian way of life. Certainly the overall developmental trajectory of Caddoan peoples resembles that of the Mississippian Southeast. After about A.D. 1100 to 1300 the people in the Caddoan area began to grow corn and other tropical cultigens; their societies show increasing evidence of social ranking; and their political and ritual organization became more complex. Their civic centers included mounds that were used as platforms for temples and as elite burial sites. These mounds were not the centers of compact towns with large resident populations, but neither were the mounds of some of the variants in the Mississippian Southeast at certain times and at certain places. Such was the case, for example, in Apalachee.

Caddoan societies were characteristically composed of dispersed farmsteads, packed more closely together at places where there was good farming along the larger rivers, and less so on the smaller tributaries. No Caddoan communities were surrounded by fortifications—but such was also the case elsewhere in the Mississippian Southeast at certain times and places. For example, the De Soto chroniclers make no mention of fortifications until they crossed the Appalachian Mountains and arrived at Chiaha, though they most certainly traversed areas where fortifications had existed a century or so earlier.

Caddoan peoples built houses comparable to those in the Mississippian Southeast, though instead of covering them with sheets of bark or cane mats, they more commonly thatched them with grass. Their principal prey animal was the white-tailed deer, though in places and at times some of those who lived on the western margin of the Caddoan area could also hunt buffalo. Most of the small animals they hunted were the same as those hunted in the Mississippian Southeast. The Caddoan people made excellent pottery in a style that was distinctively their own (see figs. 79, 83).

Some very productive salines existed in the Caddoan area, and the Caddoan people were famous salt traders. But there were other salt traders in the Southeast, as for example, the people of Joara and Tanico. The Caddoan people were like Mississippian people elsewhere in trading far and wide for exotic substances such as conch shells and copper, but the only exotic trade substances peculiar to them were cotton cloth and turquoise, which they procured in small quantities from the Southwest.

One way in which the peoples of the Caddoan area differed from the Mississippian Southeast is in the words they used to designate positions of power in their society. Most Southeastern chiefdoms, whatever the language spoken, used variants of the words *mico* (chief), *orata* (lesser chief), *heniha* (councilor, adjudicator), *yatika* (translator, speaker), and *tastanagi* (warrior). In contrast, the equivalent terms in the Caddoan area were *xinesi* (spiritual leader), *caddi* (village headman), *canaha* (subordinate headman or village elder), and *amay-xoya* (war leader or warrior).[3]

Unfortunately, the chroniclers of the De Soto expedition were not interested in documenting cultural differences. They did so only indirectly or in passing. But they were mightily interested in plundering stores of dried corn, and their difficulties in finding adequate supplies as they traveled westward may indicate variant cultural practices in the Caddoan area as well as a drier climate.

The day before the Spaniards arrived at the first town of Chaguate, a Spaniard who was ill strayed from the expedition and was lost. Moscoso suspected the Indians of Chaguate had killed him, and he sent word ahead to the chief that the lost man should be searched out and handed over. If the chief of Chaguate would bring the lost Spaniard to him, Moscoso would be his friend as before, but if he did not, he would be an enemy and the Spaniards would raze the land of Chaguate. With this threat, the chief came and reminded Moscoso that he had voluntarily come to see De Soto at Utiangüe, pledging his loyalty, and he had no reason to do the Spaniards any injury. His people had sheltered the lost man, and he had intended to hand him over to Moscoso when he reached the main town of Chaguate. Moscoso explained that he had expected to find the chief in the town in which they were then located. But when he did not find him there, he had assumed the chief had run away, as had so many others.

The chief of Chaguate led Moscoso and his men to the town where he was living, a day's travel away.[4] While traveling from one of these towns to the other, they passed by a salt lake—probably Saline Bayou (fig. 76)—which was fed by brine that came from spring-fed pools, where the Indians extracted a great quantity of salt.[5] This was near the town itself, and during the six days in which the Spaniards remained in this town, they extracted some salt from

Fig. 76. Saline Bayou. (Arkansas Archaeological Survey)

the brine. It is possible that during these six days, they sent out small parties of horsemen to explore the country, possibly including the area around present-day Hot Springs.[6]

When Moscoso questioned the people of Chaguate about what lay to the west, he found that their knowledge did not extend very far in that direction. But they did tell Moscoso that in three days' journey he would come to the province of Aguacay. Seemingly the people of Chaguate did not mention what lay to the south, the Felsenthal region of Arkansas and Louisiana, populated by small societies who were hunter-gatherers but nonetheless built mounds.[7]

With this knowledge about Aguacay, Moscoso and his army departed from Chaguate traveling directly westward. On the day they departed, unbeknownst to Moscoso, Francisco de Guzmán, bastard son of a gentleman of Seville, absented himself from the expedition and remained behind. Guzmán had joined the expedition in Spain with a good supply of fine clothing, excellent weapons, and three horses. According to Garcilaso, his problem was that he was an inveterate gambler.[8] He had remained behind in Chaguate because he had bet and lost a beautiful young Indian mistress whom he loved, and he was distressed over the prospect of giving her up.[9] It was not until the second day on the trail that Moscoso realized that Guzmán and his mistress were missing. He sent word to the chief of Chaguate that Guzmán was to be handed over to him at Aguacay.[10] Moscoso held some Indians of Chaguate hostage—presumably his guides—and he threatened that if Guzmán was not returned to him, he would assume the Indians had killed him, and he in turn would execute his hostages.[11] The messengers returned with the news that Guzmán was with the chief, who was treating him well, and he did not want to rejoin the expedition.[12]

On July 4 the expedition reached Aguacay, a polity located on the Little Missouri River and its tributaries.[13] The day before reaching this town they were met on the trail by fifteen Indians who carried a present of skins, fish, and roasted venison.[14] But when they reached the town of Aguacay—probably on the upper Little Missouri River—they found that all the inhabitants had fled.[15] They remained at this town for some days and made several forays into the countryside, capturing several men and women. These captives told them about the existence of a body of water that the Spaniards interpreted as being the South Sea—that is, the Pacific Ocean. They noted that in Aguacay the Indians extracted salt from sand, which they took from a vein of earth like slate (perhaps the slate bedrock common in this locale), and their manner of making it was like what they had observed earlier at Cayas.[16]

It is clear enough that Moscoso and his men intended to travel directly west, where, based on what Cabeza de Vaca had said, they believed Mexico lay.[17] But the people they captured at Aguacay told them they would only find populated areas if they traveled southwest-by-south, where there were large towns well supplied with food. They told the Spaniards that directly toward the west they would find great stretches of sand, no people, and no corn.[18]

On the day they departed from Aguacay (probably July 16), they came to a small town subject to the chief, which was located near an unusual saline, a salt marsh. This was probably the Hickman Salt Works site (fig. 77) on the western side of the Saline River. That evening, the Spaniards extracted some salt from the brine. The next day, they traveled further, bivouacking at the end of the day between two ridges in a forest of open trees. The next day they continued, coming to the small town of Pato, perhaps located on the south side of the lower Little River.

On the fourth day of travel, they came to the first town of Amaye, a chiefdom that lay between Little River and Red River, in the vicinity of present-day Ogden, Arkansas. When they interrogated an Indian they captured there, he told them that after a journey of a day and a half they would come to Naguatex.

Fig. 77. Hickman salt marsh. The white area near the center of the picture is crystallized salt on the ground and on vegetation. A brackish pool and salt marsh lies in the left portion of the picture. The high ground to the upper right shows evidence of both Indian and Euro-American salt-makers. (Arkansas Archaeological Survey)

During this time all of their travel would be through country that was continuously occupied, with no wilderness areas in between.[19]

Naguatex

They departed from Amaye on July 20, and at the end of the day they bivouacked beside a brook in a luxurious grove of trees. They were between the provinces of Amaye and Naguatex, probably in the general vicinity of present-day Fulton, Arkansas. They noticed that several Indians had come to spy on them, and some of the horsemen went after them, killing six of them and capturing two. When Moscoso interrogated the captives through his interpreters, they said they had been sent by the chief of Naguatex to find out what manner of people these strangers were. They said the chief of Naguatex and the chiefs "under his protection" had decided to wage war on the intruders.[20]

While they were interrogating these two men, they saw bands of armed Indians coming at them from two directions. When these Indians saw that they had been spotted, they began to shout loudly and rushed to attack the Spaniards.

But when the horsemen rode out and began doing them injury, the Indians turned and fled, and in fleeing many of them were killed. In coming out to repulse this attack, the horsemen forgot about the footmen they had left back in the camp. Two additional parties of Indians sprang out of concealment to attack these footmen, but the footmen resisted, and these Indians fled also.

After the Indians had retreated and the horsemen had regrouped, the Spaniards heard loud cries at a distance of a crossbow shot from where they were. Moscoso ordered twelve horsemen to ride over and see what was going on. They found two horsemen and four footmen who had gotten separated from those who went out on the first attack. They were surrounded by a great many Indians who attacked them as they were returning to camp. The two horsemen were hard put defending the four footmen.[21]

With the arrival of reinforcements, many of these Indians were killed, but they captured one and took him back to camp, where he was interrogated. When asked who was waging war against the Spaniards, the man said it was the chief of Naguatex—who was obviously a paramount chief—and his allies, the chief of Amaye and the chief of Hacanac. The latter was said to be the chief of a large province, with many "vassals." The Spaniards never reached the territory of Hacanac, and its location is unknown, though perhaps it comprised the cluster of late prehistoric sites that lay to the south, in the general vicinity of present-day Shreveport, Louisiana.

Moscoso ordered his men to cut off this Indian's nose and his right arm. He was to return to the chief of Naguatex to tell him that the next day the Spaniards would come to his country, and if he wished to fight, he should wait until they arrived.

The next day they traveled into the principal town of Naguatex, which was very large. This was probably in the vicinity of present-day Garland, in the Spirit Lake locality. This included the Battle Mound, one of the largest platform mounds in the southeastern United States. Moscoso asked where the chief was and was told he was on the other side of the river—the Red River—that ran through Naguatex. Moscoso marched his men to the Red River, and when they reached it they saw many Indian warriors lined up on the opposite side.

Since he could see no obvious place where the river could be forded and since several of his men were wounded, Moscoso decided it would be good for them to rest for a few days. Because the weather was very hot, he established a camp near the town of Naguatex. The camp was near a brook—possibly Field Bayou—in a grove of large trees about a quarter of a league from the Red River.

They captured several Indians of Naguatex and interrogated them. When asked whether it was possible to ford the Red River, they said it was possible to do so in certain places at certain times. Ten days later Moscoso sent out two of his captains, each commanding fifteen horsemen, and they went with guides to search for fords upstream and down and to determine where the population lay on the opposite side of the river. They found a ford and crossed the river against strong opposition from the Indians. On the western side of the river they found a large town and a great quantity of food. The horsemen then returned to report to Moscoso.[22]

The chiefdom of Naguatex lay in the Great Bend of the Red River, south of present-day Fulton, Arkansas, where the river takes a sharp turn to the south. Its towns lay along the river between the mouth of Little River to the north and the mouth of Big Cypress Creek to the south. The Red River dominated the lives of the people of Naguatex quite as much as the Mississippi River dominated the lives of the people who lived near it. The Red is an active, meandering river like the Mississippi, only more so. It forms levee ridges, oxbow lakes, and backswamps as the Mississippi does, but because the reddish brown soils along the Red River swell remarkably when wet and shrink just as remarkably when dry, the meandering Red River powerfully impacts the land adjacent to it. For example, only about half of the forty-nine mounds archaeologically documented for this area at the turn of the century still exist. This means that in the course of the last hundred years the Red River has probably destroyed some of the localities on both sides of the river visited by Moscoso and his men.

These hazards aside, the Red River meander zone was an exceedingly rich area in which to live. The levee ridges along the oxbow lakes were especially attractive to the people of Naguatex. The soil was rich and easily tilled, and the oxbow lakes teemed with fish, frogs, turtles, and seasonal waterfowl. And in the floodplain forests they could obtain the same game animals, nuts, roots, seeds, and fruits as in similar forests east of the Mississippi River. They undoubtedly procured most of their deer in the upland oak-pine forests to the east, west, and south of the meander zone of the river.[23] One particularly valuable resource in the Caddoan area was the Osage orange tree—regionally known as bois d'arc—the best wood in North America for making bows. Then as later, the people in the Big Bend region may have traded Osage orange wood to Indians in other localities.

On or about August 1 Moscoso sent an Indian messenger to the chief of Naguatex, telling him he should come and make an appearance. If the chief would promise to obey, he would be forgiven for what he had done in the past.

But if he did not come, Moscoso would search him out and punish him. Two days later the Indian messengers returned and said the chief would come the next day. On the same day this message was received, many Indians came to visit, including some of the principal men. The chief had sent them to try to read Moscoso's mood, so he could decide whether to come or not.

The next day (about August 4) some Indians came and announced that the chief of Naguatex was on his way, and then they immediately departed. Two hours later the chief arrived, surrounded by many attendants, who had formed themselves into two long parallel columns. When they reached the place where Moscoso waited, they halted, and the chief walked in the space between the two columns to where Moscoso was. All the Indians were weeping in the ritualistic manner in which the people of Tula had wept.[24]

The chief of Naguatex asked to be forgiven for what he had done. He acknowledged that Moscoso was a greater lord than he, and indeed Moscoso seemed to be lord of the realm of nature, and his men seemed to be immortal. The chief said he had listened to bad advice from a brother of his who was killed in the fighting. He promised henceforth to obey. Moscoso then pardoned him, saying that in the future they would be friends.[25]

Four days later, on or about August 9, Moscoso and his army departed from their camp and went to the place where they intended to ford the Red River. But when they got there, they found that the water in the river had risen greatly. This astonished the Spaniards, because it was in the summer season and it had not rained where they were for over a month. The Indians informed them that the river often rose in this way when it had not rained locally. The Spaniards thought this might mean the Gulf of Mexico was nearby and the river had risen because a high tide had backed up into it. But the Indians said the water always came from upstream, and they had no knowledge of the sea.[26]

In fact, the Spaniards were located at the upper end of water that was impounded by the Great Raft (see map 8), a vast, ancient logjam in the general vicinity of present-day Shreveport, Louisiana, that effectively dammed up the Red River. This logjam raised the level of the river up to fifteen feet higher than its modern level, and a substantial rain anywhere along the river could back water up for a considerable distance upstream. This raft forced the Red River into multiple channels, and it created large backswamps on both sides of the impounded stretch of the river. The Red River reaches far to the west, with its headwaters in western Texas and Oklahoma. When a rain occurred on the western part of the river, the river could rise quite surprisingly downstream. The Red River could not be navigated by steamboats until 1873, when the Great Raft was broken up and cleared out.[27]

The Spaniards had no choice but to return to their camp. A week later the level of the water had fallen, and they again set forth. They departed from their camp on or about August 16, forded the river, and came to a town whose people had all run away. They bivouacked in an open field, and Moscoso sent word to the chief of Naguatex to come and meet with him and to supply him with guides for the journey. Several days later, the chief had still not come. So Moscoso ordered two captains to go out in different directions to burn down towns and capture as many Indians as they could. They did so, burning down houses and stores of food and capturing many Indians. The chief then sent six of his principal men as well as three others who could serve the Spaniards as guides and translators in the region they were entering.

Aays

After staying for several days in this town of Naguatex on the western side of the river, Moscoso and his men departed.[28] They traveled for three days and came to a small town of four or five houses. They were now in Nisohone, a place that seemed "miserable" because it was thinly populated and very poor in corn.[29] Nisohone appears to have been on the lower Sulphur River. It seems to have been separated from Naguatex by an uninhabited wilderness.

Two days after departing from Nisohone, the Spaniards realized their guides were misleading them. It seemed to them that when they wished to go toward the west, the guides would lead them toward the east, and finally they found themselves on no trail at all, struggling through dense woods. Moscoso ordered that two of these guides be hanged from a tree. Then they relied upon a woman who had been taken prisoner at Nisohone, who guided them back to the trail. Two days later they came to Lacane, which seemed to them to be a very poor place. Lacane was probably located somewhere on Big Cypress Creek basin, perhaps in what is now the basin of Lake o' the Pines.[30]

It seemed to the Spaniards that the further they went from Naguatex, the poorer the country became.[31] And indeed, as they traveled west they departed from a zone with a comfortable annual rainfall of forty to sixty inches and entered a zone where the rainfall was sometimes less than forty inches per year and was subject to droughts—the bane of corn cultivators. Moreover, the average wind velocity in this drier zone increased from eight miles per hour to

Fig. 78. Post oak savannah near La Grange, Texas. Photograph by David H. Riskind. (Texas Parks and Wildlife Department)

twelve miles per hour. Particularly in treeless areas, these hot summer winds dry the soil alarmingly. As they traveled west, the oaks, hickories, and pines thinned out, and eventually the pines disappeared as they skirted a north-south band of post oak savannah (fig. 78), with scattered oaks and hickories surrounded by grassland (see map 4).[32] In such country it was extremely difficult for simple cultivators to grow corn reliably, and the Spaniards, always looking for where their next meal would come from, judged this land to be "miserable" and "wretched." (The quality of land is very much in the eye of the beholder. In later times, Spanish travelers who set out from further west or southwest judged this same land to be excellent.)

In this part of the expedition it is difficult to know whether the Indian guides were truly misleading the Spaniards, or whether the Spaniards merely thought they were being misled. The problem is that the Spaniards appear to have thought they could reach Mexico by traveling west, as Cabeza de Vaca had done. But unlike Cabeza de Vaca and his three comrades, Moscoso and his men were an army: they *had* to go where they could find stores of corn, and this could only be toward the south. Their Indian guides may have been caught on the horns of this dilemma.

At Lacane they captured an Indian who said that the land of Nondacao was very populous, with houses scattered about as one finds them in mountain-

Fig. 79. A Wilder engraved bottle (height 9⅛") from the Carpenter site, Camp County, Texas, probably a locality of Nondacao. The engraved lines were filled with red ocher. (Robert L. Turner Jr.)

ous regions, and one could find plenty of corn there. Nondacao was possibly further west, up Big Cypress Creek, perhaps in present-day Camp County, Texas (fig. 79). When they reached this place, the chief of Nondacao and his Indians approached the Spaniards weeping, as had been done in Naguatex and other places. The Spaniards took this to be their way of showing that they had consented to obey their new overlords. The Indians of Nondacao gave the Spaniards a great abundance of fish. In summer in east Texas, when the level of the rivers fell, the Indians easily caught catfish, gar pike, freshwater drum, and other fish that were impounded in shallow pools of water.[33]

They departed from Nondacao with the intention of going to Soacatino, which they had been told was a large province.[34] But first they went to Aays, which took five days. Aays was possibly on a tributary of the upper Sabine River, perhaps in present-day Wood County, Texas, though possibly even further west. The Aays Indians were said to hunt buffalo in certain seasons of the year. This proposed location places the Aays within easy reach of the Black-land Prairie (see fig. 81), an area covered with rather dense medium-to-tall little bluestem grass and Texas needle grass in a band that runs from west of present-day Texarkana down almost to San Antonio, where bison were present in notable numbers from A.D. 1200 to 1600.[35]

When Moscoso and his men appeared, the Aays were completely taken by surprise. When they spotted the Spaniards, they shouted—and presumably one of the Spaniards' Indian guides translated—that they should kill the cows that were coming.[36] The Aays seemingly had no forewarning about the Spaniards at all, and they had never seen horses, so they referred to them with their word for bison, which the chroniclers invariably recorded as *vaca*, "cow." The Aays mounted an immediate resistance. As soon as fifty or a hundred of them assembled, they would come to the trail to fight the Spaniards. Then others would attack from another direction. When the Spaniards would pursue one group, another group would pursue the Spaniards. This fighting lasted throughout most of the last day of travel before reaching the province of Aays. Several Spaniards and horses were wounded, though not seriously, but great damage was done to the Aays people.

Garcilaso, without naming it, refers to a province where the Spaniards found a settlement pattern they had not seen before. These were clusters of four or five houses situated on hill tops, which he compared to the houses of "melon growers" in Spain. They were flimsily constructed, perhaps in comparison to houses seen earlier on the route. Inside, the Spaniards found quantities of buffalo meat and also recently skinned buffalo hides. This may be a description of the province of Aays.[37] It is quite possible that Aays were ancestral to the Eyeish, who lived near present-day San Augustine in the eighteenth century and spoke a markedly different dialect of Caddoan than did neighboring Caddoan-speakers, or perhaps even a non-Caddoan language. In later times, the Caddo perceived the Eyeish as being in some sense inferior to themselves. It is likely that the Aays were some of the peoples on the western margin of the Caddoan area who lived in small, temporary shelters and who subsisted mainly by hunting and gathering.[38]

This may also have been the area in which some Indians challenged the Spaniards to one-on-one combat in a way that was reminiscent of incidents that occurred while they were in peninsular Florida. This seemed to happen in places where the Indians had no concept of the Spaniards' military might and where the level of native military organization was less than the Spaniards encountered among the Mississippian chiefdoms. In one such incident, recorded by Garcilaso, the Spaniards had bivouacked at the end of a day's march. They observed a single Indian emerge from some trees and approach them. He carried a bow and had a quiver of arrows on his back. Because he was alone and seemingly peaceable, they took little note of him. They assumed he was bringing a message from his chief to Moscoso. But when he was about fifty feet from the Spaniards, he swiftly took an arrow from his quiver, nocked it in his bow, and shot it with great velocity. The Spaniards scattered left and right, some dropping to the ground, and the arrow missed them all, but it flew on toward several female Indian slaves who were beneath a tree, preparing food. The arrow struck one of the women in the back and passed completely through her body and entered the body of another woman and stuck there, killing both of them. Then the Indian turned and fled with great speed toward the woods. The cry went up among the Spaniards, "Kill him, kill him!" and Baltasar de Gallegos, who happened to be on his horse, sped after the man and killed him.[39]

In another incident recorded by Garcilaso, the Spaniards observed two Indians who for the better part of the day walked along parallel to the Spaniards' line of march, at about two hundred yards distance. First one would take the lead, and then the other, so that they took turns guarding their rear. When their peculiar behavior was reported to Moscoso, he ordered his men to avoid them as if they were madmen. It became clear that they wanted two Spaniards to come out and engage in combat with them. At about nightfall, a party of horsemen rode into camp, and they asked about the two Indians. They were told about Moscoso's order, but Juan Páez, a native of Segovia, disobeyed the order and rode out to engage them. One of the Indians withdrew and stood behind a tree, so the contest would be one-on-one. The single Indian in the open waited for the charging horseman to come in range and then fired a single arrow, which struck Páez at his left elbow and completely pierced his armor. Because of the shock of the arrow, Páez could not move his arm, and when the reins fell from his hand (he held his lance in his right hand), his horse immediately halted. His companions realized the danger he was in, and rushed forward to attack the two Indians. The Indians ran toward some woods, but the horsemen lanced them to death before they could get to safety.[40]

Guasco

The day they departed from Aays, the guide they had been following from Nondacao told them he had heard the chief of Nondacao say that the Indians of Soacatino had seen other Spaniards. This news encouraged Moscoso and his men. They assumed that these other Spaniards had come from Mexico, which would mean there was indeed a viable route from this place back to Spanish colonial society. Their great fear, having found so little of value in La Florida, was that in their attempt to escape they would get lost in some uninhabited region.[41]

But their brighter outlook was short-lived. Two days later they began to suspect that the old man whom the chief of Nondacao had sent with them as

a guide was deliberately misleading them. He was leading them off the trail in order to take shortcuts, or so he said. But they noticed that they seemed to be going in circles.[42] When Moscoso interrogated the man, he said he did not know where they were. Moscoso ordered him tied to a tree and set a mastiff on him. When the dog seized him and shook him violently, the man begged for mercy. He admitted that the chief of Nondacao had considered the Spaniards his enemies and had ordered the old man to lead them astray, so they would die of hunger.[43] Since the chief had ordered it done, he had no choice but to obey. Moscoso was so angered with this that he ordered that all the dogs be loosed on the man, and they killed and devoured him in a short time.[44]

Another Indian they had with them guided them to Soacatino, and they arrived there the next day. Soacatino was possibly on the upper reaches of the Neches River in present-day Van Zandt, Smith, or Henderson County. They found it to be a very poor land, thickly forested, and with little corn.[45] When the Spaniards interrogated the Indians of Soacatino about whether they knew of any other Spaniards, they said they had heard that some of them were traveling about to the south.[46]

From Soacatino they marched southward for twenty days through a sparsely inhabited region where there was little corn.[47] And what corn the Indians did have, they buried in the forests, so the Spaniards had to go out searching for it after having spent long days on the trail.[48] Finally they reached the province

Fig. 80. Museum diorama at Caddoan Mounds State Historic site, Neches Valley, Texas. Painting by Nola Montgomery; sculpture by Peggy Maceo. Photograph by Nola Montgomery. (Texas Parks and Wildlife Department)

of Guasco, where they found a good quantity of corn.[49] Guasco appears to have been on the Neches River, perhaps as far south as where present-day Highway 21 crosses the river. The people of Guasco possessed pieces of cotton cloth and turquoise they had traded from Indians further west.[50]

It is not altogether clear why Guasco was seemingly an island of relative plenty (fig. 80) in the middle of an area the Spaniards judged to be miserable and wretched. A finger of southern floodplain forest extends along the Neches River, but also along the Angelina and Sabine Rivers. Through this area ran a strong east-west trail that became the Camino Real in the Mission period (and even later it became Highway 21), and the intersection of this trail with the Neches River may have made for an economically and politically favored location.[51]

At Guasco the Spaniards were still intent on investigating the report they had heard of Spaniards to the south. They went from Guasco to the south or southeast to Naquiscoza, probably in the Angelina River basin. Here they interrogated some Indians who denied having seen any Spaniards. Moscoso ordered them tortured, whereupon they said that further on—at the province of Nazacahoz, probably also in the Angelina River basin—some Spaniards had come from the west and then returned in the direction from whence they had come. The Spaniards reached Nazacahoz in two days and captured some In- dian women. One of them said she had seen Spaniards before. She said she had been captured by them but had managed to escape.

Moscoso sent a captain with fifteen horsemen to take the woman to where she said she had seen the Spaniards. They were to see if they could find any trace of horses or of Spaniards. But after traveling for less than a day, the Indian woman seemed to admit that she had lied.[52] With this, the Spaniards concluded that all the reports they had heard about Spaniards in the vicinity were lies.

At this point they were not far from where Cabeza de Vaca and his com- rades had spent several years living among the Indians, which may have ac- counted for the rumors. But it is also possible that these reports of other Span- iards were products of their own wishful thinking abetted by statements by Indians who were being tortured or threatened with torture. In fact, their route had been so circuitous, the Indians may even have been repeating rumors that had reached them about Moscoso's army itself.[53] Since the land was so poor in corn, and since they could get no information indicating that people lived west- ward of Naquiscoza or Nazacahoz, they returned to the northwest to Guasco.

The River of Daycao

The people of Guasco told the Spaniards that ten days' journey to- ward the west was the River of Daycao, where they sometimes went to hunt deer in the woods. On the opposite side of this river they had seen people mov- ing about, but they did not know who they were. The Spaniards loaded up all the corn they could find for a journey through an uninhabited area and set out for the River of Daycao. After traveling for about six days south by southwest, probably following the trail that became the Camino Real, they halted, per- haps having reached as far as the Navasota River.[54] From this point Moscoso sent ten horsemen ahead to see what they could find. With orders to return in eight or nine days, they followed a trail to the River of Daycao and crossed to the other side. There they came upon some Indians living in very small huts, who took flight as soon as they saw the Spaniards, leaving everything they owned behind. But what they left behind was poor and miserable. The land it- self was very poor, and the Spaniards found very little corn.[55] Again they had entered post oak savannah (see fig. 78) like that at Aays. The people of the River of Daycao lived entirely (or nearly so) by hunting and fishing.[56] In their mode of livelihood, they are reminiscent of the Aays.[57]

Which stream may be identified as the River of Daycao? If one takes literally

Fig. 81. Blackland Prairie, Bell County, Texas. Photograph by David H. Riskind. (Texas Parks and Wildlife Department)

Fig. 82. The Brazos River near Columbia, Texas. Photograph by Roland Harper, August 26, 1918. (William Stanley Hoole Special Collections Library, University of Alabama)

the statement that the River of Daycao lay at ten days' travel from Guasco— estimating that the Indians could average ten or so miles per day—the River of Daycao could possibly have been the Brazos. If we take literally the statement that the army marched for six days and halted, at about fifteen miles per day this would place their stopping point at the Navasota River. The party of horsemen sent forward could have again skirted Blackland Prairie (fig. 81) and easily have reached the Brazos River (fig. 82). It must be said that the

Brazos was a very long distance for the people of Guasco to travel to hunt deer. Perhaps, though, their bringing back deerskins—as well as perhaps dried venison—made hunting at such a distance cost-effective.

The hunters of Guasco could only have traveled such long distances through sparsely populated country. And herein is possibly a clue to the reason why people in the Caddo area built no fortifications around their towns for all the many centuries of their existence. With only sparse populations in the dry area to the west, in the coastal plain to the south, and in the Felsenthal region to the east, they simply had fewer enemies with which to contend than did peoples elsewhere in the Mississippian Southeast.

The party of horsemen captured several of these Indians from the River of Daycao and returned with them to where Moscoso and the others were staying.[58] When the Spaniards tried to question their captives about what they might find further west, they found that the people of Daycao spoke a language none of their interpreters could understand. The implication was as frightening as it was clear: if they continued traveling westward, they would not be able to find stores of corn, and even more important, they would not be able to gain any additional information about the lay of the land from Indian informants.[59]

Several of the place-names the Spaniards encountered on the western margin of their explorations are definitely Caddo words. This is most particularly the case with *Naguatex*, which in Caddo means "the place of salt." Naguatex was not at a place where salt naturally occurred (the salines are to the north and northeast), but for people who lived to the west and south of the Big Bend area, Naguatex middlemen were probably the source of the salt they received in trade. *Nondacao* has a secure Caddo etymology—"the place of the bumblebee"—and so does *Soacatino*—"red squirrel." Both *Naquiscoza* and *Nazacahoz* begin with the Caddo locative *na-*, and they are probably Caddo words. *Nisohone* may begin with the same locative, and may therefore be a Caddo word. *Hacanac* may be a Caddo adjective with an unknown meaning.

Lacane is problematic. The Caddo language does not contain the consonant *l*, though it would seem unusual for a non-Caddo-speaking group to be wedged between two societies of probable Caddo speakers—Nisohone and Nondacao. But it should be noted that the gentleman of Elvas renders this word as "la Came"; hence, the *l* may be from the Spanish definite article.

Other problematic words are *Guasco*, which could be Caddo on phonological grounds, but it has no known Caddo etymology.[60] And *Aays* (Háish) is a word that modern Caddo speakers use to designate a cultural group that has lived among them since the very early eighteenth century, though this word has no Caddo etymology and may not derive from a Caddo antecedent. The Háish may be a people of unknown linguistic affiliation who coalesced with Caddo-speakers in the late seventeenth century.

Return to the Mississippi River

Moscoso assembled his captains and royal officials to discuss what they should do next. They found themselves in the inhospitable country of east Texas with the prospect of even more inhospitable country to come. If they continued traveling westward, they would find nothing to eat and no one to talk to. The corn they had carried with them was giving out. It was already early October, and if they remained where they were much longer, they would find themselves marching through rain and snow.[61]

Most of them were of the opinion they should return to the "great river of Guachoya," the Mississippi, where they expected they would find plenty of corn at Anilco or in that neighborhood. During the winter they could build some boats, and the following summer they could sail down the river to the Gulf and in this way reach Mexico. They knew of the difficulties and hazards of this plan, but they could now see they had no other choice.

The land beyond the River of Daycao seemed to be the land about which Cabeza de Vaca had spoken when he returned to Spain. He said it was a land where the Indians wandered about "like Arabs," with no fixed dwelling places. They subsisted solely on the game they killed, on roots, and the fruit of prickly pears.[62] In such a place Moscoso and his men would not survive the winter.

According to the Gentleman of Elvas, Moscoso expressed a longing for a place where he could get a full night of sleep free from Indians yelling at them in the darkness. He was ready to quit this land of hardship and difficulty. Most of the others no doubt felt the same. The Spaniards decided they would immediately begin their long walk back to the Mississippi River.[63]

But when this decision was announced to the army, there was some dissension. Several of the men thought a journey by sea would be difficult and dangerous because they lacked the necessary equipment. And because of something Cabeza de Vaca had told Charles V, some of them still expected that if they traveled to Mexico by land they might yet discover a rich society before reaching Mexico. Cabeza de Vaca had said that where he had first seen cotton cloth, he had next seen gold, silver, and precious gems. Their course had been inland, and because they were under the impression that Cabeza de Vaca's course had been along the coast, they believed they had not yet traversed the country where he had gone. Already at Guasco they had seen cotton shawls and turquoises that the natives had said came from the west. Cabeza de Vaca had said that from the coast he had traveled northward, to the interior. Hence, if they continued in a westerly direction, they should eventually come to the land that Cabeza de Vaca had traversed.[64] These men were bitterly disappointed that they had not discovered riches, and they would have preferred to continue on, risking death rather than depart from La Florida empty-handed.

The decision, however, had already been made by Moscoso and his principal men, and the dissidents could do nothing to reverse the decision. But there were hard feelings. One of the malcontents said he would be willing to put out one of his own eyes if he could have the privilege of putting out one of Moscoso's.[65]

They returned on the same general trail by which they had come.[66] On the first part of their return journey (perhaps as far as Naguatex), they suffered from the same kind of small alarms and attacks and resistance they had met on their entry.[67] The Indians would lie on the ground near the trail and cover themselves with grass. As the Spaniards passed near, they would then rise up suddenly, fire their arrows, and take to their heels. Often small parties of Indians would attack from two, three, or even four places simultaneously, and in so doing they killed and injured several soldiers, Indian slaves, and horses.

The story of one of these attacks is told by Garcilaso. Alvaro de San Jorge was riding his horse across a stream when an Indian who was concealed in some bushes rose up and fired an arrow at him. The arrow penetrated his mail breeches, passed through his right thigh, and continued on through his saddletree and saddle blanket and sank into his horse, nailing his leg to the horse. The startled and wounded horse ran bucking and jumping out of the stream, trying to dislodge both San Jorge and the arrow in his side. Men who were nearby rushed to give assistance, and seeing San Jorge's predicament, they steadied his horse and led it to the camp, which was nearby. There they cut the arrow in two between his thigh and the horse's saddle. The horse's wound was superficial, but they were amazed that a cane arrow could have done so much damage.[68]

But the story does not stop there. According to Garcilaso, San Jorge had the reputation of being an effective medic. He was reputed to possess a God-given ability to heal wounds by using oil (probably olive oil), wool, and incantations. But all of his oil and wool had burned up during the battle at Mabila, and because of this he had quit offering his services. He himself had been wounded two other times in the course of the expedition. One arrow had struck him in the instep of his foot and had come out at the heel. He had been four months in recovering from this wound. On another occasion he had been struck in the knee by an arrow, the point of which had been made from deer antler. The point had broken off in his knee and had to be extracted. When the surgeon performed this operation, it caused San Jorge so much pain that he flew into a rage, swearing to the surgeon that even if he were dying, he would never call on him again. The surgeon replied that, well enough, if San Jorge were dying it would do no good to call on him because he would not come. True to his word, San Jorge would not call on the surgeon for help with the wound in his thigh, and the surgeon would not go to help him.

So now if San Jorge was to be healed, he would have to heal himself. Instead of oil he used pork lard, and in place of wool, he used the ravelings of old Indian shawls. Treating his wound in this way, he recovered in a very few days. The army had paused for the wounded and exhausted men to recover. And when they started moving again, San Jorge mounted his horse and rode from one part of the army to another shouting: "Give me death, Christians, because I have been a traitor and an evil companion, for believing that the strength of my cures lay in oil and wool, I have made no attempt to heal you and in consequence have permitted more than a hundred and fifty of you to perish." [69] He presumably resumed his role as healer for the rest of the expedition.

On the return journey the army had difficulty finding enough corn to eat. They had devastated the food stores of the land they had passed through, and the Indians had attempted to hide any corn that remained. They regretted having torched the towns of Naguatex, but when they returned there they were surprised to find that the Indians had rebuilt their houses and had a good supply of corn.

On the return journey the Gentleman of Elvas took particular notice of the pottery of Naguatex. He commented that it was made of a fine clay (*barro coado*) and was very similar to that which was made in the towns of Estremoz and Montemor in eastern Portugal.[70] The vessels in question may have been double-shouldered, Belcher engraved bowls (fig. 83), which resemble the Iberian *cazuela*, or else the Belcher ridged cooking or storage jar. Neither of these vessel types was manufactured outside the Great Bend area of the Red River.[71]

As their long trek back to the Mississippi River proceeded, the weather worsened. It grew cold, and it rained and snowed, making the creek and river crossings more difficult. The Spaniards kept up as strenuous a pace as they could, but crossing even small streams was difficult, so that they were often

Fig. 83. A Belcher engraved *cazuela*. (Arkansas Archaeological Survey)

delayed. They were by now almost altogether dressed in deerskin and fur garments, which were slow to dry out when they became wet. They had made these skins into short jackets, which served as shirt, doublet, and cloak, and they went bare-legged, with no stockings, shoes, or sandals.[72]

The Indians continued their small ambushes and attacks both day and night. If any Spaniards strayed from the army, the Indians would attack them from ambush. They would creep into camp at night—crawling along the ground like snakes, as the Spaniards said—to suddenly attack both men and horses. On one night they killed two sentinels in this way.[73]

The Indians continued to impress the Spaniards with their valor. According to another of Garcilaso's stories, some of Moscoso's men got his permission to capture some Indian slaves. When the army broke camp and moved out, a number of horsemen and infantry remained behind in concealment to ambush and seize some of the Indians who would come to scavenge. In this way they easily captured fourteen Indians, who did not resist. But when they divided their catch among themselves, Maestro Francisco, who was their Genoese shipwright, was not content with the two slaves who were given to him. He wanted a third one. The others tried to persuade him to be satisfied with two, but he would not yield. Finally the others gave in, partly because Francisco was the only one among them who was capable of supervising the building of the boats that could carry them to Mexico. Francisco may have justified his selfishness on the grounds that he was an unwilling participant in the expedition. De Soto, with considerable foresight, had forced him to come along.

Soon afterward, on their way to catch up with the army, they spotted a single Indian approaching. Juan Páez impetuously galloped toward him, and the Indian, in order to escape being trampled, ran beneath the shelter of a tree. As Páez rode his horse by the tree, he thrust his lance at the Indian with no effect. But the Indian fired an arrow that struck his horse near the left stirrup. The horse stumbled for about twenty feet and fell dead. Then Francisco de Bolaños made a pass at the Indian, and again his lance thrust was ineffective. The Indian shot Bolaños's horse in the same way he had that of Páez, and this horse likewise stumbled along for some way and fell dead.

With this, a third Spaniard, Juan de Vega (a native of Badajoz) galloped forward. Both Juan Páez and Francisco Bolaños rushed at the Indian on foot, but the man realized the charging horseman was the most serious threat, and if he could kill or disable the horse, he would be able to flee on foot. Even though the two men were running at him, he ran from the tree to attack Vega. He fired an arrow at the horse, but Vega had equipped his horse with a breastplate of three thicknesses of hide (probably buffalo). The arrow penetrated this breastplate, wounding the horse, but not so much that the horse was disabled. Thus Vega was able to lance the man and kill him. They expected the Indian to be a big strong warrior, but he was small, thin, and wizened.[74]

When the army reached Chaguate, Moscoso attempted to persuade Francisco de Guzmán, who had remained there with his Indian concubine, to return to the expedition. He attempted this through the chief of Chaguate, but the chief said Guzmán wished to remain in Chaguate. Moscoso wrote Guzmán a letter and sent it to him with paper and some ink so that he could reply. In the letter Moscoso told Guzmán that he and the others were going to depart from La Florida, and that he, Guzmán, was a Christian, who should not remain among infidels. If he returned to the expedition he would be forgiven, and if the Indians were forcing him to remain there he should indicate this in writing. But the Indian who took the letter to Guzmán returned with the same letter, and on its back, chillingly mute, the paper bore only Guzmán's signature as proof that he was still alive.[75] Moscoso sent out twelve horsemen to look for him, but Guzmán had spies who warned him, and they were not able to find him. Because the Spaniards were short of corn, they had no time to look for him any more, and they continued their march.[76]

When they reached the Arkansas River they crossed to the northern side at Ayays, as they had before when they traveled from Utiangüe to Anilco. Proceeding down the river, they came to the town of Chilano, which they had missed on their previous journey.[77]

The return journey was hard on the Spaniards. They suffered from exhaustion, lack of sleep, and exposure. Many of them succumbed to an unidentified illness and died. Some of the horses also sickened and died. The unfortunate Indian slaves got the worst of the starvation and exposure, and many of them died. Most were left along the way unburied, or only half buried.

Only the pigs did well. In fact, Garcilaso relates that on this return journey the Spaniards came across a sow that had been left behind. She had given birth to thirteen piglets, which had now grown large. The Indians had supposedly nocked their ears. Each nock was different, and the Spaniards concluded that the Indians had divided them among themselves.[78]

They were now approaching the Mississippi River, which they had been so anxious to leave behind them a few months earlier. But on their return the river seemed like a haven.[79] When they reached Anilco, they were surprised and disappointed to find that the supply of corn was very scant. They learned that while they had been at Guachoya earlier, it was at planting time, and after the massacre ordered by De Soto, the people of Anilco had been afraid to go out and plant their fields.[80] When the Spaniards searched the settlements surrounding the principal settlement, they found them to be empty of corn.[81]

Aminoya

The lack of corn was a serious blow to the Spaniards. Anilco had been the most abundant province they had encountered on the lower Arkansas River, and they had expected to find plenty of food there. Some of them said that just as they had feared, it was a bad idea to have returned from the River of Daycao. They should have continued westward by land. It seemed that only a miracle could deliver them by sea. They had neither a pilot nor a map. They did not know where the Mississippi River entered the Gulf, and they knew very little about the Gulf itself. They had no cloth for sails, and they did not have the proper materials for building boats that could withstand the rigors of the journey they faced. Moreover, they did not have enough corn to support them while they built their boats. Some of them feared they would experience the same fate as Narváez's men: starvation, cannibalism, torture by the Indians, and drowning. Some of them commended themselves to God and prayed for deliverance.[82]

They felt that such deliverance had come when some Indians of Anilco arrived and told them about a chiefdom that was new to them. This was Aminoya, which was two days' journey away. It was a fertile province, but the people of Anilco, being at war with Aminoya, did not know whether any stores of corn could be found there. They said, however, the warriors of Anilco would be only too glad to go along and assault Aminoya.

To investigate, Moscoso sent out a captain with a detachment of horsemen and footmen, along with some warriors of Anilco. When they reached Aminoya, they found that its principal settlements were two large towns standing near the Mississippi River, both well supplied with corn. They also managed to capture a large number of Indians. The Spaniards took up residence in one of the towns of Aminoya and immediately sent word back for Moscoso and the others to come forward.

16

Winter, 1542–1543

Early in December 1542 Moscoso and his men departed from Anilco and set out for Aminoya. It was a difficult journey because it was so cold and wet. Trudging through a relentless rain, they had to cross many expanses of water, often wading through standing water. They gave thanks to God whenever they were lucky enough to find some high land on which to spend the night.[1]

A wind from the north blew down upon them, and it grew very cold. Their suffering was greater because they were so poorly clothed. They were wearing deerskin shoes—probably moccasins made for them by Indian women—which as soon as they became wet were waterlogged. So, too, did their long deerskin shirts—their only garments—become waterlogged when wet, giving them no insulation against the cold.[2]

Many in the army fell ill, and a great number of the Indian slaves died. Many of the Spaniards were ill with a disease that made them notably lethargic. The Portuguese André de Vasconcelos da Silva died. So did two brothers—nicknamed "the Sotis"—who were his kinsmen.[3] Nuño de Tovar, who had gotten on De Soto's bad side through his affair with Leonor de Bobadilla on the voyage from Spain to Cuba, also died.

380

Arriving at Aminoya, they found it to be composed of two towns, a half a league apart, situated a quarter of a league from the Mississippi River. Both towns were fortified with palisades.[4] The Spaniards picked the best of the two towns and occupied it. They tore down the second town, salvaging building materials to build additional shelters in the first.[5] They plundered all of the corn in the second town and carried it to the first—a total estimated at six thousand fanegas—nine thousand bushels—and they also found stores of nuts and dried fruits.[6]

Archaeologists have not yet located the site of Aminoya. It would seem to have been located somewhere between about the present-day Desha-Phillips county line and present-day Old Town. From some of the events that occurred during the winter of 1542–43, as well as during the later passage down the river, the southern part of this area would seem to be the more likely location of the two towns of Aminoya.[7]

The Spaniards found excellent wood for shipbuilding at Aminoya. A Portuguese from Ceuta, who had learned to saw lumber while he had been a prisoner at Fez, taught his skills to others. Maestro Francisco supervised construction of seven bergantines, which he calculated would be sufficient to satisfy their purpose. He was assisted by several Basque carpenters who hewed planks and knees for the ship. According to Garcilaso, they built four large sheds to serve as a boatyard so the weather would not hinder construction. In an all-out effort, all of the Spaniards, both of high and low degree, worked on the boats.[8]

They collected together every scrap of expendable iron, including all the iron chains used on their Indian slaves and all the steel shot. They set up a forge and converted all of this iron into nails. The two caulkers (one Genoese, the other Sardinian) were able to partially caulk the boats with fiber from a local plant whose growing habit reminded them of daffodils. They called it *henequén* (i.e., the yellowish fiber extracted from the yucca or agave plant). But in fact the plant was probably button snake-root—*Eryngium yuccifolium* or *E. aquaticum*—from whose leaves the Southeastern Indians extracted a *henequén*-like fiber. The problem was that this fiber could also be used to make serviceable rope, and there was not enough of this *henequén* available for both uses. As a result, they had to partly caulk the edge-joined planking of the boats with the ravelings of old and worn Indian shawls. Because of the location in which they built the boats, they were unable to obtain an essential boat-building material—pitch, the sap of pine trees, used for waterproofing.

Then as now, huge pine forests blanketed parts of the Southeast, but pine trees do not grow in the moist soils of the southern floodplain forest, where Aminoya was located.[9]

One of their number was a cooper, but he fell ill and almost died, which greatly worried them, because without him they would not have been able to construct the casks in which to keep a supply of fresh water on their boats. Fortunately, his health improved, and although he was sick for a long while, he recovered in time to make for each bergantín two quarter casks (*piparote*), so called because the volume of four of them equaled that of a regular water cask (*pipa*).[10]

Moscoso ordered the Indians in the vicinity to bring a supply of fiber shawls to be sewn together to make sails. Fortunately, the people of Guachoya, Anilco, and Taguanate (located at two days' travel upriver and presumably on the western side of the river) came often, bringing shawls, cordage, and a great quantity of fish.

The cooperation of the Indians was fortunate, saving the Spaniards from having to go to their towns and take the supplies by force. This would have been almost impossible for them to do because of the high water caused by the excessive rain of that winter. When the water was high, Aminoya became isolated on an island—no doubt a levee ridge—not more than about two or three leagues in diameter. Under such conditions, they could not have used their horses to assault the Indians, and without horses they would not have had enough military advantage to be effective.

The Spaniards had to use their utmost ingenuity to complete the building of the boats. They made hawsers out of mulberry bark. After using their iron stirrups to fashion anchors for the boats, they equipped their saddles with makeshift stirrups made of wood.[11]

The sixteenth-century bergantín is not to be confused with the brigantine, a later vessel that was a medium-size, two-masted vessel with square sails on its foremast. The sixteenth-century bergantín was a large service boat normally towed behind a mother ship and used for coastal and riverine reconnaissance, and for loading and unloading people and freight. They were open, flat-bottomed boats that were powered both by oars and by sail carried on one or two masts. Garcilaso says that the boats the Spaniards built were not truly bergantines, but only large boats (*unas grandes barcas*), which had portions of their prows and poops decked over for ships' stores. The flooring in the center of the boats was left loose so it could be removed to bail out the water that seeped in. They had axial stern rudders and probably had single masts that were lateen-rigged.

The dimensions of the boats Moscoso's men built are unknown. They were powered by seven benches of oarsmen, and they carried about fifty passengers each. Perhaps a length of thirty feet or so would not be far amiss. They probably drew about three feet of water.[12]

According to a story by Garcilaso, when they had first entered the town of Aminoya, Captain Espindola and Alonso de Carmona came upon an old woman who had been unable to flee. She asked where they planned to stay when the Great River overflowed its banks, as it did every fourteen years, flooding everything. This was the fourteenth year since the last flood. She told them that when the river flooded, the Indians would take refuge in the upper parts of their houses. But Espindola and Carmona dismissed this as nonsense.[13]

But time would prove the old woman right. The heavy rains of early winter had ceased, and by March it had not rained significantly in Aminoya for a month. And yet even so, the waters of the Mississippi began to rise as snow melted in the north.[14] On Palm Sunday, March 18, floodwater entered the town of Aminoya.[15] It rose until the entire distance between Aminoya and Anilco was covered with water.[16] The Indians told the Spaniards that the water extended for another nine leagues on the other side of Anilco. Aminoya was higher than surrounding land, but still the water in places rose to the stirrups of the Spaniards' horses. They piled up wood in great heaps and coaxed their horses onto them, giving them some refuge from the high water. They also piled up wood inside the houses to give themselves a place to stand above the water level, and eventually they had to climb up in the upper parts of the houses, just as the old woman had reportedly said they would have to do. The houses at Aminoya may have had upper rooms that were used for storage as well as for refuge in high water.[17] When the Spaniards left their houses, they could travel on horseback where the land was higher, but elsewhere they had to go in dugout canoes. The river remained out of its banks for about two months, and they were unable to do any work on the bergantines during this period.[18]

Garcilaso has a story concerning the high water that, if true, gives us a glimpse of the aftermath of the massacre at Anilco. According to the story, Moscoso ordered a squad of twenty men under the command of Gonzalo Silvestre to go to Anilco in canoes to procure cordage and caulking material for the boats. They went there in four dugout canoes, tied together in pairs to prevent them from capsizing.[19] Anilco itself was on a large island of high ground—a geological formation known as the Grand Prairie—surrounded by miles of water on all sides. Silvestre claimed that the reason he was picked for this assignment was that he had held a son of the chief of Anilco captive when they had journeyed to the River of Daycao but had delivered him back to the chief upon their return, and the chief was grateful to him for this. While they were at Anilco, according to Silvestre, the boy served as interpreter. One of the matters they discussed was the massacre the Spaniards had perpetrated against Anilco, in which the warriors of Guachoya had removed the remains of the chief's ancestors from the temple, dumped them on the ground, desecrated them, and then set fire to Anilco. The chief was vehement with rage as he spoke of the revenge he would take against Guachoya once the Spaniards had left the country.[20]

Throughout the winter the Indians kept coming to where the Spaniards were at work on the bergantines. The Spaniards were suspicious of their motives. They thought that because some of the Indians' fields were near the river, they may have suspected that the Spaniards were going to use these boats to search out their fields and seize their food.[21] Moscoso began to fear that the Indians were planning an attack, perhaps intending to take advantage of the flood. He ordered his men to capture one of the Indians who had come to visit and to hold him secretly until the others had departed. This they did, and they later tortured the captive, questioning him about any attack the Indians might be planning. The tortured man said that the chiefs of Guachoya, Anilco, Taguanate, and others—about twenty chiefs in all—were in fact planning to attack the Spaniards with a great number of warriors.[22] Three days before the attack they planned to deliver a great quantity of fish, a gesture designed to put the Spaniards off their guard. On the day of the attack they would send some men with similar gifts. But these bearers of gifts, and others, were to set the houses on fire, having first seized the Spaniards' lances, which they kept propped against the doors of their houses. At the same time, the chiefs and their warriors would be waiting in hiding nearby and would launch a sudden attack when they could see that the town was on fire. They were the ones who would take care of the horsemen. Moscoso ordered that their prisoner be put under close guard.

On the day specified by the Indian whom they had tortured, thirty men came from Guachoya with gifts of fish. Moscoso had them seized, and then he ordered his men to cut off their right hands and their noses (see fig. 20). The Guachoya men submitted with stolid courage to this maiming. They walked up to the chopping block one after another, and scarcely had one hand been chopped off than another was laid on the chopping block.[23] Moscoso sent them home with instructions to tell the chief of Guachoya that he should come and attack any time he wished, and he should bring all his allies. Moscoso's strategy, just as De Soto's had been, was to bluff Guachoya with the threat that he would not be able to devise any surprise that Moscoso could not anticipate.[24]

Moscoso's brutal action had the effect he desired. The intimidated chiefs of Anilco and Taguanate came to him and tried to excuse themselves. The conspiracy fell apart. A few days later the chief of Guachoya came, accompanied by one of his principal men and some of his subjects. It appears that he had not been party to the conspiracy.[25] He told Moscoso he had reliable information that Anilco and Taguanate had plotted to make war on the Spaniards. As soon as some Indians came from Anilco to visit, Moscoso asked them whether this was true. When they admitted that it was true, he handed them over to the principal men of Guachoya, who led them outside the town and executed them. Soon afterward, some Indians came from Taguanate and they too confessed to being party to the plot. Moscoso ordered that their right hands and noses be cut off, and he sent them back to their chief.[26]

Garcilaso says that the chief of Quigualtam (or Quigualtanqui) played a role in this conspiracy. He is thought to have been a young and aggressive chief, and it is clear that he was much feared in the Mississippi Valley. He may have urged his former enemies to lay aside their old animosities to form an alliance to expel or kill the Spaniards.[27]

The actions of the Spaniards against Anilco and Taguanate pleased the people of Guachoya very much, and they began to come to the Spaniards frequently with gifts of shawls, fish, and even some hogs bred from several sows that had gotten loose when the Spaniards had been at Guachoya. The chief of Guachoya struck a deal with the Spaniards that as soon as the floodwater went down they would launch a great attack against Taguanate. At the appointed time the Guachoyas came in canoes. A party of Spanish cavalry and infantry went with the Guachoyas, who guided them to Taguanate. They attacked the town, capturing men, women, and a quantity of shawls.[28]

The water of the river began to fall in late April, but only very slowly. Even as late as May 20, after the water had receded from the town, the land was so muddy the Spaniards could not get around except by going barefoot and bare legged.[29]

Construction of the bergantines was completed in June, about six months after it began.[30] But the men were anxious about how they would get the boats down to the water. For lack of iron, it had been necessary to make their nails very short, which meant the planks had to be sawed thin. Now they were afraid that overland transport would break in the bottoms and open up the ships. But there seemed to be no other choice but to try to do it this way, since, according to the Indians, there would not be any more high water until the next winter, when the northern snows melted again. Fortunately, however, the water did rise for a second time, high enough to reach the bergantines, so they could be floated to the river from the places where they had been built.[31]

In the course of the winter the Spaniards had seized all the corn from the Indians of Aminoya and had thereby reduced them to starvation. Pressed by hunger, they began coming to where the Spaniards were to beg for a little corn. Many of them were extremely emaciated, and a number of them died of starvation. But Moscoso, fearing that the Spaniards' own supplies would not last, imposed very severe penalties on anyone who gave food to the Aminoyas. In the end, however, seeing that there were plenty of hogs remaining and that the Aminoyas were in such wretched condition and were humbling themselves to the Spaniards, Moscoso relented and allowed his men to give them some corn out of pity. But this the Spaniards later regretted, because when they loaded up their boats they had rather less corn than they would have liked.[32]

17

Flight down the Mississippi River

With the seven boats moored in the river, the Span-
iards began making final preparations to depart. They killed all their hogs,
butchered them, and salted the meat.[1] With about fifty horses remaining, they
culled out the worst of them, tied them to stakes, and opened their veins. This
saddened the men because the horses had served them so well on the expedition. But sentiment could not stand in the way of survival: their supply of salt
pork and corn for the voyage was insufficient.[2] Therefore, they butchered the
horses they had killed, boiled the meat, and dried it in the sun.[3] They retained
twenty-two of the best horses to take with them down the river in case a situation might arise in which they would be needed.

The day before they departed from Aminoya they had to decide what to do
with over five hundred Indian slaves who remained alive. They could not
take all of them in the boats. Moscoso told his men they could choose to load
the slaves in the boats and start out with them, but because of the limited
amount of water they could carry, they would have to maroon them once they
reached saltwater. Many of the Spaniards felt it would be cruel to use their
slaves in this way, to abandon them in a land stranger and more hostile than
the one they were already in.[4]

But Moscoso privately told some of the Spaniards who were in his good favor (a minority, according to the Gentleman of Elvas) to load their personal slaves into the boats and they would take them to Mexico. The rest of the Spaniards were not told this, but they later discovered Moscoso's duplicity.

Moscoso, as governor and commander in chief, commanded the lead boat, and his two brothers, Juan de Alvarado and Cristóbal Mosquera, commanded the next ranked boat. The comptroller, Juan de Añasco, and the factor, Luís Hernandez de Biedma, commanded the third boat. Captain Juan de Guzmán and the treasurer commanded the fourth, while Captains Arias Tinoco and Alonso Romo de Cardeñosa took the fifth. Pedro Calderón and Francisco Osorio were in command of the sixth. And Juan de Vega of Badajoz and presumably an unnamed person commanded the seventh. Each boat had two captains, so that if one were incapacitated, the other could be in charge.[5]

On the morning of July 2, 1543, they rowed their boats out into the channel of the Mississippi River (see map 8).[6] On board the ships were 322 Spaniards.[7] Behind each boat was towed a small dugout canoe that they used for various purposes. Several of the large canoes were tied together in pairs, into which the twenty-two horses were loaded with their front feet in one canoe and their hind feet in the other.[8]

Left standing on the bank, abandoned to the mercy of the local Indians, were several hundred male and female Indian slaves, most of them weeping because they feared imminent death and possible torture at the hands of the local Indians. Many of the younger ones among them spoke Spanish, and some of them were nominal Christians.[9]

The boats were well built, but the Spaniards worried about the thin planks and the short nails, and they worried because they had had no pitch with which to treat the planks. Moreover, they had no decks with which to keep out water from high seas. They only had planks athwart the boats on which the sailors could stand and manipulate the sails, and these planks gave some protection to those below. Each boat was equipped with seven pairs of oars, and except for the commanders, all persons took their turn on the oars. In addition to the oarsmen, they proceeded down the river under sail, which they occasionally had to unfurl when they wanted to slow down.[10]

Unlike the Mississippi River of today, the stream the little fleet of boats entered was still a wild river. On the insides of the Mississippi's great looping bends, the foliage was mostly willow trees and, in swampy areas, cypress trees. On the outsides of the bends, mature forest stood like a sheer wall. This included stands of cane as much as thirty feet high. The extreme activity of the meandering river shortened the lives of the trees that lay in its vast meander zone, so that many of the trees were only moderately tall. The higher ground was covered with black ash, elm, hickory, walnut, maple, and honey locust. Closer to the river there were cottonwood trees trailing vast skeins of vines, and white-limbed sycamore trees, visited by raucous flocks of green-and-yellow Carolina parakeets foraging for seeds. Nearly all of the smooth-bark trees were loaded with mistletoe.

As the current bore them down the river, the press of necessity forced decision after decision upon them, and any bad choice could have meant death. The water ran swiftest—as much as five miles per hour—on the outside of the bends in the river. In their haste to get down river, they must have been tempted to steer their boats through this swift current. But these were also the places where the river cut constantly into the banks, creating vast overhanging ledges of earth supporting large trees (see fig. 57). Inevitably, as time went on, these massive ledges slumped into the river, casting trees and soil hissing into the river. As the soil was dissolved by the current, the trees went floating down the river, and because the wood was green, they were often submerged. When their limbs and roots were just below the surface of the water, they could rip the bottom out of a boat in the wink of an eye.

Each time the little fleet bore down upon an island in the river, the Spaniards had to turn to the more navigable side of the island. If they picked the wrong side, their boats could have run aground on sandbars or tangles of driftwood. The dense fogs that sometimes form on the Mississippi could have compounded all of these hazards.[11]

On the first day of their journey they passed by Guachoya, whose people had built a large arbor near the bank of the river, where the Spaniards might come ashore. Many of the Guachoyas were in canoes along the river bank. But Moscoso declined to go ashore, and they continued on well out in the channel of the river. For a time, the Guachoyas paddled their canoes along with the fleet until they came to an arm of the river that branched off to the right (i.e., to the west), and here the people of Guachoya said that the province of Quigualtam lay nearby, on the eastern side of the river.

This seems to be a reference to a lateral channel of the Mississippi River, probably Bayou Macon, which was an important lateral channel of the river until the building of the levees.[12] This lateral channel hived off from the Mississippi River somewhere in the vicinity of present-day Arkansas City. And it should be noted that a similar channel to the left—that is, to the east—was Deer Creek, with an entrance in this same general vicinity. It led to the Yazoo River and the territory of Quigualtam. The people of Guachoya begged

Moscoso to go with them to attack Quigualtam. But Moscoso was suspicious. Earlier the Guachoyas had told the Spaniards that Quigualtam lay three days away, while now they were saying that the territory was nearby, and because of this discrepancy Moscoso smelled a trap.

But it seems unlikely that the people of Guachoya were party to a conspiracy. Rather, it seems to have been a question of what they had originally meant by saying it took three days to reach Quigualtam. It is possible they meant that it would take three days to travel to Quigualtam's central town. Whether these were three days by river, or by travel overland, or by a combination of both is not known. But from events that had transpired, it is evident that the northern extent of Quigualtam's power came quite close to the territory of Guachoya, and perhaps that is what they now meant when they said that Quigualtam was nearby.

The Spaniards kept their boats out in the swifter part of the current, which was very powerful, and assisted by their oars and sails, they made very good speed. At the end of this first day they came to shore on the western side of the river, pulling up next to a woods. They were at this time somewhere northwest of present-day Winterville, Mississippi. They spent the night in the boats.[13]

The Canoes of Quigualtam

The next day, July 3, they traveled for an unknown distance down the river and spotted a town. The people of the town fled at their approach, but they managed to capture an old woman. She told them that the town belonged to a chief named Huhasene, who was subject to Quigualtam. She also told them that Quigualtam was waiting for them with many warriors.

The horsemen were put ashore, and they rode down along the river and found some houses with a good supply of corn, dried fruit, dressed deer skins (some painted with colors), and animal skins. All of the Spaniards went to this place, and they spent the rest of the day there gathering and processing the corn they needed.[14] It is impossible to be sure where they were at this time, but a location in present-day northern Washington County, Mississippi, is a good possibility.

While they were there, a large number of Indians came upriver in canoes. They drew near to each other on the opposite side of the river in a rather careless battle formation. Under orders from Moscoso, crossbowmen manned two canoes and paddled over to attack them. The Indians in the canoes fled, but when they saw that the Spaniards could not catch up with them they became bolder. As soon as the Spaniards in the canoes turned around and began to return to their comrades, the Indians in the canoes pursued them. A second group of Indians ran along the river bank, and when they reached a second town near a bluff of the river, the Indians on foot and the ones in the canoes united and made as if they would take a stand there. But when Moscoso ordered the men to go in the dugout canoes and attack this second town, the Indians all fled. Moscoso ordered them to burn the town. The Spaniards then cast off and guided their boats downstream to a place in the river flanked by a large open field, probably a cornfield. They put ashore, and the Indians did not dare attack them.[15] Here they spent the night.

The next morning, July 4, as they were getting under way, a great number of Indians appeared on the river in a fleet of as many as a hundred canoes, some of which were very large, holding sixty or seventy men.[16] The larger canoes had twenty-five to thirty paddlers on each side, as well as twenty-five to thirty warriors positioned between them in a line from poop to prow.[17] In addition, the paddlers had their own bows and arrows, which they could take up and shoot when they were not paddling. The crews on the canoes sang songs regaling their exploits in battle, and the tempo of their songs set the pace of their paddle strokes. At the fastest tempo, they could move through the water very rapidly.[18] The canoes carrying the commanders of the fleet had awnings like the Spaniards had seen before to shade them from the sun and rain. Some of the larger vessels were decked out in colors, so that the canoe itself, the paddles, the bows and arrows, and the clothing worn by the warriors and the crew were all of a single color. Many of the canoes were smaller, perhaps with less impressive crews, but all the canoes moved in disciplined ranks. It was a magnificent, if terrifying, spectacle.[19]

The fleet of canoes came to within two crossbow shots of the Spanish boats. They sent a small canoe with three men in it to approach the Spanish fleet. These were spies whose intent was to observe the nature of the boats and how the Spaniards were armed. One of them told Moscoso that his chief, Quigualtam, had sent him to inform Moscoso that whatever the people of Guachoya had told him about Quigualtam was false. The Guachoyas had revolted, and they were enemies of Quigualtam.[20] As for their part, Quigualtam wished to serve the Spaniards. Moscoso indicated to the man that he believed what he said and that he appreciated the friendship of Quigualtam.

The three men then paddled their canoes back to the fleet. When they reached the others, the entire fleet of Indians closed in on the Spaniards, yelling and threatening them. Moscoso ordered Juan de Guzmán, who had been captain of the footmen, to take some men in the small canoes to disperse the fleet of Indians. Guzmán took twenty-five men in four or five of the small canoes.[21] As soon as the Indians saw these canoes approaching, they divided their fleet into two parts and waited silently. When the Spaniards approached, the two groups of canoes suddenly closed in on Guzmán and the lead canoes. Attacking furiously, many of the Indians dove into the water and reached up to hold the gunwales of their own large canoes to make them more stable. Others swam underwater and seized the gunwales of the Spanish canoes and overturned them. When they fell into the water, the Spaniards who wore the heaviest armor sank immediately to the bottom. Those who grabbed hold of a canoe to stay afloat were attacked by the Indians, swinging their paddles and war clubs.[22]

When the men in the bergantines saw this attack, they lowered their sails and attempted to go and render aid, but the current of the river was so strong they could not turn back. Of the men who went with Guzmán, only four Spaniards in the canoe that was nearest the boats managed to swim back to them. They were Pedro Morón, Alvaro Nieto, Juan Coles, and Hernán Suárez de Mazuelas. Eleven men were killed, and the rest were not accounted for.[23] Those who survived said they saw Indians pull Juan de Guzmán aboard the stern of one of their canoes, but they could not tell whether he was alive or dead. Also among the dead was Juan de Vargas, a son of Don Carlos Enríquez, as well as several other important men.[24] Juan Terrón, notorious for having thrown his pearls away in a fit of exasperation while crossing the Blue Ridge Mountains, reached one of the bergantines, but before he could be pulled aboard, he died from multiple arrow wounds.[25]

Encouraged by their victory over Guzmán and his comrades in the canoes, the warriors of Quigualtam began to close in on the boats and attack them.[26] They came first to the boat commanded by Calderón, the rear guard. Loosing a cloud of arrows at Calderón's boat, they wounded twenty-five people almost instantaneously. The four men in Calderón's boat who wore armor were now stationed at the sides of the boat. All the others, including those manning the oars, took refuge in the bottom of the boat. With this, the boat began to turn crosswise against the current and to drift about. One of the men in armor ran back to the tiller, and he forced another to take it and steer while he protected him from arrows with his shield.[27]

As the Indians pursued them, they continued singing their war songs. According to the Indian slaves in the boats, the songs praised the courage of the Indians and cast vituperation on the cowardice of the Spaniards. They frequently mentioned the name of chief Quigualtam, but no one knew whether he was present in one of the canoes.[28] In the songs, the Spaniards were cowards and thieves who were now fleeing, but all of them were doomed. In one of their songs they said that while the Spaniards traveled on land their dead bodies had provided food for dogs and birds, and now that they were in the water they would be food for the fishes. At the end of each song they would send up a tremendous shout.[29]

Had they been more aggressive, the warriors of Quigualtam could have prevailed over the Spaniards. But they would approach no closer than an arrow flight to the bergantines, where they could hit the boats with their arrows while minimizing injury to themselves. The Spaniards themselves had very few offensive weapons. Their arquebuses had not been effective, but even if they had been, all of their powder was expended, and they had made them into nails.[30] There was not more than one working crossbow per boat, and these were in poor condition. All they had were swords, knives, and shields. All the armored men could do was to stand as targets for the Indians' arrows. Thus, the Indians could—if only they would—draw very near to the bergantines to shoot their arrows.

After Quigualtam's canoes attacked Calderón's boat, they proceeded on to the next one and assaulted it for a half an hour. The Spaniards, seeing what was about to happen, draped their sleeping mats along the sides of their boats. These fiber mats were double woven, with a weave so tight that arrows could not penetrate them. The Indians proceeded from one boat to another, attacking each in order, perhaps trying to find one that was more vulnerable than the others. When the Indians saw that their arrows would not penetrate the sleeping mats, they began to shoot up into the air, so their arrows would arc down into the Spanish boats from above. In this way they succeeded in wounding some of the Spaniards.[31] For the remainder of the day, the swift fleet of canoes kept circling the Spanish boats in a clockwise direction.[32]

The Indians then made a move to attack the more defenseless men who were in the paired canoes carrying the horses. The horses had some protection from the shields and animal skins that were tied around them.[33] When the men in the bergantines saw what the Indians were up to, they converged their boats and surrounded the horse-laden canoes, giving them some protection.

The pursuit by the canoes of Quigualtam pressed so hard upon the Spaniards that they were nearing complete exhaustion. Nonetheless, they decided not to pull ashore for the night but to continue on down the channel of the river to see if they could get beyond the domain of Quigualtam. Darkness fell, and as they drifted down the river, they began to think that they had left Quigualtam behind. But then, very close by in the darkness, a terrifyingly loud shout went up—the fleet of Indians was still in pursuit. This situation continued all through the night and until noon the next day—July 5—when the canoes at last ceased their pursuit. The Indians of Quigualtam had presumably reached the southern limit of their territory. The fleet turned around and began paddling upriver, shouting the name of Quigualtam.[34] When Don Antonio de Mendoza, viceroy of New Spain, was later told of this incident, he is reported to have said: "Truly, my lords, Quigualtanqui must have been a real man."[35]

The Mouth of the Mississippi River

The Spaniards enjoyed a short rest, but then they entered the territory of another polity, whose name they never learned. Here they were attacked by a fleet of fifty canoes, who were no less aggressive than those of Quigualtam. The Indians in this attack managed to board one of the rear-guard boats that lagged behind the others. They managed this by first climbing into the small canoe the boat was towing. The Spaniards fought these Indians off with their swords and knives, but they could not prevent them from taking away an Indian woman (whether they captured or rescued her is unknown), and they wounded several Spaniards.[36] These Indians ceased their attack and retreated when the other boats began approaching.

The men in the tandem canoes carrying the horses were exhausted from paddling night and day. When they ceased paddling, allowing themselves to rest, they would fall behind the boats and the Indians would attack them. The boats would then have to slow down and wait for them to catch up. They became such an impediment, Moscoso gave the order that they were to go ashore and kill the horses. When they saw a suitable place, they pulled in to shore, unloaded the horses, and killed most of them. They butchered them, salted the meat, and loaded it into the boats. Apparently they accomplished all of this during the afternoon of July 5.[37]

After loading the meat into the boats, they reembarked and proceeded down the river. Four or five of the horses were still alive on the shore. Perhaps they had gotten loose from the Spaniards, who could not afford the time to retrieve them. Some of the Indians in the pursuing fleet went ashore and approached these horses, which began to neigh and to run about. This reportedly frightened the Indians so much that they ran and jumped into the water.[38]

The second fleet of Indian canoes continued pursuing the Spaniards down the river, coming up behind them and firing arrows at them. They kept up the attack all that night and until ten o'clock the next day, July 6. At this time they evidently came to the southern limit of their territory, and like the canoes of Quigualtam, they turned their canoes around and paddled back upstream.[39]

Soon after this second fleet ceased their attack, perhaps later in the day of July 6, a fleet of seven canoes came out from a small town that was located near the river. They followed the Spaniards down the river, shooting arrows at them. But they were few in number and caused little damage. After pursuing the boats in this way for a short distance, these Indians left off their attack and paddled back upstream.[40]

After this third attack, the Spaniards proceeded down the river with no further trouble from Indians until they reached a point quite near the mouth of the river. It is likely that they traveled the remaining distance during daylight hours, mooring their boats close to shore each night. Near where the river emptied into the Gulf, the river divided into two arms, each of which was very wide.[41] They chose one of the arms, and when they came to within a half a league of where it emptied into the Gulf of Mexico, they anchored to rest up for the ordeals they were yet to face.[42] They probably reached this point on July 16.

The men were very tired. They had been taking their turns at the oars since July 2, when they had set out from Aminoya. Many of them had been wounded by Indian arrows. For many days they had eaten nothing but parched corn, which they had boiled. They parceled it out in daily portions of a third of a helmetful to each person. Evidently their store of meat had been completely consumed several days before reaching the coast.

The river had grown very wide. Both banks were lined with marshes grown up with what seemed to be tall reeds, but which, when they approached shore, they saw were actually large trees. Along the way they saw a huge island made of a tangled mass of trees carried down the current of the river and lodged there. While they were anchored and taking their rest, they killed and butchered nine or ten of the hogs they were carrying.[43]

It was during this interlude that a small number of Indians came by both water and land to assault them one last time. Several canoes sallied out from the reeds to threaten the Spaniards. These Indians looked different from those they had seen before. They were as large as "Philistines," and their skin was very dark from constant exposure to the sun. Their main mode of subsistence appears to have been fishing. One of these Indians stood on the prow of his canoe and berated them. As the story of this encounter is told by Garcilaso, one of the Spaniards' Indian slaves was able to translate some of the words the man uttered, and his violent gestures made the rest of his meaning plain: "Thieves, vagabonds, and loiterers who without honor or shame travel along this coast disquieting its inhabitants, depart from this place immediately by one of the two mouths of the river, if you do not want me to destroy you all and burn your ships. And see to it that I do not find you here tonight, for if I do, no man of you will escape with his life. . . . If we possessed such large canoes as yours . . . we would follow you to your own land and conquer it, for we too are men like yourselves."[44]

The Spaniards were concerned that these Indians might become emboldened enough to launch an effective attack. Moscoso ordered several armed men to go out in the canoes they were towing and do what they could against the Indians who were also in canoes. But even though the Spaniards almost broke their arms trying to paddle up close to the Indians, the Indians kept their canoes about an arrow shot's distance away. The Indians circled about in the water, feinting and turning as if to skirmish. The more the Spaniards pursued, the more injury the Indians did to them. But in the end they drove the Indians off.[45]

One of the soldiers in this fracas was wounded by a weapon they had not seen before in their wanderings. It was a six-foot spear that had been thrown by a man wielding a spear-thrower (fig. 84). The dart, or spear, was made of

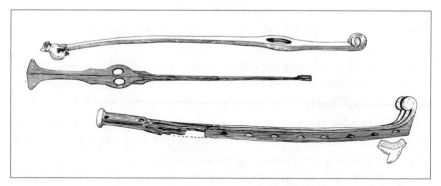

Fig. 84. Wooden artifacts recovered from Key Marco, Florida. *Above:* a spear-thrower with a knob and one finger hole, and with the hook for the spear carved in the form of a cat; *middle:* a spear-thrower with a flaring knob and two finger holes; *below:* a war club with a long groove in which sharks' teeth had been glued. Frank Hamilton Cushing, *A Preliminary Report on the Explorations of Ancient Key-Dweller Remains on the Gulf Coast of Florida*, Proceedings of the American Philosophical Society, vol. 25, no. 153 (Philadelphia, 1897), plate 32.

cane, and it had a barbed, deer-horn point with two lateral prongs. It was a fish spear. The point had completely penetrated the Spaniard's thigh, and when his comrades removed it, great damage was done to his leg, and he later died.[46]

In reaction to the Spanish attack on the Indians in canoes, the Indians on land came running through a swamp and a thicket of trees. They were armed with war clubs that were set with very sharp fish bones—perhaps sharks' teeth. (Several such clubs set with sharks' teeth were found in 1896 at the Key Marco site [see fig. 84] in southern Florida.[47]) They fought courageously with the Spaniards who went out to engage them. When approached, they would flee as fast as horses, turning this way and that, never getting further than an arrow-shot from the pursuing Spaniards. None of them were injured, but they injured several of the Spaniards.[48] Eventually they withdrew. It would seem that these Indians near the mouth of the Mississippi River, with their antique implements, were as marginal to the Mississippian Southeast as were the Indians who lived to the south of Tampa Bay.

Moscoso and his men had spent at least fifteen days—from July 2 until July 16—rowing down the river.[49] For three of these days—July 4 until July 6—they had been under very severe attack, and they had remained in the channel of the river both day and night. They had had to slaughter their horses, placing them at a severe disadvantage in case they were forced to travel by land. Many of the men had suffered arrow wounds. But they could give thanks that they had escaped from La Florida with their lives.

18

To Mexico

On July 18, 1543, the Spaniards cast off from where they had anchored near the mouth of the Mississippi River and sailed downstream toward the Gulf of Mexico (see map 8).[1] They dropped their anchors near the shore, just short of open sea, and one boat went out to the deepest part of the river and sounded it, finding that it had a maximum depth of forty brazas—about 220 feet.[2]

Moscoso asked all the men to state their opinions on how they ought to proceed. The fundamental question was whether they should cut their journey short and sail directly for Mexico or play it safe by skirting the coastline.

According to Garcilaso, one of those who favored sailing directly to Mexico was Juan de Añasco, who claimed to possess great knowledge of navigation and sailing. He had retrieved the astrolabe from Mabila after the fire; he had improvised a forestaff; and from memory he had drawn a sea chart on a deerskin. He said he had seen the sailing chart then in use for the Gulf of Mexico, and the coast ran east and west to the Rio de Las Palmas—today the Soto la Marina River—and from there to Mexico it ran north and south. A state-of-the-art sailing chart for the Gulf of Mexico would have been no more than a crude sketch of the shoreline with named landmarks visible from shipboard written in around the shoreline. And Añasco's chart from memory was surely even more schematic. Both the metal astrolabe and the wooden cross staff were used to measure the angular elevation of the sun at noon, and from this one could determine one's latitude, though errors of one half to two degrees were common when such measurements were taken at sea. There is a question whether Añasco even possessed the navigational information necessary to make such measurements. Techniques of estimating longitude were extremely crude in the sixteenth century, often little better than guesses.[3] Añasco told them that if they sailed along the Gulf coast, within sight of land, the distance would be much greater than if they sailed directly. Their progress would be so slow that winter might overtake them. But if they sailed directly, with favorable weather, they might reach Mexico in ten or twelve days.[4]

The majority of the men had little confidence in Añasco's knowledge of navigation, and they were opposed to his plan. It was safer, they said, to sail within sight of land because their ships were not strongly built, and they had no decks; if a storm blew up they would take on too much water and sink. And if they were becalmed, they carried so little water in their casks, they could die of thirst. Even if their ships were strongly built, they said, it would not be wise to sail across open sea without a proper pilot or a proper sailing chart. A clear majority of the men favored this decision, and they did in fact proceed along the coastline.[5] When some of the men made light of Añasco's claim to knowledge of the sea, he threw his forestaff and chart overboard in a rage, keeping only the astrolabe. But the men in one of the other boats retrieved them from the water.[6]

Just as they were about to pull up their anchors, the cable holding Moscoso's boat snapped, and his anchor was lost. But even though they were near land, they could not retrieve the anchor by diving for it, because the water was so deep. This distressed Moscoso and the men in his boat, because without an anchor, they were in jeopardy. But some of the hidalgos had kept the bridles of their horses, and by attaching one of these bridles to a heavy grinding stone for corn, they improvised an anchor.[7]

The Gulf Coast

On July 18 they set sail on a calm sea. Moscoso's boat led the way. But when he was two to three leagues offshore, the others closed up and asked him why he was putting so far to sea. If he intended to leave the coast, he should say so, because if he did so without getting the approval of all, then each of the boats would go its own way. Moscoso replied that he would not do anything without hearing the opinions of all. He said he only wanted to get offshore so that they could sail all night more safely, and the next day they would return to sight of land.[8]

They continued under sail all that first day, and all that night, and all the next day, July 19. Until vespers on July 19 they were sailing in freshwater, and it seemed marvelous to them that freshwater should occur so far at sea.[9] The volume of the Mississippi River is so great, and the coast is so shallow, that freshwater lies for a great distance along the shore, extending very far out into the Gulf. That night they saw some small islands to their right, and they made for them, anchoring there for the night.[10] They were possibly the Isles Dernieres.

Juan de Añasco continued to argue in favor of sailing by open sea, emphasizing how much shorter their voyage would be. Because the men were eager to reach Mexico, more and more of them were persuaded to Añasco's position, until a majority supported the more direct route. Accordingly Moscoso led the way into the open sea, where they sailed for two days—July 20 and 21. On July 21 their drinking water began to run low, but when they tried to return to land, they could not do so because the wind was blowing offshore.[11] Feeling themselves to be in danger, they cursed Juan de Añasco for giving them such bad advice. They cursed Moscoso for having listened to Añasco. Each of the captains said he would not venture out of sight of land again no matter what Moscoso or anybody else said. As for Moscoso, he could go wherever he wished. Then the wind shifted a little for the better, and all of them began to row as hard as they could. On the afternoon of July 21 they reached an unsheltered beach, possibly the coast of present-day Vermillion Parish, Louisiana. But later in the day the wind veered to the south, blowing as a crosswind along the coast, and it began driving the boats toward shore. The wind was very strong, and their small anchors, when cast, straightened out and began dragging. As the water grew shallow, Moscoso ordered all to jump into the water and tip the bergantines seaward when the waves passed by. They had to keep up this exhausting work until the wind died down.[12]

After the danger had passed, they went ashore and used some hoes to dig holes, which filled up with fresh water. They were able to dig these water holes only a few feet from the edge of the sea, and a very shallow hole would do.[13] Much relieved, they filled up their water casks.[14]

On July 22 they cast off and sailed for two days. More than once they came to small barren islands that were densely covered with birds. They collected the eggs and young birds in great numbers, though when they ate them both tasted strongly of shellfish. At several places they were able to collect shell-fish.[15] They put ashore on July 23 in the mouth of a small creek, which was like an estuary. The entrance to the creek sheltered them from a south wind that was contrary to the direction in which they were sailing. They had possibly pulled up in a creek on the coast of present-day Cameron Parish, Louisiana. While this contrary wind blew, they remained at anchor for four days.[16]

On July 28 the sea was calm enough that they could row out to sea. They sailed uneventfully until about evening, when the wind blew very hard, driving them to shore, and they regretted having decided to cast out from the little creek in which they had had such safe anchorage. After it became dark, the storm blew in very hard. In the wind and rain the boats strayed from each other. The two of them that were furthest out to sea came upon the coast at a distance of two leagues from the others, and they sailed into an inlet. This was possibly the mouth of Sabine Pass. The other five boats were blown ashore along the coast about a league to a league and a half apart. None of them had any idea where the others were. They were on an unsheltered beach that still ran east and west. Again their anchors straightened out and dragged, and they were blown toward the beach. The men could not keep the boats upright using the oars alone, even though there were seven or eight men to the oar. Again, the men had to jump out into the water, and as the waves struck against their boats, they pointed them toward the sea as best they could. The men inside the boats used bowls to bail the water that shipped in over the gunwales. To add to their terror and distress, the men were attacked by great swarms of mosquitoes that stung them unremittingly.[17]

The next morning, about July 29, the wind died down and the sea became calm. But the clouds of mosquitoes remained. The white sails were so covered with them they appeared to be black. The men who were manning the oars could not endure rowing unless others fanned the mosquitoes off of their bodies. Now that the terror of the storm abated, they had the luxury of being distressed by the bites of the insects. As they were all slapping ridiculously at each other, they began to laugh.[18]

During the course of this same day, all five of the boats proceeded down the coast and put in to the estuary where the other two boats had anchored. They remained here for two days—about July 30 and 31. While in this estuary they found on the beach a kind of pitch that had come from the sea. They called it "copee," thinking it to be the resin of a tree (*Clusia rosea* and *C. minor*) that grows in Venezuela. But what they found was probably coagulated oil from a seep in the Gulf of Mexico. They used this to coat the planking of their boats, which had been leaking and sorely needed it.[19]

They resumed their voyage on about August 1 and continued sailing the next day, when they put in at a large bay, where they remained for two days (about August 3 and 4). Six men took a canoe one day and paddled up this bay without being able to come to its head. The coast where they were still ran east and west. At this point they were possibly in Galveston Bay.

On the day they departed—about August 5—a south wind was blowing. Though it was not a favorable wind, it was only blowing lightly, and so they determined to sail anyway. But even though they rowed very hard this day and all of the following day, they made very little progress. They put in behind a small island and cast anchor. They possibly sailed through San Luis Pass at the southern end of Galveston Island. It was fortunate they did put in, because a serious storm blew up. They remained behind the shelter of this island for fourteen days—from about August 7 to about August 20. Fortunately, the fishing was very good, and they caught an abundance of fresh fish using both nets and line-and-hook. One man who threw out a baited hook made the mistake of tying the line to his arm. A very large fish struck the bait and pulled him out into the water up to his neck. Fortunately, the man remembered his knife, which he used to cut the line and save his life. At the end of their stay, they were grateful when the weather turned fair. They were so very grateful, they formed a procession and walked along the beach thanking God and praying to Him to take them to a land where they could serve Him better.[20]

They embarked from their safe haven behind the island and sailed for six days, keeping within sight of the coast. When they went ashore, they dug holes and collected fresh water to replenish their casks.[21] It is impossible to say where they went day by day on this leg of their journey, but certainly they sailed off the coasts of Matagorda Island, St. Joseph Island, Mustang Island, and Padre Island.

One day Juan de Añasco declared that he was of the opinion they were nearing the Río de las Palmas (see map 3), where he believed the coast took a north-south direction.[22] This river was the landmark they were all looking for.[23] Añasco advised them to put out to sea at this point so they could save time in reaching the Río de las Palmas. That night they remained out to sea, and the next morning they could see across the water palm trees and the coast running from north to south. Later in the day, at around noon, they saw mountains in the distance. Mariners of the day knew that when one started out at the Florida peninsula and sailed westward along the Gulf coast, these mountains of Tamaulipas were the first that could be seen from the coast. From these observations, they inferred that during the night (September 8) they had passed by the mouth of the Río de las Palmas.[24]

Pánuco

They were all jubilant. The Río de las Palmas was not very far from the Río de Pánuco, their destination in Mexico.[25] They were off the coast of present-day Tamaulipas and nearing their destination. All the boats drew close to each other, and they discussed how they should proceed. Some of the men were of the opinion they should not sail at night, fearing they might pass by the mouth of the Río de Pánuco as they had the Río de las Palmas. But others argued that with such a favorable wind as they then had, they could not afford to lose any time. They compromised by running at night with their sails half reefed.[26] Two of the boats, however, perhaps with men more eager than the others, ran with full sails.

The next morning, on September 10, the first of the five boats running under half-sail, captained by Calderón, saw muddy water in the sea. They tasted it, and it was fresh. This had to be the effluent of a sizable river. They ran for a quarter of a league before approaching the mouth of the river. In the distance they could see that water was breaking over a shoal where the river emptied into the sea, but because none of them were familiar with this coast, they were in doubt about how to approach land. They decided to enter directly into the port. Just before entering the current of the river, they turned in toward land and successfully entered the port.[27]

As they neared shore, they saw Indian men and women dressed in Spanish clothing. When these people approached, the Spaniards asked where they were. The Indians answered in Spanish that this was the Río de Pánuco and the town of Pánuco was located fifteen leagues inland. This was what they wanted to hear. Many of them leapt from the boat and went ashore to kiss the ground and give thanks to God that they had reached safety at last.[28] When the other four boats saw Calderón at anchor, they too came in to port.

The two boats that had run at full sail had passed through the muddy effluent of the Río de Pánuco in early dawn without having seen it. One of these ships was captained by Juan Gaytán, the treasurer, and the other was captained by Juan de Alvarado and Cristóbal Mosquera.[29] Those on board these two ships saw the five ships behind them tack and turn toward land. When they went further out into the Gulf in an attempt to turn back and rejoin the others, they found themselves heading into a strong north wind on a choppy sea.[30] Fearing that they would be separated from the others, they turned their ships in to the coast, where they anchored.[31]

But a storm blew in, and their anchors would not hold. They rode out the storm through the night, thinking it would abate the next day, but it did not. The mast of Gaytán's boat was struck by a strong gust of wind, knocking it out of the mortar box where it was attached to the keel, and it was with great difficulty that the men inserted it again.[32] Because the boats had no decks, they began taking on water. They considered running down the coast to find a refuge. But in the boat of Alvarado and Mosquera there was a twenty-year-old named Francisco who had sailed along this coast while serving as a ship's page. He said that where they were the coast was a soft sand, but further south toward Vera Cruz the coast was rocky, and if they went aground there the boats would be destroyed. It would be better to run the boats aground where they were. Their boats were small, and if they ran them ashore with sufficient skill, they might escape damage.[33]

Alvarado and Mosquera decided they would run their ship up on the beach. They sailed as near to Gaytán's ship as they could safely approach, and they signaled and indicated by signs what they intended to do. The people on the other boat agreed this was the best course for them to take. As Garcilaso tells the story, only Gaytán, in his capacity as royal treasurer, questioned whether it was wise to risk the boat he captained, because it was valuable. But the other men on board with him had a different conception of "valuable." They said they all had a stake in the boat because they had all labored at sawing planks and at making charcoal for the forge. But they reminded Gaytán that he had excused himself from such labor because he was the treasurer. Therefore, what had he to lose in the destruction of the boat? Should all who were on board die for the sake of the boat? Gaytán had a deep scar on his neck, which he had received in a quarrel with a comrade in Tunis in 1535, and some of the men on board cursed the man who had wounded him for not doing a better job at cutting his throat.[34]

Gaytán did not reply to these taunts. The soldiers on board moved quickly to man the sails, and Domingo de Acosta, a Portuguese, took the rudder. They turned the boat toward the coast and ran it up on the sand.[35] When they hit the bank, the only casualty was Gaytán, who for some reason leaped from the poop and on landing in the sand injured his naked shoulder against the rudder. When the surf receded, the boat was ten feet from the edge of the water.

The others remained inside the boat. They tipped it over on its side and leaped out. Then some of them righted the boat so it would not be swamped by the surf. With the help of the surf they eased it further up on the sand, and shored it up in case they might later have to return to it.[36]

The boat of Alvarado and Mosquera came ashore in a similar manner, about two arquebus shots away. They unloaded their gear and began discussing what to do next. The first order of business was to find out what had happened to the other boats. For all they knew, they had been lost. Someone would have to walk up the coast and look for them. The men were exhausted. They had spent the previous night without sleeping, and they had not eaten for a very long time. They did not know how far they would have to walk, and they did not know whether they might encounter rivers, creeks, and hostile Indians along the way. Gonzalo Quadrado Xaramillo (who had been the one who went forward and scouted Mabila) volunteered for the mission, and Francisco Múñoz of Burgos volunteered to accompany him. They were without shoes or leggings, and for weapons they had only their swords and shields. For food, they were given some saddlebags with a small quantity of corn and salt pork, both of which had been poorly cooked.[37]

The men who remained behind on the beach sent out three small squads of men to reconnoiter the countryside. Antonio de Porros led a squad down the coast to the south; Alonso Calvete led one up the coast to the north; and Gonzalo Silvestre led one inland. All were ordered not to venture so far away that they could not be reinforced in case they found themselves in trouble. One of the squads sent along the coast soon returned with a piece of ceramic ware that had been made in Spain, and the other one also soon returned with a broken ceramic bowl made in Spain. These discoveries made the men very happy.[38]

Silvestre and the squad that went inland made an even happier discovery. As Garcilaso tells the story, they had not gone far when they came upon a freshwater lagoon that extended for more than a league. There they saw four or five canoes of Indians out fishing. Silvestre and his men took cover, and then spread out and eased their way through some trees in a wing formation, as if they were hunting for horses. As they moved along paralleling the coast of the lagoon, keeping under cover, they spied two Indians who were gathering fruit from a guava tree. Silvestre and the others fanned out and crept forward, crawling on their bellies. When they had the two Indians surrounded, they all jumped up at once and rushed them. One of the Indians raced to the lagoon, plunged in, and swam away. But the other one was caught. The terrified man shouted *"Bredos! Bredos!"* over and over again. This sounded like the

Spanish word *bledos*—wild amaranth, an edible green. It is used in such deprecating expressions as *No me importa un bledo*, "I don't care a straw!" The Spaniards cursed their captive, saying "Go to the Devil, you dog. What should we want with *bredos?*"[39] They bound the man securely so he could not escape.

The Spaniards also seized two baskets of guavas the two Indians had been collecting. At a nearby hut they found a small quantity of corn, a turkey, a rooster and two hens, and a small quantity of preserves made from maguey leaves.[40]

Silvestre and his squad took their captive and the food they had found back to the boats. When the men at the boats saw the turkey and the chickens they began to jump for joy, for these farm animals indicated even more strongly that they were near where Spaniards lived. They again questioned their captive, asking him to tell them where they were. Finally, one of their number who had spent some time in Mexico and who knew something of the native languages, thought he recognized something in what the Indian said. He held up a pair of scissors and asked the Indian what they were. The Indian, now somewhat calmer, said *tiselas*, and with this the men were jubilant. Clearly the Indian had uttered a variant of the Spanish word *tijeras*, "scissors."

They next established that the Indian was a vassal of a Spaniard named Cristóbal de Brazos. Unable to correctly pronounce "Brazos," the man had been saying what sounded like "bredos." As they questioned him further they learned that Cristóbal de Brazos lived in Pánuco, which was some distance from where they were, but their captive's cacique lived only about a league away. This cacique, the man said, spoke Spanish, and he had learned to read and write. They sent the captive to go to his cacique and tell him where they were, and to bring back pen and paper. The man was back in less then four hours. He brought the pen and paper, and also the cacique, who brought along eight men loaded down with fruit, fish, and bread made from cornmeal. The Spaniards thanked him and gave him a gift of dressed deerskins they had brought along with them. They quickly wrote a letter to Moscoso and dispatched it by an Indian runner. They remained for several days near where they had come ashore, and each day the cacique came to talk with them about their exploits during the expedition.[41]

Two days after the other five boats had cast anchor in the Río de Pánuco, Gonzalo Quadrado Xaramillo and Francisco Múñoz found them. The men from the five boats were overjoyed, having feared that the other two boats had been lost with all who were on board. The next day the letter from the others reached Moscoso, who immediately sent back a reply saying that after resting they should all come to Pánuco, and there they would decide what to do next.[42]

Moscoso's group started sailing up the Río de Pánuco in the five boats. But they did not have enough wind to their advantage. Moreover, the current in the river was strong and the channel crooked. After a great deal of effort they were able to make very little progress. The men abandoned the boats to the sailors (who presumably continued taking them upstream) and they walked to Pánuco.[43]

The people in Pánuco had been told by Indian messengers that Moscoso and his men were coming. When they arrived, Moscoso and his men headed straight for the church to pray and give thanks for having been delivered from La Florida. They must have been a spectacle, clothed as they were in ragged cassocks, breeches, and shoes made of dressed deerskins. There were 311 of them—eleven fewer than had departed from Aminoya.[44]

The alcalde mayor of Pánuco invited Moscoso into his home. The others were taken into other houses in Pánuco in numbers of up to six or ten, according to the size of the house. They dined well on chicken, bread from cornmeal, and the various fruits that grew there.[45]

Pánuco was a small town with perhaps seventy Spanish households. The houses were made of cut stone and the roofs were thatched. There was no gold or silver nearby, and the land was not productive; hence, there was little in the way of a money economy. The people at Pánuco did a little stock farming, and some were planting mulberry trees for silk production. The Spanish people at Pánuco were supported mainly by tribute paid them in cotton cloth, fowls, and corn. Almost everyone wore clothing made of cotton cloth manufactured locally, and only the wealthier citizens wore cloth that had been woven in Castile.[46]

The alcalde mayor of Pánuco immediately sent word to the viceroy in Mexico City, Don Antonio de Mendoza, that about three hundred survivors of the De Soto expedition were in Pánuco, and he had undertaken to provide supplies for them because they were on a mission for His Majesty. This news was a great surprise to people in Mexico City, who had assumed that De Soto and all his men had perished. It seemed miraculous that they could have remained alive for such a long time in such a hostile land.[47]

The viceroy sent out an order that whenever it should be required, food and Indian porters would be supplied to these men. According to the order, if supplies and services were refused, Moscoso and his men were authorized to take them by force if necessary, and they would suffer no penalty. The survivors of the expedition noted that this order that they be generously treated was followed so thoroughly that as they traveled from place to place, the people would often come out for some distance from their town to meet them and give them food.[48]

Eight days after they had run their ships up on the beach, the men from the two wayward boats arrived at Pánuco. Like the others, they were haggard, sunburned, and lean as wolves.[49] Moscoso and his men rested in Pánuco for up to a month. They were well provided for, and perhaps because of Mendoza's order, their hosts did not hurry them along. The alcalde mayor used the store of cotton cloth that had been paid to him in tribute to clothe the men. Those few who still had coats of mail traded them for horses. But most had to travel by foot beyond Pánuco.[50]

Once they had reached safety, some of the Spaniards began having second thoughts about decisions and actions that had been made during the course of the expedition. As they looked about them, they saw that Pánuco was a frontier town in a land that lacked some of the advantages of the land they had just abandoned. Here they had to wear cotton clothing, but in La Florida they could wear clothing of fine dressed deerskin and "marten." In La Florida they would not have to plant mulberry trees for silk production, because there they grew wild. La Florida had an abundance of fine nut trees, wild fruit trees, and wild grapes. The land was exceedingly fertile and could be used to grow any sort of grains and vegetables, and there were vast pastures for livestock.[51] In La Florida there were freshwater pearls and seed pearls. Moreover, a diligent search in La Florida might reveal gold and silver mines, for such discoveries had surely been made in Mexico. With these thoughts, some of the men began to imagine they had been cheated out of rich estates in La Florida. It seemed that they had left a rich land to come to a poor land, where they had to accept handouts. Some of the men began to sink into depression and self-pity, and finally anger.

Fights began breaking out among the survivors, no doubt set off by real or imagined injuries they had suffered during the course of the expedition. Their greatest anger was directed at the officers of the Royal Exchequer and the captains and soldiers of Seville. They were the ones who had argued so strongly after De Soto died that they should abandon La Florida. They were the ones who persuaded Moscoso that they should try to escape by traveling overland to New Spain—a disastrous decision that had caused all to suffer and many to die. Had they sent out two bergantines, as De Soto proposed, they might have sailed to Mexico, Cuba, or Santo Domingo, so that assistance could have been provided to them in establishing a colony.[52]

As they fought among themselves, according to Garcilaso, several suffered knife wounds, and a few were killed. As the story was told, the captains and officials of the king were under such threat, they dared not come out of the houses in which they were lodged. The survivors were in such a fury that the townspeople of Pánuco could not control them.[53]

Mexico City

The alcalde mayor of Pánuco informed the viceroy of these disturbances. The viceroy ordered that Moscoso and the men should proceed as soon as possible to Mexico City. According to Garcilaso, they were told to proceed in groups of ten to twenty each, with each group being all of one faction, so they would not kill each other en route.[54]

As they traveled to Mexico City, people along the way continued to supply the men with lodging and food. If any of the survivors were ill, the people would carry him in a sedan chair from town to town. Mendoza's order of hospitality was enforced by the caciques, whose orders in turn were enforced by Indians called *tapiles*, who carried "rods of justice" in their hands. They insured that provisions and services were forthcoming all along the way.[55]

When they were about twenty leagues from Mexico City they were met by a Portuguese who had been sent by Mendoza. The man brought a quantity of sugar, raisins, pomegranates, and other foods that would be beneficial to those who were sick.[56] They arrived in Mexico City after four days of travel.[57] The inhabitants of the city came out to meet them and took them into their homes in groups of five or six, and under order of the viceroy, they gave them clothing as they could afford to do so.[58]

According to Garcilaso, a man named Xaramillo, a native of Extremadura, went to the plaza to see the survivors. He found there a kinsman, very likely Gonzalo Quadrado Xaramillo, and invited him and seventeen others into his house. He dressed them all in clothing made of black cloth from Segovia and provided each of them with a bed, mattress, sheet, blanket, and pillow, all of which must have seemed like the greatest of luxuries.[59]

Many of the survivors went to kiss the hand of the viceroy, who took some of them into his own house. He, too, clothed the men in his charge. As the Gentleman of Elvas tells the story, when it came time to eat, the viceroy sorted the men out according to social status. The persons of highest status ate at the viceroy's table, while the men of lower status ate at another table. The viceroy was told who each man was so he could treat him accordingly. Those men who stayed at the houses of artisans and citizens of lower status, however, were not segregated. Both hidalgos and peasants ate at the same table.[60] Garcilaso, on the other hand, says the viceroy treated them all without distinction.

These were men who were excessively conscious of honor and social standing. They were apt to feel insulted with the slightest breach of etiquette, and they were more than ready to fight when this occurred. According to Garcilaso, one of the survivors, Diego de Tapia, who was very small in stature, was approached by a citizen of Mexico City. Seeing that Tapia was dressed in animal skins, and perhaps emboldened because of his small size, the man told him that he owned a cattle farm, and if Tapia wanted to, he could have a job on this farm. Tapia bristled, saying that he was going to Peru, where he would in time own twenty farms, and if the man wished, he could come to Peru and work for him. Hearing this, the citizen of Mexico walked away without saying another word, knowing that another word could get him into a situation from which he might not be able to extricate himself.

The people in Mexico City were greatly interested in the experiences of the survivors, and they were interested in the objects they had managed to bring out of La Florida. Whether for their novelty or their intrinsic value, they wanted to have these things for their own. They bought the few pearls the survivors had. They bought dressed deerskins and furs, even those that had been greatly soiled through use as clothing and blankets.[61] When the people of Mexico City began displaying these bits of La Florida on their persons, some of the survivors again began to question whether they had been foolish to abandon that land.[62]

The survivors' anger and resentment again boiled over, and they began lashing out at each other, and again some were killed and wounded. The viceroy defused some of this anger by saying he was persuaded that La Florida was a rich country, and he would like to colonize it, and if any of the survivors wanted to return they could most assuredly do so. Some of them said they wanted to return, but many of them in fact hated La Florida and wanted nothing more to do with it.[63]

The viceroy seemingly was truly interested in La Florida. He and his son, Don Francisco de Mendoza, closely questioned the survivors about their exploits and about the land and people they had seen. The survivors gave them oral accounts of their adventures, and it is likely that some were asked to provide written accounts.[64] The viceroy was particularly interested in the quality of the land and in its natural products. He concluded that La Florida should be colonized, but he found that few of the survivors had any real enthusiasm for doing so.[65]

19

After the Expedition

In the spring of 1540, De Soto's plan had been to make a great expeditionary thrust from Apalachee to the northeast, and then to loop around to the southwest to Ochuse, at Pensacola Bay, where he could be resupplied. Just before launching his expedition from Apalachee into the interior, De Soto ordered Diego Maldonado and Gómez Arias to sail to Havana. They were to take news of the expedition to Isabel de Bobadilla. In Havana they were to purchase food, clothing, and ammunition and load this onto De Soto's caravel and two bergantines, as well as onto additional ships they might purchase. At the proper time, they were to sail to the harbor of Ochuse to rendezvous with the army. From Ochuse, according to the plan, the expedition could take whatever course seemed best.

Maldonado and Arias did what they were commanded to do. The prospects for the expedition's success seemed favorable when they sailed out of Apalachee Bay, and in Cuba they purchased supplies and provisions, plus all that would be needed to establish a colony—tools, seeds, and farm animals. They sailed in the fall of 1540 and arrived at Ochuse, where they cast anchor and waited. And waited. When no one appeared, Maldonado and Arias split up and sailed in opposite directions along the Gulf coast, looking for signs of De Soto and his men. Whenever they put ashore at a likely place, they would cut signs into the bark of trees as signals of their having been there, and they left written messages in the hollows of trees informing De Soto of what they had done and what they planned to do. When winter set in, after finding no traces of the expedition, they had no choice but to turn around and sail back to Havana.[1]

In the summer of 1541 Maldonado and Arias again went out to look for signs of life. They sailed all along the Gulf coast to Mexico, finding not a trace of the expedition. Then they sailed up the Atlantic coast, again finding nothing. In 1542 they renewed the search and again found no signs of life. Could La Florida have so completely swallowed up an army of more than six hundred people?

In 1543 Maldonado and Arias again sailed along the Gulf coast, doggedly looking for signs of their comrades. When they reached Vera Cruz in the middle of October, they finally found the survivors, who told them the grim tale of the expedition. Maldonado and Arias then sailed back to Havana with word that half the army had perished and De Soto himself had died. De Soto's army had discovered no rich society, and they had chosen to abandon the land without planting a colony. Doña Isabel de Bobadilla had lost her husband, and their fortune was ruined.[2]

The Survivors

For the people who had gone with De Soto, the expedition had been a disaster. All had suffered greatly from the rigors of surviving in a land of belligerent chiefdoms who doggedly resisted the invaders. At best the participants lost all or a great part of their personal fortunes in the venture; at worst they lost their lives. De Soto had taken about 600 people with him from Cuba to Florida. There are different estimates of how many of these survived, but the number is somewhere between 300 and 350. The Gentleman of Elvas puts it at 311 (probably omitting slaves), and this may be close to the actual figure. The names of 257 of these survivors are now known with good authority.[3]

Those who possessed high social status or were servants of high-status people had a better survival rate than those of low status. All three of the royal officials survived: Juan Gaytán, the treasurer; Juan de Añasco, the *contador;* and Luís Hernández de Biedma, the factor. Both of those who served as De Soto's field marshals survived—Luís de Moscoso and Baltasar de Gallegos. Eight of those who served as captains survived. De Soto's personal servants fared well: his page Juan de Viota, his aide Juan López Cacho, and his secretary Rodrigo

Rangel. Two scribes survived, as did Ana Méndez, a maidservant of Don Carlos Enríquez.[4]

Where did they go after they reached Pánuco? The destinations of eighty-six of these survivors are presently known. Most of this number—fifty-nine—remained in Mexico to continue seeking their fortunes. Eighteen of them went on to Peru, where several saw military action in the uprising of Gonzalo Pizarro. They too continued their quest for riches.

Gómez Suárez Porcallo de Figuerora y de la Cerda returned to his father's estate in Cuba. Whether through uncommon sagacity or because he quarreled with De Soto, Porcallo's father had chosen to end his participation in the expedition before they departed from Tampa Bay.[5] As the wealthiest man in Cuba, he had an alternative the other men did not possess.

At least fifteen of the eighty-six returned to Spain, sometimes after ventures in other parts of the New World.[6] Some of the ones returning to Spain harbored a decided rancor for the New World. They had all suffered greatly during the course of the expedition, and they had lost the fortunes they had invested in the venture.[7]

The fates of the survivors were various. Juan de Añasco remained a while in Mexico, before going on to Peru, where he was for a time in charge of running the Guadalcanal mines. He died in Peru.[8]

Gómez Arias Dávila was one of the few survivors who later prospered. He went from Mexico to Nicaragua, where he was selected to go with a contingent of men to Peru to fight in the uprising of Gonzalo Pizarro. He was rewarded by being granted the right to collect tribute from the Chupacho Indians, and he became governor of the Guánaco province.[9]

Luís de Moscoso remained in Mexico. In 1543 he asked to be granted the encomienda of the Indians of Xochimilco. Later he was accused of living illegally with his cousin, Leanor de Alvarado, who bore him a son.[10] According to Garcilaso, Moscoso married this woman.[11] Rodrigo Rangel recorded De Soto's new will in Havana, and on December 6, 1543, he witnessed the intent of Isabel de Bobadilla to inventory De Soto's assets. Rangel returned to Mexico, where he became alcalde major of Pánuco.[12]

Francisco Maldonado and Juan López Cacho returned to Spain.[13] So did Peria, a Vizcayan, who later played a role in the affairs of New Granada in what is now Colombia.[14] Gonzalo Silvestre went to Peru to serve with those who were sent to help put down the uprising of Gonzalo Pizarro. Here he became acquainted with the young Inca mestizo, Garcilaso de la Vega, to whom he told stories of the De Soto expedition. Later he returned to Spain, where he was a citizen of Villa de Herrera.[15] Gonzalo Quadrado Xaramillo returned to Spain where he joined the Franciscan brotherhood.[16]

Isabel de Bobadilla vs. Hernán Ponce de León

For the people who were closest to De Soto—his wife and his compañero—the failure of the expedition would pit them against each other in a bitter legal struggle.

The first full account of De Soto's death reached Havana in December 1543. Rodrigo Rangel arrived in Havana at this time, and he carried the news to Doña Isabel.[17] Doña Isabel drew up an inventory of property owned by herself and De Soto.[18] Much of it was sold at auction. She took all the proceeds from the auction as well as De Soto's papers and returned to Spain, where she became embroiled in a lawsuit instituted by Hernán Ponce de León. The testimony in the court proceedings reveals details about the relationship between De Soto and Ponce de León, as well as about some of the events in Cuba just before the expedition sailed to La Florida.

Ponce de León sought to recover compensation from De Soto's estate for money and goods he claimed had been taken from him illegally, by force. It was well established in the course of these proceedings that as young men Ponce de León and De Soto had formed a partnership in Nicaragua, and they had reaffirmed this partnership in Cuzco on June 26, 1535. The legal problem before the court was to set a value on what they owned jointly.

Ponce de León swore that he had decided to end his partnership with De Soto before he departed from Peru to return to Spain. He contended that in Cuba De Soto had coerced him into handing over half of a treasure in gold and silver he had in his possession at the time, as well as a ship he had purchased in Peru in partnership with another person. The sum of treasure he had with him he set at eight thousand castellanos.

Ponce de León contended that De Soto had no right to this money because before he had departed from Peru he, Ponce, had empowered the licenciate Pedro Vázquez, who was a judge there at that time, to dissolve the partnership between himself and De Soto. Diego del Castillo, who made a deposition in Ponce de León's lawsuit, affirmed that De Soto had acknowledged to him that he did in fact know this legal action had been instituted by Hernán Ponce de León.[19] According to Ponce de León, after he landed in Cuba, whether by choice or force of circumstance, De Soto not only would not agree to a settlement, he berated Pedro Vázquez so threateningly that the latter was too frightened and cowed to take any action against De Soto.[20]

Ponce de León contended, moreover, that after De Soto had assumed the governorship of Cuba, he, Ponce, had sent Diego Gómez de Marcado to Havana with a message to De Soto that he wished to dissolve their partnership. When Ponce de León sailed from Peru to Spain, he claimed that he intended to pass by Cuba without landing, but bad weather had forced him to seek refuge in the harbor of Havana.[21] He said that because De Soto was governor of Cuba, he, Ponce de León, knew he would be at a decided disadvantage if a dispute arose between them.

Hard words passed between De Soto and Ponce de León in Havana. Ponce de León stated that he told De Soto he wished to dissolve their partnership. He contended that De Soto should be content to keep all that he had taken from Peru to Spain, and for his part, he should have for his own all that had been left in Peru. But De Soto wanted the partnership to continue. He asserted that all he had negotiated in Spain procuring the right to conquer La Florida had been on behalf of the two of them, and Ponce de León had a right to half of all that they would discover and acquire in La Florida. By the same token, De Soto contended he had a right to half of what Ponce de León had accumulated in the three years he had remained in Peru. Diego Gutiérrez de los Ríos and Luís de Moscoso served as go-betweens while they were negotiating.

In Havana, De Soto and Ponce de León then came to a seeming agreement to keep their partnership in force. De Soto had a document drawn up by the notary Francisco Cepero, and they both signed it. It was at this time that Ponce de León handed over to De Soto the 8,000 or so castellanos. Ponce de León also claimed that De Soto had commandeered a ship in which he had a half interest worth 750 castellanos, as well as a fine tent made of Peruvian wool and cotton. De Soto took the ship with him to La Florida, and he took the tent for his personal use on the expedition.

After De Soto departed for La Florida, Ponce de León secretly had a document drawn up by Mancio Zapata, royal notary in Havana, asserting that the agreement he and De Soto had recently signed was invalid because he had been threatened by De Soto.[22] One of De Soto's threats was that he would force Ponce de León to go on the expedition to La Florida. Ponce de León contended that given De Soto's great powers as governor of Cuba, anyone, no matter how courageous, would have been intimidated.[23] In his deposition, Luís de Moscoso verified that Ponce de León had in fact signed the agreement with De Soto against his will.

Ponce de León testified that when Isabel learned he had registered his secret repudiation with Mancio Zapata, she had sent Juan de Rojas, whom De Soto had left behind as his lieutenant, to the ship where Mancio Zapata was. Rojas threatened Zapata, forcing him to hand over the document Ponce de León had signed. Doña Isabel immediately dispatched a caravel carrying this document and other information to De Soto.[24] However, by the time this caravel arrived at Tampa Bay, De Soto had already departed for the interior. Pedro Calderón, who had been left in charge at Tampa Bay, took the documents to De Soto when he later went to Apalachee.[25]

Doña Isabel concealed from Ponce de León the fact that she had seized the document. She bided her time until a ship that was in Havana harbor bound for Spain had departed, leaving Ponce de León with no way out, and then she sent a letter to him asking why he had behaved so badly. As acting governor, she ordered him not to leave Havana until he had renounced his secret legal action. She had a document drawn up, and thus intimidated, Ponce de León signed it, repudiating his repudiation.

A substantial part of Ponce de León's suit argued that De Soto had spent prodigally in Spain, wasting much of the money that belonged to Ponce de León. He contended that it was bad judgment for De Soto to have spent it on an expedition to La Florida, which ended in ruin as had the expeditions of all those who had preceded him there.[26] But many of those who gave depositions in the suit denied these charges. They said De Soto had no choice but to spend a lot of money on such a large expedition, and they affirmed that La Florida was a rich land, and if De Soto had not died, he would surely have founded a colony there.

Isabel enlisted the testimony of several individuals to counter assertions made by Ponce de León. Hernando Pizarro testified that when De Soto departed from Peru for Spain, Ponce de León remained behind in De Soto's house in Cuzco, with benefit of their joint possessions and slaves. Pedro Cataño testified that he had heard that the property they held jointly in Peru amounted to about two hundred thousand ducats.[27] Deponents testified that before departing from Peru, Ponce de León had sold the house he owned with De Soto to Don Diego de Almagro for a reputed four thousand castellanos, and that debts had been owed to De Soto and Ponce de León, but it was difficult to establish exact amounts.

Rodrigo Rangel contradicted Ponce de León's contention that he planned to sail past Cuba without landing there. Rangel testified that De Soto told him he had received a letter from Ponce de León saying he was coming to Havana to discuss their partnership. Alonso Martín, who was the pilot on Ponce de León's ship, also testified that Ponce de León went to Havana to talk with De Soto.[28] However, Diego Gutiérrez de los Ríos contradicted them, saying that Ponce de León meant to sail directly to Spain.

Several deponents testified that in Cuba they had heard letters read, which Ponce de León had sent from Spain to Isabel, stating that he had paid debts De Soto owed. This implied that Ponce de León was behaving as if the partnership were still in effect even after De Soto had returned to Spain.

Several of Ponce de León's witnesses implied that his protestations about the ship De Soto seized were blown out of proportion. They said the ship was in such poor condition it could not have made it back to Spain. It was such a poor ship that De Soto had to scuttle it after unloading it in La Florida. Moreover, De Soto had sent back to Ponce de León a very good ship, the *Magdalena*, in which he could proceed to Spain.[29]

It is notable that many of the survivors of the expedition from whom Ponce de León sought depositions in Mexico did not publicly vilify or denounce De Soto; rather, they said he had too good a character to have done many of the things Ponce de León charged him with. And several said that if De Soto had lived—and especially if he had reached Quigualtam—he would have established a colony, because La Florida was a rich land.[30] It was good for cattle, wheat, and wine, and everyone expected that mines of precious metals would eventually be discovered there.[31] And some of them asserted that should a new expedition be sent to La Florida, they would be willing to join it.[32]

Hence, for De Soto's wife and compañero, the fruit of the expedition was that they would fight it out in the courts over who had intended what, and when, and who had behaved honorably or dishonorably, and most important, they contended over who had a claim to the dregs of a great fortune—extracted from the blood of the native people of Central America and Peru—that De Soto had largely squandered on his entrada into La Florida. The documents do not reveal how the lawsuit was ultimately resolved.

The Decline of the Southeastern Chiefdoms

For Spain, the De Soto expedition was a disappointment, but not a serious setback. It did not add to Charles V's treasury, but neither did it cost him very much. The long-term cost was that Spain now had to worry about who would control the continent De Soto had explored. In this vast land a competing European power could found a colony and threaten future Spanish interests there as well as in Mexico. In particular, Spain was afraid that a competing European power would discover a road from La Florida to Zacatecas, in northern Mexico, where Spain had discovered and was exploiting one of the richest silver deposits in the world.

For the native chiefdoms of the Southeast, the De Soto expedition was an unimaginable calamity. It was the beginning of a long decline, the beginning of the end of the world they had built for themselves. There were two causes for their initial decline: military assault (and consequent destabilization) and epidemic diseases brought from the Old World to the New.

The military impact of the De Soto expedition on the Indians was much greater in some places than in others. The greatest impact surely fell on the subjects and allies of chief Tascaluza. Losing twenty-five hundred to three thousand of their fighting-age men was a stupendous loss of life for chiefdom-level societies. The losses sustained by the Indians at the battle of Napituca in northern Florida, at Chicaza in northern Mississippi, and at Anilco in Arkansas must also have been substantial, although there is no way either to set a figure on their losses or to compare them with those at Mabila.

In addition to killing Indians in direct military actions, the De Soto expedition may have destabilized the balanced hostilities that appear to have prevailed among chiefdoms all across the Southeast. This low-level, "Texas draw" Mississippian warfare must have occasioned relatively few casualties before the Spaniards first arrived. But when De Soto struck a substantial military blow against a particular native society, the traditional enemies of this society could well have been tempted to step up their own hostilities by mounting heavier than normal attacks. Such destabilization may have occurred at Anilco, where De Soto ordered his army to launch a surprise attack against this town to terrorize and intimidate them and their neighbors. When the expedition revisited Anilco several months later, they found that the people had not been able to put in a corn crop, and they were starving. Other forms of destabilization may have occurred elsewhere along the route. One wonders, for example, what transpired between Pacaha and Casqui after the Spaniards departed. De Soto negotiated what he took to be a peace between these two polities, but one cannot imagine that this peace lasted very long once De Soto and his army moved on.

The losses of life the Indians of the Southeast suffered as a direct result of Spanish military actions and through the heightened military actions of their traditional enemies pale in comparison to their losses from being exposed to the germs and viruses that the invading Europeans and Africans unwittingly carried in their blood and breath. Microbial and viral parasites are most numerous where a species is oldest, and for our species that is the Old World. We largely evolved in Africa, where an extraordinary variety of germs and viruses exists today. From there our species gradually spread to all parts of the Old World, and only about fifteen thousand years ago to the New World. The tiny bands of migrants who were the ancestors of the Indians took passage from the Old World to the New through Siberia and Alaska, and because their numbers were so small, and because human parasites are so few in the Arctic, the New World they came to occupy was relatively free of the germs and viruses that attack humans. Moreover, most of the diseases that afflict our species did not become infectious among us until after the invention of agriculture and pastoralism, that is, more recently than fifteen thousand years ago, after the Indians became isolated in the New World. Many diseases, in fact, infected our species as a consequence of the close relationship that developed between Old World peoples and domesticated animals—dogs, cattle, sheep, goats, pigs, and horses. And the infectious epidemic diseases—smallpox, measles, flu, and so on—did not become problematic until after the development of cities, where there were large enough populations for lethal germs and viruses to become endemic.

In the microparasitical contest between Europeans and Africans on the one hand, and Indians on the other, the Indians had very little on their side. Syphilis may have been present among the Indians, but it is by no means certain that it was, because the germ that causes syphilis closely resembles the germ that causes yaws, a disfiguring Old World disease. So far as anyone knows with certainty, no germs or viruses were transferred from the Indians of the Southeast to the European and African invaders. The transfer was very much in the opposite direction. Europeans and Africans brought with them smallpox, measles, typhoid, diphtheria, mumps, and many other diseases. Many of these were diseases that Europeans and Africans normally contracted as children and survived. But among "virgin soil" populations, such as the American Indians, some of these diseases inflicted frightful mortality rates. A single outbreak of smallpox could easily carry away a third of an entire population. And repeated infections caused a cumulative drop in population by a factor of 90 to 95 percent or even more. It was disease more than anything else that enabled Spanish armies numbering in the hundreds to conquer Aztecs and Incas numbering in the millions. It was disease that devastated New World societies, leaving the survivors too demoralized and disorganized to effectively resist the military and cultural onslaught of the invaders.[33]

The Indians of the Southeast were impacted by Old World diseases, but precisely which diseases were the main culprits is not known. Because most of the diseases killed so quickly—in days or weeks—they inflicted few traumata to the bones of the victims (who in any case often went unburied and were eaten by scavengers), and this means that archaeologists and biological anthropologists can tell us little about the epidemics. It is only in the richer historical records of later times, beginning in the eighteenth century, that the diseases in specific epidemics can be identified. But the steepest population decline in the New World occurred in the poorly documented sixteenth and seventeenth centuries.

The next question is when exactly did the epidemics strike, and most particularly, did any of the Old World pathogens reach the Indians before De Soto arrived? Might Juan Ponce de León, Lucas Vázquez de Ayllón, Pánfilo de Narváez, or other Spaniards have introduced pathogens among people living on the coast, who then transmitted them to people living in the interior? Or might pathogens have been introduced even earlier by Norse voyagers or Bristol fishermen coming ashore on the coast of Newfoundland or New England?[34]

Epidemic disease would be a handy explanation for the collapse of some of the large Middle Mississippian chiefdoms at about A.D. 1350 to 1450. But this would mean the diseases would have been introduced by Europeans—Norsemen—making contact in the far north. Such epidemics, in advance of exploration of the interior and colonization, surely occurred in later times. For example, the Indians of the Massachusetts Bay area were struck by an epidemic in 1616–17 that evidently spread southward from an origin at a French outpost in Nova Scotia, an event the Massachusetts colonists, who arrived three years later, regarded as divine providence.[35] Such an occurrence in the Southeast is a theoretical possibility, but there is at present no evidence for epidemics from the north reaching the Southeast, and certainly archaeological confirmation is lacking for such an epidemic in the fourteenth or fifteenth century.

A far more likely direction from which early infections could have come was the Caribbean. Smallpox was definitely introduced into Hispaniola in 1518 and quickly became virulent. By 1519 it had spread to Cuba, and from there it was taken to Mexico. There is some evidence of early native voyaging in canoes between Cuba and Florida, and it is *possible* the disease reached Florida and the mainland in this way. There is, however, no archaeological confirmation that it did. Alvar Núñez Cabeza de Vaca reports that Indians died along the Texas coast of a "stomach ailment" in 1528, but again there is no archaeological confirmation that this disease spread to depopulate the interior.[36]

Well before the time of European exploration, the archaeological record in many parts of the Southeast attests to chiefdoms rising to prominence, and sometimes forming into larger social entities—complex or paramount chiefdoms—and then declining, and in extreme cases, ceasing to exist. In the Savannah River basin, for example, between A.D. 800 and 1600 there were many instances of such societies undergoing cycles of growth and decline. In fact, between 1350 and 1450 the entire Savannah River basin gradually emptied out, the only exception being some towns that remained on the headwaters of the river. This vacated area became the wilderness of Ocute that so discomfited the members of the De Soto expedition. The causes of all these changes were complex: chiefdoms could decline because of power struggles within, struggles with enemies from without, resource depletion, and climatic worsening. The Savannah River chiefdoms were particularly impacted by dry periods occurring at about 1300–40, 1370–1400, 1440–85, and 1565–75. But even these droughts do not seem to have caused regionwide depopulation of the sort that would have been caused by a pandemic.[37]

Other indirect evidence against a pandemic in the Southeast before 1539 is the fact that De Soto encountered seemingly vital populations from Apalachee northward. Indeed, some of these societies had enough numbers to pose a significant military threat to the Spaniards. The only explicit observation by members of the De Soto expedition of the deleterious effects of disease on the Indians was at Cofitachequi. The chroniclers report that a pestilence had struck Cofitachequi two years before they arrived, and there seemed to have been substantial loss of life. Certainly Cofitachequi was not as formidable in 1540 as the people of Ocute had led the Spaniards to expect it would be.

Unfortunately, there are many difficulties in interpreting this incident. If a virulent epidemic had struck Cofitachequi, then why had it not similarly affected people living elsewhere in the Southeast? Would the buffer zones have been sufficient to impede the spread of the disease? And if the pathogen causing the disease was brought in by Lucas Vázquez de Ayllón's colonists, why did it take twelve years to reach Cofitachequi? Or perhaps the Spaniards misinterpreted what the people of Cofitachequi told them. That is, perhaps the loss of life in Cofitachequi was exacerbated by a drought, which in turn caused starvation.[38] Severe drought may also have impacted the people of Casqui and Pacaha. Between 1565 and 1575 the Carolina area is known to have experienced a severe drought, and they may have been feeling the initial effects as early as 1539–43.[39] It is also possible that the disease that affected Cofitachequi was a slow-moving disease—perhaps a venereal disease or a disease, such as typhus or malaria, transmitted by an animal intermediary.

It is possible that members of the De Soto expedition themselves carried pathogens into the Southeast, but there is no conclusive proof that they did. The one place where the chroniclers mention that members of the expedition were dying from illness was in the winter of 1542, when they returned to

Arkansas after an arduous march to east Texas and back, and after having suffered hunger and prolonged exposure to cold, wet weather. Whatever this illness was, some of them died of it, and the pathogens causing the illness may have been present among them for the entire duration of the expedition.

After the founding of St. Augustine in 1565, Spain began a continuous colonial presence in the Southeast. In the tiny towns and missions of Spanish Florida, both sexes and all ages of Spaniards were present, and there was a continuous coming and going of people from the stewpot of diseases endemic in the Caribbean and in Europe. Moreover, there was at least some traffic between these towns and missions and Indian towns in the interior. Hence, it is likely that the principal impact of epidemics on the Indians of the Southeast was during the last quarter of the sixteenth century and the first quarter of the seventeenth century, and mounting archaeological evidence confirms this.

There are still many questions to be answered about the Indians' demographic decline. Following the De Soto expedition, the next Spanish expedition to penetrate the interior was led by Tristán de Luna y Arellano in 1559–61. At least one of Luna's colonists was a survivor of the De Soto expedition. After Luna's colonists began starving at Pensacola Bay, he looked to the interior to find a native society that could produce enough food to feed his people. It is surely significant that he did not attempt to find succor in the domain of Tascaluza, the center of power on the Alabama River twenty years earlier, at the time of the De Soto expedition. Tascaluza's chiefdom had been seriously damaged from the battle that was fought at Mabila. And indeed, there is every indication that by the time of the Luna expedition, Tascaluza's chiefdom had completely disintegrated. Even the people of Nanipacana located on the Alabama River in present-day Wilcox or southwestern Dallas County, where Luna's colonists settled, complained to him of their decline as a consequence of the actions of "a certain captain," who can have been no other than De Soto.[40]

When his colonists began starving at Nanipacana, Luna sent a detachment of soldiers to Coosa, which was remembered as a very rich province. When this detachment reached Coosa, they found that this chiefdom was still extant, but they said it was not the abundant province they expected to find. Moreover, one of Coosa's tributaries, the Napochies, were in active rebellion and had in fact killed some of Coosa's subjects.[41] But while Coosa had seemingly suffered some decline by 1560, the paramount chief of Coosa still had enough clout in 1567 to organize a coalition of chiefs and to threaten Juan Pardo so effectively that he aborted his expedition in the Tennessee Valley.[42]

Although the evidence is imperfect, in 1566–68 Juan Pardo saw less robustness in the chiefdom of Cofitachequi than he saw in the paramount chiefdom of Coosa. Cofitachequi was still a town in 1566–68, but there is no evidence of a chief approaching the stature of the cacica whom De Soto had encountered.[43]

To date, the best evidence on the effects of Old World diseases on Indians in the Southeast is from the paramount chiefdom of Coosa and from neighboring areas in South Carolina, Georgia, and Alabama. Archaeologists have unearthed several kinds of evidence for rapid depopulation in the territory of Coosa. This includes the discovery of graves containing the remains of several individuals interred together. Except in instances of retainer burial, Mississippian peoples ordinarily buried only a single individual in a grave. The discovery of several multiple burials in the territory of the paramount chiefdom of Coosa, therefore, suggests that many people were dying at one time.[44]

Moreover, in the several decades following the De Soto expedition, the total number of towns and villages in Coosa decreased, and eventually the territory of Coosa was abandoned by the people, who began migrating down the Coosa River, probably concentrating their population as they moved. These concentrations or coalescences of population appear to have migrated further down the river episodically, about every thirty or forty years, and with each move the number of towns became fewer. The chiefdom of Coosa, with its many towns on the Coosawattee River at the time of De Soto's expedition, had, by the early eighteenth century, coalesced into a single town near present-day Childersburg, Alabama.

By the middle of the seventeenth century, few people lived in eastern Tennessee in the former territory of the paramount chiefdom of Coosa. By the early eighteenth century, several of the towns situated in this area at the time of the De Soto expedition had moved to the area near the junction of the Coosa and Tallapoosa Rivers in Alabama. For a time, the central and northern parts of the former territory of the paramount chiefdom of Coosa became a wilderness.[45]

Severe depopulation and coalescence were evident in the late sixteenth century among the formerly dense populations along the Mississippi River. By 1673, when Marquette and Joliet explored the Mississippi River down to the mouth of the Arkansas River, Casqui, Pacaha, Quizquiz, Aquixo, and Quigualtam were nowhere to be seen. The great fleets of riverine warriors were no more. In the late seventeenth century the principal native populations appear to have been concentrated near the mouth of the Arkansas River and in the area of present-day Natchez, Mississippi. However, small communities of people living back away from the channel of the river probably escaped the notice of the Frenchmen in their canoes.[46]

Regionwide archaeological sampling of Caddoan settlements has not been done, and as a consequence reliable estimates of Caddoan population just prior to the De Soto expedition cannot be made. Nonetheless, several drastic changes in cultural usages in the Caddoan area in the late sixteenth century argue that the Caddoans experienced the same precipitous decline in population as did other areas in the Southeast. They ceased building and maintaining mounds, and they ceased interring their elaborate elite burials in shafts in mounds. Some areas, such as the Arkansas River basin in Oklahoma, were abandoned, and along with this, Caddoan people developed a more mobile way of life based on employing their newly acquired horses to hunt buffalo. In other places in the Caddoan area, the survivors of collapsed populations coalesced, seemingly in the same way as in other parts of the Southeast.[47]

The general archaeological picture of the Southeastern chiefdoms between about 1550 and 1650 is the same everywhere. The populations declined sharply; some areas became very thinly populated, or even abandoned; the construction and maintenance of platform mounds ceased; and the level of ritual and artistic elaboration decreased. From Apalachee to Cofitachequi to Chiaha to Coosa to Pacaha to Tanico to Naguatex the general picture is the same. Some areas, such as the Cherokee-speaking people of the Appalachian Mountains and the Caddoan-speaking people of the Red and Ouachita Rivers, may have for a time been spared the worst, but in the end the germs and viruses exacted their terrible toll everywhere. The severe drought between 1549 and 1577 may have caused a dietary shortfall, but the principal killers were the diseases.[48]

What was the extent of this population collapse? It is very difficult to give a quantitative answer. Early estimates of the native population of North America were quite low because at the time these estimates were made the role of Old World disease was not appreciated. For example, early in the twentieth century, James Mooney estimated the sixteenth-century Indian population north of Mexico at 1,153,000, and he estimated the population of the Southeast (his South Atlantic, Gulf, and Caddoan populations) at 178,000.[49] In recent years the pendulum has swung the other way. Henry Dobyns, for example, using estimates of population that could theoretically have been supported by his estimates of available foodstuffs, corroborated by his projections of population decline of as much as 20 to 1, places the population of America north of Mexico at 18 million—an estimate that is 15.6 times higher than Mooney's. Dobyns's estimate for the eastern United States (an area somewhat larger than Mooney's) is 9,258,000.[50] Many scholars, however, argue that these estimates are far too high.

Must we strike a mean between these two extremes, or is there some other way to arrive at a more trustworthy estimate? Again, the excellent quality of archaeological evidence for the paramount chiefdom of Coosa allows for better estimates. Several of the late prehistoric towns of Coosa have been extensively excavated, and the majority of them have been sampled, so that estimates of the total population can be obtained, and likewise the total number of towns of the paramount chiefdom of Coosa can be estimated. Using such information, the population of the paramount chiefdom of Coosa is estimated to have been 30,000 to 50,000 individuals, and the average town had about 600 people. The sixteenth-century population of the central towns of Coosa alone, plus the Abihka towns in the vicinity of present-day Rome, Georgia, is estimated to have been 11,947. In 1715 a census of descendants of these same Coosa-Abihka towns shows 1,733 individuals—a decline of 6.47 to 1, a far lower rate of decline than that proposed by Dobyns.[51]

Using early censuses, head counts, and estimates, Peter Wood has estimated that the total Indian population of the Southeast in 1685 was about 200,000 people.[52] If the 6.47-to-1 rate of decline in Coosa may be applied across the board in the Southeast, perhaps we can use Wood's figure to estimate the sixteenth-century population of the Southeast at 1,294,000.

In some places, at least for a time, some populations of native people remained in place. This was the case in the territory of the paramount chiefdom of Ocute, where the large towns were abandoned and people dispersed to live in very small villages in the surrounding uplands. This was also the case in the territory of Cofitachequi, where the name "Cofitachequi" continued in use until the late seventeenth century. But the name Cofitachequi had disappeared from the map by the early eighteenth century. The population collapsed along the lower Tallapoosa River in Alabama, but societies there may have continued to have a sense of continuity into the early eighteenth century. And a small population remained at Ichisi, in central Georgia, until the early eighteenth century, when the area was abandoned.

Several kinds of archaeological evidence indicate that the Southeastern chiefdoms began undergoing major structural failure within a few decades of the De Soto expedition. The construction of mounds—perhaps the most characteristic artifacts of the chiefdoms—evidently ceased by the end of the sixteenth century. Mounds continued to be used after this time in some places, but very few were built anew or enlarged. Likewise, by the early seventeenth century, the ordering of polities into hierarchies of small and large towns ceased in most places. In particular, the large mound sites were abandoned. In addition, the elaborate shell and copper status markers no longer show up in burials. By the middle of the seventeenth century, a little more than a century after the seven Spanish bergantines made their desperate run down the Mississippi River, all of these changes had occurred in most places. This implies that the uppermost echelons of the chiefdoms had failed by this time, leaving the survivors to organize themselves along simpler lines.

The Lost World of the Southeastern Chiefdoms

Precious little of the world De Soto and his men explored has survived the ravages of time. Hardly anything remains on the landscape today that one can experience directly with one's senses to conjure up anything of the chiefdoms of the sixteenth-century Southeast. If the people of the Southeastern chiefdoms had built stone houses that could have survived the centuries, their place in the history of the early South might not have evaded scholars for so long. But the building materials of the Southeastern chiefdoms were impermanent: earth, wood, cane, bark, thatch, and clay. And to make things even more perishable, they lived in a land of ample rain and acidic soils.

The material fallout of everyday life in the chiefdoms is there in the soil for archaeologists to excavate and interpret. But these artifacts (mostly broken into pieces), as well as traces of human behavior in the soil, do not speak to us directly and familiarly. They only yield their meaning through archaeological interpretation, and such interpretation is all too often cast in language that the layman is unwilling or unable to penetrate.

The only obvious remains left by the chiefdoms of the Southeast are their platform and burial mounds. These were the symbolic centers of their social worlds, and their falling into disuse is one of the most significant indications of the demise of an entire way of life. Many of these mounds have been destroyed in the past century and a half by farmers, by builders of dams for hydroelectric power and flood control, and by other large-scale earth-disturbing endeavors. But a few of the mounds remain, and they are today not only precious repositories of archaeological information on the ancient chiefdoms but also the material objects that most directly evoke the world of the Mississippian chiefdoms and of the Spaniards who so abruptly entered their lives as harbingers of a long decline. A few of these mounds have been preserved (often after being partially or wholly reconstructed) and some of them have been enhanced with small museums and visitors centers. These include the Lake Jackson mounds near Tallahassee, Florida (ancestors of members of the Apalachee chiefdom); the Lamar mounds at the Ocmulgee National Monument at Macon, Georgia (chiefdom of Ichisi); the Town Creek mounds near

Mt. Gilead, North Carolina (probably subsidiary to the paramount chiefdom of Cofitachequi); the Etowah mounds at Cartersville, Georgia (chiefdom of Itaba, subsidiary of the paramount chiefdom of Coosa); Moundville, Alabama (chiefdom of Apafalaya); the Chucalissa mounds at Memphis, Tennessee (subsidiary of the chiefdom of Quizquiz and the paramount chiefdom of Pacaha); the Monks mound and several smaller mounds at the Cahokia site in East St. Louis; the Parkin mound site at Parkin, Arkansas (chiefdom of Casqui); the Spiro mounds at Spiro, Oklahoma (probably ancestral to members of the chiefdom of Cayas); and the George C. Davis mounds near Alto, Texas (whose people were probably ancestral to those of the chiefdom of Guasco).

The sixteenth-century Spanish explorers of the Southeast—De Soto as well as Tristán de Luna in 1559–61 and Juan Pardo in 1566–68—left behind only the thinnest scatter of material remains. They were premodern people, whose material possessions were few, and everything they possessed was carried on the back of a human, a horse, or a mule. Only in the past fifteen years or so have archaeologists learned to recognize some of the artifacts these people carried (fig. 85). The most notable of these are certain types of glass beads (Nueva Cadiz and chevron); the copper Clarksdale bells they attached to the trappings on their horses; sword fragments from various sites and a complete sword from the King site in northern Georgia, probably the site of Apica (the first "Piachi" in Rangel's narrative); horseshoes; large-headed wrought-iron nails; small iron chisels and wedges; and points from crossbow bolts. In two places— the locales of Nondacao in east Texas and Pacaha in northeastern Arkansas— archaeologists have excavated ceramic "stemmed vessels" made by the Indians (fig. 86). Seemingly these are copies of chalices or stemmed cups the Indians may have seen the Spaniards using.[53] The entire collection of these Spanish-era artifacts could almost be accommodated on the top of a good-sized conference table. When plotted on a map (map 9), the sites where they have been found generally fall on or near the routes that have recently been reconstructed for the travels of De Soto, Luna, and Pardo.

Assailed by Old World diseases, the populations of the Southeastern chiefdoms collapsed. But a small percentage of the total population survived, and their genetic descendants still live in the Southeast, as well as in Oklahoma, and in fact today their genes are scattered to the four winds. Some contemporary Southeastern Indians claim to be "full-bloods," but it is to be doubted that there are many, if any, who do not possess genes that originated in other parts of the world. There is no reason to think that members of De Soto's expedition—either European or African—refrained from having sexual intercourse with Indian women. And the same is true of later times. Many of the Indians

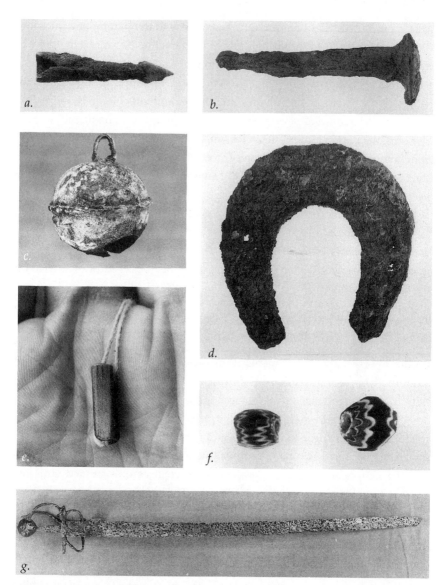

Fig. 85. Selected sixteenth-century European artifacts found at archaeological sites in the Southeast. They are shown in various scales. *a.* Iron point from a crossbow bolt (length 1⅝″), Governor Martin site (Anhayca, Apalachee), (Florida Division of Historical Resources); *b.* Large-headed wrought-iron nail (length 2⅝″), Berry site (Joara), (North Carolina Division of Archives and History, Western Office); *c.* Clarksdale bell (diameter 1⅜″), Little Egypt site (a locality of Talisi), (Marvin T. Smith); *d.* Horseshoe (length 5⅛″), Hightower site (a locality of Talisi), (University of Alabama Museums); *e.* Nueva Cadiz bead (length ⅝″), Moundville locality (Apafalaya), (University of Alabama Museums); *f.* Chevron beads (length 5/16″), Parkin site (Casqui), (Marvin T. Smith); *g.* Sword (length 40″), King site ("Piachi," i.e., possibly Apica), (Richard Polhemus).

Fig. 86. A "chalice" vessel (height 5″) from the Johns site in Camp County, Texas, probably a locality of Nondacao. White kaolin clay was rubbed into the incised lines. (Robert L. Turner Jr.)

of the Southeast observed matrilineal descent, and one's paternity was far less important socially than one's maternity. Hence, there is every reason to think that the children who were born of these unions were incorporated into the native societies. In fact, they and their descendants are likely to have been biologically better able to survive the diseases that continued to strike the Indians until our present century.

Genetic descendants of the chiefdoms still live in certain parts of the Southeast today—on the Seminole and Mikasuki reservations in Florida, on the Qualla Boundary in North Carolina, and on the Choctaw Reservation near Philadelphia, Mississippi. There are even places where modern variants of the names of societies that appear in the documents of the sixteenth-century expeditions are still in use for Indian groups today. These are names like Catawba (Cataba), Chickasaw (Chicaza), Alabama (Alibamo), Koasati (Coste), and Tunica (Tanico). But such continuities of name are deceiving. Though the names that people use to refer to themselves may continue to be used for hundreds of years, the societies to which the names refer may, over the course of time, change almost unrecognizably. The Southeastern Indians who survived into the eighteenth century had to organize their lives in terms of social and cultural structures that were very different from the social and cultural structures of the sixteenth-century chiefdoms.

At the turn of the eighteenth century the survivors of the epidemics found themselves faced by unprecedented challenges. The populations of the fiercely independent chiefdoms had declined to a fraction of their original number. They suffered an incalculable loss of knowledge and traditional practices. Old

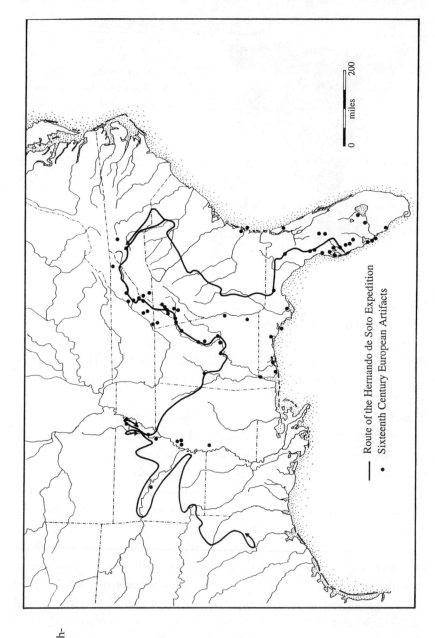

Map 9.
Archaeological site
locations of sixteenth-
century European
artifacts. (Courtesy,
Marvin T. Smith)

—— Route of the Hernando de Soto Expedition
• Sixteenth Century European Artifacts

miles
0   200

ways of minimizing the level of violence between chiefdoms and within chiefdoms undoubtedly broke down. Life in the Southeast must have become less predictable and palpably more hazardous. Catholic missionaries in Spanish Florida and in French Louisiana devoted their lives to trying to win the Indians over to a new religion, new languages, and new ways of thinking and doing. An even more severe threat was posed by the English, who came on the cutting edge of a new, cheap, and highly effective way of organizing and running the world economy. The English came to trade and to make money, using an economic system whose by-product was an inevitable, progressive erosion of the economic and social institutions of the native people (fig. 87).

In the eighteenth century the Southeastern Indians had to put themselves together into new societies in which they could cope with the inhospitable new world in which they found themselves. Quite naturally, they tried to

Fig. 87. Indian hunters in early eighteenth-century Georgia. The hunter at left wears a painted deerskin matchcoat and is armed with a bow and arrow. The Indian on the right wears a European trade blanket, and he is armed with a flintlock gun. He has a copper kettle in his pack basket, and he holds a rum bottle. (Royal Library, Copenhagen)

organize themselves as much as possible in terms of their old beliefs and social arrangements. The traditional ways were strongest in places where the
Spanish and the French were dominant. The principal examples of such traditionalist societies were the Apalachees, Caddos, and Natchez. In the early seventeenth century the Apalachee chiefs realized that their bases of authority
were eroding, and they invited the Spanish missionaries into their towns to
strengthen their positions, to give them some stability. In 1633 the Spaniards
established a mission system in Apalachee, and it endured until 1704 (fig. 88),
when the English crushed it in a matter of a few months.[54] The Apalachees retained some of their old myths into the early eighteenth century, myths that
justified the legitimacy of their ruling chiefs.[55] But the presence of Lamar pottery from the interior in seventeenth-century Apalachee archaeological sites is
testimony that they were absorbing people who were migrating south from
the old territory of Ocute, and probably from Ichisi and Toa as well.

In the west, large areas that had been occupied mainly by Caddoan-
speaking peoples were abandoned, and the survivors clustered together in
several places. In the territory of Naguatex, the Kadohadacho confederacy
formed (fig. 89). Other Caddoan-speaking people moved out onto the Plains,

Fig. 88. San Luís, the principal Apalachee mission, ca. 1680–1700, in present-day
Tallahassee. Based upon archaeological and historical evidence, it depicts the plank-
and-thatch church on a market day. Drawing by Edward Jones. (Florida Division of
Historical Resources)

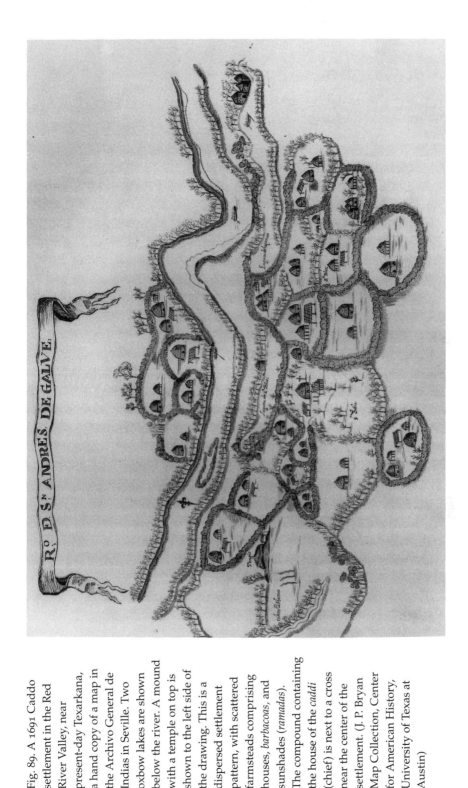

Fig. 89. A 1691 Caddo settlement in the Red River Valley, near present-day Texarkana, a hand copy of a map in the Archivo General de Indias in Seville. Two oxbow lakes are shown below the river. A mound with a temple on top is shown to the left side of the drawing. This is a dispersed settlement pattern, with scattered farmsteads comprising houses, *barbacoas*, and sunshades (*ramadas*). The compound containing the house of the *cadi* (chief) is next to a cross near the center of the settlement. (J. P. Bryan Map Collection, Center for American History, University of Texas at Austin)

fashioning a new way of life based upon the horse and the buffalo. In eastern Texas, in the area of Guasco, the Hasinai confederacy formed. And a third Caddo population, smaller than the other two, settled around the French trading post at present-day Natchitoches, Louisiana. For a time, some of the Caddos maintained temples in which sacred fires burned perpetually, and they were governed by a hereditary elite.[56]

By far the most extreme example of the traditionalist coalescent societies were the Natchez, who were located in the territory of the unnamed chiefdom that sent a fleet of canoes in pursuit of Moscoso and his men after they got away from the canoes of Quigualtam. The principal town of the Natchez lay near the present-day town of the same name in the state of Mississippi. The Natchez kept up their mounds into the early eighteenth century, and their chief, the Great Sun, lived in a house built on top of one of the mounds. They, too, kept a perpetual fire burning in a temple. On certain ritual occasions they carried the Great Sun about on a litter, in much the same way, though less grandly, as the chief of Coosa was carried. Finally, and most extraordinarily, they practiced retainer burial into the early eighteenth century. When a notable person died, several individuals stepped forward to be strangled (fig. 90) and

Fig. 90. Natchez mortuary ceremony for Tattooed-Serpent, a high-status person. In the background is a mound with a temple on top, surmounted by carved wooden birds. The corpse of Tattooed-Serpent is being carried on a litter. The eight seated individuals are to be strangled and buried along with the corpse of Tattooed-Serpent. Drawing in Antoine Simon Le Page du Pratz, *Histoire de la Louisiane*, vol. 3, opposite p. 55. (Hargrett Rare Book and Manuscript Library, University of Georgia Libraries)

then buried along with the notable individual.[57] The Natchez have long been regarded by scholars either as possessing unique social arrangements in the annals of humankind, or else as representing survivals of the Mississippian way of life. Neither of these interpretations is accurate. The Natchez did retain some archaic social institutions, but they had absorbed peoples from shattered societies, as had all the other native societies in the early eighteenth-century Southeast; and the early French observers who described the Natchez misperceived and misunderstood their social system.

None of these traditionalist societies had much staying power. The Apalachee were crushed in 1704 by a series of raids by English colonists and their Indian mercenaries from the Carolina colony. The Natchez were extirpated in 1729–30, after having revolted against the French colonists. The Caddos lay far to the west of the English sphere of influence, and this gave them some insulation from the new economic and political forces. But as the eighteenth century wore on, they gradually gave up their old-time ways.

The majority of the descendants of the Southeastern chiefdoms organized themselves in a different way. They have been called "confederacies," "tribes," "nations," and so on, but in fact we still do not have an adequate vocabulary to describe these peoples. For convenience we can call them "coalescent" societies. They were all, in varying degrees, coalescences of peoples from different societies, cultures, and languages. But what is more important, they made more accommodation than did the traditionalists to the new economic system spearheaded by the English, and to a lesser extent by the French. They entered into a series of new occupations—professional hunter, mercenary, slave catcher, horse thief, prostitute, and so on. In this way they could purchase the guns, ammunition, cloth, and tools on which their existence came to depend.

These coalescent societies included people like the Catawbas, who coalesced in the territory of Cofitachequi, absorbing people from shattered societies in North Carolina, South Carolina, and backcountry Virginia.[58] The descendants of the paramount chiefdom of Coosa coalesced—along with many other peoples—to form the Upper Creeks on the Coosa and Tallapoosa Rivers in central Alabama, and the Lower Creeks on the lower Chattahoochee River on the boundary of Alabama and Georgia.[59] The Chickasaws coalesced near Tupelo, Mississippi, just north of the territory of old Chicaza; more than any other Southeastern Indians, they embraced the interests of the English deerskin and slave traders, and for a time they were the scourge of all the other native peoples around them. The Choctaws coalesced in the area encircled by the great bend of the upper Pearl River, in Mississippi, in an area that previously had very little population, absorbing peoples from the Yazoo Basin and also peoples from the east.[60] The Quapaw, composed mainly of Dhegiha Siouan-speaking peoples, coalesced near the mouth of the Arkansas River, and their origins are still debated.[61]

Some of the Cherokee-speaking people continued living in the mountains, where they became known as the Middle and Valley Cherokees. Other Cherokee-speaking people—the Overhills—moved down to occupy choice agricultural lands on the Little Tennessee River that had been vacated by the subjects of the paramount chiefdom of Coosa. Other Cherokee-speakers may have lived on the headwaters of the Savannah and Chattahoochee Rivers. These Cherokees, known as the Lower Towns, may also have coalesced with some remnant populations from Georgia and South Carolina. These Lower Towns may have absorbed some people who spoke languages other than Cherokee.

Whereas the traditionalists retained ritual and religious practices that strove to keep the old hierarchical social order alive, the coalescent societies developed ways of maintaining a new equality among the various components of their society. This difference was noted by René-Robert Cavelier de La Salle and his comrades on their two expeditions into the Mississippi Valley. When La Salle visited the Quapaws in 1682, they enacted on his behalf an elaborate greeting ritual that symbolically put all concerned on an equal footing with each other. But when some of La Salle's people visited the Caddoans in 1687, the greeting ritual was intent on dramatizing hierarchy, the divine rights of chiefs, as it were.[62]

The discontinuities in Southeastern Indian culture between the sixteenth century and the eighteenth century were very great. For some decades after the boats of the survivors of the De Soto expedition made their hurried way down the Mississippi River, the native peoples remembered the Spaniards. In 1559, when Tristán de Luna sent a party of men to Nanipacana, which was not far down the Alabama River from old Mabila, the people complained that they had once been great, but they had suffered terribly from Spaniards (i.e., De Soto) who had been there years before Luna arrived.[63] In 1567, when members of the Juan Pardo expedition reached Satapo, on the Little Tennessee River, the Indians told him that a Spaniard—De Soto—had been there earlier and had killed many people. Years later, a member of the Pardo expedition claimed to have seen at Satapo pictures of Spanish lancers the Indians had painted on the walls of their houses.[64]

Memories of the De Soto expedition were still alive as late as the spring of 1606, when Fray Martín Prieto was sent from St. Augustine to the province of

Potano in northern Florida, near the towns of Potano and Utinamocharra on the De Soto route. His missionizing was met with a great deal of opposition by the Indians, and eventually he learned that the chief of this place, a very old man, had suffered greatly at the hands of De Soto and his men. Prieto went to talk to this chief, but when he entered the chief's house the man turned his face to the wall, foamed at the mouth in rage, and ordered his subjects to give Prieto a beating and throw him out.[65] Obviously, his memory of De Soto was quite vivid. When Thomas Nairne, a Carolinian diplomat with wide experience with the Indians of the Southeast, visited the Chickasaws in 1708, he said they were the only Indians he had met who had any memory of De Soto. "Some old men here show the way they [the Spaniards] entered and Departed out of their Nation with the Hill where they Encampt."[66]

In the cultural and social discontinuity that came with the disintegration of the chiefdoms, not only was De Soto's memory largely forgotten by the Indians, but so was their own former world of hierarchical societies. By the end of the eighteenth century, many Southeastern Indians professed to have no knowledge of who had built the platform mounds. The naturalist William Bartram traveled extensively in the Southeast in 1765–66 and 1773–77, and he noted many mounds in the course of his travels. But in his *Travels*, published in 1791, Bartram concluded that the mounds had been built by an ancient "nation" who inhabited the land before they were conquered by Cherokees and Creeks. The mounds were so ancient, wrote Bartram, "that the Cherokees, Creeks, or the nation they conquered, could render no account for what purpose these monuments were raised."[67]

By the late eighteenth century, the Southeastern Indians had not only forgotten who had built the mounds, they had no memory of a social order based on hierarchy and inherited authority. James Adair, who lived among the Southeastern Indians as a trader from about 1735 to 1768, and who knew them well, says of the Indians that they "have no such titles or persons as emperors, or kings; nor an appelative for such, in any of their dialects. Their highest title, either in military or civil life, signifies only a *chieftain*; they have no words to express despotic power, arbitrary kings, oppressed, or obedient subjects. . . . The power of their chiefs is an empty sound. . . . It is reputed merit alone, that gives them any titles of distinction above the meanest people."[68] Adair evidently told some of his Indian friends about the Aztecs, and they denied that there had ever been "red emperors, and great empires in America."[69] One surmises that had Adair given them a description of the chiefs of Cofitachequi, Coosa, Tascaluza, and Pacaha, their reaction would have been similar.

By the late nineteenth and early twentieth centuries, the dilution of the

Fig. 91. A Cherokee log cabin on the Qualla Reservation, North Carolina. Photograph by James Mooney in the late nineteenth century. The man pictured here may be Swimmer, Mooney's principal informant. (National Anthropological Archives, Smithsonian Institution)

cultural components of the chiefdoms had proceeded even further (fig. 91). Mounds figured into several of the myths James Mooney collected from the Cherokees at the end of the nineteenth century. They told stories of mounds in which fires perpetually burned and from which spirit warriors could suddenly emerge to fight the enemies of the Cherokees. They also retained a memory of a special class of people they called the *Ani-kutani,* who possessed hereditary privileges and whose eminence depended upon their being descended from spiritual beings in the Upper World. The Cherokees remembered them as excessively haughty people who victimized other Cherokees, and for this reason the Cherokees had exterminated them. This myth of the Ani-kutani may have been a vestigial memory of an older, more hierarchical Cherokee social order.[70]

Vestigial mounds have been built on the ceremonial grounds of Southeastern Indians in Oklahoma in this century. They are roughly circular in shape, and no more than a foot or two high. But small as they are, they were built in close relation to other ceremonial structures, and they were ascended by dancers in certain of the dances performed in the course of the summer Green Corn Ceremony.[71]

The question often arises, most particularly in the state of Arkansas, as to whether any of De Soto's pigs escaped and were ancestors of the wild hogs of the later South. It is a reasonable question, because no domesticated animal reverts to the wild as readily as pigs do. They are adaptable and aggressive, and they can defend themselves against predators. Mature boars fight by thrashing their heads from side to side, and in so doing they can inflict painful wounds with their tusks—their elongated, curved canine teeth. When aroused, they open and close their mouths with great rapidity, and the frightful popping sound this makes is often enough to inspire an intruder to run as fast as possible or take to the trees.

There were many occasions in which pigs could have gotten separated from De Soto's herd and stranded in the wilderness. For example, when they crossed the Savannah River several pigs were swept downstream and lost. And when the Chicazas set fire to the Spanish camp in early spring of 1541, the small piglets were able to squeeze through cracks in their burning sty and escape, and some of them may have got away. After Moscoso and the army returned from their failed foray into east Texas and were building their boats at Aminoya, some Indians of Guachoya brought them pigs that had been born to a sow that had remained behind. Pigs could have escaped almost anywhere along the route, but they could have been founders of the lineage of southern wild hogs only if a male and female escaped together, or if a pregnant sow escaped and gave birth to a male.

It can be said that there is no uncontestable evidence that the wild hogs of the South have De Soto's hogs in their ancestry, and there is some indirect evidence that they do not. That is, hogs are extremely fecund, and in the wild they multiply very rapidly. Yet there is no evidence that wild hogs were numerous in the early eighteenth-century South, as they surely would have been if they had been breeding there since the sixteenth century.[72]

Finally, we might ask what remains of the leafy theater in which the drama of the De Soto expedition unfolded—the varied, magnificent old-growth forest that stretched from Florida and the Atlantic coast westward into eastern Texas? Large areas of the Southeast are today covered in forest, but only vestiges of true old-growth forest remain. Tiny remnants of Florida scrub remain in present-day Highland County, Florida. Only a few thousand protected acres of old-growth longleaf pine and wiregrass forest survive at places like the Ichauway research center in Baker County, Georgia. The oak-hickory-pine forest of the Appalachian Mountains can be seen in places in the Great Smoky Mountains National Park, but conspicuously missing are the chestnut trees that once dominated this forest. These were all killed by a fungus that infected them early in the twentieth century. Very small tracts of the southern floodplain forest are preserved in places like the Delta National Forest in Mississippi.

In these precious remnants of this once vast southeastern forest of the sixteenth century, one can walk today and imagine knights from Spain on a doomed quest, pitted against the agile warriors of chiefdoms whose rulers were said to be descendants of the Sun.

Afterword

I have tried to depict the reality of the De Soto expedition in a smooth narrative, leaving out the clutter of intricate scholarly judgments and arguments that underlay my particular interpretation. But the fact is, as all De Soto scholars know, that while the De Soto expedition may be depicted as a historical event that flows like a river from its source to its end, it flows in a scholarly streambed of obdurate shoals, difficult passages, obstructions, and dead-end cut-offs. This afterword is intended for readers who are interested in this streambed.

The Documentary Sources

Most of what can currently be known about the De Soto expedition comes from four chronicles: three are firsthand, or substantially firsthand, and one is a secondary account. Of the three firsthand De Soto chronicles, the one that modern De Soto scholars have most relied on in reconstructing the day-by-day movements and activities of the expedition is the one produced by Rodrigo Rangel, De Soto's secretary.[1] It is reasonable to think that one of Rangel's duties was to prepare a record of the expedition for the time when De Soto would be required to give an accounting of himself before royal officials. But with De Soto dead, it was Rangel himself who gave a report on the expedition before the Audiencia Real in Santo Domingo. At that time he was commanded to give his written account of the expedition to Gonzalo Fernández de Oviedo y Valdés, who was royal historian of the Indies. Thus, Oviedo had access to both written and oral information from Rangel. One infers from the detailed, day-by-day information in Rangel's account that it is based upon a diary that was written during the course of the expedition. A serious problem in assessing the veracity of the Rangel account is that Rangel's original diary is not known to have survived. Thus, we only know Rangel's narrative through Oviedo, who drew on Rangel's information to write a narrative that is included in book 17 of his *Historia general y naturel de las Indias.* Lacking Rangel's diary, there is no way to directly assess changes, deletions, and distortions introduced by Oviedo. It is clear that Oviedo occasionally inserts his own words into the narrative. In some instances, one can recognize Oviedo's voice, as for example, when he castigates De Soto for committing adultery when he was at Casqui and Pacaha, and when he faults him for having continued the expedition past Cofitachequi.[2] Occasionally one is unsure whether one is reading Rangel's or Oviedo's words. For example, is it Rangel or Oviedo who is responsible for the probably erroneous first of two uses of the Piachi place-name (i.e., the one that occurs near Ulibahali)?[3]

But for all these uncertainties, the Rangel chronicle recounts many more day-by-day events than any of the other chronicles, and except for Oviedo's moralizing and second-guessing, it appears to be a straightforward narrative of what Rangel thought happened. For these reasons, I have used the Rangel account to lay out the fundamental shape of the expedition, for as long as his narrative lasts. And I have used the other chronicles for corroboration and amplification.

It is a minor tragedy that the last two chapters of Rangel's account are missing. A list of the contents of these two chapters is included in Oviedo's *Historia,* but the texts are missing. Either Oviedo never finished the writing of these two chapters, or else they were lost before publication. The consequence of this is that for the final twenty-three months of the expedition, our reconstructed chronology has many gaps, and often one can only estimate within the space of several days when particular events occurred.

Rangel's account was not published in Spanish until 1851, when a new edition of book 17 of Oviedo's *Historia* saw print. The first English translation was published in 1904. The literal English translation recently prepared by John Worth is to be preferred over previous translations.[4]

The only chronicle that still exists in manuscript form is that of Luys Hernández de Biedma, who was factor for the expedition and was therefore responsible to the crown. This account was written in 1544, seemingly from memory, on the occasion of his testifying before the Consejo de Indias, and it is signed by Biedma. Because it was written from memory rather than from a journal, Biedma's is an occasion-by-occasion, rather than a day-by-day, account. It is less than half the length of what has survived of Rangel's narrative, but because Biedma, of all the chroniclers, remembered the broadly figured directions in which they traveled for days or weeks at a time, his account is crucial in reconstructing the route, and on occasion he reports details missing from the other accounts. For example, only Biedma describes the cane fence the people of Casqui built around the cross De Soto ordered erected, and only he describes the reed houses of the hunters who lived to the northwest of Pacaha.[5] Biedma's account is a straightforward report to royal officials, with little commentary or obvious embellishment.

The string of incidents recounted by Biedma accords well with that of Rangel, though the events are described in far less detail, and they are not attached to dates. But the Biedma document is not without its problems. One major problem is that while Biedma is generally to be relied on for directions traveled, he says that when they started out from where they landed, they went westward before turning northwestward. Since they landed on the west coast of Florida, such a turn would have required them to walk on water. I can only conclude that this is an error or blunder of Biedma or his copyist. That is, he wrote the opposite of what was intended.[6] There are also a few discrepancies between Biedma and other chronicles. Biedma, for example, says that De Soto's men first noted the Indians building semisubterranean houses at Capachequi, while the Gentleman of Elvas puts this observation at the next stop to the north, at Toa.[7] Occasionally the variant spellings of place-names in Biedma would seem to have been copyists' errors. For example, the Biedma account has *Viranque* for Rangel's *Utiangüe* and Elvas's *Autiamque*.[8] The *V* is probably a copyist's error.

The Biedma account was first published in a French translation in 1841; then in Spanish in 1857; and in an English translation by Buckingham Smith in 1866. Again, the best translation into English is by John Worth.

The last of the three primary accounts was written in Portuguese by an anonymous gentleman of the town of Elvas. It was first published by André de Burgos in 1557 at Evora, Portugal, fourteen years after the survivors reached Mexico, and was the first of the chronicles to be published. The author—

usually referred to simply as Elvas—wrote an account describing the events of specific days, implying that he based his narrative on a journal. He does not mention as many Indian towns by name as does Rangel, nor as many dates. As one might expect in an independent source, his spellings of Indian place-names often vary from Rangel's, and his dates are sometimes at variance with Rangel's by a day or more. The most common chronological nonconformity is that Elvas tends to set the dates of events one day earlier than Rangel, and less commonly one day later. Several dates in Elvas's chronicle are evidently copyist's errors: for example, Elvas has them arriving at Calahuchi on October 25 instead of October 5; he has them departing from Cofitachequi on May 3 instead of May 13; he has them departing from Mabila on March 18 instead of March 14; De Soto asks the Chicaza chief for porters on March 8 instead of March 3; and he has them arriving at Pacaha on June 19 instead of June 29.[9]

Because of the anonymous authorship of the Elvas narrative, it is even more difficult to critically assess the veracity of this text than it is the Rangel narrative. In a foreword, André de Burgos claims that the manuscript was written in Portuguese by a gentleman of Elvas who experienced all that he wrote about, and Burgos claims not to have altered the text.[10] But even a casual reading of the narrative suggests that there are at least two voices. One is that of a military man with an Extremaduran frame of reference who was loyal to De Soto and close enough to him to have some insight into the inner working of the expedition. The other is that of a person with some literary pretensions who set Indian speeches into the style of the chivalric romances popular in Portugal at that time. In addition, whether on the part of the military man or some other, the text reflects the sensibility of someone who had knowledge of the geography of eastern Portugal.[11]

Elvas's narrative is more than twice as long as that of Rangel's surviving text, and his recording of noteworthy or interesting incidents is more elaborated than Rangel's. In addition to drawing on one or more written records, Elvas must have drawn upon his own memory for some of the incidents, and he did so soon enough after the events that one can have some confidence in the accuracy of his memory. In addition, some of what he wrote about was surely the experience of others told to him orally.

When the narrative of Elvas is compared to that of Rangel, one sees that both recount the same events in the same order, with no major contradictions. The principal difference is that Elvas's account is more elaborated, and the elaborations often contain ethnological and geographical information. Only he, for example, tells of the Indians of Chiaha storing bear fat in gourds, a practice Southeastern Indians continued into the eighteenth century.[12]

What is one to make of this concordance between the Elvas and Rangel narratives? Are we to conclude that the two texts corroborate each other, or on the contrary, that one of them is derived from or cribbed from the other? Before this can be considered, it is most important to realize that De Soto's army was both small and premodern. Numbering only a few hundred men, and with many of them related to each other by ties of blood, marriage, and neighborhood, and with a leadership of only a dozen or so royal officials and officers, the expedition was far more a collective experience than would be the case with a modern army. As De Soto's men—and particularly the officers—discussed their daily experiences, they must have come to agreement on what their most notable experiences were. Much of what they remembered about the expedition was shaped by their collective experiences, and the stories they told are properly termed legends. Each saw the expedition through his own eyes, but also through the eyes of his comrades. And the stories they settled upon were highlighted by the situation in which they found themselves. Thus, they told many stories about the actions of De Soto, who had the power of life and death over them, and they told stories about the Indians against whom they were pitted in a life-or-death struggle. And as premodern men, they were inordinately interested in marvelous occurrences, prophesies, and religious stories.[13] One would expect to find, therefore, a great deal of agreement in the written accounts by participants in this expedition, far more agreement, for example, than one would expect to find in the accounts of the soldiers who participated in General Sherman's Civil War march to the sea.

The question of whether the close agreement between the Elvas and Rangel narratives may be taken as corroboration or as an indication that one was derived from the other has been the subject of scholarly debate. Patricia Galloway has argued that Elvas "lifted information and even phraseology" from Rangel, and specifically from Oviedo's version of Rangel rather than the original diary.[14] Her theory is that André de Burgos procured a copy of Oviedo's version of Rangel when he was in Seville and took it to Portugal where one of the Portuguese participants on the expedition used it as an aide memoire, to which he added his own reminiscences.

It is not implausible, Galloway argues, that Burgos could have seen Oviedo's manuscript. Burgos was a publisher in Seville from 1542 until 1548, and Oviedo was in Spain off and on between 1546 and 1549, attempting to get a new edition of his *Historia* (containing the Rangel narrative) published. It would seem that Burgos knew Oviedo, for in 1545 he published a second edition of Oviedo's *Don Claribalte*, a romance. But adducing evidence that Burgos *could* have seen the manuscript falls far short of proving that he stole or otherwise procured a copy of the manuscript, took it to Portugal with him in 1549 when he set up a publishing house at Evora, waited until after Oviedo was dead, and then used it in the way Galloway has suggested.

Martin and Ivana Elbl argue, on the other hand, that Galloway convicts Burgos in a rush to judgment. Burgos may have published *Claribalte* without Oviedo's permission, and they suggest that Oviedo was somewhat embarrassed by the work and may not have wanted it reprinted. Moreover, Burgos was in debt and going out of business when Oviedo was in Seville and, as such, would not have been an attractive publisher for his revised *Historia*. The Elbls conclude that it is very unlikely that Burgos could have obtained a copy of Oviedo's manuscript of the Rangel narrative.[15]

Has Galloway any evidence that is more than circumstantial? She argues that the Rangel and Elvas narratives are structurally similar, each consisting of a recounting of the journey followed by a summary of geography and natural history. But this argument is vitiated by the fact that so many chronicles of exploration have been cast in this form; it hardly sustains the argument for direct borrowing. For example, John Lawson's account of his travels in the Carolinas in 1699–1700 follows this same form.[16]

Whereas I take the agreement between the Rangel and Elvas narratives to be evidence that they are two different accounts of the same string of experiences, Galloway takes this to be proof that Elvas is cribbed from Rangel. Since these antithetical conclusions follow from precisely the same evidence, other kinds of evidence must be sought.

Galloway argues that similarities in figures of speech used in the two chronicles argue for plagiarism. For example, both Rangel and Elvas describe the mulberry fiber shawls worn by the native women and tell of their habit of wearing one shawl wrapped around the waist, forming a skirt, while draping another over one shoulder and tying it at the right side, leaving the right shoulder exposed. Rangel compares this to the manner in which Bohemians or Egyptians wear their clothing, while Elvas compares it to Gypsies, both of them referring to the same cultural phenomenon in Europe, though using slightly different terms of ethnic identity. This does not necessarily mean, however, that Elvas stole this description from Rangel. If Indian dress was notably similar to the dress of Gypsies, Bohemians, or Egyptians, why should it be surprising that both chroniclers should use this comparison in their attempt to describe it? This may even have been a comparison generally agreed upon by the Spaniards when they first encountered Indians dressed in this fashion. Who can say?

To give another example, Galloway argues that cribbing is indicated because both Elvas and Rangel use the Aztec word *petaca* to describe the boxlike, covered baskets they procured at Cofitachequi and Joara. But sixteenth-century Spaniards used several Amerindian words to refer to New World things, for example, *macana* (war club), *piragua* (long, narrow, flat-bottomed boat), and *barbacoa* (a framework elevated on poles or posts). Both chroniclers, and presumably all the Spaniards on the expedition, used these widespread loanwords.

Galloway's contention that the Elvas narrative is derived from the Rangel narrative is weakened by their use of variant place-names. If Elvas is derived from Rangel, we might ask why their place-names do not agree more closely? Where Rangel has *Utinamocharra*, Elvas has *Utinama*; Rangel has *Aguacaleyquen* and Elvas *Caliquen*; Rangel has *Napituca* and Elvas *Napituca*; Rangel has *Apalu* and Elvas *Hapaluya*; Rangel has *Toa* and Elvas *Toalli*; Rangel has *Canasoga* and Elvas *Canasagua*; Rangel has *Quitamaya* and Elvas *Catamaya*.

I have already noted that while Rangel's and Elvas's dating of many events in the course of the expedition are identical, there are also quite a few events that are dated differently. Some of these differences can be explained as copyists' errors. But the dates that are off by a single day would seem to be more plausibly explained in terms of a second diarist who was not as scrupulous about dating his entries as was Rangel.

Finally, Galloway herself notes that Rangel seemingly allotted only one of the two missing chapters of his narrative to events that occurred between the third winter and the arrival of the survivors in Mexico City. In contrast, Elvas allots sixteen chapters to this stretch of time, a full 35 percent of his narrative. If Elvas was dependent on Rangel, then how is it that he gets along so handily without him in the last third of his narrative, and with no change in style, structure, or tone?[17]

I see no merit to Galloway's argument that Elvas's chronicle is derived from Rangel's, and several indications that it was not so derived. To the extent that Elvas and Rangel agree, they corroborate each other. But this still leaves us with the puzzle of the anonymous authorship of the Elvas narrative. Ivana and Martin Elbl have argued that the text was possibly prepared for publication by a young and inexperienced scholar of the Vasconcelos family in Evora or Elvas. The identity of the soldier who was responsible for the narrative is still unknown. But despite this uncertainty, the Elbls conclude that the Elvas chronicle is "at least as authentic as Oviedo, and infinitely more so than Garcilaso."[18]

The Elvas narrative was translated into English in 1609. It was translated into

French in 1685, and this French translation was again translated into English in 1686. As such, the Elvas narrative was the first of the De Soto chronicles to become accessible to English readers. The first modern English translation of Elvas's chronicle—and one that still has not been improved upon—is that of James A. Robertson in 1933, published by the Florida State Historical Society along with a facsimile of the original Portuguese text.

The fourth De Soto chronicle was written by a man who was a true son of the colonial society that was built on the wreckage of the Inca empire, the fruit of a conquest in which Hernando de Soto was a principal actor. Gómez Suárez de Figuerora was the son of the conquistador Sebastián Garcilaso de la Vega y Vargas and his concubine, Chimpu Oclla, an Inca princess. He was born in 1539, the year in which De Soto sailed from Havana to Tampa Bay and launched his expedition into La Florida. In later life the boy considered himself to have noble ancestry on both sides of his family. On his father's side he could trace his lineage to distinguished soldiers and poets, including his great-uncle Garcilaso de la Vega, who under Italianate influence was one of the founders of modern Spanish poetry. His mother was a niece of Huayca Capac, cousin of both Atahualpa and Huascar, the last Inca kings. For his entire life, the boy attempted to gain social advantage from his doubly elite ancestry. In later life he took the name of his father (as well as that of his great-uncle), styling himself Garcilaso de la Vega, el Inca. Scholars generally refer to him as Garcilaso.[19]

Garcilaso grew up in Cuzco and was bilingual, speaking both Quechua and Spanish. He spent his childhood and adolescence in a time of notable social turmoil. This included the revolt of Gonzalo Pizarro, who rebelled against royal authority. In 1548 Gonzalo Pizarro was defeated and executed. Garcilaso's father had at first sided with Gonzalo Pizarro, but he shifted his allegiance to the royal side before it was too late. Garcilaso's father's house was a place where many Spaniards visiting Cuzco were entertained, including one Gonzalo Silvestre, who had been a member of the De Soto expedition. When Garcilaso was thirteen, he met Silvestre, and it was at this impressionable age that he first heard stories of the expedition.[20] It seems that his father also allowed Garcilaso to have full access to the Inca relatives of Chimpu Occlo, and it was thus that Garcilaso also heard many stories about the culture and glory days of the Inca empire. As a child he played games in the Inca fortress of Sacsahuaman, north of Cuzco. As a young man he witnessed firsthand the erosion of Inca traditions and their replacement by Spanish and Christian traditions.

When Garcilaso's father died in 1559, he left his son a bequest of four thousand pesos in order that he could study in Spain. Soon after the death of his father, Garcilaso went to Spain, never to return to Peru. He took up residence with his father's brother, Alonso de Vargas, in the small town of Montilla, about thirty miles south of Córdoba. Here he lived a moderately privileged life, and to all appearances he was respected by the townspeople.[21] As a young man he had a military career, but not a particularly distinguished one.

Garcilaso had received a rudimentary education in Peru, including the study of Latin. While in Montilla, he evidently improved his education considerably, perhaps under the tutelage of clergy. He read widely, and he especially read the writers of the Italian Renaissance. After his uncle died, Garcilaso became more serious about intellectual matters. In the early 1580s he began translating the Jewish philosopher León Hebreo's *Dialoghi d'amore* from Italian into Spanish. Published in 1590, this work was a notable literary achievement, and Garcilaso evidently owes much to Hebreo for his writing style. Perhaps Garcilaso felt some affinity for this man who was born in Lisbon but fled to Italy when the Jews were expelled in 1492.

By 1586 Garcilaso was at work writing an account of De Soto's expedition into La Florida, though he probably began toying with the idea of writing it many years earlier. Gonzalo Silvestre had returned to Spain and lived not so far from Montilla, at Las Posadas, about twenty miles southwest of Córdoba, and Garcilaso visited him several times, writing down his stories of the De Soto expedition. Although in his book Garcilaso leaves anonymous his principal source of information, there is no question that it was Silvestre. Many of the incidents in *La Florida* are told from the point of view of Silvestre. Garcilaso knew him for about twenty years in Spain, and when Silvestre died, Garcilaso was named one of the executors of his estate. Garcilaso does not explain why he leaves his principal informant anonymous. Although scholars have speculated rather wildly about his motive, in the absence of new information, we cannot say what it was.

Why did Garcilaso undertake to write *La Florida?* One of his stated purposes was that as both a Spaniard and an Indian he had a particular interest in the De Soto expedition. He realized that if he were to die, no one else would go to the trouble of recording Silvestre's stories for posterity. And if Silvestre were to die, Garcilaso would have no other source of testimony about the expedition, or so he said.[22] A second motive, not so explicitly stated, was that he wished to persuade his countrymen that La Florida was a fit place to colonize, that the natives were capable of being Christianized, and that Spain had a duty to protect them from Protestants.[23] Finally, much of what Garcilaso did was motivated by his feeling that though he was a nobleman on two counts, he never attained the status he felt was rightfully his. He was always proud of his Indian ancestry, but he wanted no one to doubt that he was a Spaniard. And if he was an author of admired writings, the very model of a Renaissance scholar, could anyone doubt that he was a Spaniard?

He moved to Córdoba in 1591, and here he completed work on *La Florida*. He sought to obtain a royal license to publish the book in 1599, but it was not until 1605 that it was published by Pedro Crasbeeck in Lisbon.[24]

Of all the De Soto chronicles, *La Florida* is by far the one that is the most self-consciously literary. It is also the least chronological. Garcilaso divides his work into six books. The first book covers the background and preliminaries to the expedition, as well as the passage of the fleet from Spain to Cuba. Each of the next four books deals with a year of the expedition. And the sixth book tells of the journey down the Mississippi River and around the Gulf coast to Pánuco.

Most of the calendar dates mentioned by Garcilaso are in the first book, and these dates are closer to Rangel's dates than are dates cited later. He has the fleet departing from San Lúcar on April 6, 1538, whereas they departed on April 7; his date of April 21 as the day of their arrival in the Canaries is accurate; he has them sailing from Havana on May 12, 1539, whereas they departed on May 18; and he has them sighting land on May 31, whereas they actually sighted land on May 25. As the expedition went on, his dates frequently were off by two or three weeks.

Even more seriously, Garcilaso transposes place-names and ethnonyms from one place to another, confuses geographical features, and gets some events notably out of chronological order. For example, he transposes events in northern Florida that must have occurred at the Suwannee River to the Santa Fe River—two quite different streams. He erroneously applies the name Acuera to Ocale; the name Ocale to Potano; the name Ochile to Aguacaleyquen; the name Vitachuco to Napituca; and the name Altapaha to Ichisi. These are just a few examples.

Thus, the inadequacies of Garcilaso's chronology are much greater than and are qualitatively different from those of Elvas, whose anachronisms can more readily be seen as copyists' errors and as the product of a none too fastidious diarist. Garcilaso's anachronisms, on the other hand, are consistent with his having derived almost all the content of *La Florida* from the oral testimony of an informant, just as he claims in his preface. He refers to this person—Gonzalo

Silvestre—as his "author." In addition to Silvestre's oral testimony, Garcilaso notes that he had access to two brief written accounts of the expedition, both from memory. One was about ten pages in length by Juan Coles, and the second, eight and a half pages long, by Alonso de Carmona. Garcilaso says that neither Coles nor Carmona places the events he describes in chronological order.[25] Neither of these documents is known to have survived.

Using modern terminology, Garcilaso's La Florida would seem to be a work of oral history. Moreover, it is an oral history that was unabashedly cast in the literary conventions of its time. In spite of his protestations to the contrary, Garcilaso was a literary man; even though he claimed to abjure the chivalric romances he read as a young man, insisting that La Florida contained no fictions, one has to read only a few pages of it to find examples of what Miguel de Cervantes was burlesquing at the very time Garcilaso was writing. (There is no evidence, by the way, that Garcilaso was cognizant of Cervantes' work.)[26]

Garcilaso mentions having read Cabeza de Vaca's Naufragios and a few other printed sources, but there is no real evidence that he had access to Rangel's manuscript, nor to Oviedo's version of Rangel's manuscript, nor, most surprisingly, to Elvas's published account. But lack of evidence does not deter Patricia Galloway from asserting that La Florida was probably based on Elvas's narrative, and specifically that Garcilaso used the Elvas narrative as a means of eliciting information from Silvestre.[27] But if Garcilaso used the Elvas narrative in this way, why did he not rely on it to establish chronology, or at least get events, places, and peoples in their proper sequence? The problems in using Garcilaso as a source are great, as I have indicated, but Galloway's attempt to sweep La Florida away with a single groundless supposition does nothing but muddy the waters.

An even more determined attempt to deny any historicity to La Florida has been made by David Henige. Henige argues that because Garcilaso was a pre-Enlightenment scholar, who lived in a time when chivalric romances were popular, La Florida is to be regarded as a work of this genre, and as such, it is nothing more than "pseudohistory." Henige argues that while we cannot deny that Gonzalo Silvestre existed, we may doubt anything he told Garcilaso about his experience in La Florida.[28] The fact is, however, that it is amazing just how much of the real story is told in Garcilaso's work, despite his literary embellishments, the secondhand nature of his reporting, and the passage of time between the events and his writing. We cannot take Garcilaso at anything approaching face value, but neither can we peremptorily dismiss him.

La Florida is about four times the length of Elvas's narrative, and it is more than nine times as long as Rangel's surviving narrative. What use can we make of this work? It cannot be used to establish the route of the expedition. The chronology is minimal, and even when it is not, it is at variance with Rangel and Elvas. Places and names are sometimes scrambled, as are events. Hence, *La Florida* cannot be used in helping to reconstruct what might be thought of as the skeleton of the expedition. Likewise, almost all of Garcilaso's estimates of numbers—personnel, casualties, distances traveled—are exaggeratedly high and cannot be trusted.

Garcilaso's descriptions of native customs, particularly those that imply an acquaintance with their beliefs or categories of thought, must be read with skepticism. Patricia Galloway is probably correct in noting that Garcilaso took the Inca culture he learned as a boy to be the lens through which the Southeast should be viewed.[29] While the basic assumptions of Garcilaso's Inca belief system were probably more congruent with those of the Indians of La Florida than was the belief system shared by Rangel, Elvas, and Biedma, the Inca world that Garcilaso understood was far more complex and elaborate than anything that existed in La Florida.

Likewise, one can strip away from the Indians of *La Florida* all of the speechifying and noble posturing that would do justice to a Renaissance courtier. Garcilaso was intent on depicting the Indians of La Florida as being fit subjects for colonization and Christianization; hence, he often depicts them as so many stage actors.

What remains in *La Florida* are incidents that Silvestre either witnessed himself or heard described around campfires at the end of the day. The stories that stayed with him would have been the ones that were particularly notable, and they would have undergone modification as they were told and retold. It would be absurd to claim that any of Garcilaso's stories are the primary stuff of experience. They are properly called legends, containing representations of events that happened, but codified in the perceptions, language, and storytelling framework of sixteenth-century Spanish military men. What Garcilaso can add to a reconstruction of the De Soto expedition is not the skeleton, nor the flesh, but the skin, the colorful surface of life. A greyhound accidentally falls off a ship and is lost at sea, only to be later saved by a fisherman, who subsequently refuses to return the dog to his owner, arguing that finders are keepers, losers are weepers. Juan López Cacho rides a horse that was a toast-colored bay, with a black mane and tail. In a fierce battle with Indians, Nuño de Tovar's ash lance is pierced by an Indian's arrow, forming a cross.

La Florida was translated into French in 1670, and it was reprinted several times in the eighteenth century. This French translation was then translated into English in 1881. The first adequate English translation was made by John G. Varner and Jeannette J. Varner, published by the University of Texas Press in 1951. A translation that is somewhat more literal than that of the Varners was prepared in the 1930s by Charmion Shelby. The manuscript of Shelby's translation was used by the U.S. De Soto Expedition Commission in its researches, but it was not published until 1993 by the University of Alabama Press.

Eugene Lyon has discovered a one-page summary of De Soto information from a fifth source in a *legajo* of documents in the AGI relating to Pedro Menéndez de Avilés's conquest of La Florida.[30] The source of this account is Fray Sebastián de Cañete, one of the religious who went on the De Soto expedition. It is a highly condensed summary of information, completely lacking in chronology. It confirms several matters described in the other chronicles (e.g., the large quantity of pearls in the temple at Cofitachequi), the finding of Juan Ortiz (though his name is omitted or forgotten), the huge size of chief Tascaluza, the death of De Soto at Guachoya, and so on. Much of this manuscript is devoted to describing the resources of La Florida, the economy of the Indians, and also their social practices. If, as Lyon believes, this is a fragment of a much longer document, the discovery of the longer document could be most useful because of the seeming richness of the descriptive content. But if, as John Worth believes, this document is a secondhand summary of oral testimony of Cañete and an unidentified person, seemingly over twenty years after the expedition, then no further information from Cañete is likely to be forthcoming.[31]

It is, however, quite possible that one or more additional accounts of the De Soto expedition could turn up in the future. Many of the participants were literate. And there are indications that other documents did exist and may still exist. For example, Garcilaso says that he sent the manuscript of *La Florida* to "a chronicler of the Catholic Majesty"—possibly Ambrosio de Morales, but more likely Antonio de Herrera—who later wrote to Garcilaso saying he had compared the manuscript of *La Florida* to a written account of the expedition given by survivors to Don Antonio de Mendoza, viceroy of New Spain, and that he judged the two to be consistent.[32] The account in question could have been that of Rangel or Biedma, but it could just as well have been by some other author or authors.

The only map that can be said to be a map of the De Soto expedition is the quill-and-ink sketch that bears an inscription stating that it is from the papers of Alonso de Santa Cruz, who was a cosmographer for Charles V.[33] The map represents the lower Atlantic coast from the Cape of Santa Elena—a place-name associated with the Ayllón colony—down to the Florida peninsula and around the Gulf coast to Pánuco, where the survivors of the expedition found refuge. From bays and inlets along the coast, the map shows many rivers running rather haphazardly and sometimes oddly into the interior. The Appalachian Mountains are incorrectly shown running east-west, and the Ozark and Ouachita Mountains are also poorly represented. Many of the place-names mentioned in Rangel, Biedma, and Elvas are shown on the map, though often with spellings that match none of those used in the chronicles.

The author of the map is unknown, but he may have been Alonso de Santa Cruz.[34] What is more pertinent is what the author's sources were. The outline of the Atlantic and Gulf coasts resembles state-of-the-art maps in Spain in the 1540s, and it was no doubt copied from one of them. The map contains no information from the Tristán de Luna expedition, which would seem to place its composition between about 1544 and 1561. The author of the map could have had access to the manuscripts by Rangel and Biedma, as well as Elvas's printed work. Alternatively, the author of the map could have derived most of his information from one or more of the survivors.

Perhaps the most notable characteristic of the map is that many more place-names are shown west of the Mississippi River than are shown east of the river. Of all the place-names from the De Soto documents, only about 35 percent of those east of the Mississippi River are shown on the "De Soto map." In contrast, about 76 percent of those west of the Mississippi River are shown. Why the difference? Barbara Boston has surmised that writing in the names on the eastern side of the Mississippi would have unduly crowded the map. But this is not persuasive—there is plenty of room.[35]

It would seem that two hypotheses could explain this east-west difference. One is that the mapmaker worked solely with information from manuscript sources, including some or all of the ones mentioned above. In composing the map, he started out from the better-known part of North America—the coast of Mexico—and proceeded toward the lesser-known part, spotting in information as he worked backward along the route. But as he proceeded east of the Mississippi River, his confidence in his enterprise faltered. A second hypothesis is that the mapmaker got most of his information from a veteran of the expedition who drew the interior locations from memory, and his memory was more accurate for the latter part of the route than for the earlier part. Remarkably, no place-names from De Soto's route are shown in peninsular Florida and only two—Cofaq (perhaps Cofaqui) and Capalar (perhaps Capachequi)—in southern Georgia. Until this map is better understood, it cannot be used as evidence in reconstructing the route of the De Soto expedition.

A number of documents pertaining to De Soto and to the expedition have come to light over the years. They have been collected together and published along with the four chronicles in *The De Soto Chronicles,* edited by Lawrence A. Clayton, Vernon James Knight Jr., and Edward C. Moore. The most important of these are the king of Spain's concession of La Florida to conquest by De Soto; a letter written at Tampa Bay by De Soto to officials in Santiago, Cuba; a letter from these same officials to Charles V; and an inventory of De Soto's possessions following his death. These documents add relatively little, however, to our understanding of the conduct of the expedition.[36]

A considerable quantity of legal documents were created in the wake of the expedition, most particularly in connection with the Isabel de Bobadilla–Hernán Ponce de León legal battle. Irene A. Wright photocopied several hundred pages of these documents and transcribed and translated many of them. These were turned over to the U.S. De Soto Expedition Commission, and they are now housed in the National Anthropological Archives in the Smithsonian Institution. From what I have seen of these documents, they have much to say about the background of the expedition and its aftermath, as well as the personalities of the participants, but very little about the expedition itself or of the native peoples. Still, there is much of historical value to be gleaned from these documents, and research on them would be in order.

History of Research on the De Soto Route

Reconstructing the route of the De Soto expedition across the southeastern landscape has been one of the most difficult problems in early American history. As we have seen, the quantity and specificity of the documentation are quite limited, and because the social and cultural texture of the native peoples of the Southeast had changed drastically between the time of the expedition and the time historical research was first attempted, it became impossible to reconstruct the route using documentary sources alone. If native place-names had been in the same locations in the eighteenth and nineteenth centuries as they were in the sixteenth century, reconstructing the De Soto route would have been child's play. Many sixteenth-century place-names disappeared from the map without a trace. But a more difficult problem is that many of them were not in the same locales in the eighteenth century as they were in the sixteenth century. Only as archaeology has achieved a mature level of development in the Southeast—in the past two decades or so—has it become possible to combine documentary and archaeological information and thus to make feasible a reasonably accurate solution to the De Soto route.

The earliest attempts to reconstruct De Soto's route were, by necessity, based almost exclusively on documentary information. In addition to using one or more of the basic chronicles, early scholars used state-of-the-art maps of various scales. They read the chronicles and tried to situate the rather broadly defined movements of the expedition, location by location, on a map. In a few instances, scholars who possessed intimate understandings of particular locales may have brought to bear information based on local experience and oral traditions. Taking the route that my colleagues and I have reconstructed as the standard, none of the early route reconstructions can be said to come close to the entire length of De Soto's route. Some do, however, get close to the route at specific locations, though one is hard put to know whether these "hits" are due to a particularly intelligent reader of the sources, or else luck. Only the most influential of these early route reconstructions will be discussed here.[37]

The earliest reconstructions of De Soto's route appear on maps. Several early printed maps, such as the 1584 map by Ortelius, use place-names from the De Soto expedition more or less as decorations. But in 1718 the French cartographers Claude and Guillaume Delisle produced one of the most influential early maps of the central and eastern United States, and on this map is reconstructed a De Soto route from the point of landing to Moscoso's return to the Mississippi River. The Delisles had access to both the translation of Elvas by Samuel de Braë and the translation of Garcilaso by Pierre Richelet. Their spelling of Cofitachequi is like that of Elvas (i.e., Cutifaqui), and it would seem that wisely or luckily they relied upon Elvas for their information.

The Delisles' representation of the Florida peninsula is so inaccurate, one cannot determine where they located the landing place. But according to their map, De Soto traveled from this landing place to Apalachee, in the vicinity of present-day Tallahassee, where the historic location of the descendants of these people was well known to the eighteenth-century French colonists. The general location of Apalachee was one on which all subsequent route reconstructions would agree (map 10). What is astonishing about the Delisles' route is that they place Cofitachequi on the Catawba-Wateree-Santee River, a correct location that would not be duplicated again until the work of Mary Ross in 1930.[38] The Delisles place Chiaha on the upper Ocmulgee River; Tascaluza was near the Black Warrior River; Mabila would seem to have been at

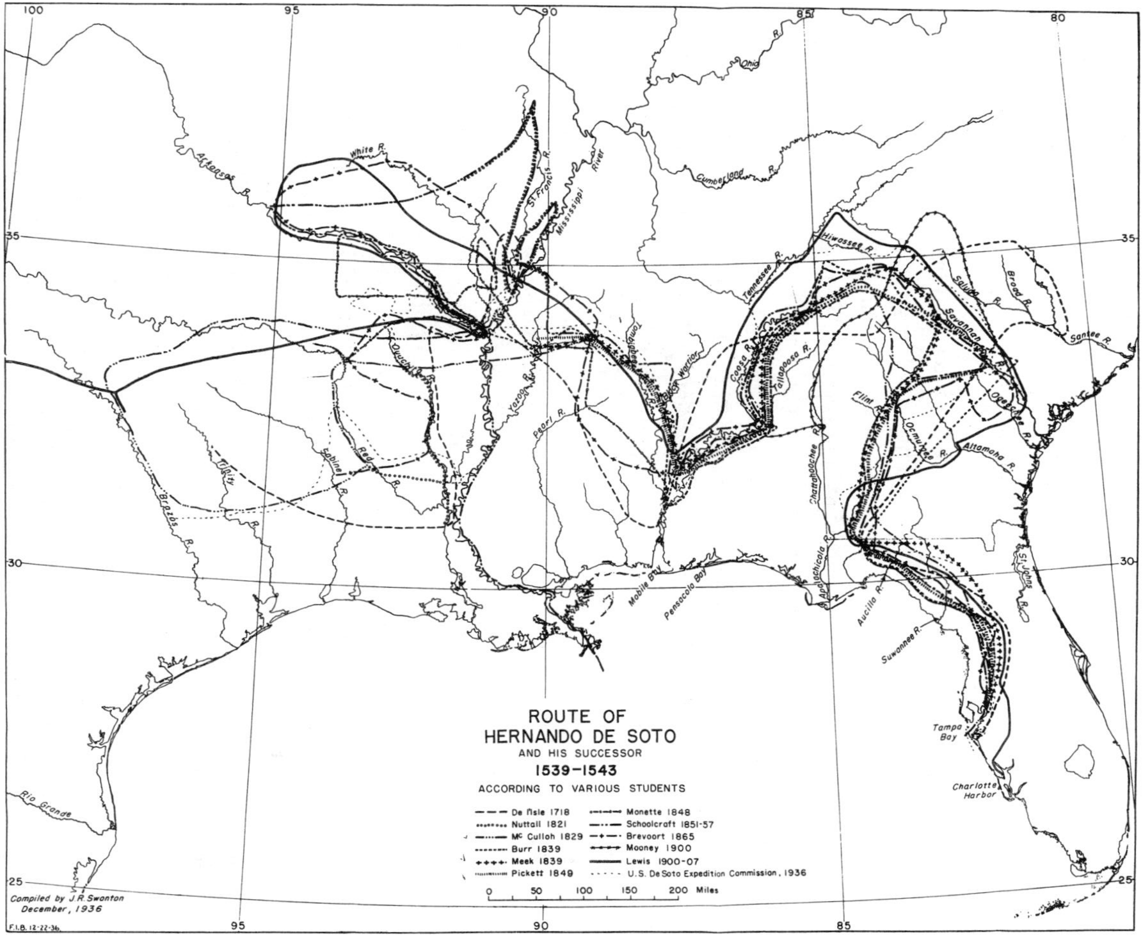

Map 10. Various reconstructions of the route of the Hernando de Soto expedition. (Reprinted from *Final Report of the United States De Soto Expedition Commission*, House Document No. 71, 76th Congress, 1st Session [Washington, D.C.: GPO, 1939], map no. 2.)

ROUTE OF
HERNANDO DE SOTO
AND HIS SUCCESSOR
1539–1543

ACCORDING TO VARIOUS STUDENTS

De l'Isle 1718   Monette 1848
Nuttall 1821   Schoolcraft 1851-57
Mc Culloh 1829   Brevoort 1865
Burr 1839   Mooney 1900
Meek 1839   Lewis 1900-07
Pickett 1849   U.S. De Soto Expedition Commission, 1936

0   50   100   150   200 Miles

Compiled by J.R.Swanton
December, 1936

the head of Mobile Bay; the crossing of the Mississippi River was below the mouth of the St. Francis River, at Pointe d'Oziers, opposite an eighteenth-century Quapaw town; Casqui and Pacaha were seemingly on the St. Francis River; Guachoya was just below the mouth of the Red River; and Lacane was on the Trinity River.[39]

Thomas Nuttall, a gifted early naturalist, published his interpretation of a portion of De Soto's route in a book on his travels in the Arkansas territory. In 1818–19 Nuttall traveled down the Ohio and Mississippi Rivers to the Arkansas territory. He had read an abridged English translation of Garcilaso, and he mentions the expedition in several places in his book, but most particularly in an appendix on the native peoples. Nuttall places De Soto's crossing of the Mississippi River at the lower Chickasaw Bluff at present-day Memphis; he equates Casqui with the later Kaskaskia Indians of Illinois; Chalaque with the Cherokee; Tanico with the Tunica; Quipana with Quapaw; Quigualtam with Natchez; and Naguatex with Natchitoches.[40] He may have been correct in seeing the similarity between *Tanico* and *Tunica*, and many later scholars seconded his equating Quigualtam with Natchez, as well as Chalaque with Cherokee.

In 1829 J. H. McCulloh Jr. published a route reconstruction accompanied by a map. Relying on both Garcilaso and Elvas, he attempted to locate the route mainly in terms of the locations of nineteenth-century place-names. Consequently, his route in places is quite far afield from where De Soto went. He places the landing at Tampa Bay; Aute was at the head of the Bay of St. Marks; Altapaha was on the Alapaha River; Achalaqui (which he equates with Cherokees) was seemingly on the upper Flint River; Cofitachequi was on the Ocmulgee River; Xuala was in present-day Hall County, Georgia; Guaquili was on the head of the Chattahoochee River; Guasili was on the Etowah River; Talisi was at the elbow of the lower Tallapoosa River; Mabila was on the north side of the Alabama River, east of Boguechitto Creek; Ochuse was at Mobile Bay; Zabusta was on the Black Warrior River; the crossing of the Mississippi was below the mouth of the Arkansas River; Pacaha was on the Red River.[41] In 1835 Theodore Irving, a nephew of Washington Irving, published a popular book on the De Soto expedition that generally follows the route of McCulloh and Nuttall.[42]

Albert James Pickett, in his *History of Alabama* (1851), proposed several locations on the route that were influential for later scholars. He located Cofitachequi at Silver Bluff, just south of present-day Augusta, Georgia, citing George Galphin, an Indian trader who claimed to have been told by Indians in 1736 that it was at this location. He located Chiaha at present-day Rome,

Georgia; Coosa at its eighteenth-century location on the Coosa River; Talisi at the later site of Tukabatchee, in the elbow of the Tallapoosa River; Mabila at Choctaw Bluff, twenty-five miles upstream from the confluence of the Tombigbee and Alabama Rivers; and like many other early investigators, he located Guachoya near the mouth of the Arkansas River.[43]

Another state historian, J. F. H. Claiborne, was particularly interested in the De Soto route in the state of Mississippi, and his work influenced later scholars. Claiborne drew upon the knowledge of local residents concerning trails and geographic features. He placed the crossing of the Tombigbee where an old trail intersected with the river at Lincecum's Shoals, near the present-day town of Waverly. (He was under the mistaken impression that De Soto's army forded the Tombigbee; actually they crossed it in a piragua.) He placed Chicaza at Pontotoc Ridge, where the eighteenth-century Chickasaws were located. Remnants of the fortifications of these eighteenth-century Chickasaw towns were still in evidence in Claiborne's day.[44]

James Mooney of the Smithsonian Institution added his authority to several locations others had proposed along the route, and he proposed some new ones of his own. He accepted Pickett's location of Cofitachequi at Silver Bluff on the Savannah River, a location that had been seconded by Cyrus Thomas, the chief archaeologist at the Smithsonian Institution. Mooney also agreed with the supposition that *Chalaque* referred to the Cherokees, and he thought their location was probably on the headwaters of the Keowee River. He thought Guaquili was a Cherokee town, but Joara (Xuala) was "Siouan" (i.e., Catawban), which he located on the upper Broad River in western North Carolina. He located Guasili at the Nacoochee mound in present-day White County, Georgia. From here he thought De Soto proceeded down the Chattahoochee River to Chiaha, near Columbus, Georgia.[45] Mooney is one of the earliest scholars to attempt to locate sites on the route by correlating them with known archaeological sites.

The first scholar to rely primarily on Rangel in a route reconstruction was the historian T. H. Lewis. But even using Rangel, documentary sources alone were not enough to achieve an accurate route reconstruction. Unlike all his predecessors, Lewis argued that De Soto's landing was at Charlotte Harbor. The River of Mocozo was the Myakka River; Anhayca was on the Apalachicola River; the Bay of the Horses was Ochlockonee Bay; the White Fountain was Radium Springs, near present-day Albany, Georgia; the Ocmulgee was the eastward flowing river; Cofitachequi was on the Savannah River; Joara (Xuala) was at Qualla, on the modern Cherokee Reservation in North

Carolina; Chiaha was on Bussell Island; Coste was on an island upstream from Chattanooga; Coosa was below the junction of the Coosa and Tallapoosa Rivers; Mabila was west of the Cahaba River and north of the Alabama River; Chicaza was in Pontotoc County, Mississippi; the crossing of the Mississippi River was in Tunica County, Mississippi; Casqui was on the St. Francis River near the mouth of Tyronza River; Coligua was on the White River; Anilco was on the lower Arkansas River; Guachoya was near Arkansas City; Aguacay was near Arkadelphia; the River of Daycao was the Brazos; and Aminoya was in Desha County, Arkansas.[46] West of the Mississippi River, many of Lewis's locations have proven to be close to the mark.

The amateur Alabama archaeologist James Y. Brame Jr. proposed a number of site locations in 1928 that were subsequently influential. He placed Chiaha on Burns Island, in the Tennessee River near present-day Chattanooga. And further down the Tennessee River he placed Coste on the upper end of Pine Island. From there the route crossed Sand Mountain to go to the Coosa River. Itaba was at an archaeological site on Hatchet Creek; Tuasi was at Montgomery; Talisi was at Durant's Bend, near Selma; Mabila was near the point where Clarke, Wilcox, and Marengo Counties meet; and Apafalaya was on the Tombigbee River below Demopolis.[47]

John R. Fordyce, a businessman in Hot Springs and Little Rock, Arkansas, made a number of site proposals that affected later scholarship. As early as 1932 he collaborated with Brame and John R. Swanton. Fordyce placed the crossing of the Mississippi above the mouth of the Arkansas River; Pacaha was a little below present-day Memphis; the route went up the Ouachita River past Hot Springs; the Ouachita River then became the River of Cayas; Anilco was on the lower Ouachita River; and Guachoya was on the Mississippi River just to the east of Anilco.[48]

The U.S. De Soto Expedition Commission

By far the most elaborate prearchaeological attempt to reconstruct the route of the De Soto expedition was set in motion by an act of the 74th Congress, approved on August 26, 1935. Its purpose was to memorialize the four-hundredth anniversary of "the first and most imposing expedition ever made by Europeans into the wilds of North America." A commission was to be appointed to study the expedition so that highway markers could be established and the expedition could be properly celebrated. Accordingly, on December 26, 1935, President Franklin Roosevelt appointed to this commission the following persons: the Honorable W. G. Brorein of Tampa, Florida; Caroline Dorman of Chestnut, Louisiana; Colonel John R. Fordyce of Hot Springs and Little Rock, Arkansas; V. Birney Jones of Columbus, Mississippi; Andrew O. Holmes of Memphis, Tennessee; Walter B. Jones of the University of Alabama; and John R. Swanton of the Smithsonian Institution. This committee later elected Swanton as its chairman, Fordyce as its vice-chairman, and Jones as its secretary. The commission further elected a fact-finding committee consisting of John R. Swanton (chairman), Caroline Dorman, and John R. Fordyce. To this fact-finding committee fell the task of establishing where the route lay.

The commission held three meetings in 1936—in Washington, D.C., at Tampa, Florida, and at Tuscaloosa, Alabama—and they submitted an interim report to the House of Representatives on April 30, 1937. They sponsored Irene A. Wright to search out and translate De Soto documents in Spain, and they employed Charmion Shelby to translate Garcilaso's *La Florida*. Several members of the commission carried out field investigations, but these were probably little more than visits to mound sites and investigations of landscape features. The fact-finding committee made its final report on December 28, 1938, delivering its scholarly findings on De Soto's route and making various recommendations about how the expedition might be memorialized. This report was published in 1939 as House Document no. 71 of the 78th Congress, 1st session.[49]

While Swanton communicated frequently by mail with Dorman and Fordyce, it is not to be doubted that he is the sole author of the *Final Report*. It was up to Swanton to uphold scholarly objectivity and to "mediate between competing local enthusiasms." To date the story of how this was done has not been researched.[50] However, it is clear that Swanton became interested in the historical problem of the De Soto expedition at an early date. He carried out ethnological field work on the Indians of the Southeast between 1907 and 1919, and again in 1929, and he published several important ethnological works on them. He realized early in his research the importance of the De Soto route in Southeastern Indian studies.

As early as November and December 1931, he visited site locations in Arkansas and Louisiana, and in February and March 1934 he visited sites in Georgia, Florida, and North Carolina. By 1935 he had corresponded about the route with such scholars as Carl E. Guthe, John R. Fordyce, and Irene A. Wright.[51] Swanton also began reaching conclusions about the route as early as 1911–12, including some that he still held at the time the *Final Report* was published.[52] Prior to the researches of the commission he had published his opinion that De Soto had crossed the Oconee River at Carr Shoals; Joara was at Towns Hill in northwestern South Carolina; De Soto crossed the mountains via present-day Highlands, North Carolina, to Franklin; and thence went through Black Gap to Guasili at the Peachtree archaeological site on the Hiwassee River.[53]

In working out the route, Swanton relied first upon Rangel, and then for corroboration upon Elvas and Biedma. He relied upon Garcilaso the least. He was well aware of documents of the Luna and Pardo expeditions, but evidently he did not attempt detailed reconstructions of the activities of Luna and Pardo.

What he depended upon next was the locations of "Indian tribes and towns" with respect to topographic features on maps. Some geographical features were unambiguous (e.g., the crossing of the Mississippi River and the Appalachian Mountains). An assumption that was to prove disastrous for Swanton was that "the Indian tribes encountered by De Soto and his successor Moscoso, preserved the same locations down to the late seventeenth and early eighteenth centuries when English and French explorers and traders visited them."[54] While named groups did maintain some residential continuity in northern Florida and in eastern Texas, they did not in most parts of the interior South.

On the rare occasions in which the chroniclers state league measurements, Swanton used the legua legal of 2.6 miles to the league. And like other scholars before and since, Swanton notes that the league estimates in Elvas appear to be rather wild guesses. When estimating distances in terms of days traveled, Swanton seems to have used a figure of twelve to fifteen miles per day.[55]

The key locations in Swanton's route may be summarized as follows (see map 10). The landing was at Tampa Bay, specifically Terra Ceia Island. The Santa Fe River was the River of Discords, and Olustee Creek was the River of Aguacaleyquen. The principal town of Apalachee was in or near present-day Tallahassee, and the Bay of Ochuse was "probably Pensacola." The expedition crossed the Flint River near Bainbridge. Both Toa and Ichisi were west of the Flint River. Altamaha, Ocute, Cofaqui, and Patofa were on the Ocmulgee River. The wilderness of Ocute thus lay between the Ocmulgee River and the Savannah River, and the Oconee River lay in the middle of this wilderness. Cofitachequi was where Pickett placed it—at Silver Bluff. And the route through the mountains was the same as what he had worked out prior to his appointment to the commission, as discussed above.

He follows Brame in placing Chiaha on Burns Island, Coste on Pine Island, and Coosa at its eighteenth-century location on the Coosa River. Swanton appears to have had a particularly high confidence in this location for Coosa. He places Talisi at Durant's Bend, and Mabila in present-day southern Clarke County, Alabama. Apafalaya was on the lower Black Warrior River. The expedition crossed the Tombigbee River at the Aberdeen or Cotton Gin Port crossing, and Chicaza was at the eighteenth-century Chickasaw towns near Tupelo, Mississippi.

The crossing of the Mississippi River was made at some point between the mouths of the St. Francis and Arkansas Rivers. Pacaha lay near the mouth of the St. Francis River. Swanton follows Fordyce in placing Coligua near present-day Little Rock, and the River of Coligua was the Arkansas River. Tanico and Cayas were on the upper Ouachita River, near Hot Springs; Tula was near Caddo Gap; and Guachoya was near Ferriday, Louisiana. He follows Nuttall in identifying Quigualtam with the Natchez.

He follows Dorman in placing Naguatex at a series of mound sites on the Red River above present-day Shreveport; Nondacao was on the Sabine River; the Hais were where the mission of Nuestra Señora de los Dolores de los Ais was located in the seventeenth century. The River of Daycao was the Trinity River.

Swanton did not claim finality for his route. He was quite aware that the discovery of new manuscripts, and most particularly the expansion of Southeastern archaeology, which was only in its infancy in the 1930s, could require the route to be redrawn. Time has proven him right on both counts. His route has not fared at all well with respect to archaeological research. The simplest use of archaeology in reconstructing De Soto's route is to sample or excavate a site that has been proposed as a site visited by the expedition. In 1948 David L. De Jarnette and Asael Hansen excavated the site that Swanton said was Coosa, and they found that the site dates to the eighteenth century and no earlier.[56] With this determination, one of the linchpins of Swanton's route fell away. At about the same time, Ripley P. Bullen excavated the Terra Ceia site, where Swanton had placed Uzita. Bullen reported that he did not find the evidence that should have been present if this was where the landing occurred, and he argued that the geography of the Terra Ceia site does not fit the requirements of the De Soto narratives.[57] With this, another of Swanton's linchpins fell away, leaving his reconstruction of the route badly shaken.

These negative findings opened the door to calling the Swanton route into question generally, and it was an invitation for scholars—both professional and amateur—to publish arguments for and against sites and segments of the route. Such arguments were not immune to the "local enthusiasms" mentioned by Swanton. In the two and half centuries that had passed since the

Delisles' map was published, rival claimants for De Soto place-names had developed across the Southeast, and they had been memorialized on historical markers and attached to pieces of real estate. For example, a rather intemperately argued case was made echoing Lewis's old argument that the landing was at Charlotte Harbor rather than at Tampa Bay.[58]

Combining Archaeological and Historical Evidence

A decisive turn in De Soto research did not come with a mere archaeological refutation of a few of Swanton's proposed site locations, but rather with the gradual development of (1) more thorough regional archaeological surveys and a more precise geographical plotting of archaeological phases, (2) more precise dating and ultimately an understanding of where sites were located in 1539–43, and just as important, where sites were *not* located, and (3) the identification of diagnostic European artifacts of the sixteenth century.

An early example of this more sophisticated use of archaeological evidence in De Soto research was included by Philip Phillips, James A. Ford, and James B. Griffin in their report of a massive survey of the lower Mississippi Valley carried out between 1940 and 1947. On the basis of his grasp of Late Mississippian phases in the valley, Phillips argued that Swanton's crossing of the river was too far south. He argued that a good fit between historical and archaeological evidence could be had at Commerce Landing, a few miles south of present-day Memphis.[59] Dan and Phyllis Morse pressed this approach even further and made some very precise identifications. Namely, they located the capitol town of the Casqui province at the Parkin site; they identified Aquijo with the Walls phase; and they placed Pacaha at Pecan Point.[60]

A further use of archaeological evidence was made in the 1970s. Stephen G. Baker presented evidence that the province of Cofitachequi was on the Wateree-Santee River, as Mary Ross had argued, and not on the Savannah River, as Swanton had argued. Baker used historical evidence from the seventeenth century along with archaeological evidence to make his case.[61] This was a significant achievement, although Baker located the center of the Cofitachequi polity too far downriver.

In the late 1970s notable advances were made in bringing archaeological evidence to bear on De Soto's route through Alabama. George E. Lankford III proposed a new route for De Soto, and he collaborated with the archaeologists Cailup (aka Caleb) Curren Jr. and Keith J. Little. Curren and Little had excavated a sixteenth-century Spanish context site in northern Alabama.[62] This group brought a notable collection of sixteenth-century Spanish artifacts to the attention of the profession, including a complete sword that was found by amateurs at the King site in northwestern Georgia. But even more important was their realization that the commonly accepted archaeological chronology of the De Soto expedition in Alabama was incorrect. The consensus before their research was that the De Soto expedition dated to the time of the Alabama River phase (i.e., the Burial Urn Culture), after a population collapse had occurred and after mound building had ceased. But their sampling of several sites persuaded them that the De Soto expedition dated to the end of the previous Moundville III phase.[63] Subsequent research has sustained their conclusions.

The identification of diagnostic sixteenth-century artifacts proceeded hand in hand with this pioneering research combining archaeological and historical evidence. The first breakthrough was Jeffrey P. Brain's identification of the small copper Clarksdale bells as markers of the sixteenth-century explorers.[64] And Marvin Smith began identifying certain chisels and spikes as well as a variety of glass beads as indicators of Spanish contact.[65]

One final development in the late 1970s that made a new scholarly attack on the De Soto expedition possible was a theoretical innovation. Namely, it was at this time that regional analysis became a concern of Southeastern archaeologists. The purpose of regional analysis was to go beyond the mere classifying of sites into phases on the basis of cultural similarities. An effort was now being made to discern social, economic, and political entities that encompassed numbers of sites. The identification of such an entity by Marvin Smith and Stephen Kowalewski was a particularly happy development: in the course of time it became apparent that they had found one of De Soto's provinces—the paramount chiefdom of Ocute.[66]

Hence, by about 1980 a number of pieces of the De Soto puzzle were on the board. Putting them together, however, was not so easy. Partly on the basis of the recovery of Clarksdale bells recovered from a mound at Clarksdale, Mississippi, Jeffrey P. Brain, Alan Toth, and Antonio Rodriguez-Buckingham argued that De Soto's crossing of the Mississippi River was near Friars Point, Mississippi.[67] But this site location has proven to be inconsistent with the locations of archaeological sites and the actions that occurred on the western side of the river. Their proposed location for De Soto's crossing of the Mississippi River has relatively little support today. Similarly, Marvin Smith would be the first to say that his early attempt to use the locations of the discoveries of sixteenth-century artifacts as a way of reconstructing De Soto's route has not held up.[68]

A More Accurate De Soto Route

In 1977–78 I was fortunate enough to have been awarded a senior fellowship at the Center for the History of the American Indian, at the Newberry Library in Chicago. It was a year in which I could assess what I understood about the native peoples of the Southeast and, even more important, what I did not understand. In 1976 I had published *The Southeastern Indians,* an introduction to the culture of the native peoples of the Southeast, surveying their prehistory, their social and cultural institutions, and their history.[69] But I was acutely aware of an enormous hiatus in the history of the early Southeast. I could not begin to provide an answer to the question of what were the connections between the elaborate, mound-building Mississippian cultures of the late prehistoric Southeast and the far different peoples of the eighteenth- and nineteenth-century Southeast—the Cherokees, Choctaws, Chickasaws, Creeks, Catawbas, and others. Standard histories of the South contained virtually nothing on the sixteenth century, and precious little on the seventeenth century. Furthermore, I knew of evidence that by the 1700s the Indians themselves had little understanding or memory of changes they had undergone since the 1500s. It became clear to me that filling in this hiatus was the most crucial problem in the social history of the early Southeast.[70]

In researching a social history of the southeastern region of the United States from, say, 1500 to 1750, where was one to begin? Clearly, the most considerable body of historical information for the sixteenth century was from the De Soto expedition. I realized that if one could reconstruct the activities of this expedition accurately enough, it would become possible to link this information together with a considerable body of information archaeologists had been collecting for over a century. If a sufficiently accurate route could be worked out, it would become possible to put together a picture of the social geography of the sixteenth-century Southeast—a map of who lived where. From this point of reckoning, it would then become possible to recede back into the past to examine how the sixteenth-century native societies had evolved from earlier Mississippian antecedents and to proceed forward in time to show how this 1539–43 Southeastern world gave way, fell apart, and reorganized itself into the peoples of the eighteenth-century South.

In the winter quarter of 1980, I taught a seminar at the University of Georgia whose principal players were myself and two graduate students, Chester DePratter and Marvin Smith. We committed ourselves to trying to work out a more accurate De Soto route. But we soon ended in a mire. It became clear to us that the De Soto documents alone, even when we tried to combine them with archaeological evidence known to us, did not furnish enough information to allow us to lay a line on a map with any degree of confidence. On the basis of these documents we could construct equally plausible arguments for taking the expedition in several directions from any particular location. Something more was needed.

Our first breakthrough came when DePratter called to our attention a document he had come upon in 1978–79, when he had spent a year in research supported by a predoctoral fellowship at the Newberry Library. He had elected to write his dissertation on Mississippian social organization, combining archaeological and early historical information. From the North Carolina State Archives he had obtained a copy of a neglected document of the Juan Pardo expedition of 1566–68. This document was written by Juan de la Bandera, Pardo's notary, and had been translated but seemingly not analyzed by Herbert E. Ketcham. Now from a quick reading of the document, we could see that Pardo had gone to visit several towns in the interior that De Soto had visited twenty-six years earlier. Furthermore, Bandera's account contained far more details than we had in any of the De Soto documents. We realized that if we could determine where Pardo had gone, we would have what no previous De Soto scholars had ever had—corroboration for several native town locations in the interior. If we could succeed in this, it might make it possible to start De Soto out from Apalachee, known to be in the Tallahassee area, and from there to trace his route to the towns Pardo visited.

Our De Soto seminar quickly turned into a Pardo seminar, and by the time the quarter ended, we felt confident that enough information was contained in the long Bandera account and in other Pardo documents to reconstruct Pardo's route. In the course of the next few months, greatly aided by Paul Hoffman, who prepared transcriptions and fresh translations of all the Pardo documents, we were able to work out a reconstruction of this route.[71]

We now realized that we could not limit our researches to the De Soto documents. All of the documentation on the sixteenth-century southeastern interior had to be utilized. In addition to Pardo, this included the activities of Lucas Vázquez de Ayllón in 1526, Pánfilo de Narváez in 1528, and most particularly, Tristán de Luna y Arellano in 1559–61. To be taken seriously, any reconstruction of De Soto's route would have to be congruent with the activities of these additional Spanish explorations.

Our experience with the route of the Pardo expedition helped us when we began anew on De Soto. We had a keener appreciation of the importance of supplies of native food in shaping the course of an expedition. Wherever Spaniards might wish to go in the sixteenth-century Southeast, they *had* to go where the native food was. This meant that, all things being equal, they would favor traveling from population center to population center. We began requiring that all the Indian towns and polities on our route match the locations of archaeological sites and site clusters with known sixteenth-century occupations. And using Rangel and Elvas, we determined to try to do this in a day-by-day fashion, as we had been able to do with Pardo. In some instances our route crossed areas in which little archaeological survey had been done. Such locations then became "tests" for the plausibility of our reconstructed route. For example, when we worked out the segment of the De Soto route from Apalachee to Chiaha, we did not know whether a sixteenth-century occupation existed on the upper Flint River, where we located Toa. But John Worth subsequently carried out a survey of this section of the Flint River and found evidence that such a population was indeed present there.[72]

The first segment of the De Soto route we worked out was that from Apalachee to Chiaha.[73] As our research proceeded, we refined several methodological principles. One was that we were committed to what Vernon J. Knight Jr. once termed the "long string approach." That is, route reconstructions of short stretches of the route are less persuasive than those of long stretches of the route. Without having a likely location for Chiaha, for example, we could not name a plausible location for Coste, and without a location for Coste, we could not locate Tali. Using a day-by-day itinerary, the location of any one site places constraints on where other sites can be located.

The importance of maps showing the distribution of sixteenth-century archaeological sites cannot be overestimated. Ironically, the absence of such sites on the maps was at times more important in our route reconstructions than the presence of sites. This is because on several occasions the De Soto expedition crossed extensive areas of "wilderness" (i.e., areas where no people lived). One such wilderness was located between Ocute and Cofitachequi. One of the first triumphs of our new route is that we placed the wilderness of Ocute on both sides of the Savannah River, where modern archaeological research has amply borne out the conclusion that this area was abandoned after about A.D. 1450. This alone is a mortal blow to the eastern part of Swanton's route, which places the wilderness of Ocute on both sides of the Oconee River, which is now known to have been heavily populated in 1540, and it places Cofitachequi on the Savannah River, in an area we now know to have been vacant in the sixteenth century.[74]

One of the difficulties in reconstructing the De Soto route is the problem of statements in the documents estimating distances between named points and distances traveled per day. Some of the chroniclers' distances between points appear to be simple multiples of estimated travel days given them by Indian informants, as for example, the estimated distance from Mabila to Ochuse. The league distances in the Elvas chronicle are so obviously out of line with other kinds of information, one is tempted to conclude that they were after-the-fact estimates or guesses that were added to the account either by Elvas or some other person.

Estimates of distances traveled for the Pardo route were quite different. Juan de la Bandera reports the number of leagues traveled—most commonly five—on most days. When we began fitting the Pardo route to a map, we achieved the best fit using the Spanish legua común (3.45 miles to the league) rather than the legua legal (2.63 miles to the league), the measure used by the U.S. De Soto Expedition Commission. Thus, on average days, Pardo appears to have traveled about 17 miles per day.[75] In extrapolating this rate of speed to our De Soto research, we took into account that De Soto's army was larger than Pardo's, and he was driving a herd of pigs everywhere he went. Hence, when we came up with a rough estimate of a day of travel for De Soto, we settled on 15 miles per day, the same figure that was used by the U.S. De Soto Expedition Commission.[76] Our principal way of using this number was to maintain that any segment of De Soto's trail—proposed by whomever—that required a consistent daily rate of travel in excess of 15 miles per day was suspect. This is the case, for example, when one places the landing place at Charlotte Harbor. Traveling from Charlotte Harbor to Potano (whose location is corroborated by the French Huguenot documents) would have required a daily rate of travel far in excess of 15 miles per day. And if one were to locate Potano further south, to make it consistent with a 15-miles-per-day travel time from Charlotte Harbor, then such a location for Potano would no longer be consistent with activities described in the French Huguenot documents.[77]

We worked out our reconstruction of De Soto's route a segment at a time, publishing our results to put them before professionals and laymen in the hope that criticism and debate would bring new information and interpretations forward. After the Apalachee to Chiaha segment, we next worked out

the route of the expedition from Chiaha to Mabila, though at the time of publication we had considerably more confidence in our route from Chiaha to
northern Georgia than we did from northern Georgia to Mabila.[78] As a preliminary to working out this segment, we had to come up with a provisional
reconstruction of the activities of Tristán de Luna in 1559–61. Luna visited
Atache (De Soto's Atahachi), Apica (possibly De Soto's duplicate "Piachi"),
Ulibahali, and Coosa. A crucial step in working out the Luna route was the realization that the River of the Napochies was the Tennessee River, and the
Napochies were probably located in the vicinity of present-day Chattanooga.
No previous scholar had been able to make any sense of Luna's movements,
although some of them lamely proposed the Mississippi River as the River of
the Napochies.[79]

The next segment of the De Soto route was that between Mabila and the
Mississippi River. This was a difficult segment, because we did not have a
firm location for Mabila, and thus we did not have a starting point as securely
located as Apalachee or Chiaha. All we could say is that our grasp of the
documents and the modus operandi of the expedition placed Mabila in the
vicinity of the lower Cahaba River, and perhaps at the site of Old Cahawba.
Nonetheless, as we proceeded westward, we worked out good locations for
the several towns of Apafalaya, a vicinity location for Chicaza, and a very
good fit with Quizquiz and with the towns and geographical features on the
western side of the Mississippi River.[80]

Unquestionably, locating the site of Mabila is the most important piece of
the puzzle that archaeologists might be able to bring to the table. If this location could be established, it would firm up our reconstruction of the route
both coming and going. At the time of writing, the most that can be said is that
existing archaeological evidence does not contradict our proposal that Mabila
could be at the Old Cahawba site. The recent discovery of a Nueva Cadiz bead
in the Moundville area is encouraging.[81] Locating the winter encampments at
Chicaza and Utiangüe are other questions that may in time yield to an archaeological solution.

As we worked at reconstructing the particulars of De Soto's route, we also
worked at locating sixteenth-century native polities and in gaining further insight into their social structure and dynamics. From the outset, we designed
this project to be an exercise in writing social history in the Braudelian manner, not merely an exercise in establishing historical particulars. Prior to our
research, Southeastern archaeologists had realized that the native peoples of
the Southeast were organized into chiefdoms, but for the most part their mod-

els were based on chiefdoms from other parts of the world, particularly Polynesia. It was our opinion, however, that our conception of Southeastern chiefdoms should be based, insofar as possible, on early historical information. Chester DePratter broached this question in his dissertation, in which he marshaled early historical evidence on such matters as territorial size, warfare patterns, the ideology of power, succession to office, the form and function of temples, and so on.[82] Perhaps the most novel part of DePratter's dissertation is his perception that the chiefdoms of the Southeast were unstable. Their evolutionary trajectory was not a simple path of onward and upward forever, but rather it was a picture of rises and falls, though the causal mechanisms were obscure.[83]

My principal contribution to this effort was a close reading of the Pardo documents. In particular, it became clear that Bandera documented three distinct levels of command in Southeastern chiefdoms, with the top level being the one I termed "paramount chief." I also perceived that whatever the political activities of a paramount chiefdom, they incorporated people who were culturally different and linguistically different. And these were not merely abstract theoretical models. I was able to locate them in space, and to some degree in time.[84] Marvin Smith became particularly interested in the way in which the chiefdoms in the interior Southeast collapsed as a consequence of epidemic diseases and other factors, as well as the manner in which survivors coalesced to form new societies.[85] By 1984 we felt that for the province of Coosa we had enough understanding of De Soto's movements and enough understanding of native social structure to venture an analysis. We published our analysis of Coosa as a substantive contribution, but also as a demonstration of what our work on De Soto could contribute to writing a social history of the early Southeast.[86]

Two segments of the route remained to be worked out: the route west of the Mississippi River and the segment from the landing site to Apalachee. As a preliminary to working out the western part of the route, my wife and I drove the route as closely as we could in our automobile. I attempted to match my route reconstruction with features of the landscape. As we visited with archaeologists along the way, I tested my ideas of where the route lay against their detailed archaeological knowledge of particular locales.[87]

Soon after making this reconnaissance of the western route, I published a brief statement of my reconstruction that stimulated quite a bit of scholarly discussion in Arkansas.[88] The University of Arkansas sponsored two symposia on the De Soto expedition and published proceedings containing most of the conclusions and issues attendant to the western route.[89] The quality of the archaeological record is quite good in Arkansas, and the scholarly give-and-take was exciting. Particularly notable contributions to working out the western route were made by David Dye, Dan and Phyllis Morse, Ann Early, and Frank Schambach.[90]

Working out the route in Florida was particularly difficult. The peninsula of Florida is quite symmetrical, and the relief is low. Eventually I concluded that Swanton was correct in placing the landing at Tampa Bay, but that his locations for where the horses and men were put ashore and his location for the base camp were incorrect. I worked up a scenario that fit the geography, and I presented this at a meeting of the American Society for Ethnohistory.[91] The state of Florida was particularly generous in supporting archaeological research on the route, and much of this research was directed by Jerald T. Milanich. At some point we realized that our thinking on the route was congruent enough that we might collaborate. We worked out the Florida route from the point of landing to Apalachee, and we placed this into a larger archaeological and historical context.[92]

Commissions and Controversies

After our research was well in motion, a number of commissions and agencies became interested in the particulars of the De Soto route. In large part, this flurry of activity was stimulated by the 500th anniversary of Columbus's discovery of the New World, and to a lesser extent by the 450th anniversary of the De Soto expedition. For a period of years leading up to 1992, scholars in several fields became interested in all things Hispanic. These activities stimulated public interest in the De Soto expedition, funded research and outreach programs to the public, and stimulated sometimes bitter controversy over where monuments of the De Soto route should be officially located.

Florida, the state with the greatest historical awareness of the Spanish era in southern history, and the state with perhaps the greatest awareness of De Soto, was the first to sponsor a task force. In 1983, at the initiative of Governor Bob Graham, the Florida Division of Recreation and Parks and the College of Liberal Arts of the University of Florida sponsored a conference to establish De Soto's route through Florida. Chaired by Michael Gannon, this task force reached a consensus on the general corridor the expedition followed from present-day Inverness, in central Florida, northward to Tallahassee and the Georgia border. This route was subsequently memorialized by installing De

Soto Trail signs at five-mile intervals and with interpretive pavilions at significant points along the trail. But opinion among scholars at the conference was so sharply divided on whether the landing was at Charlotte Harbor or Tampa Bay, the southern part of the route was not memorialized.[93] The state of Florida was unusually generous in providing funding for archaeological research that subsequently clarified several particulars about the route of De Soto in northern Florida.

The Alabama De Soto Commission was initiated by Governor George Wallace, who authorized it in an executive order on September 13, 1985. Douglas Jones, director of the Alabama Museum of Natural History, was appointed director and chairman of the commission, which was to conduct its business over a five-year period. Douglas Jones's father—Walter B. Jones—had been a member of the U.S. De Soto Expedition Commission in the 1930s. The State of Alabama appropriated funds for the conduct of the commission's business, as well as for modest undertakings of archaeological research. The commission began its work with a very carefully worked out set of goals.

Perhaps the highest ambition of the Alabama De Soto Commission was to locate the site of Mabila. But by the end of 1986 it became clear that among commission members there were two irreconcilable hypotheses about where Mabila might be located. My hypothesis was that it was probably in the vicinity of the lower Cahaba River, perhaps at the Old Cahawba site (1Ds32) located on the western side of the mouth of the Cahaba River. This site was known to have been the locus of a mound, and historical information suggested that the site was once surrounded by an earthwork. The second hypothesis, agreeing with the Swanton route, was that Mabila lay far down the Alabama River, in southern Clarke County, probably at the Doctor Lake site (1Ck219).

In archaeological testing carried out in the winter of 1986–87 at the Old Cahawba site, Vernon James Knight Jr. established that the site was surrounded by a semicircular ditch whose two ends abutted the Alabama River. The ditch was about ten feet wide and four feet deep. Earth had been piled up on the inside of the ditch about a foot high, and a palisade had been built out of posts averaging about six inches in diameter, spaced at about a foot apart. Clay daub reinforced with split cane was found in the ditch that once may have covered the outside of the palisade. Several larger posts were found inside the palisade that may have served as reinforcement or as some other defensive structure. Some evidence of burned structures was found at the site. The site appears to have been occupied for a relatively short time, and the pottery is a local variety of Pensacola phase. Testing around the site indicates that there is very little cultural debris outside the fortification, suggesting that the people lived inside the palisade wall.[94] This is consistent with Mabila being a frontier town, as stated in the documents. In short, this excavation does not prove that Old Cahawba was the site of Mabila, but neither does it contradict that hypothesis.

Beginning in 1819, the first capital of Alabama was built at the Old Cahawba site. A semicircular street—Arch Street—was built around the native defensive ditch, and a cotton warehouse was built inside the area enclosed by the ditch. Because the town was subject to frequent and severe flooding, no doubt exacerbated by cotton cultivation, in 1826 the capital was moved temporarily to Tuscaloosa. But Cahawba remained a viable town, and during the Civil War the cotton warehouse was converted into Castle Morgan, a Confederate prison for captured Union troops. But the floods continued, and by the 1870s most of the population of Old Cahawba had abandoned the town. In time, the area filled up with squatters.

By 1987 it was clear that the Alabama De Soto Commission had before it two proposed routes for the De Soto expedition through Alabama, with no way of reconciling them. One was the route worked out by my associates and me; the other was by Caleb Curren and his associates.[95] Some local citizens of Childersburg, Alabama, where Swanton had located Coosa, added their voices to the controversy. Both the Colonial Dames of America and the Alabama Historical Association had erected markers at Childersburg memorializing Coosa.[96] The commission also gave some attention to a third Alabama De Soto route proposed by Alan Blake, based mainly on geological information.[97] In 1988 the commission, by a majority vote, decided to memorialize a highway route that lay near the one my colleagues and I had reconstructed.[98] But in August 1989, some members of the commission prepared a minority report in which they asserted that the evidence for the route approved by the commission was insufficient to justify setting up highway markers.[99] Nonetheless, the route was memorialized according to a plan drawn up by the commission, and highway markers and exhibits were set up. Despite the skill and good humor that Douglas Jones brought to the chairmanship of the commission, it ended hopelessly divided.

In Georgia, in 1989, Governor Joe Frank Harris signed an executive order creating the Georgia De Soto Trail Commission. James B. Langford Jr. was appointed chairman. With little controversy, the commission voted in favor of establishing a highway route that generally follows my route. The Georgia

Department of Natural Resources sponsored several public symposia on De Soto, and an exhibit devoted to the expedition was installed at the Etowah mounds visitors center. A research committee within the commission established a series of ranked priorities for archaeological research at sites on the route in Georgia, but no money was appropriated by the state.[100]

Our proposed route for De Soto's expedition through Georgia ran into two patches of pro-Swanton sentiment. One came from an environmental group, Swamp of Toa, Inc., whose principal purpose was to protect the wetlands of which the Chickasawhatchee Swamp is a part. Because this is where Swanton located Toa, the environmental group attached the name Toa to the swamp. However, name or no name, the simple fact is that if one is to achieve a good fit with inhabited and uninhabited areas in 1540, Toa has to have been located much further up the Flint River.[101]

The second pro-Swanton argument came from W. S. Eubanks Jr., who argued that the Savannah River basin was not a wilderness in 1540, that Cofitachequi was indeed located on the Savannah River at Silver Bluff, that our conception of the Spanish land league was muddled, and that Guasili was at the Peachtree mound site in present-day Cherokee County, North Carolina.[102] To this David G. Anderson replied by citing massive archaeological evidence that the Savannah River was indeed abandoned in 1540.[103] Along with this, Roland Chardon defended his research, which we had followed, on the Spanish league.[104] For our part, Marvin Smith and I addressed Eubanks's claim that a great quantity of sixteenth-century European artifacts from the Peachtree mound site proved that De Soto had visited the site, and that it must perforce be the site of Guasili. We determined that by far the greater proportion of the artifacts from the Peachtree site date to the eighteenth century; a few date to the seventeenth century; and a very small number—as documented in a photograph of three Nueva Cadiz beads owned by a local collector—are probable sixteenth-century European artifacts. Such artifacts are quite portable, and their presence does not prove that De Soto visited the Peachtree site.[105] Eubanks went on to found his own journal—*Soto States Anthropologist*—published by the Waypoint Foundation, and this became a vehicle for his views for a number of years.

The state of Mississippi appointed a De Soto Trail Commission with Delma Furniss (state representative from Coahoma County) as chairman. The commission sponsored a symposium on the route in Columbus, Mississippi, in December 1989. A consensus was reached by participants at the symposium that Chicaza was probably located on the drainage of Tibbee Creek and its tributaries. But this symposium had placed before it two different reconstructions of the expedition's route from Chicaza to the Mississippi River. One was by my colleagues and me, and the other was put forth by Jeffrey Brain and Richard Weinstein. Brain and Weinstein's route, similar to the route of the U.S. De Soto Expedition Commission, goes west from Chicaza across the Mississippi delta to Sunflower Bend or Friar's Point. One crucial piece of information, the full distribution of Mississippi archaeological sites, was not sufficiently developed at the time of the conference to enable the issue to be decided. The expedition crossed a wide uninhabited wilderness between Chicaza and Quizquiz. If either of the two proposed routes proves to cross populated country, then it can be excluded. But even lacking such information, the fact remains that when one places De Soto's crossing of the Mississippi River in present-day Coahoma County, it is impossible to achieve a good fit for the route on the Arkansas side with respect to documentary evidence, archaeological evidence, and geographical evidence. In contrast, all of these sources of information can be accommodated by a crossing in De Soto County.[106]

The Mississippi De Soto Trail Commission never issued a final report. However, a study of the distribution of late prehistoric and early protohistoric sites by David Morgan contains some interesting information. One notable finding is that in the sixteenth century hardly anyone lived in the broad band of hills in central and northern Mississippi, between the watersheds of the Tombigbee and Mississippi Rivers. Hence, it would seem that this finding would equally support Coahoma County or De Soto County as the location for Quizquiz. But one of the notable characteristics of Quizquiz is that after crossing an extensive wilderness, at Quizquiz the expedition quite abruptly came upon a notably tight cluster of towns. When one examines Morgan's map of Mississippi showing the distribution of late prehistoric and early protohistoric sites, the cluster of sites in De Soto County is much tighter than are the sites in Coahoma County.[107]

In the state of Louisiana, no formal commission was appointed. Instead, an ad hoc committee was formed of prominent Louisiana archaeologists and historians. Apparently, they met on only one occasion—September 10, 1988—to determine "the most logical" route of De Soto and Moscoso. The highway route they agreed upon generally follows the Swanton route, though with some of the native polities repositioned to avoid some of the obvious contradictions of the Swanton route. Thus, Guachoya is located about where Swanton placed it, north of present-day Ferriday, in southern Tensas Parish; Anilco was near Harrisonburg instead of Jonesville; Quigualtam is located in the greater Natchez area; Naguatex was along the Red River, upstream from

Natchitoches, and a proposed direct historical connection is made between the two place-names; and the Aays were near Nacogdoches or the Angelina River, approximately where Swanton placed them, and again this is on the basis of the location of where the Hais were in the eighteenth century. Aminoya was near Lake St. Joseph in northern Tensas Parish, and the second fleet of Indian canoes to attack the survivors are identified as Houma.[108] Using eighteenth-century place-names to establish the route was one of the mistakes that so badly misled John Swanton.

The state of Arkansas appointed no De Soto trail commission. Rather, when I felt I had worked out an approximate solution to the route through Arkansas, I published it in 1985 in a brief article in the newsletter of the Arkansas Archaeological Survey.[109] This was then debated among members of the survey and others in Arkansas. To facilitate scholarly debate and to place the issues before the public, the University Museum of the University of Arkansas sponsored two symposia—in 1988 and 1990—and a volume containing most of the scholarly presentations at these two symposia was edited by Gloria A. Young and Michael P. Hoffman.[110]

The implications of my route are rather great for the state of Arkansas. De Soto and his men spent almost half of the expedition zigzagging through the territory within its borders. In contrast, the Swanton route only takes De Soto and his men quickly through the southeastern quadrant of Arkansas. These considerations may help explain why I encountered so little entrenched pro-Swanton sentiment in Arkansas, in marked contrast to other parts of the Southeast.[111]

Primarily stemming from the initiative of Bob Graham, first as governor and later as senator of Florida, the governors of Alabama, Arkansas, Florida, Georgia, Louisiana, Mississippi, North Carolina, South Carolina, Tennessee, and Texas approved the establishment of a regional De Soto Trail Commission in 1988. Douglas E. Jones, who chaired the Alabama De Soto Commission, also served as chairman of this regional commission. Its purpose was to promote research on the expedition and to coordinate state initiatives with the Department of Interior's National Park Service in studying and planning a De Soto National Historic Trail. The most important action of the regional commission came in 1989, when a majority of representatives of the various states voted to adopt a De Soto highway trail through the Southeast that closely followed the route my colleagues and I reconstructed.[112]

In 1987 Senator Bob Graham and Representative Charles E. Bennett introduced legislation in the U.S. Senate and House of Representatives authorizing the study and identification of a De Soto historic trail (Public Law 100–187). It then fell to the National Park Service to conduct a study to determine whether it was feasible to designate the De Soto route as a national historic trail in accordance with its standards for such trails. The National Park Service contracted with me to supply them with a map and a synopsis of the expedition as I understood it at that time. For each town or locality on my route, I was to indicate whether the location was positive, probable, possible, or problematic. Of the entire route, only one location—the 1539–40 winter camp at the Governor Martin site in Tallahassee—could be judged to be positive; a fair number of locations were probable; but the majority, lacking archaeological confirmation, could only be listed as possible or problematic.[113] The National Park Service Advisory Board determined that the De Soto trail could not be designated a national historic trail because it failed to meet two of three requisite criteria. First, because too few sites along the trail are positively documented, it can be argued that a scholarly consensus on the route does not exist. And because the route cannot be positively located, there is little potential for public use.[114]

Appended to the final report of the National Historic Trail Study is a series of letters from the public that provide a representative sample of the kind of debate my route has engendered.[115] These range from serious, reasoned scholarly argumentation to unabashed local boosterism and defense of in-place De Soto monuments, as well as some downright loopy claims of understanding the mysteries of the De Soto expedition. For obscure reasons, the De Soto expedition excites strange passions in people. For example, one gentleman, a dowser from Natchez, Mississippi, whose instrument is a bent coat hanger, offered his services to De Soto researchers, promising to pinpoint locations on a map.[116] All he asked in return was a "souvenir" from one of the sites, and some recognition.

On November 16, 1990, an act (Public Law 101–607) was passed in the 101st Congress establishing a federal De Soto Expedition Trail Commission. The purpose of the commission was to encourage research on De Soto's route and on the native societies he encountered. The commission was allotted four years in which to do its work. It was to consist of nineteen members, appointed by the secretary of the interior. The act authorized an appropriation of $250,000 for the operation of the commission and $750,000 for research. However, it fell victim to federal cost-cutting or else to a wariness of the kind of contention and argumentation that soured some of the state commissions. The money was never appropriated, and the commission never met.

In addition to the pointed and often particularistic criticism already discussed, our research has also come under broader attack. Lewis Larson tried to argue that Juan Pardo did not depart in a northerly direction from Santa Elena, but rather southward, and therefore the Pardo route I set forth along with Marvin Smith and Chester DePratter was off by a mere 110 degrees. While Larson coyly declined to discuss the implications of his alternative direction for Pardo's departure from Santa Elena, his argument was simply that if we were wrong on Pardo, our De Soto route was robbed of corroboratory evidence for the locations of native towns in the interior.[117] However, Larson cites the available primary documents selectively, and he was too trusting of secondary sources and sixteenth-century maps. He does not place the Pardo route into the larger historical and archaeological context. It was not difficult for us to refute his proposed reorientation of Pardo's route.[118]

Another species of broad attack on our research has been methodological. C. Clifford Boyd Jr. and Gerald F. Schroedl chose to attack our route through the Tennessee Valley.[119] My colleagues and I immediately published a detailed reply to all of their criticisms.[120] A far more sweeping methodological attack came from David Henige. Certain that we cannot have done what we claim to have done, he comes close to criticizing us for the buttons on our overcoats.[121] My colleagues and I published immediate rebuttals to his criticisms.[122]

I do not wish to impute a false solidity to the new routes of exploration of De Soto, Luna, and Pardo. I have resisted referring to the new routes as hypotheses—as have some of my colleagues—because I do not regard them as propositions that can be neatly proved or disproved. They are interpretive reconstructions that aim for a best fit with available historical and archaeological information. In the interest of achieving successively better fits, I have already made a number of modifications in the initial formulations. In some cases, these changes have been instances of coming up with more adequate ways of making sense of existing information. I saw and understood things that I did not see before. For example, when DePratter, Smith, and I published our paper on Pardo's route, I was not confident in our accounting for the excursion that Pardo took beyond Chiaha, and I subsequently worked out a better route, one that made more sense with respect to geographical details and known archaeological sites and that explained some puzzling linguistic anomalies.[123] I was similarly dissatisfied with the segment of De Soto's route from Chiaha to Tali when our initial reconstruction was published. And again, I subsequently worked out a solution that was more consistent with a series of river crossings and the locations of archaeological sites.[124]

Still other changes in our initial routes have been made possible through discoveries of new information, both archaeological and documentary. For example, on the basis of John Worth's archaeological survey of the Flint River, we moved De Soto's second crossing of the Flint River a few miles upstream from our initial location, and we also moved our proposed location for the chiefdom of Toa upstream.[125] Other archaeological discoveries have persuaded me that I was right in the first place. For example, a criticism that was once made when I placed Apafalaya at the Moundville archaeological complex was that not a single Spanish artifact had ever been found in this area, even though about 10 percent of this large site has been excavated. But subsequently, an avocational archaeologist found a Nueva Cadiz bead in the Moundville area.[126]

Ultimately, the archaeological discoveries that will be most beneficial in refining the route will be the discovery of more sites like the Governor Martin site in Tallahassee, where the 1539–40 winter camp was located. The general location of Anhayca (Apalachee) had been known to archaeologists and historians for many decades. Because of this, it was discouraging that the discovery of the actual site was so long in coming, and when it was discovered, it was almost by accident.[127] But because the site has now been pinpointed, more confidence can be had in De Soto's approach to Anhayca in 1539, as well as his route when he departed from Anhayca in the spring of 1540 and traveled northward.

If the long time required to discover the site of Anhayca was discouraging, the recent discovery of what may be the site of Joara is encouraging. I, for one, had little hope that Joara would ever be found. In our initial reconstruction of De Soto's route through the Appalachian Mountains, we placed the town of Joara at the McDowell site (31MC41) near Marion, North Carolina. However, the recent discovery of an unusual amount of sixteenth-century Spanish ceramics and hardware at the Berry site (31Bk22), about twenty miles to the northeast of our initial location, strongly argues that this is the site of Joara.[128] If this is, in fact, the site of Joara—and only extensive excavation will make such a determination possible—it means that the route De Soto took through the mountains must be moved slightly eastward. It now appears that De Soto crossed the mountains by following the North Toe River rather than the French Broad River. And it also appears that Juan Pardo may have crossed the mountains by a different route, possibly along the Pigeon River.[129]

In quite a different quarter, archaeologists at Pensacola Bay (Ochuse) recently discovered the remains of one of Tristán de Luna's ships that sank in a hurricane.[130] It is notable that not so long ago Mobile Bay was thought to be a possible location for Ochuse. Thus, as the reconstructed routes of sixteenth-century Spanish explorers are situated successively closer to places they actually visited, more and more evidence of the sites where these Spaniards spent varying lengths of time may be expected to be forthcoming. I do not think it is at all far-fetched that in coming years we may expect to find one or more of the following: Mabila, Chicaza, Utiangüe, and Aminoya. And of these, the site that will do the most in anchoring a very long stretch of the De Soto route will be the site of Mabila.

Notes

Works frequently cited have been identified by the following abbreviations:

B   Luys Hernández de Biedma, "Relation of the Island of Florida . . . 1539," trans. John E. Worth, in DC, 1:223–46.

DC   Lawrence A. Clayton, Vernon James Knight Jr., and Edward C. Moore, eds., *The De Soto Chronicles: The Expedition of Hernando de Soto to North America in 1539–1543,* 2 vols. (Tuscaloosa: University of Alabama Press, 1993).

DWM   Gloria A. Young and Michael P. Hoffman, eds., *The Expedition of Hernando de Soto West of the Mississippi, 1541–1543* (Fayetteville: University of Arkansas Press, 1993).

E   Gentleman of Elvas, *True Relation of the Hardships Suffered by Governor Fernando de Soto and Certain Portuguese Gentlemen during the Discovery of the Province of Florida,* vol. 2, trans. and ed. James Alexander Robertson (DeLand, Fla.: Florida State Historical Society, 1933).

FC   Charles Hudson and Carmen Chaves Tesser, eds., *The Forgotten Centuries: Indians and Europeans in the American South, 1521–1704* (Athens: University of Georgia Press, 1994).

FR   John R. Swanton, *Final Report of the United States De Soto Expedition Commission,* House Document No. 71, 76th Congress, 1st Session (Washington, D.C.: GPO, 1939). Reprinted in 1985 by Smithsonian Institution Press, with an introduction by Jeffrey P. Brain.

G   Garcilaso de la Vega, *The Florida of the Inca,* trans. John Grier Varner and Jeannette Johnson Varner (Austin: University of Texas Press, 1951).

LA   Mark Williams and Gary Shapiro, eds., *Lamar Archaeology: Mississippian Chief-doms in the Deep South* (Tuscaloosa: University of Alabama Press, 1990).

R   Rodrigo Rangel, "Account of the Northern Conquest and Discovery of Her-nando de Soto," trans. John E. Worth, DC, 1:247–310.

T&T   David H. Dye and Cheryl Anne Cox, eds., *Towns and Temples along the Missis-sippi* (Tuscaloosa: University of Alabama Press, 1990).

PREFACE

1. Powell's painting can be seen on the jacket cover of David J. Weber's invaluable survey *The Spanish Frontier in North America* (New Haven: Yale University Press, 1992).

Lytle's novel was published in 1941 (and reprinted by the University of Alabama Press in 1990), in the wake of the scholarship and publicity stimulated by the work of the U.S. De Soto Expedition Commission. Lytle's novel ends with De Soto's body being placed in the Mississippi River.

Lily Peter, *The Great Riding: The Story of De Soto in America* (Fayetteville: University of Arkansas Press, 1983).

2. David Hackett Fischer, "The Braided Narrative: Substance and Form in Social History," in *The Literature of Fact,* ed. Angus J. S. Fletcher (New York: Columbia University Press, 1976), 109–33.

3. Fernand Braudel, *On History,* trans. Sarah Matthews (Chicago: University of Chicago Press, 1980), esp. 25–54.

4. Roland Chardon, "The Elusive Spanish League: A Problem of Measurement in Sixteenth-Century New Spain," *Hispanic American Historical Review* 60 (1980): 294–302; Roland Chardon, "The Linear League in North America," *Annals of the Association of American Geographers* 70 (1980): 129–53.

5. Chester B. DePratter, Charles M. Hudson, and Marvin T. Smith, "The Route of Juan Pardo's Explorations in the Interior Southeast, 1566–68," *Florida Historical Quarterly* 62 (1983): 138.

6. This estimate of De Soto's rate of speed is about the same as the figure that appears to have been favored by Swanton (FR, 104).

7. FR, 107–8.

CHAPTER 1: Separate Worlds

1. Throughout this chapter I have relied heavily on J. H. Elliott, *Imperial Spain, 1469–1716* (New York: St. Martin's Press, 1963).

2. Elliott, *Imperial Spain,* 13; David J. Weber, *The Spanish Frontier in North America* (New Haven: Yale University Press, 1992).

3. Elliott, *Imperial Spain,* 77.

4. Ibid., 30.

5. Ibid., 37–38.

6. Ibid., 104–6.

7. Ibid., 111–18.

8. Ibid., 45–47; James Lockhart, *The Men of Cajamarca: A Social and Biographical Study of the First Conquerors of Peru* (Austin: University of Texas Press, 1972), 18–21.

9. Lockhart, *Cajamarca*, 79; D. K. Abbass, "Horses and Heroes: The Myth of the Importance of the Horse to the Conquest of the Indies," *Terrae Incognitae* 18 (1986): 21–41. Abbass, while at pains to argue that it was a myth that the horse was important in the conquest, in fact only presents evidence that the horse could not be used in *all* situations, that not *all* Indians were afraid of them, and that the Spaniards may have loved their horses too much.

10. Elliott, *Imperial Spain*, 57–58.

11. Ibid., 62–63.

12. Ibid., 68.

13. J. H. Elliott, "The Discovery of America and the Discovery of Man," in *Spain and Its World, 1500–1700*, ed. J. H. Elliott (New Haven: Yale University Press, 1989), 42–64. John Worth informs me that in seventeenth-century Florida the word was spelled "Chichimeco."

14. Elliott, *Imperial Spain*, 55.

15. Ibid., 59–63.

16. Ibid., 71–72.

17. Bartolomé Bennassar, *The Spanish Character: Attitudes and Mentality from the Sixteenth to the Nineteenth Centuries*, trans. Benjamin Keen (Berkeley: University of California Press, 1979), 27–46.

18. Ibid., 47–68.

19. Ibid., 146–77.

20. Ibid., 213–36. Sixteenth-century Spaniards were not alone in having been greatly concerned with questions of honor. See J. G. Peristiany, ed., *Honour and Shame: The Values of Mediterranean Society* (Chicago: University of Chicago Press, 1966). And it was a cultural complex that would have been quite intelligible to people in the Old South, as may be seen in Bertram Wyatt-Brown, *Southern Honour: Ethics and Behavior in the Old South* (Oxford: Oxford University Press, 1982).

21. Charles Hudson, *Elements of Southeastern Indian Religion*, Iconography of Religions, sect. 10, fascicle 1 (Leiden: E. J. Brill, 1984).

22. Alvar Núñez Cabeza de Vaca, *The Narrative of Alvar Núñez Cabeza de Vaca*, trans. Fanny Bandelier (Barre, Mass.: Imprint Society, 1972), 27, 99–101; T. M. Hamilton, *Native American Bows*, Missouri Archaeological Society, Special Publication, no. 5, 2d ed. (Columbia: Missouri Archaeological Society, 1982), 1–57; Frank Schambach, "A Probable Spiroan Entrepôt in the Red River Valley in Northeast Texas," manuscript.

23. Wayne Van Horne, "The Warclub: Weapon and Symbol in Southeastern Indian Societies," Ph.D. diss., University of Georgia, 1993.

24. Eugene Lyon, "The Cañete Fragment: Another Narrative of Hernando de Soto," in *The Hernando de Soto Expedition*, ed. Jerald T. Milanich (New York: Garland, 1991), 453–54. John Worth is of the opinion that this document is a notary's summary of oral testimony by Cañete.

25. John Phillip Reid, *A Law of Blood: The Primitive Law of the Cherokee Nation* (New York: New York University Press, 1970).

26. Van Horne, "The Warclub."

27. David G. Anderson, "Stability and Change in Chiefdom-Level Societies: An Examination of Mississippian Political Evolution on the South Atlantic Slope," LA, 187–213; Anderson, *The Savannah River Chiefdoms: Political Change in the Late Prehistoric Southeast* (Tuscaloosa: University of Alabama Press, 1994).

28. William H. Baden, "The Impact of Fluctuating Agricultural Potential on Coosa's Sociopolitical and Settlement Systems" (paper presented at the annual meeting of the Southeastern Archaeological Conference, Knoxville, Tenn., November 1995).

29. Anderson, "Stability and Change."

30. Elliott, *Imperial Spain*, 52–59.

31. Ibid., 57–59; Paul E. Hoffman, "Introduction: The De Soto Expedition, a Cultural Crossroads," DC, 1:1–3.

32. Peter Martyr, *De Orbe Novo*, ed. and trans. F. A. MacNutt (New York, 1912), 2:24–25.

33. Paul E. Hoffman, *A New Andalucia and a Way to the Orient: The American Southeast during the Sixteenth Century* (Baton Rouge: Louisiana State University Press, 1990), 6.

34. Ibid., 10.

35. Ibid., 4–17.

36. Ibid., 48.

37. Martyr, *De Orbe Novo*, 2:24–25.

38. Ibid., 12–21, 35, 48. Martyr denies that they were cannibals (2:24).

39. Hoffman, *A New Andalucia*, 38.

40. Ibid., 51–59.

41. Ibid., 66–68.

42. Louis DeVorsey Jr., "Early Maps and the Land of Ayllón," in *Columbus and the Land of Ayllón: The Exploration and Settlement of the Southeast*, ed. Jeannine Cook (Darien, Ga.: Darien News, 1992), 17–22.

43. Hoffman, *A New Andalucia*, 84–86.

44. Paul E. Hoffman, "Narváez and Cabeza de Vaca in Florida," FC, 53–54.

45. Rochelle A. Marrinan, John F. Scarry, and Rhonda L. Majors, "Prelude to de Soto: The Expedition of Pánfilo de Narváez," in *Columbian Consequences*, ed. David H. Thomas (Washington, D.C.: Smithsonian Institution Press, 1990), 2:71–82.

46. Cabeza de Vaca, *Narrative*, 38–39.

CHAPTER 2: Hernando de Soto

1. David Ewing Duncan, *Hernando de Soto: A Savage Quest in the Americas* (New York: Crown Publishing, 1995), 3–4.

2. James Lockhart, *The Men of Cajamarca: A Social and Biographical Study of the First Conquerors of Peru* (Austin: University of Texas Press, 1972), 199.

3. Miguel Albornoz, *Hernando de Soto: Knight of the Americas* (New York: Franklin Watts, 1986), 13.

4. E, 5; Rocío Sánchez Rubio, "El Adelantado Don Hernando de Soto," trans. Eduardo Kortright, DC, 1:387.

5. Paul E. Hoffman, "Hernando de Soto: A Brief Biography," DC, 1:421–27. The origin of such companies is obscure. See Lockhart, *Cajamarca*, 70–74.

6. John Hemming, *The Conquest of the Incas* (New York: Harcourt, Brace, Jovanovich, 1970), 26–27; Duncan, *Hernando de Soto*, 102–3.

7. Hemming, *The Conquest of the Incas*, 23–177; Hoffman, "Hernando de Soto," DC, 1:434–40; Duncan, *Hernando de Soto*, 116–200.

8. Lockhart, *Cajamarca*, 82–89, 193–94.

9. AGI, Justicia 750, Pieza 2A. This and other documents cited here from the Archivo General de Indias (AGI) in Seville were copied and translated by Irene Wright in the 1930s. They are housed in the National Anthropological Archive, Smithsonian Institution. See the afterword, this volume.

10. Lockhart, *Cajamarca*, 197.

11. Testimony of Cristóbal Calcanas, AGI, Justicia 750B, Pieza 7.

12. Testimony of Diego Gutiérrez de los Rios, AGI, Justicia 750B, Pieza 7. Ponce de León later set the figure at 130,000 *castellanos*, claiming that this was all the gold and silver the two of them had accumulated up to this point.

13. E, 6–7.

14. "Conveyance of Dower by the Widow of Pedrárias Dávila to Hernando de Soto, in Consideration of the Espousal of her Daughter," DC, 1:357.

15. G, 5; Hoffman, "Hernando de Soto," DC, 1:448–49.

16. AGI, Justicia 750B, Pieza 7; "Letter of Hernando de Soto Respecting Concessions He Desires Shall Be Obtained for Him at Court," DC, 1:358.

17. Elvas says De Soto took 180,000 cruzados to Spain. A portion of this was paid to the emperor, including an investment of 600,000 reales in the silks of Granada (E, 6). For *juros*, see Lockhart, *Cajamarca*, 55.

18. Lockhart, *Cajamarca*, 197–98.

19. Hoffman, *A New Andalucia*, 87–88; "Concession Made by the King of Spain to Hernando de Soto of the Government of Cuba and Conquest of Florida, with the Title of Adelantado," DC, 1:359–65.

20. Alvar Núñez Cabeza de Vaca, *The Narrative of Alvar Núñez Cabeza de Vaca*, trans. Fanny Bandelier (Barre, Mass.: Imprint Society, 1972).

21. E, 8–9.

22. Ibid., 9–11.

23. Hoffman, *A New Andalucia*, 89–90.

24. E, 12. After the expedition, Luís de Moscoso claimed he had counseled De Soto several times not to proceed with the expedition to La Florida (AGI, Justicia 750, Pieza 2A).

25. Lockhart, *Cajamarca*, 196.

26. Ibid., 190–91; Hoffman, "Hernando de Soto," DC, 1:457.

27. Lockhart, *Cajamarca*, 199–200, 24–25. No children were born from De Soto's union with Isabel.

28. E, 7.

29. FR, 80; "Authorization for Doña Isabel de Bobadilla to Bring Three Slave Women to the Island of Cuba for Her Service," DC, 1:469–70.

30. Ignacio Avellaneda, *Los Sobrevivientes de la Florida: The Survivors of the De Soto Expedition*, Research Publications of the P. K. Yonge Library of Florida History, no. 2 (Gainesville: University of Florida Libraries, 1990), 68.

31. E, 11.

32. Ibid., 12.

33. Ibid., 14.

34. Ibid., 15.

35. Avellaneda, *Los Sobrevivientes*, 6–7.

36. Ibid., 6, 38–39.

37. Ibid., 69–73.

38. E, 13.

39. Garcilaso says there were eight ships, and he claims to name all of them, plus two bergantines that are unnamed (G, 21–22). Elvas says De Soto delivered seven ships to the appointed captains (E, 15).

40. G, 23.

41. Hoffman, "Hernando de Soto," DC, 1:453; Garcilaso sets this at April 6 (G, 23).

42. E, 16–17.

43. G, 24.

44. Ibid., 24–25.

45. Ibid., 25–26.

46. Ibid., 26–27.

47. Ibid., 28.

48. E, 16–17, 329.

49. G, 29.

50. G, 28.

51. Ibid., 28.

52. E, 17–18.

53. G, 30–31.

54. E, 30–31.

55. Ibid., 17–18.

56. Ibid., 21–23.

57. Ibid., 19.

58. Ibid., 20–21.

59. G, 40.

60. E, 21.

61. Ibid., 25.

62. Ibid., 22–23. Garcilaso, ever the apologist, says most of the Indians of Cuba hanged themselves because the easy, tropical climate made them lazy and they did not want to labor (G, 41–42).

63. G, 39–40. I am grateful to John Worth for advice on *juegos de cañas*.

64. Ibid., 41.

65. Ibid., 42–43.

66. Ibid., 44; E, 30. Both Elvas and Rangel say the herd of pigs was large.

67. E, 23–26.

68. Garcilaso, who sets the number of men at 350, says De Soto and the cavalry departed from Santiago at the end of August (G, 44).

69. E, 24–25.

70. Ibid., 25–26.

71. Ibid., 26–27.

72. Ibid., 30–31.

73. Ibid.

74. Estimates of how many Indians they brought back from La Florida ranged from two to five. Testimony of Rodrigo Rangel, Alonso Martín, Catalina Ximénez, Pedro Calderón, and Monso Gutiérrez de Cardona in AGI, Justicia 750, Pieza 2A. Garcilaso says they spent two months exploring the coast. Only Garcilaso says De Soto sent Añasco back to explore the coast on a second occasion, this time for three months (G, 45).

75. G, 45.

76. E, 29–30; Duncan, *Hernando de Soto*, 239.

77. G, 46.

78. AGI, Justicia 750, Pieza 2A.

79. G, 46–47.

80. Ibid., 47.

81. Ibid., 47–48.

82. E, 31.

83. G, 48–49.

84. AGI, Justicia 750, Pieza 2A.

85. Ibid. According to later testimony, the tent soon wore out.

86. "Will of Hernando de Soto," DC, 1:366–72.

87. G, 50–51.

CHAPTER 3: La Florida

1. R, 252; E, 31. Garcilaso names one ship too many (G, 54–55). He says they departed on May 12 (G, 54). A detailed argument for a landing at Tampa Bay may be found in Jerald T. Milanich and Charles Hudson, *Hernando de Soto and the Indians of Florida* (Gainesville: University Press of Florida, 1993), 39–70. For a discussion of ships, see Roger C. Smith, *Vanguard of Empire: Ships of Exploration in the Age of Columbus* (New York: Oxford University Press, 1993), 34–49, 126–27.

2. E, 31. Elvas puts their distance from shore at one league.

3. R, 254.

4. E, 32–33.

5. B, 225.

6. R, 253.

7. Ibid.

8. Ibid.

9. R, 254. In 1897 the depth of this channel was 25.5 feet (Milanich and Hudson, *Hernando de Soto*, 46–47). Because of a modern warming trend, the depth was perhaps 3 feet shallower in 1539. Donald J. Colquhoon and Mark J. Brooks, "New Evidence from

the Southeastern U.S. for Eustatic Components in the Late Holocene Sea Levels," *Geo-archaeology* 1 (1986): 276.

10. G, 59.

11. R, 253. Unfortunately, Rangel does not say whether this village was the "village of Ozita," where De Soto had first arrived. Elvas puts the distance at two leagues (E, 31).

12. R, 254. Garcilaso is probably incorrect in saying this man's name was Hirrihigua (G, 60).

13. Roger Hanlon, Frederick Bayer, and Gilbert Voss, *Guide to the Mangroves, Button-wood, and Poisonous Shoreline Trees of Florida, the Gulf of Mexico, and the Caribbean Region,* Sea Grant Field Guide Series, no. 3, University of Miami Sea Grant Program (Miami, 1975), 1–29; Jedfrey M. Carlton, *A Guide to Common Florida Salt Marsh and Mangrove Vegetation,* Florida Marine Research Publications, no. 6, Florida Department of Natural Resources (St. Petersburg, 1975), 1–30.

14. E, 32.

15. Ibid.

16. R, 254.

17. G, 60.

18. R, 254; E, 32.

19. Elvas says they were put ashore only two leagues from where the village subject to Ozita was located (E, 31). Elvas spells it "Uzita," and he seems to imply that De Soto remained at the landing place (E, 33).

20. R, 255.

21. E, 31; Milanich and Hudson, *Hernando de Soto,* 61.

22. Rangel says they departed from Havana with 570 men and with about 130 sailors manning the ships (R, 254). The 570 may not include women (at least two) and servants. Rangel says they departed from Havana with 243 horses and 19 or 20 died en route. Elvas says they landed with 213 horses (E, 31). Biedma says they landed 620 men and 223 horses (B, 225).

23. Terence Wise, *The Conquistadores* (London: Osprey, 1980), 14, 18, plates B and C.

24. E, 32.

25. Ibid., 33; Milanich and Hudson, *Hernando de Soto,* 66–67; Jerald T. Milanich and Charles H. Fairbanks, *Florida Archaeology* (New York: Academic Press, 1980), 204–10; Jeffrey M. Mitchem, "Redefining Safety Harbor: Late Prehistoric/Protohistoric Archaeology in West Peninsular Florida," Ph.D. diss., University of Florida, 1989, 2:550–605.

26. E, 34; Milanich and Hudson, *Hernando de Soto,* 67–68.

27. E, 33. Elvas evidently errs when he says the men and horses reached Uzita on June 1.

28. R, 252, 255.

29. E, 34.

30. Hernando de Soto, "Letter of Hernando de Soto at Tampa Bay to the Justice and Board of Magistrates in Santiago de Cuba," DC, 1:375–77.

31. G, 107, 109, 113, 146.

32. Robert M. Denhardt, *The Horse in the Americas* (Norman: University of Oklahoma Press, 1948).

33. G, 147, 327–28, 409.

34. Jeffrey M. Mitchem and Bonnie G. McEwan, "New Data on Early Bells from Florida," *Southeastern Archaeology* 7 (1988): 39–49. Archaeologists have generally interpreted Clarksdale bells as hawks' bells that were carried by early Europeans as gifts for the Indians. It is known that members of the Narváez expedition gave "little bells" to the Indians as gifts while they were with their horses in Florida and later, after they had killed their horses for food and had been shipwrecked on the Texas coast (Alvar Núñez Cabeza de Vaca, *The Narrative of Alvar Núñez Cabeza de Vaca,* trans. Fanny Bandelier [Barre, Mass.: Imprint Society, 1972], 19, 46–47). Presumably the bells could have been tied to the trappings of horses as well as to the legs of hawks. But it is notable that of all the goods given to Indians by Juan Pardo, bells are not included, and Juan Pardo and his men had no horses with them—they traveled on foot. See Charles Hudson, *The Juan Pardo Expeditions: Exploration of the Carolinas and Tennessee, 1566–1568* (Washington, D.C.: Smithsonian Institution Press, 1990), 134–44.

35. John G. Varner and Jeannette Johnson Varner, *Dogs of the Conquest* (Norman: University of Oklahoma Press, 1983), 93.

36. Reginald Lennard, *Rural England, 1086–1135: A Study of Social and Agrarian Conditions* (Oxford: Clarendon Press, 1966), 252–55; George Duby, *Rural Economy and Country Life in the Medieval West,* trans. Cynthia Postan (Columbia: University of South Carolina Press, 1968), 81, 141; Charles Wayland Towne and Edward Norris Wentworth, *Pigs: From Cave to Corn Belt* (Norman: University of Oklahoma Press, 1950), 7–8, 36–53.

37. Julius Klein, *The Mesta: A Study in Spanish Economic History* (Cambridge: Harvard University Press, 1920), 20–28; Edmund Cody Burnett, "Hog Raising and Hog Driving in the Region of the French Broad River," *Agricultural History* 20 (1946): 86–103.

38. R, 255; E, 35.

39. G, 74–75.

40. E, 37–38.

41. G, 76–77.

42. Ibid., 79.

43. R, 255; E, 36, 38; G, 78–79. According to Elvas, Juan Ortiz stated: "Sirs, I am a Christian; do not kill me. Do not kill these Indians, for they have given me my life" (E, 38). Biedma says they learned of Ortiz's existence from some Indians they captured soon after landing. Ortiz was said to be held by Indians who lived eight leagues from their camp (B, 225).

44. G, 80.

45. B, 225.

46. Ibid.; G, 79.

47. G, 62. Garcilaso says three Spaniards went ashore.

48. Ibid.; Garcilaso says Ortiz was about eighteen years old when he was captured. According to Garcilaso, Ortiz's life was spared when he was first captured because of the chief's wife and three daughters, who pleaded that he be allowed to live (G, 63).

49. G, 83.

50. Ibid., 64–65.

51. Ibid., 81, 82.

52. Ibid., 65.

53. Garcilaso says "lions" would enter the temples and eat the bodies (G, 65). It is possible he is referring to panthers, but panthers are not scavengers.

54. Ibid., 66.

55. Elvas calls the weapon a "club" (E, 41); G, 66–67.

56. G, 67.

57. E, 39–41.

58. G, 68.

59. According to Garcilaso, the chief resolved to kill Ortiz on account of his old anger over his mutilation and the horrible execution of his mother (G, 68–69).

60. E, 42.

61. According to the ever-romantic Garcilaso, Mocozo wished to marry the girl who helped Ortiz (G, 70).

62. E, 43–44.

63. Ibid., 44.

64. Ibid., 45.

65. Ibid.

66. G, 76.

67. E, 45–46.

68. G, 83.

69. Ibid., 81.

70. According to Garcilaso, Hirrihigua complained to Urriparacoxi about Mocozo's holding his former prisoner, Ortiz, and he wanted him returned. But Urriparacoxi either could not or would not order that he be returned to him (G, 72–73).

71. E, 46–47; B, 226. Elvas has this as "Paracoxi." Biedma confirms that they all paid tribute to him. Note the dominance of an interior chief over coastal chiefs. Biedma says Urriparacoxi was twenty leagues inland (B, 226).

72. E, 47–48.

73. G, 86–87.

74. Rangel spells them "Orriygua" and "Ezita" (R, 256). Caploey may be the Pojoy of later documents.

75. Ibid.

76. Ibid.

77. Ibid.

78. Ibid., 257.

79. Rangel has it "Orriparacogi" (R, 257).

80. Ibid.

81. G, 88.

82. R, 257. The soils around Tampa Bay are the Myakka-Immokalee-Waveland association. All have severe limitations on the plants they can support.

83. E, 49. Elvas says there were fifty horsemen and thirty to forty foot soldiers.

84. G, 90–91.

85. R, 257–58.

86. E, 49.

87. G, 97–98.

88. Ibid., 98–99.

89. R, 258; E, 50; G, 100.

90. G, 99–100.

91. Ibid., 92–95. Garcilaso spells this "Urribarracuxi" (G, 92).

92. Garcilaso says they traveled the sixteen or seventeen leagues from Mocozo to Urri-paracoxi in four days. He says the distance from Ozita was twenty-five leagues (G, 95).

93. E, 50–51. Gonzalo Silvestre claimed to have been one of those sent back. He claimed they covered the twenty-five leagues in two days (G, 96).

CHAPTER 4: Apalachee

1. Garcilaso says the detachment consisted of Gonzalo Silvestre and three other horsemen (G, 96).

2. R, 258.

3. Ibid.

4. B, 226. Elvas says Ocale was toward the west from Urriparacoxi (E, 51). In actuality, it was to the northwest.

5. Hernando de Soto, "Letter of Hernando de Soto at Tampa Bay to the Justice and Board of Magistrates in Santiago de Cuba," DC, 1:375–77.

6. E, 51. Randolph J. Widmer, *The Evolution of the Calusa: A Nonagricultural Chiefdom on the Southwest Florida Coast* (Tuscaloosa: University of Alabama Press, 1988), 3–5, 40–41.

7. R, 258. Elvas says De Soto left thirty cavalry and seventy infantry behind at Tampa (E, 51). Garcilaso puts it at forty cavalry and eighty foot soldiers in addition to the sailors who manned the ships (G, 101).

Garcilaso says the ships in the harbor were a caravel and two brigantines (G, 101).

8. E, 51.

9. G, 102.

10. E, 46.

11. De Soto, "Letter of Hernando de Soto at Tampa Bay," DC, 1:375–77.

12. G, 101. Garcilaso says twenty cavalry were sent (with Gonzalo Silvestre) with news that De Soto would follow "when four more days had passed" (G, 101).

13. Biedma says they headed toward the west (B, 226), but this is obviously an error. Jerald T. Milanich and Charles Hudson, *Hernando de Soto and the Indians of Florida* (Gainesville: University Press of Florida, 1993), 76. See also p. 443, this volume.

14. E, 33; G, 282–83, 271.

15. Paul A. Delcourt, Hazel R. Delcourt, Dan F. Morse, and Phyllis A. Morse, "History, Evolution, and Organization of Vegetation and Human Culture," in *Biodiversity of the Southeastern United States,* ed. William H. Martin, Stephen G. Boyce, and Arthur C. Echternacht (New York: John Wiley, 1993), 47–79.

16. Garcilaso implies that they visited Mocozo's main town (G, 102).

17. R, 259.

18. Randall B. Brown, Earl L. Stone, and Victor W. Carlisle, "Soils," in *Ecosystems of Florida,* ed. Ronald L. Myers and John J. Ewel (Orlando: University of Central Florida

Press), 1990, 36–41; Don Stap, "Along a Ridge in Florida: An Ecological House Built on Sand," *Smithsonian*, September 1994, 36–44.

19. Evidently they traveled across a stretch of Candler-Apopka-Astatula association soils. In the eighteenth century Indians in Florida knew that one had to carry a water supply for both men and horses when crossing this area. See Bernard Romans, *A Concise Natural History of East and West Florida* (New Orleans: Pelican Publishing, 1961), 24–25.

20. R, 259. The local soils are of the Arredondo-Kendrick-Miller association, some of which are fertile.

21. Milanich and Hudson, *Hernando de Soto*, 73–76, 128–29.

22. Katherine C. Ewel, "Swamps," in *Ecosystems of Florida*, ed. Ronald L. Myers and John J. Ewel (Orlando: University of Central Florida Press, 1990), 281–322.

23. R, 259–60. There is a discrepancy in the number of cavalry remaining with De Soto when Rangel returned to camp. Rangel says his absence left only ten men with De Soto. But then he says the fourteen reinforcements he brought forward raised the number of men with De Soto to twenty-six. Assuming that Rangel returned with the fourteen men, this leaves a discrepancy of one. Perhaps De Soto was the one who was not accounted for.

24. Ibid., 260.

25. E, 52.

26. R, 260; G, 107–13.

27. De Soto sent two riders back from the swamp of Ocale on two different occasions: first, to order thirty lancers forward and to order the army to move forward, and second, two days later, to warn the army to speed up. The incident recounted by Garcilaso is clearly the first of these (G, 107–13).

28. Ibid., 114–15.

29. Garcilaso confuses the swamp near the main towns of Urriparacoxi with the swamp of Ocale. That is to say, the swamp Garcilaso describes (G, 104–22) was not three leagues from Urriparacoxi—the distance was closer to three days' travel. Garcilaso's treatment of this swamp crossing seems curiously overblown. He allots, for example, far too many days to the episode.

30. Ibid., 104; Milanich and Hudson, *Hernando de Soto*, 87–91.

31. G, 105.

32. Ibid. Cabeza de Vaca mentions no swamp crossing before reaching the Withlacoochee (Alvar Núñez Cabeza de Vaca, *The Narrative of Alvar Núñez Cabeza de Vaca*, trans. Fanny Bandelier [Barre, Mass.: Imprint Society, 1972], 17).

33. G, 121.

34. Ibid., 105. Garcilaso says *two* trees had fallen across the river, presumably one from either bank, and they built a footbridge connecting the two trees (G, 105).

35. Ibid., 105–6.

36. Ibid., 106. Garcilaso says the horse crossing was three crossbow shots upstream from the bridge.

37. R, 260–61. Obviously, this refers to the effective range of a crossbow, not the maximum range.

38. Ibid.

39. Ibid; G, 107.

40. Garcilaso incorrectly identifies this place as Acuera (G, 116).

41. R, 261. Elvas says they captured three Indians (E, 53). Biedma says three or four (B, 226).

42. B, 226.

43. G, 116.

44. R, 261.

45. Ibid.

46. E, 53.

47. These soils are of the Arredondo-Kendrick-Milhopper association. General Soil Map of Florida, United States Department of Agriculture, 1982; Milanich and Hudson, *Hernando de Soto*, 91–110.

Biedma says Ocale was 15 to 20 leagues from Urriparacoxi (B, 226). From present-day Lacoochee to Camp Izard is about 45 miles. At 15 leagues this suggests a league measurement of about 3 miles to the league. At 20 leagues it is a league of about 2.25 miles to the league. Biedma also appears to say that Ocale was 10 or 12 leagues from the coast (B, 226).

Garcilaso places Acuera (i.e., Ocale) at 20 leagues to the north of Urriparacoxi. The direction is correct, but the straight line distance is about 32 miles (9.2 leguas comúnes), and their actual travel distance was about 40 miles (11.5 leguas comúnes), but it must have *seemed* much longer than that.

Note that I assume, for reasons already given, that everywhere Garcilaso uses "Acuera" he should have used "Ocale."

48. G, 117–18.

49. Ibid., 118–19.

50. Garcilaso puts the number of Spanish dead at fourteen and the number of Indian dead at fifty (G, 120).

51. Milanich and Hudson, *Hernando de Soto*, 96–98. In his letter, De Soto says Acuera was located three days from Urriparacoxi and two days from Ocale. These estimated travel times are consistent with the locations I propose for these places. John Worth informs me that in the early seventeenth century, an Acuera province with two missions was located on the Oklawaha River, a bit north of Lake Weir.

52. R, 261; Milanich and Hudson, *Hernando de Soto*, 131.

53. E, 53–54.

54. "A mortar cannon or mortar made of a log, with a pestle like a window bar" (E, 54).

55. Ibid., 54–55.

56. Ibid., 54.

57. R, 262; E, 55. Again, this place-name may be a title (*holata* is Timucuan for "chief"). There was an eastern and a western trail they could have taken upon departing from Ocale. I favor the eastern trail. Milanich and Hudson, *Hernando de Soto*, 136, 146.

58. This trail is shown on a military map of Florida compiled in 1839 by order of Gen. Zachary Taylor. Itarraholata was probably in the vicinity of Charley Emathla's town, present-day Emathla.

59. G, 121.

60. Ibid., 122.

61. Milanich and Hudson, *Hernando de Soto,* 140. Again, these are the Arredondo-Kendrick-Milhopper soils. Political relations among peoples of the Alachua archaeological culture in 1539 are unknown.

62. R, 262. Elvas puts the number at twenty-eight (E, 55). It is not clear whether these slaves were seized at Potano or at Malapaz, but Elvas appears to imply they were seized the night they were at Potano (E, 56).

63. E, 56.

64. R, 262; E, 56. In Garcilaso's version of this story, the man jumped into a river, but Bruto jumped in after him and tore him to pieces in the water (G, 126).

65. G, 126.

66. R, 262; Milanich and Hudson, *Hernando de Soto,* 154–56.

67. Garcilaso mistakenly calls Aguacaleyquen "Ocale" (122).

68. B, 226; G, 122.

69. R, 263.

70. The largest village appears to have been Uriutina. Garcilaso mistakenly calls it "Ochile" (G, 129). Garcilaso says the province was ruled by three brothers, though he did not know the basis on which the province had been divided up. Garcilaso quotes Juan Coles as saying that the territory of Yustega measured two hundred leagues from one side to the other (G, 137).

71. Brent R. Weisman, *Excavations on the Franciscan Frontier: Archaeology at the Fig Springs Mission* (Gainesville: University Press of Florida, 1992), 28–34; Milanich and Hudson, *Hernando de Soto,* 148–51.

72. G, 125–26.

73. E, 57–58.

74. R, 263.

75. E, 58; R, 263–64.

76. Elvas says they departed from Aguacaleyquen on September 10. Rangel says they departed on September 9, but he has them arriving at two different towns on Friday, September 12, "the next day." Hence, Elvas is to be trusted on the date of departure from Aguacaleyquen. Note that Elvas's dates often are a day later than Rangel's.

Water in the Ichetucknee must have been high to have made a bridge necessary. The Ichetucknee is principally fed from springs, and one can ordinarily skirt around the uppermost spring. But in wet weather Rose Creek runs into the Ichetucknee, making it a continuous stream.

77. Garcilaso mistakenly calls this town "Ochile" (G, 129). Only Garcilaso describes this as a frontier town with dispersed hamlets nearby, and only he describes De Soto's taking it by force with a vanguard of cavalry (G, 129–30).

78. R, 264. This was probably either a men's house or else a house of an important chief. Garcilaso says it was the latter, describing it as being 120 feet long and 40 feet wide, with many rooms inside, and with four doors opening in the cardinal directions (G, 130).

79. Milanich and Hudson, *Hernando de Soto,* 161.

80. R, 264.

81. E, 58.

82. Garcilaso appears to lump together Uzachile and Napituca, calling both "Vitachuco," apparently derived from "Ivitachuco," the first major town of Apalachee. But when Garcilaso uses "Vitachuco," it most often appears that he is referring to Napituca (G, 129–68).

83. G, 134–35.

84. Ibid., 135–38.

85. Milanich and Hudson, *Hernando de Soto,* 161–62.

86. R, 264.

87. It is possible that Napituca lay some miles to the south of present-day Live Oak. According to Garcilaso, the town of Napituca had two hundred large, strong houses, with many smaller hamlets scattered about (G, 138).

88. Ibid.

89. Elvas says fourteen or fifteen Indians came to talk with De Soto (E, 59).

90. R, 264.

91. G, 139–40.

92. Ibid., 139–42; E, 59.

93. G, 143–44.

94. E, 60.

95. Garcilaso says the headdresses were half a fathom high, and he says they were meant to make the men seem taller than they were (G, 145).

96. R, 265.

97. G, 146–47.

98. Ibid., 147.

99. Ibid., 148.

100. Ibid., 145.

101. Garcilaso says the smaller lake was only a league in circumference. The larger one was half a league wide; it was so long it looked like a river, and they did not know where it ended (G, 145).

102. Ibid., 148–49.

103. E, 61.

104. G, 149.

105. E, 62.

106. R, 265.

107. Ibid. Elvas sets the total of Indian prisoners at about two hundred (E, 63).

108. R, 265–66.

109. Ibid.

110. Elvas says the man was an Indian interpreter (E, 62). Garcilaso says he was chief Vitachuco, who as we have seen, was incorrectly named and appears to be several chiefs combined into one (G, 163), though probably he was the chief of Napituca.

111. G, 163–64.

112. Ibid., 166.

113. E, 63; G, 166–67.

114. G, 167.

115. Garcilaso says four were killed (G, 167).

116. Ibid., 163–64.

117. Another possible location for the place at which they came to the river was the vicinity of Ellaville. Future archaeological research should make it possible to decide between the two possible crossings. Note that Garcilaso transposed the Suwannee River with the Ichetucknee or the Santa Fe River. Clearly it is the Suwannee that has banks "twenty-eight feet in height and as sheer as a wall" (G, 123). Such steep banks are especially notable in the vicinity of Dowling Park.

118. R, 266.

119. G, 123.

120. Ibid., 123–24.

121. Ibid., 168–69.

122. R, 266; G, 169. Garcilaso spells Uzachile "Osachile" (G, 175). Elvas spells Apalu "Napaluya" (E, 64).

123. G, 169.

124. Ibid. Garcilaso describes temple mound construction at Uzachile (G, 170–71), but such mounds do not occur in this territory. He may have transposed information on mounds at Apalachee to Uzachile.

125. R, 266.

126. G, 175.

127. "Asile" is the preferred spelling. Rangel has "Agile"(R, 266), whereas Elvas has "Axille" (E, 66).

128. Rangel (or Oviedo) denies that Herrera wanted to assault her. Rather, he says the woman wanted to get free and run away (R, 267).

129. Ibid., 267; E, 66.

130. R, 267. Garcilaso says the river was about forty feet wide (G, 177).

131. G, 175–81.

132. Elvas has "Vitachuco" (E, 66).

133. G, 181–82.

134. Ibid., 182.

135. Elvas has this as "Uzela" (E, 67). Milanich and Hudson, *Hernando de Soto*, 214–15.

136. R, 267.

137. Ibid.

138. Rangel spells Anhayca "Iviahica" (R, 267), obviously a mistranscription of "Iniahica." Biedma has "Yniahyco" (B, 227).

139. R, 267; E, 67.

140. B, 227.

141. This comes to 121.6 leagues using the legua legal and to 92.5 leagues using the legua común. It would seem that Biedma was either using the legua legal, or overestimating how far they had traveled.

CHAPTER 5: Winter, 1539–1540

1. G, 184. Charles Ewen, "Anhaica: Discovery of Hernando de Soto's 1539–1540 Winter Camp," in *First Encounters, Spanish Explorations in the Caribbean and the United*

States, 1492–1570, ed. Jerald T. Milanich and Susan Milbrath (Gainesville: University of Florida Press, 1989), 110–18.

2. G, 193–94.

3. William Bartram, *The Travels of William Bartram,* ed. Frances Harper (New Haven: Yale University Press, 1958), 104–5, 363.

4. G, 259–60. The best soils are those of the Dothan-Orangeburg-Fuquay association (General Soil Map of Florida, United States Department of Agriculture, 1982); Andrew F. Clewell, "The Vegetation of Leon County, Florida," in *The Leon County Bicentennial Survey Report: An Archaeological Survey of Selected Portions of Leon County, Florida,* ed. Louis Daniel Tesser, Bureau of Historic Sites and Properties, Miscellaneous Project Report Series, vol. 1, no. 49 (Tallahassee: Florida Department of State, 1980), 386–440.

5. John H. Hann, *Apalachee: The Land between the Rivers* (Gainesville: University Press of Florida, 1988), 126–33.

6. G, 184, 255.

7. Ibid., 170–71. Garcilaso mistakenly places mounds at Uzachile, where none have been discovered by archaeologists.

This description of the Apalachee chiefdom is based on John F. Scarry, "The Apalachee Chiefdom: A Mississippian Society on the Fringe of the Mississippian World," FC, 156–78.

8. Hann, *Apalachee,* 70–117.

9. G, 185.

10. Garcilaso says they penetrated fifteen to twenty leagues to the north. He felt the nature of this country of Apalachee was so at variance with what Alvar Núñez Cabeza de Vaca reported—that it was rough, covered with forests, swamps, rivers, thinly populated and sterile—that he concluded Narváez had explored near the coast and did not go as far inland as had De Soto (G, 185). In fact, Narváez's path from his landing to the north may have taken him nearer the coast than De Soto's, but beyond the Withlacoochee, his path was probably much the same as De Soto's (G, 186).

11. Garcilaso, probably exaggerating, says there were forty horsemen and fifty foot soldiers (G, 187).

12. E, 67–68. Garcilaso calls this place "Aute" (G, 187). It is likely he got this place-name from reading the narrative of Alvar Núñez Cabeza de Vaca, who reports a town by this name between Apalachee and the coast. Jerald Milanich and Charles Hudson, *Hernando de Soto and the Indians of Florida* (Gainesville: University Press of Florida, 1993), 219.

13. G, 187.

14. Garcilaso says this man misled them because he began to be ashamed that he had served his enemies so well (G, 187).

15. Ibid., 189.

16. Ibid., 190.

17. R, 267. Garcilaso describes it as a broad bay (G, 192). Rangel says Narváez's camp was 8 leagues from Anhayca (R, 267). Biedma says it was about 9 leagues distant (B, 227). Actual distance to the coast was about 24 miles (i.e., 9.1 leguas legales; 6.9 leguas comúnes).

18. Milanich and Hudson, *Hernando de Soto,* 219–20.

19. G, 192.

20. R, 267; E, 78; G, 192.

21. G, 192.

22. B, 227; G, 192–93.

23. G, 252–53.

24. B, 228. Yupaha may have been a tributary society of this female chief, whose chiefdom was Cofitachequi.

25. G, 254.

26. Ibid.

27. E, 71–72.

28. R, 268.

29. G, 195.

30. Ibid., 196.

31. E, 68. Garcilaso incorrectly has this date as October 20 (G, 196).

32. Garcilaso says the swamp was 11 leagues from Anhayca (G, 197). The actual distance was about 34 miles (9.8 leguas comúnes; 12.9 leguas legales). In several instances Garcilaso gives this day's travel as 13 leagues (45 miles by leguas comúnes; 34.2 miles by leguas legales) (G, 197).

33. G, 197.

34. On the return trip Garcilaso again transposes the topography of the Suwannee River to the Santa Fe River, which he here calls the River of Ochali (G, 201).

35. E, 68–69.

36. G, 200.

37. Ibid., 213.

38. Ibid., 198–99.

39. Ibid., 213–14.

40. Garcilaso says they traveled 20 leagues on both the sixth and seventh days. By the end of the seventh day, they had traveled 107 leagues, more or less (G, 214).

41. Ibid., 215.

42. Ibid., 216.

43. Ibid., 219–20.

44. Garcilaso says they made thirteen leagues on this day (G, 220).

45. Garcilaso says they did not enter it because they did not want to encounter its inhabitants (G, 220). In truth, the town was probably considerably east of the trail they were following.

46. Garcilaso says they made fifteen leagues this day (G, 220).

47. Ibid.

48. Garcilaso says these were hostages to be held until they could determine whether the Indians had attacked Calderón (G, 221). But this was untrue. Elvas says, probably erroneously, that the twenty women were taken at "Itarraholata and Potano" (68–69). This is doubtful because on foot the women could not have kept up with the Spanish horsemen.

49. G, 221.

50. Garcilaso calls this "Hirrihigua" (G, 223).

51. R, 268.

52. Garcilaso says they spent nine days traveling (minus one at the Suwannee River and one at the Withlacoochee River) in which they covered 150 leagues (G, 225). Elvas says they were ten days in getting to Tampa Bay (E, 68–69).

53. What happened to the captured women and children is not clear. Garcilaso says they were released to return to Mocozo (G, 225). Elvas, who is probably to be trusted, says they were sent in the caravel to Havana to be given to Doña Isabel (E, 68–69).

54. R, 268. Garcilaso no doubt exaggerates. He says they gave the Indians twenty-five tons of cassava, cloaks, loose coats, doublets, breeches, hose, shoes, buskins, canvas shoes (*alpargates*), curiasses, bucklers, pikes, lances, steel helmets, sails, tackle, pitch, oakum, tallow, ropes, panniers, hampers, anchors, and cables, and quantities of iron and steel (G, 227–28).

55. G, 228–29.

56. B, 227. Garcilaso's numbers are far too high—seventy lancers and fifty footmen (G, 232).

57. G, 238–40.

58. Ibid., 243.

59. Ibid., 245; R, 268.

60. Garcilaso erroneously says Añasco arrived at the Bay of the Horses six days before Calderón arrived in Apalachee (G, 246).

61. B, 227.

62. E, 68–69. Rangel incorrectly gives his arrival date as Saturday, November 19 (R, 268).

63. R, 267. Rangel said each of them acted as if he were a Mucio Scévola of Rome (R, 267).

64. Hann, *Apalachee*, 71.

65. Seemingly describing the same incident, Garcilaso says it involved seven horsemen and occurred in February 1540. He says the Spaniards came upon one woman and two men (G, 250–52).

66. E, 69–70; R, 267.

67. G, 251–52.

68. Ibid., 255.

69. Ibid., 256.

70. Ibid., 206.

71. Ibid., 258–59.

72. Ibid., 259.

73. Clewell, "Vegetation of Leon County," 387–89; G, 194. Garcilaso says he was eight leagues away (G, 203).

74. G, 204–5.

75. Garcilaso, perhaps to explain why Capafi's people would carry him on a litter, wrote that Capafi was so corpulent he had to go about on hands and knees (G, 205).

76. Garcilaso says it was six leagues from Anhayca (G, 207).

77. G, 206–9.

78. Ibid., 210.

79. B, 228.

80. Both Elvas and Garcilaso say it was sixty leagues from Apalachee (E, 71; G, 247).

81. G, 248; E, 71.

82. Elvas spells it "Ochus" (E, 71). This place was revisited by Tristán de Luna y Arellano in 1559–61. "Ochuse" is the preferred spelling. See Charles Hudson, Marvin T. Smith, Chester B. DePratter, and Emilia Kelley, "The Tristán de Luna Expedition, 1559–1561," *Southeastern Archaeology* 8 (1989): 31–45.

Garcilaso says they captured two men—a chief and his kinsman (G, 248).

83. R, 268.

84. B, 228.

85. E, 71.

86. G, 249–50; B, 228; E, 72.

87. G, 249.

88. Garcilaso says the rendezvous was to occur in October (G, 249). Biedma says De Soto allowed himself six months to complete his explorations (B, 228).

89. B, 228.

90. E, 71.

CHAPTER 6: Cofitachequi

1. Elvas says this uninhabited area was 60 leagues in extent (E, 73). Perhaps what he had in mind was the distance between Apalachee and Toa, an actual distance of about 160 miles—60.8 leguas legales or 46.2 leguas comúnes.

2. Lewis H. Larson, *Aboriginal Subsistence Technology in the Southeastern Coastal Plain during the Late Prehistoric Period* (Gainesville: University Presses of Florida, 1980), 35–65.

3. R, 268; B, 228. Garcilaso places this departure at the end of March (G, 263). Unless otherwise noted, the route they followed is based on Charles Hudson, Marvin T. Smith, and Chester B. DePratter, "The Hernando de Soto Expedition from Apalachee to Chiaha," *Southeastern Archaeology* 3 (1984): 65–77.

4. R, 268. Rangel erroneously has this as "Guacuca." Bacuqua was an Apalachee frontier town that lay to the north of Anhayca. John H. Hann, *Apalachee: The Land between the Rivers* (Gainesville: University Press of Florida, 1988), fig. 2.1.

If they went west of Lake Iamonia they traveled nineteen miles, an easy day's travel for horsemen. If they went east of Lake Iamonia, they traveled twenty-six miles, a long day's travel for horsemen.

5. R, 269. The distance from Anhayca to the Flint River near Newton, Georgia, is about 63 miles. The horse vanguard averaged 25.2 miles per day in this travel.

6. E, 73; B, 228. At four days, the foot soldiers would have had to average 15.75 miles per day. At five days, they would have had to average 12.6 miles per day.

7. R, 269; E, 73.

8. Charles M. Hudson, John E. Worth, and Chester B. DePratter, "Refinements in Hernando de Soto's Route through Georgia and South Carolina," in *Columbian Consequences*, ed. David Hurst Thomas (Washington, D.C.: Smithsonian Institution Press, 1990), 2:107–19.

9. B, 228.

10. R, 269.

11. G, 263. The Magnolia Plantation site is 9Du1.

12. Hudson et al., "Refinements," 109. John E. Worth, "Mississippian Mound Centers along Chickasawhatchee Swamp," *LAMAR Briefs* 13 (1989): 7–9. For what it is worth, Garcilaso was under the impression this was a town of Apalachee (G, 267).

13. Garcilaso says they went no more than two hundred feet from the camp (G, 264).

14. Ibid., 266.

15. Ibid., 265.

16. E, 74.

17. R, 268. Hudson et al., "Refinements," 110.

18. Hudson et al., "Refinements, 110–11. Their distance traveled was forty-five miles, requiring them to travel fifteen miles per day.

19. The passage in Rangel describing travel from Capachequi to Toa is ambiguous (R, 268–70). I believe this to be the most reasonable interpretation of what he says.

20. E, 74.

21. The archaeological culture of this middle sixteenth-century chiefdom on the Chattahoochee River is Stewart phase.

22. B, 228.

23. R, 269–70. Biedma remembered this incident incorrectly as one in which they had built bridges across two rivers, but he specifically says their usual way of building bridges was to lash pine trees together (B, 228).

24. R, 270; B, 228. Biedma has "Otoa"; Elvas has "Toalli." The town they came to was possibly the Red Neck Hunting Club site. See Hudson et al., "Refinements."

25. John E. Worth, "Archaeological Investigation of a Mississippian Fall-Line Chiefdom on the Middle Flint River" (paper presented at the annual meeting of the Southeastern Archaeological Conference, New Orleans, La., October 1988). Worth has identified Toa with the Lockett phase, A.D. 1450–1550. Worth recovered a fragment of a crystalline quartz bead from the Hartley-Posey mound that may be a sixteenth-century Spanish artifact.

26. William W. Baden, "The Impact of Fluctuating Agricultural Potential on Coosa's Sociopolitical and Settlement Systems" (paper presented at the annual meeting of the Southeastern Archaeological Conference, Knoxville, Tenn., November 1995).

27. LA, passim; David J. Hally, "An Overview of Lamar Culture," in *Ocmulgee Archaeology, 1936–1986*, ed. David J. Hally (Athens: University of Georgia Press, 1994), 114–53.

28. R, 271; E, 74–76.

29. Without explaining, Rangel says some of De Soto's knights and gentlemen wished to remain behind under another captain, whom he does not name (R, 270).

30. E, 77; R, 270.

31. This was the southern fork of a trail shown on the 1847 Bonner map. See Hudson et al., "Refinements."

32. R, 270.

33. Rangel says they traveled twelve leagues (R, 270). Garcilaso erroneously calls Ichisi "Altapaha," confusing it with Altamaha. He also errs in saying that De Soto took both horsemen and footmen in getting there (G, 267–69).

34. Being surprised by De Soto sometimes indicates that a chiefdom was at war with the chiefdom De Soto visited last. But De Soto departed from Toa very quickly, probably outrunning any messengers who might have been sent. Also, the chronicles do not say whether the people of Toa knew of the existence of the Spaniards, though it is difficult to see how they could not have known.

The Bullard Landing site (9TW1), in the Ocmulgee River flood plain near Warner Robins, is quite like the island town of Ichisi encountered by De Soto. It was a small village of earth-covered houses, with no palisade, and it probably occupied an island in the river in 1540. This particular site, however, may lie too far upriver to be the town in question. Mark Williams and Don Evans, *Archaeological Excavations at the Bullard Landing Site (9TW1)*, LAMAR, Institute Publication 24, LAMAR Institute, 1993.

35. R, 270.

36. E, 77.

37. B, 229.

38. E, 77.

39. R, 270.

40. Elvas implies that the Ocmulgee River and the creek in which Benito Fernández drowned were one and the same. His being ignorant of this detail may indicate he was not a member of the vanguard (E, 76–77).

41. R, 270; E, 78. Rangel only reports three questions.

42. R, 270–71.

43. Elvas says De Soto replied to them he was "a son of the sun" and he came from where the sun dwelled (E, 78).

44. Marvin T. Smith and David J. Hally, "Chiefly Behavior: Evidence from Sixteenth-Century Spanish Accounts," in *Lords of the Southeast: Social Inequality and the Native Elites of Southeastern North America*, ed. Alex W. Barker and Timothy R. Pauketat, Archaeological Papers of the American Anthropological Association, no. 3, 1992, 99–109.

45. R, 271.

46. This was possibly the Cowart's Landing site, 9Bi14. Elvas says there were many villages along the river (E, 79).

47. R, 271. Garcilaso telescopes this course of travel up the Ocmulgee and Oconee Rivers, and he places Chalaque upstream from "Alapaha" (G, 269).

48. R, 271–72. Hale G. Smith, ed., *Analysis of the Lamar Site (9Bi7) Materials at the Southeastern Archaeological Center*, mimeographed report, Florida State University, 1973.

49. R, 272. Elvas says it was set up "very high in the middle of a public place" (E, 79). The archaeological culture of the Lamar site is Cowart's phase.

50. R, 272; E, 79.

51. E, 79.

52. Charles Hudson, Marvin T. Smith, and Chester B. DePratter, "The Hernando de Soto Expedition: From Apalachee to Chiaha," *Southeastern Archaeology* 3 (1984): 70.

53. E, 79; R, 272.

54. B, 229.

55. Ibid.

56. It should also be kept in mind that this observation was made by Biedma, who

drew his account from memory. He may have confused the Oconee and Ocmulgee Rivers (B, 229).

57. Paul E. Hoffman, *A New Andalucia and a Way to the Orient: The American Southeast during the Sixteenth Century* (Baton Rouge: Louisiana State University Press, 1990), 71–72, 328.

58. B, 229.

59. This village is presently unlocated.

60. R, 272.

61. Garcilaso (271–74) calls Ocute the "province of Cofa," evidently a place based on a faulty memory of "Cofaqui" (see below).

62. R, 272.

63. B, 229.

64. Ibid.

65. R, 272.

66. G, 273. Garcilaso says De Soto left it at the first town of "Cofa." This may have been Altamaha (Shinholser site), though it could just as well have been at Ocute or Cofaqui.

67. R, 272.

68. Ibid.

69. E, 79.

70. Charles Hudson, "The Social Context of the Chiefdom of Ichisi," in *Ocmulgee Archaeology, 1936–1986,* ed. David J. Hally (Athens: University of Georgia Press, 1994), 175–80. The archaeological culture of Ocute is Dyar phase.

71. E, 81. Garcilaso was under the impression that Cofaqui was "Cofa's" elder brother. Perhaps he was thinking of the uncle-nephew relationship between Cofaqui and Patofa (G, 273). Garcilaso says that while De Soto was there, Cofaqui slept in a different town (G, 275).

72. Presumably, Patofa was Cofaqui's sister's son. Rangel calls the province "Cofaqui" (273); Elvas calls it "Patofa" (84).

73. R, 273. Rangel calls him "Tatofa." There is no evidence in the documents that Patofa had a town separate from Cofaqui's. If he did, it is likely it was at the Scull Shoals site, a few miles up the Oconee River from the Dyar site.

74. E, 82–83.

75. G, 280.

76. E, 84.

77. B, 229. Garcilaso says Cofitachequi lay on the other side of a wilderness that took seven days to cross (G, 276).

78. Garcilaso says this occurred at midnight of the night before they were to depart (G, 280).

79. Ibid.

80. R, 273.

81. Ibid; E, 84.

82. E, 85; R, 273; G, 277.

83. G, 278. Garcilaso erroneously says the club was made of palm wood.

84. Garcilaso implies that this principal man was none other than Patofa (G, 278). The other chroniclers do not corroborate this.

85. Ibid., 279.

86. This departure date is not mentioned in the chronicles, but this date is consistent with the Gentleman of Elvas's statement that it took them nine days to cross the wilderness (i.e., reach the Broad River) (E, 86). But note that Garcilaso says they delayed departing one day because of Perico (G, 281). J. R. Swanton set the departure date at April 16 (FR, 169).

87. G, 283.

88. B, 229.

89. R, 274. Hudson et al., "Refinements." This was a distance of about sixty-five miles, which they could have traveled in four and a fraction days, traveling at less than sixteen miles per day. Elvas says the Savannah River was two crossbow shots wide (E, 85).

90. Elvas says the line of horses formed downstream from the foot soldiers (E, 85).

91. R, 274.

92. E, 85.

93. R, 274. Elvas says this river was two crossbow shots wide (E, 85).

94. Hudson et al., "Refinements."

95. E, 85.

96. R, 274.

97. G, 286.

98. E, 86. Perico may have acquired some facility in Spanish by this time.

99. E, 99.

100. R, 274.

101. G, 284.

102. The archaeological designations for the late prehistoric culture of the Savannah River are Rembert phase and Hollywood phase. David G. Anderson, *The Savannah River Chiefdoms: Political Change in the Late Prehistoric Southeast* (Tuscaloosa: University of Alabama Press, 1994), 157–234.

103. Ibid., 323–32.

104. E, 87. Garcilaso lists Juan de Añasco but, seemingly in error, includes André de Vasconcelos, Juan de Guzmán, and Arias Tinoco (G, 287).

105. R, 275; B, 230; G, 288. Elvas and Garcilaso say they were issued half a pound per person per day (E, 88; G, 288). According to Garcilaso, Alonso de Carmona said they killed only four of the large hogs (G, 294).

106. Elvas says De Soto sent the Indians home (E, 88); Garcilaso says he gave them gifts (G, 295).

107. G, 290–91. Utrera is a village about twenty miles southeast of Sevilla. Presumably the buns baked there were distinctive.

108. Garcilaso says they found some "cow horns" in this town (G, 292). Garcilaso is the only chronicler who says the Indians of Patofa sacked the temple of Hymahi and killed and scalped many Indians of all ages and sexes (G, 292–96).

109. B, 230.

110. R, 275; E, 89.

111. E, 89; G, 294.

112. E, 89. Rangel says the army stopped only two leagues short of Hymahi with their horses exhausted (R, 275). Garcilaso says the distance to Hymahi was more than twelve leagues (G, 293).

113. R, 275; E, 89–90. Rangel calls it *pinol* (R, 275). Biedma says the quantity was fifty *fanegas* (B, 230).

114. B, 230; R, 275.

115. Elvas seems to imply that this execution by burning prompted one of the Indians to talk (E, 90).

116. R, 276.

117. One wonders where he captured this woman, because the Broad River was mostly uninhabited.

118. Elvas recorded Lobillo's name as "Juan Rodriguez" (E, 90).

119. R, 276; E, 90.

120. E, 90; R, 276.

121. The total distance from Hymahi to Cofitachequi was 35 miles. With his vanguard De Soto may have traveled as much as 25 or 30 miles on the first day. The next day he covered the remaining 5 to 10 miles.

122. R, 278.

123. G, 296–97.

124. Chester B. DePratter, "Cofitachequi: Ethnohistorical and Archaeological Evidence," in *Studies in South Carolina Archaeology: Essays in Honor of Robert L. Stephenson,* ed. Albert C. Goodyear III and Glen T. Hansen, Anthropological Studies 9 (Columbia: South Carolina Institute of Archaeology and Anthropology, 1989), 143–44.

125. Garcilaso says there were six of them. They were between forty and fifty years old and appeared to be "town magistrates" (G, 297).

126. E, 90; Karen M. Booker, Charles M. Hudson, and Robert L. Rankin, "Place Name Identification and Multilingualism in the Sixteenth-Century Southeast," *Ethnohistory* 39 (1992): 416–21.

127. G, 298.

128. Garcilaso says the Indians normally asked this question when the Spaniards entered a new province (G, 298).

129. Charles Hudson, *The Juan Pardo Expeditions: Exploration of the Carolinas and Tennessee, 1566–68* (Washington, D.C.: Smithsonian Institution Press, 1990), 64–67.

130. Biedma likewise says she was the lady's niece (B, 230). Elvas says she was her sister (E, 91). Garcilaso says she had "inherited"—presumably her office—and was ready for marriage (G, 298). He also says the Spaniards were "enamored of her great beauty, which was perfect in the extreme" (G, 303).

131. E, 99. By this time some of the Spaniards were not inclined to believe what Perico said because they had caught him in so many lies.

132. Ibid., 91.

133. G, 300. Garcilaso compares this to Cleopatra's meeting with Marc Antony at the River Cydnus (G, 299).

134. Ibid., 300.

135. Ibid., 301.

136. E, 92; R, 278; B, 230.

137. G, 302. Garcilaso says De Soto removed a gold ring with a ruby from his finger and gave it to the lady (G, 302). This grand gesture seems unlikely, to say the least.

138. E, 93; R, 278; G, 300.

139. E, 93; G, 303.

140. R, 278–79. Later, another formidable woman lived at this site: during the Civil War this was the location of Mulberry Plantation, whose mistress was the diarist Mary Chestnut.

141. G, 301.

142. Ibid., 329.

143. Ibid., 303. Alonso de Carmona confirms that seven horses were lost.

144. R, 279.

145. G, 310.

146. Ibid., 311.

147. Ibid.

148. Ibid.

149. Ibid., 312; E, 109.

150. G, 313.

151. R, 279.

152. Biedma mentions a rosary with "jet" beads (B, 231).

153. G, 329. The place-name Santa Elena had no firm referent in the early sixteenth century. In 1565 it was affixed to a Spanish town at Port Royal Sound, South Carolina. Hoffman, *A New Andalucia,* map 6.

154. R, 280.

155. E, 94.

156. B, 231. Elvas puts the coast at two days' travel (E, 95). Biedma seems to imply that a survivor of the Ayllón expedition was among them (B, 231).

157. G, 330. Biedma puts the quantity of pearls at 6.5 to 7 arrobas (B, 231).

158. R, 280. Garcilaso says Talimeco was a league away (G, 311).

159. R, 280.

160. Ibid.

161. Ibid. Garcilaso says the town of "Talomeco" was situated at *en un alto sobre la barranca del río* (an eminence overlooking a gorge of the river) (G, 314). DePratter, "Cofitachequi," 144.

162. G, 315; DePratter, "Cofitachequi," 147.

163. G, 314.

164. Garcilaso says the structure measured forty by one hundred feet (G, 315).

165. The wooden clubs were (1) clubs with the upper end spiked with diamond-shaped points; (2) like broadswords; (3) like small flax swingles, with the first two-thirds round, and the last third widening to the shape of a shovel; (4) like battle-axes (one with a blade of copper, with a four-cornered point on its back; the other made of chipped flint). This last type is reminiscent of the Mississippian bi-lobed arrow.

166. G, 317–18. Garcilaso also says the temple roof was decorated on the outside with

pearls and marine shell (G, 316). There is no archaeological confirmation of this use of shells.

167. Elvas puts the quantity of pearls at fourteen arrobas. He also mentions "pearls" made into "babies and birds"—probably shell gorgets (E, 93–95).

168. G, 319; R, 280.

169. G, 316–24. Garcilaso says they were stored in *salas,* or chambers (G, 321).

170. Elvas describes the dressed deerskins (E, 93). Garcilaso mentions the panther and "marten" furs (G, 320).

171. E, 93; G, 298, 300. According to Garcilaso, Alonso de Carmona says there were four large houses at Talimeco stacked with bodies of people who died of the plague. However, Carmona may have only been describing a mortuary temple (G, 325).

172. DePratter, "Cofitachequi," 147–48; Randolph J. Widmer, "The Structure of Southeastern Chiefdoms," FC, 138.

173. E, 99.

174. R, 279. In the Pardo documents this town is spelled "Ilasi"; in Oviedo it is consistently spelled "Ilapi." "Ilasi" is preferred.

175. R, 279. According to Garcilaso, there were two deposits of corn in Cofitachequi of six hundred bushels each, and at Ilasi there were two thousand bushels (G, 300).

176. G, 304. Garcilaso says the woman who absconded was the true chieftainess, a widow who lived twelve leagues away.

177. B, 230.

178. G, 304–10.

179. Ibid., 310.

180. E, 94–95.

181. Ibid., 97.

182. Ibid., 96.

183. Ibid., 97.

184. Ibid., 98–99. The archaeological culture of Cofitachequi is Mulberry phase. DePratter, "Cofitachequi," 144–50.

185. Hudson, *Juan Pardo,* 81–83.

CHAPTER 7: Coosa

1. B, 231.

2. E, 98.

3. R, 280; B, 231. The chroniclers disagree on their date of departure. Rangel says they departed on Wednesday, May 13, but Wednesday fell on May 12. Elvas says they departed on May 3—clearly incorrect because they first arrived on May 2 (E, 98). Biedma says they were at Cofitachequi for ten or eleven days. Reckoning from May 2, Biedma would therefore place their departure date at May 12 or 13. Wednesday, May 12 would seem to be the most likely date of departure.

4. Garcilaso says she remained behind (G, 328).

5. Elvas says they traveled through one hundred leagues of her land (E, 99).

6. R, 280.

7. Charles Hudson, *The Juan Pardo Expeditions: Exploration of the Carolinas and Tennessee, 1566–1568* (Washington, D.C.: Smithsonian Institution Press, 1990), 84–85.

8. G, 328.

9. E, 99–100. Elvas says the number of turkeys was seven hundred, surely an exaggeration (100).

10. R, 280.

11. Elvas says it took them seven days to reach "Chalaque," making for an average of 16.4 miles per day (E, 99).

12. R, 280.

13. G, 325.

14. Hudson, *Juan Pardo,* 75, 83–84, 91–94.

15. This assumes that Guaquili is the same as Guaquiri of the Pardo expedition. There is no way to know the location of the place where De Soto departed from on May 17. If the place was near Otari, the distance to Guaquili would have been about 38 miles, and he would have had to average 19 miles per day. If the place was near Yssa, the distance would have been about 23 miles to Guaquili, and he would have averaged 11.5 miles per day. His point of departure could, of course, have been at some point in between these two proposed locations.

16. R, 280–81. Whether these were in fact dogs has been the subject of much speculation. It has been suggested, for example, they may have been opossums or raccoons, both of which were minor prey animals of the Indians and neither of which was familiar to De Soto and his men.

17. G, 331. "Joara," used in the Juan Pardo documents, is the preferred spelling. "Guaquili" appears as "Guaquiri" in the Pardo documents.

18. Recent work at the Berry site has prompted me to modify De Soto's route across the Appalachian Mountains. David G. Moore and Robin A. Beck Jr., "New Evidence of Sixteenth-Century Spanish Artifacts in the Catawba River Valley, North Carolina" (paper presented at the annual meeting of the Southeastern Archaeological Conference, Lexington, Ky., November 1994); John E. Worth, "Exploration and Trade in the Deep Frontier of Spanish Florida: Possible Sources for Sixteenth-Century Spanish Artifacts in Western North Carolina" (paper presented at the annual meeting of the Southeastern Archaeological Conference, Lexington, Ky., November 1994).

19. G, 330–31; Hudson, *Juan Pardo,* 83–91. The archaeological culture of the chiefdom of Joara is Burke phase. See Robin A. Beck Jr., "From Joara to Chiaha: Spanish Exploration of the Appalachian Summit Area, 1540–1568" (paper presented at the annual meeting of the Southeastern Archaeological Conference, Knoxville, Tenn., November 1995).

20. G, 325.

21. Ibid.

22. Ibid., 326.

23. Ibid., 327.

24. R, 281; G, 326.

25. R, 281.

26. Ibid. Some of the *petacas* may have been covered with leather.

27. Ibid.

28. Ibid.

29. Beck, "From Joara to Chiaha." Either Rangel or Oviedo inferred the course of the Mississippi River with the help of a no longer extant map by Alonso de Chaves. Rangel writes that the Río del Espíritu Santo empties into a great salt bay at thirty-one degrees north of the equator (R, 281). But the Mississippi does not empty into a bay, and its mouth is at twenty-nine degrees.

30. Garcilaso says three slaves escaped after they departed from Joara—two blacks and a Moor (333).

31. R, 281–82.

32. G, 333.

33. R, 281–82.

34. Ibid., 281.

35. E, 102.

36. Ibid. The black slave's name is not given, but perhaps it was Rodriguez.

37. G, 333.

38. Garcilaso says they were worth more than six thousand ducats (G, 334).

39. G, 334–35.

40. R, 282; Beck, "From Joara to Chiaha."

41. Elvas spells it "Guaxulle" (E, 102). Garcilaso spells it "Guaxule" (G, 333).

42. G, 335.

43. R, 282. Elvas says there were three hundred dogs, which the Indians themselves were not accustomed to eat (E, 102). Garcilaso's description of Guasili is extravagant (e.g., it had three hundred houses and a mound [G, 335–36]).

44. R, 282.

45. Hudson, *Juan Pardo,* 94–101; Roy S. Dickens Jr., *Cherokee Prehistory: The Pisgah Phase in the Appalachian Summit Region* (Knoxville: University of Tennessee Press, 1976); Dickens, "An Evolutionary-Ecological Interpretation of Cherokee Cultural Development," in *The Conference on Cherokee Prehistory,* comp. David G. Moore (Swannanoa, N.C.: Warren Wilson College, 1986), 81–94; Hudson, "Some Thoughts on the Early Social History of the Cherokees," in *The Conference on Cherokee Prehistory,* comp. David G. Moore (Swannanoa, N.C.: Warren Wilson College, 1986), 139–53.

46. Elvas spells it "Canasagua" (E, 102). Garcilaso compares the river to the Guadalquivir at Seville (G, 336).

47. R, 282; E, 102–3. Canasoga was possibly at 40Gn9 or 40Gn11. See Beck, "From Joara to Chiaha."

48. R, 282.

49. Ibid.

50. E, 103.

51. Ibid.; G, 331. Elvas confirms that from Canasoga to Chiaha it was five days (E, 103). Biedma says it took four days (B, 231).

52. B, 231.

53. E, 106.

54. Biedma calls this the Río del Espíritu Santo (B, 231). Garcilaso incorrectly says the island was five leagues long (G, 336).

55. R, 283; B, 232.

56. E, 105.

57. Hudson, *Juan Pardo,* 101–4. Karen M. Booker, Charles M. Hudson, and Robert L. Rankin, "Place Name Identification and Multilingualism in the Sixteenth-Century Southeast," *Ethnohistory* 39 (1992): 426–33.

58. E, 106.

59. Elvas calls it "walnut oil" (E, 104). Rangel says it was "walnut and acorn oil" (R, 282).

60. They called this gruel *mazamorras.*

61. E, 106.

62. Ibid.

63. G, 339–40.

64. Ibid., 338–39.

65. R, 282; E, 106.

66. E, 107.

67. R, 283.

68. E, 109. Rangel does not mention a chief of Coste coming to Chiaha (R, 284). And in fact, he says De Soto did not send out men to go to Chisca until they reached Coste. But this must be erroneous, because it does not allow for the wounded men to come down-river in canoes, as is specifically mentioned by the Gentleman of Elvas (E, 112).

69. G, 337. Garcilaso says the Chiscas were thirty leagues from Chiaha (G, 336).

70. E, 109–10.

71. G, 338. Rangel may also be incorrect in saying that the Spaniards first witnessed the extraction of pearls at Coste (R, 284).

72. Biedma says they were there twenty-six or twenty-seven days (B, 232). Unless otherwise noted, the route from Chiaha to Mabila is based on Charles Hudson, Marvin T. Smith, and Chester B. DePratter, "The Hernando de Soto Expedition: From Apalachee to Chiaha," *Southeastern Archaeology* 3 (1984): 65–77.

73. E, 110; R, 283; G, 337.

74. The route from Chiaha to Tali follows that in Charles Hudson, "The Hernando de Soto Expedition, 1539–1543," FC, 84–85.

75. R, 283.

76. Biedma spells it "Costehe" (B, 232). He seems to say that several towns of Coste were on islands.

77. R, 283.

78. B, 232. Elvas is incorrect in saying it took seven days to reach Coste (E, 110). Actual trail time was five days.

79. G, 341.

80. E, 110–12.

81. G, 340. Garcilaso says they saw copper mines, and they were of the opinion a search would turn up veins of silver and gold (G, 340).

82. E, 112–13. Rangel, however, says they came back with "good news" (R, 284). But if they had seen strong indications of gold, surely De Soto would have gone in pursuit of it.

83. G, 340.

84. Jefferson Chapman, Hazel R. Delcourt, and Paul A. Delcourt, "Strawberry Fields, Almost Forever," *Natural History,* September 1989, 50–59.

85. Samuel Cole Williams, ed., *Early Travels in the Tennessee Country, 1540–1800* (Johnson City, Tenn.: Watauga Press, 1928), 470–78.

86. Richard R. Polhemus, "Mississippian Architecture: Temporal, Technological, and Spatial Patterning of Structures at the Toqua Site (40 MR6)," master's thesis, University of Tennessee, 1986.

87. Ibid.

88. Hudson, *Juan Pardo,* 38–40, 105–6; Hudson, "Juan Pardo's Excursion beyond Chiaha," *Tennessee Anthropologist* 12 (1987): 74–87. At the time I wrote these two works, my reconstruction of the De Soto route placed Tali in the vicinity of Loudon, Tenn. By modifying De Soto's approach to Coste, and placing Tali at the Toqua site, much of the puzzlement about events at Satapo in the above publications clears up.

89. E, 114.

90. R, 284; E, 114. Elvas says this food was sent out by order of the chief of Coosa (E, 114).

91. R, 284.

92. G, 343.

93. E, 115. Garcilaso says the men wore feather headdresses half a fathom high, and they were arranged in squadrons, with twenty men in a row, making a fine spectacle (G, 343).

94. G, 345.

95. E, 116–17; G, 342.

96. E, 117. Rangel specifies *ciruelas* (plums), while Elvas mentions *amexeas* of Spain (i.e., plums) as well as "plums of the country" (i.e., persimmons). What these small sour apples can have been is unclear because no apples are native to the Southeast.

97. Marvin T. Smith, "Coosa: The Rise and Fall of a Southeastern Chiefdom, A.D. 1000–1775," typescript.

98. Charles Hudson et al., "Coosa: A Chiefdom in the Sixteenth-Century Southeastern United States," *American Antiquity* 50 (1985): 723–37; David J. Hally, Marvin T. Smith, and James B. Langford Jr., "The Archaeological Reality of de Soto's Coosa," in *Columbian Consequences,* ed. David Hurst Thomas (Washington, D.C.: Smithsonian Institution Press, 1990), 2:121–38; Hally, "Overview of Lamar Culture," 167–73.

99. E, 118; R, 284–85.

100. G, 342–44. Garcilaso says the Indians only emptied out half their town for the Spaniards.

CHAPTER 8: Tascaluza

1. G, 346.

2. Garcilaso has his name as "Falco Herrado" (G, 346).

3. Ibid., 347.

4. R, 285; E, 119. Elvas spells it "Tallimuchase."

5. Elvas spells it "Itaua" (E, 119).

6. R, 285. Adam King, "De Soto's Itaba: Reoccupation of an Ancient Chiefly Capital" (paper presented at the annual meeting of the Southeastern Archaeological Conference, Knoxville, Tenn., November 1995).

7. E, 119–20.

8. Ibid., 120.

9. Elvas says it was thirty women (E, 121).

10. R, 285; E, 121. Elvas says he went looking for grapes.

11. C. Roger Vance, "A Study of Lamar Ecology on the Western Edge of the Southern Piedmont," LA, 145–46.

12. R, 285; E, 121. Rangel calls this second village "Piachi," a name that indubitably belonged to a town they came to several weeks later. One wonders whether this second town downriver from Ulibahali was not in fact Apica, a town known to have been in this general location in 1559–60, at the time of the Tristán de Luna expedition. That is, Rangel's "Piachi" may be a mistranscription of some version of "Apica." Charles Hudson, Marvin T. Smith, Chester B. DePratter, and Emilia Kelley, "The Tristán de Luna Expedition, 1559–1561," *Southeastern Archaeology* 8 (1989): 40.

13. David J. Hally and James B. Langford Jr., *Mississippian Period Archaeology of the Georgia Valley and Ridge Province*, Laboratory of Archaeology Series, Report No. 25 (Athens: University of Georgia, 1988); Patricia Kelly, "The Architecture of the King Site," master's thesis, University of Georgia, 1988.

14. R, 287. Elvas spells the town name "Toasi," and he says they were given thirty Indian women.

15. R, 287–88; B, 232.

16. E, 121–22. Garcilaso says Talisi was heavily fortified with a wooden palisade and was on a peninsula in the bend of a great river (G, 346).

17. R, 288; B, 232.

18. R, 288.

19. Ibid.

20. G, 348.

21. R, 288.

22. G, 380.

23. E, 123.

24. R, 288; B, 232.

25. R, 288; E, 123.

26. R, 288.

27. Garcilaso is the only chronicler who mentions a river-crossing before reaching Tascaluza, but he incorrectly says it was just after departing from Talisi. He may also be incorrect in saying the river could not be forded and they had to cross it on rafts and canoes (G, 349).

28. R, 288; E, 123. Elvas says two leagues (E, 123).

29. R, 288.

30. Ibid., 290. Garcilaso was under the impression that Atahachi was not Tascaluza's principal town (G, 349).

31. R, 291; G, 349.

32. G, 356.

33. E, 124; R, 291. Garcilaso says it was a chamois banner with a yellow field with three blue bands across, and the shape was like banners carried by cavalry men in Spain. He says it was the first such banner they had seen (G, 349).

This order was founded in Jerusalem in the eleventh century as the Hospitallers of St. John of Jerusalem. In 1309 they acquired Rhodes, on Cyprus, became an independent state, and became the scourge of Muslim shipping in the eastern Mediterranean. Suleyman the Magnificent drove them from Cyprus in 1523. They wandered for a time, and in 1530 they acquired a Maltese archipelago and resumed their attacks on Muslim shipping. They played a prominent role in crushing the Turkish navy in the Battle of Lepanto in 1571. *Encyclopedia Britannica*, 1992, 6:915–16.

34. E, 124.

35. G, 346. But Garcilaso is incorrect in saying the chief of Coosa accompanied De Soto to Talisi to force them to obey him.

36. Vernon J. Knight Jr., "A Summary of Alabama's De Soto Mapping Project and Project Bibliography," Working Paper No. 9, Alabama De Soto Commission, 1988.

37. B, 232; E, 124–25.

38. E, 160.

39. R, 291.

40. G, 350.

41. Ibid.

42. R, 291.

43. Ibid. The boots were *borceguís* (buskins, half-boots).

44. Ibid. Again Garcilaso neglects to mention that De Soto made Tascaluza a hostage. He says he went with De Soto voluntarily (G, 350).

45. G, 351.

46. B, 233. Biedma remembered it as a plumed fly-whisk large enough to shield him from the sun (B, 233).

47. Erhard Rostlund, "The Myth of a Natural Prairie Belt in Alabama: An Interpretation of Historical Records," *Annals of the Association of American Geographers* 47 (1957): 392–411; Alice Simms Tores and E. Gibbs Patton, "Forest, 'Prairie,' and Soils in the Black Belt of Sumter County, Alabama, in 1832," *Ecology* 47 (1966): 75–80; Thomas H. Wilson, "Natural History of the Black Belt Prairie," *Journal of the Alabama Academy of Science* 52 (1981): 10–19; Evan Peacock, "Some Additional Notes on Forest Reconstruction in the Black Belt," *Mississippi Archaeology* 27 (1992): 1–18.

48. R, 291. Garcilaso calls this place "Tascaluza," and he thought it to be Tascaluza's main town. He says it was on a peninsula in the river and says incorrectly that they traveled for three days at four leagues per day (G, 351).

49. B, 232–33.

50. R, 292.

51. Ibid., 292; E, 126.

52. E, 127.

53. G, 351. Whether Juan de Villalobos is the one who went out to search for the slave is not clear.

54. E, 127; B, 233.

55. R, 292.

56. B, 233.

57. G, 351.

58. E, 127; G, 352.

59. R, 292. In fact, abundant chestnut trees occurred somewhat to the north and to the east of what is believed to have been Tascaluza's territory.

60. Ibid. Elvas says De Soto had fifteen cavalry and thirty infantry (E, 128).

61. None of the chroniclers mentions these individuals at this point, but they were mentioned after the battle began.

62. E, 128; G, 383; R, 292.

63. E, 139.

64. G, 361.

65. Ibid., 353, 361.

66. B, 233. Garcilaso says eight o'clock (G, 353).

67. B, 233; G, 353.

68. G, 353–54.

69. Ibid., 354.

70. Elvas says he was sent there three or four days earlier (E, 128).

71. Ibid.; G, 355.

72. B, 233.

73. G, 357.

74. B, 233.

75. E, 128.

76. R, 292.

77. E, 128–29.

78. Ibid., 129. Rangel says all the people with Soto went inside (R, 292).

79. E, 129.

80. R, 292. Rangel calls this dance an *areyto*—a West Indian word for dance.

81. B, 233; G, 356.

82. E, 129; B, 233; G, 359.

83. E, 129.

84. Ibid.

85. Ibid., 130.

86. B, 233; R, 292.

87. E, 130.

88. Ibid., 130–31; R, 292; B, 235. Garcilaso says this man must have been the "Captain general" of Mabila (G, 359). Elvas says he was wounded on the back (E, 131).

89. B, 233.

90. R, 292.

91. G, 360.

92. R, 292.

93. G, 360–61. If the people of Mabila were matrilineal, this boy may have been a nephew (i.e., sister's son) of the dead man.

94. B, 235.

95. E, 131.

96. R, 293.

97. E, 131.

98. G, 361.

99. R, 293.

100. Ibid.

101. Ibid.

102. E, 132.

103. Ibid.

104. Ibid.

105. B, 235.

106. Ibid.

107. G, 362.

108. Ibid., 361.

109. R, 294. Elvas says there were only a friar, a clergyman, one of De Soto's servants, and a female slave (E, 86–87). Garcilaso claims there were three crossbowmen and five halberdiers (G, 366).

110. E, 133.

111. Ibid., 134.

112. B, 233.

113. G, 360.

114. R, 293.

115. G, 362.

116. Don Carlos was married to one of De Soto's nieces (G, 364).

117. R, 293; G, 364.

118. G, 377–78.

119. E, 133.

120. G, 363. Garcilaso says they fought for three hours in this way.

121. G, 363–64.

122. E, 134–35.

123. G, 380.

124. Ibid., 364.

125. Ibid., 365.

126. B, 235.

127. E, 136; R, 293–94.

128. G, 379.

129. Ibid., 370–71.

130. E, 136. This "pond" may be helpful in locating the site of Mabila. The "pond" may have been a cutoff channel of a river, a spring-fed pool, or perhaps a barrow pit.

131. R, 293–94; G, 366; E, 136.

132. G, 367. Garcilaso says De Soto fought standing up in his stirrups for five hours.

133. Ibid., 368; R, 294.

134. E, 137.

135. Ibid; G, 368.

136. R, 294; G, 369.

137. G, 370.

138. Ibid., 372–73.

139. B, 235; G, 373. In Garcilaso's version of this incident, this man was stupefied in the battle, and when he came to his senses he hung himself from the tree in the palisade. According to Garcilaso, several trees were left growing among the posts of the palisade (G, 373).

140. G, 373.

141. B, 235.

142. R, 294; E, 138.

143. R, 294. Elvas puts the figures at 150 Spanish wounded (bearing a total of 700 arrow wounds) and 18 killed, and he says 12 horses died and 70 were wounded (E, 137–38). Biedma says more than 20 Spaniards died, and 250 were wounded with 760 arrow wounds (B, 235). Garcilaso says 47 Spaniards died during and after the battle; 22 died in the aftermath; and 45 horses died (G, 377).

144. R, 294; E, 137; G, 377–79. Instead of Captain Diego de Soto, Rangel lists Francisco de Soto, a nephew of Hernando (R, 294).

145. G, 374.

146. R, 294.

147. E, 137. Garcilaso puts the number of Indian dead at more than 11,000. He says 2,500 were found dead in the town. In the fires in the houses, 3,500 were killed, mostly women. And they found 2,000 dead and wounded Indians within four leagues of the town (G, 379–80).

148. G, 380.

149. Ibid., 372.

150. Ibid.

151. Ibid., 371–72.

152. One would like to know from which chiefdom Tascaluza first obtained this information. Was it Apalachee? Ocute? Ichisi? Toa? Coosa? Luís de Moscoso took one of these women back to Mexico, where she was much admired (G, 356).

153. G, 357.

154. Ibid., 380.

155. Ibid., 381.

156. Ibid., 381–82.

157. Ibid., 357.

158. Hudson et al., "Tristán de Luna," 36.

159. Ibid.

160. G, 376.

161. B, 236; G, 376–77.

162. E, 91; G, 383.

163. G, 384.

164. Ibid.

165. R, 294.

166. E, 138.

167. B, 236. Elvas says it was six days away (E, 138). Garcilaso says it was less than thirty leagues away (G, 384).

168. G, 384. Garcilaso says twenty leagues inland.

169. Hudson et al., "Tristán de Luna," 31–32.

170. G, 385.

171. E, 138.

172. B, 236.

173. G, 385–86.

174. R, 294; E, 139.

175. G, 387.

176. Ibid., 385.

177. Ibid., 388.

178. B, 236.

179. Charles Hudson, Marvin T. Smith, and Chester B. DePratter, "The Hernando de Soto Expedition: From Mabila to the Mississippi River," T&T, 181–83. See also the afterword, this volume.

CHAPTER 9: Chicaza

1. B, 236; R, 294. Charles Hudson, Marvin T. Smith, and Chester B. DePratter, "The Hernando de Soto Expedition: From Mabila to the Mississippi River," T&T, 181–207.

2. E, 140.

3. R, 296. Rangel erroneously has this date as November 28 (R, 294). Elvas erroneously has it as November 18 (E, 139). Garcilaso erroneously has them going directly to Chicaza (G, 395).

4. Paul D. Welch, *Moundville's Economy* (Tuscaloosa: University of Alabama Press, 1991), 23–26. This discussion of Moundville owes much to a personal communication from Vernon J. Knight Jr. summarizing a decade of his research at the site.

5. Vincas Steponaitis, "Contrasting Patterns of Mississippian Development," in *Chiefdoms: Power, Economy, and Ideology*, ed. Timothy Earle (Cambridge: Cambridge University Press, 1991), 193–212.

6. Welch, *Moundville's Economy*, 194–95.

7. Rangel's spelling is "Talicpacana" (R, 296). It is transcribed in Elvas as "Taliepataua" (E, 140). The most plausible spelling is "Taliepacana."

8. Welch, *Moundville's Economy*, 70.

9. R, 296. It is not clear whether De Soto's men visited this village. There is at present no known large village site on the opposite side of the Black Warrior River between 1Ha7/8 and Moundville. Since 1Ha7/8 is located on the southern end of Martin's Creek, a relict channel of the Black Warrior, it is possible the village in question was on the opposite side of this channel.

10. Ibid. The second village may have been at 1Ha107.

11. G, 393.

12. R, 296; E, 140.

13. The date of this move is not given, but it probably was around November 22. Elvas erroneously calls Mozulixa "Zabusta" (E, 91).

14. G, 394.

15. E, 140.

16. G, 395.

17. Rangel says sixty men embarked in it (R, 296). Garcilaso says they built two boats, and ten cavalry and forty infantry were in each of the two boats (G, 395). Perhaps they transported two boatloads of thirty men each to the other side of the river.

18. E, 140; R, 296.

19. Only Garcilaso says that a small number of horsemen were loaded into the piragua.

20. G, 395–96. Hudson et al., "The Hernando de Soto Expedition," T&T, 188.

21. R, 296.

22. Hudson et al., "The Hernando de Soto Expedition," T&T, 181.

23. R, 296.

24. E, 141.

25. Welch, *Moundville's Economy,* chap. 4.

26. Ibid., 134–78.

27. R, 296. This was either at 1Tu42/43 or at 1Tu46/47, and considering trail time, it was probably the latter.

28. B, 236; R, 296; E, 140–41. The Gentleman of Elvas refers to it as a "province," though he spells it "Pafallaya." The Snow's Bend site is 1Tu2/3.

29. R, 296.

30. Elvas says they marched five days through a wilderness before reaching Chicaza (E, 141).

31. R, 296.

32. Ibid.

33. Alternatively, they could have followed a trail south of Luxapallila Creek, perhaps following near the course of the present-day Gulf, Mobile, and Ohio Railroad. But doing so would have necessitated crossing a wide expanse of water.

34. I am grateful to Rufus A. Ward Jr. for alerting me to the fact that in 1817 Mr. H. Young, Andrew Jackson's engineer, recommended that the military road from Nashville to New Orleans cross the river at this point. Major Pitchlynn, a local resident, told Young this was the place where the Choctaws would cross the river on rafts when the water was high. See H. Young to Andrew Jackson, September 30, 1817, a manuscript on file at Natchez Trace Parkway Headquarters, Tupelo, Mississippi.

35. Rangel says they were waving white flags (R, 297). But such an act would be odd in light of the fact that in the native Southeast white ordinarily symbolized peace.

36. E, 141.

37. R, 297; E, 141. Garcilaso omits mention of this river crossing. Elvas says the crossing was on December 17.

38. E, 141.

39. Hudson et al., "The Hernando de Soto Expedition," T&T, 194.

40. R, 297.

CHAPTER 10: Winter, 1540–1541

1. Charles Hudson, Marvin T. Smith, and Chester DePratter, "The Hernando de Soto Expedition: From Mabila to the Mississippi River," T&T, 197.

2. R, 297.

3. E, 142.

4. John H. Blitz, *Ancient Chiefdoms of the Tombigbee* (Tuscaloosa: University of Alabama Press, 1993).

5. G, 398.

6. E, 142.

7. Elvas erroneously has these names as "Nicalasa" and "Alimamu" (E, 142). "Alibamo" is the preferred spelling.

8. E, 142; B, 236.

9. Blitz, *Ancient Chiefdoms*, 39–184. Lyon's Bluff is 22Ok1; Lubbub Creek is 1Pi33&85.

10. E, 142–43.

11. B, 236.

12. R, 297. Note, however, that in the early eighteenth century, the Chickasaws used the word *currus* to refer to the Algonquian-speaking people of the north. Thomas Nairne, *Nairne's Muskhogean Journals: The 1708 Expedition to the Mississippi River*, ed. Alexander Moore (Jackson: University Press of Mississippi, 1988), 37.

13. Vincas P. Steponaitis, "Contrasting Patterns of Mississippian Development," in *Chiefdoms: Power, Economy, and Ideology*, ed. Timothy Earle (Cambridge: Cambridge University Press, 1991), 216–26.

14. R, 297. Elvas has this as "Saquechuma" (143). Hudson et al., "The Hernando de Soto Expedition," T&T, 197.

15. R, 297. Talapatica is neither identified nor located.

16. E, 144–46.

17. R, 297. Elvas says they were to depart on March 9 (E, 146).

18. B, 236.

19. R, 297–98. This was the *modorra*, the second, or sleeping, watch (E, 146).

20. B, 236. Garcilaso says the fire was kept in the form of faggots woven of a certain grass, so that they held fire like arquebus fuses (G, 399).

21. G, 399.

22. E, 147.

23. R, 298.

24. B, 236–37.

25. G, 399.

26. Ibid., 401.

27. E, 149; G, 403.

28. E, 148–49.

29. R, 298. Biedma says thirteen or fourteen (B, 237); Elvas says eleven (E, 149); Garcilaso says forty (G, 403).

30. E, 149.

31. B, 237. Elvas says fifty (E, 149); Garcilaso also says fifty (G, 403).

32. E, 149; G, 404. Biedma says more than three hundred were killed (B, 237).

33. G, 404.

34. Ibid., 404–5.

35. Ibid., 411.

36. Ibid., 407.

37. R, 298; B, 237; E, 150.

38. G, 405–6.

39. Ibid., 406; R, 298; E, 150. Elvas says it was half a league distant (E, 151).

40. G, 406.

41. R, 298; G, 408.

42. R, 298; E, 151.

43. G, 408.

44. R, 298.

45. E, 151; B, 237.

46. E, 152.

CHAPTER 11: Quizquiz, Casqui, Pacaha

1. R, 299. Elvas says they departed on April 25.

2. B, 237. Rangel spells it "Limamu" (R, 299); Elvas spells it "Alimamu" (E, 152). Garcilaso says they traveled in a northerly direction from Mabila to Pacaha (G, 450).

3. R, 299; E, 153; B, 237.

4. R, 299.

5. G, 415.

6. E, 153; R, 299; B, 237.

7. Garcilaso says it was four hundred feet square—probably an exaggeration (G, 416).

8. G, 417.

9. E, 153.

10. B, 237.

11. R, 299.

12. G, 417.

13. B, 237–38.

14. G, 417–18.

15. Ibid., 418.

16. Ibid., 416–17.

17. Ibid., 417.

18. Ibid., 419.

19. E, 155.

20. G, 416.

21. Ibid., 419–20.

22. E, 155. Biedma says seven or eight men died and twenty-five or twenty-six more were wounded (B, 237–38). Elvas says many were wounded and fifteen died (E, 155).

23. R, 299. Only Garcilaso says the Spaniards killed many Indians when they stormed the fort (G, 419).

24. B, 237. It should be noted, however, that the resident population of Lubbub Creek had been quite small, and the site had outer and inner palisades. Hence, the Alibamo fort may have been a similar refuge fort.

25. E, 155.

26. G, 415.

27. E, 156; B, 237. Only Garcilaso says they remained at this place for four days, ravaging the countryside for vengeance (G, 420–21). Garcilaso says the Indian casualties were more than two thousand.

28. B, 238.

29. Dan F. Morse and Phyllis A. Morse, *Archaeology of the Central Mississippi Valley* (New York: Academic Press, 1983), 1–15.

30. R, 299; B, 238. Elvas says they marched seven days (E, 156). Garcilaso calls this place "Chisca" (G, 423–27). Scholars have proposed etymologies in various Indian languages for *Quizquiz*, including Choctaw for "the cougar's anus" and "to cast out," and Chickasaw for "great cougar." See David H. Dye, "Reconstruction of the De Soto Expedition Route in Arkansas: The Mississippi Alluvial Plain," in *The Expedition of Hernando de Soto West of the Mississippi, 1541–1543* (Fayetteville: University of Arkansas Press, 1993), 55–56.

To this, I am compelled to add that the resemblance between *Quizquiz* and *Kaskaskia* is intriguing.

31. E, 156. Quizquiz comprised some of the towns of the Walls phase, which lay on the eastern side of the Mississippi River at and below present-day Memphis.

32. Morse and Morse, *Central Mississippi Valley*, 201–69; Gerald P. Smith, "The Walls Phase and Its Neighbors," T&T, 140–45. The Irby site is 22DS515.

33. G, 423–25.

34. E, 157.

35. Ibid. Dye, "Reconstruction," 42.

36. B, 238.

37. There is no evidence that De Soto ever talked with this chief directly. His principal town may have been located elsewhere.

38. B, 238.

39. Dye, "Reconstruction," 42. Lake Cormorant is 22DS501; Woodlyn is 22DS517; Walls is 22DS500.

40. E, 158.

41. Garcilaso attributes this fact to Juan Coles (G, 423).

42. R, 300; E, 159; Dye, "Reconstruction," 43.

43. G, 428.

44. E, 159.

45. G, 428.

46. For once, Garcilaso sets the low estimate. His estimate is six thousand (G, 428).

47. E, 159; R, 300.

48. E, 161.

49. Ibid.

50. B, 238.

51. G, 429.

52. B, 238. If construction began on May 22 and was finished on June 17, it took twenty-seven days. Elvas says they were there thirty days (E, 161). Garcilaso, far off the mark, says it took twenty days to build the piraguas (G, 429).

53. R, 300.

54. E, 162. Half a league is 1.3 (legua legal) to 1.7 miles (legua común). The actual width of the river at this point is about 1.5 miles.

55. B, 238. Biedma estimated the river to be nearly a league wide. A *braza*, the span of one's arms, was about 5.5 feet.

56. E, 163.

57. G, 428.

58. Dye, "Reconstruction," 43–44.

59. E, 162.

60. Morse and Morse, *Central Mississippi Valley*, 309. Aquijo is archaeologically identified as Horseshoe Lake phase.

61. E, 163–64.

62. Elvas appears to have been one of the men in the piraguas (E, 163–64).

63. Ibid.

64. Morse and Morse, *Central Mississippi Valley*, 296; Dye, "Reconstruction," 45. The Pouncey site is 3CT34.

65. Morse and Morse, *Central Mississippi Valley*, 296.

66. R, 300.

67. Ibid.; E, 165; Dye, "Reconstruction," 46.

68. E, 165. David Dye has them traveling directly northwest through deep swamp to a place where no known Parkin phase sites exist ("Reconstruction"). A more reasonable route was to the west through shallower backswamps to the St. Francis River, where many large and small Parkin phase sites are known to exist.

69. Rangel initially spells this "Quarqui," clearly a mistranscription (R, 300). Biedma spells it "Icasqui" (B, 239).

70. E, 166.

71. Ibid. This pattern of compact towns separated by agricultural fields atop a levee ridge exactly matches the Parkin phase settlement pattern. See Phyllis A. Morse, "The Parkin Site and the Parkin Phase," T&T, 118–34.

72. E, 187.

73. Ibid., 166.

74. Ibid. Elvas uses the word *amexea* ambiguously. At times he uses it to mean "plum," but later in his account he says the *amexeas* of La Florida had four or five pits (i.e., they were persimmons). If he is here referring to persimmons, he may be referring to two different varieties, *Diospyros virginiana* and *D. texana*. If not, he is referring to Chickasaw plums as opposed to persimmons.

75. G, 430.

76. E, 166.

77. G, 430.

78. Ibid., 434.

79. B, 238.

80. E, 167–69. This implies there were no trees in the town to shade the people inside.

81. Morse, "The Parkin Site," T&T, 118–25. The chiefdom of Casqui is archaeologically identified as Parkin phase.

82. E, 169–70.

83. B, 239; G, 432.

84. David G. Anderson, "Political Change in Chiefdom Societies: Cycling in the Late Prehistoric Southeastern United States," Ph.D. diss., University of Michigan, 1990, 536–59.

85. G, 432. Archaeologists have in fact excavated an unusual, large charred posthole on top of the Parkin mound. Morse, "The Parkin Site," T&T, 121.

86. G, 432.

87. R, 300.

88. G, 431.

89. Ibid., 432–33.

90. Ibid.

91. Ibid.

92. E, 170–71; R, 301.

93. B, 239.

94. G, 434–35.

95. E, 171.

96. R, 301; E, 171.

97. G, 435.

98. E, 171.

99. Dan F. Morse, "The Nodena Phase," T&T, 78. The Pacaha chiefdom comprised a cluster of Nodena phase sites.

100. G, 436.

101. R, 301; B, 231; G, 436. The exact timing of De Soto's going from Casqui to Pacaha is unclear. The chief of Casqui said it should only take one day, but this is the rate at which his own people traveled. Biedma says they were two days getting there (B, 231). Rangel says they departed on Sunday, June 26, and arrived on Wednesday, June 29— four days in all (R, 301). Elvas says he entered the town and took up lodging there on Wednesday, June 19, the first digit of the date being in error (E, 174). Perhaps they arrived at Pacaha on June 28 but only took up lodging there on June 29.

102. G, 436.

103. E, 174; G, 436.

104. B, 239–40.

105. Dan Morse, "The Nodena Phase," T&T, 78. These sites included 3CT9 and 3CT43, which with the Bradley site occupied two kilometers of Bradley Ridge.

106. E, 172.

107. G, 437.

108. Ibid., 438–39.

109. Ibid., 439–40.

110. B, 240.

111. E, 174.

112. R, 301. "De más primores en la gente, excepto la da Cofitachequi."

113. Morse, "The Nodena Phase," T&T, 69–97.

114. Robert L. Rankin, "Language Affiliations of Some de Soto Place Names in Arkansas," in *The Expedition of Hernando de Soto West of the Mississippi, 1541–1543,* ed. Gloria A. Young and Michael P. Hoffman (Fayetteville: University of Arkansas Press, 1993), 210–20.

115. E, 172–73.

116. Ibid., 176.

117. Ibid., 175.

118. Ibid.

119. Ibid., 175–76.

120. Phyllis A. Morse, "The Parkin Archaeological Site and Its Role in Determining the Route of the de Soto Expedition," in *The Expedition of Hernando de Soto West of the Mississippi, 1541–1543,* ed. Gloria A. Young and Michael P. Hoffman (Fayetteville: University of Arkansas Press, 1993), 64.

121. E, 178.

122. G, 440–41.

123. Garcilaso says they fled because of what the people of Pacaha threatened to do to them after the Spaniards departed. The Casquis had been defeated so often, they were terrified even of defeated Pacahas (G, 442).

124. G, 442.

125. E, 178.

126. R, 301.

127. E, 179.

128. G, 445.

129. Ibid.

130. R, 301.

131. Ibid.

132. E, 179–80.

133. R, 301.

134. Ibid.

135. Ibid.

136. Ibid.

137. Ibid.

138. E, 180.

139. Ibid., 180–81.

140. Ibid.; R, 302.

141. R, 302.

142. Ibid.

143. Ibid., 302–3.

144. G, 446.

145. B, 241.

146. Ibid.

147. G, 447.

148. Ibid. Elvas says De Soto appeased them by saying that among Christians both sides were equally valued, and they should consider it so.

149. G, 448.

150. E, 183. Elvas says Pacaha gave De Soto two of his sisters (E, 183). Garcilaso says both were wives of Pacaha whom De Soto had captured upon entering the main town. And he says the Spaniards felt that Pacaha did not want them back because the Spaniards had defiled them (G, 448–49).

151. B, 240.

152. E, 165.

153. William P. Cumming, *The Southeast in Early Maps* (Chapel Hill: University of North Carolina Press, 1958), plate 5, pp. 113–15.

154. B, 240.

155. Ibid. Elvas says seven days (E, 182).

156. Dye, "Reconstruction," 50–51.

157. B, 240; E, 182.
Elvas calls it "Caluza." Biedma spells it "Caluzi" (241). Note that earlier the Chicazas had directed the Spaniards to a very populous province called Caluza (R, 297). Clearly this was a different place.

158. B, 240–41.

159. Dan F. Morse, "Protohistoric Hunting Sites in Northwestern Arkansas," in *The Protohistoric Period in the Mid-South: 1500–1700*, ed. David H. Dye and Ronald C. Brister, Proceedings of the 1983 Mid-South Archaeological Conference, Archaeological Report No. 18 (Jackson: Mississippi Department of Archives and History, 1986), 89–94.

160. E, 182. How far they traveled is not known. If they averaged from three leagues (10.3 miles) to five leagues (17.25 miles) per day they could have gone as far as 83 to 138 miles from Pacaha. They perhaps got as far as present-day Craighead or Lawrence County, Arkansas.

161. Morse and Morse, *Central Mississippi Valley*, 312.

162. G, 449–50. Garcilaso says they found "brass."

163. James E. Price and Cynthia R. Price, "Protohistoric/Early Historic Manifestations in Southeastern Missouri," T&T, 59–68; Dye, "Reconstruction," 50.

164. B, 241; E, 182.

165. Charles J. Bareis and James W. Porter, eds., *American Bottom Archaeology* (Urbana: University of Illinois Press, 1984); Thomas E. Emerson and R. Barry Lewis, eds., *Cahokia and the Hinterlands: Middle Mississippian Cultures of the Midwest* (Urbana: University of Illinois Press, 1991); James B. Stoltman, ed., *New Perspectives on Cahokia: Views from the Periphery*, Monographs in World Archaeology, no. 2 (Madison: Prehistory Press, 1991).

166. Stephen Williams, "The Vacant Quarter and Other Late Events in the Lower Valley," T&T, 170–80.

167. G, 450.

1. E, 182; R, 303. Rangel incorrectly says they departed on June 29.

2. B, 241. Elvas incorrectly says they were in Pacaha forty days. Actually, they were there thirty days (E, 183).

3. E, 183.

4. R, 304. It is notable that they traveled from Pacaha to the territory of Casqui in one day. Elvas appears to be in error in saying De Soto's army reached the principal town of Casqui in one day (E, 184).

5. E, 184.

6. R, 304; E, 184; David H. Dye, "Reconstruction of the de Soto Expedition Route in Arkansas: The Mississippi Alluvial Plain," in *The Expedition of Hernando de Soto West of the Mississippi, 1541–1543*, ed. Gloria A. Young and Michael P. Hoffman (Fayetteville: University of Arkansas Press, 1993), 51. The Rose site is 3CS27.

7. R, 304.

8. Ibid.

9. E, 184.

10. Dye, "Reconstruction," 51. The Big Eddy site is 3SF9.

11. R, 304. Elvas spells it "Aquiguate" (E, 184).

12. E, 184. Garcilaso incorrectly says the people remained in this town and offered hospitality to the Spaniards (G, 450).

13. R, 304. The Grant site is 3LE15.

14. B, 241; E, 184.

15. E, 184–85. Garcilaso says it was divided into three districts and the Spaniards occupied two of them (G, 450–51).

16. G, 451.

17. Quiguate is archaeologically identified as Kent phase. John House, "Dating the Kent Phase," *Southeastern Archaeology* 12 (1993): 21–32.

18. E, 185–86.

19. Ibid.

20. Rangel seems to imply that they did not learn there were other large populations living on the St. Francis until later. Or perhaps he means they did not see this with their own eyes until later (i.e., during the winter of 1542–43), while they were at Aminoya (R, 304).

21. B, 241.

22. E, 187.

23. G, 451–52. Garcilaso says the soldier who informed on Gaytán was Pablos Fernández, the "adjutant general," a native of Valverde.

24. Biedma may incorrectly say they were at Quiguate for eight or nine days (B, 241).

25. Ibid.

26. R, 304; E, 188.

27. E, 188.

28. Garcilaso calls this place "Colima." He incorrectly locates it five days down the River of Casqui from Quiguate (G, 453). The Magness site is 3IN8.

29. E, 188–89; R, 304.

30. E, 189. Elvas says they were given only two buffalo skins (E, 189). But Biedma says they found a large quantity of both green and cured buffalo skins (B, 241).

31. E, 189–90.

32. Coligua is archaeologically identified as Greenbrier phase. Dan F. Morse and Phyllis A. Morse, *Archaeology of the Central Mississippi Valley* (New York: Academic Press, 1983), 298–300.

33. Elvas says these buffalo were at a distance of only five or six leagues, an estimate that is suspect (E, 189).

34. R, 304.

35. E, 189.

36. B, 241.

37. Ibid.

38. E, 189.

39. Scott Akridge, "De Soto's Route in North Central Arkansas," *Fieldnotes: News- letter of the Arkansas Archaeological Society* 211 (1986): 3–7.

40. Rangel spells it "Palisma" (R, 304). Elvas says they reached it after five days (E, 190), whereas in fact they reached it in three.

41. E, 190.

42. R, 304; B, 241. Elvas spells it "Tatilcoya" (E, 190), as does Biedma (B, 241).

43. R, 304–5.

44. E, 191; B, 241. Rangel was under the impression that "Cayase" was a large stock- aded town they had missed as they had traveled up the river (R, 305).

45. E, 191–92.

46. G, 454.

47. R, 305.

48. E, 192–93. Garcilaso's account of this salt-making appears to be garbled. He im- plies that it was the Spaniards who discovered this salt-encrusted sand. He says it was blue in color, and they tried to extract the blue from the white, thinking they could make saltpeter and thus make powder for their arquebuses. They spent several days making a quantity of this salt. Some of the men ate it to excess and died from a surfeit, or so says Garcilaso. Garcilaso says they called this place Provincia de la sal—the province of salt (G, 453–54).

49. Frank F. Schambach, "Some New Interpretations of Spiroan Culture History," in *Archaeology of Eastern North America: Papers in Honor of Stephen Williams*, ed. James B. Stoltman, Archaeological Report No. 25 (Jackson: Mississippi Department of Archives and History, 1993), 187–230. See also Michael P. Hoffman, "The Protohistoric Period in the Lower and Central Arkansas River Valley in Arkansas," in *The Protohistoric Period in the Mid-South, 1500–1700,* ed. David H. Dye and Ronald C. Brister, Proceedings of the 1983 Mid-South Archaeological Conference (Jackson: Mississippi Department of Archives and History, 1986), 24–30.

50. E, 192.

51. Ibid., 193–94.

52. Ibid., 194; B, 241. Elvas spells it "Tulla."

53. E, 194.

54. R, 305. Biedma says he took twenty horsemen (B, 242).

55. Ibid.

56. G, 456.

57. Ibid., 455.

58. Ibid., 455–56. Garcilaso may have interviewed this man. He says that at the time he was finishing his book in 1591, Reynoso was living in Spain (G, 456).

59. B, 242.

60. Ibid. Rangel says four or five horses were wounded (R, 306).

61. Biedma set Tula casualties at thirty or forty (B, 242).

62. Ibid.

63. Charles Hudson, "Reconstructing the De Soto Expedition Route West of the Mississippi River," DWM, 147.

64. Ibid.; E, 195–96.

65. Tula has been archaeologically identified as Fort Coffee phase. Ann M. Early, "Finding the Middle Passage: The Spanish Journey from the Swamplands to Caddo Country," in *The Expedition of Hernando de Soto West of the Mississippi, 1541–1543,* ed. Gloria A. Young and Michael P. Hoffman (Fayetteville: University of Arkansas Press, 1993), 71–75. More recently, Frank Schambach has argued that the very concept of "Fort Coffee phase" is deficient and erroneous. He argues that the Tulas were Caddoan people who in 1541 were occupying an area that had previously been occupied by Arkansas Valley tradition people. One possible problem is that because it contains an *l*, "Tula" cannot be a word from a Caddoan language. Schambach, "Some New Interpretations," 221–24.

66. R, 305; E, 196.

67. R, 305; G, 458.

68. E, 196. Biedma and Garcilaso say they were formed into three squadrons (B, 242; G, 458).

69. G, 459.

70. Ibid.

71. Ibid., 461–63. Silvestre claimed the Indian said, "peace be with you" before he fell to the ground. This is an odd claim, since not even the Indians could understand the language of the Tulas.

72. G, 462–64.

73. Ibid., 465–66.

74. Ibid., 465.

75. E, 197.

76. G, 457.

77. E, 198–99.

78. B, 242.

79. G, 457.

80. Ibid., 458.

81. Schambach, "Some New Interpretations," 221–24; Wallace Chate, "Caddo Names in the de Soto Documents," DWM, 225.

82. E, 197–98.

83. Ibid., 198.

84. Ibid.

85. Ibid., 199–200.

86. Ibid., 200.

87. B, 242.

88. Ibid.; E, 199. Only Biedma says there were large towns toward the west, specifically the northwest. These towns would seem to have been in the old western territory of the Arkansas Valley tradition. But who might the occupants of this territory have been in 1541?

89. E, 199; B, 242.

90. E, 200. Elvas estimated the distance to be eighty leagues.

91. Elvas incorrectly says the time was over three years (E, 200).

92. Ibid.

93. E, 200–201.

94. B, 242.

95. R, 305; E, 201.

96. R, 305; B, 242; E, 201. Elvas says they were on the trail for five days, whereas in fact, it took them four days to reach Quipana (E, 201).

97. E, 201; Hudson, "Reconstructing the De Soto Expedition Route," DWM, 146–47.

98. E, 201.

99. None of the chroniclers specifically says they spent time in Quipana, but it can be inferred from the days given by Rangel. Quipana was said to be six days from Utiangüe, yet they arrived in Quipana on October 22 and in Utiangüe on November 2—a span of eleven days.

100. E, 201; B, 242–43; R, 305. Only Elvas mentions the town of Anoixi. It was probably deserted when they got there.

101. Elvas spells it "Catamaya" (E, 202).

102. R, 305; E, 202.

103. R, 305. Here the narrative of Rodrigo Rangel ends.

CHAPTER 13: Winter, 1541–1542

1. Biedma calls Utiangüe "Viranque," obviously a mistranscription (B, 243). Elvas calls it "Autiamque" (E, 199); Garcilaso has it as "Utiangüe" (G, 466). He says it was situated between two streams in a plain (G, 467).

2. Utiangüe and other polities along the lower Arkansas River are identified as Quapaw phase, or more appropriately, Menard phase. Dan F. Morse and Phyllis A. Morse, *Archaeology of the Central Mississippi Valley* (New York: Academic Press, 1983), 300–301.

3. Garcilaso says they repaired the palisade, which already encircled the town (G, 467). No doubt their worry about fire was a lesson learned from the Chicazas.

4. E, 202–3. Their building a palisade suggests that they may have built other palisades (e.g., at the base camp at Ozita).

5. G, 469–70.

6. Ibid., 470. Garcilaso says the chief was lame, and one must wonder whether this is not simply another case of a chief being carried on a litter.

7. E, 204.

8. Ibid.

9. G, 471.

10. E, 234.

11. B, 243.

12. E, 205–6.

13. Garcilaso says they also killed some deer in hunts in which the Spaniards had to be on the ready for combat with the Indians (G, 468).

14. Ibid.

15. E, 205–6.

16. Garcilaso mistakenly calls this province "Naguatex." He places it twenty leagues from Autiamque, but he does not say in which direction (G, 471).

17. Ibid., 471–72.

18. B, 243.

19. E, 207.

CHAPTER 14: Guachoya

1. Elvas spells it "Nilco" (E, 206). Biedma spells it "Anilcoyanque" (B, 234). Garcilaso is mistaken both about their departure date and about where they went next. He says they departed on the first of April and went to Naguatex, a chiefdom they entered much later, as they were attempting to reach Mexico (G, 475).

2. Elvas says they had three hundred fighting men (E, 206).

3. Ibid., 207. Could this have been Perico?

4. Ibid.

5. Elvas specifically says this was the river that ran past Cayas and Utiangüe (E, 212).

6. E, 208.

7. Ibid.

8. Ibid., 207–9.

9. Elvas says the chief's town was two leagues from Tianto (E, 209).

10. Ibid., 210; G, 485.

11. E, 210. Biedma calls it one of the best in all of La Florida (B, 234).

12. E, 210.

13. Ibid., 210–11. It is not known whether *margaridetas* were Nueva Cadiz, chevron, or some other type of bead.

14. Ibid., 211.

15. Ibid., 212.

16. G, 486.

17. Biedma spells it "Guachoyanque" (B, 234). Elvas reiterates that the same river that flowed through Cayas and Utiangüe flowed through Anilco, and this River of Cayas emptied into the Mississippi River, which flowed through Pacaha and Aquixo and ran "hard by the province of Guachoya" (E, 212). Elvas further says that at Guachoya the

river was half a league wide, sixteen *brazas* deep, and very swift (E, 219). Garcilaso says it was a quarter of a league wide and nineteen fathoms deep (G, 503).

18. E, 212.

19. Ibid., 212–13.

20. B, 234.

21. E, 213. This could, of course, indicate that Guachoya was on good terms with Quigualtam. Alternatively, it may mean that the Guachoyas regarded Quigualtam as the lesser of two evils.

22. Elvas specifically says "down river" (E, 213).

23. Garcilaso says the town contained two large "hills" (i.e., mounds) and three hundred houses, with half the houses on one mound and the other half on the other; the space in between the mounds was a plaza (G, 487).

24. Elvas notes that in Coosa the Mississippi (actually the Tennessee–French Broad) was called *mico* (chief). Note the social implications of this (i.e., it was the river into which all others flowed). At the port "the river was called *Ri*" (E, 214). It is unclear whether this is a word they got from Juan Ortiz or a word they learned from captives.

25. Marvin D. Jeter, "Tunicans West of the Mississippi: A Summary of Early Historic and Archaeological Evidence," in *The Protohistoric Period in the Mid-South, 1500–1700,* ed. David H. Dye and Ronald C. Brister (Jackson: Mississippi Department of Archives and History, 1986), 49–58.

Guachoya included some of the sites of the Hog Lake phase.

26. E, 214–15.

27. Garcilaso says this chief was also called "Guachoya" (G, 459).

28. Ibid., 490.

29. Garcilaso calls him "Quigualtanqui" (G, 496).

30. E, 216.

31. G, 490–91.

32. E, 217; B, 243.

33. Frank F. Schambach, "The End of the Trail: Reconstruction of the Route of Hernando de Soto's Army through Arkansas and East Texas," in *The Expedition of Hernando de Soto West of the Mississippi, 1541–1543,* ed. Gloria A. Young and Michael P. Hoffman (Fayetteville: University of Arkansas Press, 1993), 102.

34. De Soto evidently took to his sickbed in the last week of April. Garcilaso is in error in saying that De Soto first felt a slight fever on June 20, 1542 (498); on this date he had been dead for a month.

35. E, 219.

36. Ibid., 217–19.

37. Gayle J. Fritz and Tristam R. Kidder, "Recent Investigations into Prehistoric Agriculture in the Lower Mississippi Valley," *Southeastern Archaeology* 12 (1993): 1–14; Jeffrey P. Brain, "Late Prehistoric Settlement Patterning in the Yazoo Basin and Natchez Bluffs Regions of the Lower Mississippi Valley," in *Mississippian Settlement Patterns,* ed. Bruce D. Smith (New York: Academic Press, 1978), 331–68; Jeffrey P. Brain, *Winterville: Late Prehistoric Culture Contact in the Lower Mississippi Valley,* Archaeological Report No. 23 (Jackson: Mississippi Department of Archives and History, 1989); Stephen Williams

and Jeffrey P. Brain, *Excavations at the Lake George Site, Yazoo County, Mississippi, 1958–1960* (Cambridge: Peabody Museum of Archaeology and Ethnology, 1983).

38. G, 496.

39. E, 219–20.

40. Ibid., 220.

41. Garcilaso erroneously has them going downstream from Guachoya (G, 491).

42. Elvas says they were so confused they did not fire an arrow (E, 221–22).

43. Ibid., 222.

44. Ibid., 223.

45. Ibid., 224.

46. Biedma says Guachoya and Anilco were at continual war with each other (B, 243).

47. G, 487.

48. Ibid., 493.

49. Ibid., 494.

50. Garcilaso is inaccurate on many points. He says De Soto ordered this raid to see whether Anilco could aid him in building the boats. And he says De Soto himself took part in the raid (G, 494).

51. Ibid., 496–97.

52. AGI, Justicia 750, Pieza 2B. San Jorge remembered the name as "Tigualta."

53. De Soto was at least three weeks on his deathbed. Garcilaso has him dying within seven days of falling ill (G, 498–99).

54. E, 224–25.

55. G, 498.

56. E, 226–27. De Soto had demoted Moscoso during the winter at Chicaza (G, 498).

57. G, 499. Garcilaso says he died at the age of forty-two.

58. Elvas says they did not do so because they were worried about being lost in a strange land (E, 227). Garcilaso says they greatly mourned him, as they would a father (G, 501).

59. E, 231–32.

60. It should be noted that Quigualtam did not, in fact, believe everything that was told to him.

61. E, 228. Garcilaso says they buried him where the Indians dug dirt to plaster their dwellings. They galloped their horses over the ground to conceal it, pretending great festivity and rejoicing to deceive the Indians (G, 502).

62. G, 502.

63. Ibid.

64. E, 228–29. Garcilaso says they first sounded the river to find the deepest part. He also says they placed the body in a thick live oak tree, which they hollowed out and then nailed boards over (G, 503–4).

65. E, 229–30.

66. Ibid., 230. Garcilaso may have garbled this incident. According to him, as they were departing from Guachoya they noted that an Indian boy of sixteen or seventeen had voluntarily gone with them. When Moscoso, fearing that he was a spy, interrogated him (but not through Juan Ortiz, as Garcilaso mistakenly says), he learned that the boy

was orphaned and adopted by a relative of the chief of Guachoya, who reared him as one of his own. But this man was ill, and the boy was told that since the man loved him so, he was to be killed and interred with him. The boy said that even though he loved the man, he did not love him enough to go to the grave with him. He would rather be a slave than be dead (G, 511–12).

67. E, 231.

68. Ibid.

69. They missed the people living on the Chattahoochee River in Georgia and on the headwaters of the Savannah River, as well as the small societies living on the coast of Georgia and South Carolina. The thoroughness with which they went from population center to population center can best be seen in the state of Arkansas. See Dan F. Morse, "Archaeology and the Population of Arkansas in 1541–1543," in *The Expedition of Hernando de Soto West of the Mississippi, 1541–1543*, ed. Gloria A. Young and Michael P. Hoffman (Fayetteville: University of Arkansas Press, 1993), 29–35.

70. E, 232–33; B, 243.

CHAPTER 15: The River of Daycao

1. Catalte is identified with the Tillar archaeological complex. Marvin D. Jeeter, "The Protohistoric 'Tiller Complex' of Southeast Arkansas" (paper presented at the annual meeting of the Society for American Archaeology, Minneapolis, Minn., April 1982).

Garcilaso says they departed from Guachoya on July 5 (G, 510). He says they marched rapidly and had no intention of colonizing, and for this reason they did not learn the names of the provinces through which they passed.

2. E, 234–36. Chaguate is identified as having been a polity of the Middle Ouachita region. Ann M. Early, "Finding the Middle Passage: The Spanish Journey from the Swamplands to Caddo Country," DWM, 76. Quipana, which lay between Tula and Utiangüe, was also a Middle Ouachita region polity.

3. Timothy K. Perttula, *"The Caddo Nation": Archaeological and Ethnohistoric Perspectives* (Austin: University of Texas Press, 1992), 3–18, 68–71; Perttula, "Caddoan Area Archaeology since 1990," typescript.

4. They arrived there on June 21. Biedma correctly states the travel time from Guachoya to the principal town of Chaguate was seventeen days (B, 243).

5. Ibid. Both the Hardman site (3CL418) and the Bayou Sel site (3CL27) lay on Saline Bayou. Early, "Finding the Middle Passage," DWM, 76. Ann Early, ed., *Caddoan Saltmakers in the Ouachita Valley: The Hardman Site*, Arkansas Archaeological Survey Research Series, no. 43 (Fayetteville, Ark.: Archaeological Survey, 1993).

The first European salt works in Arkansas were established at this very productive saline. Frank F. Schambach, "The End of the Trail: Reconstruction of the Route of Hernando de Soto's Army through Southwest Arkansas and East Texas," DWM, 83.

6. E, 237. Even though the last two chapters of Rangel's account are missing, outlines of the chapters are extant, and they mention "hot rivers and salt which is made from the sand" (R, 306).

7. B, 243; Frank Schambach, ed., *Coles Creek and Mississippi Period Foragers in the*

Felsenthal Region of the Lower Mississippi Valley, Research Series No. 40 (Fayetteville: Arkansas Archaeological Series, 1991).

8. G, 477. Garcilaso, probably on the authority of Gonzalo Silvestre, calls him "Diego de Guzmán," but he notes that Alonso de Carmona calls him "Francisco" (G, 481).

9. Garcilaso says she was the daughter of a chief (G, 477).

10. E, 237; G, 477.

11. G, 478.

12. Ibid. Garcilaso says Moscoso became suspicious that Guzmán had been killed and sent a messenger to him with a letter, asking him to respond. But here Garcilaso has out of place the incident reported by the Gentleman of Elvas on the return journey.

13. There are at least twenty mound sites in a forty-mile stretch of the river through which the expedition passed, and many were occupied during the sixteenth century. Schambach, "End of the Trail," DWM, 83.

14. E, 237–38. This gift of venison was unusual; the Indians seldom gave it to the Spaniards.

15. Schambach places the principal town somewhat further west, near present-day Nashville ("End of the Trail," DWM, 83).

16. E, 238; Schambach, "End of the Trail," DWM, 84.

17. G, 510; E, 257. In fact, they went westward only from Guachoya to Aguacay and then from Naguatex to Aays; the remainder of their journey was south by southwest.

18. B, 243.

19. The Hickman Salt Works site is 3SV69. Amaye appears to be a polity of the Texarkana phase. Schambach, "End of the Trail," DWM, 85–87.

20. E, 239.

21. Ibid., 241.

22. Ibid., 241–42. Naguatex is identified as the principal chiefdom of the Belcher phase. Belcher phase sites lay between present-day Fulton, Arkansas, and Shreveport, Louisiana. Schambach, "End of the Trail," DWM, 88–89. Naguatex probably included the Foster, Friday, McClure, Battle, Cedar Grove, and perhaps Egypt sites; Hacanac possibly included the Belcher, Mounds Plantation, Vanceville, and Werner sites. See map in Perttula, *"Caddo Nation,"* 98.

23. Frank B. Schambach and Frank Rackerby, eds., *Contributions to the Archaeology of the Great Bend Region,* Arkansas Archaeological Survey Research Sources 22 (Fayetteville: Arkansas Archaeological Survey, 1982), 1–12. Naguatex is identified as a polity of the Belcher phase. The major pottery types are Belcher Engraved, Hodges Engraved, Glassell Engraved, Foster Trailed-Incised, Belcher Ridged, and Karnack Brushed-Incised.

24. E, 243–44. Elvas says, incorrectly, that Tula lay to the east of Naguatex and that it was not far away. In fact, it was to the north northwest, and it was 130 to 175 miles away. Garcilaso has the arrival at Naguatex out of sequence (G, 475–76).

25. E, 244–45.

26. Ibid., 245–46.

27. Schambach, "End of the Trail," DWM, 94–95.

28. E, 247. From this point onward, it becomes difficult to even approximately estimate the dates on which events occurred.

29. Biedma spells it "Nisione" (B, 244). Nisohone is identified as comprising a town or polity of the Texarkana phase. I am grateful to Timothy Perttula for informing me that little archaeological research has been done on the Sulphur River and it is not currently known whether the "Texarkana" people living there were comparable in their agricultural productivity to those living on the Red River.

30. E, 247. Elvas spells it "Lacane." Charles Hudson, "Reconstructing the De Soto Expedition Route West of the Mississippi River," DWM, 149–52. Lacane was probably a town of the Titus phase. There are several clusters of sites along Big Cypress Bayou, each with slight differences in ceramics and lithics. Perttula, "Caddo Nation," 104, 114. Only a single platform mound—the Camp Joy site (41UR142)—is known to have been in use in the Cypress Creek Basin in the sixteenth century (Timothy Perttula, personal communication).

31. B, 244.

32. Walter Prescott Webb, *The Great Plains* (New York: Ginn, 1931), 10–24.

33. E, 247–48. Nondacao was probably a town of the western area of the Titus focus. Robert L. Turner Jr., "The Tuck Carpenter Site and Its Relation to Other Sites within the Titus Focus," *Bulletin of the Texas Archaeological Society* 49 (1978): 1–110. In many Caddoan sites, fish constituted as much as 40 percent of the faunal remains. Perttula, "Caddoan Area Archaeology."

34. B, 244.

35. Biedma spells it "Hais" (B, 244). Garcilaso has it as "Auche" (G, 512). Nancy Adele Kenmotsu, James E. Bruseth, and James E. Corbin, "Moscoso and the Route in Texas: A Reconstruction," DWM, 127–28. I am grateful to Timothy Perttula for suggestions that led to this placement of Aays.

36. B, 244.

37. G, 516. It is also possible this was a description of the people of the River of Daycao. For Garcilaso, all or most of the country west of the Red River was "the province of the herdsmen" (i.e., hunter-gatherers).

38. Kenmotsu et al., "Moscoso," 110–11, 128.

39. G, 516–17.

40. Ibid., 518–19.

41. E, 249–50.

42. G, 513–14.

43. E, 250. Biedma confirms that the chief of Nondacao ordered this (B, 244). Garcilaso also appears to describe this same incident of torture (G, 514–15).

44. G, 515.

45. B, 244. Biedma spells it "Xacatin." Timothy Perttula informs me that little is known about the late prehistoric archaeology of this stretch of the Sabine River.

46. E, 250.

47. Biedma says they traveled "eastward"—probably southeastward—from Soacatino. He confirms that here they were told about other Spaniards (B, 244). Soacatino is identified as a village or polity of the Frankston phase.

48. These must have been short days' marches, perhaps because of their difficulty in finding food.

49. E, 251. Guasco is identified as a polity of the Frankston phase. There were at least

two Frankston platform mound centers, the A. C. Saunders mound and the Pace McDonald mound, both on the Neches River in present-day Anderson County. Perttula, "*Caddo Nation*," 116–17.

50. Kenmotsu et al., "Moscoso," 119–21.

51. I am grateful to James Corbin and to Timothy Perttula for emphasizing the importance of the Camino Real trail.

52. E, 251–52. Elvas says they had gone three or four leagues. Naquiscoza and Nazacahoz were probably towns of the Angelina phase, although the Angelina phase is currently poorly defined.

53. B, 244. Garcilaso reports that they went through the province of "Guancane," where they found the Indians had placed wooden crosses atop their houses (G, 482). Seemingly he speculates that they got the idea of displaying the cross from Cabeza de Vaca, not from a direct visit but by word of mouth and imitation.

Garcilaso has them visiting the "Guancane" out of sequence, before coming to Guachoya instead of afterward. Cabeza de Vaca does not include the ethnonym "Guancane" in his narrative. The closest he comes is "Guaycones," which he lists without further elaboration. Alvar Núñez Cabeza de Vaca, *The Narrative of Alvar Núñez Cabeza de Vaca,* trans. Fanny Bandelier (Barre, Mass.: Imprint Society, 1972), 102.

54. B, 244. Kenmotsu et al., "Moscoso," illus. 24.

55. E, 252–53. Elvas puts the amount of corn they found at less than half an *alqueire,* an alqueire being a dry measure of 1.38 liters (E, 253). Garcilaso incorrectly says Moscoso sent out three contingents of twenty-four horses each in three different directions (G, 520).

56. B, 244.

57. Kenmotsu et al., "Moscoso," 110–11.

58. Elvas says they brought back two (E, 253). Biedma says three or four (B, 244).

59. E, 253.

60. Wallace Chafe, "Caddo Names in the De Soto Documents," DWM, 222–25.

61. E, 254; B, 244–45.

62. This assumes that Cabeza de Vaca's oral report was like what he wrote in his *Relación,* which was not published until 1542.

63. E, 254. Biedma says they intended to return to the town where De Soto died (B, 244–45).

64. E, 255–56. Donald E. Chipman, *Spanish Texas, 1519–1821* (Austin: University of Texas Press, 1992), 30–31.

65. E, 256–57. Elvas says, without explanation, that two days after saying this, this man left the command.

66. B, 245. Only Garcilaso says that on their return they took a trail "to the right" (i.e., to the south) of the route by which they had come. He says this route was shorter, but because it did not pass through populated areas, they did not have benefit of food and guides (G, 521–22). It *is* possible they took such a shortcut while going from Guasco to Naguatex.

67. This segment of the route appears to be what Garcilaso calls the "province of the herdsmen" (G, 522).

68. Ibid., 523. Garcilaso erroneously spells his name "Sanjurge." Ignacio Avellaneda, *Los Sobrevivientes De La Florida: The Survivors of the De Soto Expedition,* Research Publications of the P. K. Yonge Library of Florida History (Gainesville: University of Florida Libraries, 1990), 50.

69. G, 524–25.

70. E, 259.

71. Schambach, "End of the Trail," DWM, 104–5. I am grateful to Martin and Ivana Elbl for this translation.

72. G, 529.

73. Ibid., 525.

74. Ibid., 526–28.

75. E, 257–58.

76. Ibid., 258.

77. Ibid. Elvas spells it "Aays."

78. G, 530.

79. Ibid., 531.

80. E, 258–59.

81. Ibid.

82. Ibid., 259–69.

CHAPTER 16: Winter, 1542–1543

1. Elvas says they departed from Anilco at the beginning of December (E, 261). He does not say how many days it took them to reach Aminoya.

2. G, 560, 529.

3. E, 259–60. Garcilaso says fifty Spaniards and an equal number of Indians died (G, 533). Four out of five of the Indian slaves belonging to Gonzalo Silvestre died (G, 556).

4. B, 245.

5. G, 534.

6. E, 261–62. Garcilaso says each of the two towns had two hundred houses, and a moat of water from the river surrounded the towns, making an island of them (G, 531). He may be confused here about the effects of the flood on Aminoya. Alonso de Carmona put the corn at eighteen thousand bushels (G, 532).

7. I am grateful to John H. House for helpful discussion of this proposed location of Aminoya.

8. G, 537–39.

9. E, 264; B, 245; G, 538. From the roots of *Eryngium,* Southeastern Indians procured one of their most important medicines.

10. E, 265.

11. Ibid., 264–66.

12. G, 552, 564–65. Roger C. Smith, *Vanguard of Empire: Ships of Exploration in the Age of Columbus* (New York: Oxford University Press, 1993), 126–28; Smith, "Ships in the Exploration of *La Florida,*" *Gulf Coast Historical Review* 8 (1992): 19–29.

13. G, 534–35.

14. According to Garcilaso, the water began to rise on March 8 or 10 (G, 553).

15. Ibid., 554.

16. Garcilaso says Aminoya was sixteen leagues upstream from Guachoya (G, 534). He also says it was seven leagues from Aminoya to where the river that ran past Anilco (i.e., the Arkansas River) entered the Mississippi (G, 546).

17. Ibid., 554–55. It is in the context of this flood that Garcilaso makes the point that the houses of native lords were on top of artificial mounds, which lent them grandeur and also protection from high water.

18. E, 266. Garcilaso says they continued to work on the boats (G, 559).

19. Here Garcilaso contradicts himself in saying that Anilco was twenty leagues from Aminoya (G, 555).

20. Ibid., 557–58.

21. E, 264–65.

22. Garcilaso contradicts this by saying that the chief of Anilco came to the Spaniards and informed them of a plot by Quigualtam, after the flood water had gone down (G, 561).

23. Ibid., 564.

24. E, 268.

25. Garcilaso says Guachoya was envious and jealous of the attention the Spaniards paid to Anilco, his enemy (G, 539). He also says that in a face-to-face altercation, the war chief of Anilco challenged the chief of Guachoya to one-on-one combat (G, 542–47).

26. E, 269.

27. G, 539–42. Garcilaso may be untrustworthy on this matter. Clearly Garcilaso is wrong in saying it was Anilco who advised Moscoso of the existence of the conspiracy.

28. E, 269. The use of horsemen implies that Taguanate was on the western side of the Mississippi River. Possibly it was at the Old Town site.

29. G, 560.

30. B, 245.

31. E, 269–70.

32. Ibid., 271.

CHAPTER 17: Flight down the Mississippi River

1. E, 271. Garcilaso confirms that they salted this pork, and he says they loaded a dozen and a half of the live animals into the boats in case they came upon a suitable place to found a colony. He also says they gave a boar and two sows to each of the local friendly chiefs so they could breed them (G, 565).

2. E, 271.

3. G, 565.

4. Garcilaso claims they had eight hundred slaves when they reached Aminoya, but all but twenty-five or thirty had died during the winter; they took all the survivors with them (G, 570).

5. Ibid., 569–70. There may be some errors in Garcilaso's list of boat commanders.

6. Garcilaso says they floated their boats into the water on the day of St. John the Baptist. They then spent the five days before the eve of Saints Peter and Paul killing the

hogs and loading the boats. They disembarked on the Day of the Apostles (G, 566). Garcilaso would seem to be incorrect in saying they set forth as the sun was sinking on the Day of the Apostles (570). But they may have set out very early on the morning of the day they departed.

7. Garcilaso says there were fewer than 350 Spaniards out of almost 1,000 in the beginning (G, 570).

8. Biedma puts the number of horses at twenty-six (245).

9. E, 272–73.

10. G, 570, 579, 586.

11. Thomas Nuttall, *Journal of Travels into the Arkansas Territory during the Year 1819* (Philadelphia, 1821), 43–63.

12. Stanley Faye, "The Forked River," *Louisiana Historical Quarterly* 25 (1942): 930–933. Before the levees were built, the Mississippi River branched into several lateral channels, the St. Francis River being the one furthest north. Today, only the Atchafalaya River has resisted domestication by the U.S. Corps of Engineers.

13. E, 274–75. At 4 miles per hour, their distance could have been in the realm of 6:00 A.M. to 4:00 P.M., 40 miles; 6:00 A.M. to 7:00 P.M., 52 miles; 4:00 A.M. to 9:00 P.M., 68 miles. Garcilaso says that on the first day and two nights of their journey they were in the territory of Guachoya, who did not attack them (G, 570–71).

14. It is possible, though it seems unlikely, they also spent the day of July 4 in this place.

15. E, 275–76.

16. Biedma puts the size of this fleet at forty to fifty large canoes, some with as many as eighty men (B, 245). Garcilaso says a large fleet of canoes appeared to attack the Spaniards on the second day (G, 571). He may be confused about the fleet on the day before, which mounted no serious attack, or he may be confused—as already discussed—about their time of departure.

17. G, 575.

18. Garcilaso surely exaggerates when he says they could rival the speed of a galloping horse (G, 575).

19. Ibid., 575–76.

20. It is possible that Guachoya had once been tributary to Quigualtam.

21. B, 245. Garcilaso says there were fifty-two Spaniards in four canoes (G, 585).

22. E, 277–78. Garcilaso's account of how this attack began is quite different from that of the Gentleman of Elvas. According to Garcilaso, the attack on the Indian canoes was made by a small canoe taken out by Estevan Añez, a vainglorious young man from Villanueva de Bacarrota, who got five young men to go with him. They pretended they wanted to go to the front of the fleet to speak with Moscoso, but instead they made for the Indians in the canoes. Garcilaso says the Indians formed a crescent, and as the Spaniards approached the right arm of the crescent, they swept in and rammed the canoe, overturning it (G, 586–87).

23. Biedma sets the number of dead at twelve (B, 245). "Alonso de Argote's Recollections of the De Soto Expedition, 1557," AGI, Patronato 77, Num. 1, Ramo 1, trans. John Worth.

24. E, 278–79.

25. G, 587–88.

26. According to Garcilaso the attack began about noon (G, 587–88).

27. E, 279–80.

28. Garcilaso sometimes spells his name "Quigualtanqui" (G, 577).

29. Ibid., 576.

30. Ibid., 579. Biedma says they had no arquebuses or crossbows left (B, 245).

31. E, 280–81.

32. G, 577–78.

33. Ibid., 578. It is likely they injured and killed some of these horses.

34. E, 281–82; G, 589. Garcilaso erroneously says this attack (and perhaps subsequent ones) went on continuously for ten days.

35. G, 589.

36. E, 282. Garcilaso says they got away with a canoe with five sows, which was towed behind this brigantine (G, 583).

37. Garcilaso says they also found corn, dried fruit, dressed deerskins, and animal skins at this place. But he may have the earlier visit to the town at Huhasene mixed up with the killing of the horses (G, 579–81). He does not, in fact, mention that they butchered some of the last remaining horses.

The place where they killed the horses may be the place where Gonzalo Silvestre claimed to have found a strip of "marten skins" 1.5 yards wide and 8 yards long, with strings of pearls sewn to it (G, 580).

38. E, 282–83.

39. Ibid., 283.

40. Ibid.

41. Elvas says each arm was about a league and a half wide (E, 284).

42. Ibid.

43. G, 590.

44. Ibid., 595.

45. E, 285–86. Again, Garcilaso's account differs from that of the Gentleman of Elvas (G, 596).

46. G, 597–98.

47. Marion Spjut Gilliland, *The Material Culture of Key Marco Florida* (Gainesville: University Presses of Florida, 1975), 123, 133, plate 80.

48. E, 285.

49. Elvas says they spent seventeen days on the river, a correct count using his July 2 starting date and his July 18 date for when they sailed a quarter of a league to enter the Gulf (E, 283). But Biedma says they were nineteen days on the river (B, 245). Garcilaso says they were nineteen days and one additional night on the river (G, 591).

CHAPTER 18: To Mexico

1. Elvas contradicts himself in saying they remained at anchor for a few days. Perhaps he meant they were at anchor for part of the sixteenth and for all of the seventeenth (E, 286).

2. Ibid.

3. G, 600, quoting Alonso de Carmona. David B. Quinn, *North America from Earliest Discovery to First Settlements: The Norse Voyages to 1612* (New York: Harper and Row, 1975), 75–81.

4. E, 286–87.

5. Ibid., 288.

6. G, 600.

7. E, 288. Garcilaso says they recovered the anchor (G, 599).

8. E, 289. It is impossible to follow the movements of the fleet in the Gulf of Mexico with any precision. They put to sea on July 18 and landed at the mouth of the Pánuco River on September 10. Hence they were fifty-five days en route from the mouth of the Mississippi River to the mouth of the Pánuco. Elvas incorrectly says it took fifty-two days (E, 300). The total distance along the coast was about 780 miles. For at least twenty-two days they were at anchor; they were in motion for no more than thirty-three days. Thus, they averaged about 23.6 miles per day. This is not a firm figure because occasionally they ventured out away from the coast and ran under sail all night.

On the day they reached the Rio de las Palmas, Garcilaso says they had been at anchor for twenty-three days and at sea for thirty days (G, 603), estimates that are seemingly close to the actual figures.

9. E, 290.

10. Ibid. Garcilaso says they had to take on water every three days (G, 601).

11. Biedma says they were out of sight of land for three days and three nights, and all the while sailed through water so fresh they could drink it (B, 246).

12. E, 290–91.

13. G, 601.

14. E, 291–92.

15. G, 601–3.

16. E, 292.

17. Ibid., 292–93.

18. Ibid., 293–94.

19. Ibid., 294. Garcilaso says it was slabs of bitumen resembling tar. The slabs weighed from eight to fourteen pounds. Garcilaso may be incorrect in saying they spent eight days in this place. Only Garcilaso says that eight Indians in a canoe visited them peaceably while they tarred their brigantines (G, 601).

The "De Soto map" shows a *p[unt]o de copei* on the Texas coast.

20. E, 295.

21. Ibid., 296.

22. This geographical notion of Añasco is puzzling. At this point they were in the general vicinity of present-day Brownsville, Texas. But here the coast runs north-south, and in fact it had already run in this direction for quite some distance. Perhaps the missing days not accounted for by Elvas were in this leg of their journey.

23. G, 603.

24. E, 296–97.

25. Elvas spells it "Panico" (E, 297).

26. E, 297.

27. Ibid., 297–98.

28. Ibid., 298.

29. G, 603.

30. Ibid.

31. E, 299.

32. G, 604.

33. Ibid., 605.

34. Ibid., 606–7. It would seem that Gonzalo Silvestre was on board Gaytán's boat. This Juan Gaytán was the nephew of a famous swordsman, also named Juan Gaytán.

35. Ibid.

36. Ibid., 608.

37. Ibid., 609–10.

38. Ibid., 611. Garcilaso says one piece was made in Talvera and the other in "Malasa" (probably Málaga).

39. Ibid., 612–13.

40. Ibid., 612.

41. Ibid., 615–16.

42. Ibid., 617.

43. E, 300–301.

44. Ibid., 301–2.

45. Ibid., 302.

46. Ibid.

47. Ibid., 303.

48. Ibid.; G, 617.

49. G, 616–18.

50. E, 304–5.

51. G, 618–19.

52. Ibid., 619–20.

53. Ibid., 620.

54. Ibid., 621.

55. E, 306.

56. Ibid. Both Juan Coles and Alonso de Carmona said these gifts came from the Brotherhood of Charity of Mexico, at the order of the viceroy (G, 618).

57. G, 622.

58. Ibid., 621.

59. Ibid., 622–23.

60. E, 307. Garcilaso says the viceroy treated them all without distinction (G, 623).

61. Garcilaso may have got an exaggerated idea of the value of the skins and furs from Gonzalo Silvestre. Silvestre claimed to have visited the house of the factor, Gonzalo de Salazar, who purchased Silvestre's old sword for his collection, and he said he would have paid Silvestre fifteen hundred pesos for the "marten" skin decorated with pearls, which Silvestre had stolen on their flight down the Mississippi River. But Silvestre had already given the skin to his host in Pánuco (G, 626–27).

62. Ibid., 624.

63. Ibid., 624–25.

64. Ibid., 627–28.

65. Ibid., 629–30.

CHAPTER 19: After the Expedition

1. G, 631–33.

2. Ibid., 633–34.

3. Ignacio Avellaneda, *Los Sobrevivientes de la Florida: The Survivors of the De Soto Expedition*, Research Publications of the P. K. Yonge Library (Gainesville: University of Florida Libraries, 1990), 6–10.

4. Avellaneda, *Los Sobrevivientes*, 71.

5. G, 630.

6. Avellaneda, *Los Sobrevivientes*, 73.

7. G, 630. Garcilaso includes in this number Juan de Añasco, Juan Gaytán, Baltasar de Gallegos, Alonso Romo de Cardeñosa, Arias Tinoco, and Pedro Calderón. But Añasco is known to have died in Peru, and Garcilaso is probably wrong on some of the others named here.

8. Avellaneda, *Los Sobrevivientes*, 13–14.

9. Ibid., 15.

10. Ibid., 41.

11. G, 631. Garcilaso says she was rich and illustrious.

12. Avellaneda, *Los Sobrevivientes*, 47.

13. Ibid., 35, 36.

14. Ibid., 45.

15. Ibid., 53.

16. G, 630.

17. AGI, Justicia 750B, Pieza 7.

18. Deposition of Francisco de Castejon, AGI, Justicia 750, Pieza 2A; "Inventory of the Assets Left by the Adelantado Hernando de Soto following his Death, 1543," DC, 1:489–98.

19. AGI, 50–2–55/10; AGI, Justicia 750, Pieza 2B.

20. AGI, Justicia 750, Pieza 2A.

21. Several of De Soto's men, when interviewed in Mexico, verified that this was indeed true. Others denied it, saying the weather was fair when Ponce de León arrived. AGI, Justicia 750, Pieza 2A.

22. Ibid.

23. Ibid.

24. Ibid. Some extra horses were sent to De Soto on this caravel.

25. Ibid.

26. Ibid.

27. AGI, Justicia 750B, Pieza 7.

28. Ibid.

29. AGI, Justicia 750, Pieza 2A.

30. Ibid.

31. Ibid.

32. Some of them may have provided one impetus behind the Tristán de Luna expedition. And some may have, in fact, gone with Luna.

33. Alfred W. Crosby Jr., *The Columbian Exchange: Biological and Cultural Consequences of 1492* (Westport, Conn.: Greenwood Press, 1972), 35–63; William H. McNeill, *Plagues and Peoples* (New York: Doubleday, 1976), chaps. 1–5.

34. David B. Quinn, *North America from Earliest Discovery to First Settlements: The Norse Voyagers to 1612* (New York: Harper and Row, 1977), 20–70.

35. McNeill, *Plagues*, 210.

36. Henry F. Dobyns, *Their Numbers Become Thinned: Native American Population Dynamics in Eastern North America* (Knoxville: University of Tennessee Press, 1983), 250–62.

37. David G. Anderson, *The Savannah River Chiefdoms: Political Change in the Late Prehistoric Southeast* (Tuscaloosa: University of Alabama Press, 1994), 274–89.

38. Randolph Widmer, "The Structure of Southeastern Chiefdoms," FC, 137–39.

39. Anderson, *The Savannah River Chiefdoms*, 619; Barbara A. Burnett and Katherine A. Murray, "Drought, Death, and de Soto: Bioarchaeology of Depopulation," DWM, 227–36.

40. Charles Hudson et al., "The Tristán de Luna Expedition, 1559–1561," *Southeastern Archaeology* 8 (1989): 41.

41. Charles Hudson, "A Spanish-Coosa Alliance in Sixteenth-Century North Georgia," *Georgia Historical Quarterly* 72 (1988): 599–626. Paul Hoffman has pointed out that the statements of Luna's men need not be taken as proof that Coosa had declined. That is, the discrepancy between descriptions of Coosa in the De Soto and Luna documents may be a case of explorers' rhetoric as opposed to settlers' rhetoric. Paul Hoffman, "Did Coosa Decline between 1540 and 1560?" (paper presented at the annual meeting of the Southeastern Archaeological Conference, Knoxville, Tenn., November 1995).

42. Charles Hudson, *The Juan Pardo Expeditions: Exploration of the Carolinas and Tennessee, 1566–1568* (Washington, D.C.: Smithsonian Institute Press, 1990), 39–46.

43. For a second opinion on the robustness of Cofitachequi in the late sixteenth and seventeenth centuries, see Chester B. DePratter, "The Chiefdom of Cofitachequi," FC, 197–226.

44. Several individuals were buried on a single occasion in elite retainer burials, but these are easily distinguished from the multiple burials of the late sixteenth century.

45. Marvin T. Smith, "Aboriginal Depopulation in the Postcontact Southeast," FC, 257–65.

46. Ann F. Ramenofsky, *Vectors of Death: The Archaeology of European Contact* (Albuquerque: University of New Mexico Press, 1987), 42–71.

47. Timothy K. Perttula, "The Long-Term Effects of the de Soto Entrada on Aboriginal Caddoan Populations," DWM, 237–53.

48. Barbara A. Burnett and Katherine A. Murray, "Death, Drought, and de Soto: The Bioarchaeology of Depopulation," DWM, 227–36.

49. James Mooney, "The Aboriginal Population of America North of Mexico," Smith-

sonian Miscellaneous Collections, vol. 80, no. 7 (Washington, D.C.: Smithsonian Institution, 1928), 2–13, 33.

50. Dobyns, *Their Numbers Become Thinned,* 34–44.

51. Smith, "Aboriginal Depopulation," FC, 268–69.

52. Peter H. Wood, "The Changing Population of the Colonial South: An Overview by Race and Region, 1685–1790," in *Powhatan's Mantle: Indians in the Colonial Southeast,* ed. Peter H. Wood, Gregory A. Waselkov, and M. Thomas Hatley (Lincoln: University of Nebraska Press, 1989), 39.

53. Robert L. Turner Jr. first suggested that these stemmed vessels may have been modeled after Spanish cups or chalices in his article "The Tuck Carpenter Site and Its Relation to Other Sites within the Titus Focus," *Bulletin of the Texas Archaeological Society* 49 (1978): 98–103. See also Gregory Perino, *The Banks Village Site: Crittenden County, Arkansas,* Memoir of the Missouri Archaeological Society, no. 4 (Columbia: Missouri Archaeological Society, 1966), 56, 131.

54. John H. Hann, "The Apalachee of the Historic Era," FC, 327–54.

55. John Gregory Keyes, "Change in the Mythology of the Southeastern Indians," master's thesis, University of Georgia, 1993.

56. Timothy Perttula, *"The Caddo Nation": Archaeological and Ethnohistoric Perspectives* (Austin: University of Texas Press, 1992), 12–18.

57. Robert S. Neitzel, *Archaeology of the Fatherland Site: The Grand Village of the Natchez,* Anthropological Papers of the American Museum of Natural History, vol. 51, pt. 1 (New York: American Museum of Natural History, 1965).

58. Charles Hudson, *The Catawba Nation* (Athens: University of Georgia Press, 1970), 5–28; James H. Merrell, *The Indians' New World: Catawbas and Their Neighbors from European Contact through the Era of Removal* (Chapel Hill: University of North Carolina Press, 1989).

59. Vernon James Knight Jr., "The Formation of the Creeks," FC, 373–92.

60. Patricia Galloway, "Confederacy as a Solution to Chiefdom Dissolution: Historical Evidence in the Choctaw Case," FC, 393–420.

61. Michael P. Hoffman, "The Terminal Mississippi Period in the Arkansas Valley and Quapaw Ethnogenesis," T&T, 208–26; Dan F. Morse, "The Nodena Phase," T&T, 94–97.

62. George Sabo III, "Rituals of Encounter: Interpreting Native American Views of European Explorers," *Arkansas Historical Quarterly* 51 (1992): 54–68.

63. Hudson et al., "Tristán de Luna," 35–36.

64. Hudson, *Pardo,* 105–6.

65. Luís Gerónimo de Oré, *The Martyrs of Florida,* trans. Maynard Geiger, Franciscan Studies, no. 18 (New York: Joseph F. Wagner, 1936), 112–14.

66. Thomas Nairne, *Nairne's Muskhogean Journals: The 1708 Expedition to the Mississippi River,* ed. Alexander Moore (Jackson: University Press of Mississippi, 1988), 36–37.

67. William Bartram, *The Travels of William Bartram,* ed. Francis Harper (New Haven: Yale University Press, 1958), 330–31.

68. James Adair, *The History of the American Indians* (London, 1775), 428.

69. Ibid., 211.

70. Hudson, *Pardo*, 189.

71. John R. Swanton, "The Interpretation of Aboriginal Mounds by Means of Creek Indian Customs," Annual Report of the Board of Regents for 1927 (Washington, D.C.: Smithsonian Institution, 1928), 495–506; W. L. Ballard, *The Yuchi Green Corn Ceremonial: Form and Meaning*, American Indian Studies Center (Los Angeles: University of California, 1978).

72. Bob Lancaster, "The Adelantado's Pigs," *Arkansas Times*, January 1986, pp. 65–76.

AFTERWORD

1. John R. Swanton, for example, calls the Rangel narrative "basal"; he says that after Rangel, Elvas is the source to be most relied on in reconstructing the route (FR, 10).

2. R, 301.

3. Ibid., 285, 291.

4. Ibid., 247–310. Edward Gaylord Bourne, *Narratives of the Career of Hernando de Soto*, 2 vols. (New York: A. S. Barnes, 1904). Rangel's name was spelled "Ranjel" by Oviedo; hence it is spelled this way in much of the literature on the De Soto expedition.

5. B, 239–41.

6. Ibid., 226.

7. Ibid., 338.

8. Ibid., 243.

9. For a handy summary of dated events during the expedition, see FR, 305–36.

10. E, 43.

11. Martin Malcolm Elbl and Ivana Elbl, "The Gentleman of Elvas and His Publisher," in *Studies in the Historiography of the Hernando de Soto Expedition*, ed. Patricia Galloway (Lincoln: University of Nebraska Press, in press).

12. E, 88.

13. George E. Lankford, "Legends of the Adelantado," DWM, 173–90.

14. Patricia Galloway, "The Incestuous de Soto Narratives," in Galloway, *Studies in the Historiography*.

15. Elbl and Elbl, "The Gentleman of Elvas."

16. John Lawson, *A New Voyage To Carolina* (Chapel Hill: University of North Carolina Press, 1967).

17. Galloway, "Incestuous de Soto Narratives."

18. Elbl and Elbl, "The Gentleman of Elvas."

19. Donald G. Castanien, *El Inca Garcilaso de la Vega* (New York: Twayne, 1969), 17–18; John Grier Varner, *El Inca: The Life and Times of Garcilaso de la Vega* (Austin: University of Texas Press, 1968); Galloway, "Incestuous de Soto Narratives."

20. Frances G. Crowley, "Garcilaso de la Vega, the Inca," DC, 2:1–24.

21. Castanien, *El Inca*, 31–35.

22. Ibid., xxxvii.

23. Ibid., 62–63.

24. Ibid., 40–42.

25. G, xxxvii–xlii.

26. Ibid., xxxiii.

27. Galloway, "Incestuous de Soto Narratives."

28. David Henige, "The Context, Content, and Credibility of *La Florida del Ynca*," *The Americas* 43 (1986): 1–23.

29. Galloway, "Incestuous de Soto Narratives."

30. Eugene Lyon, "The Cañete Fragment: Another Narrative of Hernando de Soto," DC, 1:307–10.

31. John Worth, personal communication.

32. G, xlii; Castanien, *El Inca,* 67–68.

33. Barbara Boston, "The 'De Soto' Map," *Mid-America* 23 (1941): 236–50.

34. Ibid., 248–50.

35. Ibid., 244.

36. DC, 1:357–81, 463–98.

37. For a more extensive examination of early research on the De Soto route, see John R. Swanton's chapter in FR, 12–46.

38. Mary Ross, "With Pardo and Boyano on the Fringes of Georgia's Coast," *Georgia Historical Quarterly* 14 (1930): 267–85. Ross got Cofitachequi on the correct river system, but not in the correct location on that river.

39. William P. Cumming, *The Southeast in Early Maps* (Chapel Hill: University of North Carolina Press, 1958), plate 47, 186–87; Jean Delanglez, "The Sources of the Delisle Map of America, 1703," *Mid-America* 25 (1943): 275–98.

40. Thomas Nuttall, *Journal of Travels into the Arkansas Territory during the Year 1819* (Philadelphia: Thomas M. Palmer, 1821), 247–94.

41. J. H. McCulloh Jr., *Researches, Philosophical and Antiquarian, Concerning the Aboriginal History of America* (Baltimore, 1829), 523–31.

42. Theodore Irving, *The Conquest of Florida under Hernando de Soto* (London, 1835), 2 vols. A revised edition was issued in one volume by George P. Putnam, New York, 1869.

43. Albert James Pickett, *History of Alabama* (Charleston, 1851), 1:1–53.

44. J. F. H. Claiborne, *Mississippi as a Province, Territory, and State* (Jackson, Miss., 1880), 1:2–11.

45. James Mooney, *The Myths of the Cherokee,* Bureau of American Ethnology, Annual Report No. 19 (Washington, D.C.: GPO, 1901), 23–27.

46. Theodore H. Lewis, "The De Soto Expedition through Florida," *American Antiquarian* 12 (1900): 351–57; 13 (1901): 107–11, 242–47.

47. James Y. Brame Jr., "De Soto in Alabama, 1540," *Arrowpoints* 13 (1928): 38–39, 47–54, 63–71.

48. John R. Fordyce, "Trailing De Soto" (paper presented at the Conference on Midwestern Archaeology, St. Louis, Mo., May 1929); "The Explorations of Hernando de Soto in the Southern Part of the United States," *Military Engineer* 28 (1936): 1–7, 113–19.

49. FR, v–xii.

50. William C. Sturtevant, foreword in FR, v–vi.

51. Ibid.

52. John R. Swanton, "De Soto's Line of March from the Viewpoint of an Ethnologist,"

Proceedings of the Mississippi Valley Historical Association for the Year 1911–12, ed. Benjamin F. Schambaugh (Cedar Rapids, Iowa: Torch Press, 1912), 147–57.

53. FR, 44.

54. Ibid., 103.

55. Ibid., 104–8.

56. David L. De Jarnette and Asael T. Hansen, *The Archaeology of the Childersburg Site, Alabama*, Notes in Anthropology No. 6, Department of Anthropology (Tallahassee: Florida State University, 1960).

57. Ripley P. Bullen, *The Terra Ceia Site, Manatee County, Florida*, Florida Anthropological Society, Publication No. 3 (Gainesville: Florida Anthropological Society, 1951); Bullen, "De Soto's Ucita and the Terra Ceia Site," *Florida Historical Quarterly* 30 (1952): 317–23.

58. Warren H. Wilkinson, *Opening the Case against the U.S. De Soto Commission's Report*, Papers of the Alliance for the Preservation of Florida Antiquities, vol. 1, no. 1 (Jacksonville Beach, Fla., 1960); Rolfe F. Schell, *De Soto Didn't Land at Tampa* (Ft. Myers Beach, Fla: Island Press, 1966).

59. Philip Phillips, James A. Ford, and James B. Griffin, *Archaeological Survey in the Lower Mississippi Alluvial Valley, 1940–1947*, Papers of the Peabody Museum of Archaeology and Ethnology, vol. 25 (Cambridge, Mass.: Peabody Museum of Archaeology and Ethnology, 1951), 391.

60. Phyllis A. Morse, *Parkin: The 1978–1979 Archaeological Investigations of a Cross County, Arkansas, Site*, Arkansas Archaeological Society, Research Series No. 13 (Fayetteville: Arkansas Archaeological Society, 1981); Dan F. Morse and Phyllis Morse, *Archaeology of the Central Mississippi Valley* (New York: Academic Press, 1983), 305–13. All except their location for Pacaha have stood up to subsequent research.

61. Steven G. Baker, "Cofitachique: Fair Province of Carolina," master's thesis, University of South Carolina, 1975.

62. George E. Lankford III, "A New Look at De Soto's Route through Alabama," *Journal of Alabama Archaeology* 23 (1977): 10–36; Keith J. Little and Cailup B. Curren Jr., "Site 1CE308: A Protohistoric Site on the Upper Coosa River in Alabama," *Journal of Alabama Archaeology* 27 (1981): 117–40.

63. George E. Lankford III, Cailup B. Curren Jr., and Keith J. Little, "De Soto's Route through Alabama—An Update" (paper presented at the annual meeting of the Southeastern Archaeological Conference, New Orleans, La., November 1980); Cailup B. Curren Jr., "The Alabama River Phase: A Review," in *Archaeology in Southwestern Alabama: A Collection of Papers*, ed. Caleb Curren (Camden, Ala.: Alabama-Tombigbee Regional Commission, 1982), 103–14.

64. Jeffrey P. Brain, "Artifacts of the Adelantado," *Conference on Historic Site Archaeology* 8 (1975): 129–38.

65. Marvin T. Smith, "European Materials from the King Site," *Southeastern Archaeological Conference Bulletin* 18 (1975): 63–66; Marvin T. Smith and Mary Elizabeth Good, *Early Sixteenth-Century Glass Beads in the Colonial Trade* (Greenwood, Miss.: Cottonlandia Museum Publications, 1982).

66. Marvin T. Smith and Stephen A. Kowalewski, "Tentative Identification of a Prehistoric Province in Piedmont Georgia," *Early Georgia* 8 (1979): 1–13.

67. Jeffrey P. Brain, Alan Toth, and Antonio Rodriguez-Buckingham, "Ethnohistoric Archaeology and the De Soto Entrada into the Lower Mississippi Valley," *Conference on Historic Site Archaeology* 7 (1974): 232–89.

68. Marvin T. Smith, "The Route of De Soto through Tennessee, Georgia, and Alabama: The Evidence from Material Culture," *Early Georgia* 4 (1976): 27–48; Smith, "The Early Historic Period (1540–1670) in the Upper Coosa River Drainage of Alabama and Georgia," *Conference on Historic Site Archaeology Papers* 11 (1977): 151–67.

69. Charles Hudson, *The Southeastern Indians* (Knoxville: University of Tennessee Press, 1976).

70. Charles Hudson, "The Crucial Problem in the Early History of the Southeastern Indians" (paper presented at the annual meeting of the Southern Anthropological Society, Lexington, Ky., April 1978). I presented revisions of this paper at the Chancellor's Symposium, University of Mississippi, Oxford, Miss., October 6, 1980, and at the Key Symposium of the Southern Anthropological Society, Fayetteville, Ark., April 12, 1985. It was published as "An Unknown South: Spanish Explorers and Southeastern Chiefdoms," in *Visions and Revisions: Ethnohistoric Perspectives on Southern Cultures,* ed. George Sabo and William Schneider, Proceedings of the Southern Anthropological Society, no. 20 (Athens: University of Georgia Press, 1987), 6–24.

71. Chester B. DePratter, Charles M. Hudson, and Marvin T. Smith, "The Route of Juan Pardo's Explorations in the Interior Southeast, 1566–1568," *Florida Historical Quarterly* 62 (1983): 125–58.

72. John E. Worth, "Mississippian Occupation on the Middle Flint River," master's thesis, University of Georgia, 1988.

73. Charles Hudson, Marvin T. Smith, and Chester B. DePratter, "The Hernando de Soto Expedition: From Apalachee to Chiaha," *Southeastern Archaeology* 3 (1984): 65–77.

74. Charles Hudson, "The Uses of Evidence in Reconstructing the Route of the Hernando de Soto Expedition," De Soto Working Paper No. 1, Alabama De Soto Commission, 1987.

75. DePratter et al., "Juan Pardo's Explorations," 138.

76. FR, 104–6.

77. Hudson, "Uses of Evidence," 3.

78. Chester B. DePratter, Charles M. Hudson, and Marvin T. Smith, "The Hernando de Soto Expedition: From Chiaha to Mabila," in *Alabama and the Borderlands: From Prehistory to Statehood,* ed. R. Reid Badger and Lawrence A. Clayton (Tuscaloosa: University of Alabama Press, 1985), 108–27.

79. Hudson et al., "The Tristán de Luna Expedition, 1559–1561," 31–45.

80. Charles Hudson, Marvin T. Smith, and Chester B. DePratter, "The Hernando de Soto Expedition: From Mabila to the Mississippi River," T&T, 181–207.

81. John Wm. Adkinson, "Early Spanish Bead Found in Tuscaloosa County," *Stones and Bones Newsletter* 33 (1991): 2–3.

82. Chester B. DePratter, "Late Prehistoric and Early Historic Chiefdoms in the Southeastern United States," Ph.D. diss., University of Georgia, 1983.

83. Ibid., 204–21.

84. Charles Hudson, *The Juan Pardo Expeditions: Exploration of the Carolinas and Tennessee, 1566–1568* (Washington, D.C.: Smithsonian Institution Press, 1990), 51–124.

85. Marvin T. Smith, *Archaeology of Aboriginal Culture Change in the Interior Southeast: Depopulation during the Early Historic Period* (Gainesville: University Presses of Florida, 1987).

86. Charles Hudson, Marvin Smith, David Hally, Richard Polhemus, and Chester DePratter, "Coosa: A Chiefdom in the Sixteenth-Century Southeastern United States," *American Antiquity* 50 (1985): 723–37.

87. Joyce Rockwood Hudson, *Looking for De Soto: A Search through the South for the Spaniard's Trail* (Athens: University of Georgia Press, 1993).

88. Charles Hudson, "De Soto in Arkansas: A Brief Synopsis," *Field Notes: Newsletter of the Arkansas Archaeological Society* 205 (1985): 3–12.

89. Young and Hoffman, DWM.

90. See Young and Hoffman's chapters in DWM.

91. Charles Hudson, "The Hernando de Soto Expedition: The Landing" (paper presented at the annual meeting of the American Society for Ethnohistory, New Orleans, La., November 1984).

92. Jerald T. Milanich and Charles Hudson, *Hernando de Soto and the Indians of Florida* (Gainesville: University Press of Florida, 1993).

93. Letter from Michael Gannon to author, January 30, 1985.

94. Letter from Vernon J. Knight Jr. to author, February 7, 1987. I have not seen a report on results from testing at the Doctor Lake site.

95. The most accessible version of Curren's route, as well as a critique of my work, may be seen in Keith J. Little and Caleb Curren, "Conquest Archaeology of Alabama," in *Columbian Consequences,* ed. David Hurst Thomas (Washington, D.C.: Smithsonian Institution Press, 1990), 2:169–95. My critique of their work may be seen in Charles Hudson, "Critique of Little and Curren's Reconstruction of De Soto's Route through Alabama," De Soto Working Paper No. 12 (Tuscaloosa: University of Alabama State Museum of Natural History, 1989).

96. "Childersburg Group Organizes to Prove Town Is Oldest in U.S.," *Birmingham News,* May 12, 1987; "City Resents Omission from Trail," *Birmingham Post-Herald,* July 22, 1988; letter from John W. Washam Jr. and B. J. Meeks to Douglas Jones, August 22, 1988.

97. Alan Blake, "A Proposed Route for the Hernando de Soto Expedition, Based on Physiography and Geology," De Soto Working Paper Nos. 2, 3, and 4 (Tuscaloosa: University of Alabama State Museum of Natural History, 1987–88).

98. Minutes of the meeting of the Alabama De Soto Commission, May 20, 1988.

99. This report is included in "Some Letters Concerning the National Park Study for a De Soto Historic Trail," ed. Douglas E. Jones, De Soto Working Paper No. 13 (Tuscaloosa: University of Alabama State Museum of Natural History, 1987), 9–33.

100. 1990 Annual Report, Georgia De Soto Trail Commission.

101. Charles Erwin, "De Soto in the Swamp of Toa," *Journal of Southwest Georgia History,* in press.

102. W. S. Eubanks Jr., "Studying De Soto's Route: A Georgian House of Cards," *Florida Anthropologist* 42 (1989): 369–80.

103. David G. Anderson, "The Mississippian Occupation and Abandonment of the Savannah River Valley," *Florida Anthropologist* 43 (1990): 13–35.

104. Roland Chardon, "Response to Eubanks," *Florida Anthropologist* 43 (1990): 43–44.

105. Charles Hudson and Marvin Smith, "Reply to Eubanks," *Florida Anthropologist* 43 (1990): 36–42. See also Russell K. Skowronek, *Return to Peachtree* (Cullowhee, N.C.: Western Carolina University, 1991).

106. Letter from author to Jeffrey P. Brain and Richard Weinstein, January 18, 1990; letter from author to Gov. Bill Clinton, February 11, 1991.

107. David Morgan, *The Mississippi De Soto Trail Mapping Project,* Mississippi Department of Archives and History Report No. 26 (Jackson: Mississippi Department of Archives and History, in press). See also Kenneth F. Styer, "An Evaluation of Controlled Surface Collections from Three Potential De Soto Contact Sites in Western Mississippi," master's thesis, University of Mississippi, 1991.

108. "De Soto's Route through Louisiana: Consensus of the ad hoc Louisiana De Soto Commission," undated document.

109. Hudson, "De Soto in Arkansas: A Brief Synopsis," 3–12.

110. Gloria A. Young and Michael P. Hoffman, eds., *The Expedition of Hernando de Soto West of the Mississippi, 1541–1543* (Fayetteville: University of Arkansas Press, 1993).

111. But see Samuel D. Dickinson, "The River Cayas, the Ouachita or the Arkansas River?" *Field Notes: Newsletter of the Arkansas Archaeological Society* 209 (1986): 5–11.

112. *De Soto Trail: De Soto National Trail Study,* Final Report prepared by the National Park Service as required by the National Trail Study Act of 1987 (Atlanta: National Park Service, Southeast Regional Office, 1990), 59.

113. Charles Hudson, "A Synopsis of the Hernando de Soto Expedition, 1539–1543," in *De Soto Trail,* 77–126.

114. *De Soto Trail,* 145.

115. Ibid., 149–82.

116. Carl McIntire, "De Soto Tracer Seeks 'Divine' Inspiration," *Clarion-Ledger,* Jackson, Miss., n.d.

117. Lewis Larson, "The Pardo Expedition: What Was the Direction at Departure?" *Southeastern Archaeology* 9 (1990): 140–46.

118. Chester B. DePratter, Charles Hudson,, and Marvin Smith, "The Juan Pardo Expedition: North from Santa Elena," *Southeastern Archaeology* 9 (1990): 140–46.

119. C. Clifford Boyd Jr. and Gerald F. Schroedl, "In Search of Coosa," *American Antiquity* 52 (1987): 840–44.

120. Charles Hudson et al., "Reply to Boyd and Schroedl," *American Antiquity* 32 (1987): 845–56.

121. David Henige, "Proxy Data, Historical Method, and the de Soto Expedition," DWM, 155–69; "Life after Death: The Posthumous Aggrandizement of Coosa," *Georgia Historical Quarterly* 78 (1994): 687–715.

122. Charles Hudson, Chester B. DePratter, and Marvin T. Smith, "Reply to Henige," DWM, 255–69; Charles Hudson et al., "De Soto in Coosa: Another Reply to Henige," *Georgia Historical Quarterly* 78 (1994): 716–34.

123. Charles Hudson, "Juan Pardo's Excursion beyond Chiaha," *Tennessee Anthropologist* 12 (1987): 74–87.

124. Charles Hudson, "The Hernando de Soto Expedition, 1539–1543," in *The Forgotten*

Centuries: Indians and Europeans in the American South, 1521–1704, ed. Charles Hudson and Carmen Chaves Tesser (Athens: University of Georgia Press, 1994), 84–86.

125. Charles M. Hudson, John E. Worth, and Chester DePratter, "Refinements in Hernando de Soto's Route through Georgia and South Carolina," in *Columbian Consequences*, ed. David Hurst Thomas (Washington, D.C.: Smithsonian Institution Press, 1990), 2:108–11.

126. Adkinson, "Early Spanish Bead."

127. Charles Ewen, "Soldier of Fortune: Hernando de Soto in the Territory of Apalachee, 1539–1540," in *Columbian Consequences*, ed. David Hurst Thomas (Washington, D.C.: Smithsonian Institution Press, 1990), 2:83–91.

128. David G. Moore and Robin A. Beck Jr., "New Evidence of Sixteenth-Century Spanish Artifacts in the Catawba River Valley, North Carolina" (paper presented at the annual meeting of the Southeastern Archaeological Conference, Lexington, Ky., November 1994).

129. Robin A. Beck Jr., "From Joara to Chiaha: Spanish Exploration of the Appalachian Summit Area, 1540–1568" (paper presented at the annual meeting of the Southeastern Archaeological Conference, Knoxville, Tenn., November 1995).

130. Roger C. Smith et al., *The Emanuel Point Ship: Archaeological Investigations, 1992–1995, Preliminary Report*, Bureau of Archaeological Research, Division of Historical Resources (Tallahassee: Florida Department of State, 1995).

Index